KINANTHROPOMETRY AND EXERCISE PHYSIOLOGY LABORATORY MANUAL

Volume Two: Physiology

Kinanthropometry is the study of human body size, shape and form and how those characteristics relate to human movement and sporting performance. In this fully updated and revised edition of the classic guide to kinanthropometric theory and practice, leading international sport and exercise scientists offer a clear and comprehensive introduction to essential principles and techniques.

Each chapter guides the reader through the planning and conduct of practical and laboratory sessions and includes a survey of current theory and contemporary literature relating to that topic. The book is fully illustrated and includes worked examples, exercises, research data, chapter summaries and guides to further reading throughout.

Volume Two – *Exercise Physiology* – covers key topics such as:

- Neuromuscular aspects of movement
- Skeletal muscle function
- Oxygen transport, including haemotology, pulmonary and cardiovascular functions
- Metabolism and thermoregulation
- $\dot{V}O_2$ kinetics
- Physiological economy, efficiency and 'fitness'
- Physiological limitations to performance
- Assessment of energy expenditure, perceived exertion and maximal intensity.

The *Kinanthropometry and Exercise Physiology Laboratory Manual* is essential reading for all serious students and researchers of sport and exercise science, kinesiology and human movement.

Roger Eston is Professor of Human Physiology and Head of the School of Sport and Health Sciences at Exeter University.

Thomas Reilly is Professor of Sports Science and Director of the Research Institute for Sport and Exercise Sciences at Liverpool John Moores University.

KINANTHROPOMETRY AND EXERCISE PHYSIOLOGY LABORATORY MANUAL

Tests, procedures and data
Third Edition

Volume Two: Physiology

Edited by
Roger Eston

and

Thomas Reilly

Routledge
Taylor & Francis Group

LONDON AND NEW YORK

First edition published 1996
by E & FN Spon, an imprint of the Taylor & Francis Group
Second edition published 2001
by Routledge
Third edition published 2009
by Routledge
2 Park Square, Milton Park, Abingdon, Oxon, OX14 4RN

Simultaneously published in the USA and Canada
by Routledge
270 Madison Avenue, New York, NY 10016

Routledge is an imprint of the Taylor & Francis Group, an informa business

© 1996 E & FN Spon, 2001, 2009 Roger Eston and Thomas Reilly for selection and
editorial matter; individual contributors, their contribution

Typeset in Sabon by Pindar New Zealand (Egan Reid) Ltd, Auckland
Printed and bound in Great Britain by TJ International Ltd, Padstow, Cornwall

British Library Cataloguing in Publication Data
A catalogue record for this book is available from the British Library.

Library of Congress Cataloging-in-Publication Data
Kinanthropometry and exercise physiology laboratory manual : tests, procedures, and
data / edited by Roger Eston and Thomas Reilly. — 3rd ed.
      p. ; cm.
   Includes bibliographical references and index.
   1. Anthropometry—Laboratory manuals. 2. Exercise—Physiological aspects—
Laboratory manuals. I. Eston, Roger G. II. Reilly, Thomas, 1941-
   [DNLM: 1. Biomechanics—Laboratory Manuals. 2. Anthropometry—methods—
Laboratory Manuals. 3. Exercise—physiology—Laboratory Manuals. 4. Kinesiology,
Applied—methods—Laboratory Manuals. WE 25 K51 2009]
   GV435.K56 2009
   599.94—dc22   2008018782

ISBN 13:978-0-415-43723-3 pbk
ISBN 13: 978-0-415-43722-6 hbk

ISBN 10:0-415-43722-9 hbk
ISBN 10:0-415-43723-7 pbk

ISBN 978-0-415-46671-4 set

CONTENTS

ILLUSTRATIONS

FIGURES

TABLES

LIST OF CONTRIBUTORS FOR
EXERCISE PHYSIOLOGY

Vasilios Baltzopoulos
Institute for Biomedical Research into
Human Movement & Health
Manchester Metropolitan University
Manchester, UK

Tim Cable
Research Institute for Sport and Exercise
Sciences
Liverpool John Moores University
Liverpool, UK

Carlton B. Cooke
Carnegie Faculty of Sport and Education
Headingley Campus
Leeds Metropolitan University
Leeds, UK

Jonathan H. Doust
School of Sport, Exercise and Leisure
Roehampton Institute
University of Surrey
Surrey, UK

Roger Eston
School of Sport and Health Sciences
St Lukes Campus
University of Exeter
Exeter, UK

James Faulkner
School of Sport and Health Sciences
St Lukes Campus
University of Exeter
Exeter, UK

Nigel Gleeson
School of Health Sciences
Queen Margaret University
Edinburgh, UK

Andrew M. Jones
School of Sport and Health Sciences
St Lukes Campus
University of Exeter
Exeter, UK

John Leiper
Department of Biomedical Sciences
University of Aberdeen
Aberdeen, UK

Don P. MacLaren
Research Institute for Sport and Exercise
Sciences
Liverpool John Moores University
Liverpool, UK

Ron Maughan
School of Sport and Exercise Sciences
Loughborough University
Loughborough, UK

Thomas Reilly
Research Institute for Sport and Exercise
Sciences
Liverpool John Moores University
Liverpool, UK

Lee M. Romer
School of Sport and Education
Brunel University, Uxbridge
Middlesex, UK

Susan Shirreffs
School of Sport and Exercise Sciences
Loughborough University
Loughborough, UK

Anni T. Vanhatalo
School of Sport and Health Sciences
St Lukes Campus
University of Exeter
Exeter, UK

John G. Williams
Department of Kinesiology
West Chester University
West Chester, PA, USA

Edward M. Winter
The Centre for Sport and Exercise Science
Sheffield Hallam University
Collegiate Crescent Campus
Sheffield, UK

PREFACE

The third edition of this twin-volume text covers both anthropometry (Volume 1) and exercise physiology (Volume 2). These volumes are complementary in covering areas related to sport and exercise sciences, physical therapy and healthcare professionals. Across all the content is an emphasis on tests, protocol and procedures, data collection and analysis and the correct interpretation of observations.

The subject area referred to as kinanthropometry has a rich history, although the subject itself was not formalised as a discipline until the International Society for Advancement of Kinanthropometry (ISAK) was established in Glasgow in 1986. The Society supports its own international conferences and publication of proceedings linked with these events. Until the publication of the first edition of *Kinanthropometry and Exercise Physiology Laboratory Manual: Tests, Procedures and Data* by the present editors in 1996, there was no laboratory manual that would serve as a compendium of practical activities for students in this field. Accordingly, the text was published under the aegis of ISAK in an attempt to make good the deficit.

Kinanthropometrists concern themselves with the relation between structure and function of the human body, particularly within the context of movement. Kinanthropometry has applications in a wide range of areas including, for example, biomechanics, ergonomics, growth and development, human sciences, medicine, nutrition, physical therapy, healthcare, physical education and sports science. Initially, the idea for the book was motivated by the need for a suitable laboratory resource that academic staff could use in the planning and conduct of class practicals in these areas. The content of the first edition in 1996 was designed to cover specific teaching modules in kinanthropometry and other academic programmes, mainly physiology, within which kinanthropometry is sometimes subsumed. It was intended also to include practical activities of relevance to clinicians, for example in measuring metabolic functions, muscle performance, physiological responses to exercise, posture and so on. In all cases the emphasis was placed on the anthropometric aspects of the topic. By the time of the second edition in 2001, all the original chapters were updated and seven new chapters were added, mainly concerned with physiological topics. Consequently, it was decided to separate the overall contents of the edition into two volumes, one focusing on anthropometry practicals, whilst the other contained largely physiological topics.

It seems that 6–7 years is a reasonable life cycle for a laboratory-based text in a field that is expanding. In the third edition, the structure of the previous two volumes has been retained, without the need for any additional new chapters. Nevertheless, all chapters in both volumes have been altered and updated, some more radically than others needed to be. New content is reflected in the literature trawled, the new illustrations included and changes in details of some of the practical laboratory exercises.

The content of both volumes is oriented towards laboratory practicals, but offers much more than a series of laboratory exercises. A comprehensive theoretical background is provided for each topic so that users of the text are not obliged to conduct extensive literature searches in order to place the topic in context. Each chapter contains an explanation of the appropriate methodology and, where possible, an outline of specific laboratory-based practicals. Across all the content is an emphasis on tests, protocol and procedures, data collection and handling and the correct interpretation of observations. The last two chapters in Volume 1 are concerned with basic statistical techniques and scaling procedures, which are designed to inform researchers and students about data analysis. The information should promote proper use of statistical techniques for treating data collected on human participants as well as avoid common abuses of basic statistical tools. Nevertheless, there is a common emphasis on rigour throughout all the chapters in each volume and guidance on the reduction of measurement error.

The content of Volume 2 emphasizes exercise physiology, but still includes kinanthropometric aspects of the selected topics where appropriate. Practical activities of relevance to clinicians are covered; for example, in measuring metabolic and cardiovascular functions, assessing muscle performance, and haematological responses to exercise. The novel topics introduced at the time of the second edition have all been retained, whilst the material has been refreshed by inclusion of new authors.

Many of the topics included within the two volumes called for unique individual approaches and so a rigid structure was not imposed on contributors. Nevertheless, in each chapter there is a clear set of aims for the practicals outlined and an extensive coverage of background theory. As each chapter is independent of the others, there is an inevitable reappearance of concepts across chapters, including those of efficiency, metabolism, maximal performance, measurement error and issues of scaling. Nevertheless, the two volumes represent a collective set of experimental sessions for academic programmes in kinanthropometry and exercise physiology.

It is hoped that this third edition in two volumes will stimulate improvements in teaching and instruction strategies in kinanthropometry and physiology. In this way, editors and authors will have made a contribution towards furthering the education of the next generation of specialists concerned with the relation between human structure and function, in terms of both well-being and performance.

Roger Eston
Thomas Reilly

INTRODUCTION

The third edition of this twin-volume text covers both anthropometry (Volume 1) and exercise physiology (Volume 2). These volumes are complementary in covering areas related to sport and exercise sciences, physical therapy and healthcare professionals. Across all the content is an emphasis on tests, protocol and procedures, data collection and analysis and the correct interpretation of observations.

The first edition of this book was published as a single volume in 1996. The book has been used widely as a laboratory manual in both undergraduate and post-graduate programmes and in the continuous education and development workshops of a number of professional bodies. The subject area referred to as kinanthropometry has a rich history although the subject itself was not formalised as a discipline until the International Society for Advancement of Kinanthropometry (ISAK) was established in Glasgow in 1986. The Society supports its own international conferences and publication of Proceedings linked with these events. Until the publication of the first edition of *Kinanthropometry and Exercise Physiology Laboratory Manual: Tests, Procedures and Data* by the present editors in 1996, there was no laboratory

manual that would serve as a compendium of practical activities for students in this field. Accordingly, the text was published under the aegis of ISAK in an attempt to make good the deficit, later expanded into two volumes to reflect related areas and topics.

Kinanthropometrists are concerned about the relation between structure and function of the human body, particularly within the context of movement. Kinanthropometry has applications in a wide range of areas including, for example, biomechanics, ergonomics, growth and development, human sciences, medicine, nutrition, physical therapy, healthcare, physical education and sports science. Initially, the idea for the book was motivated by the need for a suitable laboratory resource that academic staff could use in the planning and conduct of class Practicals in these areas.

The content of the first edition in 1996 was designed to cover specific teaching modules in kinanthropometry and other academic programmes, mainly physiology, within which kinanthropometry is sometimes subsumed. It was intended also to include practical activities of relevance to clinicians; for example, measuring metabolic functions, muscle performance, physiological responses to exercise, posture and so on. In all cases the emphasis was placed on the anthropometric aspects of the topic. By the time of the second edition in 2001, all the original chapters were updated and seven new chapters were added, mainly concerned with physiological topics. Consequently, it was decided to separate the overall contents of the edition into two volumes, one focusing on anthropometry Practicals whilst the other contained largely physiological topics.

In the current revised edition, the ways in which anthropometry and physiology complement each other on academic programmes in the sport and exercise sciences are evident in the practical laboratory sessions across the two volumes. The structure of the previous two volumes has been retained, without the need for any additional new chapters. Nevertheless all chapters in both volumes have been altered and updated – some more radically than others needed to be. New content is reflected in the literature trawled, the new illustrations included and changes in the detail of some of the practical laboratory exercises. New authors are also included where appropriate. The most radical changes in Volume 1 have been introduced by the new authors in Chapters 1, 8 and 10. The initial chapter on body composition analysis has been re-vamped to acknowledge developments in this field and discard some of the field methods now deemed obsolete or discredited. Chapter 8 has been restructured and contains further information on growth and development and aerobic metabolism in children, in accordance with recent developments in the field. Chapter 10 has been re-worked so that the ubiquitous use of SPSS in data analysis is more directly recognised. In Volume 2, the new authors have also introduced substantial changes to Chapters 3, 9 and 10. The third chapter on lung function has been restructured and contains more recent population-specific regression equations for predicting lung function. Chapter 9 has been reworked and introduces new concepts and content, particularly in perceived exertion,

and Chapter 10 has been rewritten to reflect the considerable and significant advances in knowledge regarding oxygen uptake kinetics and critical power in the last eight years.

We regret, earlier in 2008, the death of William Duquet co-author of Chapter 2 with J. E. L. Carter. Completion of the chapter was his last professional contribution to the literature on kinanthropometry before his passing. Apart from his many likeable and personable characteristics – especially as a caring mentor and tutor – he will be remembered for the methodical manner in which he approached and conducted his professional work. This chapter should stand as a tribute by which we can remember him.

As with the very first edition, the content of both volumes is oriented towards laboratory Practicals, but offers much more than a series of laboratory exercises. A comprehensive theoretical background is provided for each topic so that users of the text are not obliged to conduct extensive literature searches in order to place the topic in context. The book therefore serves as a 'one-stop shop' for writing up the assignments set on each topic. Each chapter contains an explanation of the appropriate methodology and, where possible, an outline of specific laboratory-based Practicals. Across all the content is an emphasis on tests, protocol and procedures, data collection and handling and the correct interpretation of observations. The last two chapters in Volume 1 are concerned with basic statistical techniques and scaling procedures, which are designed to inform researchers and students about data analysis. The information should promote proper use of statistical techniques for treating data collected on human participants as well as avoid common abuses of basic statistical tools. Nevertheless, there is a common emphasis on rigour throughout all the chapters in each volume and guidance on the reduction of measurement error.

Many of the topics included within the two volumes called for unique individual approaches and so a rigid structure was not imposed on contributors. Nevertheless, in each chapter there is a clear set of aims for the Practicals outlined and an extensive coverage of background theory. As each chapter is independent of the others, there is an inevitable reappearance of concepts across chapters, including those of efficiency, metabolism, maximal performance, measurement error and issues of scaling. Nevertheless, the two volumes represent a collective set of experimental sessions for academic programmes in kinanthropometry and exercise physiology.

It is hoped that this third edition in two volumes will stimulate improvements in teaching and instruction strategies in kinanthropometry and physiology. In this way, editors and authors will have made a contribution towards furthering the education of the next generation of specialists concerned with the relation between human structure and function.

Roger Eston
Thomas Reilly

PART ONE

NEUROMUSCULAR ASPECTS OF MOVEMENT

CHAPTER 1

SKELETAL MUSCLE FUNCTION

Vasilios Baltzopoulos and Nigel Gleeson

1.1 AIMS

The aims of this chapter are to:
* describe specific aspects of the structure and function of the muscular system and the role of muscles in human movement;
* provide an understanding of how neuro-muscular performance is influenced by training, ageing and gender-related processes;
* provide an understanding of how neuromuscular performance is influenced by joint angle and angular velocity;
* describe the assessment of muscle performance and function by means of isokinetic dynamometry;
* provide an understanding of the value and limitations of isokinetic dynamometry in the assessment of asymptomatic and symptomatic populations.

1.2 INTRODUCTION

Human movement is the result of complex interactions between environmental factors and the nervous, muscular and skeletal systems. Brain cell activities within the cerebral cortex are converted by supraspinal centre programming into neural outputs (central commands) that stimulate the muscular system to produce the required movement (Enoka 2002). In this chapter specific aspects of the structure and function of the muscular system are considered as part of the process for producing movement. Knowledge of basic physiological and anatomical principles is assumed.

1.3 PHYSIOLOGICAL ASPECTS OF MUSCLE AND JOINT FUNCTION

1.3.1 Basic structure and function of skeletal muscle

Each skeletal muscle contains a large number of muscle fibres assembled together by collagenous connective tissue. A motoneuron and the muscle fibres it innervates represent a motor unit. The number of muscle fibres in a motor unit (innervation ratio) depends on the function of the muscle. Small muscles, such as the extraocular muscles, which are responsible for fine movements, have approximately 5–15 muscle fibres per motor unit. Large muscles, such as the gastrocnemius, required for strength and power events, have innervation ratios of approximately 1:1700–1900. A muscle fibre comprises a number of myofibrils surrounded by an excitable membrane, the sarcolemma. The basic structural unit of a myofibril is the sarcomere, which is primarily composed of thick and thin filaments of contractile proteins. The thick filaments are mainly composed of myosin; the thin filaments are composed of actin and the regulatory proteins tropomyosin and troponin, which control the interaction of actin and myosin.

Nerve action potentials propagated along the axons of motoneurons are transmitted to the postsynaptic membrane (sarcolemma) by an electrochemical process. A muscle action potential is propagated along the sarcolemma at velocities ranging from 1 to ~4 m·s⁻¹. This conduction velocity can be measured with surface electromyography (see, for example, Farina and Merletti, 2004). It depends on a number of anatomical, physiological and recruitment factors, and it has also been reported that it can be increased to approximately 6 m·s⁻¹ with resistance training (Kereshi *et al.* 1983). The muscle action potential causes Ca^{2+} release that disinhibits the regulatory proteins of the thin filaments. This allows the myosin globular heads to attach to binding sites on the actin filaments and form cross-bridges. The interaction of the actin and myosin filaments causes them to slide past one another and generate force, which is transmitted to the Z discs of the sarcomere. This is known as the sliding filament theory. The details of the exact mechanism responsible for the transformation of adenosine triphosphate energy from a chemical to a mechanical form in the cross-bridge cycle are not completely known (e.g. Pollack 1983), despite recent advances in the understanding of cross-bridge kinetics (Horiuti 1997; Spudich 2001) and the effects of previous stretch history (Herzog *et al.* 2006; Herzog 2004, 2005). For a detailed discussion of the electrochemical events associated with muscular contraction the reader is referred to the text by MacIntosh *et al.* (2005).

1.3.2 Motor unit types and function

Based on animal experiments, motor units are usually classified according to contractile and mechanical characteristics into three types (Burke 1981):

Type S: Slow contraction time, low force level, resistant to fatigue

Type FR: Fast contraction time, medium force level, resistant to fatigue

Type FF: Fast contraction time, high force level, fatiguable

Morphological differences are also evident between the different motor unit types. For example, motoneuron size, muscle fibre cross-sectional area and innervation ratio are increased in fast compared with slow type motor units. Whether this classification scheme is also relevant for human muscle motor units has been questioned, especially concerning the relation of force level and contractile speed (Bigland-Ritchie *et al.* 1998) and activation frequency and fatiguability (Fuglevand *et al.* 1999).

Another scheme classifies the muscle fibres in the different motor units as Type I, IIa and IIb, based on myosin ATPase. An alternative subdivision is slow twitch oxidative (SO), fast twitch oxidative glycolytic (FOG) and fast twitch glycolytic (FG), based on myosin ATPase and anaerobic/aerobic capacity (Brooke and Kaiser 1974). More recently, muscle fibres have been classified according to some molecular properties based on myosin heavy chain (MHC) isoforms (Bottinelli and Reggiani 2000; Ennion *et al.* 1995). The relative distribution of different motor unit types is determined by genetic factors. Elite endurance athletes demonstrate a predominance of slow or Type I fibres. Fast twitch fibres predominate in sprint or power event athletes.

The muscle fibres in a motor unit are all of the same type, but each muscle contains a proportion of the three motor unit types (Nemeth *et al.* 1986). In normal physiological human movements, motor units are activated in a relatively standard sequence (S-FR-FF) (orderly recruitment) that is determined mainly (but not entirely) by the motoneuron size of their motor unit according to the size principle (Henneman 1957; Enoka and Stuart 1984; Gustafsson and Pinter 1985). The force exerted by a muscle depends on the number of motor units activated and the frequency of the action potentials (Harrison 1983). The orderly recruitment theory, based on the size principle, indicates that recruitment is based on the force required, not the velocity of movement. Thus slow motor units are always activated irrespective of velocity. Most human movement is performed within the velocity range of the slow fibres (Green 1986), although there is evidence of selective activation of muscles with a predominance of fast twitch motor units during rapid movements (Behm and Sale 1993).

1.3.3 Training adaptations

Resistance training results in neural and structural adaptations, which improve muscle function. Neural adaptations include improved central command that generates a greater action potential (Komi et al. 1978; Sale 1992) and a better synchronization of action potential discharge in different motor units (Semmler 2002). Structural adaptations include increases in the cross-sectional area of muscle fibres (hypertrophy) and possibly an increase in the number of muscle fibres through longitudinal fibre splitting. There is no conclusive evidence for development of new fibres (hyperplasia) in humans. The structural changes that are induced by resistance training result in an overall increase in contractile proteins and therefore muscle force capacity (MacDougall et al. 1982). Adaptation of specific motor unit types depends on resistance training that stresses their specific characteristics: this is known as the principle of specificity. There is also some evidence suggesting that limited transformation between slow- and fast-twitch muscle fibres is possible with long-term specific training (Simoneau et al. 1985; Tesch and Karlsson 1985).

1.3.4 Effects of age and gender on muscle performance

Gender differences in muscle function parameters have been examined extensively. The absolute muscular force in males is approximately 30–80% higher than in females, depending on the type of test and segments examined and specific characteristics of the sample (Morrow and Hosler 1981; Heyward et al. 1986; Kanehisa et al. 1994, 1996). Because of gender differences in anthropometric parameters such as body mass, lean body mass, muscle mass and muscle cross-sectional areas that affect strength, muscular performance should be expressed relative to these parameters. Research on the relationship between body mass and maximum muscular force or moment is inconclusive, with some studies indicating high significant correlations (Beam et al. 1982; Clarkson et al. 1982) and others indicating no significant relationship (Morrow and Hosler, 1981; Kroll et al. 1990). Maximum muscular force expressed relative to body mass, lean body mass or muscle mass is similar in males and females, but some studies indicate that differences are not completely eliminated especially in upper-extremity muscles (Frontera et al. 1991).

Maximum force is closely related to muscle cross-sectional area in both static (Maughan et al. 1983) and dynamic conditions (Schantz et al. 1983). Research on maximum force relative to muscle cross-sectional area in static or dynamic conditions indicates that there is no significant difference between gender (Schantz et al. 1983; Bishop et al. 1987) although higher force to cross-sectional area ratios for males have also been reported (Maughan et al. 1983; Ryushi et al. 1988). Other studies have shown that differences in muscle force per cross sectional area depend on the muscle group tested (e.g. Kanehisa et al. 1994).

However, instrumentation and procedures for measurement of different anthropometric parameters *in vivo* (for example cross-sectional area, moment arms, lean body mass, muscle mass) are often inaccurate. Therefore, the findings of muscle function studies must always be considered relative to the inherent problems of procedures, instrumentation and *in vivo* assessment of muscle performance and anthropometric parameters.

Muscular force decreases with advancing age (Dummer *et al.* 1985; Bemben 1991; Frontera *et al.* 1991). This decline has been attributed mainly to changes in muscle composition and physical activity (Bemben 1991; Frontera *et al.* 1991) and other morphological or mechanical factors (e.g. Morse *et al.* 2005). Furthermore, the onset and rate of force decline is different in males and females and upper-lower extremity muscles (Dummer *et al.* 1985; Aoyagi and Shephard 1992). These differences are mainly due to reduction in steroid hormones in females after menopause and involvement in different habitual-recreational activities. Generally there is a decrease of approximately 5–8% per decade after the age of 20–30 (Shephard 1991; Aoyagi and Shephard 1992). However, it is important to emphasize that most of the morphological and mechanical changes are reversible with training (Reeves *et al.* 2003, 2004, 2005; Morse *et al.* 2007).

1.4 MECHANICAL ASPECTS OF MUSCLE AND JOINT FUNCTION

1.4.1 Muscular actions

Muscular activation involves the electrochemical processes that cause sliding of myofilaments, shortening of the sarcomere and exertion of force. The overall muscle length during activation is determined not only by the muscular force, but also by the external load or resistance applied to the muscle. The ratio of muscular force: external load determines three distinct conditions of muscle action:

Concentric action: muscular force is greater than external force and consequently overall muscle length decreases (i.e. muscle shortens) during activation.

Isometric action: muscular force is equal to external force and muscle length remains constant.

Eccentric action: external force is greater than muscular force and consequently muscle length is increased (muscle lengthening) during activation.

During all three conditions, sarcomeres are stimulated and attempt to shorten by means of actin-myosin interaction (sarcomere contraction). The use of the term 'contraction' to describe shortening should be adopted to describe the shortening of sarcomeres only, not changes in length of the whole muscle-tendon. During eccentric activation, for example, the muscle-tendon is lengthened and therefore terms such as 'eccentric contraction' or 'isometric contraction' may be misleading (Cavanagh 1988), even if there is some evidence that in certain eccentric actions the contractile element actually shortens.

In attempting to examine whole muscle function it is important to consider the different component parts of the muscle; that is both the functional contractile (active) and the elastic (passive) components. A simplified mechanical model of muscle includes three components that simulate the mechanical properties of the different structures. The contractile component (CC) simulates the active, force-generating units (i.e. sarcomeres), the series elastic component (SEC) simulates the elastic properties of the sarcolemma and the parallel elastic component (PEC) simulates the elastic properties of the collagenous connective tissue in parallel with the contractile component (Komi 1984, 1986; Chapman 1985).

Muscle architecture describes the organization of muscle fibres within the muscle. The angle between the muscle fibres and the line of action from origin to insertion is defined as the pennation angle. The pennation angle and the number of sarcomeres that are arranged in series or in parallel with the line of action of the muscle are important factors affecting muscle force (e.g. Maganaris and Baltzopoulos 1999; Maganaris *et al.* 1998).

1.4.2 Force-length and force-velocity relationships in isolated muscle

In muscles isolated from the skeletal system in a laboratory preparation, the force exerted at different muscle lengths depends on the properties of the active (CC) and passive components (SEC and PEC) at different muscle lengths. The force exerted by the interaction of actin and myosin depends on the number of the available cross-bridges, which is maximum near the resting length of the muscle. The force exerted by the passive elastic elements (SEC and PEC) is increased exponentially as muscle length increases beyond resting length (Figure 1.1). The total force exerted is therefore the sum of the active and passive forces, and although at maximum length there is no active component force because of minimum cross-bridge availability, the total force contributed by the elastic components alone may be even greater than the maximum CC force at resting length (e.g., Baratta and Solomonow 1991).

The effect of the linear velocity during muscle shortening or lengthening on the force output has been examined extensively since the pioneering work of Hill (1938). With an increase in linear concentric velocity of muscle shortening, the force exerted is decreased non-linearly because the number of cross-bridges formed, and the force they exert, are reduced (Figure 1.2). Furthermore, different types of muscle fibres have different force and velocity characteristics (Bottinelli *et al.* 1996; Widrick *et al.* 1996) so their relative distribution in a muscle will affect its force-velocity relationship and in general a higher output at faster angular velocities indicates a higher percentage of FF-FR motor units. When the linear eccentric velocity of muscle lengthening is increased on the other hand, the force exerted is increased or maintained at approximately similar levels that are significantly higher than the isometric or concentric forces (e.g. Wilkie 1950; Rijkelijkhuizen *et al.* 2003).

1.4.3 Muscle function during joint movement

Examination of the mechanical properties of isolated muscle is of limited use when considering how muscles function during movements in sports or other activities in humans. Movement of body segments results from the application of muscular

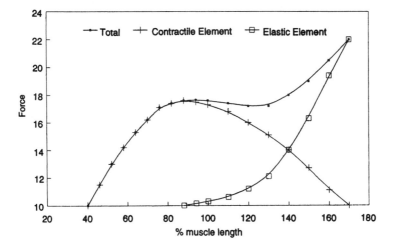

Figure 1.1 Force-length relationship in isolated muscle showing the contribution of the contractile and the elastic elements on total muscular force.

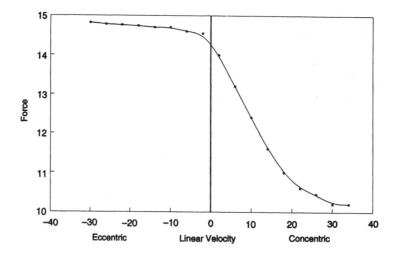

Figure 1.2 Force-velocity relationship of isolated muscle during concentric, isometric and eccentric muscle action.

force around the joint axis of rotation. It is therefore important to consider the relationship between muscle function and joint position and motion (Bouisset 1984; Kulig *et al.* 1984). The movement of the joint segments around the axis of rotation is proportional to the rotational effect of the muscular force (moment). This is measured in Newton·metres (N·m) and is defined as the product of muscular force (in newtons) and moment arm; that is, the perpendicular distance (in metres) between force line and the axis of rotation of the joint (Figure 1.3). In the isokinetics literature the term 'torque' is also used instead of 'moment' to describe the rotational effect of force. In engineering applications these two terms normally describe different configurations of force application, but in the context of strength-testing they are used interchangeably, although when referring to the joint and muscle as opposed to the dynamometer mechanics, the term 'moment' is more appropriate (Baltzopoulos 2008), so this term is used consistently throughout this chapter. Other physiological, mechanical and structural factors that were described earlier also affect muscle function in a joint system (Figure 1.4).

Joint motion results from the action of several muscle groups. Individual muscles

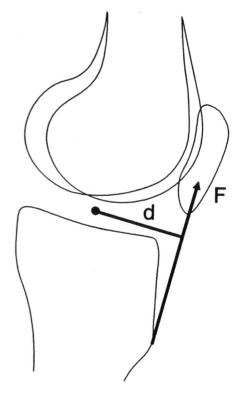

Figure 1.3 The moment arm (d) of the knee extensor group is the shortest or perpendicular distance between the patellar tendon and the assumed joint centre (in this case the tibiofemoral 'contact' point). The muscular moment is the product of the force (F) along the patellar tendon and the moment arm (d).

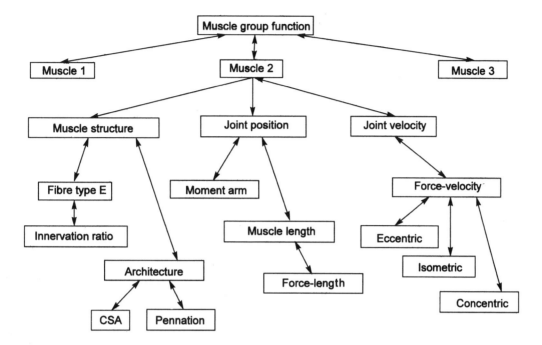

Figure 1.4 The main physiological and mechanical factors that affect the function of a muscle group. This simple model is not exhaustive and any interactions between the different factors are not indicated for simplicity.

in the group may have different origin or insertion points; they may operate over one or two joints and have a different architecture. The moment arm of the muscle group is also variable over the range of motion of the joint. Therefore, assessment of dynamic muscle function must consider these factors. It must be emphasized that relationships such as force-length or force-velocity refer to individual muscles, whereas joint moment-angle and joint moment-angular velocity relationships refer to the function of muscle groups around a joint. For example, the moment of the knee extensor group (rectus femoris, vastus lateralis, vastus medialis, vastus intermedius) at different knee joint angular velocities and positions can be examined during voluntary knee extension using appropriate instrumentation. These terms must not be confused with the force-velocity and force-length relationships of the four individual muscles. These can be examined only if the muscles were separated from a cadaveric joint in the laboratory. More recently, measurement of the tendon force using special tendon force transducers or estimation from the measured joint moment and then distribution of the tendon force to the individual muscles based on their physiological properties, such as cross-sectional areas, allowed the calculation of muscle force-velocity relationships *in vivo* from joint moment-angular velocity measurements (e.g. Komi *et al*. 1992; Finni *et al*. 2003).

1.4.4 Measurement of dynamic muscle function – isokinetic dynamometry

The most significant development for the study of dynamic muscle and joint function was the introduction of isokinetic dynamometry in the 1960s (Hislop and Perrine, 1967; Thistle *et al*. 1967). All modern isokinetic dynamometers have electromechanical mechanisms that maintain the angular velocity of a joint constant once a preset target velocity is reached. This is achieved by providing a resistive moment that is equal to the muscular moment throughout the range of constant joint angular velocity movement. This is referred to as optimal loading. Older passive systems (e.g. Cybex II) permitted isokinetic concentric movements only, but all the current active systems (e.g. Biodex, CONTREX, Isomed, Cybex Norm, KinCom) provide both concentric and eccentric isokinetic conditions, with maximum joint angular velocities up to 8–9 rad·s^{-1} (~500 deg·s^{-1}) for both concentric and eccentric actions (see Figure 1.5). It is important to note that it is the joint angular velocity that is controlled and kept constant, not the linear velocity of the active muscle group and the muscle fascicles (Hinson *et al.* 1979; Ichinose-Muraoka *et al.* 2000). Most commercial isokinetic systems have accessories that allow testing of all the major joints of the upper and lower limbs and the back. Apart from isolated joint tests, workplace manual activities such as lifting and handling materials and equipment can be simulated on adapted dynamometers using dedicated attachments. Methodological problems, such as subject positioning, alignment of joint and dynamometer axes during movement and motivation during the test, require standardized protocols. Mechanical factors such as the effect of gravitational moment or the control of the acceleration of the segment affect measurement of muscular moment but appropriate correction methods have been developed and must be used routinely (Baltzopoulos and Brodie 1989; Baltzopoulos 2008). Excellent test reliability and computerized assessment of muscle function permit widespread application of isokinetics for testing, training and rehabilitation.

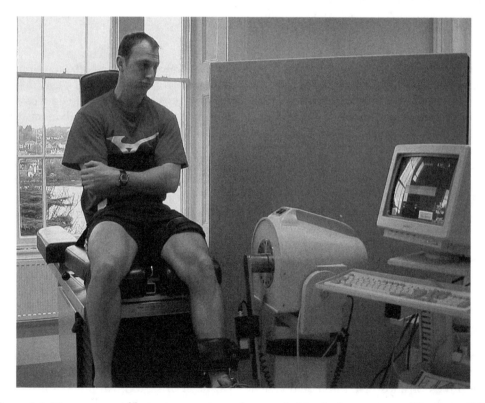

Figure 1.5 Measurement of knee extensor strength on an isokinetic dynamometer (Kin Com, 500H Chattex, Chattanooga, TN, USA).

1.4.5 Moment-angular velocity relationship

The moment exerted during concentric actions is maximum at slow angular velocities and decreases with increasing angular velocity (e.g. Seger and Thorstensson 2000; Lanza et al. 2003; Croce and Miller 2006). Some authors have reported a constant moment output (plateau) for a range of slow angular velocities (Lesmes et al. 1978; Perrine and Edgerton, 1978; Wickiewicz et al. 1984; Thomas et al. 1987) whereas others have found a continuous decrease from slow to fast concentric angular velocities (Thorstensson et al. 1976; Coyle et al. 1981; Westing et al. 1988). Although the plateau has been attributed to neural inhibition during slow dynamic muscular activation, it is also affected by training level and test protocol (Hortobagyi and Katch 1990). This plateau at slower velocities is also present in the in situ force-velocity relationship (e.g Edman et al. 1997; Devrome and MacIntosh, 2007). The rate of decrease at higher angular velocities is affected by activity, gender and the physiological/mechanical factors discussed above. The maximum concentric moment of the knee extensors decreases by approximately 40% from 1.47 to 4.19 rad·s^{-1} (60 to 240 deg·s^{-1}), whereas decrease in the knee flexor moment varies between 25% and 50% (Prietto and Caiozzo 1989; Westing and Seger, 1989). The eccentric moment remains relatively constant with increasing angular velocity and approximately 20% higher than the isometric moment. There are considerable differences in muscular moment measurements at different concentric-eccentric angular velocities between the large number of studies on dynamic muscle function. These result mainly from differences in methodology, anthropometric, physiological and mechanical parameters (Cabri 1991; Perrin, 1993).

The moment-velocity relationship is influenced by the physiological principles of isolated muscular action and the mechanical factors affecting muscle function in a joint system. Figure 1.4 is a simple representation of the different mechanical and physiological factors that affect the function of a muscle group during joint movement. Direct comparisons of the moment-angular velocity relationship during isokinetic eccentric or concentric joint motion with the force-linear velocity relationship of isolated muscle is of limited use, given the number of variables affecting muscle and joint function (Bouisset 1984; Bobbert and Harlaar 1992). In fact, recent studies have highlighted this important issue related to the applicability of the classical in vitro force-velocity to the function of intact human muscles during natural human movement. It has been shown consistently, both in animals and humans, that muscle-tendon forces during the ground contact phase in movements containing stretch-shortening actions is considerably higher than the force that would be predicted by the application of the classic isolated muscle force-velocity relationship or even the force measured in isolated joint tests using dynamometry (Gregor et al. 1988; Komi et al. 1992; Finni et al. 2001). The main reasons for this force potentiation in the instantaneous force-velocity in vivo are the activation levels and the storage of elastic energy during the eccentric phase that is recovered during the subsequent concentric phase, increasing the force output above the level predicted by the classic in vitro force-velocity relationship obtained by contractions performed at constant stimulation or loading (isotonic) and no pre-stretch conditions.

1.5 ISOKINETIC DYNAMOMETRY APPLICATIONS

1.5.1 Measurement issues—indices of neuromuscular performance and relationships to functional capability

The utility of 'isokinetic' machinery that offers controlled patterns of movement and loading of the musculoskeletal system as an effective mode of conditioning has been established in the literature. The most significant aspects of isokinetic training are velocity-specific adaptations and the transfer of improvements to angular velocities, other than the training velocity. Training at intermediate velocities 2.09–3.14 rad·s^{-1} (120–180 deg·s^{-1}) produces the most significant transfer to both slower and faster angular velocities (Bell and Wenger 1992; Behm and Sale 1993). Eccentric training at 2.09 rad·s^{-1} improves muscle function in both slower (e.g. 1.05 rad·s^{-1}) and faster (e.g. 3.14 rad·s^{-1}) angular velocities (Duncan *et al.* 1989). There is no conclusive evidence for improvements in eccentric muscle function after concentric training and vice-versa.

Isokinetic dynamometry has also become a favoured method for the assessment of dynamic muscle function in both clinical, research and sports environments. Several indices, such as peak moment, are used in the literature to characterize individual, group or larger population performance. The validity and related limitations to this mode of assessment have continued to receive critical scrutiny in the literature (e.g. Kellis and Baltzopoulos 1999; Iossifidou and Baltzopoulos 2000; Arampatzis *et al.* 2004; Tsaopoulos *et al.* 2006).

A preliminary evaluation of the potential relevance of performance assessments using isokinetic dynamometry may be done by considering the specificity of this mode of testing in relation to the criterion physical activity. The extent of congruence with the reference activity may be evaluated on varying levels that include identification and assessment of the involved muscle group; simulation of the activity's movement pattern and muscle action type during testing; and simulation of the movement velocity during testing (Sale 1991). The muscle group of interest may be tested using anatomical movements that employ this muscle group as an agonist. Further test specificity in terms of simulation of the movement pattern may be limited because, while commercially available isokinetic dynamometers are capable of

testing uni-lateral single-joint movements, most are not suitable for testing the multi-joint movements that are common to many sports. Similarly, replication of the stretch-shortening cycle (eccentric-concentric) pattern of muscular action, which occurs in many sports activities, is limited to those commercially available isokinetic dynamometers that offer assessment of both concentric and eccentric types of muscular action. This limitation may further extend to compromised replication of the temporal sequencing of these types of muscular action during testing.

Attempted replication of the eccentric component of sport-specific movements may offer increased potential for injury during the testing of symptomatic and asymptomatic individuals completing rehabilitation or conditioning programmes. The latter also demands that greater attention be given by the test administrator to accommodation and habituation responses of the participant to the test protocols. Isokinetic dynamometers are often compromised in their ability to replicate sport-specific movement velocities, for example offering concentric muscle action test velocities up to only 65% (~7 rad·s^{-1}) of the maximum unloaded knee extension velocity (~12 rad·s^{-1}) (Thorstensson *et al.* 1976) and up to 20% (~3.4 rad·s^{-1}) of the maximal eccentric action velocity of the knee flexors during sprint running (~17 rad·s^{-1}) (Sale 1991).

Thus in general, isokinetic movement-loading patterns are probably not congruent with the movements associated with most sporting activities. Even when assessments of strength capabilities by means of isokinetic dynamometry and net joint moments might have been shown to have offered apparently appropriate validity and reliability characteristics (please see later sections for more detailed considerations of these issues), these estimates of strength performance may not offer sufficient sensitivity of measurement or concurrent validity to properly reflect differences or changes in functional performance. Indeed, there is only a limited amount of published research relating isokinetically-derived net joint moments to functional athletic performance. For example, while isokinetic joint moments have been shown to be correlated significantly with vertical jumping performance (Pua *et al.* 2006) and sprinting performance over short distances (Dauty *et al.* 2003), and be capable of differentiating between contralateral limb and age-related functional performance capabilities in soccer players (Rahnama *et al.* 2003; De Ste Croix *et al.* 2003), there is little evidence of net joint moments being capable of consistently tracking conditioning-related effects on functional activities. In general, evidence from the literature suggests that inferences about functional performance capabilities based on assessments using isokinetic dynamometry should be made with caution.

The validity of isokinetic dynamometry is complicated by many factors that interact to influence the externally registered estimate of the net moment or work associated with a joint system. Strength performance constitutes only one aspect of the cascade of the neuromuscular and musculoskeletal machinery necessary to achieve temporal neuromuscular control and coordinated rapid production of force. The relative importance of absolute strength to the sports performance of interest will be influenced by moment-velocity and power-velocity relationships (Fenn and Marsh 1935; Hill, 1938) interacting with sport-specific neuromuscular recruitment and activation patterns (Edman 1992). As alluded to earlier, the magnitude of the correlation between indices of isokinetic neuromuscular performance and functional performance has been shown to be variable and accounts for only low to moderate portions of the shared variance. During the rehabilitation of high-performance soccer players from musculoskeletal injury and dysfunction through to full functionality and return to match-play, absolute strength performance of the involved musculature varied relatively little across the period of rehabilitation

(15–20% change relative to post-injury asymptomatic functional performance and time of return to match-play) (Rees and Gleeson 1999; Bailey *et al.* 2007). In contrast, indices of temporal neuromuscular control (electromechanical delay [see Gleeson 2009, Chapter 2]; rate of force development and static and dynamic proprioception [discussed later]) demonstrated relatively dramatic performance changes over the same period (70–85%; Bailey *et al.* 2007), suggesting a more potent role for the latter factors in functional performance. Overall, these limitations suggest that isokinetic assessment should constitute at most one component of a wider multivariate assessment model of neuromuscular capacity for performance prediction in different sports (Cabri 1991; Perrin 1993) or in the assessment of the time at which 'safe' return to play may be considered for the athlete rehabilitating from injury (Rees and Gleeson 1999).

The sensitivity of measurement associated with indices of performance and criterion test protocols may be defined as the ability to detect small changes in an individual's performance, or relative positional changes of an individual's performance within a sub-sample (Gleeson and Mercer 1996; Mercer and Gleeson 2002). The capability to discriminate between subtle changes or differences in performance relates directly to the precision (error), reliability and reproducibility characteristics of the measurements derived from the isokinetic test protocol. Within the context of a given application, the selection of minimum or threshold reliability and reproducibility criteria to meet the demand for appropriate measurement precision will, in turn, regulate the selection of suitable protocol characteristics (e.g. required number of replicates, inter-replicate time duration and mode of action). For example, in an investigation involving a 'case study' design, less stringent criteria for the precision of measurement may be appropriate for the discrimination of gross muscle dysfunction in the clinical setting where relatively large differences or changes in performance may be expected. By comparison, relatively greater precision may be needed to interpret correctly the effects of intervention conditioning in an elite strength-trained athlete, whose performance levels may vary by only ±5% over the competitive season (Mercer and Gleeson 2002).

Within an intended measurement application, there are typically several competing demands within the design of a measurement protocol that may affect the assessment of isokinetic strength and its subsequent suitability for meaningful evaluation and interpretation. The desire to increase measurement precision, reliability and sensitivity to suit the intended application by using more elaborate protocols involving multiple-trials may be hampered by logistical and financial constraints, or indeed, reduced tolerance of the participant being assessed to the demands of the test protocol. The net effect of the interaction of such demands may be considered to be the utility of the isokinetic dynamometry protocol. Of the factors that impinge on utility, those that relate to reproducibility and reliability afford the most control of measurement quality by the test administrator.

Research data suggest that, in many measurement applications, the precision and sensitivity associated with many frequently used indices of isokinetic leg strength that are estimated by means of single-trial protocols are not sufficient to differentiate confidently between either performance change within the same individual or individuals within a homogeneous group. While such limitations may be addressed by the use of protocols based on three to four inter-day trials for the index of peak moment, other indices, which demonstrate reduced reliability and reproducibility characteristics (e.g. the ratio of knee flexion to extension peak moment), may require many more replicates to achieve the same level of precision and sensitivity. Here, the measurement utility of the index may not be sufficient to justify its proper

deployment. Such issues are important for the utility of all aspects of dynamometry and the reader is directed to more complete reviews (e.g. Mercer and Gleeson 2002).

1.5.2 Data collection and analysis considerations

One of the most important considerations for precise, accurate and valid measurements when testing muscle function is the positioning of the subject. The length of the muscle group tested, the contribution of the elastic components, the effective moment arm, the development of angular velocity, inhibitory effects by the antagonistic muscle groups are all influenced by positioning and segment-joint stabilization during the test. Furthermore, contributions from biarticular muscles affected by the angle of adjacent joints (e.g. ankle joint angle during knee flexion tests due to the likely contribution of the gastrocnemius to knee flexion moment at different lengths) are also possible. For these reasons, the above factors and parameters must be controlled and standardized between tests, to allow precise measurements, valid comparisons and high test sensitivity. It is important to emphasize that not only the tested joint, but also the adjacent joints (e.g. hip and ankle joint angle during knee flexion or extension tests) must be controlled and standardized by careful positioning, sabilization and subject instructions. The positioning and sabilization of the subject is also important for another reason related to the alignment of the joint and dynamometer axes of rotation. This is essential because all the measurements are based on the assumption that the two axes are perfectly aligned during the test and it has been shown that considerable individual errors up to ~17% in the joint moment can result from axes misalignment (Arampatzis et al. 2004, 2007). For these reasons it is essential to align the joint axis of rotation with the axis of rotation of the dynamometer very accurately during submaximal or maximal contraction conditions (i.e. not during rest because there is always some movement between segment and dynamometer during contraction) and close to the expected position of maximum joint moment, in order to minimize as much as possible the error close to the measurement positions (Baltzopoulos 2008). Another important factor for accurate measurements in isokinetic dynamometry is the joint angular velocity. The recorded dynamometer moment is only equal to the joint moment exerted by the muscles when the angular velocity is constant, but the duration of constant angular velocity (isokinetic) period varies and is reduced significantly at high velocity tests (e.g. Iossifidou and Baltzopoulos 1996). For this reason it is essential to record and check the angular velocity so that moment measurements are only taken from the constant velocity or isokinetic range of motion. In some isokinetic systems the angular velocity output is not provided or it is not easily accessible and in these cases it is necessary to calculate the angular velocity from the angular position data, for example. It is important to understand that although the dynamometer will show a moment output throughout the range of motion, only the moment data in the constant angular velocity (isokinetic) period should be used for assessment (Baltzopoulos 2008).

Isokinetic testing of an isolated joint does not employ a natural movement. Accurate instructions are required concerning the operation of the isokinetic dynamometers and the testing requirements together with adequate familiarization. Eccentric conditions, particularly fast angular velocities, require special attention in order to avoid injury in novices or subjects with musculoskeletal weaknesses.

Simple isometric measurements can be performed using force transducers or cable tensiometers, hand dynamometers or myometers and simple free weights or resistive exercise equipment (Watkins 1993). The force output using these devices depends on the point of attachment to the limb, the moment arm of muscle group and the joint position. It is therefore essential to express joint function in terms of moment ($N \cdot m$); that is, as the product of the force output of the measuring device (N) and the perpendicular distance (m) between the force line and the joint axis of rotation. Accurate determination of the joint centre is not possible without complicated radiographic measurements and therefore an approximation is necessary. An example is the use of the most proximal points on the femoral epicondyles in the knee as landmarks to indicate the joint axis of rotation.

Computerized, isokinetic dynamometers allow more accurate positioning of the subject, the joint tested and assessment of muscle function. However, the cost of these devices may prohibit their use as tools in teaching. The moment recorded by isokinetic dynamometers is equal to the total (or resultant) moment exerted around the joint's axis of rotation. Although the main component of this total joint moment is the moment exerted by the active muscle group, there are also contributions from the antagonist muscles and other structures, such as the joint capsule and ligaments. Moment is the product of force and moment arm (distance from the axis of rotation) and during a knee extension test; for example, the moment exerted by the quadriceps is the product of the force exerted by the patellar tendon on the tibia and the moment arm, that is the perpendicular or shortest distance between the patellar tendon and the assumed centre of the knee joint (Figure 1.3). The moment arm is variable over the range of movement (Figure 1.6), being minimum at full knee extension and flexion and maximum at approximately 0.78 deg of knee flexion (Baltzopoulos 1995a). Moment arms at different joint positions are usually measured directly on the subject using radiography or derived indirectly from previous studies. As an example calculation, if the isometric moment of the knee extensors of a subject with body weight of 800 N (body mass 81.5

kg) was 280 Nm at 0.87 rad (50 deg) of knee flexion, and assuming that the moment arm at this joint position is 0.035 m, then the muscular force exerted by the patellar tendon was 8000 N or 10 times the body weight (BW) of that subject. This method can be applied to the moment measurements from isokinetic or isometric tests in order to obtain the actual muscular force exerted (assuming that any contributions from the antagonist muscles have been accounted for – see, for example, Kellis and Baltzopoulos 1997). This is usually expressed relative to body weight to allow comparisons. Using a similar method, it was estimated that the maximum muscular force exerted during isokinetic knee extension ranged from 9 BW at 0.52 rad·s⁻¹ (30 deg·s⁻¹) to 6 BW at 3.66 rad·s⁻¹ (210 deg·s⁻¹) (Baltzopoulos 1995b).

Another important aspect of muscle function assessment is the general acceptance that most physiological variables, including strength, would be influenced to a large extent by body size and dimensions because of dimensionality theory and should, therefore, be related to different anthropometric parameters, such as body mass, lean body mass, body height, muscle cross-sectional area and so on (Jaric 2003). However, the nature of these relationships varies and therefore, the expression (normalization) of maximum performance parameters, such as joint moment as a ratio relative to anthropometric variables without considering the underlying relationship between the two parameters, may lead to erroneous conclusions. This ratio is usually obtained by dividing the mean force, for example, by the mean body mass, without considering the regression line between force and body mass. A ratio relationship assumes that the regression line crosses the origin of the axes (i.e. the intercept is approximately zero). If despite a high correlation, a ratio relationship does not exist between moment and body mass then expressing the moment relative to body mass (N·m·kg⁻¹) is representative of subjects with body mass close to the mean body mass. However, this will overestimate or underestimate the moment for subjects with

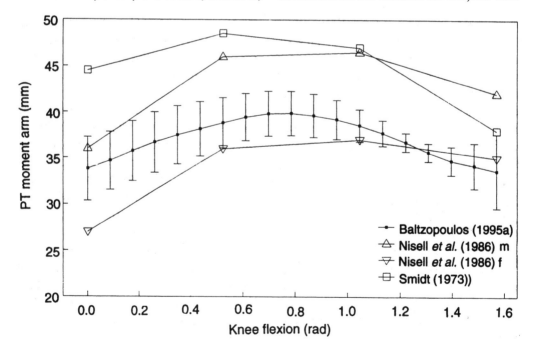

Figure 1.6 The patellar tendon moment arm during knee extension from different studies.

body mass further away from the mean body mass. In fact, the magnitude of the error in estimating the maximum moment from the ratio instead of the regression line, depends on the intercept (i.e. difference between regression and ratio lines) and the deviation of the subject's body mass from the mean body mass (see Winter and Nevill 2009). Different strength variables (e.g. muscle force or joint moment) would also require different treatment based on dimensionality theory. For example, Jaric *et al.* (2002) have shown that, according to a simple mechanical model based on geometrical similarity, force was proportional to mass raised to a power of ~0.67 whereas moment was related to mass as a simple ratio standard (exponent ~1.00), showing that moment expressed relative to mass as a simple ratio Nm kg^{-1} is an appropriate method for normalizing joint moment to body or muscle size.

1.5.3 Assessment of short-term muscle power and fatigue using isokinetic dynamometry

The work capacity of a muscle or muscle group may be determined by calculating the total area under one or a series of moment-angular position curves. Power is determined by assessing the time required to complete the relevant period of work. The limits of the range of motion would obviously affect the work so these must be set accurately and consistently. Many isokinetic dynamometry systems have software that is capable of determining these indices of performance. Protocols have been used to assess the capability of the neuromuscular system to produce all-out short-term work by means of varying simultaneous contributions from the ATP-PC and glycolytic energy pathways (Kannus *et al.* 1991; Abernethy *et al.* 1995). Depending on the methodology used for the assessment of power during single or repeated muscle actions, isokinetic indices of peak or mean power may be compromised by the intrusion of the effects of acceleration

and deceleration periods associated with limitations to the angular velocity control mechanisms (Iossifidou and Baltzopoulos 2000). Furthermore, the restricted frequency of analogue to digital conversions in commercially available dynamometers would tend to filter the highest frequencies of changes to work patterns and associated power outputs. The effects of these limitations may be minimized by the sampling of analogue raw data signals directly from the transducers within an isokinetic dynamometry system. Alternatively, interfacing the transducers or the analogue signals provided by specially installed interface cards (e.g. Cybex Norm system) directly to external data acquisition systems would allow more suitable analogue to digital sampling frequencies to be imposed that better reflect the nature of inherent and rapid fluctuations in performance data.

Various isokinetic dynamometry protocols involving a series of muscle actions have been used to assess the effects of fatigue on neuromuscular performance. Protocols have ranged from 50 uni-directional maximal voluntary actions of the knee extensor muscle group (Thorstensson *et al.* 1976) to bi-directional (reciprocal) all-out exercise tasks consisting of 25–30 reciprocal maximal voluntary actions of the knee extensors and flexors of the leg at moderate movement velocities (3.14 rad·s^{-1}) with no rest between movements (Burdett and van Swearingen 1987; Baltzopoulos *et al.* 1988; Montgomery *et al.* 1989; Mathiassen 1989; Gleeson and Mercer 1992). In the case of bi-directional protocols, total work and indices of fatigue may be determined during both extension and flexion movements involving eccentric and concentric muscle activations. The latter indices may be calculated automatically using the dynamometer's software or using data derived from external transducers. A least squares regression may be applied to the actual work done in all repetitions and the index of fatigue can be determined as the ratio of the work done in the last repetition compared to the first repetition and expressed as a percentage. Alternatively, Thorstensson *et al.* (1976) defined endurance as the moment from the last three in a series of 50 contractions as a percentage of the initial three contractions and Kannus *et al.* (1992) reported that the work performed during the last 5 in a series of 25 repetitions and the total work performed were valuable markers in the documentation of progress during endurance training. The isokinetic protocols may be designed to reflect the 'worst-case' scenario for fatiguing exercise within the context of the sport of interest (Gleeson *et al.* 1997), be associated with a particular duration in which a bioenergetic pathway is considered to have prominence (Sale 1991), or indeed, be designed to provoke exercise-induced muscle damage (Gleeson *et al.* 2003; Marginson *et al.* 2005).

Indices of leg muscular fatigue demonstrate significantly greater variability in inter-day assessments of reproducibility compared with indices of strength (9.1% vs 4.3%, respectively) (Burdett and van Swearingen 1987; Gleeson and Mercer 1992). The ability to reproduce exactly the pattern of work output and fatigue responses over repeated day-to-day trials appears to be compromised. The latter trend may be due, in part, to an intrusion of conscious or unconscious work output pacing strategies as suspected for this and other exercise modalities during tests of similar duration (Perrin 1986; Burke *et al.* 1985). The inflated variability associated with the assessment of isokinetic endurance parameters may be explained by the problems of subjects having to sustain a higher degree of self-motivation to maximum effort throughout 30 repetitions lasting approximately 40 seconds, compared with the relatively short duration of three maximal voluntary muscle actions associated with strength assessment protocols. As the series of bi-directional agonist-antagonist muscle group actions associated with the fatigue test protocols progresses, it may be that inherently higher variability of the interaction of motoneuron recruitment, rate coding, temporal patterning

and co-activation phenomena and, ultimately, changes to the recorded net moment about the joint of interest (Milner-Brown *et al.* 1975; Enoka 2002) may underscore these findings. While the dynamometer provides a 'safe' environment in which to stress the musculoskeletal system with high-intensity fatiguing exercise tasks, the 'work-rest' duty cycles and motor unit recruitment patterns associated with the isokinetic testing cannot faithfully mimic the loading during the sports activity. The results from such isokinetic tests of muscle endurance must be interpreted cautiously.

1.5.4 Clinical applications of isokinetic dynamometry

Isokinetic dynamometry provides a relatively controlled and risk-free environment in which to stress or assess the neuromuscular capabilities associated with a joint system. Clinical applications of isokinetic dynamometry include assessment of contralateral and agonist-antagonist muscle group performance in symptomatic populations and prophylactic assessments of asymptomatic populations.

Net joint moments and performance scores for the uninjured extremity are often used as the standard for return of the injured extremity to a normal state. However, this marker for a safe return to play may be compromised by the influence of limb dominance or the effect of neuromuscular specificity of various sport activities on bilateral strength relationships. Bilateral differences in performance capabilities may be negligible in healthy non-athletes or in participants in sports that involve symmetrical action. However, bilateral differences in strength performance of up to 15% have been reported in asymmetrical sport activities (Perrin *et al.* 1987). Importantly, in most circumstances involving sports injury, prospective pre-injury performance scores for both involved and contralateral limbs are likely to be unavailable to the clinician. Furthermore, the condition of the contralateral 'control' limb is often compromised substantively by physiological deconditioning, involving changed motor unit recruitment patterns associated with reduced volume and intensity of habitual exercise, and injury-related bilateral autogenic and arthrogenic inhibitory effects between the involved and contralateral control limbs. This often serves to lessen the utility of concurrent contralateral limb comparisons because of the consequent masking of the extent of the pre-injury baseline performance of the contralateral limb. Furthermore, the latter may be compromised as an optimal marker for a safe 'return to play' because it may have been actually associated with the occurrence of the injury. Figure 1.7 illustrates the dilemma faced by the clinician in assessing a safe 'return to play' for the injured athlete.

The bilateral assessment of the injured athlete presents further hindrances to the proper interpretation of performance scores. The injury may cause unilateral restriction to the range of motion available for isokinetic assessment. While this may be an interesting clinical finding in itself, comparisons of the neuromuscular performance of contralateral limbs through unequal ranges of motion could be compromised. The intrusion of different levels of pre-stretch and metabolic potentiation under these circumstances would be expected to alter falsely the differential in the level of net joint moments that would otherwise have been observed in the comparison of the performance between involved and contralateral limbs. Similarly, the differential movement patterns would confound contralateral comparisons of average moment and work values. Variations or modifications in placement of the fixation point between

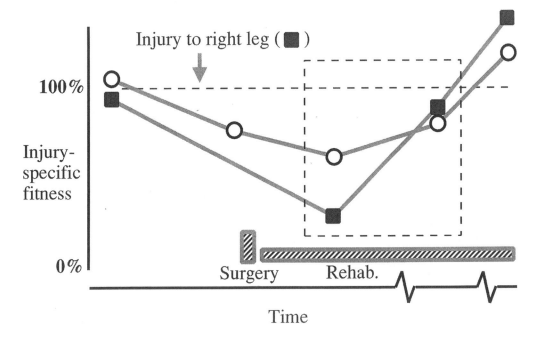

Figure 1.7 A schematic diagram illustrating the dilemma faced by the clinician in assessing safe return-to-play for the injured athlete. The figure shows the progression of performance associated with both the involved (square markers) and contralateral (circular markers) limbs prior to and following injury to the right limb. Pre-injury levels of performance are associated with injury. Post-injury conditioning should exceed pre-injury levels of performance for protection from the threat of injury. The clinician has data and contralateral limb comparisons within the dashed box available to help in the decision of when it is safe to return to play (see text).

the dynamometer and the patient may affect the recorded peak or average moment. It is essential that appropriate anatomical measurements or mapping techniques be used in these circumstances to minimize the intrusion of these aspects of technical error (Gleeson and Mercer 1996). Similarly, situations in which further inference about *in vivo* knee joint mechanics is to be derived from net joint moments measured externally require careful evaluation of likely sources of error. For example, mechanical compliance of the isokinetic dynamometer's lever-arm interacting with that of the lower leg system influence knee joint kinematics under active and passive loading, whereas characteristics of protocols used to estimate the origin of the centre of joint rotation introduce errors to the computation of the length of the patellar tendon moment arm and in the measurement of active knee extension moment (Tsaopoulos *et al.* 2006).

Bilateral asymmetries and imbalances in muscle performance capabilities associated with the knee joint have been offered as important factors in the aetiology of many musculoskeletal injuries (Hewett *et al.* 2001; Decker *et al.* 2003; Griffin *et al.* 2006).

Concentric knee flexion/extension peak moment ratios range from 0.4 to 0.6 and are mainly affected by activity, methodological measurement problems and gravitational forces in particular (Appen and Duncan 1986; Fillyaw *et al.* 1986; Figoni *et al.* 1988). Studies that have used peak moment data uncorrected for the effect of gravitational forces tend to demonstrate higher ratios and a significant increase with increasing angular velocity. Gravity corrected moment ratios tend to be approximately constant at different angular velocities (Appen and Duncan 1986; Fillyaw *et al.* 1986; Baltzopoulos *et al.* 1991). During joint motion in sport or other activities, concentric action of agonist muscles requires eccentric action of the antagonist muscles to control the movement and facilitate joint stability. For this reason, ipsilateral antagonist eccentric/agonist concentric muscle group

moment ratios have been proposed as being more representative of joint function during sport activities (Aagaard *et al.*1995). The latter indices of performance capability have been evaluated against conceptual models for the dynamic sabilization of joints systems at functional and clinically-relevant joint positions (e.g. Kellis 1998; Coombs *et al.* 2002). However, definitive experimental evidence derived from prospective randomized control trials of whether correction of bilateral asymmetries and imbalances in muscle performance capabilities reduces the risk of musculoskeletal injury remains elusive.

It is intuitively appealing for isokinetic dynamometry to offer the capability to discriminate and potentially diagnose pathologies in muscle-tendon units and bony articulations of a joint system. Various artefacts in the moment-angular position curves have been attributed to conditions such as anterior cruciate ligament deficiency, and chondromalacia patella (Perrin 1993). There are many factors including subject-dynamometer positioning, limb fixation characteristics, the compliance of soft tissue and padding of the dynamometer, injury-related neuromuscular inhibitory and pain responses, differential accommodation, habituation and warm-up effects that influence neuromuscular performance (Gleeson and Mercer 1996; Minshull *et al.* 2007). These factors contribute to the technical and biological variability in the recorded net moment associated with the interaction between a given assessment protocol, patient and the dynamometry system. Figure 1.8 illustrates 95% confidence limits constructed around a single moment-angular position curve derived from maximal voluntary muscle actions of the knee extensors and flexors at 1.05 rad·s^{-1}. The limits are estimated from empirical data from reproducibility and single-measurement reliability studies involving asymtomatic participants (Gleeson and Mercer 1992, 1994; Mercer and Gleeson, 2002). Potential anomalies to the moment-angular position curve would typically need

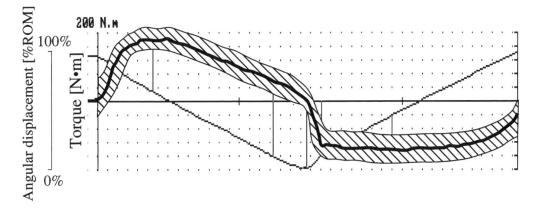

Angular displacement [%ROM]

Torque [N•m]

200 N.m

100%

0%

Figure 1.8 95% confidence limits constructed around a single moment-angular position curve derived from maximal voluntary muscle actions of the knee extensors and flexors at 1.05 rad·s-1. The limits are estimated from empirical data from reproducibility and single-measurement reliability studies involving asymtomatic participants (Gleeson and Mercer 1992, 1994).

to exceed such limits consistently before further investigation was warranted.

1.5.5 Assessment of proprioception performance using isokinetic dynamometry

An important function of skeletal muscle is to contribute both sensory and moment-generating machinery to a model for dynamic joint stability, which comprises primary ligamentous restraints interacting with other static sabilizers (osseous geometry, capsular structures and meniscii) and with dynamic sabilizers (Fu 1993). In the functionally stable knee, such restraints interact to maintain joint stability. Optimal functioning relies on a complex integration of numerous contributory factors, which offer an inherent enhancement to the awareness of joint position and motion sensation. Proprioception can be thought of as a complex neuromuscular process that involves both afferent and efferent signals and allows the body to maintain stability and orientation during both static and dynamic activities (Lephart *et al.* 1992).

Proprioceptive input is derived from mechanoreceptors located in the skin, joint capsules, ligaments, and musculotendinous units, which relay afferent feedback to the central nervous system (CNS) for continuous processing. Different types of afferent joint receptors have been identified: Ruffini receptors, Paciniform, Golgi Tendon Organs (GTO) and nociceptive type fibres, which are high threshold and slowly adapting in the detection of pain. These receptors may play a role in the regulation of muscle stiffness around the joint by means of the gamma-muscle spindle system and ultimately contribute to the control of joint stiffness and functional stability (Johannsen *et al.* 1986; Johannsen 1991). Information from proprioceptive receptors offers sensory awareness in the form of both feed-back and feed-forward mechanisms. Feed-back processes are thought to regulate motor control continually through reflex pathways and be associated with reactive muscle activity. Feed-forward neuromuscular control involves planning movements based on sensory information from past experiences and is responsible for preparatory muscle activity (Swanik *et al.* 1997). It is possible that a protective feed-back reflex would be too slow to provide protection in a rapid ligamentous injury scenario (Pope *et al.* 1979; Rees and Gleeson 1999; Minshull *et al.* 2007). Thus sensory awareness in the form of both feed-back and feed-forward mechanisms may underpin the integrity and sabilization of the joint as well as the co-ordination of complex movement systems (Hasan and Stuart 1988; Krauspe *et al.* 1992). For example, the main function of ligamentous afferents may be to provide a continuous preparatory adjustment (or pre-programming) of intrinsic muscle stiffness through the reflex-mediated stiffness.

Proprioceptive performance has been assessed in the contemporary clinical literature using tests such as the ability to reproduce passive positioning of the injured and contralateral limbs (Lattanzio and Petrella1998). These tests are undertaken at relatively slow angular velocities of movement. More recently, dynamic proprioception assessments have been developed which may be more applicable to the dynamic model of knee joint stability (Rees and Gleeson

1999; Walters-Edwards *et al.* 2006; Bailey *et al.* 2007). These tests involve the ability to regulate volitional force and results are expressed as the discrepancy between the blinded attainment of a prescribed force (e.g. 50% maximal voluntary muscle force of the knee flexors) and subsequent reproduction of this target force. Figure 1.9 shows data from a single trial of a blinded attainment of a prescribed force. In controlled clinical trials involving anterior cruciate ligament (ACL)-deficient populations, the patterns of change in the dynamic proprioception performance of the musculature of the knee joint prior to and following bone-patella tendon-bone ACL reconstruction surgery and subsequent rehabilitation, appear to predict improvements in the functional stability of the knee joint.

The isokinetic dynamometry system and its associated control software offers a useful facility for employing both the traditional

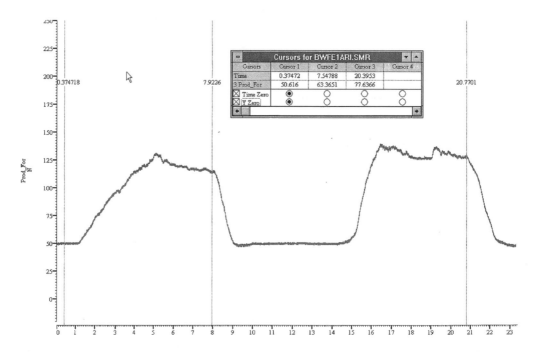

Figure 1.9 Example data from a single trial of an assessment involving the ability to regulate volitional force (measured by the net moment). Performance is expressed as the discrepancy between the blinded attainment of a prescribed force (for example, 50% maximal voluntary muscle force of the knee flexors, static [left force-time curve]) and subsequent reproduction of this target force (right force-time curve).

clinical tests of joint proprioception (reproduction of passive positioning of the involved and contralateral limbs) and more recent dynamic proprioception tests.

The practical exercises in this chapter describe assessment of knee joint function at different joint angular velocities and positions.

Similar parameters of muscle function during maximal voluntary activation (isokinetic or isometric) can be assessed in different groups of subjects using other muscle groups to examine the effects of age, sex and sport and the relationship of muscle function with various anthropometric measures.

1.6 PRACTICAL 1: ASSESSMENT OF MUSCLE FUNCTION DURING ISOKINETIC KNEE EXTENSION AND FLEXION

1.6.1 Purpose

The purpose of this practical is to assess the maximum muscular moment (dynamic strength) of the knee extensor and flexor muscles at different concentric and eccentric knee joint angular velocities. This practical requires an isokinetic dynamometer for data collection. As these devices are very expensive, they may not be available in all laboratories. Data collected from a group of young female age group swimmers using a Biodex dynamometer are presented in Tables 1.1, 1.2 and 1.3. These can be used for data analysis and discussion of the topics examined in this practical.

Table 1.1 Body mass, lean body mass and height of subjects (n =10)

Subject no.	Body mass (kg)	Lean body mass (kg)	Height (m)
1	51.6	39.5	1.57
2	49.4	38.1	1.57
3	58.1	41.2	1.69
4	48.1	37.0	1.62
5	62.5	46.0	1.62
6	58.7	42.9	1.55
7	54.5	38.9	1.52
8	46.5	37.2	1.62
9	68.4	54.1	1.76
10	56.2	39.4	1.53
Mean	55.4	41.4	1.60
SD	6.8	5.5	0.07

Table 1.2 Knee flexion moment (Nm) during isokinetic eccentric and concentric angular velocities

	Angular velocity (rad·s⁻¹)ᵃ							
	Eccentric				Concentric			
	4.19	3.14	2.09	1.05	1.05	2.09	3.14	4.19
Subject no.								
1	65	61	63	59	52	52	42	39
2	69	71	74	71	57	49	38	38
3	76	83	80	82	67	67	50	45
4	63	61	59	56	43	47	39	34
5	77	81	84	78	68	64	52	47
6	93	90	89	92	69	57	43	42
7	56	65	63	59	50	61	47	39
8	65	72	70	68	54	50	37	29
9	104	110	116	118	96	108	98	105
10	88	90	86	81	62	60	50	44

ᵃ1 rad·s⁻¹ is equal to an angular velocity of 57.2960 deg·s⁻¹.

Table 1.3 Knee extension moment (N·m) during isokinetic eccentric and concentric angular velocities

	Angular velocity (rad·s⁻¹)ᵃ							
	Eccentric				Concentric			
	4.19	3.14	2.09	1.05	1.05	2.09	3.14	4.19
Subject no.								
1	137	140	139	132	123	105	105	101
2	128	131	134	130	122	104	78	83
3	179	183	195	186	169	141	116	105
4	152	153	151	144	132	108	82	72
5	179	184	173	169	157	115	96	87
6	180	185	187	191	168	128	98	87
7	171	169	173	166	154	119	97	84
8	159	157	161	112	131	103	82	71
9	253	249	245	238	202	162	139	121
10	159	179	175	169	152	118	98	85

1.6.2 Procedure

1 Record all data in the appropriate data sheet for this Practical (Figure 1.10)

| | | | Joint Angular Velocity (rad s^{-1}) | | | | | | | | |
| | | | Eccentric | | | | | Concentric | | | |
Side	Action	Parameter	4.19	3.14	2.09	1.05	0	1.05	2.09	3.14	4.19
R	EXT	Maximum Moment (Nm)									
		Angular Position (rad))									
	FLX	Maximum Moment (Nm)									
		Angular Position (rad)									
		FLX/EXT Moment Ratio									
L	EXT	Maximum Moment (Nm)									
		Angular Position (rad)									
	FLX	Maximum Moment (Nm)									
		Angular Position (rad)									
		FLX/EXT Moment Ratio									
	L/R EXT Moment Ratio										
	L/R FLX Moment Ratio										

Figure 1.10 Data collection sheet (R = right, L = left, EXT = extension, FLX = flexion).

2 Calibrate equipment according to the manufacturer's instructions. Record date, subject name, sex, age, body mass, height and training status.
3 Measure or estimate other anthropometric parameters if required (for example lean body mass, cross-sectional area of muscle groups, segment circumference and volume, muscle mass etc).
4 Allow the subjects general warm-up/stretching exercises. Position the subject on the dynamometer without attaching the input arm. A sitting position with the hips flexed at approximately 1.74 rad (100 degrees) is recommended. A supine position may be preferable in order to increase muscular output and simulate movements where the hip angle is approximately neutral.
5 Attach the input arm of the dynamometer on the tibia above the malleoli and ensure that there is no movement of the leg relative to the input arm. Generally a rigid connection is required between the segment and the various parts of the input arm.
6 Align carefully the approximate joint axis of rotation with the axis of the dynamometer by modifying the subject's position and/or the dynamometer seat adjustments whilst the subject is performing a submaximal contraction (near the expected position of maximum joint moment if possible). For the knee test specifically, align the lateral femoral epicondyle with the dynamometer axis during the submaximal contraction, separately for the knee extension and flexion tests, and ensure that it remains in alignment for most of the test range of movement and in particular during the

expected maximum moment position. The alignment must be performed accurately using a physical or light-based pointer.

7 Secure all the other body parts not involved in the test with the appropriate straps. Ensure that the thigh, opposite leg, hips, chest and arms are appropriately stabilized. Make a note of the seat configuration and the joint positions in case you need to replicate the test on another occasion.

8 Provide written, clear instructions to the subject concerning the purpose of the test and the experimental procedure. Explain in detail the requirement for maximum voluntary effort throughout the test and the use of visual feedback to enhance muscular output. Allow the subject to ask any questions and be prepared to explain in detail the test requirements.

9 Familiarize the subject with the movement. Allow at least five submaximal repetitions (extension-flexion throughout the range of movement) at all the test angular velocities.

10 Allow the subject to rest. During this period, enter the appropriate data on the computer system, set the range of movement and perform the gravity correction procedure according to the instructions provided by the manufacturer of the dynamometer.

11 Start the test and allow five to six reciprocal repetitions (extension followed by flexion). The order of the test angular velocity should be randomized. Visual feedback and appropriate test instructions are adequate for maximum effort. If other forms of motivation are required (e.g. verbal encouragement) then make sure they are standardized and consistent between subjects.

12 After the test is completed, note the maximum moment for knee extension and flexion and the angular position where the maximum was recorded, on the data sheet for this practical. Ensure that the maximum moment was recorded during constant angular velocity (isokinetic) conditions by plotting the angular velocity together with the moment graph (superimposed) if allowed by the dynamometer software. If this is not possible then calculate the angular velocity from the angular position data. Allow 1–2 minutes rest and perform the test at the other angular velocities. Repeat the procedure for the other side.

1.6.3 Data analysis

1 Plot the maximum moment of the knee extensors and flexors against the angular velocity of movement (moment-angular velocity relationship).

2 Compare the increase/decrease of the moment during the eccentric and concentric movements with previously published studies examining this relationship.

3 Discuss the physiological/mechanical explanation for these findings.

4 Calculate the flexion/extension ratio by dividing the corresponding maximum moment recorded at each speed and plot this ratio against angular velocity. What do you observe? Explain any increase or decrease at the different eccentric and concentric velocities.

5 Plot the angular position (knee flexion angle) of the maximum moment at different angular velocities. Is the maximum moment recorded at the same angular position

at different angular velocities? What is the physiological/mechanical explanation for your findings?

6 If data for both sides have been collected, then calculate the bilateral moment ratio (left joint moment/right joint moment) at the different angular velocities. See if you can explain any bilateral differences.

7 Establish the relationship between maximum moment, body mass and lean body mass. Can you express the maximum moment relative to body mass or lean body mass as a ratio? Explain the rationale for your answer.

1.7 PRACTICAL 2: ASSESSMENT OF ISOMETRIC FORCE-JOINT POSITION RELATIONSHIP

1.7.1 Purpose

The purpose of this practical is to assess the maximum isometric moment (static strength) of the knee extensor muscles at different knee joint positions. Isometric force can be measured using relatively inexpensive instruments that are commercially available.

1.7.2 Procedure

Record all data in the appropriate data sheet for this practical.

1 Record date, subject name, sex, age, body mass, height and training status.

2 Measure or estimate other anthropometric parameters if required (for example lean body mass, cross-sectional area of muscle groups, segment circumference and volume, muscle mass etc).

3 After some general warm-up/stretching exercises, position the subject on a bench lying on his/her side. A position with the hips flexed at approximately 1.74 rad (100 degrees) is recommended. An extended position may be preferable to increase muscular output and simulate movements where the hip angle is approximately neutral.

4 Secure all the other body parts not involved in the test with appropriate straps. Ensure that the thigh, opposite leg, hips, chest and arms are appropriately stabilized. Make a note of the joint positions in case you need to replicate the test on another occasion. Attach the tensiometer or portable dynamometer to the limb near the malleoli. Ensure that the instrument is perpendicular to the tibia and on the sagittal plane (i.e. the plane formed by the tibia and femur). The movement must be performed on a plane parallel to the ground in order to avoid the effect of the gravitational force on the measurements. If the test is performed with the subject seated in a chair then the measurements of muscular moment are affected and must be corrected for the effect of the gravitational moment. For details of this procedure see Baltzopoulos and Brodie (1989).

5 Provide written, clear instructions to the subject concerning the purpose of the test and the experimental procedure. Explain in detail the requirement for maximum voluntary effort throughout the test and the use of feedback to enhance muscular output.

6 Familiarize the subject with the movement and allow at least two submaximal repetitions. An important aspect of isometric testing is the gradual increase of muscular force, avoiding sudden, ballistic movements. Allow the subject to ask any questions and be prepared to explain and demonstrate the test requirements.

7 Position the knee at approximately 90 degrees of knee flexion, start the test and maintain maximum effort for 5–7 seconds. Verbal and/or visual feedback and appropriate test instructions are adequate for maximum effort. Ensure that feedback is standardized and consistent between subjects.

8 After the test is completed, note the maximum force recorded. Measure the distance between the point of application and the joint centre of rotation and calculate the moment for knee extension as the product of force and moment arm. Record the isometric moment and the angular position where the maximum was recorded, on the data sheet for this practical. Allow a 1- to 2-minute rest and perform the test at angular position intervals of 10 degrees until full extension.

1.7.3 Data analysis

1 Plot the maximum moment of the knee extensors against the angular joint position (moment-joint position relationship).

2 Explain the increase/decrease of the moment during the range of movement and compare these findings with previously published studies examining this relationship in other muscle groups.

3 Establish the physiological/mechanical explanation for these findings.

4 Calculate the muscular force from the equation: Moment = Force × Moment Arm. The moment arm of the knee extensors at different joint positions is presented in Figure 1.6. Is the force-position similar to the moment position relationship? What are the main determinants of these relationships during knee extension and other joint movements such as knee and elbow flexion?

1.8 PRACTICAL 3: ASSESSMENT OF KNEE JOINT PROPRIOCEPTION PERFORMANCE: REPRODUCTION OF PASSIVE JOINT POSITIONING

1.8.1 Purpose

The purpose of this practical is to assess the error associated with the passive reproduction of a series of blinded target knee flexion angles in a sagittal plane. Knee flexion angles can be measured using the isokinetic dynamometer goniometer system and movement of the lever input arm can be achieved manually or in an automated fashion under software control as appropriate.

1.8.2 Procedure

1 Calibrate equipment according to the manufacturer's instructions. Record date, subject name, sex, age, body mass, height and training status.

2 Measure or estimate other anthropometric parameters if required (for example lean body mass, cross-sectional area of muscle groups, segment circumference and volume, muscle mass etc).

3 Allow the subject general warm-up/stretching exercises. Position the subject on the dynamometer without attaching the input arm. A sitting position with the hips flexed at approximately 1.74 rad (100 degrees) is recommended. A supine position may be preferable in order to increase muscular output and simulate movements where the hip angle is approximately neutral.

4 Select a random assessment order for involved and contralateral limbs. Align carefully the approximate joint axis of rotation with the axis of the dynamometer by modifying the subject's position and/or the dynamometer seat adjustments. For the knee test, align the lateral femoral epicondyle with the dynamometer axis and ensure that it remains in alignment throughout the test range of movement.

5 Attach the input arm of the dynamometer on the tibia above the malleoli and ensure that there is no movement of the leg relative to the input arm. Generally, a rigid connection is required between the segment and the various parts of the input arm.

6 Secure all the other body parts not involved in the test with the appropriate straps. Ensure that the thigh, opposite leg, hips, chest and arms are appropriately stabilized. Make a note of the seat configuration and the joint positions in case you need to replicate the test on another occasion.

7 Provide written, clear instructions to the subject concerning the purpose of the test and the experimental procedure. Explain in detail the requirement for a blinded presentation of the target knee flexion angle (the participant should be blindfold or a screen should be placed so as to visually obscure the knee position). In the case of automated control of the input arm movement and associated knee flexion, the participant may need to wear earphones in order to minimize the intrusion of the dynamometer's motor noise and potential cueing of knee position. Allow the subject to ask any questions and be prepared to explain in detail the test requirements.

8 Familiarize the subject with the procedures and allow at least three practice repetitions. Potential distractions to the participant should be minimized and the least possible number of investigators should be present in the laboratory in addition to the participant during data capture.

9 The participant's musculature should remain passive throughout the test procedures. Enter the appropriate data on the computer system, set the blinded target knee flexion angle by using the on-screen visual display of knee flexion angle (this should be blinded from the participant) and either moving the input arm manually or using the control software to 'drive' the input arm into position (select in random order from several angles spanning the knee range of motion). Ensure that each movement is initiated from a different knee flexion angle selected at random to minimize potential cueing effects. Attempt to standardize the movement velocity of the input arm to 5 deg·s^{-1} or to that which is permitted by the dynamometers control software. Once the blinded target knee flexion angle is achieved, maintain this target position for 5 seconds. Move the input arm to another position selected at random. After a 15-second period, initiate movement

of the input arm at the standardized velocity throughout the knee joint range of movement. The initial direction of movement (either towards or further away from the target angle before returning from the extreme of the range of motion) should be selected at random. During this movement, the participant should indicate the position at which equivalence of knee joint angle with the blinded target angle is achieved.

10 Repeat the ipsilateral assessment process at the other knee flexion angles of interest in random order. Repeat the whole series of assessments.

11 Repeat the whole assessment protocol on the contralateral limb.

1.8.3 Data analysis

1 Calculate the average error for joint position estimation across selected target knee flexion angles and duplicate trials.

2 Determine performance differences associated with contralateral limb comparisons.

3 Are there systematic differences in performance at the extremes and mid-range of the knee joint range of motion?

4 What improvements to the test procedures could be made to further limit the intrusion of potential cueing effects?

5 Discuss the physiological/mechanical basis for the findings.

6 Where the dynamometer system permits 'closed-chain' joint loading, repeat the above procedures. Discuss potential differences in responses between in knee joint proprioception performance under 'closed-chain' (weight-bearing) and 'open-chain' (non-weight-bearing) joint loading conditions.

1.9 PRACTICAL 4: ASSESSMENT OF KNEE JOINT PROPRIOCEPTION PERFORMANCE: REPRODUCTION OF NET JOINT MOMENT

1.9.1 Purpose

The purpose of this practical is to assess the error associated with reproduction of a series of blinded target net moments in the knee flexors in a sagittal plane. This protocol was designed to assess the ability of the subject to actively regulate or control the force production in the knee flexors. Knee flexion moments can be measured using the isokinetic dynamometry system at 0 degrees per second (static or isometric mode).

1.9.2 Procedure

1 Calibrate equipment according to the manufacturer's instructions and record date, subject name, sex, age, body mass, height and training status.

2 Measure or estimate other anthropometric parameters if required (for example lean body mass, cross-sectional area of muscle groups, segment circumference and volume, muscle mass etc).

3 Allow the subject general warm-up/stretching exercises. Position the subject on the dynamometer without attaching the input arm. A sitting position with the hips flexed at approximately 1.74 rad (100 degrees) is recommended. A supine position may be preferable in order to increase muscular output and simulate movements where the hip angle is approximately neutral.

4 Select a random assessment order for involved and contralateral limbs. Align carefully the approximate joint axis of rotation with the axis of the dynamometer during contraction by modifying the subject's position and/or the dynamometer seat adjustments. For the knee test, align the lateral femoral epicondyle with the dynamometer axis and ensure that it remains in alignment throughout the test range of movement.

5 Attach the input arm of the dynamometer on the tibia above the malleoli and ensure that there is no movement of the leg relative to the input arm. Generally a rigid connection is required between the segment and the various parts of the input arm.

6 Secure all the other body parts not involved in the test with the appropriate straps. Ensure that the thigh, opposite leg, hips, chest and arms are appropriately stabilized. Make a note of the seat configuration and the joint positions in case you need to replicate the test on another occasion.

7 Assessments may be undertaken in random order at several knee flexion angles of interest; for example, 0.44 rad (25 deg), 0.87 rad (50 deg) and 1.31 rad (75 deg).

8 Assess peak moment associated with maximal voluntary muscle actions of the knee flexors at each of the above knee flexion angles.

9 Provide written, clear instructions to the subject concerning the purpose of the test and the experimental procedure. Explain in detail the requirement for a blinded presentation of the target knee flexion moment (the participant should be blindfold or a screen should be placed so as to visually obscure the knee musculature and any feed-back from the computer control software to minimize the intrusion of the potential cueing of effort). Allow the subject to ask any questions and be prepared to explain in detail the test requirements.

10 Familiarize the participant with the procedures and allow at least three practice repetitions. Enter the appropriate data on the computer system.

11 Using the previously measured Peak Moment, participants should be requested to produce muscle actions eliciting a blinded target knee flexion moment of 50% Peak Moment under verbal direction from the test administrator. On attainment of the prescribed force level, the participant should be requested to maintain this prescribed moment for 3 seconds. The subject should then be requested to relax the involved musculature for a period of 15 seconds after which they are required to reproduce the prescribed force within a period of 5 seconds. The participant should be requested to indicate verbally perceived equivalence between the prescribed target moment and reproduced force levels before relaxing immediately the involved musculature to place a marker on the moment-time record. Following a 120-second recovery period, this procedure should be repeated.

12 Repeat the whole assessment protocol on the contralateral limb.

1.9.3 Data analysis

1 The observed discrepancy between the prescribed and reproduced force levels may be expressed as a percentage of Peak Moment (moment error [%]). The percentage error may be calculated as the mean of the two intra-session replicates and defined as the quotient of the difference between prescribed and perceived force divided by the maximal voluntary knee extensor strength multiplied by 100.

2 Calculate the average moment error across selected knee flexion positions and duplicate trials.

3 Determine performance differences associated with contralateral limb comparisons.

4 Are there systematic differences in performance at the extremes and mid-range of the knee joint range of motion?

5 What improvements to the test procedures could be made to further limit the intrusion of potential cueing effects?

6 Discuss the physiological/mechanical basis for the findings.

7 Repeat the assessments at blinded target knee flexion moments of 75% peak moment and 25% peak moment in random order and suggest what effect this would have on moment error.

FURTHER READING

Books:

Lieber R. (2002) *Skeletal muscle structure, function & plasticity: the physiological basis of rehabilitation* (2nd Edition). Lippincott Williams & Wilkins; London. ISBN 0781730619

Brown L. (ed) (2000) *Isokinetics in Human Performance.* Human Kinetics; Champaign, IL.

Chan K. M., Maffulli N., Korkia P., Li R. C. T. (eds) (1996) *Principles and Practice of Isokinetics in Sports Medicine and Rehabilitation.* Lippincott Williams & Wilkins; London.

Dvir Z. (2004) *Isokinetics: Muscle testing, interpretation and clinical applications, (2nd Edition.).* Churchill Livingstone; St Albans, UK.

Jones D., Round J. and de Haan A. (2004) *Skeletal muscle from molecules to movement: a textbook of muscle physiology for sport, exercise, physiotherapy and medicine.* Elsevier; Edinburgh.

Lephart S. M. (2000) *Proprioception and Neuromuscular Control in Joint Stability,* Human Kinetics; Champaign, IL.

Websites:

IOS Press: http://www.iospress.nl/loadtop/load.php?isbn=09593020

European Interdisciplinary Society for clinical and sports applications: http://www.eiscsa.com/

http://www.isokinetics.net/

REFERENCES

Aagaard P., Simonsen E. B., Trolle M., Bangsbo J. and Klausen K. (1995) Isokinetic hamstring/quadriceps strength ratio: influence from joint angular velocity, gravity correction and contraction mode. *Acta Physiologica Scandinavica;* **154**: 421–7.

Abernethy P., Wilson G. and Logan P. (1995) Strength and power assessment. *Sports Medicine;* **19**: 401–17.

Aoyagi Y. and Shephard R. (1992) Aging and muscle function. *Sports Medicine;* **14**: 376–96.

Appen L. and Duncan P. (1986) Strength relationship of knee musculature: effects of gravity and sport. *Journal of Orthopaedic and Sports Physical Therapy;* **7**: 232–5.

Arampatzis A., Karamanidis K., De Monte G., Stafilidis S., Morey-Klapsing G. and Brüggemann G.-P. (2004) Differences between measured and resultant joint moments during voluntary and artificially elicited isometric knee extension contractions. *Clinical Biomechanics*; **19**: 277–83.

Arampatzis A., De Monte G. and Morey-Klapsing G. (2007) Effect of contraction form and contraction velocity on the differences between resultant and measured ankle joint moments. *Journal of Biomechanics*; **40**: 1622–8.

Bailey A. K., Gleeson N. P., Rees D., Roberts S. N. J., Eston R. and Richardson J.,B. (2007) The effects of non-concurrent strength and endurance rehabilitation on the neuromuscular and musculoskeletal performance of knees treated with autologous chondrocyte implantation (ACI). In: (Orthopaedic Sports Medicine Committee, eds) *ISAKOS Media Collection (Volume 1)*. www.isakos.com International Society of Arthroscopy, Knee Surgery and Orthopaedic Sports Medicine; San Ramon, CA.

Baltzopoulos V. (1995a) A videofluoroscopy method for optical distortion correction and measurement of knee joint kinematics. *Clinical Biomechanics*; **10**: 85–92.

Baltzopoulos V. (1995b) Muscular and tibio-femoral joint forces during isokinetic knee extension. *Clinical Biomechanics*; **10**: 208–14.

Baltzopoulos V. (2008) Isokinetic dynamometry. In: (C. J. Payton and R. M. Bartlett, eds) *Biomechanical Evaluation of Movement in Sport and Exercise*. Routledge; Oxon: pp. 103–28.

Baltzopoulos V. and Brodie D. (1989) Isokinetic dynamometry: applications and limitations. *Sports Medicine*; **8**: 101–16.

Baltzopoulos V., Eston R. G. and MacLaren D. (1988) A comparison of power outputs on the Wingate test and on a test using an isokinetic device. *Ergonomics*; **31**: 1693–9.

Baltzopoulos V., Williams J. and Brodie D. (1991) Sources of error in isokinetic dynamometry: effects of visual feedback on maximum torque output. *Journal of Orthopaedic and Sports Physical Therapy*; **13**: 138–42.

Baratta R. and Solomonow M. (1991) The effects of tendon viscoelastic stiffness on the dynamic performance of isometric muscle. *Journal of Biomechanics*; **24**: 109–16.

Beam W., Bartels R. and Ward R. (1982) The relationship of isokinetic torque to body weight in athletes. *Medicine and Science in Sports and Exercise*; **14 (2)**: 178 (Abstract)

Behm D. and Sale D. (1993) Velocity specificity of resistance training. *Sports Medicine*; **15**: 374–88.

Bell G. and Wenger H. (1992) Physiological adaptations to velocity-controlled resistance training. *Sports Medicine*; **13**: 234–44.

Bemben M. (1991) Isometric muscle force production as a function of age in healthy 20- to 74-yr-old men. *Medicine and Science in Sports and Exercise*; **23**: 1302–9.

Bigland-Ritchie B., Fuglevand A. J. and Thomas C. K. (1998) Contractile properties of human motor units: is man a cat? *Neuroscientist*; **4 (4)**: 240–9.

Bishop P., Cureton K. and Collins M. (1987) Sex differences in muscular strength in equally trained men and women. *Ergonomics*; **30**: 675–87.

Bobbert M. and Harlaar J. (1992) Evaluation of moment angle curves in isokinetic knee extension. *Medicine and Science in Sports and Exercise*; **25**: 251–9.

Bottinelli R. and Reggiani C. (2000) Human skeletal muscle fibres: molecular and functional diversity. *Progress in Biophysics and Molecular Biology*; **73 (2–4)**: 195–262.

Bottinelli R., Canepari M., Pellegrino M. A. and Reggiani C. (1996) Force-velocity properties of human skeletal muscle fibres: myosin heavy chain isoform and temperature dependence. *Journal of Physiology*; **495 (2)**: 573–86.

Bouisset S. (1984) Are the classical tension-length and force-velocity relationships always valid in natural motor activities? In: (M. Kumamoto, ed) *Neural and Mechanical Control of Movement*. Yamaguchi Shoten; Kyoto: pp. 4–11.

Brooke M. and Kaiser K. (1974) The use and abuse of muscle histochemistry. *Annals of the New York Academy of Sciences*; **228**: 121–44.

Burdett R. G. and van Swearingen J. (1987) Reliability of isokinetic muscle endurance tests. *Journal of Orthopaedic and Sports Physical Therapy;* **8 (10):** 485–9.

Burke E. J., Wojcieszak I., Puchow M. and Michael E. D. (1985) Analysis of high intensity bicycle tests of varying duration. *Exercise Physiology: Current Selected Research;* **1:** 159–70.

Burke R. (1981) Motor units: anatomy, physiology, and functional organization. In: (V. Brooks, ed) *Handbook of Physiology.* American Physiological Society; Bethesola: pp. 345–422.

Cabri J. (1991) Isokinetic strength aspects of human joints and muscles. *Critical Reviews in Biomedical Engineering;* **19:** 231–59.

Cavanagh P. (1988) On muscle action versus muscle contraction. *Journal of Biomechanics;* **21:** 69 (Abstract)

Chapman A. (1985) The mechanical properties of human muscle. In: (L. Terjung, ed) *Exercise and Sport Sciences Reviews.* Macmillan; New York: pp. 443–501.

Clarkson P., Johnson J., Dexradeur D. *et al.* (1982) The relationship among isokinetic endurance, initial strength level and fibre type. *Research Quarterly for Exercise and Sport;* **53:** 15–19.

Coombs R., Garbutt G. and Cramp M. (2002) Comparison of conventional and functional hamstring-quadriceps moment ratios through a 90° range of leg motion. *Journal of Sports Sciences;* **20:** 3–4.

Coyle E., Feiring D., Rotkis T. *et al.* (1981) Specificity of power improvements through slow and fast isokinetic training. *Journal of Applied Physiology;* **51:** 1437–42.

Croce R. V. and Miller J. P. (2006) Angle- and velocity-specific alterations in torque and semg activity of the quadriceps and hamstrings during isokinetic extension-flexion movements. *Electromyography and Clinical Neurophysiology;* **46 (2):** 83–100.

Dauty M., Potiron-Josse M. and Rochcongar P. (2003) Consequences and prediction of hamstring muscle injury with concentric and eccentric isokinetic parameters in elite soccer players. *Annales de Readaptation et de Medecine Physique;* **46:** 601–6.

Decker M. J., Torry M. R., Wyland D. J., Sterett W. I. and Steadman J. R. (2003) Sex differences in lower extremity kinematics, kinetics and energy absorption during landing. *Clinical Biomechanics;* **18:** 662–9.

De Ste Croix, M. B. A., Deighan M. A. and Armstrong N. (2003) Assessment and interpretation of isokinetic muscle strength during growth and maturation. *Sports Medicine;* **33:** 727–43.

Devrome A. N. and MacIntosh B. R. (2007) The biphasic force-velocity relationship in whole rat skeletal muscle *in situ. Journal of Applied Physiology;* **102:** 2294–2300.

Dummer G., Clark D., Vaccano P. *et al.* (1985) Age-related differences in muscular strength and muscular endurance among female masters swimmers. *Research Quarterly for Exercise and Sport;* **56:** 97–102.

Duncan P., Chandler J., Cavanaugh D. *et al.* (1989) Mode and speed specificity of eccentric and concentric exercise. *Journal of Orthopaedic and Sports Physical Therapy;* **11:** 70–5.

Edman P. K. A. (1992) Contractile performance of skeletal muscle fibres. In: (P. V. Komi, ed) *Strength and Power in Sport.* Blackwell Scientific Publications; Oxford: 96–114.

Edman K. A. P., Mansson A. and Caputo C. (1997) The biphasic force-velocity relationship in frog muscle fibres and its evaluation in terms of cross-bridge function. *Journal of Physiology;* **503 (1):** 141–56.

Ennion S., Sant'Ana Pereira J., Sargeant A. J., Young A. and Goldspink G. (1995) Characterization of human skeletal muscle fibres according to the myosin heavy chains they express. *Journal of Muscle Research and Cell Motility;* **16 (1):** 35–43.

Enoka R. M. (2002) *Neuromechanics of Human Movement.* Human Kinetics; Champaign, IL.

Enoka R. and Stuart D. (1984) Henneman's `size principle': current issues. *Trends in Neurosciences;* **7:** 226–8.

Farina D. and Merletti R. (2004) Methods for estimating muscle fibre conduction velocity from surface electromyographic signals. *Medical and Biological Engineering and Computing;* **42 (4):** 432–45.

Fenn W.O. and Marsh B.S. (1935) Muscular force at different speeds of shortening. *Journal of Physiology;* **85:** 277–97.

Figoni S., Christ C. and Massey B. (1988)

Effects of speed, hip and knee angle, and gravity on hamstring to quadriceps torque ratios. *Journal of Orthopaedic and Sports Physical Therapy*; **9**: 287–91.

Fillyaw M., Bevins T. and Fernandez L. (1986) Importance of correcting isokinetic peak torque for the effect of gravity when calculating knee flexor to extensor muscle ratios. *Physical Therapy;* **66**: 23–9.

Finni T., Komi P. V. and Lepola V. (2001) *In vivo* muscle mechanics during normal locomotion is dependent on movement amplitude and contraction intensity. *European journal of applied physiology;* **85**: 170–6.

Finni T., Ikegawa S., Lepola V. and Komi P. V. (2003) Comparison of force-velocity relationships of vastus lateralis muscle in isokinetic and in stretch-shortening cycle exercises. *Acta Physiologica Scandinavica;* **177**: 483–91.

Frontera W., Hughes V., Lutz K. and Evans W. (1991) A cross-sectional study of muscle strength and mass in 45- to 78-yr-old men and women. *Journal of Applied Physiology;* **71**: 644–50.

Fu F. H. (1993) Biomechanics of knee ligaments. *Journal of Bone and Joint Surgery;* **75**A: 1716–27.

Fuglevan, A. J., Macefield V. G. and Bigland-Ritchie B. (1999) Force-frequency and fatigue properties of motor units in muscles that control digits of the human hand. *Journal of Neurophysiology;* **81** (4): 1718–29.

Gleeson N. P. (2009) Assessment of neuromuscular performance using electromyography. In (R. G. Eston and T. Reilly, eds.) *Kinanthropometry Laboratory Manual (3rd Edition): Exercise Physiology (Chapter 2).* Routledge; Oxon: pp. 41–71.

Gleeson N. P. and Mercer T. H. (1992) Reproducibility of isokinetic leg strength and endurance characteristics of adult men and women. *European Journal of Applied Physiology and Occupational Physiology;* **65**: 221–8.

Gleeson N. P. and Mercer T. H. (1994) An examination of the reproducibility and utility of isokinetic leg strength assessment in women. In: (F. I. Bell and G. H. Van Gyn, eds) *Access to Active Living: 10th*

Commonwealth and International Scientific Congress. University of Victoria; Victoria, B.C: pp. 323–7.

Gleeson N. P. and Mercer T. H. (1996) Influence of prolonged intermittent high intensity running on leg neuromuscular and musculoskeletal performance. *The Physiologist;* **39**: A-62.

Gleeson N. P., Mercer T. H., Morris K. and Rees D. (1997) Influence of a fatigue task on electromechanical delay in the knee flexors of soccer players. *Medicine and Science in Sports and Exercise;* **29**: (Suppl.) S281.

Gleeson N. P., Eston R. E., Marginson V. and McHugh M. (2003) Effects of prior concentric training on strength performance following exercise-induced muscle damage. *British Journal of Sports Medicine;* **37**: 119–25.

Green H. (1986) Muscle power: fibre type recruitment metabolism and fatigue. In: (N. Jones, N. McCartney and A. McComas, eds) *Human Muscle Power.* Human Kinetics; Champaign, IL: pp. 65–79.

Gregor R. J., Roy R. R., Whiting W. C., Lovely R. G., Hodgson J. A. and Edgerton, V. R. (1988) Mechanical output of the cat soleus during treadmill locomotion: *in vivo* vs. in situ characteristics. *Journal of Biomechanics;* **21**: 721–32.

Griffin L. Y., Albohm M. J., Arendt E. A., Bahr R, Beynnon B. D., Demaio M., Dick R. W., Engebretsen L.; Garrett W. E. Jr., Hannafin J. A., Hewett T. E., Huston L. J., Ireland M. L., Johnson R. J., Lephart S., Mandelbaum B. R., Mann B. J., Marks P. H., Marshall S. W., Myklebust G., Noyes F. R., Powers C., Shields C. Jr., Shultz S. J., Silvers H., Slauterbeck J., Taylor D. C., Teitz C. C., Wojtys E. M. and Yu B (2006) Understanding and preventing non-contact anterior cruciate ligament injuries. *American Journal of Sports Medicine;* **34**: 1512–32.

Gustafsson B. and Pinter M. (1985) On factors determining orderly recruitment of motor units: a role for intrinsic membrane properties. *Trends in Neurosciences;* **8**: 431–3.

Harrison P. (1983) The relationship between the distribution of motor unit mechanical properties and the forces due to recruitment and to rate coding for the generation of muscle force. *Brain Research;* **264**: 311–15.

Hasan Z. and Stuart D. G. (1988) Animal solutions to problems of movement control: the role of proprioceptors. *Annual Reviews in Neuroscience;* **11**: 199–223.

Henneman E. (1957) Relation between size of neurons and their susceptibility to discharge. *Science;* **126**: 1345–7.

Herzog W. (2004) History dependence of skeletal muscle force production: Implications for movement control. *Human Movement Science;* **23**: 591–604.

Herzog W. (2005) Force enhancement following stretch of activated muscle: critical review and proposal for mechanisms. *Medical and Biological Engineering and Computing;* **43** (2): 173–80.

Herzog W., Lee E. J. and Rassier D. E. (2006) Residual force enhancement in skeletal muscle. *Journal of Physiology;* **574**: 635–42.

Hewett T. E., Myer G. D. and Ford K. R. (2001) Prevention of anterior cruciate ligament injuries. *Current Women's Health Report;* **3**: 218–24.

Heyward V., Johannes-Ellis S. and Romer J. (1986) Sex differences in strength. *Research Quarterly for Exercise and Sport;* **57**: 154–9.

Hill A. (1938) The heat of shortening and the dynamic constants of muscle. *Proceedings of the Royal Society of London;* **126B**: 136–95.

Hinson M., Smith W. and Funk,, S. (1979) Isokinetics: a clarification. *Research Quarterly;* **50**: 30–5.

Hislop H. and Perrine J. (1967) The isokinetic concept of exercise. *Physical Therapy;* **47**: 114–17.

Horiuti K. (1997) The cross-bridge mechanism studied by flash photolysis of caged ATP in skeletal muscle fibers. *Japanese Journal of Physiology;* **47**: 405–15.

Hortobagyi T. and Katch F. (1990) Eccentric and concentric torque-velocity relationships during arm flexion and extension. *European Journal of Applied Physiology;* **60**: 395–401.

Ichinose-Muraoka Y., Kawakami Y., Ito M., Kanehisa H. and Fukunaga T. (2000) *In vivo* estimation of contraction velocity of human vastus lateralis muscle during 'isokinetic' action. *Journal of Applied Physiology;* **88** (3): 851–6.

Iossifidou A. N. and Baltzopoulos V. (1996) Angular velocity in eccentric isokinetic dynamometry. *Isokinetics and Exercise Science;* **6** (1): 65–70.

Iossifidou A. N. and Baltzopoulos V. (2000) Inertial effects on moment development during isokinetic concentric knee extension testing. *Journal of Orthopedic Sports Physical Therapy;* **30** (6): 317–23.

Jaric , S. (2003) Role of body size in the relation between muscle strength and movement performance. *Exercise and Sport Sciences Reviews;* **31** (1): 8–12.

Jaric S., Radosavljevic-Jaric S. and Johansson H. (2002) Muscle force and muscle torque in humans require different methods when adjusting for differences in body size. *European Journal of Applied Physiology;* **87** (3): 304–7.

Johannsen H. (1991) Role of knee ligaments in proprioception and regulation of muscle stiffness. *Journal of Electromyography and Kinesiology;* **1**: 158–79.

Johannsen H., Sjolander P. and Sojka P. (1986) Actions of γ-motoneurons elicited by electrical stimulation of joint afferent fibers in the hind limb of the cat. *Journal of Physiology (London);* **375**: 137–52.

Kanehisa H., Ikegawa S. and Fukunaga T. (1994) Comparison of muscle cross-sectional area and strength between untrained women and men. *European Journal of Applied Physiology and Occupational Physiology;* **68**: 148–54.

Kanehisa H., Okuyama H., Ikegawa S. and Fukunaga T. (1996) Sex difference in force generation capacity during repeated maximal knee extensions. *European Journal of Applied Physiology and Occupational Physiology;* **73**: 557–62.

Kannus P., Jarvinen M. and Lehto M. (1991) Maximal peak torque as a predictor of angle-specific torques of hamstring and quadriceps muscles in man. *European Journal of Applied Physiology and Occupational Physiology;* **63**: 112–18.

Kannus P., Cook L. and Alosa D. (1992) Absolute and relative endurance parameters in isokinetic tests of muscular performance. *Journal of Sport Rehabilitation;* **1**: 2–12.

Kellis E. (1998) Quantification of quadriceps and hamstring antagonist activity. *Sports Medicine;* **25**: 37–62.

Kellis E. and Baltzopoulos V. (1997) The effect

of antagonist moment on the resultant joint moment during concentric and eccentric efforts of the knee extensors. *European Journal of Applied Physiology;* 76: 253–9.

Kellis E. and Baltzopoulos V. (1999) *In vivo* determination of the patella tendon and hamstrings moment arms in adult males using videofluoroscopy during submaximal knee extension and flexion. *Clinical Biomechanics;* 14 (2): 118–24.

Kereshi S., Manzano G. and McComas A. (1983) Impulse conduction velocities in human biceps brachii muscles. *Experimental Neurology;* 80: 652–62.

Komi P. (1984) Biomechanics and neuromuscular performance. *Medicine and Science in Sports and Exercise;* 16: 26–8.

Komi P. (1986) The stretch-shortening cycle and human power out-put. In: (N. Jones, N. McCartney and A. McComas, eds) *Human Muscle Power.* Human Kinetics; Champaign, IL: 27–39.

Komi P., Viitasalo J., Rauramaa R. and Vihko V. (1978) Effects of isometric strength training on mechanical, electrical and metabolic aspects of muscle function. *European Journal of Applied Physiology;* 40: 45–55.

Komi P.V., Fukashiro S. and Järvinen M. (1992) Biomechanical loading of Achilles tendon during normal locomotion. *Clinics in Sports Medicine;* 11: 521–31.

Krauspe R., Schmidt M. and Schaible H. G. (1992) Sensory innervation of the anterior cruciate ligament. *Journal of Bone Joint Surgery (Am);* 74: 390–7.

Kroll W., Bultman L., Kilmer W. and Boucher J. (1990) Anthropometric predictors of isometric arm strength in males and females. *Clinical Kinesiology;* 44: 5–11.

Kulig K., Andrews J. and Hay J. (1984) Human strength curves. In: (R. Terjung, ed) *Exercise and Sport Sciences Reviews.* Macmillan; New York: 417–66.

Lanza I. R., Towse T. F., Caldwell G. E., Wigmore D. M. and Kent-Braun J. A. (2003) Effects of age on human muscle torque, velocity, and power in two muscle groups. *Journal of Applied Physiology;* 95 (6): 2361–9.

Lattanzio P. J. and Petrella R. J. (1998) Knee proprioception: A review of mechanisms, measurements, and implications of muscular fatigue. *Othopaedics;* 21: 463–70.

Lephart S. M., Kocher M. S., Fu F. H., Borsa P. A. and Harner C. D. (1992) Proprioception following anterior cruciate ligament reconstruction. *Journal of Sports Rehabilitation;* 1: 188–96.

Lesmes G., Costill D., Coyle E. and Fink W. (1978) Muscle strength and power changes during maximum isokinetic training. *Medicine and Science in Sports and Exercise;* 10: 266–9.

MacDougall J., Sale D., Elder G. and Sutton J. (1982) Muscle ultrastructural characteristics of elite powerlifters and bodybuilders. *European Journal of Applied Physiology;* 48: 117–26.

MacIntosh B., Gardiner P. E. and McComas A. J. (2005) *Skeletal Muscle: Form and Function;* Human Kinetics; Champaign, IL.

Maganaris C. N. and Baltzopoulos V. (1999) Predictability of *in vivo* changes in pennation angle of human tibialis anterior muscle from rest to maximum isometric dorsiflexion. *European Journal of Applied Physiology and Occupational Physiology;* 79 (3): 294–7.

Maganaris C. N., Baltzopoulos V. and Sargeant A. J. (1998) *In vivo* measurements of the triceps surae complex architecture in man: Implications for muscle function. *Journal of Physiology;* 512 (2): 603–14.

Marginson V., Rowlands A. R., Gleeson N. P. and Eston R.G. (2005) Comparison of the symptoms of exercise-induced muscle damage after an initial and repeated bout of plyometric exercise in men and boys. *Journal of Applied Physiology;* 99: 1174–81.

Mathiassen S. E. (1989) Influence of angular velocity and movement frequency on development of fatigue in repeated isokinetic knee extensions. *European Journal of Applied Physiology and Occupational Physiology;* 59 (1/2): 80–8.

Maughan R. Watson J. and Weir J. (1983) Strength and cross-sectional area of human skeletal muscle. *Journal of Physiology;* 388: 37–49.

Mercer T. H. and Gleeson N. P. (2002) The utility of measurement and evaluation in evidence-based clinical practice. *Physical Therapy in Sport;* 3 (1): 27–36.

Milner-Brown H., Stein R. and Lee R. (1975) Synchronization of human motor units: possible roles of exercise and supraspinal reflexes. *Electroencephalography and Clinical Neurophysiology*; 38: 245–54.

Minshull C., Gleeson N., Walters-Edwards M., Eston R. and Rees D. (2007) Effects of acute fatigue on the volitional and magnetically-evoked electromechanical delay of the knee flexors in males and females. *European Journal of Applied Physiology*; 100: 469–78.

Montgomery L. C., Douglass L. W. and Deuster P. A. (1989) Reliability of an isokinetic test of muscle strength and endurance. *Journal of Orthopaedic and Sports Physical Therapy*; 10 (8): 315–22.

Morse C. I., Thom J. M., Reeves N. D., Birch K. M. and Narici M. V. (2005) *In vivo* physiological cross-sectional area and specific force are reduced in the gastrocnemius of elderly men. *Journal of Applied Physiology*; 99 (3): 1050–5.

Morse C. I., Thom J. M., Mian O. S., Birch K. M. and Narici M. V. (2007) Gastrocnemius specific force is increased in elderly males following a 12-month physical training programme. *European Journal of Applied Physiology*; 100 (5): 563–70.

Morrow J. and Hosler W. (1981) Strength comparisons in untrained men and trained women athletes. *Medicine and Science in Sports and Exercise*; 13: 194–7.

Nemeth P., Solanki L., Gordon D., Hamm T. M., Reinking R. M. and Stuart D. G. (1986) Uniformity of metabolic enzymes within individual motor units. *Journal of Neuroscience*; 6: 892–8.

Perrin D. H. (1986) Reliability of isokinetic measures. *Athletic Training*; 10: 319–21.

Perrin D. (1993) *Isokinetic Exercise and Assessment*. Human Kinetics; Champaign, IL.

Perrin D., Robertson R. and Ray R. (1987) Bilateral isokinetic peak torque, torque acceleration energy, power, and work relationships in athletes and nonathletes. *Journal of Orthopaedic and Sports Physical Therapy*; 9: 184–9.

Perrine J. and Edgerton V. (1978) Muscle force-velocity and power-velocity relationships under isokinetic loading. *Medicine and Science in Sports and Exercise*; 10: 159–66.

Pollack G. (1983) The cross-bridge theory. *Physiological Reviews*; 63: 1049–113.

Pope M. H., Johnson R. J., Brown D. W. and Tighe C. (1979) The role of the musculature in injuries to medial collateral ligament. *Journal of Bone and Joint Surgery (Am)*; 61: 398–402.

Prietto C. and Caiozzo V. (1989) The *in vivo* force-velocity relationship of the knee flexors and extensors. *American Journal of Sports Medicine*; 17: 607–11.

Pua Y. H., Teik-Hin K. M. and Teo Y. Y. (2006) Effects of allometric scaling and isokinetic testing methods on the relationship between countermovement jump and quadriceps torque and power. *Journal of Sports Sciences*; 24: 423–32.

Rahnama N., Reilly T., Lees A. and Graham-Smith P. (2003) Muscle fatigue induced by exercise simulating the work rate of competitive soccer. *Journal of Sports Sciences*; 21: 933–42.

Rees D. and Gleeson N. P. (1999) The scientific assessment of the injured athlete. *Proceedings of the Football Association – Royal College of Surgeons Medical Conference*. Edinburgh, October.

Reeves N. D., Narici M. V. and Maganaris C. N. (2003) Strength training alters the viscoelastic properties of tendons in elderly humans. *Muscle and Nerve*; 28: 74–81.

Reeves N. D., Narici M. V. and Maganaris C. N. (2004) Effect of resistance training on skeletal muscle-specific force in elderly humans. *Journal of Applied Physiology*; 96: 885–92.

Reeves N. D., Maganaris C. N. and Narici M. V. (2005) Plasticity of dynamic muscle performance with strength training in elderly humans. *Muscle and Nerve*; 31 (3): 355–64.

Rijkelijkhuizen J. M., De Ruiter C. J., Huijing P. A. and De Haan A. (2003) Force/velocity curves of fast oxidative and fast glycolytic parts of rat medial gastrocnemius muscle vary for concentric but not eccentric activity. *Pflugers Archiv European Journal of Physiology*; 446 (4): 497–503.

Ryushi T., Hakkinen K., Kauhanen H. and Komi P. (1988) Muscle fibre characteristics, muscle cross-sectional area and force production in strength athletes, physically active males and females. *Scandinavian Journal of Sports Sciences*; 10: 7–15.

Sale D. G. (1991) Testing strength and power. In: (J. D. MacDougall, H. A. Wenger and H. J. Green, eds) *Physiological Testing of the High Performance Athlete* (2nd Edition). Human Kinetics; Champaign, IL: pp. 21–106.

Sale D. G. (1992) Neural adaptation to strength training. In: (B. V. Komi, ed) *Strength and Power in Sports*. Blackwell Scientific Publications; Oxford: pp. 249–65.

Schantz P., Randal-Fox A., Hutchison W., Tydén A. and Astrand P. O. (1983) Muscle fibre type distribution of muscle cross-sectional area and maximum voluntary strength in humans. *Acta Physiologica Scandinavica*; 117: 219–26.

Seger J. Y. and Thorstensson A. (2000) Electrically evoked eccentric and concentric torque-velocity relationships in human knee extensor muscles. *Acta Physiologica Scandinavica*; 169 (1): 63–9.

Semmler J. G. (2002) Motor unit synchronization and neuromuscular performance. *Exercise and Sport Sciences Reviews*; 30 (1): 8–14.

Shephard R. (1991) Handgrip dynamometry, Cybex measurements and lean mass as markers of the aging of muscle function. *British Journal of Sports Medicine*; 25: 204–8.

Simoneau J., Lortie G., Boulay M., Marcotte M., Thibault M.C. and Bouchard C. (1985) Human skeletal muscle fibre type alteration with high-intensity intermittent training. *European Journal of Applied Physiology*; 54: 250–3.

Spudich J. A. (2001) The myosin swinging cross-bridge model. *Nature Reviews Molecular Cell Biology*; 2: 387–92.

Swanik C. B., Lephart S. M., Giannantonio F. P. and Fu F. H. (1997) Reestablishing proprioception and neuromuscular control in the ACL-injured athlete. *Journal of Sport Rehabilitation*; 6: 182–206.

Tesch P. and Karlsson P. (1985) Muscle fibre type and size in trained and untrained muscles of elite athletes. *Journal of Applied Physiology*; 59: 1716–20.

Thistle H., Hislop H., Moffroid M. and Lohman E. (1967) Isokinetic contraction: a new concept of resistive exercise. *Archives of Physical Medicine and Rehabilitation*; 48: 279–82.

Thomas D., White M., Sagar G. and Davies C. (1987) Electrically evoked isokinetic plantar flexor torque in males. *Journal of Applied Physiology*; 63: 1499–502.

Thorstensson A., Grimby G. and Karlsson J. (1976) Force-velocity relations and fibre composition in human knee extensor muscle. *Journal of Applied Physiology*; 40: 12–16.

Tsaopoulos D. E., Baltzopoulos V. and Maganaris C. N. (2006) Human patellar tendon moment arm length: Measurement considerations and clinical implications for joint loading assessment. *Clinical Biomechanics*; 21 (7):657–67.

Walters-Edwards M., Minshull C., Gleeson N. P., Rees D., Bailey A., Nordvall M. (2006) The effects of serial fatiguing tasks and acute recovery on indices of neuromuscular and sensorimotor performance of the knee flexors in females. *Proceedings of the 11th Annual Congress of the European College of Sport Science*. Lausanne, July.

Watkins M. (1993) Evaluation of skeletal muscle performance. In: (K. Harms-Ringdahl, ed), *Muscle Strength*. Churchill Livingstone; London: pp. 19–36.

Westing S. and Seger J. (1989) Eccentric and concentric torque-velocity characteristics, torque output comparisons, and gravity effect torque corrections for the quadriceps and hamstring muscles in females. *International Journal of Sports Medicine*; 10: 175–80.

Westing S., Seger J., Karlson E. and Ekblom B. (1988) Eccentric and concentric torque-velocity characteristics of the quadriceps femoris in man. *European Journal of Applied Physiology*; 58: 100–4.

Wickiewicz T., Roy R., Powell P., Perrine J. and Edgerton R. (1984) Muscle architecture and force velocity in humans. *Journal of Applied Physiology*; 57: 435–43.

Widrick J. J., Trappe S. W., Costill D. L. and Fitts R. H. (1996) Force-velocity and force-power properties of single muscle fibers from elite master runners and sedentary men. *American Journal of Physiology – Cell Physiology*; 271 (2): 40–2, C676–C683

Wilkie D. (1950) The relation between force

and velocity in human muscle. *Journal of Physiology (London);* **110**: 249–54.

Winter E. M. and Nevill A. M. (2009) Scaling: adjusting for differences in body size. In (R. G. Eston and T. Reilly, eds.) *Kinanthropometry Laboratory Manual (3rd Edition): Anthropometry (Chapter 11).* Routledge; Oxon: pp. 300–320.

CHAPTER 2

ASSESSMENT OF NEUROMUSCULAR PERFORMANCE USING ELECTROMYOGRAPHY

Nigel Gleeson

2.1 AIMS

The aims of this chapter are:

- to describe the application of electromyography (EMG) to the study of neuromuscular performance;
- to describe the relationship between physiological and recorded EMG signals;
- to provide an understanding of how the fidelity of the recorded EMG signal may be influenced by factors intrinsic to the muscle and by factors that may be controlled by the test administrator;
- to describe some of the characteristics of the EMG recording instrumentation;
- to evaluate the value and limitations of using EMG in the assessment of temporal neuromuscular control;
- to describe factors that affect the validity and reliability of measurements derived from EMG techniques.

2.2 INTRODUCTION

Muscle is an excitable tissue that responds to neural stimulation by contracting and attempting to shorten within its articular system. The many functions that are served by associated changes to the stiffness or movement of a joint system permit effective and safe interaction with our environment. Any mechanical response to a stimulus for action is preceded by an asynchronous pattern of neural activation and an electrical response from the muscle fibres. EMG is a technique for recording the changes in the electrical potential of a muscle when it is activated by a motor nerve impulse.

The fundamental structural and functional unit of neuromuscular control (Enoka 1994; Aidley 1998) is the motor unit consisting of a single motor nerve fibre (efferent a-motoneuron) and all the muscle fibres that are innervated by it. These can be distributed throughout a large portion of the volume of the muscle (Nigg and Herzog 1994). Each muscle is comprised of multiple motor units. The contractile force produced by the whole muscle is partly determined by the number of motor units activated by neural stimulation and by the rate at which stimulation occurs.

Stimulation of the muscle fibre at the neuromuscular junction (motor end-plate) elicits a reduction of the electrical potential of the cell and initiates a propagation of an action potential throughout the muscle fibre.

The electrical waveform resulting from this depolarization is known as the motor (fibre) action potential (MAP). Each nerve impulse produces synchronous contraction in all the muscle fibres of the motor unit before being followed by a wave of ionic repolarization. The spatial and temporal summation of MAPs from the fibres associated with a given motor unit is termed a motor unit action potential (MUAP). Repeated neural stimulation elicits a train of MUAPs (MUAPT) (Basmajian and De Luca 1985) and the summation over time of these trains from the various motor units is referred to as the physiological EMG signal (Figure 2.1). Of the electrical and mechanical events that follow neural activation, it may be somewhat easier to detect the electrical events. Electromyography is a fundamental tool in functional anatomy and clinical kinesiology for objectively assessing and recording when a muscle is active (Grieve 1975). It is commonly used to evaluate the roles of specific muscles in movement situations (Basmajian and De Luca 1985), to present biological feedback for the improvement of motor performance and to investigate the effects of neuromuscular conditioning.

There are two basic methods of recording muscular activations involving invasive intramuscular or surface (interferential) electromyography (please see sub-section 2.4, 'EMG Electrodes,' for more detailed information). The latter will be the focus of discussions within this chapter, as the technique arguably offers its greatest utility for applications within sports medicine and science. The technique requires neither the training in specialist clinical imaging techniques, such as ultrasound to insert needle electrodes with anatomical precision, nor offers the risk of electrodes breaking that would be expected during intramuscular electromyography during aggressive dynamic manoeuvres.

While EMG offers important and useful applications of kinanthropometric interest, it is also fraught with potential limitations that threaten to detract from its utility. The recorded EMG signal is an intrinsically complex history of the muscular electrical activity that can be influenced at any given time by many variables. It is thus a proxy of the physiological EMG signal. Its interpretation is considered to be even more complex.

2.3 FACTORS INFLUENCING THE ELECTROMYOGRAPHIC SIGNAL

The primary factors that have an influence on the recorded signal, and ultimately its interpretation, can be segregated into intrinsic and extrinsic factors. 'Intrinsic' factors reflect physiological, anatomical and biochemical characteristics within the muscle. 'Extrinsic' factors include the external system for detecting and recording the EMG signals. In this respect, the quality of the recorded EMG signal and its proper interpretation are very much dependent on the electrode type, structure and placement. However, depending on the application, the recorded EMG signal and its interpretation can also be influenced by other components of this system during modification of the signal (amplifier) and the storage of the resulting waveform (digital recording system).

2.3.1 The musculature and intrinsic factors influencing the recorded EMG signal

Intrinsic factors include the following: the number of active motor units at any specified time of the muscle action; fibre-type composition of the muscle; blood flow in the muscle; fibre diameter; depth and location of the active fibres within the muscle relative to the electrode detection surfaces; amount of tissue between the surface of the muscle and the electrode; firing characteristics of the motor units (firing rates of the motor units and potential for synchronization); and the characteristics of the twitch of the motor unit.

These factors contribute in various ways to changes in the amplitude and frequency content (spectrum) of the EMG signal by

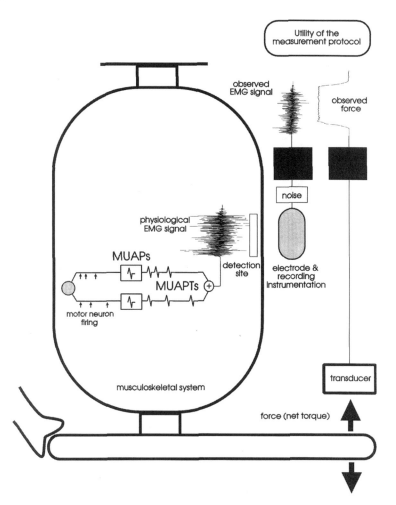

Figure 2.1 A schematic representation of the electromechanical sequelae of neural activation of the muscle.

means of spatial filtering and changes to the conduction velocity. For example, the fibre diameter may influence the amplitude, shape and conduction velocity of the action potentials that constitute the signal; increased distance of the fibres of active motor units from the detection electrode hinders the detection of separate MUAPs. Also, the type and amount of subcutaneous tissue modifies the characteristics of the signal by rejecting some of the high-frequency components of the signal, especially during the recording of surface EMG.

Limitations in current technology and knowledge mean that for the most part such intrinsic factors cannot be controlled. The contributions of some of the factors (for example, the depth and location of the active fibres within the muscle relative to the electrode detection surfaces) would be expected to add to the background experimental error or noise associated with the measurement of the recorded EMG signal. Others, for example fibre diameter and firing characteristics of the motor units, may be influenced systematically by changes to the neuromuscular system associated with specific conditioning interventions. The relative importance of these factors to the utility of the EMG signal remains elusive.

2.3.2 The system for detecting the EMG signals: extrinsic factors

Electrode configuration describes the shape and area of the electrode detection surfaces and determines the number of active motor units that are registered by the detecting electrodes. The distance between the electrode detection surfaces determines the bandwidth or the range of frequencies that the differential electrode configuration will be capable of detecting. The location of the electrode with respect to the musculotendinous junction and the motor end-plates in the muscle moderates the amplitude and frequency characteristics of the detected signal. The location of the electrode on the surface of the muscle, with respect to the anatomical border of the muscle, regulates the potential for cross-talk. The term 'cross-talk' is used to describe the interference of EMG signals from muscles other than the ones under the electrode (Basmajian and De Luca 1985). The orientation of the detection surfaces relative to the pennation characteristics of the muscle fibres influences the value of the measured conduction velocity of the action potentials and ultimately the frequency content and amplitude of the signal. Extrinsic factors such as those listed above, can be controlled by the test administrator. Optimized practice should increase the utility, validity and reliability (reproducibility) of measurements involving EMG.

Other aspects of the EMG instrumentation can contribute to the utility of the measurement. The following sections overview key aspects of instrumentation used to optimize detection and recording of the EMG signal.

2.4 EMG ELECTRODES

The EMG can be recorded by means of invasive and surface electrodes. Invasive EMG is necessary for recording activity in deep muscles, but involves the use of indwelling (fine wire) electrodes that are inserted with a hypodermic needle. While the fine wire electrodes have a very small diameter (approximately 0.025 mm), which means that they are relatively painless in use, several problems limit the potential use of such invasive procedures in sports medicine and science. These include ethical issues relating to possible breakage during dynamic manoeuvres and associated risks of infection. The method also requires clinical imaging techniques, such as ultrasound, to overcome the difficulties of locating deep muscles precisely. High electrode impedance, potential distortion of the recorded signal due to deformation and changes in the effective length of the electrode and damage to adjacent muscle fibres during insertion are technical issues, which have also contributed to the fact that these procedures are rarely deployed outside specialist research applications or where indicated clinically. Fine wire electrodes have been advocated clinically when the patient is obese, oedematous or in cold conditions, but are rarely used even under such circumstances (Engbaek and Mortensen 1994).

Surface EMG techniques generally permit access to electrical signals from superficial muscles only. Both active and passive surface electrodes require placement on the surface of the skin above the musculature of interest. Active surface electrodes require a power supply to operate and thus demand electrical isolation. This type of surface electrode has the advantage of not requiring any skin preparation or electrode gels, but they are likely to increase the overall noise level during the amplification of the EMG signal (De Luca and Knaflitz 1990).

Passive surface electrodes are routinely used for monitoring neuromuscular transmission in a bipolar configuration in which the difference in potential between two adjacent electrodes is utilized to reduce mains-related interference during subsequent amplification (see later section). Paediatric electrodes are often recommended due to their increased current density. These are generally up to 10 mm in diameter although

10 mm × 1 mm rectangular-shaped electrodes are likely to interact with greater numbers of muscle fibres. Disposable, self-adhesive, electrocardiogram (ECG) surface electrodes are of the Ag/AgCl type consisting of a silver metal base coated electrolytically with a layer of ionic compound and silver chloride, and pre-gelled with electrolyte gel. This type of electrode is electrochemically stable and reduces polarization potentials that cause signal distortion. A full discussion of electrode characteristics can be found in Geddes and Baker (1989).

The detection of the activity of single motor units has been of interest for research as well as diagnostic applications. Traditionally, detection has been confined to the use of invasive needle electrodes. These electrodes selectively record the signature of the compound action potentials (MUAP) from the multiple motor fibres associated with the motor unit or motor units in closest proximity to an electrode's tip. High density, multi-channel surface electromyography has been developed recently. Using this technique, spatial and morphological features of MUAPs can be detected by two-dimensional arrays of electrodes, multi-channel amplifiers and specialized signal decomposition processing procedures. The approach offers non-invasive techniques for quantifying the number of motor unit action potentials (MUAPs) appearing in the surface electromyogram, motor unit recruitment and firing rates, and thus potentially valuable information about the level of activation of the motoneuron pool. Although these techniques have not yet become routinely used in contemporary scientific and clinical practice, they continue to receive scrutiny in the literature (Disselhorst-Klug et al. 1999; Gazzoni et al. 2004; Kleine et al. 2007) and potentially offer useful additional approaches to the evaluation of patterns of muscle activation.

When not located within a fixed array, surface electrodes are subject to movement artefacts that in turn disturb the electrochemical equilibrium between the electrode and skin, and therefore cause a change in the recorded electrode potential. Electrode gel minimizes this change by moving the metal and electrolyte away from the skin so that movement of the electrode does not disturb the metal-electrolyte junction; thereby the potential is unaltered. Electrode gel contains Cl- as the principal anion in order to maintain good contact. Lewes (1965) showed that electrolyte gel with high chloride and abrasive content is unnecessary with the input impedance of an amplifier in excess of 2 mega ohms (MΩ). Reduction of impedance at the electrode-skin barrier is important to minimize induced currents from external electrical and electromagnetic sources. Without skin preparation, skin impedance can be in the order of 100 kilo ohms (kΩ) depending on the measuring technique. Impedance has components of resistance, capacitance and inductance making it frequency-dependent. In tissue such as muscle, fat and skin, the capacitance and resistance are significant components (Basmajian and De Luca 1985).

It is usually desirable to reduce skin impedance and contact resistance by means of appropriate skin preparation. Many techniques have been used to reduce electrode-skin impedance and motion artefacts. Medina et al. (1989) and Tam and Webster (1977) measured offset potential and showed a decrease with 'light' abrasive skin preparation. More invasive methods include a skin-puncture technique with a micro-lancet (Burbank and Webster 1978) and scratching with a needle and the reverse side of a sterile lancet to break the superficial layer of dead skin (Okamoto et al. 1987). De Talhouet and Webster (1996) suggested that stripping skin layers with Scotch tape could reduce that motion artefact incurred by stretching of the skin, which was considered to be the least skin preparation technique employed prior to application of electrodes. Patterson (1978) found no significant difference in electrode-skin impedance between acetone and alcohol when each was used as a solvent for degreasing the skin. However, Almasi and Schmitt (1974) suggested differences in electrode-skin impedance between the sexes and in addition, wide and systematic variation depending on where the electrodes were placed on the body. All strategies should aim to minimize (less than 10 k ohm and preferably less than 5 k ohm), standardize and maintain the measured impedance (measured across the expected signal frequency range) between sets of recording electrodes after the electrode sticker and sterilized electrode have been attached. These precautions will maximize the detected EMG signal compared to the noise inherent in the remainder of the recording instrumentation. The latter is particularly important where high performance (high input impedance) amplifiers are not available.

2.4.1 Positioning of the electrodes

Whatever the type of surface EMG electrode, the location of the electrodes is of fundamental importance. This should be away from the location of the motor end-plate (De Luca and Knaflitz 1990). The amplitude and frequency spectrum of the EMG signal are affected by the location of the electrode with respect to the innervation zone, the musculotendinous junction and the lateral edge of the muscle. The preferred location is in the mid-line of the belly of the muscle between the nearest innervation zone and the musculotendinous junction. The EMG signal with the greatest amplitude is typically detected in this location. The latter process requires the use of an external device to elicit activation of the muscle. Where a stimulator is not available, electrodes may be placed over the mid-point of the muscle belly (Clarys and Cabri, 1993) and this may offer a reasonable approach to the standardization of the recorded signal. Further consistency is afforded to the recorded EMG signal by placing the two detector electrodes with the line between them parallel to the direction of the muscle fibres or pointing to the origin and insertion of the muscle where the muscle

fibres are not linear or without a parallel arrangement (Clarys and Cabri 1993).

Since surface EMG electrodes are susceptible to cross-talk, the separation of the electrodes determines the degree of localization of the detected signal. A standard electrode separation distance of 10 mm has been recommended (Basmajian and De Luca 1985). Furthermore, as discussed previously, several factors have the potential to influence the spatial filtering, amplitude and frequency characteristics of the detected signal. These include the depth and location of the active fibres within the muscle with respect to the electrode detection surfaces, the amount of tissue between the surface of the muscle and the electrode and the fibre diameter. Thus, even subtle deviations in the positioning of the detecting electrodes relative to the motor units and muscle fibres originally contributing to the physiological signal may alter the spatial filtering characteristics of the detection volume, may be sufficient to place a new set of active motor units within the detection volume of the electrode and remove some of the motor units from the detection volume. Incorrect positioning would be expected to produce additional error or noise in the recorded EMG signal as well as in associated indices of neuromuscular performance. Under the most unfavourable circumstances of relative migration of the electrode and active fibres, this could actually invalidate the recorded EMG signal. This potential for error raises concern for inter-trial assessments of the same muscle, where electrodes are re-affixed on each test occasion or during dynamic muscle actions where there is inevitability about relative movement between a specific detecting electrode and the active muscle fibre population. Tattooing of the skin at the site of the electrode position or preserving the geography of the site by mapping on an acetate sheet the electrode position relative to moles, small angiomas and permanent skin blemishes would be expected to facilitate signal stability and comparability across inter-trial assessments of the neuromuscular performance of the same musculoskeletal system.

2.5 OVERVIEW OF HARDWARE

A typical physiological recording system will consist of an isolated connection to the participant, signal conditioning in terms of amplifiers and filters, and an analogue-to-digital converter before collection and storage on the PC.

As outlined earlier, where the electrode assembly connects directly to the participant circuit, an isolation barrier is necessary for electrical-participant connection safety. These terms are defined under the relevant safety requirements for medical electrical equipment (for example, see British Standards Institute documentation, BS EN 60601–1: 2006 Medical electrical equipment. General requirements for basic safety and essential performance. BSI British Standards, London, UK [http://www.bsi-global.com/] and international equivalents: for example, see International Electrotechnical Commission IEC 60601–2-26: 2003. Geneva, Switzerland [http://www.iec.ch/]). The safety implication for the amplifier circuitry is that the participant circuit is electrically isolated from the amplifying equipment and the connection provides no path to ground. An isolation transformer and a frequency modulator often provide this isolation barrier. After passing through a transformer with a low primary-to-secondary ratio, the modulated carrier is demodulated and the original signal is recovered. This isolated input demands that the electrical potential of the participant is floating, the participant is isolated from earth and the mains equipment is under a single fault condition and protected by an allowable participant leakage current.

2.5.1 Signal amplification

The detected EMG signal will have amplitude in the order of 5–9 mV when recorded by means of surface electrodes. This relatively low-level signal typically requires amplification to match the electrical characteristics of a variety of suitable signal recording instrumentation systems. The gain describes this process and is calculated as the ratio of output to input voltages. The gains used in EMG are typically high and vary in the range from 100 to 10 K depending on the instrumentation system and application.

There are several important aspects concerning design of amplifiers that are critical to the meaningful collection of the surface EMG signal and related physiological data (Basmajian and De Luca 1985). The amplifier should be situated close to the participant during the recordings in order to minimize noise that can be produced from many sources and appear as mains interference across the amplifier's input terminals. The source of this interference can be the participant or the environment or instrumentation being used in the participant environment. In particular, these sources can principally be due to electrostatic or electromagnetic induction from mains or radio-frequency sources. Electrical currents may be induced from an electrostatic source, and the participant can act as a plate of a capacitor that may have its other plate as the alternating current source potential, or objects such as other equipment, the operating table or people nearby. These capacitative-linked electrostatic potentials will vary as the potential path to ground varies with the object and they may appear as 50-Hz interference at the input of the amplifier. In addition, interference occurs close to cables carrying alternating current due to the constantly changing flux linkage across a conductor within its field. An electromagnetically induced current flowing at the same frequency as the source would be produced. Further, 50-Hz interference can be introduced due to earth-loop interference where two earth points have slightly different potentials and a leakage current can flow due to the potential difference between the two. Finally, radio-frequency greater than 100 kHz can enter the recording system by a number of routes. This may be through the mains mixed with 50 Hz current, or directly propagated through the air. These interference effects can all be accentuated by high electrode impedance. If the electrode impedance is low the induced current, due to the interference, will not cause a significant drop in potential at the input of the amplifier, which, in turn, will be exhibited as minimal 50-Hz interference on the input signal.

Good amplifier design aims to reduce interference; all biological amplifiers are of a differential type with a good Common Mode Rejection Ratio (CMRR). The CMRR is a measure of how well the amplifier rejects any interference or common mode signal that will appear at both input terminals of a differential amplifier. The amplifier magnifies the difference between the voltage appearing at the two input terminals (a tri-phasic wave derived from the bi-phasic wave associated with each electrode from the bipolar electrode configuration) so that that the common mode signal is rejected (Basmajian and De Luca 1985). The CMRR is defined as:

CMRR = amplifier gain for a signal voltage / amplifier gain for a common mode voltage

When expressed in decibels then:
CMRR (dB) = 20log10(CMRR).

Another feature of a biological amplifier that ensures faithful reproduction of the signal of interest is the high input impedance of the amplifier. The high input impedance ensures that most of the signal voltage is presented at the input of the amplifier. If the input impedance was similar to that of the skin and tissue impedance, a high proportion of the signal voltage would be lost due to the potential drop across the electrodes. Therefore, the signal voltage at the input to the amplifier would be much less.

2.6 RECORDING OF DATA

Many systems have been used to record the amplified EMG signal. In contemporary practice, analogue-to-digital conversion and computer processing are the most commonly used recording methods. Where excessive connection cabling threatens to intrude on the ecological validity of the recording of EMG during sports manoeuvres, radio telemetry and portable digital data loggers have also been used to transmit and provide intermediate storage for EMG signals, respectively.

The highest frequency expected in the spectrum of the evoked muscle compound action potential is of the order of 500 Hz – 1 kHz when using surface electrodes. This will be higher when using wire electrodes (~ 1 kHz) and much higher with needle electrodes (10 kHz). In order to prevent erroneous measurement of the sampled signal (aliasing), the rate of digitization must be at least twice that of the highest frequency expected in the sample. This is termed the *Nyquist* frequency. Any frequency above the *Nyquist* frequency will be recorded as an artefact. This would suggest that an analogue-to-digital sampling rate of at least 2 kHz should be deployed so as not to introduce additional error into the recorded signal during surface EMG, for example. Ideally, the sampling rate should be several times higher than the *Nyquist* frequency (Basmajian and De Luca 1985). However, depending on the application and the number of EMG recording channels for instance, the need to use such high sampling rates may exceed the capacity of some systems used routinely in contemporary practice. An alternative strategy would be to digitally filter the signal with an anti-aliasing hardware filter in order to make sure only frequencies below this optimum frequency pass into the recording system. Wherever possible, from a technical and logistical perspective, it may be prudent to attempt to record the EMG signal in an unadulterated fashion in the first instance. Recording in this way would involve maintaining the analogue-to-digital sampling rates at a level to ensure a significant margin of 'safety' between the highest frequency expected in the detected signal and the *Nyquist* frequency, and no additional filtering save that intrinsically linked with the detection site. This procedure would preserve the integrity of the original recorded signal and make it available for a variety of appropriate post hoc manipulations involving software-derived digital filtering and data smoothing procedures.

The recorded EMG offers potential utility when used in conjunction with other markers of neuromuscular and musculoskeletal performance to investigate the temporal and sequential activation of the musculature associated with exercise. A critical evaluation and comparison of all applications that have used EMG in this way would be impracticable. In the next section, selected applications will be described and potential limitations to their successful deployment highlighted.

2.7 SELECTED APPLICATIONS UTILIZING EMG TECHNIQUES

2.7.1 Assessment of temporal musculoskeletal and neuromuscular control

In many sports and daily activities, precise motor acquisition and rapid reaction time are as important as the capacity to produce force. This is perhaps best illustrated when considering the protection from injury offered to a joint system by the musculature associated with its movement. A conceptual model that defines the limits of normal joint movement comprises primary ligamentous restraints interacting with the other static sabilizers (osseous geometry, capsular structures, and menisci) and with the dynamic muscle sabilizers (Fu 1993). An unfavourable interaction of the dynamic and static sabilizing factors may predispose sports participants to increased threat of ligamentous disruption (Gleeson *et al.* 1997a). The time-course of

ligamentous rupture can be very rapid (300 ms; Rees 1994).

Optimal functioning of the dynamic muscle sabilizers of the joint system may be fundamental to limit or prevent the severity of ligamentous injury. The neuromuscular system has a limited reaction time response to dynamic forces applied to the joint. Electromechanical delay (EMD) is defined as the time delay between the onset of muscle activity and onset of force generation (Norman and Komi 1979). The EMD is determined by the time taken for the contractile component to stretch the series elastic component (SEC) of the muscle (Winter and Brookes 1991). It represents an important aspect of neuromuscular reaction time, during which there could be unrestrained development of forces of sufficient magnitude to damage ligamentous tissue in synovial joints (Huston and Wojtys 1996; Mercer *et al.* 1998; Gleeson *et al.* 2000; Shultz *et al.* 2001). The importance of this index of performance can be exemplified further by recognizing that factors such as muscle fatigue can cause increases in EMD latency of up to 70%. This dramatic loss of performance has been shown in studies involving acute bi-lateral cycling fatigue tasks (Zhou *et al.* 1996), single-leg control trials involving prolonged cycling fatigue tasks (Mercer *et al.* 1998), isokinetic fatigue trials (Gleeson *et al.* 1997b) and under more ecologically-valid fatigue trials involving the simulation of metabolic and mechanical stresses of team games and high-intensity running (Gleeson *et al.* 1998). The extent of this change in EMD performance may also be influenced by the loading of viscoelastic structures, which can cause creep within the affected tissue and a modulation of the neuromuscular performance characteristics of the associated musculature (Chu *et al.* 2003; Solomonow *et al.* 2003; Solomonow 2004; Sbriccoli *et al.* 2005).

The visco-elastic behaviour may be indicative of transient impairment to joint musculoskelatal robustness. According to this model, it is possible that fatigue-related slowing of excitation-contraction coupling or altered visco-elastic behaviour of collagen within the SEC of muscle and ligamentous structures of the knee may be reflected in an increased EMD. This alteration to temporal neuromuscular control has been observed in maximal voluntary actions of the musculature associated with the knee joint using EMG and static force assessment techniques.

2.7.2 Assessment of EMD involving static and dynamic muscle activations

While EMD may offer potentially important insights into the neuromuscular and musculoskeletal performance of a joint system, attempts to estimate the precise time at which a muscle begins and ends being activated and at which net torque is provided by the joint system to do useful work are fraught with difficulties. The latter have not yet been completely resolved in the literature and offer a threat to the validity of the measurement. In addition, the protocols deployed to assess EMD are associated with technical and biological variability (noise) that may decrease measurement reproducibility and reliability and ultimately compromise the specificity, sensitivity and utility of the measurement (Minshull *et al.* 2008). Nevertheless, the measurement of EMD serves as a useful model from which to appreciate some of the limitations associated with the assessment of neuromuscular performance by way of EMG.

2.7.3 Measurement techniques

The validity of the measurement protocol used to assess EMD and other neuromuscular indices of performance may be inexorably linked to how well it mimics the stresses imposed on the neuromuscular system by 'real world' activity. In the case of ligamentous injury to the joint system, this has been observed in a spectrum involving high- and low-velocity episodes of joint movement (Rees 1994).

It may be appropriate therefore to attempt to assess EMD across this joint movement velocity-spectrum of joint movements. Of fundamental importance to the assessment of EMD involving both static and dynamic muscle actions is the determination of whether any segment of the muscle in the vicinity of the electrode becomes active. This requires that the recorded surface EMG signal should not be substantively contaminated by cross-talk from adjacent muscles and that the amplitude of the EMG signal exceeds the amplitude of the noise in the detection and recording equipment. The issue of cross-talk is particularly important because the amplitude of the signal being analyzed is relatively low at the initiation of muscular activity (Figures 2.2 and 2.3) and progressively emerges from the background noise level. Similar problems afflict the detection of significant force (net torque) generation relative to the electrical noise inherent in the transducer. While the placement of the electrode in the mid-line of the belly of the muscle may offer considerable protection against the intrusion of cross-talk in the detection of minimal signal, it may not always be a sufficient precaution (De Luca and Knaflitz 1990). The assessment of EMD associated with dynamic muscle actions (for example, assessments involving isokinetic dynamometry; Vos *et al.* 1991) may be more susceptible to issues such as cross-talk, since there is a greater potential for repetitive deviations in the positioning of the detecting electrodes relative to the motor units and muscle fibres contributing to the physiological signal at any time.

2.7.4 Factors influencing the measurement of EMD

The delay between the detected EMG signal and the force would be expected to depend on several physiological and mechanical factors including the fibre-type composition and firing rate dynamics of the muscle and the viscoelastic properties of the muscle and tendon tissues. It may also be influenced

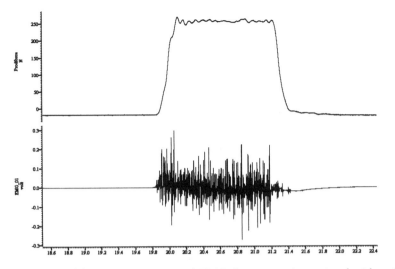

Figure 2.2 A time plot of force (upper trace) and EMG (lower trace) associated with a single static maximal voluntary muscle action of the m. biceps femoris at 0.44 rad of knee flexion.

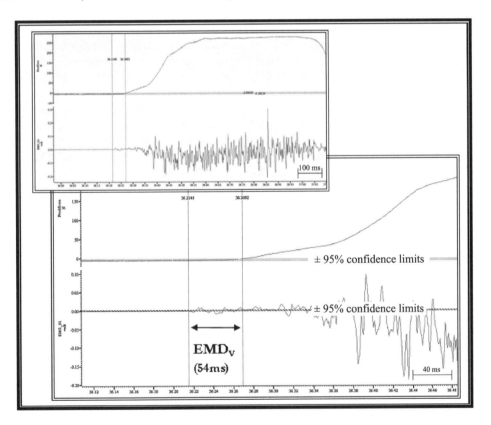

Figure 2.3 A time plot of force (upper trace) and EMG (lower trace) associated with the initial phase of a single static maximal voluntary muscle action of the m. biceps femoris at 0.44 rad of knee flexion. The time difference between left vertical line (muscle activation) and right vertical line (initiation of force response) may be defined as the electromechanical delay (EMD; 54.0 ms) (see text).

by protective neuromuscular inhibitory mechanisms associated with joint injury, deconditioning and limited MU recruitment patterns (Doyle *et al.* 1999; Rees and Gleeson 1999). In general, a muscle consisting of a greater percentage of fast-twitch muscle fibres may be expected to have a shorter time delay between the EMG signal and the registration of force. The signal propagation velocity and the interactive effect of this with differential positioning of the detection surfaces of the electrodes relative to the sites of innervation of the muscle may further influence the estimate of EMD. This may influence inter-individual comparisons of EMD in particular. It may also contribute a limitation to the precision with which estimates of EMD can be made in intra-individual comparisons where the detection surfaces have been relocated and reference cannot be made to anatomical mapping of electrode positioning.

A standardized approach to the discrimination of the recorded EMG signal and joint net torque from background noise is to consider each recorded signal as a stochastic variable in which 95% confidence limits can be constructed around the mean noise amplitude (Minshull *et al.* 2007).

The onset of electrical activity may be defined as the first point in time at which the electrical signal has exceeded consistently the 95% confidence limits of the isoelectric line associated with the background electrical noise amplitude and quiescent muscle, and which would be the first deviation of the recorded electrical signal that would be considered congruent with physiological activation of the muscle. A similar approach can be deployed to detect significant force generation relative to the background noise of the transducer and associated instrumentation. For example, the onset of muscle force may be defined as the first point in time at which the force record has exceeded consistently the 95% confidence limits associated with the electrical noise amplitude of the load cells (see Figure 2.3 and Figure 2.4 [discussed later]). This approach would generally improve upon the quality of outcome measures derived by means of visual inspection of signals.

2.7.5 Electromechanical delay and fatiguing exercise

There is accumulating evidence from the recent literature (Horita and Ishiko 1987; Mercer and Gleeson 1996; Zhou *et al.* 1996; Gleeson *et al.* 1997b; Gleeson *et al.* 1998; Mercer *et al.* 1998; Minshull *et al.* 2007) that fatiguing exercise increases EMD during maximal voluntary muscle actions in the knee extensors and flexors. Other reports involving sub-maximal muscle actions have suggested the opposite (Vos *et al.* 1991). The processes involved in the conversion of excitation into muscle force can potentially contribute to the fatigue-related changes in the force-generating capability observed in the current study. However, it has been proposed that the majority of the EMD is determined by the time taken to stretch the SEC (Norman and Komi 1979), most of which is situated at the connective tissue attachments at the end of the muscle fibres (McComas, 1996). Therefore, the potential fatigue-related impairment of EMD may be attributed to a complex interaction of neuromuscular and biomechanical factors. The rate of shortening of the SEC of muscle, most of which is situated at the connective tissue attachments at the end of the muscle fibres (McComas 1996) may be the primary cause of EMD in a given muscle (Norman and Komi 1979). This compliance predominates over tendon compliance during movement requiring sub-maximal tension development (Alexander and Bennet-Clark 1977). However, the limb segment orientation and moment of inertia and unfavourable joint position for net muscle torque development near to full knee extension, may present substantive challenges to the whole musculotendinous unit. Thus, any increases in compliance of the musculotendinous unit associated with the exercise would tend to increase the EMD. Increased muscle temperature may be an important moderator in the latter process (Zhou *et al.* 1998). Temperature changes are associated with an increase in neural propagation velocity and an increase in compliance in the connective tissue (Shellock and Prentice 1985). Since the time to shorten the SEC of muscle substantially exceeds the time leading to the activation of cross-bridges during concentric muscle actions (Norman and Komi 1979), the influence of increased compliance may prevail and contribute to increase in EMD.

Furthermore, habituated exposure to scenarios where knee joint stability may be under threat might condition the neuromuscular system of individuals at functional joint angles. The subsequent formation of pre-programmed responses that provide fast compensatory reactions to joint perturbations (Latash 1998) may quickly harness the SEC and enhance EMD performance. However, under conditions of muscle fatigue and sustained loading, this capability may be diminished due to a reduction of the effectiveness of the fastest, most powerful motor units, impairing the temporal capability of the muscle to 'gather in' a more compliant SEC of the muscle.

It is assumed that the asymptomatic, well-conditioned and motivated individual undertaking exercise involving maximal voluntary muscle actions is able to recruit heavily from populations of larger high-threshold fast-acting motor units to contribute to the measured neuromuscular performance. Larger high-threshold fast-contracting motor units have been observed to be recruited preferentially over the slow-contracting types in tasks demanding rapid ballistic muscle actions (Grimby and Hannerz 1977; Sale 1992) and it is known that normal recruitment order according to the Henneman 'size-principle' may be violated under some conditions (Enoka 1994). This premise cannot be assured under all circumstances involving volitional efforts. For example, it is unclear how well orderly recruitment is preserved under conditions of fatigue (Enoka

1994). It is possible that under conditions of fatigue or involving sub-maximal muscle actions, the determination of 'voluntary' EMD reflects variable contributions from slow acting, fatigue-resistant motor units since these motor units are recruited first according to the 'size principle' under most circumstances.

Although not yet widely used in contemporary clinical and scientific practice, evoked M-wave and fused tetanic responses from the knee extensor and flexor muscle groups by means of magnetic stimulation of the femoral nerve and anterior horn cells associated with the sciatic nerve (L4-L5), respectively, may offer interesting insights into the ultimate physiological performance capability of these muscle groups (Figure 2.4). It is interesting to note that under conditions of muscle activation in which the musculature is not protected by central and peripheral nervous system inhibitory responses, EMD latency responses are significantly reduced compared to their volitional counterparts in all asymptomatic and symptomatic populations with musculoskeletal injury (Minshull *et al.* 2007). The latter population has shown some of the greatest reductions in latency between volitional and evoked EMD performance (up to 70% reduction in latency compared to volitional performance) (Rees and Gleeson 1999).

Other techniques for the estimation of temporal neuromuscular control have been proposed, which offer utility under both static and dynamic assessment conditions. The estimation of EMD by means of cross-correlation techniques entails constructing a linear envelope without phase shift with respect to the raw, rectified EMG signal data. Subsequently, the phase difference between the linear envelope and the force recorded during static or dynamic muscle actions is established by cross-correlation procedures (Vos *et al.* 1990; Vos *et al.* 1991). The technique offers an estimate of EMD performance based on a large proportion of the rising phase of the force production and EMG response (for

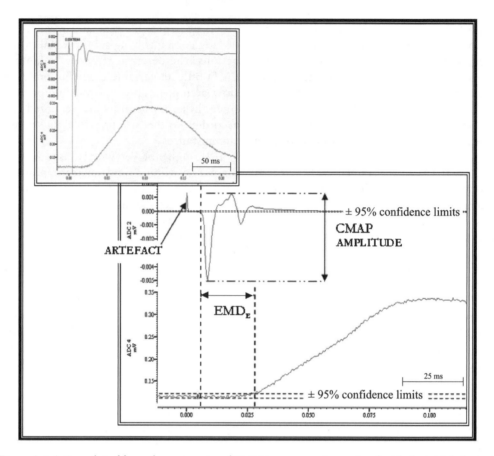

Figure 2.4 A time plot of force (lower trace) and EMG (upper trace) associated with the initial phase of a single evoked M-wave response from the knee flexor muscle group (m. biceps femoris) at 0.44 rad of knee flexion by means of magnetic stimulation anterior horn cells associated with the sciatic nerve (L4-L5). The time difference between stimulation (0.0 ms) and the left vertical dashed line (muscle activation) represents latency of neural propagation (5.8 ms). The time difference between muscle activation and the right dashed vertical line (initiation of force response) may be defined as the electromechanical delay (EMD; 22.5 ms [i.e. 28.3 ms – 5.8 ms]) (see text).

example, between 0% and 75% of peak force, Figure 2.5) and therefore provides a 'holistic' view of the muscle activation characteristics that may be averaged over several cycles of muscle activation and relaxation. The EMD may be defined as the delay at which the highest correlation is observed (Figure 2.6). It may be considered particularly effective in assessment conditions involving voluntary muscle activations and in which there are difficulties associated with precisely controlling the dynamic movements, for example in assessments involving bi-

directional isokinetic dynamometry (Gleeson *et al.* 1997b).

2.8 MEASUREMENT UTILITY: PRINCIPLES OF MEASUREMENT AND EVALUATION IN INDICES OF NEUROMUSCULAR PERFORMANCE INVOLVING EMG

While appreciation of factors that threaten to compromise the fidelity of the recorded EMG signal is fundamental to the integrity

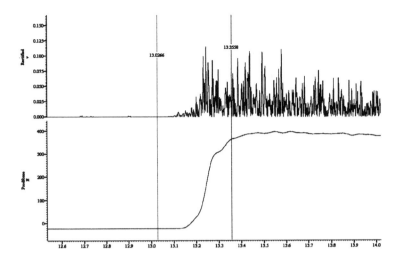

Figure 2.5 A time plot of force (lower trace) and EMG (rectified, raw, upper trace) associated with the initial phase (0–75% of peak force) of a single static maximal voluntary muscle action of the m. biceps femoris at 0.44 rad of knee flexion. The phase difference between muscle activation initiation of force response may be measured using cross-correlation techniques (see text).

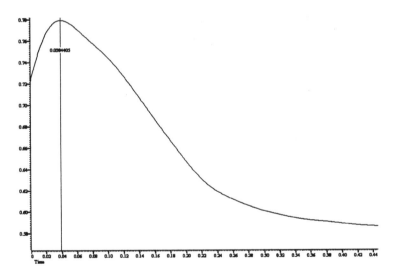

Figure 2.6 Cross-correlation (r, vertical axis) between force and EMG associated with the initial phase (0–75% of peak force) of a single static maximal voluntary muscle action of the m. biceps femoris at 0.44 rad of knee flexion. An index of EMD may be defined as the time (phase difference) at which the highest correlation is observed (vertical line, 38 ms).

of the index of neuromuscular performance, other measurement issues contribute equally to the utility of the index within a specific measurement context. The assessment of indices of neuromuscular performance, such as EMD, has been deployed in a variety of measurement environments.

Contemporary empirical and scientific research spans a continuum of demands that includes the examination of difference in performance capabilities within a single test session and evaluation of treatment interventions over time. The goal of these evaluations may be to ascertain the extent of contralateral differences between injured and non-injured limbs within one test occasion (intra-session), or to monitor changes in performance associated with a programme of conditioning or physical therapy (inter-day) within an individual or within a group of participants. Each research application (e.g. intra-session vs inter-day) presents unique challenges in the selection of an appropriate test protocol to enable confident discrimination between performances (Altman 1991).

A fundamental attribute of any test of performance capacity must be that it offers at least a minimal level of measurement precision commensurate with its intended use (Mercer and Gleeson 2002). The extent of the need for precision of measurement can be considerable. For example, following peripheral magnetic stimulation of motor nerves, neurological abnormality may need to be diagnosed on the basis of EMG-derived contralateral transmission latency differences of only 1.5 ms, which corresponds typically to an 11% deficit (Chokroverty *et al.* 1993). Furthermore, discrimination of changes in the performance levels of the elite strength athlete may be similarly demanding of experimental design sensitivity, given that neuromuscular performance might be expected to vary by only ± 5% over the competitive season (Gleeson and Mercer 1992). Consequently, the selected indices of performance need to offer reliability characteristics that ensure sensitivity to a given level of change in performance capability expected within the particular research setting (Mercer and Gleeson 2002).

In scenarios involving inter-group treatment comparisons, participant numbers can be manipulated to achieve a desired level of experimental power (Lipsey 1990). However, contemporary clinical practice frequently dictates the necessity for a case study approach. Important clinical decisions regarding whether or not an individual is fully rehabilitated, or may return to sport without excessive risk of re-injury are often made on an individual basis (Rees 1994).

Moreover, any given 'diagnostic' index of performance should be associated with reliability characteristics that ensure the proper discrimination of scores of particular individuals from those within a group. This would facilitate the effective targeting of limited clinical resources towards sub-populations of patients with particular needs from within larger patient groups (Gleeson and Mercer 1996). Investigations of this nature demand stringent criteria for precision of measurement in order to make meaningful performance comparisons (Mercer and Gleeson 2002). Appropriate protocol considerations include the number of inter- and intra-trial replicates that might be required; estimates of which are calculated on the basis of the reproducibility and reliability characteristics of the performance indices of interest. Without careful consideration of issues potentially detracting from measurement precision, it is easy to overestimate the available precision of measurement and to not account fully for the biological variability inherent in repeated neuromuscular performance assessments (Mercer and Gleeson 2002).

2.8.1 Reproducibility and reliability

Once repeated exposures to the criterion test elicit negligible increases in performance, subjects may be considered to have become habituated to the criterion test and its associated environment. This process may be verified using repeated measures analysis of variance (ANOVA) techniques for sub-samples of appropriate size (Verducci 1980; Kirkendall *et al.* 1987; Thomas *et al.* 2005). The process of learning will include an accommodation phase in which the specific movements, neuromuscular patterns and demands of the test will become familiar to the subject. Subsequent multiple measurements on the criterion test will be prone to random measurement variability or error, with smaller variations being indicative of greater reliability, consistency or reproducibility of the criterion test (Verducci 1980; Sale 1991;

Mercer and Gleeson 2002; Thomas *et al.* 2005).

2.8.2 Variability in performance

The two principal sources of variability in the index of neuromuscular performance are biological variation, which is the relative consistency with which a subject can perform, and experimental error, which describes variations in the way the assessment is conducted (Sale 1991). Examples of these categories of variation include time-of-day effects on indices of neuromuscular performance (Reilly *et al.* 1993) and technological/instrumentation variation, respectively (Mercer and Gleeson 2002). Selected contributions to the latter sources of variation have been considered in the previous sections. The goal of the test administrator may be considered to be to dilute error variance to best reveal the true performance score, consequently permitting the proper interpretation of the effects of physiological intervention or adaptation.

In situations where the assessment of reliability of the criterion test is intended to be reflected mainly in terms of the consistency or reproducibility of observed scores, it may be estimated effectively using coefficient of variation (V%) corrected for small sample bias (Sokal and Rohlf 1981). This process would allow the quantification of variability in performance for an individual and subsequently the minimum number of intra-subject replicates that would be required to attain a criterion measurement error or precision. Group mean estimates of the reproducibility of the index of EMD and related latencies of volitional muscle activation have ranged between 3.2% and 10.1% for repeated inter-day assessments (Viitasalo *et al*, 1980; Gleeson *et al.* 1998; Minshull *et al.* 2002).

Reliability models relating to the fluctuations of a participant's repeated test scores within the context of sub-sample performance variability may be estimated using the intra-class correlation coefficient (R_I). This estimate of reliability is based on partitioning models in ANOVA, but is susceptible to misinterpretation where significant inter-subject heterogeneity exists. There have been reports of superior single measurement reliability (intra-class correlation coefficient) characteristics associated with magnetically evoked estimates compared with the equivalent volitional estimates of EMD performance in asymptomatic young adult populations (0.84 vs 0.80, respectively) (Minshull *et al.* 2002). Scores of greater than 0.80 have been considered acceptable in clinical contexts (Currier 1984), whereas this criterion may be entirely inappropriate when attempting to discriminate amongst a group of high-performance athletes demonstrating homogeneous performance characteristics. Bland-Altman plots and the construction of 95% confidence limits associated with repeated measurements of EMD may also be useful in estimating the reproducibility responses in this context (Bland and Altman 1986; Nevill *et al.* 2009).

As alluded to earlier, sensitivity or precision of a criterion test may be defined as the ability to detect small changes in an individual's performance, or relative positional changes of an individual's performance within a sub-sample. This discrimination ability relates directly to the reliability of the test and may be estimated and further quantified using SEM in conjunction with R_I and the sub-population standard deviation (a measure of homogeneity/heterogeneity) (Mercer and Gleeson 2002). For given levels of error variance associated with the performance of each individual, greater heterogeneity and separation between measurements of individuals within a group would be expected to enhance measurement sensitivity and the capability for detecting differences amongst the performances of those individuals. Furthermore, in 'case study' interventions, assuming an appropriate current trainability phenotype, sensitivity should be enhanced in situations where there is greatest potential for improvement in performance. This includes situations in which the individual has undertaken limited prior strength conditioning or is rehabilitating following injury. The reader is directed to more complete reviews of measurement issues relating to the assessment of neuromuscular performance (Mercer and Gleeson 2002).

2.8.3 Measurement objectivity and standardization

Objectivity is the degree to which a test measurement is free from the subjective influences and concomitant additional variability due to the differential styles of test administrators (Thomas et al. 2005). Standardization of all aspects of the test administration, including for example, the test administrator, test instrumentation, calibration of the instrumentation, subject positioning and restraint, lever-arm length, delivery and content of test instructions, will minimize the intrusion of measurement error from extraneous variables and enhance reliability (Sale 1991).

2.8.4 Measurement validity

A criterion test that does not yield consistent results is compromised in its validity because the results cannot be depended upon (Thomas et al. 2005). As such, the identification of protocols that will confer appropriate test reproducibility and reliability is a prerequisite for establishing test validity. Validity of a test or measurement instrument refers to the degree of soundness or appropriateness of the test in measuring what it is designed to measure (Vincent 2005). The validity of the index of EMD may be ascertained by a logical analysis of the measurement procedures or an estimate of its concurrent validity may be obtained by correlating measurements with those from other established factors contributing to muscle contractile performance, such as predominance of a particular isoform of myofibrillar protein (Thomas et al. 2005). The

relevance and relative importance of the use of EMD within sports medical applications may be estimated by considering its likely predictive validity (Thomas et al. 2005). The predictive validity of EMD as a discriminator of predisposition to musculoskeletal injury may be supported if individuals who reported knee injury had demonstrated prior insufficiency in EMD capability compared to uninjured counterparts, or compared to their own uninjured limb.

2.8.5 Utility of the protocol

A fundamental attribute of any assessment of EMD must be that it offers at least a minimal level of measurement rigour and integrity commensurate with its intended use. The utility of the test protocol may be considered to be the net outcome from several competing demands (Gleeson and Mercer 1996).

Within the context of a given application, the selection of threshold reproducibility and reliability criteria to meet the demand for appropriate measurement rigour will in turn regulate the selection of suitable protocol characteristics (for example, required number of replicates, inter-replicate time duration and mode of action). The logistical constraints, time-related pressures and costs associated with replicate testing of the same individual may be considerable in the context of case study investigations. Furthermore, the concerns regarding the subject waning in motivation as a result of multiple replicate testing over protracted periods may compromise the validity of a test involving maximal voluntary muscle actions. The proper manipulation of the inter-replicate periods to minimize the effects of confounding physiological adaptation factors, such as potentiation or fatigue, would tend to further lengthen the test period and exacerbate the problem.

Factors that contribute to the measurement utility of EMD, and which may be directly manipulated by the test administrator, need to be fully appraised and optimized. This category includes factors such as electrode positioning, number of replicates, inter-replicate interval, presentation of test instructions, and isolation of the involved muscle groups. Other factors, such as the available EMG instrumentation, associated technological error, and biological variation in performance, are relatively immutable. The net overall effect of factors that tend to enhance measurement rigour but detract from ease of administration of testing and participant tolerance to testing may be to override any practical use for the measurement in relation to its intended purpose. These issues remain a substantive challenge for the administrator of the test.

2.9 PRACTICAL 1: ASSESSMENT OF ELECTROMECHANICAL DELAY OF THE KNEE FLEXORS ASSOCIATED WITH STATIC MAXIMAL VOLUNTARY MUSCLE ACTIONS

Prior to conducting this practical, ensure that any conditions imposed by the local ethics committee for experimentation in humans have been met and that any participants are asymptomatic.

2.9.1 Purpose

The purpose of this practical is to assess the EMD of the knee flexors associated with static maximal voluntary muscle actions and knee flexion angles at which key ligamentous structures are placed under mechanical strain and non-contact knee joint injuries have occurred (Rees 1994). This Practical requires appropriate surface electrodes, an EMG recording system as described previously and a dynamometry system permitting prone gravity-loaded knee flexion movements in the sagittal plane.

2.9.2 Procedures

1 Test apparatus calibration. Prior to and repeatedly during testing the technical error performance of the measurement instrument should be subject to validity assessments using inert gravitational loading. Experimentally recorded force-transducer responses should be compared to those expected during the application of standard known masses through a biologically valid range (for example 0 N – 600 N). Recorded forces should demonstrate an overall mean technical error (± standard error of the estimate) that is acceptable in the context of the assessment to be undertaken. For example, low technical error associated with the force transducer (for example, 0.2 ± 0.03 N across a total of more than 10 calibrations) facilitates the test administrator's ability to identify the point at which force generation is initiated. Similarly, where the appropriate instrumentation is available to generate known patterns of voltage potential, the calibration of the EMG signal voltage recording system can be verified.

2 Record the date, participant's name, sex, age, relevant anthropometric details and training status.

3 The detected EMG signals may be recorded with bi-polar surface electrodes (self-adhesive, silver-silver chloride, 10 mm diameter, inter-electrode distance 20 mm centre to centre) applied to the preferred leg following standard skin preparation (inter-electrode impedance < 5000 Ω). In the absence of muscle stimulation apparatus to identify sites of muscle innervation, electrodes should be placed longitudinally

distal to the belly of the m. biceps femoris on the line between ischial tuberosity and lateral epicondyle of the femur. It may also be helpful if the participant were to perform a sub-maximal voluntary muscle action in the musculature of interest. This would facilitate the identification of the palpable part of the musculature and by means of the appropriate surface anatomical land marks, would help to identify the longitudinal axis of the muscle. The reference electrode may be fixed on the pre-amplifier and placed over the lateral femoral epicondyle. The m. biceps femoris is of interest in this investigation as a contributor to the restraint of anterior tibio-femoral displacement in the knee joint and the restraint of the lateral rotation of the femur relative to the tibia, both of which are implicated in the disruption of the anterior cruciate ligament (Rees 1994). As was discussed earlier, if further assessment trials are to be conducted on the same participant, it would be prudent to make a map of the thigh of each subject to ensure the same electrode placement in subsequent trials. This could be achieved by marking on acetate paper the position of the electrodes, moles and small angiomas.

4 Following habituation to procedures, allow each participant to perform a standardized warm-up (5 minutes cycling at an exercise intensity of 120 W for males and 90 W for females followed by 5 minutes of stretching of the involved muscles).

5 Position the participant in a prone position on the dynamometer with the knee flexed passively to 0.44 rad (25°) [0° = full knee extension]. While seated positions can be used, a prone position may be preferable since it allows simulation of movements where the hip angle is approximately neutral. The lower leg should be supported at a position 0.1 m proximal to the lateral malleolus by a rigid adjustable system. The latter system should incorporate a load cell (range 2000 N) interfaced to a voltage signal recording system that provides appropriate signal amplification and analogue to digital conversion of muscle force at 2 kHz (see Figure 2.7). The signal recording system should provide temporal synchronization of the load cell and EMG signal data.

6 Align carefully the approximate joint axis of rotation with the axis of the dynamometer by modifying the participant's position and/or the adjustments of the dynamometer's seat. For this assessment involving the knee, align the lateral femoral epicondyle with the dynamometer's axis and ensure that it remains aligned throughout the participant's maximal intensity efforts.

7 Secure all the other body parts not involved in the test with the appropriate straps. Ensure that the thigh, contralateral leg, hips, chest and arms are appropriately stabilized. Record the seat configuration and the joint positions in case subsequent intra-participant comparisons are to be made.

8 Provide written, clear instructions to the participant concerning the purpose of the test and the experimental procedure. Explain in detail the requirement for muscular relaxation prior to the test and for maximum voluntary effort throughout the test, including the need to initiate the maximal force effort absolutely as rapidly as possible after receipt of the stimulus to start the muscle activation. The use of visual feedback to enhance muscular output should also be emphasized. Allow the subject to ask any questions, and be prepared to explain in detail the test requirements. Potential distractions to the participant should be minimized during data capture

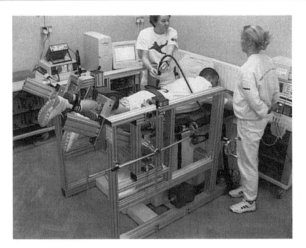

Figure 2.7 An example experimental set-up for the assessment of neuromuscular performance (EMD). The participant may be positioned prone on the dynamometer with the knee flexed passively to 0.44 rad (25°) [0° = full knee extension]. The system incorporates a load cell (range 2000 N) interfaced to a voltage signal recording system which provides appropriate signal amplification and analogue to digital conversion of muscle force at more than 2 kHz and provides temporal synchronization of the load cell and EMG signal data.

including the number of investigators present in the laboratory in addition to the participant.

9 Allow the participant to undertake a specific muscle warm-up against the resistance offered by the static immovable structure incorporating the load cell and allow at least five intermittent sub-maximal repetitions (nominally $3 \times 50\%$, $2 \times 75\%$ and $1 \times 95\%$ of maximal effort). It is worthwhile recording the latter trial as an estimate of the likely signal to noise ratios to be expected during the subsequent maximal voluntary assessments. Modifications to skin preparation, electrode to data acquisition system connections and potential intrusions from electromagnetic interference can be made at this juncture as appropriate.

10 Gravity moment correction. Compensation procedures for gravitational errors in recorded forces during maximal voluntary muscle actions in the vertical plane were undertaken just prior to testing. Angle-specific torque data generated by the effect of gravity acting on the mass of the involved lower extremity of each participant and the weight of the relevant input accessories at the prescribed knee flexion angles of 0.44 rad (25°) should be recorded with the participant resting passively. These scores should then be used to correct all subsequent force measurements as appropriate.

11 Allow the participant to rest (more than 60 s).

12 After a verbal warning, an auditory signal should be delivered to the participant randomly within a 1–4 s period. On receipt of the signal the participant should attempt to flex the knee joint as forcefully and rapidly as possible against the immovable restraint offered by the apparatus. After a suitable period of maximal voluntary muscle activation (~ 3 s) to elicit peak force (PF), another auditory signal should be delivered to the participant to cue the conscious withdrawal of muscle

activation and associated neuromuscular relaxation by the participant as rapidly as possible. This procedure can be completed twice more with an appropriate inter-trial rest period (approximately 60 s or more). The EMG and force transducer signals should be archived to hard disk for subsequent interrogated by means of software

2.9.3 Data analysis and additional practical activities

1 The EMD may be defined as the time interval from the onset of electrical activity of the biceps femoris muscle to the observed development of muscle force (Winter and Brookes 1991). An example of the assessment output is displayed in Figure 2.2 (A time plot of a single maximal voluntary muscle actions of the m. biceps femoris associated with the assessment protocol). Figure 2.3 shows a time plot of a single maximal voluntary muscle action from the onset of the EMG signal to the force generation EMD.

2 Record the time at which the onset of electrical activity occurs in the m. biceps femoris and the development of force by means of visual inspection.

3 Identify and record the peak force from the data record using the relevant software as the highest force observed during the three muscle activations.

4 Compare the observed EMD for the m. biceps femoris with values from previously published studies examining this index of neuromuscular performance.

5 In order to assess the inter-tester reliability of the visual inspection method for the determination of EMD, have three other test individuals undertake 'blinded' assessments of a random sample of force-EMG records associated with single maximal voluntary muscle actions. Undertake appropriate statistical analyses of the data (for example, intra-class correlation). Discuss factors that may contribute to measurement variability and error in the visual inspection method. For example, while the data presented in Figure 2.2 is blessed with relatively good signal to noise characteristics, how might responses, in which greater noise levels have intruded, be accurately assessed for the onset of the response of interest?

6 How might an objective determination of the onset of muscle electrical activity and force generation be achieved? Discuss the factors that may contribute to measurement error in the visual inspection method.

7 Repeat the experimental protocols with exercise intensities of nominally 50% and 75% of peak force. What differences, if any, would you expect to observe in EMD derived from maximal and sub-maximal voluntary muscle actions? Discuss the physiological basis for the recruitment of motor units during the onset of voluntary muscle activations.

8 Repeat the experimental protocols to assess EMD in the knee extensor muscle group (m. vastus lateralis or m. rectus femoris) associated with maximal voluntary muscle actions. Compare the observed EMD scores for the agonist-antagonist muscle groups. Discuss the physiological and mechanical basis on which EMD might contribute to joint stability and protection from injury. Similarly, assess this index of neuromuscular performance in the non-preferred leg and comment on ipsilateral and contralateral performance differences.

Sample data for contralateral leg comparisons are presented in Table 2.1.

9 Using the acetate sheet anatomical mapping of the electrode positions which was prepared earlier, select alternative electrode positions which should be 20 mm lateral and medial, and 40 mm proximal and distal, to the original detection site, respectively. Repeat the assessment of EMD derived from maximal and sub-maximal voluntary muscle and discuss the physiological basis for any systematic changes that might be observed in EMD performance.

10 Repeat all or selected aspects of the above protocols at different times of the day that span those used in contemporary practice (for example, 07:00 h–09:00 h, 12:00 h–14:00 h and 17:00 h–19:00 h) to assess for variations in performance. Similarly, these protocols may be repeated on different days to assess the contributions of inter-day technical and biological variation to measurement error.

11 Repeat the experimental protocols to assess EMD in the knee flexor muscle group associated with maximal voluntary muscle actions before and after an acute fatiguing task. An example of a fatigue task may involve a 'work recovery' cycle of 5-s static maximal voluntary exercise at the knee flexion angle used for the assessment followed by 5-s recovery, which is repeated throughout a 60-s period. Investigate the effects of the acute fatigue task on the observed EMD scores for the muscle group of interest and the recovery. Data illustrating the effects of an acute fatigue task on the EMD values for the m. biceps femoris at 0.44 rad knee flexion are presented in Table 2.1.

Table 2.1 Example EMD (ms) data associated with static maximal voluntary muscle actions of the m. biceps femoris at 0.44 rad knee flexion in male high performance soccer players (n = 12) presenting with unilateral recurrent m. biceps femoris injury (caput longus, greater than three episodes of serious injury [4 weeks absence from training or match-play]). Data were collected according to the procedures described in 'Practical activities' for the contralateral and involved legs, prior to and after an acute fatigue task (60 s duration, 5 s static maximal voluntary muscle action, 5 s passive recovery) (Gleeson and Rees, unpublished data).

Contralateral leg; pre-fatigue (ms).	Involved leg; post-fatigue (ms).	Contralateral leg; pre-fatigue (ms).	Involved leg; post-fatigue (ms).
45.4	56.1	78.5	88.2
39.2	49.8	67.8	73.2
30.5	37.5	56.8	64.2
37.6	45.2	89.7	102.3
52.5	60.4	63.2	73.3
47.5	52.1	58.2	64.8
34.7	39.9	41.7	48.8
36.7	47.8	51.3	60.0
47.8	55.0	64.5	69.8
45.7	48.9	72.1	73.7
37.9	54.2	56.2	59.3
40.9	46.1	49.6	55.5

2.10 PRACTICAL 2: ASSESSMENT OF ELECTROMYOGRAPHIC SIGNAL AMPLITUDE AND FORCE OF THE KNEE FLEXORS ASSOCIATED WITH STATIC VOLUNTARY MUSCLE ACTIONS

2.10.1 Purpose

The purpose of this practical is to assess the relationship between electromyographic signal amplitude and force of the knee flexors associated with static voluntary muscle. This practical requires appropriate surface electrodes, an EMG recording system as described previously and a dynamometry system permitting prone gravity-loaded knee flexion movements in the sagittal plane.

The previous practical activities show that the EMG signal can be detected with minimal insult to the participant. The EMG is therefore a favourable alternative for more direct methods of assessing muscular effort in many applications. However, considerable controversy exists in the contemporary literature regarding the description of the EMG signal-force relationship. This Practical introduces the reader to the description of the EMG signal-force relationship in a relatively large muscle group (m. biceps femoris) associated with static muscle actions.

2.10.2 Procedures

1 Test apparatus calibration should be undertaken in accordance with schedules described in the previous experimental procedures.

2 Record the date, participant's name, sex, age, relevant anthropometric details and training status.

3 The detected EMG signals may be recorded with bi-polar surface electrodes (self-adhesive, silver-silver chloride, 10 mm diameter, inter-electrode distance 20 mm centre to centre) applied to the preferred leg following standard skin preparation (inter-electrode impedance < 5000 Ω). Electrodes should be placed longitudinally distal to the belly of the m. biceps femoris on the line between ischial tuberosity and lateral epicondyle of the femur. The reference electrode may be fixed on the pre-amplifier and placed over the lateral femoral epicondyle. The m. biceps femoris is of interest in this investigation as a contributor to knee flexion performance.

4 Following habituation to procedures, allow each participant to perform a standardized warm-up (5 minutes cycling at an exercise intensity of 120 W for males and 90 W for females followed by 5 minutes of stretching of the involved musculature).

5 Position the participant in a prone position on the dynamometer with the knee flexed passively to 0.44 rad (25°) [0° = full knee extension]. While seated positions can be used, a prone position may be preferable since it allows simulation of movements where the hip angle is approximately neutral. The lower leg should be supported at a position 0.1 m proximal to the lateral malleolus by a rigid adjustable system. The latter system should incorporate a load cell (range 2000 N) interfaced to a voltage signal recording system that provides appropriate signal amplification and analogue to digital conversion of muscle force at 2 kHz (see Figure 2.7). The signal recording system should provide temporal synchronization of the load cell and EMG signal data.

6 Align carefully the approximate joint axis of rotation with the axis of the dynamometer by modifying the participant's position and/or the adjustments of the dynamometer's seat. For this assessment involving the knee, align the lateral femoral epicondyle with the dynamometer's axis and ensure that it remains aligned throughout the participant's efforts.

7 Secure all the other body parts not involved in the test with the appropriate straps. Ensure that the thigh, contralateral leg, hips, chest and arms are appropriately stabilized. Record the seat configuration and the joint positions in case subsequent intra-participant comparisons are to be made.

8 Provide written, clear instructions to the participant concerning the purpose of the test and the experimental procedure. Allow the subject to ask any questions and be prepared to explain in detail the test requirements. Potential distractions to the participant should be minimized during data capture, including the number of investigators present in the laboratory in addition to the participant.

9 Allow the participant to undertake a specific muscle warm-up against the resistance offered by the static immovable structure incorporating the load cell and allow at least five intermittent submaximal repetitions (nominally $3 \times 50\%$, $2 \times 75\%$ and $1 \times 95\%$ of maximal effort). It is worthwhile recording the latter trial as an estimate of the likely signal to noise ratios to be expected during the subsequent maximal voluntary assessments. Modifications to skin preparation, electrode to data acquisition system connections and potential intrusions from electromagnetic interference can be made at this juncture as appropriate.

10 Gravity moment correction. Compensation procedures for gravitational errors in recorded forces during maximal voluntary muscle actions in the vertical plane should be undertaken just prior to testing. Angle-specific torque data generated by the effect of gravity acting on the mass of the involved lower extremity of each participant and the weight of the relevant input accessories at the prescribed knee flexion angles of 0.44 rad (25°) should be recorded with the participant resting passively. These values should then be used to correct all subsequent force measurements as appropriate.

11 Allow the participant to rest (more than 60 s).
    After a verbal warning, an auditory signal should be delivered to the participant. On receipt of the signal the participant should attempt to flex the knee joint as forcefully as possible against the immovable restraint offered by the apparatus. After a suitable period of maximal voluntary muscle activation (~ 3 s) to elicit peak force, another auditory signal should be delivered to the participant to cue the conscious withdrawal of muscle activation and associated neuromuscular relaxation by the participant as rapidly as possible. This procedure can be repeated once more with an appropriate inter-trial rest period (approximately 60 s or more). The EMG and force transducer signals should be archived to hard disk for subsequent interrogation by means of software. The recording of peak force as the average for the two trials serves as a reference from which various submaximal forces for each participant may be calculated (for example 10%, 20%, 30% of peak force).

13 Participants should be requested to produce in random order, muscle actions eliciting blinded target knee flexion forces of 10%, 20%, 30%, 40%, 50%, 60%, 70%,

80% and 90% of peak force under verbal direction from the test administrator. The random ordering of the prescribed forces minimizes the potential for intrusion of fatigue and other carry-over effects on the recorded scores. On attainment of the prescribed force level, the participant should be requested to maintain this prescribed net force for 3 s. The participant should then be requested to relax the involved musculature. Following a 120-s recovery period, this procedure should be repeated for the next target force prescribed at random. The procedures may be extended to include several efforts for each of the prescribed forces and several participants. The recorded force and corresponding EMG signal may be averaged over the number of repeated samples.

2.10.3 Data analysis and additional practical activities

1 The amplitude of the EMG signal for each prescribed force may be described in many ways. Parameters which may be used to describe the amplitude of the EMG signal include mean rectified amplitude, mean-squared amplitude and versions of integrated amplitude (Basmajian and De Luca 1985).

2 For each participant, plot the recorded force (as a percentage of peak force) against normalized amplitude of the EMG signal in the m. biceps femoris (amplitude associated with peak force is recorded as 100%) for all of the prescribed force levels.

3 Describe the relationship between normalized force and EMG signal amplitude for these experimental conditions. Where appropriate, use statistical techniques to assist in the quantification of the relationship as linear or non-linear. An example relationship between EMG signal amplitude and force normalized for their respective peak values is shown in Figure 2.8 for the m. biceps femoris.

4 Compare the observed relationship for the m. biceps femoris with those from previously published studies examining this aspect of neuromuscular performance. Further, examine inter-participant variability in the relationship between amplitude of the EMG signal and force associated with static voluntary muscle actions. Example data illustrating the relationship between amplitude of the EMG signal and force associated with static voluntary muscle actions of the m. biceps femoris at 0.44 rad knee flexion in three male soccer players is presented in Table 2.2.

5 Where the appropriate experimental apparatus is available, repeat the whole assessment protocol on different muscle groups, including smaller muscle groups of the arm or hand. An example relationship between EMG signal amplitude and force normalized for their respective peak values is shown in Figure 2.8 for the m. biceps brachii.

6 Discuss the factors which may moderate the relationship between the amplitude of the EMG signal and the force output associated with static muscle actions.

7 Discuss the factors which may moderate the relationship between the amplitude of the EMG signal and the force output associated with dynamic muscle actions.

Table 2.2: Example data illustrating the relationship between amplitude of the EMG signal and force associated with static voluntary muscle actions of the m. biceps femoris at 0.44 rad knee flexion in three male soccer players. Data collected are from the preferred leg according to the procedures described in 'Practical activities.' The EMG and force values have been normalized to their respective peak values.

Normalized force (%)	Normalized EMG amplitude (%) Participant 1	Normalized EMG amplitude (%) Participant 2	Normalized EMG amplitude (%) Participant 3
10	10.7 ± 2.2	9.2 ± 2.4	12.1 ± 3.8
20	17.9 ± 3.6	14.3 ± 3.7	16.1 ± 4.1
30	27.4 ± 5.1	24.4 ± 6.1	28.8 ± 5.5
40	38.1 ± 7.2	34.3 ± 8.6	40.1 ± 9.2
50	48.2 ± 7.3	44.2 ± 9.4	49.2 ± 7.9
60	57.9 ± 11.2	55.9 ± 12.7	58.9 ± 15.1
70	69.6 ± 12.8	66.1 ± 14.2	70.1 ± 12.3
80	81.7 ± 17.4	78.7 ± 18.3	82.4 ± 13.7
90	90.4 ± 19.1	91.3 ± 23.2	91.6 ± 19.3
100	98.9 ± 18.3	100.7 ± 24.1.	99.4 ± 17.6

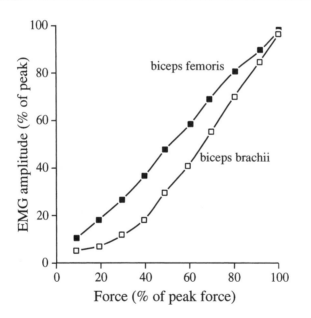

Figure 2.8 Amplitude of EMG signal-force relationship for m. biceps femoris and m. biceps brachii associated with static muscle actions. EMG and force responses have been normalized to their respective peak values. Data points represent the mean response of six trials at each prescribed force (various percentages of peak force; see text) for a single participant. Standard error bars associated with EMG amplitude are omitted for visual clarity.

FURTHER READING

Book

Payton C. and Bartlett R. (2007) Biomechanical evaluation of movement in sport and exercise. Routledge; Abingdon. ISBN: 978–0-415–43468–3 (Hb); 978–0-415–43469–0 (Pb).

Website

International Society for Electrophysiology and Kinesiology, https://www.isek-online.org/history.asp

REFERENCES

Aidley D. J. (1998) *The Physiology of Excitable Cells (4th Edition)* Cambridge University Press; Cambridge.

Alexander R. McN., and Bennet-Clark H. C. (1977) Storage of elastic strain energy in muscle and other tissues. *Nature*; **265**: 114–17.

Almasi J. J. and Schmitt C. H. (1974) Automated measurement of bioelectric impedance at very low frequencies. *Computing in Biomedical Research*; 7: 449–56.

Altman D. G. (1991) *Practical Statistics for Medical Research*. Chapman and Hall; London.

Basmajian J. V. and De Luca C. J. (1985) *Muscles Alive: Their Functions Revealed by Electromyography*, Williams & Wilkins, Baltimore. MD.

Bland J. M., Altman D. G. (1986) Statistical methods for assessing agreement between two methods of clinical measurement. *The Lancet*; i, : 307–10.

Burbank D. P. and Webster J. G. (1978) Reducing skin potential motion artefact by skin abrasion. *Medical and Biological Engineeering and Computing*; 16: 31–8.

Chokroverty S., Flynn D., Picone M. A., Chokroverty M. and Belsh J. (1993) Magnetic coil stimulation of the human lumbosacral vertebral column: site of stimulation and clinical application. *Electroencephalography and Clinical Neurophysiology*; **89 (1)**: 54–60.

Chu D., LeBlanc R., D'Ambrosia P., D'Ambrosia R., Baratta R. V. and Solomonow M. (2003) Neuromuscular disorder in response to anterior cruciate ligament creep. *Clinical Biomechanics*; **18**: 222–30

Clarys J. P. and Cabri J. (1993) Electromyography and the study of sports movements: a review. *Journal of Sports Sciences*; **11**: 379–448.

Currier D. P. (1984) *Elements of Research in Physical Therapy (2nd Edition)*. Williams and Wilkins; Baltimore, MD.

De Luca C. J. and Knaflitz M. (1990) *Surface Electromyography: What's New?* Neuromuscular Research Centre; Boston, MA.

De Talhouet H. and Webster J. G. (1996) The origin of skin-stretch caused motion artefacts under electrodes. *Physiological Measurement*; **17**: 81–93.

Disselhorst-Klug C., Rau G., Schmeer A. and Silny J. (1999) Non-invasive detection of the single motor unit action potential by averaging the spatial potential distribution triggered on a spatially filtered motor unit action potential. *Journal of Electromyography and Kinesiology*; **9 (1)**: 67–72.

Doyle J., Gleeson N. P. and Rees D. (1999) Psychobiology and the anterior cruciate ligament (ACL) injured athlete. *Sports Medicine*; **26**: 379–93.

Engbaek J. and Mortensen C. R. (1994) Monitoring of Neuromuscular Transmission. *Annals Academy of Medicine*. 23: 558–65.

Enoka R. M. (1994) *Neuromechanical Basis of Kinesiology*. Human Kinetics; Champaign, IL.

Fu F. H. (1993) Biomechanics of knee ligaments. *Journal of Bone and Joint Surgery*; 75A: 1716–27.

Gazzoni M., Farina D. and Merletti R. (2004) A new method for the extraction and classification of single motor unit action potentials from surface EMG signals. *Journal of Neuroscience Methods*; **136 (2)**: 165–77.

Geddes L. A. and Baker L. E. (1989) *Principles of Applied Biomedical Instrumentation*. John Wiley & Sons; New York.

Gleeson N. P. and Mercer T. H. (1992)

Reproducibility of isokinetic leg strength and endurance characteristics of adult men and women. *European Journal of Applied Physiology and Occupational Physiology;* **65**: 221–8.

Gleeson N. P. and Mercer T. H. (1996) The utility of isokinetic dynamometry in the assessment of human muscle function. *Sports Medicine;* **21**: 18–34.

Gleeson N. P., Mercer T. and Campbell I. (1997a) Effect of a fatigue task on absolute and relativised indices of isokinetic leg strength in female collegiate soccer players. In: (T. Reilly, J. Bangsbo and M. Hughes. eds.) *Science and Football III.* E & F.N. Spon; London: 162–7.

Gleeson N. P., Mercer T. H., Morris K. and Rees D. (1997b) Influence of a fatigue task on electromechanical delay in the knee flexors of soccer players. *Medicine and Science in Sports and Exercise;* **29** (5): S281.

Gleeson N. P., Mercer T. H., Reilly T., Rakowski S. and Rees D. (1998) The influence of acute endurance activity on leg neuromuscular and musculoskeletal performance. *Medicine and Science in Sports and Exercise;* **30**: 596–608.

Gleeson N. P., Rees D., Glover D., Minshull C. and Walters M. (2000) Effects of a fatigue task on the neuromuscular performance in the knee flexors of high-performance soccer players. In: (J. Avela, P. V. Komi and J. Komulainen eds). *Proceedings of the 5th Annual Congress of the European College of Sport Sciences.* Jyvaskyla, Finland; July: 287.

Grieve D. W. (1975) Electromyography. In: (D. W. Grieve, D. L Miller, D. Mitchelson, J. P. Paul and A.J. Smith, eds.) *Techniques for the Analysis of Human Movement.* Lepus Books; London.

Grimby L. and Hannerz J. (1977) Firing rate and recruitment order of toe extensor motor units in different modes of voluntary contraction. *Journal of Physiology;* **264**: 865–79.

Horita T. and Ishiko T. (1987) Relationships between muscle lactate accumulation and surface EMG activities during isokinetic contractions in man. *European Journal of Applied Physiology;* **56**: 18–23.

Huston L. J. and Wojtys E. M. (1996)

Neuromuscular performance characteristics in elite female athletes. *American Journal of Sports Medicine;* **24**: 427–36.

Kirkendall D. R., Gruber J. J. and Johnson R. E. (1987) *Measurement and Evaluation for Physical Educators (2nd Edition).* Human Kinetics; Champaign, IL.

Kleine B. U., van Dijk J. P., Lapatki B. G., Zwarts M. J., Stegeman D. F. (2007) Using two-dimensional spatial information in decomposition of surface EMG signals. *Journal of Electromyography and Kinesiology;* **17**: 535–48.

Latash M. L. (1998) *Neurophysiological Basis of Human Movement.* Human Kinetics; Champaign, IL: pp. 98–105.

Lewes D. (1965) Electrode jelly in electrocardiography. *British Heart Journal;* **27**: 105–15.

Lipsey M. W. (1990) *Design Sensitivity: Statistical Power for Experimental Research.* Sage Publications; London.

McComas A. J. (1996) *Skeletal Muscle: Form and Function.* Human Kinetics; Champaign, IL.

Medina V., Clochesy J. M. and Omery A. (1989) Comparison of e1ectrode site preparation techniques. *Electromyography and Clinical Neurophysiology;* **18**: 456–60.

Mercer T. H. and Gleeson N. P. (1996) Prolonged intermittent high intensity exercise impairs neuromuscular performance of the knee flexors. *Physiologist;* **39**:A–62.

Mercer T. H. and Gleeson N. P. (2002) The efficacy of measurement and evaluation in evidence-based clinical practice. *Physical Therapy in Sport;* **3** (1):1–9.

Mercer T. H., Gleeson N. P., Claridge S. and Clement S. (1998) Prolonged intermittent high intensity exercise impairs neuromuscular performance of the knee flexors. *European Journal of Applied Physiology and Occupational Physiology;***77**: 560–2.

Minshull C., Gleeson N., Walters-Edwards M., Eston R. and Rees D. (2007) Effects of acute fatigue on the volitional and magnetically-evoked electromechanical delay of the knee flexors in males and females. *European Journal of Applied Physiology;* **100**: 469–78

Minshull C., Gleeson N. P., Eston R. G., Bailey

A. and Rees D. (2008). Single measurement reliability and reproducibility of volitional and magnetically-evoked indices of neuromuscular performance in males and females. *Journal of Electromyography and Kinesiology*, published ahead of print: http://dx.doi.org/10.1016/j.jelekin.2008.07.002.

Minshull C., Gleeson N. P. and Walters M. (2002b) Reproducibility of voluntary and magnetically-evoked indices of neuromuscular performance in men and women. *Journal of Sports Sciences;* 20: 25 (Abstract).

Nevill A. M., Atkinson G. and Scott M. (2009) Statistical methods in kinanthropometry and physiology. In (R. G. Eston and T. Reilly, eds) *Kinanthropometry Laboratory Manual 3rd Edition: Anthropometry (Chapter 10)*. Routledge; Oxon: pp. 250–299.

Nigg B. M. and Herzog W. (1994) *Biomechanics of the Musculoskeletal System*. John Wiley; Chichester.

Norman R. W. and Komi P. V. (1979) Electromechanical delay in skeletal muscle under normal movement conditions. *Acta Physiologica Scandinavica;* 106: 241–8.

Okamoto, T., Tsutsumi, H., Goto Y. and Andrew, P. (1987). A simple procedure to attenuate artefacts in surface electrode recordings by painlessly lowering skin impedance. *Electromyography and Clinical Neurophysiology;* 27: 173–176.

Patterson R. P. (1978) The electrical characteristics of some commercial electrodes. *Journal Cardiology;* 11: 23–6.

Rees D. (1994) Failed ACL reconstructions. *Proceedings of the Football Association – Royal College of Surgeons, 6th Joint Conference on Sport Injury*. Edinburgh: July 2–3.

Rees D. and Gleeson N. P. (1999) The scientific assessment of the injured athlete. *Proceedings of the Football Association – Royal College of Surgeons Medical Conference*. Edinburgh; October:

Reilly T., Atkinson G. and Coldwells A. (1993) The relevance to exercise performance of the circadian rhythms in body temperature and arousal. *Biology of Sport;* 10: 203–16.

Sale D. G. (1991) Testing strength and power. In: (J. D. MacDougall, H. A. Wenger and H. J. Green, eds), *Physiological Testing of the High Performance Athlete (2nd Edition)*. Human Kinetics; Champaign, IL: 21–106.

Sale D. G. (1992) Neural adaptations to strength training. In: (P.V. Komi, ed) *Strength and Power in Sport*. Blackwell Scientific Publications; Oxford: 249–65.

Sbriccoli P., Solomonow M., Zhou B.-H., Lu Y. and Sellards R. (2005) Neuromuscular responses to cyclic loading of the anterior cruciate ligament. *American Journal of Sports Medicine;* 33: 543–51.

Shellock F. G. and Prentice W. E. (1985) Warming-up and stretching for improved physical performance and prevention of sports-related injuries. *Sports Medicine;* 2: 267–78.

Shultz S. J., Perrin D. H., Adams M. J., Arnold B. L., Gansneder B. M. and Granata K. P. (2001) Neuromuscular response characteristics in men and women after knee perturbation in a single-leg, weight-bearing stance. *Journal of Athletic Training;* 36: 37–43.

Sokal R. and Rohlf F. (1981) *Biometry (2nd Edition)*. W.H. Freeman; Oxford.

Solomonow M. (2004) Ligaments: a source of work-related musculoskeletal disorders. *Journal of Electromyography and Kinesiology;* 14: 49–60.

Solomonow M,. Zhou B.-H., Baratta R. V. and Burger E. (2003) Biomechanics and electromyography of a cumulative lumbar disorder: response to static flexion. *Clinical Biomechanics;* 18: 890–8.

Tam H. W. and Webster J. G. (1977) Minimising electrode motion artifact by skin abrasion. *IEEE Transactions of Biomedical Engneering;* BME-24: 134–9.

Thomas J. R., Nelson J. K. and Silverman S. J. (2005) *Research Methods in Physical Activity (5th Edition)*. Human Kinetics; Champaign, IL.

Verducci F. M. (1980) *Measurement Concepts in Physical Education*. C. V. Mosby; St. Louis, MO.

Vincent W. J. (2005). *Statistics in Kinesiology (3rd Edition)*. Human Kinetics; Champaign, IL.

Viitasalo J. T., Saukkonen S. and Komi P. (1980) Reproducibility of selected neuromuscular performance variables in man. *Electromyography and Clinical*

Neurophysiology; **20**: 487–501.

Vos E. J., Harlaar J. and van Ingen Schenau G. J. (1991) Electromechanical delay during knee extensor contractions. *Medicine and Science in Sports and Exercise;* **23**: 1187–93.

Vos E. J., Mullender M. G. and van Ingen Schenau G. J. (1990). Electromechanical delay in vastus lateralis muscle during dynamic isometric contractions. *European Journal of Applied Physiology;* **60**: 467–71.

Winter E. M. and F. B. C. Brookes (1991) Electromechanical response times and muscle elasticity in men and women. *European Journal of Applied Physiology;* **63**: 124–8.

Zhou S., McKenna M. J., Lawson D. L., Morrison W. E. and Fairweather I. (1996) Effects of fatigue and sprint training on electromechanical delay of knee extensor muscles. *European Journal of Applied Physiology;* **72**: 410–16.

PART TWO

OXYGEN TRANSPORT SYSTEM AND EXERCISE

CHAPTER 3

LUNG FUNCTION

Roger Eston and Lee M. Romer

3.1 AIMS

- To provide students with information regarding the assessment of lung function at rest and during different modes of exercise;
- To describe the effect of anthropometric, postural and environmental factors on lung function;
- To outline practical exercises and data to exemplify techniques of assessing lung function using open and closed circuit spirometry procedures.

3.2 ASSESSMENT OF RESTING LUNG FUNCTION

Assessment of lung function is useful for detecting, characterising and quantifying the severity of lung disease. It is mostly concerned with the testing of lung volumes and capacities observed in the resting state. The basic assessment of lung function requires the use of a spirometer. A water-sealed 'bell' spirometer, for example, functions by the fall and rise of the bell as air is inhaled and exhaled, respectively (Figure 3.1). As the bell moves down and up the movement is recorded on a rotating drum (kymograph) by a stylus/

pen, thereby providing a record (spirogram) of the ventilatory volume relative to time (Figure 3.2). It is appropriate here to describe the various lung volume classifications. The volumes can be classified as either '*static*' – referring to the volume of air with no relation to time, or '*dynamic*' – which are measured in relation to time.

3.2.1 Static lung function

The lung can be divided into four primary volumes and four capacities; the latter consist of two or more of the primary volumes (Figure 3.2). Lung volumes and capacities are measured in litres and are standardized to conditions in the lung where the gas is at body temperature, ambient pressure, saturated with water vapour (BTPS).

The volume of air inhaled or exhaled during each respiratory cycle is the *tidal volume* (V_T). The amount of air that can be inspired maximally from the end-inspiratory level during tidal breathing is termed the *inspiratory reserve volume* (IRV). The volume of air that can be expired maximally from the end-expiratory level during tidal breathing is the *expiratory reserve volume* (ERV). At rest, the IRV and ERV are usually in the range

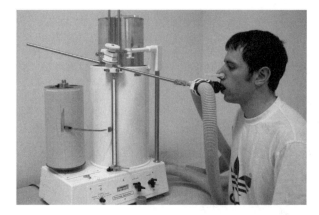

Figure 3.1 Subject breathing from a *Harvard* 9 Litre Spirometer.

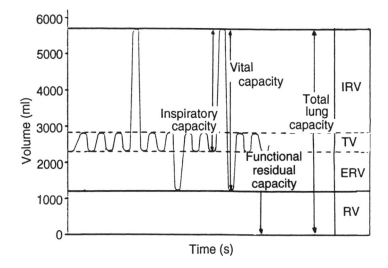

Figure 3.2 Spirogram showing the various lung volumes and capacities. IRV, inspiratory reserve volume; ERV, expiratory reserve volume; RV, residual volume; TV, tidal volume.

2.5–3.3 and 1.0–1.5 L, respectively. The IRV and ERV show large variations with posture on account of changes in the *functional residual capacity* (FRC). The FRC is defined as the volume of air in the lungs at end-expiration during tidal breathing when the elastic recoil of the lung and the thoracic cage are equal and opposite. In normal subjects the FRC while supine is reduced by about 25% compared with in the upright position because gravity acting on the chest wall and abdomen forces air out of the thorax. In the healthy upright adult, FRC is in the range 0.8–5.5 and 0.7–4.9 L for men and

women, respectively. The FRC is reduced during exercise, when it becomes termed the *end-expiratory lung volume* (EELV). The *inspiratory capacity* (IC) is defined as the volume of air that can be inhaled after a tidal expiration. It is often used to infer exercise-induced changes in EELV. The *total lung capacity* (TLC) is defined as the volume of gas in the lungs at the end of a full inspiration, or the sum of all volume compartments. In healthy adults, depending on size, the TLC is in the range 3.6–9.4 and 3.0–7.3 L for males and females, respectively.

The total volume of air that can be

moved voluntarily from the lungs from full inspiration to full expiration is the *vital capacity* (VC). It can be measured in a relaxed manner or during a forced expiration, when it is termed the *forced vital capacity* (FVC). The relaxed manoeuvre is more appropriate for patients with lung disease whose airways tend to collapse during a forced manoeuvre. In healthy adults, depending on age and size, VC is in the range 2.0–6.6 and 1.4–5.6 L for males and females, respectively. Vital capacities of 6–7 L are not uncommon for tall individuals and athletes. Ekblom and Hermansen (1968), for example, reported a VC of 7.7 L in a male Swedish national orienteering champion. The large lung volumes recorded in athletes likely reflect genetic body size effects because static lung function does not change appreciably with exercise training (see also section 3.7.1).

The volume of air remaining in the lungs after maximal exhalation is the *residual volume* (RV). Functionally, it makes sound physiological sense to have air remaining in the lungs at end-expiration as otherwise there would be complete collapse of airways and cessation of gas exchange. In healthy adults, depending on size and age, the RV is in the range 0.5–3.5 and 0.4–3.0 L for males and females, respectively. The RV tends to increase with age, whereas the IRV and ERV become proportionately smaller. The increase in RV with age is generally attributed to a loss of elasticity in the lung tissue causing early airway closure (Turner *et al.* 1968).

Measurement of FRC (and hence RV and TLC) cannot be made using spirometry, and therefore additional techniques have been developed. These include body plethysmography, nitrogen washout, helium dilution, and radiographic imaging methods (Wanger *et al.* 2005).

3.2.2 Dynamic lung function

An individual's ability to sustain high levels of airflow depends on the speed at which the volumes can be moved and the amount of air that can be moved in a given period of time. Dynamic lung function can be considered in terms of either a short period of voluntary hyperventilation or a single maximal respiratory effort. The term given to the former is *maximal voluntary ventilation* (MVV). This global test of ventilatory capacity involves rapid and deep breathing for a predetermined time, usually 15 s (MVV$_{15}$), and the result is multiplied to arrive at a volume in L min^{-1} at BTPS. The exact procedure for this measurement is explained in Practical 1. The test can be performed for longer durations (e.g. 4 minutes), when it is termed the sustained maximal voluntary ventilation, but requires supplemental carbon dioxide to prevent severe falls in the partial pressure of carbon dioxide in arterial blood (i.e. hypocapnia).

The MVV is influenced by the individual's physical size, age, sex and ethnicity. In addition, the MVV is influenced by the individual's effort, the properties of the respiratory muscles (strength, endurance and coordination), airway resistance, and the elastic properties of the lung and chest wall. Typical values for MVV in healthy, college-aged males and females are 140–180 and 80–120 L min^{-1}, respectively. Hanson (1973) reported average values of 192 L min^{-1} for the men's US Ski Team – the highest value was 239 L min^{-1}. Figure 3.3 shows a young athletic male performing the MVV test. This subject, a former amateur boxer, had an unusually high MVV of 294 L min^{-1}.

In moderately fit individuals exercising at near maximum levels, minute ventilation is appreciably less than the MVV. This difference has been termed the *breathing reserve*. Since the MVV is largely independent of fitness and training status, a highly fit individual who is capable of achieving a high level of ventilation during exercise typically has a lower breathing reserve than does a less-fit individual. Healthy individuals often achieve a ventilation of 70–80% of their MVV whilst patients with obstructive lung disease achieve levels of ventilation that are

Figure 3.3 Procedure for measuring maximal voluntary ventilation (MVV). The student photographed here (stature 1.97 m, mass 97 kg, age 24 y) had an abnormally high MVV of 294 L (BTPS).

only about 40% of their MVV (Levison and Cherniack 1968).

When the ventilatory capacity is considered in terms of a single forced expiration or inspiration, it is expressed as either the maximal flow at a defined point in the respiratory cycle or the average flow over part of the breath, usually the middle half (e.g. $FEF_{25-75\%}$, see below).

Peak expiratory flow (PEF) is the highest flow obtained during an FVC manoeuvre. It is highly effort-dependent and has poor reliability. Hence, it is normally reduced only during severe airflow limitation. The PEF in healthy adults, depending on age and size, is in the range 6–15 and 2.8–10.1 L s^{-1} in males and females, respectively.

Figure 3.4 shows a subject performing a forced expiratory test on a Vitalograph™ 'wedge' spirometer.

Figure 3.5 shows four spirometer tracings

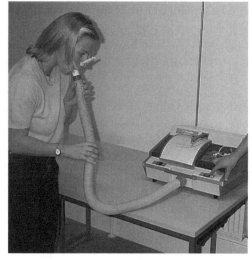

Figure 3.4 Subject performing a forced expiratory manoeuvre on a Vitalograph™ spirometer.

taken from a Vitalograph™ spirometer to illustrate some of the static and dynamic characteristics of a single 6 s forced expiratory effort in a fit, healthy male, an asthmatic male and a regular smoker. The various lung function values are shown in Table 3.1.

The amount of air expired over a specific time period of a forced expiration from a position of full inspiration is termed the *forced expiratory volume*. It is qualified by the time in seconds over which the measurement is made (e.g. $FEV_{1.0}$). In healthy adults, depending on age and size, the $FEV_{1.0}$ is in the range 1.2–5.7 and 0.8–4.2 L in males and females, respectively. In Figure 3.5, the $FEV_{1.0}$ for the healthy, non-smoking subject (A) and the asthmatic subject (B) is 5.2 and 2.9 L, respectively.

The *maximum mid-expiratory flow time* (MMEFT) is the average flow time over the middle half of the FVC. It is also called the *forced mid-expiratory flow* (FEF) for the appropriate segment of the FVC, for example $FEF_{25-75\%}$. Graphic analysis involves location of 25% and 75% volume points on the spirogram. The two points are then connected by a straight line and protracted to intersect the two time lines that are one second apart. The number of litres per second

Table 3.1 Pulmonary function values for the three spirogram tracings illustrated in Figure 3.5

Variable	Subject A (Normal)	Subject B (Asthmatic)	Subject C Pre-smoking	Subject C 10 min post-smoking
FVC (L)	6.4	6.3	5.1	4.6
$FEV_{1.0}$ (L)	5.2	2.9	3.7	3.3
$FEV_{1.0}/FVC$ (%)	81	46	73	72
$FVC_{25\%}$ (L)	1.6	1.6	1.3	1.2
$FVC_{75\%}$ (L)	4.8	4.7	3.8	3.5
$FVC_{85\%}$ (L)	5.4	5.4	4.3	3.9
$FEF_{25-75\%}$ (L s^{-1})	5.1	1.6	2.5	2.0
$FEF_{75-85\%}$ (L s^{-1})	1.5	0.8	0.7	0.5
MMEF (s)	0.65	2.0	0.95	1.05

is then measured between the points of the intersection. This method is demonstrated for subject A in Figure 3.5. The 25%, 75% and 85% FVC values are shown on the time:volume curve. In this case, the $FEF_{25-75\%}$ was calculated by taking the difference between two intersection points at time lines 0 and 1 s; i.e. 6.2 and 1.1 L. The average flow between these two points is therefore 5.1 L s^{-1}. Alternatively, but less accurately, the FEF can be calculated by dividing the change in volume by the time period between FEV at 25% FVC ($FVC_{25\%}$) and $FVC_{75\%}$ on the spirogram. Another conventional measure is the forced late-expiratory flow ($FEF_{75-85\%}$), which is calculated in a similar manner. For subject A, it was calculated as the difference between 6.7 L (at 2 s) and 5.2 L (at 1 s). The 25%, 75% and 85% FVC values are also located for the asthmatic subject (B) as a further example of this procedure. The average flow for one litre of gas starting at 200 ml after the beginning of a forced expiration ($FEF_{200-1200}$) is occasionally also used as an index of dynamic lung function.

A frequently used ratio is the forced expiratory volume in a second ($FEV_{1.0}$) expressed as a proportion of the vital capacity ($FEV_{1.0\%} = (FEV_{1.0} / FVC) \times 100$). This value provides an indication of the resistance to airflow. Often, the demarcation point for airway obstruction is the point at which less than 70% of the FVC can be expired in 1 s (but see also section 3.4.1). It can be seen from Figure 3.5 and Table 3.1 that although there is no difference between the FVC values for the healthy lung (A) and the asthmatic lung (B), the dynamic values for B are much lower in the asthmatic. It is also interesting to note the acute increase in airway resistance after smoking a cigarette (C). In this example, the student, who was a regular smoker, was tested before and 30 minutes after smoking a cigarette. Smoking resulted in a 10% reduction in FVC and a 20% reduction in mid-expiratory flow.

3.3 SOURCES OF VARIATION IN LUNG FUNCTION TESTING

Measurements of lung function are subject to several sources of variation. The variation can be attributed to technical factors such as instrumentation, procedure, observer error and so on. The variation could also be due to dysfunction or disease, or as a result of biological variation. The major focus here is on biological sources of variation. For a more detailed discussion of technical sources of variation in lung function testing we refer the reader to the position statements of the American Thoracic Society/European Respiratory Society (ATS/ERS: Miller *et al.* 2005; Wanger *et al.* 2005).

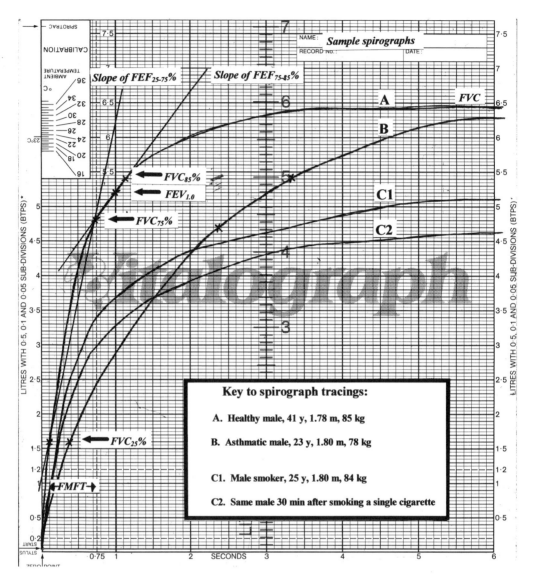

Figure 3.5 Vitalograph spirogram for a normal healthy male, an asthmatic male and a male smoker, which illustrates how the various static and dynamic lung function parameters can be calculated. (Vitalograph chart reproduced with permission of Vitalograph Ltd, Buckingham, UK.)

3.3.1 Within-subject variation

The main sources of within-subject variation in lung function parameters are body position, head position and the degree of effort exerted during the test. The FVC is 7–8% lower supine versus standing and 1–2% lower sitting versus standing (Townsend, 1984; Allen *et al.* 1985). However, obese individuals usually have higher lung volumes standing than sitting. In normal subjects the RV increases by about 20% on changing from a standing to a sitting position and by about 30% on changing from a sitting to a supine position (Blair and Hickam 1955). Systematic increases in maximal expiratory flows have been documented during neck hyperextension, as can occur if the subject bends over during the expiratory manoeuvre, due to elongation and stiffening of the trachea (Melissinos and Mead 1977). Conversely, neck flexion may decrease peak expiratory flow and increase airway resistance (Spann and Hyatt, 1971). The $FEV_{1.0}$ may be 100–200 ml lower when the effort is maximal compared to submaximal due to the effect of thoracic gas compression on lung volume (Krowka *et al.* 1987). In some subjects, repeated maximal efforts can trigger bronchospasm resulting in a progressive decrease in $FEV_{1.0}$ (Gimeno *et al.* 1972).

Another source of within-subject variation is the circadian rhythm that contributes to diurnal changes in ventilatory function. Small but significant circadian variations have been reported for FRC, PEF and $FEV_{1.0}$ in normal and asthmatic subjects (Mortola 2004). The lowest values for PEF, for example, are usually found in the morning (04:00 to 06:00 hours) and the largest values usually occur around midday (Hetzel 1981), with a peak-to-trough amplitude of the circadian rhythm of about 8% (Hetzel and Clark, 1980).

3.3.2 Between-subject variation

The main physiological and demographic factors responsible for the between-subject variation in lung function are sex, body size, age and ethnicity. These factors account for 30%, 22%, 8% and 10%, respectively, of the variation in adults (Becklake 1986). Other factors are obesity, pregnancy and level of physical activity (see also section 3.7.1).

Sitting height explains less of the variability in lung function than standing height (Ferris and Stoudt 1971; Cotes 1979). However, sitting height can be used to predict lung function in children, particularly during periods of rapid growth. Arm span measurements provide a practical substitute for stature in subjects unable to stand or those with a skeletal deformity such as kyphoscoliosis (Hibbert *et al.* 1988). Measurements of chest circumference may also improve slightly the prediction of lung function (Damon 1966).

After correcting for body size, girls appear to have higher expiratory flows than boys, but men have larger volumes and flows than women (Schwartz *et al.* 1988). With regard to age, after adult height is attained, there is either an increase (usually in young men) or little or no change in function (usually in young women) after which lung function decreases at an accelerating rate with increasing age. Ethnicity is another important determinant of lung function. Caucasians of European descent have greater static and dynamic lung volumes and greater forced expiratory flows, but similar or lower $FEV_{1.0}/FVC$ ratios in comparison to other ethnic groups. Differences due to ethnicity may be explained by differences in trunk length relative to standing height, fat-free mass, chest dimensions and strength of respiratory muscles (Jacobs *et al.* 1992). In this respect, regression equations derived from White populations using standing height as the measure of size usually over-predict values measured in Blacks by about 12% for TLC, $FEV_{1.0}$ and VC and by about 7% for FRC and RV (Cotes 1979).

3.4 PREDICTION OF LUNG FUNCTION

Reference equations provide a context for evaluating lung function in comparison to the distribution of measurements in a reference population. Linear regression is the most common model used to predict lung function in adults and, for reasons mentioned in the previous section, equations are usually based on sex, stature, age and ethnicity. However, in children and adolescents, lung volumes and stature are not linearly related. The relationship between lung volumes and stature can be linearised using a logarithmic transformation. However, the resulting regression equation is still not satisfactory for the whole age range because the relationship between trunk dimensions to height changes from birth to the end of the adolescent growth spurt. That is, the rate of growth of the trunk and its contents, including the lungs,

Table 3.2 Regression equations for the prediction of $FEV_{1.0}$ and FVC for healthy non-smoking men and women of European descent aged 18–70 years (modified from Quanjer *et al.* 1993)

Variable	Unit	Regression equation	RSD	1.64RSD
		Men		
FVC	L	$(5.76 \bullet height - 0.026 \bullet age - 4.34)$	0.61	1.00
TLC	L	$(7.99 \bullet height - 7.08)$	0.70	1.15
RV	L	$(1.31 \bullet height + 0.022 \bullet age - 1.23)$	0.41	0.67
FRC	L	$(2.34 \bullet height - 0.009 \bullet age - 1.09)$	0.60	0.99
$FEV_{1.0}$	L	$(4.30 \bullet height - 0.029 \bullet age - 2.49)$	0.51	0.84
$FEV_{1.0}/FVC$	%	$87.2 - 0.18 \bullet age$	7.17	11.8
$FEF_{25-75\%}$	L s^{-1}	$(1.94 \bullet height - 0.043 \bullet age + 2.70)$	1.04	1.71
PEF	L s^{-1}	$(6.14 \bullet height - 0.043 \bullet age + 0.15)$	1.21	1.99
$MEF_{75\%}$	L s^{-1}	$(5.46 \bullet height - 0.029 \bullet age - 0.47)$	1.71	2.81
$MEF_{50\%}$	L s^{-1}	$(3.79 \bullet height - 0.031 \bullet age - 0.35)$	1.32	2.17
$MEF_{25\%}$	L s^{-1}	$(2.61 \bullet height - 0.026 \bullet age - 1.34)$	0.78	1.28
		Women		
FVC	L	$(4.43 \bullet height - 0.026 \bullet age - 2.89)$	0.38	0.71
TLC	L	$(6.60 \bullet height - 5.79)$	0.60	0.99
RV	L	$(1.81 \bullet height + 0.016 \bullet age - 2.00)$	0.35	0.58
FRC	L	$(2.24 \bullet height + 0.001 \bullet age - 1.00)$	0.50	0.82
$FEV_{1.0}$	L	$(3.95 \bullet height - 0.025 \bullet age - 2.60)$	0.38	0.62
$FEV_{1.0}/FVC$	%	$89.1 - 0.19 \bullet age$	6.51	10.7
$FEF_{25-75\%}$	L s^{-1}	$(1.25 \bullet height - 0.034 \bullet age + 2.92)$	0.85	1.40
PEF	L s^{-1}	$(5.50 \bullet height - 0.030 \bullet age - 1.11)$	0.90	1.48
$MEF_{75\%}$	L s^{-1}	$(3.22 \bullet height - 0.025 \bullet age + 1.60)$	1.35	2.22
$MEF_{50\%}$	L s^{-1}	$(2.45 \bullet height - 0.025 \bullet age + 1.16)$	1.10	1.81
$MEF_{25\%}$	L s^{-1}	$(1.05 \bullet height - 0.025 \bullet age + 1.11)$	0.69	1.13

Height in metres, age in years. RSD is the residual standard deviation; i.e. standard deviation about the predicted value after allowing for age and height. Substitute 25 years in the equations for any adult under 25 years. The lower 5 or upper 95 percentiles are obtained by subtracting or adding the figure in the last column from the predicted mean.

is relatively greater than that of the legs. Such changes in body proportions can be resolved by taking the interaction between age and standing height into account (Quanjer *et al.* 1995).

The most commonly reported measure of how well a regression equation fits the data it describes is the residual standard deviation (RSD; standard error of the estimate). The RSD is the average standard deviation of the data around the regression line. The RSD will decrease as regression methods reduce the differences between predicted and observed values in the reference population. When the same equations are used to describe a different population, RSD will invariably be larger. Table 3.2 contains ERS prediction equations for healthy people aged 18–70 years, with a height range of 155–195 cm in males and 145–180 cm in females (Quanjer *et al.* 1993). Table 3.3 shows ERS reference equations for children aged 6–8 years (boys) and 6–16 years (girls) (Quanjer *et al.* 1995).

3.4.1 Estimation of lower limits of normal

Values below the 5th percentile or above the 95th percentile of the frequency distribution of values measured in the reference population are conventionally taken as outside the expected 'normal range' (Pellegrino *et al.* 2005). It is possible to calculate percentiles if there are sufficient measurements within each category. The value of the 5th percentile can be estimated as:

$$\text{Predicted value} - 1.64 \times \text{RSD}$$

For example, the predicted value of FVC for a 45-year-old male, stature 1.75 m, is 4.57 L according to the prediction equation of Quanjer *et al.* (1993) (see Table 3.2). The RSD is 0.61 L for this equation. Thus, the lower limit of normal (i.e. the lower 5% of the population) for a man of this age and stature would be 3.57 L ($4.57 - 1.64 \times 0.61$).

Defining a fixed $FEV_{1.0}/FVC$ ratio as a lower limit of normal (e.g. 70%) is not recommended because $FEV_{1.0}/FVC$ is inversely related to age and stature. The use of a fixed ratio will therefore result in a significant number of false-positive results in males aged >40 y and females >50 y (Hankinson *et al.* 1999), and a risk of overdiagnosis of obstructive disorders in asymptomatic elderly non-smokers (Hardie *et al.* 2002). In addition, some athletes have values for FVC that are relatively larger than those for $FEV_{1.0}$, which would result in a lower $FEV_{1.0}/FVC$ ratio. Thus, the definition of the lowest 5% of the reference population is also the preferred method to predict abnormality in this parameter.

3.5 INTERPRETATION OF LUNG FUNCTION TESTS

3.5.1 Obstruction

Obstructive ventilatory defects are characterized by a disproportionate reduction of maximal airflow from the lung with respect to the maximal volume (VC) that can be displaced from the lung. It implies narrowing of the airway during expiration and is defined as a reduced $FEV_{1.0}/VC$ ratio below the 5th percentile of the predicted value (Pellegrino *et al.* 2005). Early indications of airflow obstruction in small airways can be seen in the later stages of the volume-time curve. The slowing is reflected in a reduction in the instantaneous flow after 75% of the FVC has been exhaled ($FEF_{75-85\%}$) or in mean expiratory flow between 25% and 75% of FVC ($FEF_{25-75\%}$). Obstructive ventilatory disorders include asthma and chronic obstructive pulmonary disease (COPD). The latter term is used to describe patients with emphysema and/or chronic bronchitis.

3.5.2 Restriction

Restrictive ventilatory defects are those in which static lung volumes are diminished. Static lung volumes may be reduced by disorders which alter the elastic recoil of the lung (e.g. pulmonary fibrosis and emphysema) or the elastic properties of adjacent structures (e.g. ankylosis of joints). Static lung volumes may also be reduced by disorders of the respiratory pump (e.g. muscle weakness, muscle and motor nerve disorders and extreme obesity) or a decrease in the number of available alveolar units (e.g. atelectasis). Restrictive disorders are characterized by a reduction in TLC below the 5th percentile of the predicted value, and a normal or increased $FEV_{1.0}/VC$ (Pellegrino *et al.* 2005).

3.6 POST-EXERCISE CHANGES IN LUNG FUNCTION

In healthy nonasthmatic individuals, both the $FEV_{1.0}$ and the FVC increase during and immediately after exercise of short- and long-term duration. The most important mechanism responsible for this exercise-induced bronchodilation is withdrawal of

Table 3.3 Regression equations for the prediction of indices of lung function in healthy boys and girls of European descent aged 6–18 years (boys) and 6–16 years (girls) (modified from Quanjer *et al.* 1995)

Variable	Unit	Regression equation	RSD	1.64RSD
Boys				
$\log_e$ FEV$_{1.0}$	L	$-1.2933 + (1.2669 + 0.0174 \bullet age) \bullet height$	0.1097	0.18
$\log_e$ FVC	L	$-1.2782 + (1.3731 + 0.0164 \bullet age) \bullet height$	0.1033	0.17
FEV$_{1.0}$/FVC	%	86.21	5.58	9.15
Girls				
$\log_e$ FEV$_{1.0}$	L	$-1.5974 + (1.5016 + 0.0119 \bullet age) \bullet height$	0.1063	0.17
$\log_e$ FVC	L	$-1.4507 + (1.4800 + 0.0127 \bullet age) \bullet height$	0.1063	0.17
FEV$_{1.0}$/FVC	%	88.88	4.86	7.97

Height in metres; age in years. $\log_e$ is the natural logarithm. RSD is the residual standard deviation; i.e. standard deviation about the predicted value after allowing for age and height.

vagal parasympathetic tone to the airways. This vagal withdrawal occurs primarily reflexively via neural feedback from the activation of limb locomotor muscle mechanoreceptors at exercise onset (Kaufman and Forster 1996). The passive stretching of the airways with increasing tidal volume also contributes to airway dilation. Airway stretch results in a reduction in bronchial smooth muscle crossbridge formation by disturbing the bronchiolar smooth muscle latch state, and these reductions decrease smooth muscle stiffness and promote bronchial smooth muscle relaxation (Fredberg *et al.* 1997). In contrast to the normal bronchodilator response to exercise, most asthmatic individuals will demonstrate a post-exercise *reduction* in bronchial calibre defined as a fall in FEV$_{1.0}$ of >10% within 30 minuntes after maximum short-term exercise (Palange *et al.* 2007).

Although indices of bronchial calibre do change after exercise, the elastic characteristics of the lung and chest wall remain essentially unchanged. Thus, respiratory system compliance and TLC remain unchanged in response to exercise. Nevertheless, some studies have reported a post-exercise decrease in FVC (Miles *et al.* 1991; Rasmussen *et al.* 1988) and an increase in RV (Buono *et al.* 1981). Mechanisms that contribute to the observed transitory change in lung

volumes after exercise may include small airway narrowing consequent to reductions in maximum expiratory flow at low lung volumes, accumulation of pulmonary extravascular fluid due to increased blood volume in the lungs, and respiratory muscle fatigue.

3.7 ADAPTATIONS TO EXTERNAL STIMULI

3.7.1 Exercise training

Although lung size is influenced by the same anthropometric factors that may also predispose an individual to athletic success, it is unclear whether the function of the lung and airways can be improved by exercise training. In adults, most evidence suggests that whole-body exercise training has little or no positive effect on static lung function (Gaultier and Crapo 1997). An exception may be swimmers, who tend to have larger than average values for VC and TLC compared with the normal population (Andrew *et al.* 1972; Åstrand *et al.* 1963; Armour *et al.* 1993; Cordain *et al.* 1990). This assertion is supported by longitudinal data showing that 12 weeks of competitive swim training in already fit adults resulted in small but significant increases in VC, TLC and FRC (Clanton *et al.* 1987). In children, several studies have reported an increase in static lung volumes, over that expected from the age-dependent increase in stature, with long-term swim training (Engstrom *et al.* 1977; Zinman and Gaultier 1987), running training (Ekblom 1969) and enhanced physical education programmes (Shephard and Lavallee 1996). In a study that used an age-matched control group, a year of swim training in prepubertal girls evoked improvements in VC, FRC, TLC and airflow per unit lung volume (Courteix *et al.* 1997). In contrast with the lack of effect of exercise training on static lung function, training does appear to improve specific measures of dynamic lung function such as MVV (Davis *et al.* 1979) and maximum sustainable ventilatory capacity (Martin and Kjeldgaard 1982).

Training directed specifically at the respiratory muscles has been shown to promote small but significant improvements in lung function (McConnell and Romer 2004). For example, daily bouts of inspiratory and expiratory loading over the VC volume range increased VC and TLC by only about 4%, despite a more than 50% increase in strength of the respiratory muscles (Leith and Bradley 1976). Another study showed that VC and TLC could be increased by about 4% after a 6-week training period that involved performing multiple daily breath holds at TLC (Fanta *et al.* 1983). The mechanism responsible for the increases in VC and TLC is unclear, but may be due to an increased ability to contract the inspiratory muscles to shorter lengths. When the respiratory muscles were trained by voluntarily increasing ventilation (hyperpnoea), MVV and maximum sustainable ventilatory capacity were increased by about 15% (Leith and Bradley 1976).

3.7.2 Altitude

Like the acclimatized visitor, the high-altitude native hyperventilates relative to a normal sea-level person. This increases alveolar ventilation and limits the fall in the partial pressure of oxygen in the alveoli, thereby lessening the reduction in the oxygen pressure gradient across the alveolar membrane. At any given altitude, the ventilation of the acclimatized visitor is greater than that of the native highlander by about 20% (Minors 1985). Thus, the high-altitude native seems to have lost some respiratory sensitivity to hypoxia.

Part of the adaptive response in individuals raised at high-altitudes (>3000 m) is an increase in static lung volumes. On average, TLC is 7–15% higher in high-altitude natives compared with low-altitude natives and smaller differences have been reported for VC while larger differences have been found for FRC and RV (Frisancho 1975; DeGraff *et al.* 1970; Greksa *et al.* 1988). The larger lung volumes in high-altitude natives are not explained by race or body size (Frisancho 1975), and are not accompanied by increased airflow (Zeltner and Burri 1987). This latter finding suggests that the airways do not participate in the adaptation to high altitude. Larger lungs in high-altitude natives are probably acquired as a result of exposure to hypoxia during growth, rather than as a result of being born at high altitude (Frisancho 1975; Lahiri *et al.* 1976). Morphometric measurements of the lungs of high-altitude natives have shown alveoli that are larger and greater in number than those in lowland natives of the same body size (Saldana and Oyola 1970). The increased alveolar surface area in contact with functioning pulmonary capillaries, in combination with an increased pulmonary capillary blood volume, leads to an increased pulmonary diffusing capacity (Dempsey *et al.* 1971). The combination of increased alveolar ventilation and pulmonary diffusing capacity increases the total alveolar gas exchange in the highlander (Dempsey *et al.* 1971).

3.7.3 Diving

Pulmonary adaptations to years of diving without specialized equipment have been noted in US Navy Escape Training Tank instructors (Carey *et al.* 1956) and to a lesser extent in male recreational divers (Hong *et al.* 1970). Such changes include an increase in VC, a decrease in RV and a reduction in the RV:TLC ratio. Adaptations have also been observed in the Korean diving women known as the *Ama*. Before each dive an Ama hyperventilates then dives between 5–18 m for 20–40 s in repeated dives for approximately 3 h d^{-1}. Song *et al.* (1963) observed VC to be 125% and MVV to be 128% of predicted values. They also observed a higher inspiratory capacity (IC = V_T + EILV), but no difference in ERV between the Ama and a group of controls. The RV, expressed as a proportion of TLC, was also lower in the Ama. The reason for the increased VC was attributed to the increased IC of the Ama. As with swim training (see previous section), the reason for the difference could be attributed to an increase in the maximal shortening of the inspiratory muscles as a result of performing multiple daily sustained inhalations to TLC (Fanta *et al.* 1983). The lower RV:TLC ratio was considered to be important because it determines the maximal depth of diving.

3.8 VENTILATION

3.8.1 Pulmonary ventilation

Pulmonary ventilation refers to the mass movement of gas into and out of the lungs. It is regulated to provide the gas exchange necessary for metabolic requirements, while maintaining acid-base balance and limiting the metabolic cost of respiratory work. It is commonly assessed by measuring the total volume of air expired per minute and is abbreviated $\dot{V}_E$. Inhaled volumes are very slightly greater than exhaled volumes because more oxygen is taken in than carbon dioxide is given out. It is dependent on rate (respiratory frequency, f_R) and depth of ventilation per breath (tidal volume, V_T) such that

$$\dot{V}_E = f_R \cdot V_T$$

At rest $\dot{V}_E$ varies between 4 and 15 L min^{-1}, with typical values for f_R and V_T of 10–20 breaths min^{-1} and 0.4–0.6 L, respectively.

3.8.2 Factors affecting pulmonary ventilation

Factors affecting pulmonary ventilation relate mainly to age, body size, sex and physical fitness. Maximal pulmonary ventilation peaks at about 15 years of age for females and 25 years of age for males. The greater pulmonary ventilation in males compared to females after the age of about 15 years is primarily the result of body size. When the male hormone testosterone is secreted in larger quantities, the skeletal and muscle mass of males increases rapidly. As the rib cage enlarges, the thoracic cavity can accommodate larger quantities of air. Maximal pulmonary ventilation then decreases with age, declining to less than half the peak value (Figure 3.6). Increases in maximal ventilation from young age to adulthood are caused primarily by physical maturation. As children grow in body mass, and particularly in stature, pulmonary ventilation increases accordingly. However, adults over 25 years of age who have reached full physical growth exhibit reduced levels of maximal ventilation, even though body size remains the same or increases. The decline after young adulthood is due, in part, to a reduction in maximal metabolic demands, consequent to the physical inactivity that often accompanies ageing. There is loss of lung elastic recoil and a reduced number of elastic attachments supporting alveoli airways, causing these airways to close excessively during expiration and hence at higher lung volumes. The chest wall becomes stiffer at high lung volumes due to costal cartilage calcification, a narrowing of intervertebral distances and an increase in the anteroposterior diameter of the chest. Furthermore, the inspiratory muscles' capability to generate force is markedly reduced with age. Such reductions in chest wall stiffness and inspiratory muscle strength would be expected to limit tidal volume, and

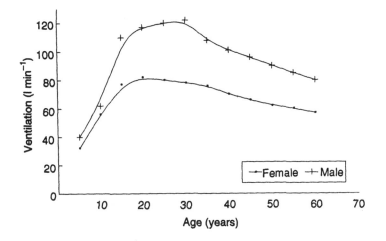

Figure 3.6 Relationship between maximal pulmonary ventilation and age for males and females. (Data from Åstrand, 1952.)

hence pulmonary ventilation, during maximal exercise in the healthy elderly (Johnson *et al.* 1991). Unfortunately, the loss of lung function with ageing does not appear to be prevented by exercise training (McClaran *et al.* 1995).

3.8.3 Alveolar ventilation and dead space

Only about two-thirds of the inspired V_T reaches the alveoli where gas exchange occurs. The volume of fresh air entering the alveolar gas compartment each minute is called the *alveolar ventilation*. The air that remains in the respiratory passages not participating in gas exchange is called the *dead space*. Expired total ventilation is therefore the sum of alveolar ventilation ($\dot{V}_A$) and dead space ventilation ($\dot{V}_D$), or

$$\dot{V}_E = \dot{V}_A + \dot{V}_D$$

If, at a total ventilation of 6.0 L min^{-1}, the respiratory frequency is 10 and the dead space volume is 0.15 L, the alveolar ventilation is

$$6.0 - (10 \times 0.15) = 4.5 \text{ L min}^{-1}$$

If the respiratory frequency is 20, and the dead space ventilation is unchanged, the alveolar ventilation becomes

$$6.0 - (20 \times 0.15) = 3.0 \text{ L min}^{-1}$$

3.8.4 Factors affecting dead space

Factors affecting the dead space include size of the subject; age; posture; position of the neck and jaw; and lung volume at the end of inspiration. It is evident that subject size affects the dimensions of the respiratory passages not involved in gas exchange such that dead space increases with body size. The average resting value of the dead space volume is about one-third of the resting V_T, which equates to about 150 and 100 ml in men and women respectively, although larger values are obtained when upright than when supine (Riley *et al.* 1959). When submerged in water, breathing through a snorkel presents a considerable challenge to gas exchange. The snorkel represents an extension of the respiratory dead space, and the tidal volume has to be increased by an amount equal to the volume of the tube if alveolar ventilation is to be maintained. During exercise, dilation of the airways may cause dead space to double, but since the tidal volume also increases, adequate alveolar ventilation, and therefore gas exchange, is maintained. Although it is not possible to measure the dead space exactly, it is possible to estimate the dead space volume using Bohr's formula, which is explained in Practical 1 of this chapter.

3.9 VENTILATORY RESPONSES TO EXERCISE

During light to moderate exercise, pulmonary ventilation increases linearly with oxygen consumption ($\dot{V}S_{O2}$), with a relatively greater increase at heavier intensities (Figure 3.7). It is not uncommon for maximal ventilation to reach values as high as 180 L min^{-1} and 130 L min^{-1} for male and female athletes, respectively. When pulmonary ventilation is expressed in relation to the magnitude of oxygen uptake, it is termed the *ventilatory equivalent* ($\dot{V}_E/\dot{V}O_2$). It is maintained at about 20–25 litres (BTPS) breathed for 1 litre (standard temperature and pressure, dry (STPD)) of oxygen consumed. With progressively increasing exercise intensities, ventilation increases disproportionately compared with the increase in oxygen consumption such that $\dot{V}_E/\dot{V}O_2$ may reach 35–40.

In children under 10 years of age, the ventilatory equivalent for oxygen is about 30 during light exercise and up to 40 during maximal exercise (Rowland and Cunningham 1997). The reason why the ventilatory equivalent is higher in children than it is in adults may be because the ventilation for a given exercise intensity is higher in children. The higher ventilation may be due, in part, to children's higher oxygen cost of exercise owing to biomechanical and respiratory inefficiencies. Consequently, ventilation would be higher to accommodate the elevated $\dot{V}O_2$. Another potential explanation is that children tend to ventilate more for a given $\dot{V}O_2$, due to age-related changes in the sensitivity to levels of carbon dioxide.

3.9.1 Breathing patterns and lung volumes

During light to moderate exercise, the increase in pulmonary ventilation is achieved by increasing both respiratory frequency and tidal volume. At higher exercise intensities, tidal volume tends to level off and an increase in respiratory frequency accounts for all of the further increase in ventilation. This breathing strategy minimizes the increase in dead space ventilation while maximizing effective alveolar ventilation. In addition to optimizing pulmonary gas exchange, this

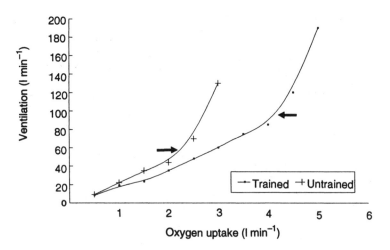

Figure 3.7 Relationship between pulmonary ventilation and maximum oxygen consumption in trained and untrained individuals. (Data from Saltin and Åstrand, 1967.)

breathing pattern minimizes airflow and, hence, the flow-resistive work of breathing. The increase in tidal volume is limited to 70% of vital capacity during heavy exercise and, in untrained healthy individuals, is accompanied by a reduction in EELV below FRC (Johnson *et al.* 1992). This breathing strategy ensures that the elastic component of the work of breathing is minimized. That is, the increase in tidal volume occurs over the most compliant portion of the respiratory pressure-volume relationship such that the least amount of negative intra-thoracic pressure has to be generated by the inspiratory muscles for a given increase in volume. The reduced EELV, achieved by activation of the expiratory muscles, means that intra-abdominal pressure is elevated allowing for the storage of elastic energy in the chest wall during expiration, which can be used to produce a significant amount of the work required during the ensuing inspiration. The reduced EELV also means that the diaphragm is lengthened at end-expiration, increasing its capability for force generation.

3.9.2 Ventilatory threshold

As exercise intensity increases, $\dot{V}O_2$ increases linearly, but blood lactate concentration changes only slightly until about 50–80% of $\dot{V}O_{2max}$ depending on training status. After this, the blood lactate concentration increases more rapidly (see Figure 10.2, Jones *et al.* (2009, Chapter 10). Because blood acidity is one factor that increases $\dot{V}_E$, the abrupt increase in $\dot{V}_E$ during incremental exercise is often used to infer the inflection point in the blood lactate curve. This has been termed the *anaerobic threshold* and procedures for its derivation are explained in detail by Wasserman *et al.* (2005) and Jones *et al.* (2009, Chapter 10). The concept is considered to be a misnomer by some experts as the physiological reasons for the rapid increase in $\dot{V}_E$ beyond the inflection point are not necessarily due to metabolic acidosis. Consequently, the disproportionate rise in

$\dot{V}_E$ is preferably referred to as the *ventilatory threshold* (T_{vent}). The T_{vent} for the trained and untrained person is indicated in Figure 3.7 by the solid arrows.

One of the most pertinent refutations of the anaerobic threshold was the study by Hagberg *et al.* (1982) on patients with McArdle's syndrome. These patients lack the enzyme myophosphorylase, which renders them incapable of catabolising glycogen and producing lactate. Hagberg *et al.* (1982) showed that these patients possess ventilatory thresholds despite the fact that there are no changes in blood lactate concentration (Figure 3.8). Further evidence stems from the finding that dietary-induced glycogen depletion prevented almost all of the exercise-induced increase in lactic acid, yet a normal hyperventilatory response persisted (Busse *et al.* 1991).

3.9.3 Acute and chronic ventilatory responses to arm and leg exercise

Ventilatory responses appear to be specific to the type of exercise performed. The ventilatory equivalent for oxygen is greater during arm exercise than during leg work (Rasmussen *et al.* 1975; Eston and Brodie 1986). As arm exercise elicits a more pronounced metabolic acidosis for any given work-rate (Stenberg *et al.* 1967) it is likely that this factor, in conjunction with a higher sympathetic outflow for arm work (Davies *et al.* 1974), contributes significantly to the higher ventilation during arm exercise. The higher ventilation during arm exercise may be an important factor in maintaining ventricular filling pressure and stroke volume in the absence of the mechanical effect of the leg muscle pump (Bevegard *et al.* 1966). Additional factors which influence ventilation during arm exercise may include (a) mechanical limitation of tidal volume by static contractions of the pectoralis and abdominal musculature; and (b) coupling/synchronization of respiratory frequency with the rhythmic movement of the arms (Mangum 1984).

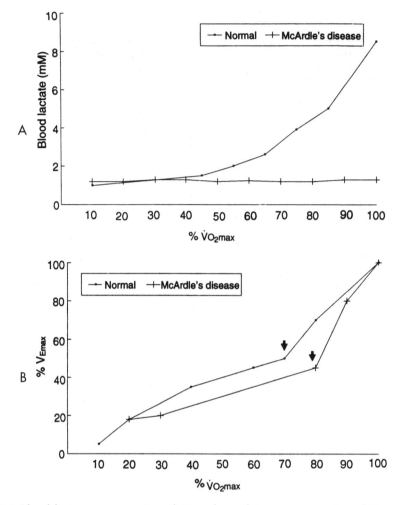

Figure 3.8 Blood lactate responses (panel A) and ventilatory responses (panel B) to continuous, progressive cycle exercise in normal controls and in patients with McArdle's syndrome during continuous, progressive exercise on a cycle ergometer. Both groups display a ventilatory threshold (arrow), despite the fact that there is no corresponding lactate threshold in the McArdle's patients. (Modified from Hagberg *et al.* 1982.)

The reduction in ventilatory equivalent for oxygen that occurs through training is also dependent on the specificity of training. Rasmussen *et al.* (1975) observed that reductions in the ventilatory equivalent for oxygen occurred only when the mode of exercise training matched the activity. In a comparison of groups trained with either arm ergometry or leg ergometry, the ventilatory equivalent was reduced only in arm exercise for the arm-trained group (from 30 to 25) and only in leg exercise for the leg-trained group (from 26 to 23). Arm training did not reduce the ventilatory equivalent for oxygen during leg exercise and vice versa.

3.9.4 Pulmonary ventilation and training

Endurance training reduces total ventilation at any given submaximal exercise intensity (Jirka and Adamus 1965; Tzankoff *et al.* 1972; Fringer and Stull 1974; Rasmussen *et al.* 1975). Proposed mechanisms for the reduction in ventilation include a reduction in circulating stimuli (such as hydrogen ions, noradrenaline and potassium), a decreased ventilatory responsiveness of the chemo-receptors to circulating stimuli, and/or a reduced central motor command owing to a delay in limb locomotor muscle fatigue. In general, the tidal volume becomes larger and the respiratory frequency is reduced with endurance training. Consequently, air remains in the lungs for a longer period of time between breaths, resulting in an increase in the amount of oxygen extracted from the inspired air. The exhaled air of trained individuals often contains only 14–15% oxygen during submaximal exercise, whereas the expired air of untrained persons may contain 18% oxygen at the same work rate. The untrained person must therefore ventilate proportionately more air to achieve the same oxygen uptake (Figure 3.7). In contrast with the effects of endurance training on the ventilatory response to submaximal exercise, ventilation at maximal exercise is increased. This is an expected response, because the parallel increase in maximal oxygen uptake results in a larger oxygen requirement and a correspondingly larger production of carbon dioxide that must be removed through increased ventilation.

3.10 PRACTICAL EXERCISES

In the following sections we suggest three laboratory Practicals to determine lung function in the resting state (Practical 1) and during exercise (Practical 2). Practical 3 describes the measurement of oxygen uptake using the closed circuit method, during which lung function measures may also be demonstrated. Each Practical contains actual data to exemplify the relationships between variables and provide examples and applications of the various formulae for assessing lung function.

3.11 PRACTICAL 1: ASSESSMENT OF RESTING LUNG FUNCTION

3.11.1 Purpose

The purpose of this Practical is to measure static and dynamic lung function in the resting state; to determine relationships between lung function and anthropometric variables; and to assess the effects of changes in posture on lung function. Data are presented in Table 3.4 to exemplify some of these measurements.

Procedures

a) Closed circuit spirometry
1   Record the subject's age, stature, body mass, and physical activity/training status.
2   Record ambient conditions (temperature, barometric pressure).
3   Record sitting height, arm span and chest circumference.
4   Measurement of inspired and expired volumes using a wet spirometer with kymograph.
    (a) Sanitize all equipment and mouthpiece.
    (b) The subject puts on a nose clip.
    (c) Procedure:
        i)   The recording pen is best placed just below half-way on the kymograph.
        ii) Set the drum rotation speed to 10 mm s^{-1}
        iii) Ask the subject to breathe normally into and out of the spirometer to allow

measurement of *tidal volume* (V_T) and *respiratory frequency* (f_R).

iv) At the end of a normal inspiration, ask the subject to inhale as deeply as possible to measure *inspiratory reserve volume* (IRV), and return to normal breathing.

v) At the end of a normal expiration, ask the subject to expire as much as possible to determine the *expiratory reserve volume* (ERV), and return to normal breathing.

vi) The subject is then requested to inhale as deeply as possible, and with minimal hesitation exhale as forcefully as possible to measure the *forced vital capacity* (FVC).

vii) *Residual volume* can be predicted from the relevant equation in Table 3.2 or it can be measured by the method explained in the laboratory practical described by Eston *et al.* (2009). This will allow *total lung capacity* (TLC) and *functional residual capacity* (FRC) to be calculated.

b) Open circuit spirometry (Vitalograph)

Measurement of FVC, $FEV_{1.0}$, $FEV_{1.0\%}$, MMEF ($FEF_{25-75\%}$), $FEF_{75-85\%}$, PEF, $FEF_{0.2-1.2}$ and MMEF time.

5   (a) Set the Vitalograph spirometer to zero.

(b) From the seated position, ask the subject to inhale as deeply as possible, place the spirometer mouthpiece into the mouth, and exhale as forcefully as possible over a period of 5–6 s. Record the best of at least three readings.

(c) Calculate the various lung function parameters as indicated in Figure 3.5.

(d) Compare individual scores with predicted scores using one of the appropriate regression equations listed in Table 3.2 and record all data.

(e) Repeat the above procedures with the subject in the supine position.

6   Measurement of *maximal voluntary ventilation* (MVV) (Figure 3.3).

(a) Predict MVV using the formula:

$$MVV = FEV_{0.75} \times 40 \text{ (Cotes, 1979)}$$

where:

$FEV_{0.75} = 0.92 \times FEV_{1.0} - 0.07$ (95% limits ±8%)

(b) Insert mouthpiece and attach the nose clip.

(c) Ask the subject to breathe as deeply and rapidly as possible for 15 s into either a Douglas bag or directly into a dry gas spirometer. Convert the values into litres per minute (BTPS).

(d) Record values on data sheet.

Table 3.4 Example of lung function parameters at rest in a 38-year-old active male

Descriptive Data

Name	RGE	Age (y)	38
Stature (m)	1.78	Mass (kg)	86.0
Sitting Height (m)	0.91	Arm span (m)	1.84

Ambient conditions

Laboratory temperature (°C)	20	P_{Bar} (mmHg)	760

(a) Resting measurements (dry spirometer)[a]

FVC (L)	$FEV_{1.0}$ (L)	$FEV_{1.0\%}$	$FEF_{25-75\%}$ ($L\,s^{-1}$)	$FEF_{75-85\%}$ ($L\,s^{-1}$)	$FEF_{0.2-1.2}$ ($L\,s^{-1}$)	MMEFT (s)	MVV ($L\,min^{-1}$)
Standing							
6.65	5.41	81.2	5.37	1.20	13.0	0.62	230
Supine							
6.32	5.10	80.6	5.21	1.10	11.0	0.81	190
Predicted values							
4.93	4.26	80.4	4.52	1.27	9.00	0.73	196.3

(b) Resting measurements (wet spirometer)[a]

V_T (L)		IRV (L)	ERV (L)	FVC (L)	RV (L)	FRC (L)	TLC (L)
Measured							
0.60		3.20	1.65	6.65	1.80	3.45	8.45
Predicted Values							
0.60		2.91	1.39	5.02	1.94	2.73	6.80

[a] All values were recorded at BTPS

7   Measurement of V_T, f_R and pulmonary ventilation ($\dot{V}_E$) at rest.
The subject sits quietly for 5 minutes. Collect expired air into a Douglas bag in the final minute. The respiratory frequency can be counted by the rise and fall of the chest wall or by movement of the respiratory valves. Tidal volume can be calculated from the following:

$$V_T = \dot{V}_{E\ BTPS} / f_R$$

8   Computation of dead space.
The volume of dead space can be calculated using Bohr's formula, which is based on the fact that the volume of oxygen for each expiration ($V_T \times F_EO_2$) is equal to the sum of the volume of oxygen contained in the dead space compartment ($V_D \times F_IO_2$) and the volume of oxygen coming from the alveolar air ($V_A \times F_AO_2$). We therefore arrive at the following formula:

$$V_T \times F_EO_2 = (V_D \times F_IO_2) + (V_A \times F_AO_2)$$

Since $V_A = V_T - V_D$, the formula may be simplified as follows:

$$V_D = V_T \times \frac{F_EO_2 - F_AO_2}{F_IO_2 - F_AO_2}$$

If the percentage of oxygen in inspired air is 21%, the percentage of oxygen in the expired air is 16%, the percentage of oxygen in the alveolar air is 14% and the depth of the breath (V_T) is 500 ml, the dead space volume (V_D) is:

$$V_D = 500 \times \frac{16 - 15}{21 - 14} = 143 \text{ ml}$$

3.11.3 Assignments

1 Examine the spirogram from the wet spirometry practical. Comment on the relative magnitude of the various volumes; e.g. compare IRV with ERV.
2 Comment on the relationship between stature, sitting height, body mass, chest circumference, arm span and the lung function measurements ($FEV_{1.0}$, FVC).
3 Compare the accuracy of the prediction of MVV by the $FEV_{0.75}$ method with the 15 s Douglas bag method.
4 Compare the measured values with the predicted values in Table 3.2.
5 Compare the spirometry values in the standing and supine position.
6 Compare the resting $\dot{V}_E$, V_T and f_R measurements with expected values. Consider the effects of body size on these measurements.
7 Calculate the relative size of each breath as a proportion of the vital capacity in the standing and supine positions (% FVC = (V_T / FVC) × 100).
8 Compare values between males and females.
9 Is there any relationship between the level of physical training and lung function values?

3.12 PRACTICAL 2: ASSESSMENT OF LUNG FUNCTION DURING EXERCISE

3.12.1 Purpose

To assess the influence of arm and leg exercise on pulmonary ventilation, alveolar ventilation, respiratory frequency, tidal volume and the ventilatory equivalent for oxygen. Some data are presented in Table 3.5 to exemplify these measurements.

Table 3.5 Example of lung function parameters at rest and during different modes of exercise in a 38-year-old active male

Descriptive Data

Name	RGE	Age (y)	38
Stature (m)	1.78	Mass (kg)	86
Sitting height (m)	0.91	Arm span (m)	1.84

Ambient conditions

Laboratory temperature (°C)	20	P_{Bar} (mmHg)	760

a) Resting values

$\dot{V}_E$ (L min^{-1})	V_T (L)	V_T (%FVC)	f_R (b/min)	O_2 (%)	CO_2 (%)	$\dot{V}O_2$ (L min^{-1})	$\dot{V}_{Eeq}$	V_D (ml)
9.1	0.70	10.0	13	15.7	4.00	0.36	25.0	172.0

b) Arm exercise

Watts	$\dot{V}_E$ (L min^{-1})	V_T (L)	V_T (%FVC)	f_R (b/min)	O_2 (%)	CO_2 (%)	$\dot{V}O_2$ (L min^{-1})	$\dot{V}_{Eeq}$
25	21.6	1.20	18.0	18	16.4	4.1	0.82	26.3
50	32.2	1.40	21.0	23	16.2	4.3	1.29	25.0
75	50.4	1.80	27.0	28	16.4	4.3	1.91	26.3
100	70.5	2.13	32.0	33	16.4	4.5	2.63	26.6
125	95.5	2.45	37.0	39	17.0	4.5	2.97	32.1
150	118.4	2.80	42.0	42	17.2	4.5	3.43	34.4

c) Leg exercise

Watts	$\dot{V}_E$ (L min^{-1})	V_T (L)	V_T (%FVC)	f_R (b/min)	O_2 (%)	CO_2 (%)	$\dot{V}O_2$ (L min^{-1})	$\dot{V}_{Eeq}$
25	16.0	1.0	15.0	16	16.3	4.0	0.63	25.4
50	24.3	1.43	21.4	17	16.0	4.0	1.03	23.6
75	29.4	1.47	22.1	20	16.0	4.1	1.24	23.7
100	38.6	1.68	25.2	23	16.3	4.2	1.51	25.7
125	47.1	1.96	29.5	24	16.5	3.9	1.80	26.2
150	53.3	2.05	30.8	26	16.4	4.0	2.05	26.0
200	69.1	2.03	30.5	30	16.6	4.4	2.44	28.3
250	96.3	2.91	43.8	33	16.8	4.6	3.18	30.2
300	130.0	3.51	52.8	37	17.0	4.6	4.02	32.3

Formulae:

$$V_T = \dot{V}_{E\,(BTPS)} / f_R$$
$$V_T \text{ as } \%FVC = (V_T/FVC) \times 100$$
$$\dot{V}O_2 = \dot{V}_{E\,(STPD)} \times ((1 - (F_EO_2 + F_ECO_2)) \times 0.265) - F_EO_2$$
$$\dot{V}O_2 = \dot{V}_E \times 0.04$$
$$\dot{V}_E = \dot{V}O_2 \times 20 - 25$$
$$V_{Tmax} = 0.74\,FVC \times 1.11$$
$$\dot{V}_{Eeq} = \dot{V}_{E\,(BTPS)} / \dot{V}O_{2\,(STPD)}$$
$$V_D = V_T \times \frac{F_EO_2 - F_AO_2}{F_IO_2 \quad F_AO_2}$$
$$F_EO_2 = \%O_2/100$$

Correction of gas volumes:

From ATPS to STPD $\dot{V}_{STPD} = \dot{V}_{ATPS} \times (273/(273 + T°C)) \times ((P_{Bar} - P_{H2O})/760)$

From ATPS to BTPS $\dot{V}_{BTPS} = \dot{V}_{ATPS} \times (310/(273 + T°C)) \times ((P_{Bar} - P_{H2O})/(P_{Bar} - 47))$

From STPD to BTPS $\dot{V}_{BTPS} = \dot{V}_{STPD} \times (310/273) \times (760/(P_{Bar} - 47))$

$PH_2O = 13.955 - 0.6584T + 0.0419T^2$

3.12.2 Procedures

1 Record the subject's age, stature, body mass and physical activity/training status.
2 Record ambient conditions (temperature, barometric pressure).
3 Perform the FVC test to obtain a spirogram for analysis of pre-exercise static and dynamic volumes.
4 Assessment of resting pulmonary values: the subject rests and breathes normally for 5 minutes. Collect expired air in the final minute in a Douglas bag. Record the respiratory frequency and compute tidal volume as described in Practical 1. Lung volumes should be recorded at BTPS (i.e. convert ambient temperature and pressure, saturdated (ATPS) to BTPS using the formula in Table 3.5).
5 Determine the oxygen and carbon dioxide fraction in the Douglas bag.
6 Incremental exercise test: exercises the subject at 25 W on the arm ergometer with increments of 25 W every 3 minutes until maximal volitional exhaustion (or 150 W). Direct expired air into a Douglas bag to obtain the oxygen and carbon dioxide fractions. Measure respiratory frequency. Measure the volume of expired air through a dry gas meter.
7 Rest the subject for 10–15 minutes.
8 Repeat the procedure described in steps 6 and 7 on a cycle ergometer at identical work-rates (for comparison of arm and leg values). Increase the work-rates by 50 W every 3 minutes until maximal volitional exhaustion. Collect expired air over the final minute of each increment.
9 Rest the subject for 5 minutes.
10 Perform the FVC test to obtain a spirogram for analysis of post-exercise static and dynamic volumes.

3.12.3 ASSIGNMENTS

1 Determine VT and the relative size of each breath in relation to the FVC for arm and leg work (%FVC = (VT /FVC) × 100).
2 Determine the ventilatory equivalent (V.Eeq) at rest, and during submaximal and maximal work intensities for arm and leg ergometry.

$\dot{V}_{Eeq} = \dot{V}_{E\,(BTPS)} / \dot{V}O_{2\,(STPD)}$

3 What do you notice about the pulmonary ventilation for arm ergometry at submaximal and maximal work-rates?
4 Are there any differences in the V.E and V.Eeq responses for trained and untrained individuals?

5 Compare the pre- and post-exercise spirogram results. What do you notice about the static and dynamic lung volumes and flow rates?

6 How accurate are the following equations for predicting $\dot{V}_E$, $\dot{V}O_2$ and V_{Tmax}?

$$\dot{V}_E = (\dot{V}O_2 \, (L \, min^{-1}) \times 20) - 25$$
$$\dot{V}O_2 = \dot{V}_E \, (L \, min^{-1}) \times 0.04$$
(Datta and Ramanathan 1969)

$$V_{Tmax} = 0.74 \, FVC - 1.11$$
(Jones 1984)

7 How does the relationship between $\dot{V}_E$ and $\dot{V}O2$ compare to previously observed values from the literature? Does $\dot{V}_E$ limit $\dot{V}O_{2max}$?

8 Compare the MVV obtained from the 15 s test to the maximum $\dot{V}_E$ obtained in the exercise test. Why is MVV usually greater than $\dot{V}_E max$?

3.13 PRACTICAL 3: MEASUREMENT OF OXYGEN UPTAKE BY CLOSED-CIRCUIT CALORIMETRY

3.13.1 Purpose

Although the closed-circuit indirect spirometry system is rarely used today, it can be used to exemplify some of the basic principles of measurement of oxygen consumption at rest and during exercise. Estimations of energy expenditure can be calculated using caloric equivalents for oxygen uptake for an RER of 0.83, i.e. 20.2 kJ L^{-1} (4.8 kcal L^{-1}). The following procedure should be used to produce spirometry tracings as exemplified in Figure 3.9.

3.13.2 Procedure

1 Rinse the spirometer with 100% oxygen and then fill with 100% oxygen.

2 Seat the subject on the arm ergometer, connect to the spirometer, and then let them breathe atmospheric air for a few minutes to familiarize with the mouthpiece and the resistance of the spirometer.

3 Direct expired air through soda lime to remove carbon dioxide.

4 Set the kymograph speed at 25 mm min^{-1}.

5 The subject then inspires oxygen from the spirometer. Initially, the expired air should be directed to the atmosphere. The spirometer should then be closed so that oxygen is breathed from and back into the spirometer. Recordings can be made for several minutes, after which time the subject should breathe normal air.

6 After a warm-up the subject should then commence arm ergometry at 50 W for 3 min. Oxygen is inspired from the spirometer for the last minute. The spirometer is then refilled with oxygen.

7 After a 20-minute rest period the mode of ergometry is switched to lower limb cycling at 50 W and the above procedure is repeated.

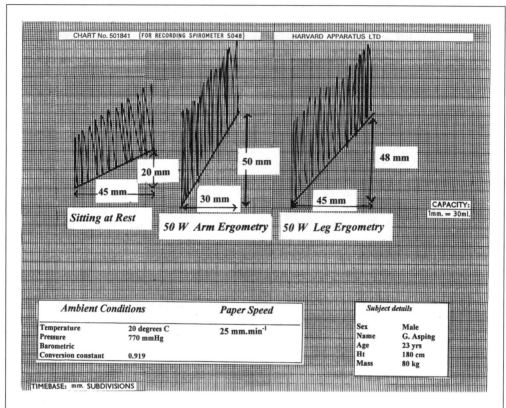

Figure 3.9 Closed circuit spirogram showing oxygen uptake at rest and during arm and leg exercise for a healthy, fit male student.

8 Oxygen uptake at STPD may be calculated using the formula below. The correction factor for converting ATPS to STPD volumes can be calculated from the formula in Practical 6.3 or from Table 6.2 (Cooke 2009).

Calculation of $\dot{V}O_2$ at STPD (ml min^{-1})

$$\frac{y \text{ (mm)} \times 30 \text{ (ml mm}^{-1}) \times \text{correction factor (CF)} \times 60 \text{ (s)}}{x \text{ (mm)} \times 2.4 \text{ (s}^{-1} \text{ mm)}}$$

Sitting at rest (20 × 30 × 0.919 × 60) / (45 × 2.4) = 306 ml min^{-1}
Arm ergometry (50 W)   (50 × 30 × 0.919 × 60) / (30 × 2.4) = 1149 ml min^{-1}
Leg ergometry (50 W)   (48 × 30 × 0.919 × 60) / (45 × 2.4) = 735 ml min^{-1}
NB: paper speed = 25 mm min^{-1} or 1 mm = 2.4 s

FURTHER READING

Books:

Dempsey J. A., Miller J. D. and Romer L. M. (2006) The respiratory system. In: (C. M. Tipton, ed). *ACSM's Advanced Exercise Physiology*. Lippincott Williams & Wilkins; London.

West J. B. (2005) *Respiratory Physiology (7th Edition)*. Lippincott Williams & Wilkins; London.

Journals:

Pellegrino R. *et al.* (2005) Interpretive strategies for lung function tests. *European Respiratory Journal*; **26**: 948–68.

Romer L. M. and Polkey M. I. (2008) Exercise-induced respiratory muscle fatigue: implications for performance. *Journal of Applied Physiology*; **104**: 879–88.

Websites:

http://www.spirxpert.com/ This is an excellent site by Phillip Quanjer covering all aspects of spirometry.

European Respiratory Society http://dev.ersnet.org/

REFERENCES

Allen S. M., Hunt B. and Green,, M. (1985) Fall in vital capacity with posture. *British Journal of Diseases of the Chest*; **79**: 267–71.

Andrew G. M., Becklake M. R., Guleria J. S. and Bates D. V. (1972) Heart and lung functions in swimmers and non athletes during growth. *Journal of Applied Physiology*; **32**: (2) 245–51.

Armour J., Donnely P. M. and Bye P. T. P. (1993) The large lungs of elite swimmers. *European Respiratory Journal*; **6**: 237–47.

Åstrand P. O. (1952) *Experimental Studies of Physical Work Capacity in Relation to Sex and Age*. E. Munksgard; Copenhagen.

Åstrand P. O., Engstrom I., Eriksson B. O., Larlberg, P., Nylander I., Saltin B. and Thoren C. (1963) Girl swimmers with special reference to respiratory and circulatory adaptation and gynaecological and psychiatric aspects. *Acta Paediatrica Scandinavica*; **S147**: 43–63.

Becklake M. R. (1986) Concepts of normality applied to the measurement of lung function. *American Journal of Medicine*; **80**: 1158–64.

Bevegard S., Freyschuss U. and Strandell T. (1966) Circulatory adaptation to arm and leg exercise in supine and sitting position. *Journal of Applied Physiology*; **21**: 37–46.

Blair E. and Hickam J. B. (1955) The effect of change in body position on lung volume and intrapulmonary gas mixing in normal subjects. *Journal of Clinical Investigations*; **34**: 383–9.

Buono M. J., Constable S. A., Morton A. R., Rotkis T. C., Stanforth P. R. and Wilmore J. H. (1981) The effect of an acute bout of exercise on selected pulmonary function measurements. *Medicine and Science in Sports and Exercise*; **13**: 290–3.

Busse M. W., Maassen N., Konrad, H. (1991). Relation between K+ and ventilation during incremental exercise after glycogen depletion and repletion in man. *The Journal of Physiology*; **43**: 469–76.

Carey C. R., Schaefer K. E. and Alvis H. J. (1956) Effect of skin diving on lung volume. *Journal of Applied Physiology*; **8**: 519–23.

Clanton T. L., Dixon G. F., Drake J. and Gadek J. E. (1987) Effects of swim training on lung volumes and inspiratory muscle conditioning. *Journal of Applied Physiology*; **62**: 39–46.

Cooke C. B. (2009) Metabolic rate and energy balance. In: (R. G. Eston and T. Reilly, eds) *Kinanthropometry and Exercise Physiology Laboratory Manual (3rd Edition): Exercise Physiology*, Routledge; Oxon, Chapter 6.

Cordain L., Tucker A., Moon D. and Stajer J. M. (1990) Lung volumes and maximal respiratory pressures in collegiate swimmers and runners. *Research Quarterly for Exercise and Sport*; **61**: 70–4.

Cotes J. E. (1979) *Lung Function: Assessment and Application in Medicine*. Blackwell Scientific; Oxford.

Courteix D., Obert P., Lecoq A. M., Guenon P. and Koch G. (1997) Effect of intensive swimming training on lung volumes, airway resistance and on maximal expiratory flow-volume relationship in prepubertal girls.

European Journal of Applied Physiology; 76: 262–9.

Damon A. (1966) Negro–White differences in pulmonary function (vital capacity, timed vital capacity and expiratory flow rate). *Human Biology;* 38: 381–93.

Datta S. R. and Ramanathan N. L. (1969) Energy expenditure in work predicted from heart rate and pulmonary ventilation. *Journal of Applied Physiology;* 26: 297–302.

Davies C. T., Few J., Foster K. G. and Sargeant T. (1974) Plasma catecholamine concentration during dynamic exercise involving different muscle groups. *European Journal of Applied Physiology;* 32: 195–206.

Davis J. A., Frank M. H., Whipp B. J. and Wasserman K. (1979). Anaerobic threshold alterations caused by endurance training in middle-aged men. *Journal of Applied Physiology;* 45: 1039–46.

DeGraff A. C., Grover R. F., Johnson R. L., Hammond J. W. and Miller J. M. (1970) Diffusing capacity of the lung in Caucasians native to 3,100 m. *Journal of Applied Physiology;* 29: 71–6.

Dempsey J. A., Reddan W. G., Birnbaum M. L., Forster H. V., Thoden J. S., Grover R. F. and Rankin J. (1971) Effects of acute through life-long hypoxic exposure on exercise pulmonary gas exchange. *Respiration Physiology;* 13: 62–89.

Ekblom B. (1969) Effect of physical training in adolescent boys. *Journal of Applied Physiology;* 27: 350–5.

Ekblom B. and Hermansen L. (1968) Cardiac output in athletes. *Journal of Applied Physiology;* 25: 619–25.

Engstrom I., Eriksson B. O., Karlberg P., Saltin B. and Thoren C. (1977) Preliminary report on the development of lung volumes in young girls swimmers. *Acta Paediatrica Scandinavica;* S217: 73–6.

Eston R. G. and Brodie D. A. (1986) Responses to arm and leg ergometry. *British Journal of Sports Medicine;* 20: 4–7.

Eston R. G., Hawes M., Martin A. D. and Reilly, T. (2009) Human body composition. In: (R. G. Eston and T. Reilly, eds) *Kinanthropometry and Exercise Physiology Laboratory Manual (3rd Edition): Anthropometry (Chapter 1).* Routledge; Oxon: pp. 3–53.

Fanta C. H., Leith D. E. and Brown R. (1983) Maximal shortening of inspiratory muscles: effect of training. *Journal of Applied Physiology;* 54: 1618–23.

Ferris B. G. and Stoudt H. E. (1971) Correlation of anthropometry and simple tests of pulmonary function. *Archives of Environmental Health;* 22: 672–6.

Fredberg J. J., Inouye D., Miller B., Nathan M., Jafari S., Raboudi S. H., Butler J. P. and Shore S. A. (1997) Airway smooth muscle, tidal stretches, and dynamically determined contractile states. *American Journal of Respiratory and Critical Care Medicine;* 156: 1752–9.

Fringer M. N. and Stull G. A. (1974) Changes in cardiorespiratory parameters during periods of training and detraining in young adult females. *Medicine and Science in Sports;* 6: 20–5.

Frisancho A. R. (1975) Functional adaptation to high-altitude hypoxia. *Science;* 187: 313–19.

Gaultier C. and Crapo R. (1997) Effects of nutrition, growth hormone disturbances, training, altitude and sleep on lung volumes. *European Respiratory Journal;* 10: 2913–19.

Gimeno F., Berg W. C., Sluiter H. J. and Tammeling G. J. (1972) Spirometry-induced bronchial obstruction. *American Review of Respiratory Disease;* 105: 68–74.

Greksa L. P., Spielvogel H., Paz-Zamora M., Caceres E. and Parades-Fernandez L. (1988) Effect of altitude on the lung function of high altitude residents of European ancestry. *American Journal of Physical Anthropology;* 75: 77–85.

Hagberg J. M., Coyle E. F., Carroll J. E., Miller J. M., Martin W. H., and Brooke M. H. (1982) Exercise hyperventilation in patients with McArdle's disease. *Journal of Applied Physiology;* 52: 991–4.

Hankinson J. L., Odencratz J. R. and Fedan K. B. (1999) Spirometric reference values from a sample of the general US population. *American Journal of Respiratory and Critical Care Medicine;* 159: 179–87.

Hanson J. S. (1973) Maximal exercise performance in members of the US Nordic Ski Team. *Journal of Applied Physiology;* 35: 592–5.

Hardie J. A., Buist A. S., Vollmer W. M., Ellingsen I., Bakke P. S. and Morkve O. (2002) Risk of over-diagnosis of COPD in asymptomatic elderly never-smokers. *European Respiratory Journal;* **20**: 1117–22.

Hetzel M. R. (1981) The pulmonary clock. *Thorax;* **36**: 481–6.

Hetzel M. R. and Clark T. J. H. (1980) Comparison of normal and asthmatic circadian rhythms in peak expiratory flow rate. *Thorax;* **35**: 732–8.

Hibbert M. E., Lanigan A., Raven J. and Phelan P. D. (1988) Relation of armspan to height and the prediction of lung function. *Thorax;* **43**: 657–9.

Hong S. K., Moore T. O., Seto G., Park H. K., Hiatt W. R. and Bernauer E. M. (1970) Lung volumes and apneic bradycardia in divers. *Journal of Applied Physiology;* **29**: 172–6.

Jacobs D. R., Nelson E. T., Dontas A. S., Keller J., Slattery M. L. and Higgins M. (1992) Are race and sex differences in lung function explained by frame size? The CARDIA study. *American Review of Respiratory Disease;* **146**: 644–9.

Jirka Z. and Adamus M. (1965) Changes of ventilation equivalents in young people in the course of three years of training. *Journal of Sports Medicine and Physical Fitness;* **5**: 1–6.

Johnson B. D., Reddan W. G., Seow K. C. and Dempsey J. A. (1991) Mechanical constraints on exercise hyperpnea in a fit aging population. *American Review of Respiratory Disease;* **143**: 968–77.

Johnson B. D., Saupe K. W. and Dempsey J. A. (1992) Mechanical constraints on exercise hyperpnea in endurance athletes. *Journal of Applied Physiology;* **73**: 874–86.

Jones N. L. (1984) Dyspnea in exercise. *Medicine and Science in Sports and Exercise;* **16**: 14–19.

Jones A. M., Vanhatalo A. and Doust J. (2009) Aerobic exercise performance. In: (R. G. Eston and T. Reilly, eds) *Kinanthropometry and Exercise Physiology Laboratory Manual (3rd Edition): Exercise Physiology (Chapter 10).* Routledge; Oxon: pp. 271–306.

Kaufman M. P. and Forster H. V. (1996). Reflexes controlling circulatory, ventilatory and airway responses to exercise. In: (L. B. Rowell and J. T. Shephered, eds.) *Handbook of Physiology.* Oxford University; New York: 381–447.

Krowka M. J., Enright P. L., Rodarte J. R. and Hyatt R. E. (1987) Effect of effort on forced expiratory effort in one second. *American Review of Respiratory Disease;* **136**: 829–33.

Lahiri S., Delaney R. G., Brody J. S., Simpser M., Velasquez T., Motoyama E. K. and Polgar C. (1976). Relative role of environmental and genetic factors in respiratory adaptation to high altitude. *Nature;* **261**:133–5.

Leith D. E. and Bradley M. (1976) Ventilatory muscle strength and endurance training. *Journal of Applied Physiology;* **41**: 508–16.

Levison H. and Cherniack R. M. (1968) Ventilatory cost of exercise in chronic obstructive pulmonary disease. *Journal of Applied Physiology;* **25**: 21–7.

McClaran S. R., Babcock M. A., Pegelow D. F., Reddan W. G. and Dempsey J. A. (1995) Longitudinal effects of aging on lung function at rest and exercise in healthy active fit elderly adults. *Journal of Applied Physiology;* **78**: 1957–68.

McConnell A. K. and Romer L. M. (2004) Respiratory muscle training in healthy humans: resolving the controversy. *International Journal of Sports Medicine;* **25**: 284–93.

Mangum M. (1984) Research methods: application to arm crank ergometry. *Journal of Sports Sciences;* **2**: 257–63.

Martin B. J. and Kjeldgaard J. M. (1982) Improvement in ventilatory muscle function with running. *Journal of Applied Physiology;* **52**: 1400–6.

Melissinos C. G. and Mead J. (1977) Maximum expiratory flow changes induced by longitudinal tension on trachea in normal subjects. *Journal of Applied Physiology;* **43**: 537–44.

Miles D. S., Cox M. H., Bomze J. P. and Gotshall R. W. (1991) Acute recovery profile of lung volumes and function after running 5 miles. *Journal of Sports Medicine and Physical Fitness;* **31**: 243–8.

Miller M. R., Burgos F., Casaburi R., Coates A., Crapo R., Enright P., van der Grinten C. P., Gustafsson P., Jensen R., Johnson D. C., MacIntyre N., McKay R., Navajas

D., Pedersen O. F., Pellegrino R., Viegi G. and Wanger J (2005) Standardisation of spirometry. *European Respiratory Journal;* **26**: 319–38.

Minors D. S. (1985) Abnormal pressure. In: (R. M. Case, ed) *Variations in Human Physiology.* Manchester University Press; Manchester: pp. 78–110.

Mortola J. P. (2004) Breathing around the clock: an overview of the circadian pattern of respiration. *European Journal of Applied Physiology;* **91**: 119–29.

Palange P., Ward S. A., Carlsen K. H., Casaburi R., Gallagher C. G., Gosselink R., O'Donnell D. E., Puente-Maestu L., Schols A. M., Singh, S. and Whipp B. J. (2007) Recommendations on the use of exercise testing in clinical practice. *European Respiratory Journal;* **29**: 185–209.

Pellegrino R., Viegi G., Brusasco V., Crapo R. O., Burgos F., Casaburi R., Coates A., van der Grinten C. P., Gustafsson P., Hankinson J., Jensen R., Johnson D. C., MacIntyre N., McKay R., Miller M.R., Navajas D., Pedersen O. F. and Wanger J. (2005) Interpretive strategies for lung function tests. *European Respiratory Journal;* **26**: 948–68.

Quanjer, Ph. H., Tammelin, G. J., Cotes J. E., Pedersen O. F., Peslin R. and Yernault, J.-C. (1993) Lung volumes and forced ventilatory flows. Report Working Party Standardization of Lung Function Tests, European Community for Steel and Coal. Official Statement of the European Respiratory Society. *European Respiratory Journal;* S16: 5–40.

Quanjer Ph. H., Borsboom G. J. J. M., Brunekreef B., Zack M., Forche G., Cotes J. E., Sanchis J. and Paoletti P. (1995) Spirometric values for white European children and adolescents: Polgar revisited. *Pediatric Pulmonology;* **19**: 135–42.

Rasmussen B. S., Klausen K., Clausen J. P. and Trap-Jensen J. (1975) Pulmonary ventilation, blood gases and pH after training of the arms and legs. *Journal of Applied Physiology;* **38**: 250–6.

Rasmussen B. S., Elkjaer P. and Juhl B. (1988) Impaired pulmonary and cardiac function after maximal exercise. *Journal of Sports Sciences;* **6**: 219–28.

Riley R. L., Permutt S., Said S., Godfrey M.,

Cheng T. O., Howell J. B. and Shepard R. H. (1959) Effect of posture on pulmonary dead space in man. *Journal of Applied Physiology;* **14**: 339–44.

Rowland T. W. and Cunningham L. N. (1997) Development of ventilatory responses to exercise in normal white children: a longitudinal study. *Chest;* **11**: 327–32.

Saldana M. and Oyola G. (1970) Morphometry of the high altitude lung. *Laboratory Investigation;* **22**: 509–12.

Saltin, B. and Åstrand P. O. (1967) Maximal oxygen uptake in athletes. *Journal of Applied Physiology;* **23**: 353–8.

Schwartz J. D., Katz S. A., Fegley R. W. and Tockman M. S. (1988) Analysis of spirometric data from a national sample of healthy 6–24 year olds (NHANES II). *American Review of Respiratory Disease;* **138**: 1405–14.

Shephard R. J. and Lavallee H. (1996). Effects of enhanced physical education on lung volumes of primary school children. *Journal of Sports Medicine and Physical Fitness,* **36**: 186–94.

Song S. H., Kang D. H., Kang B. S. and Hong S. K. (1963) Lung volumes and ventilatory responses to high CO_2 and low O_2 in the ama. *Journal of Applied Physiology;* **18**: 466–70.

Spann R. W. and Hyatt R. E. (1971) Factors affecting upper airway resistance in conscious man. *Journal of Applied Physiology;* **31**: 708–12.

Stenberg J., Åstrand P. O., Ekblom B., Royce J. and Saltin B. (1967) Hemodynamic response to work with different muscle groups, sitting and supine. *Journal of Applied Physiology;* **22**: 61–70.

Townsend M. C. (1984) Spirometric forced expiratory volumes measured in the standing versus the sitting posture. *American Review of Respiratory Disease;* **130**: 123–4.

Turner J. M., Mead J. and Wohl M. E. (1968) Elasticity of human lungs in relation to age. *Journal of Applied Physiology;* **25**: 664–71.

Tzankoff S. P., Robinson S., Pyke F. S. and Brown C. A. (1972) Physiological adjustments to work in older men as affected by physical training. *Journal of Applied Physiology;* **33**: 346–50.

Wanger J., Pedersen O. F., Brusasco V., Burgos
F., Casaburi R., Crapo R., Enright P., van
der Grinten C. P., Gustafsson P., Hankinson
J., Jensen R., Johnson D., Macintyre
N., McKay R., Miller M. R., Navajas
D., Pellegrino R. and Viegi G. (2005)
Standardisation of the measurement of lung
volumes. *European Respiratory Journal;*, **26**:
511–22.

Wasserman K., Hansen J. E., Sue D. Y., Stringer
W. W. and Whipp B. J. (2005) *Principles
of Exercise Testing and Interpretation (4th
Edition)*. Lippincott Williams and Wilkins;
London.

Zeltner T. B. and Burri P. H. (1987) The
postnatal development and growth of the
human lung. II: Morphology. *Respiration
Physiology;* **67**: 269–82.

Zinman R. and Gaultier C. (1987) Maximal
static pressures and lung volumes in young
female swimmers: one year follow up.
Pediatr Pulmonol; **3**: 145–8.

CHAPTER 4

HAEMATOLOGY

Ron Maughan, John Leiper and Susan Shirreffs

4.1 AIMS

The aims of this chapter are to:
- describe some practical issues and procedures relevant to blood sampling and handling;
- explain the rationale for haematology measurement procedures most widely used in the sport and exercise science laboratory;
- describe some of the factors that influence haematological variables and the interpretation of their physiological significance.

4.2 INTRODUCTION

A high aerobic capacity is a prerequisite for success in all endurance-based sports, and many different factors contribute to the body's ability to derive energy from oxidative metabolism. Although maximum cardiac output is often considered to be the limiting factor to oxygen transport, this is true only in the absence of another limitation (Levine 2008). For different individuals and in different situations, any of the steps in the chain of oxygen transport and use, from pulmonary function to mitochondrial enzyme activity, may determine this limit. This includes the transport of oxygen in the circulation, which in turn is influenced by the blood haemoglobin concentration and the total red blood cell mass (Ekblom *et al*, 1972). For this reason, athletes are often concerned to know their circulating haemoglobin concentration, as this is the most widely understood measure of adequacy or otherwise of an individual's iron status and is also the haematological marker that is most closely related to exercise performance. Within the normal range of haemoglobin concentration, there is generally little correlation with performance, but a fall in concentration from the individual's normal value can impair performance and values that are below the lower end of the normal range are often associated with poor performance. Although it can be argued that other markers may be of more diagnostic use, it is generally accepted that some form of haematological assessment is an important part of any routine screening of athletes being carried out as part of a sports science or sports medicine athlete support programme.

A high circulating haemoglobin concentration can confer performance advantages in many athletic events, and the recognition that reinfusion of red blood cells could increase endurance performance led to the widespread use of 'blood doping' by endurance athletes (Ekblom *et al*, 1976). This was later largely replaced by abuse of erythropoietin (EPO), the hormone that stimulates red blood cell formation, and later still by synthetic analogues of EPO. For this reason, the governing bodies of some sports have established an upper limit to the acceptable level of circulating red cells. In cycling, a male rider with a haematocrit level of 50% or more, or a female with a value of 47% or more, is deemed to have committed a doping offence, and is liable for disqualification and suspension, even though this value is within the normal range (Table 4.1). However, the Union Cycliste Internationale (UCI) has recognized that some individuals may naturally exceed these levels and has made provision for riders to submit a medical file to apply for an exemption from this ruling (UCI 2008). Therefore, haematological assessment is also an essential part of doping control in many sports.

In the exercise laboratory, an individual's haematological profile can be seen as an important descriptor alongside other variables such as age, height, weight or body fat content. Measurement of changes in blood volume or plasma volume can also be important in assessing the significance of changes in the circulating concentration of a variety of hormones, substrates, metabolites and other organic and inorganic components. Haemoconcentration or haemodilution may cause or obscure changes in the circulating concentration of the entity of interest (Kargotich *et al*. 1998). Whether or not one should correct measured concentrations for changes in the volume of distribution depends on the question that is being asked. Where the concentration in the plasma is regulated, it is normally inappropriate to correct for a change in plasma volume.

This chapter will focus on a detailed description of the practical issues relevant to blood sampling and handling, and on those haematology measurement procedures most widely used in the exercise science laboratory. More sophisticated measures used in the clinical assessment of iron status and in the physiology research laboratory will be described more briefly, as a full description of the methodology is outside the scope of a single chapter.

4.3 HEALTH AND SAFETY AND THE HUMAN TISSUES ACT

Careful antiseptic procedures should be followed at all times when collecting blood to protect the subject and the investigator,

Table 4.1 **Normal Values.** These are taken from a variety of sources. Each laboratory will establish its own reference range, which will depend on the methods used and the sample population. Samples that lie outside the reference range will normally be repeated. If an abnormal result is confirmed, further investigation may be warranted.

	Units	Men	Women
Haemoglobin	g l^{-1}	13.5–17.5	11.5–15.5
Red cell count	$\times 10^{12-1}$	4.5–6.5	3.9–5.6
Haematocrit (Hct, PCV)	l l^{-1}, %	40–52	36–48
Mean cell volume	fl	80–95	80–95
Plasma volume	ml kg^{-1} body mass	45±5	45±5
Serum iron	µmol l^{-1}	10–30	10–30
Serum transferrin	g l^{-1}	2.0–4.0	2.0–4.0
Total iron binding capacity	µmol l^{-1}	40–75	40–75
Serum ferritin	µg l^{-1}	40–340	14–150

and equal care should be applied at all times during the handling of blood samples after collection. Blood is a human tissue and is therefore covered by the Human Tissues Act (2004). The implications of this act for those working in the sport and exercise sciences have been described by Hull *et al.* (2008). The provisions of this act govern the collection and storage of human tissues, and all procedures that involve blood sampling and storage of any sample with cellular components are covered. The Act also covers other tissues that contain cellular components, but plasma and serum samples are not considered to fall within the scope of the Act. Investigators must ensure that they have ethics approval for their procedures from an institution that is licensed in accordance with the Act.

4.4 BLOOD SAMPLING AND HANDLING

Any one of several different methods and sites of blood sampling can be used in the collection of samples for analysis, but the results obtained will be affected by both sampling site and the procedures used in sample collection and subsequent processing. The chosen procedures will be determined by the needs of the investigator and the facilities available. Whatever the method used, the safety of the subject and the investigator is paramount, and appropriate sterile or antiseptic precautions must be observed. Strict safety precautions must be followed at all times in the sampling and handling of blood. It is wise to assume that all samples are infected with potentially harmful agents and to treat them accordingly. This means wearing gloves and appropriate protective clothing and following guidelines for handling of samples and disposal of waste material. Used needles, cannulae and lancets must be disposed of immediately in a suitable sharps bin: resheathing of used needles must never be attempted. Sharps – whether contaminated or not – must always be disposed of in an approved container and must never be mixed with other waste.

All other contaminated materials must be disposed of using appropriate and clearly identified waste containers. Any spillage of blood must be treated immediately.

The main sampling procedures involve collection of arterial, venous, arterialized venous or capillary blood. In most routine laboratory investigations of interest to the sports scientist, arterial blood sampling is impractical and unnecessarily invasive, and will not be considered in detail here. Where arterial blood is required, arterial puncture may be used, but in most situations, collection of arterialized venous blood, as described below, gives an adequate representation of arterial blood.

4.4.1 Venous blood

Venous blood sampling is probably the method of choice for most routine purposes: sampling from a superficial forearm or ante-cubital vein is simple, painless and relatively free from risk of complications. Sampling may be by venous puncture or by an indwelling cannula. Where repeated sampling is necessary at short time intervals, introduction of a cannula is obviously preferred to avoid repeated venous punctures. Either a plastic cannula or a butterfly-type cannula can be used. The latter has obvious limitations if introduced into an ante-cubital vein, as movement of the elbow is severely restricted. However, because it is smaller and therefore less painful for the subject, as well as being very much less expensive, the butterfly cannula is often preferable if used in a forearm vein, provided that long-term access is not required. A 21 g cannula is adequate for most purposes, and only where large volumes of blood are required will a larger size be necessary. In most situations where vigorous movements are likely, the forearm site is preferred to the elbow (Figure 4.1). A disadvantage of venous cannulation is the need to ensure that clotting of blood in the cannula does not occur. This is easily avoided by flushing with sterile isotonic saline, but this in turn requires stringent hygiene procedures. Where intermittent sampling is performed, the cannula may be flushed with a bolus of saline to which heparin (10–50 IU ml^{-1} of saline) is added, allowing the subject freedom to move around between samples. Alternatively where the subject is to remain static, as in a cycle or treadmill exercise test, a continuous slow infusion (about 0.3 ml min^{-1}) of isotonic saline may be used, avoiding the need to add heparin. Collection of samples by venous puncture is not practical in most exercise situations, and increases the risk that samples will be affected by venous occlusion applied during puncture. If repeated venous puncture is used, care must be taken to minimize the duration of any occlusion of blood flow and to ensure that sufficient time is allowed for recovery from interruption of blood flow before samples

are collected. The use of a butterfly cannula rather than a needle facilitates the collection of samples without the problems that arise from occlusion of the circulation, even when repeated sampling is not required.

The dead space of a 21-g butterfly cannula is small (about 0.4 ml), and even with the addition of a three-way tap does not exceed about 0.5 ml. However, it is essential to ensure that the dead space is completely cleared when taking samples. It is recommended that about 1–1.5 ml be withdrawn through the cannula before each sample is collected.

A disadvantage of the use of a superficial forearm vein is that flow through these veins is very much influenced by skin blood flow, which in turn depends on ambient temperature and the thermoregulatory strain imposed on the individual. In cold conditions, flow to

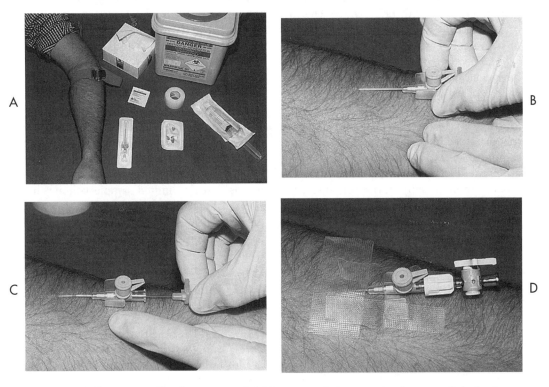

Figure 4.1 **a)** Venous sampling from a superficial forearm vein is conveniently accomplished using an indwelling plastic cannula. **b)** The cannula is inserted into the vein. If slight tension is applied to the skin, this should be completely painless. **c)** The needle is withdrawn, leaving the plastic sheath in place. This is then advanced into the vein. **d)** A three-way tap is attached to the end of the cannula, allowing samples to be withdrawn and the cannula to be flushed with saline as necessary.

the limbs and to the skin will be low, and venous blood will be highly desaturated. It is easy to observe that, where samples are taken progressively throughout an exercise task, the oxygen content of the venous blood increases progressively, reflecting the increased peripheral blood flow, especially the skin blood flow. Therefore, where sampling occurs over time, and where the degree of arterialization of the venous blood will influence the measures to be made, this may cause major problems (Leiper *et al.* 1990). A good example of such a situation is where a tracer – deuterium oxide – is added to an ingested beverage, and the rate of rise of the blood deuterium concentration is used as an index of the combined rates of gastric emptying and intestinal absorption. Deuterium enters the vascular compartment as the blood passes through the gut, and leaves as it equilibrates with body water. The rate of equilibration with body water will depend on a number of factors, but it is clear that the arterial deuterium concentration will always be higher than the venous concentration – at least until all the ingested beverage has been absorbed and complete equilibration among all body water compartments has occurred. If peripheral venous blood sampling is used, and if these measurements are made during exercise or in a situation where ambient temperature changes, the degree of arterialization of the venous blood will change, and the values for deuterium accumulation are likely to be meaningless. For some of the substrates and metabolites that are routinely measured, the difference between arterial and venous concentrations is relatively small and in many cases it may be ignored. Where a difference does occur and is of importance, the effect of a change in arterialization of the blood at the sampling site may be critical.

4.4.2 Arterialized venous blood

Where arterial blood is required, there is no alternative to arterial puncture, but for most practical purposes, blood collected from a superficial vein on the dorsal surface of a heated hand is indistinguishable from arterial blood. This reflects both the very high flow rate and the opening of arterio-venous shunts in the heated hand. Sampling can conveniently be achieved by the introduction of a butterfly cannula into a suitable vein (Figure 4.2). The hand is first heated, either by immersion up to the forearm for at least 10 minutes in hot (about 42°C) water (Forster *et al.* 1972) or by insertion into a hot air box (McGuire *et al.* 1976). If hot water immersion is used prior to exercise, arterialization – as indicated by oxygen saturation – can be maintained for some considerable time by wearing a glove, allowing this technique to be used during exercise studies. This procedure allows large volumes of blood to be collected without problems. Capillary sampling by the fingerprick method can also be used to obtain arterialized blood, but cannot guarantee a sufficient volume of blood for many procedures.

4.4.3 Capillary blood

Where only small samples of blood are required, capillary blood samples can readily be obtained from a fingertip or ear lobe. The use of micromethods for analysis means that the limited sample volume that can be obtained should not necessarily be a problem in metabolic studies. It is possible to make duplicate measurements of the concentrations of glucose, lactate, pyruvate, alanine, free fatty acids, glycerol, acetoacetate and 3-hydroxybutyrate as well as a number of other metabolites on a single 20 µl blood sample using routine laboratory methods (Maughan 1982). Provided care is taken during sampling, this method yields reliable results and the small volumes of blood used mean considerable savings in reagent costs for the analyses.

The sampling site should be arterialized, by immersion of the whole hand in hot (42°C) water in the case of the finger tip, and by the

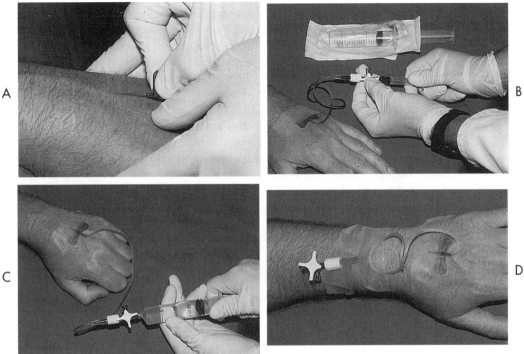

Figure 4.2 **a**) A butterfly style cannula is convenient for sampling of arterialized venous blood from a dorsal vein in a hand that has been warmed by immersion for 10 min in warm (42°C) water. **b**) Blood samples are withdrawn from the cannula as necessary via a syringe connected to the cannula by way of a three-way tap. **c**) After sampling, the cannula is flushed with saline, which should be heparinized if there is more than a short time (1–2 minutes) between samples. **d**) The cannula is taped in place, allowing the subject free use of the hand between sample collections.

use of a rubefacient in the case of the ear lobe. Samples can be obtained without stimulating vasodilatation, but bleeding is slower, the volumes that can be reliably collected are smaller, and the composition of the sample is more variable. It is essential that a free flowing sample is obtained. If pressure is applied, an excess of plasma over red cells will be obtained. Samples are most conveniently collected into calibrated glass capillaries where only small volumes are required (typically 10–100 µl). The blood must never be expelled from these tubes by mouth, because of the obvious risks involved.

Where larger volumes are required, a clean plastic or glass vessel may be used for collection and the blood then pipetted in the normal way using an automatic pipette.

Use of suitable analytical methods allows most of the metabolites of interest to be measured on samples collected in this way. More difficulty arises when larger volumes are required. Nonetheless, a volume sufficient for the measurement of haematocrit, which is normally measured in triplicate and requires a blood volume of about 150 µl, and haemoglobin (2×20 µl) in addition to the metabolites referred to above, is usually possible. However, volumes greater than about 0.5 ml present real difficulties.

4.4.4 Procedures for capillary blood sampling

As indicated above, capillary samples are commonly obtained from the ear lobe or from a digit. In most situations, the fingertip site is to be preferred. In order to ensure that a free-flowing sample can be obtained, it is helpful to immerse the hand to the wrist in hot (42°C) water or in a heated box for 10–15 minutes before the sample is collected. If necessary, the hand can be kept warm by continued immersion between samples where this is practicable. Where this is not possible, some degree of arterialization can be maintained by wearing a glove. The degree of arterialization can be verified by measurement of blood gases.

A clean laboratory coat and disposable gloves must be worn during collection and handling of samples. The sampling kit – prepared in advance – will consist of:

- Lancets (an autolet may be preferred)
- Sterile alcohol swabs
- Tissues
- Medical gloves
- Disposal facility: sharps bin for used lancets and appropriate clinical waste bags (according to local regulations).

For handling blood, collection into graduated glass capillaries is preferred. Larger volumes may be collected directly into disposable plastic containers, but such volumes are difficult to collect reliably using the fingerprick technique, and there is a real danger that clotting will occur before sufficient volume is obtained. Suitably prepared and labelled tubes for sample reception should be prepared in advance if required. For most metabolite analysis where spectrophotometric or fluorimetric analysis is used, collection of 20 µl of blood into 200 µl of deproteinizing agent is appropriate. This may be facilitated by the use of heparinized capillary tubes, which will hold about 50 µl of blood. The blood can be ejected from the capillary and 20-µl aliquots transferred using a pipette.

Subjects should be instructed to wash their hands before the procedure begins. The sampling site should be swabbed with alcohol and wiped dry with a tissue, and the cleaned area stabbed with a single prick. It is essential to ensure a free-flowing sample: the puncture wound should not be squeezed. If pressure is applied, extracellular fluid will contaminate the sample collected, and some haemolysis is also inevitable. The results will therefore be invalid. The extent to which contamination with extracellular fluid will invalidate the results depends on the measurements to be made. The first drop of blood to appear should be wiped away with a clean tissue. The capillary should be filled to about 1 cm beyond the graduation mark then the outside of the capillary should be wiped clean, and the end touched against a tissue until the bottom of the blood meniscus is aligned with the graduation mark. Transfer into the deproteinization agent is achieved by use of a rubber blow-bulb, with repeated aspiration and dispensing until all the residual blood is washed out of the capillary. Samples should always be collected in duplicate.

The site of the puncture wound should be wiped clean. If bleeding continues, a waterproof dressing should be applied. A new puncture must be made when repeated sampling is required, unless the time interval between samples is short. It is unwise to rely on continued bleeding from the same site.

4.5 BLOOD TREATMENT AFTER COLLECTION

Analysis of most metabolites can be carried out using whole blood, plasma or serum. This requires recognition of the differential distribution of most metabolites and substrates between the plasma and the intracellular space. It is important to recognize also that changes in the plasma volume during exercise or other situations may be quite different from the changes in the whole blood volume, and the effects of changes in the distribution space may require consideration. For most practical purposes, it is convenient to use whole blood for the measurement of most metabolites. The obvious exception is the free fatty acid concentration, which should be measured using plasma or serum. Glucose, glycerol and lactate are commonly measured on either plasma or whole blood. Most of the other metabolites of interest to the exercise physiologist are normally measured on whole blood. The differences become significant where there is a concentration difference between the intracellular and extracellular compartments, or where there is a change in this distribution over the time-course of an experiment.

If plasma is to be obtained by centrifugation of the sample, a suitable anticoagulant must be added. A variety of agents can be used, depending on the measurements to be made. The potassium salt of EDTA is a convenient anticoagulant, but is clearly inappropriate when plasma potassium is to be measured. Heparin is a suitable alternative in this situation. For serum collection, blood should be added to a plain tube and left for at least one hour before centrifugation: clotting will take place more rapidly if the sample is left in a warm place. If there is a need to stop glycolysis in serum or plasma samples (for example, where the concentration of glucose, lactate or other glycolytic intermediates is to be measured), fluoride should be added.

Where metabolites are to be measured on whole blood, the most convenient method is immediate deproteinization of the sample. The primary reason for deproteinization of whole blood is to inactivate the enzymes which would otherwise alter the concentrations of substances of interest after the sample has been withdrawn. A variety of agents can be used to achieve this: perchloric acid or trichloroacetic acid are equally effective. A 2.5% (0.3 N) solution of perchloric acid is recommended for general use. This can be prepared by adding 36 ml of the 70% acid to 964 ml of water.

Where blood samples are to be collected for analysis of glucose and lactate, it is convenient to add 100 µl of whole blood to 1 ml of 2.5% perchloric acid. Smaller volumes can be used, but pipetting and other measurement errors are reduced if the larger volume is used. The use of a 10:1 dilution reduces volumetric errors due to the presence of a substantial volume of precipitate. The tubes containing the acid should be prepared in advance and kept in iced water. Deproteinization should take place immediately upon collection of the sample. However, it is recommended that an anticoagulant should be used. Blood should be transferred using an automatic pipette as described below. The deproteinized sample should be kept on ice until it can be centrifuged. A note of caution: glucose is not stable in this acid medium, even when frozen at -20°C. Lactate, pyruvate and other metabolites can be stored frozen, but glucose and ammonia should be analyzed within a few hours of collection. If frozen samples are to be analyzed, they must be centrifuged again after thawing.

4.6 MEASUREMENT OF CIRCULATING HAEMOGLOBIN CONCENTRATION

Haemoglobin is the porphyrin-iron-protein compound which binds with oxygen and gives blood its characteristic red colour. Many different methods have been developed to determine the concentration of haemoglobin and its derivatives in circulating and occult blood. The techniques usually depend on reactions involving the iron component of haemoglobin or the pseudoperoxidase activity of the haem. The two most common methods currently used are the oxyhaemoglobin and the cyanmethaemoglobin techniques. The oxyhaemoglobin method is currently mainly used in conjunction with automated or semi-automated haemoglobinometers, while the cyanmethaemoglobin method is the technique of choice for manual procedures.

4.6.1 The Cyanmethaemoglobin method

In 1966 the International Congress of Haematology recommended this method be the accepted routine manual procedure for measurement of haemoglobin in blood. The main reasons for adopting this as the standard technique were:

1   The method requires dilution of blood with a single reagent.
2   All forms of haemoglobin likely to occur in the circulation are determined.
3   The colour produced is suitable for measurement in filter photometers and narrow band spectrophotometers because its absorption band at 540 nm is broad and relatively flat.
4   Standards prepared from either crystalline haemoglobin or washed erythrocytes when stored in brown glass containers and in sterile conditions are stable for at least 9 months (< 2% change in absorbance).

a) Principle

The iron of haem in haemoglobin, oxyhaemoglobin and carboxyhaemoglobin is oxidized to the ferric state by ferricyanide to form methaemoglobin. Methaemoglobin then combines with ionised cyanide to produce the stable, red cyanmethaemoglobin, which is measured photometrically at 540 nm.

Cyanmethaemoglobin solutions generally obey Beer's Law within the concentration range of interest at a wavelength of 540 nm, and a calibration curve can therefore be constructed using a reagent blank as a zero standard and a single additional standard of known concentration. Secondary standards, prepared from blood and Drabkin's reagent, can be calibrated against the commercial standard and then used for construction of the calibration curve.

The method outlined below uses a sample volume of 10 µl and a reagent volume of 2.5 ml, and the reaction is always carried out in duplicate. Smaller sample volumes can be used, but the precision of the assay, which has a coefficient of variation of about 1–2% in the hands of an experienced operator, declines with very small volumes of blood. Larger volumes are wasteful of the reagent.

b) Procedure

Drabkin's Reagent: This reagent is stable for several months when stored in a brown bottle. As cyanide is a constituent of Drabkin's solution care must be taken in preparing and storing this reagent.
1.0 g $Na\,HCO_3$
0.2 g $K_3Fe(CN)_6$
make up to 1 litre
0.05 g KCN

Standard: 180 g l^{-1} human methaemoglobin

Calibrate   The calibration curve is prepared by measuring the optical density of the Drabkin's reagent (zero standard) and of the 180 gl^{-1} standard at 540 nm without dilution. Addition of other standards will only confirm the linearity of the calibration curve.

Sample assay   In duplicate, add 10-µl sample to 2.5 ml of Drabkin's reagent and mix thoroughly; incubate at room temperature for at least 10 minutes. Read samples at 540 nm. The colour is stable for several hours if kept in the dark. Standards should be exposed to the same conditions as the samples.

4.6.2 Factors affecting measured haemoglobin concentration

Many different factors – independent of the analytical method used – will affect the measured haemoglobin concentration. The sampling site and method can affect the haemoglobin concentration, as arterial, capillary and venous samples differ in a number of respects due to fluid exchange between the vascular and extravascular spaces and to differences in the distribution of red blood cells (Harrison 1985). The venous plasma to red cell ratio is higher than that of arterial blood.

The measured haemoglobin concentration is also markedly influenced by the physical activity, hydration status and posture of the subject prior to sample collection, although the total body haemoglobin content is clearly not acutely affected by these factors. Posture is particularly important and should be standardized for a period of at least 15 minutes prior to sampling as plasma volumes will change significantly over this time (Figure 4.3a). This effect can be demonstrated reproducibly as a simple student laboratory class. Haemoglobin concentration is rather stable while a subject remains standing at rest, but increases promptly on assuming a seated or supine position. The time course of change is exponential and is largely complete within 15–20 minutes: it is then reversed with a similar time course on returning to the original posture.

Haemodynamic changes caused by postural shifts will alter the fluid exchange across the capillary bed, leading to plasma volume changes that will cause changes in the circulating haemoglobin concentration. On going from a supine position to standing, plasma volume falls by about 10% and whole-blood volume by about 5% (Harrison 1985). This corresponds to a change in the measured haemoglobin concentration of about 7 g l^{-1}. These changes are reversed on going from an upright to a seated or supine position. These changes make it imperative that posture is

controlled in studies where haemoglobin changes are to be used as an index of changes in blood and plasma volume over the time course of an experiment. However, it is common to see studies reported in the literature where samples were collected from subjects resting in a supine position prior to exercise in a seated (cycling or rowing) or upright (treadmill walking or running) position. The changing blood volume not only invalidates any haematological measures made in the early stages of exercise, it also confounds cardiovascular measures as the stroke volume and heart rate will also be affected by the blood volume.

Normal haemoglobin values for men are higher by about 20–40 g l^{-1} than those typically found in women, although it should be recognized that there is some overlap in the normal ranges for men and women. Many factors will affect the measured haemoglobin concentration. Many published reports, and most textbooks, describe a haemodilution as one of the characteristics of endurance trained athletes. This is ascribed to a disproportionate expansion of the plasma volume relative to the red cell mass. However, in a comprehensive review of the published data, and of the methodology used in these studies, Sawka and Coyle (1999) concluded that the evidence is not as convincing as might be thought. There are also problems with sample collection from athletes in daily training because of the short term changes that occur during and after a single exercise bout.

The circulating haemoglobin concentration generally increases during exercise, but the magnitude of the increase depends very much on the exercise intensity (Figure 4.4). At high exercise intensities, there is a marked fall in plasma volume due to the movement of water into the active muscle. Intracellular osmolality rises sharply due to the increased concentration of glycolytic intermediates. In prolonged exercise, at intensities of about 60–75% of maximum oxygen uptake ($\dot{V}O_{2max}$) the initial fall in plasma volume that occurs within the first few minutes of exercise is

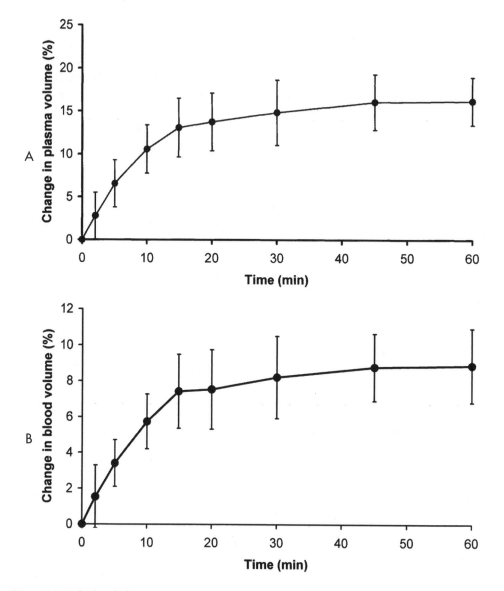

Figure 4.3 Calculated plasma volume (**a**) and blood volume (**b**) change on going from an upright to a supine position. The plasma volume change is relatively much greater than the change in blood volume: the entire blood volume change is accounted for by the changing plasma volume.

smaller in magnitude and is often reversed as exercise progresses. After prolonged hard exercise, the haemoglobin concentration is likely to be elevated, and this will return to the pre-exercise level over the few hours following exercise, with the rate and magnitude of this change being influenced primarily by the volume and composition of fluids ingested, but also by activity, posture and other factors.

However, if sampling continues beyond this time a haemodilution will be observed, and this may persist for 2–3 days (Robertson *et al.* 1988).

Hydration status clearly affects blood volume and therefore the concentration of all circulating variables, including haemoglobin concentration. The significance of this effect is clearly seen when comparing responses

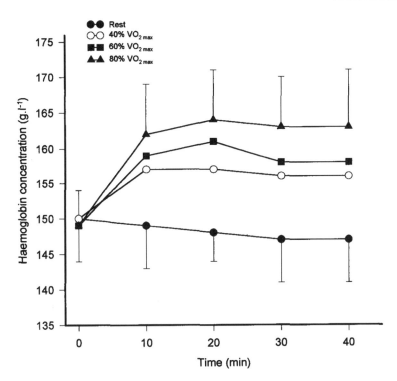

Figure 4.4 Effect of exercise intensity on measured haemoglobin (Hb) concentration. The circulating Hb concentration increases as a consequence of the plasma volume decrease: the rapid decrease in plasma volume at the onset of high intensity exercise results from a redistribution of body water rather than a loss of water from the body.

to exercise with and without fluid ingestion (Figure 4.5). The rise in haemoglobin concentration is smaller when fluid is ingested because of the better maintenance of blood volume. The dehydrated individual will have an elevated haemoglobin concentration, and care must therefore be taken to ensure euhydration if 'normal' values are to be obtained. These issues have been extensively debated in relation to the possibility that cyclists who have a naturally high haematocrit level may find that this is further increased if they allow themselves to become dehydrated, leading to ejection from competition if the value exceeds 50%.

Other factors affecting the normal values include cigarette smoking, which causes a chronic elevation of the circulating haemoglobin concentration in part due to tissue hypoxia secondary to increased carbon monoxide levels and carboxyhaemoglobin

formation. Ascent to high altitude also results in an increase in haemoglobin concentration. There is an initial fluid retention followed by diuresis. The latter may be sufficient to cause a reduction in plasma volume and a consequent increase in haemoglobin concentration and haematocrit through haemoconcentration. This is followed after a period of days to weeks by an erythropoietin-driven increase in the rate of erythropoiesis in response to hypoxia, and a true erythrocytosis with a raised haemoglobin concentration (polycythaemia). This adaptation confers a potentially increased oxygen carrying capacity on return to sea level, but the evidence that this translates to an improved exercise performance is not strong. Indigenous populations resident at an altitude of more than 1500 m have a chronic true polycythaemia.

Polycythaemia is occasionally constitutional as a familial condition. This can arise

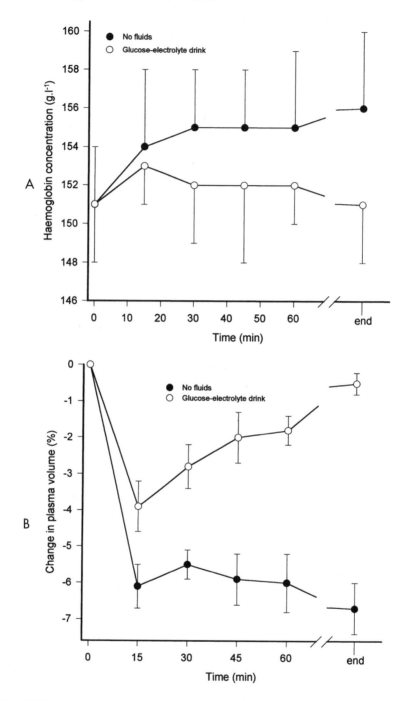

Figure 4.5 **a)** Haemoconcentration in the later stages of exercise results from an interaction of two effects: a loss of body water due to sweat loss and a redistribution of fluid between the vascular and extravascular spaces. **b)** Ingestion of fluids attenuates the change in plasma volume that occurs. These results are from a trial where fluid was ingested immediately before exercise and at intervals throughout the exercise period.

through synthesis of a haemoglobin variant with increased oxygen affinity, through increased sensitivity to erythropoietin or through a genetically determined abnormality of the erythropoietin receptor, which results in a loss of the 'off switch' for erythropoiesis. These erythropoietin-related familial polycythaemic conditions might be expected to confer increased oxygen carrying capacity and a relative increase in endurance capacity in affected individuals. More commonly, in clinical practice, polycythaemia results from cardiac, respiratory or bone marrow disorders.

4.7 MEASUREMENT OF RED CELL PARAMETERS

4.7.1 Packed Cell Volume (PCV) or spun haematocrit (Hct)

Packed cell volume is the measurement of the volume occupied by the erythrocytes compared with the overall volume of a column of the whole blood. Anticoagulated blood is spun at about 12000 g for 3–5 minutes in a glass capillary tube. The measured length of the column of packed erythrocytes is compared with that of the total length of the column of blood in the tube. Plain or heparinized micro-haematocrit capillary tubes can be used, but they must conform to the British Standard 4316 (1968) which stipulates that the capillary bore must be less than ± 2% of the mean throughout the tube. Heparinized or EDTA-treated blood should be spun in plain capillary tubes and heparinized tubes are used to collect capillary blood directly. Plain tubes may be used provided the sample is to be processed immediately, but the use of an anticoagulant is recommended in most situations to ensure that no clotting occurs. If there is any clotting of the sample, it must be discarded.

Method:

Well-mixed blood is drawn into the tube by capillary attraction without the introduction of any air bubbles. The tube should be filled to approximately $^2/_3$ to $^3/_4$ of its length. Each blood sample should be measured in triplicate. The capillary end is sealed by inserting that end into a block of 'Cristaseal' (clay type sealant) and twisting the tube into the clay. These tubes are fragile, so care must be taken to avoid breakages with the associated loss of sample and risk of injury. Haematocrit is normally measured in triplicate. After wiping the outside of the tube, place the capillary in the rotor of the micro-haematocrit centrifuge. The tube must lie in one of the channels in the rotor with the sealed end of the tube resting against the rubber rim. The safety cover is gently screwed down. The centrifuge lid is closed and the tubes spun for 5 minutes.

The spun tube is placed into the channel of the reader. The upper edge of the sealant plug is aligned with the black base line, and the meniscus of the column of blood plasma is aligned with the angled black upper line. The silver line of the movable slide on the reader is set at the level of the top of the packed erythrocyte column and the PCV reading is taken where the silver line cuts the scale on the right hand side of the instrument. It is not easy to measure more precisely than to the nearest 0.5%, and the three measurements should normally agree to within 1%. The mean of the three values should be used.

The PCV was traditionally expressed as a percentage of the whole blood volume (e.g. 45.3%), but it is now recommended that this value be expressed as litres of red cells per litre of whole blood (e.g. 0.453 l l^{-1}).

Determination of the true proportions of red cells and plasma in the blood requires suitable correction for plasma trapped between the red cells. Corrections of 2–4% are widely used, but Dacie and Lewis (1968) suggested that 1–1.5% is a more realistic figure when the standard microhaematocrit method is used. There are also differences between the central and peripheral haematocrit due to differential distribution of the red blood cells in the circulation. This can cause practical difficulties if, for example, peripheral venous blood is sampled and the degree of arterialization changes due to changes in the distribution of cardiac output (see Harrison (1985) for a discussion of this).

4.8 ANAEMIA AND THE MEASUREMENT OF IRON STATUS

Athletes are often concerned about the possibility of anaemia, which will adversely affect exercise performance, and the usual measure used to assess this is the circulating haemoglobin concentration. This has some value, as iron deficiency does not adversely affect performance until it is sufficiently severe to cause a fall in the circulating haemoglobin level (Weight *et al.* 1988). However, haemoglobin concentration is a poor index of an individual's iron status and more reliable measures should be used in any screening where there is reason to suspect that iron status might be sub-optimal. The prevalence of iron deficiency anaemia is not different between the athletic population and the general population, but whereas mild anaemia may be of little consequence to the sedentary individual, it will have a negative effect on all exercise situations where oxygen transport is a factor.

4.8.1 Erythrocyte (red cell) count

The red cell count is seldom measured outside a clinical setting, where it has diagnostic significance. Counting of red and white blood cells was, until recently, a standard laboratory practical class in most undergraduate physiology courses, but this seems now to be rare. Manual methods for cell counting involve counting individual cells in a known volume of diluted blood on a graduated microscope slide, and are tedious and time consuming. These methods have also all but disappeared from the clinical laboratory, where they have been replaced by automatic cell counters.

The Coulter counter is the most widely known of the automated systems, and

operates by passing diluted blood through a small aperture where electrical conductivity is measured. The cell membrane is an effective electrical insulator while the diluent is an electrolyte solution. Each particle displaces electrolyte, giving an electrical pulse proportional to the cell volume: counting these signals gives a measure of cell number in the measured volume of sample and of the volume of each of the cells counted. These automated procedures are more reliable than the manual methods. A measure of total red cell volume is obtained from the mean cell volume and the total red cell count.

The modern automated cell counter incorporates an autosampler and spectrophotometer which permits automated measurement of haemoglobin concentration. While this automation has considerable attractions, including a high level of accuracy in the measures of red cell count and haemoglobin concentration, care must be taken in the interpretation of the measures of cell volume. The diluent commonly used in the preparation of samples for analysis is not isotonic with normal human blood plasma: Isoton II has an osmolality of about 340 mosmol kg^{-1}, compared with an osmolality of human plasma of about 285–290 mosmol kg^{-1}. Because the red cell membrane is freely permeable to water, a rapid equilibration will take place on mixing of blood with the diluent, leading to a change in the red cell volume. (In the case of Isoton II there will be a decrease.) The measured volume is therefore different, by an amount proportional to the difference in osmolality between the plasma and the diluent, from the volume of the cells while in the circulation. In situations where the plasma osmolality changes substantially, as during intense or prolonged exercise in the heat, this will invalidate measures made using automated cell counting procedures.

4.8.2 Assessment of iron status

When anaemia is due to iron deficiency, erythropoiesis is microcytic, and the mean cell volume (MCV) is therefore low. The adequacy or otherwise of the body's iron stores is most commonly assessed clinically by measurement of the serum concentration of ferritin. Ferritin is tissue storage iron and the small proportion present in blood generally reflects total body iron stores. A low serum ferritin concentration is therefore diagnostic of tissue iron deficiency and this reduction precedes any fall in MCV and haemoglobin concentration. This early warning of impending anaemia is clearly advantageous in any routine monitoring of athletes. However, the serum ferritin concentration rises as a response to inflammatory and malignant conditions, and in such circumstances the serum concentration of ferritin may be misleadingly normal, or even raised, in the face of iron deficiency. This is not a significant problem in otherwise healthy subjects.

The serum iron concentration is also reduced in iron deficiency and this is accompanied by a rise in the total iron binding capacity, which represents transferrin, the principal iron transport protein in blood. Transferrin is normally around one third saturated with iron and a saturation of <15% is insufficient to support normal erythropoiesis, which becomes iron deficient. Although low serum iron, low transferrin saturation and increased iron binding capacity are typical of iron deficiency, the serum iron is also reduced in systemic disease even in the face of normal iron stores. This fall is usually accompanied by a reduced iron binding capacity, in contrast with the typical increase in iron deficiency.

4.8.3 Red cell turnover and cell age

Erythropoiesis takes place in the red bone marrow in postnatal life. In adults, red marrow is restricted to the cavities of the flat and proximal long bones, especially the skull, sternum, ribs, vertebrae and proximal ends of the femora. The released red cells circulate for 120 days and senescent cells are removed by macrophages of the reticuloendothelial system in liver, spleen and bone marrow. For the first 48 hours after this release, red cells contain residual RNA, which gives these immature red cells a purple tinge on a stained blood film. These reticulocytes can be more readily identified and counted by staining of a spread blood film using a supravital stain. An absolute increase in reticulocytes, which normally represent less than 1% of red cells, is indicative of increased erythropoietic activity, typically in response to acute blood loss or shortened red cell life span due to haemolysis. A more accurate assessment of total erythropoiesis is best achieved through measurement of iron turnover. This can be measured using an isotope of iron, ^{52}Fe or ^{59}Fe, which binds to transferrin *in vivo* and is cleared from plasma with a half time of 60–120 minutes when erythropoiesis is in steady-state and normal.

4.9 ALTITUDE TRAINING, BLOOD DOPING AND ERYTHROPOIETIN

Most endurance athletes are aware of the benefits of an elevated haemoglobin concentration, and can set about trying to achieve this in a number of ways. As indicated earlier, residence at high altitude results in a measurable increase in haemoglobin concentration due to an increase in body red cell mass in response to increased secretion of erythropoietin. This may be one mechanism for the perceived benefit of training at altitude. Historically, transfusion of red cells has been used to achieve an increase in body red cell mass, improved oxygen carriage and endurance performance. Transfusion of homologous blood (from a donor) carries many risks, including transfusion reactions and transmission of infections such as hepatitis. The same ends have been achieved more safely by transfusion of pre-donated autologous red cells. Because a donor who is iron replete can replenish the red cells in a donated unit (around 400 ml of blood) in one week, and because the shelf life of blood or separated red cells under appropriate conditions is up to 5 weeks, it is possible to increase the haemoglobin concentration by up to 50 g l[-1] from normal by transfusion of pre-donated autologous cells. Transfusion of as little as the equivalent of two units has been shown to improve aerobic work capacity and endurance performance under laboratory conditions. More recently erythropoietin has been employed to achieve the same ends as blood doping by transfusion. Erythropoietin manufactured by recombinant techniques has been and is readily available for clinical use, principally to treat the anaemia of chronic renal failure. When administered parenterally, along with intensive iron supplementation, to healthy individuals, it causes a predictable increase in body red cell mass, haemoglobin concentration and haematocrit, which is likely to be performance enhancing in endurance events. Should the haemoglobin be allowed to rise excessively, blood hyperviscosity results with reduced capillary perfusion. This situation, compounded by a further rise in haematocrit due to dehydration during competition, probably accounts for some cases of sudden deaths amongst competitive sportsmen using erythropoietin. Blood doping, by transfusion or pharmacological means, is banned under IOC regulations. However, neither method of blood doping can be detected by urine testing and increased haematocrit can occur in other situations, as described earlier. This topic represents a difficult challenge for governing bodies in a range of sports.

4.10 BLOOD AND PLASMA VOLUME CHANGES

4.10.1 Measurement of blood and plasma volume

Many studies require the measurement of the blood and/or plasma volume. Blood and plasma volumes can be determined using a number of different dilution methods, but all of these are relatively invasive. They also require sophisticated labelling facilities and suffer from the problem of not being amenable to repeated measurements at short time intervals.

In many investigations, it is more important to know how these measurements change over the time-course of a study than to know their absolute magnitude. Because of the practical difficulties, the indirect estimation of plasma or blood volume changes is more widely used in exercise physiology laboratories and will be discussed in greater detail here. However, a brief description of the methods for determination of blood and plasma volumes will be given first.

Detailed descriptions of methods for measurement of red cell volume and plasma volume can be found in Dacie and Lewis (1984). In principle, a small volume of tracer material is injected intravenously and its dilution measured after allowing time for mixing in the circulation. The plasma volume can thus be measured using human albumin labelled with radioactive iodine (^{131}I or ^{125}I), although it should be noted that this has limitations as there is some interchange between albumin in plasma and that in extravascular extracellular fluids. There is also some concern regarding the small risk of contamination with infective agents, especially prions, of any product prepared from donor blood. Red cells can be easily labelled with radioactive chromium, technetium or indium (^{51}Cr, ^{99m}Tc, ^{111}In) and from the dilution of labelled injected autologous red cells and the haematocrit the total blood volume and red cell volume can be calculated.

4.10.2 Estimation of blood and plasma volume changes

Because of the difficulties outlined in the previous section, changes in blood volume are usually estimated without direct measurement of the absolute volume. Changes in the concentration of an endogenous marker can be used as an index of blood volume changes. Total plasma protein and plasma albumin have been used for this purpose, but some exchange of protein across the vascular endothelium does occur in exercise, making these markers unsuitable (Dill and Costill 1974). Haemoglobin (Hb) is generally accepted as the most appropriate marker: Hb is contained within the red blood cell, and neither enters nor leaves the circulation in significant amounts over the time scale on which most exercise studies are conducted. Haemoglobin also has the added advantage of being easy and inexpensive to measure. It should be noted that the method is not suitable for use over long time scales where significant changes in the circulating Hb mass may occur or in experimental situations where there is a significant blood loss.

A change in haemoglobin concentration reflects, and can be used to calculate, a change in blood volume. Although the absolute plasma volume cannot be determined other than by dilution methods, changes in plasma volume can be calculated if both the Hb concentration and the haematocrit are known: various descriptions of the method have been published, but the most appropriate is that of Dill and Costill (1974). Use of changes in other circulating variables, such as total plasma protein, have been shown to be unreliable: proteins can enter and leave the vascular compartment during exercise (Harrison 1985). Haemoglobin, which is trapped within the red cells, does not leave the circulation.

As mentioned above, it is not appropriate to use Hct values derived from automated analyzers (such as the widely used Coulter counter) in these equations: these analyzers rely on dilution of the blood in a medium with a constant osmolality prior to analysis. The osmolality of these solutions is often very different from plasma osmolality: the commonly-used Isoton II has an osmolality of about 340 mosmol kg^{-1}. Because plasma and intracellular osmolality are not the same as that of the diluent, the measured Hct will not reflect the true *in vivo* Hct, due to changes in cell volume on being mixed with the diluent after collection. A more serious error arises if the osmolality of the plasma changes, as it almost invariably does when the plasma volume changes. In this situation, calculation of changes in plasma volume based on repeat measures of haematocrit have no validity, although there are many publications in the literature in which Coulter-derived values have been used inappropriately in this way. Although the error is small when the change in plasma osmolality is small, if the change is unknown, the error is also unknown.

4.10.3 Calculation of volume changes

Changes in blood volume (BV), plasma volume (PV) and red cell volume (RCV) can be calculated from the changes in Hb and Hct. The subscripts B and A are used to denote the first (before) and second (after) samples in the following calculations.

$$BV_A = BV_B \times (Hb_B/Hb_A)$$
$$RCV_A = BV_A \times Hct_A$$
$$PV_A = BV_A - RCV_A$$

Percentage changes in BV, PV and RCV can be calculated even though the absolute values in the above equations remain unknown.

$$\Delta BV = 100\ (BV_A - BV_B)\ /\ BV_B$$
$$\Delta RCV = 100\ (RCV_A - RCV_B)\ /\ CV_B$$
$$\Delta PV = 100\ (PV_A - PV_B)\ /\ PV_B$$

Sample calculation:
The calculations described above are demonstrated by a worked example based on the following data obtained before and after exercise:

Before: Hb = 151, Hct = 0.437
After: Hb = 167, Hct = 0.453

If the initial blood volume is assumed to be 100 ml, the blood volume after exercise is given by:

$$BV_A = 100\ (151/167)\ ml = 90.4\ ml$$

The decrease in blood volume (ΔBV) is therefore:

$$\Delta BV = ((90.4 - 100)/100) \times 100 = -9.6\%$$

The red cell volume before exercise is 43.7 ml (Hct = 0.437): after exercise the red cell volume is given by:

$$RCV_A = 0.453 \times 90.4 \text{ ml} = 41.0 \text{ ml}$$

The decrease in red cell volume is therefore:

$$((41.0 - 43.7) / 43.7) \times 100 = -6.2\%$$

The plasma volume before exercise was (1 – Hct) × 100 ml, or 56.3 ml. After exercise, the plasma volume was (90.4 – 41.0) ml, or 49.4 ml. The decrease in plasma volume was therefore 6.9 ml, or:

$$((49.4 - 56.3)/56.3) \times 100 = -12.3\%$$

Where some indication of the absolute magnitude of the volume shifts is required, an estimate of blood volume based on anthropometric data may be made. Several data sets are available, and a reasonable estimate may be that blood volume equals 75 ml kg^{-1} body mass in men and 65 ml kg^{-1} body mass in women (Astrand and Rodahl 1986).

FURTHER READING

Book:

Lewis S. M., Bain B. J., Bates I. (2006) *Dacie and Lewis Practical Haematology* (10th Edition) Churchill Livingstone; Philadelphia, PA.

Website:

The British Society for Haematology http://www.b-s-h.org.uk/

REFERENCES

Åstrand P. O. and K. Rodahl (1986) *Textbook of Work Physiology*. 3rd Edition. McGraw-Hill; New York.

Dacie J. V. and Lewis S. M. (1984) Blood volume, Chapter 9. In: *Practical Haematology*. 6th Edition. Churchill Livingstone; Philadelphia, PA.

Dacie J. V. and S. M. Lewis (1968) *Practical Haematology*. 4th Edition. Churchill; London: pp. 45–9.

Dill B. D. and D. L. Costill (1974) Calculation of percentage changes in volumes of blood, plasma, and red cells in dehydration. *Journal of Applied Physiology*; 37: 247–8.

Ekblom B., Goldbarg A. N. and Gullbring B. (1972) Response to exercise after blood loss and reinfusion. *Journal of Applied Physiology*; 33: 175–80.

Ekblom B., Wilson G. and Åstrand P.O. (1976) Central circulation during exercise after venesection and reinfusion of red blood cells. *Journal of Applied Physiology*; 40: 379–83.

Forster H. V., Dempsey J. A., Thomson J., Vidruk E. and DoPico G. A. (1972) Estimation of arterial PO2, PCO2, pH and lactate from arterialized venous blood. *Journal of Applied Physiology*; 32: 134–7.

Harrison M. (1985) Effects of thermal stress and exercise on blood volume in humans. *Physiological Reviews*; 65: 149–209.

Hull J. H. K., Ansley P. and Ansley L. (2008) Human Tissue Act: implications for sports science. *British Journal of Sports Medicine*; 42: 236–7.

Kargotich S,. Goodman C,. Keast D. and Morton A. R. (1998) The influence of exercise-induced plasma volume changes on the interpretation of biochemical parameters used for monitoring exercise, training and sport. *Sports Medicine*; 26: 101–17.

Leiper J. B., Maughan R. J. and Vist G. E. (1990) Choice of sampling site may influence the interpretation of results of blood analysis in exercising man. *Journal of Physiology*; 420 (Suppl.): 53P.

Levine B. D. (2008) V̇O2max: what do we know, and what do we still need to know? *Journal of Physiology*; 586: 25–34.

Maughan R. J. (1982) A simple rapid method

for the determination of glucose, lactate, pyruvate, alanine, 3-hydroxybutyrate and acetoacetate on a single 20μl blood sample. *Clinica Chimica Acta;* **122**: 232–40.

McGuire E. A. H., Helderman J. H., Tobin J. D., Andres R. and Berman M. (1976) Effects of arterial versus venous sampling on analysis of glucose kinetics in man. *Journal of Applied Physiology;* **41**: 565–73.

Robertson J. D., Maughan R. J. and Davidson R. J. L. (1988) Changes in red cell density and related parameters in response to long distance running. *European Journal of Applied Physiology;* **57**: 264–9.

Sawka M. N. and Coyle E. F. (1999) Influence of body water and blood volume on thermoregulation and exercise performance in the heat. *Exercise and Sports Science; Reviews;* **27**: 167–218.

UCI (2008) UCI Medical monitoring road. Accessed at: http://www.uci.ch/templates/UCI/UCI1/layout.asp?MenuId=MTUxNTQ. 20 January 2008.

Weight L. M., Myburgh K. H. and Noakes T. D. (1988) Vitamin and mineral supplementation: effect on running performance of trained athletes. *American Journal of Applied Physiology;* **47**: 192–5.

CHAPTER 5

CARDIOVASCULAR FUNCTION

Tim Cable

5.1 AIMS

- to provide students with an understanding of human cardiovascular control mechanisms during exercise;
- to discuss techniques used for the measurement of blood pressure and peripheral blood flow;
- to outline practical exercises that demonstrate the cardiovascular response to exercise, the reflexes involved in the cardiovascular response and the measurement of skin blood flow.

5.2 INTRODUCTION

During physical activity, several organs share the demand for increased perfusion. The heart must supply adequate blood to its own contracting muscle as well as to the contractile apparatus of skeletal muscle. Blood flow to the central nervous system must be maintained and skin perfusion augmented to allow for the dissipation of metabolic heat. During exercise, cardiac output, heart rate, oxygen consumption and systolic blood pressure are linearly related to the intensity of the activity performed. Indeed, during isotonic exercise in a thermally controlled environment, blood flow to skeletal muscle may be increased 25-fold. Such an increase is mediated by means of an increase in cardiac output, a redistribution of the cardiac output and a reduction in muscle vascular resistance. According to the Fick principle ($\dot{V}O_2$ = Cardiac Output [Q] × arteriovenous difference for oxygen [a-vO_2 diff]), oxygen consumption is also elevated by increasing oxygen extraction in the muscle (during exercise).

5.3 CARDIOVASCULAR ADJUSTMENTS DURING EXERCISE

5.3.1 Heart rate

Cardiac output is a function of heart rate and stroke volume. During exercise, heart rate may increase 300% above that at rest; the actual increase being dependent upon the exercise intensity. At low workloads, this increase in heart rate is mediated through a withdrawal of vagal tone (Ekblom *et al.* 1972). As exercise intensity is increased above a workload of 50% $\dot{V}O_{2max}$, the gradual rise in heart rate is mediated by both neural and humoral adrenergic activity, stimulating β_1 adrenoceptors. Evidence for such reciprocal control comes from studies in which atropine and propranolol have been infused (Ekblom *et al*. 1972). Atropine is a competitive antagonist of acetylcholine and can therefore be used to block the action of the parasympathetic system. On the other hand, propranolol, which is a β_1 and β_2 receptor blocker, can be used to block sympathetic nervous activity to the heart. These drugs can therefore be used to examine the relative importance of parasympathetic and sympathetic control of heart rate. Only at higher heart rates is the influence of vagal tone totally diminished. However, with β adrenergic blockade during exercise, the maximal heart rate achieved is some 40 beats.min^{-1} below that normally attained. Adrenergic activity is therefore a prerequisite for the increase in heart rate during heavy exercise. The withdrawal of vagal tone and the initiation of sympathetic noradrenergic activity seen rapidly after the onset of exercise are probably mediated by central command, a re-setting of the operating point of arterial blood pressure and a neural reflex mechanism originating in muscle and joint receptors (Group III fibre receptors).

During longer-term exercise, heart rate responses are probably adjusted by means of a pressure 'error' signal and the stimulation of peripheral mataboreceptors (Group IV fibre receptors) following chemical changes in the extracellular fluid of active muscles (see Figure 5.1).

5.3.2 Stroke volume

Stroke volume increases two-fold during dynamic exercise, although debate is still lively concerning the point at which maximum stroke volume is attained during incremental exercise (e.g. see Gonzalez-Alonso 2008; Warburton and Gledhill 2008). Some evidence suggests that maximum stroke volume is reached at an intensity of 50% $\dot{V}O_{2max}$ (Higginbotham *et al*. 1986), whilst other data suggest that there is a linear increase in stroke volume with exercise intensity, particularly in endurance athletes (Gledhill *et al*. 1994). The mechanisms that contribute to the increase in stroke volume include the Frank-Starling law of the heart and sympathetic neuronal activity. The Frank-Starling law of the heart states that

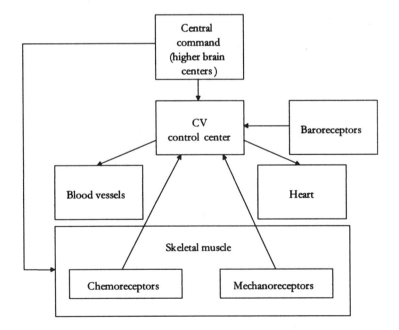

Figure 5.1 Reflexes responsible for cardiovascular control mechanisms.

the force of contraction is proportional to the initial length of the cardiac muscle fibres. Thus, the more blood that enters the ventricle during diastole, the greater the degree of stretch on the cardiac fibre and the greater the strength of contraction. The relationship only holds for work-rates up to 50% $\dot{V}O_{2max}$. Above this threshold, end diastolic volume (EDV) is reduced due to the increase in heart rate, which reduces cardiac filling time. Nevertheless, stroke volume is maintained, in spite of the decreased EDV by a greater force of contraction of cardiac fibres mediated by stimulation of β_1 adrenoceptors arising from sympathetic noradrenergic activity. Such stimulation increases the contractility of the cardiac muscle as evidenced by a reduction in end systolic volume (ESV).

During exercise, the stimulus that mediates the increased sympathoadrenal activity remains equivocal. There have been two major hypotheses (central command vs peripheral command) generated to explain the control of the sympathoadrenal response to exercise. These hypotheses are not mutually exclusive, but must be considered to be integrated in some manner. At the onset of exercise, it is thought that impulses from motor centres in the brain, as well as afferent impulses from inside the working skeletal muscle, are integrated to produce an increase in both noradrenergic and sympathoadrenal activity, which is dependent on work-rate. Throughout exercise the degree of this autonomic activity is continually adjusted by metabolic signals, and also by non-metabolic signals arising from the stimulation of pressure, volume, osmolality and temperature receptors.

During static isometric exercise there is a rapid pressor effect, an increase in mean arterial pressure and an associated increase in heart rate. During dynamic exercise, there is a more gradual (depending upon intensity) increase in mean arterial pressure and heart rate, although the change in pressure is far less than that observed during static exercise. It has long been thought that these responses occur to maintain the close match

necessary between blood flow and tissue metabolism.

5.3.3 Central command

Evidence that these haemodynamic responses are initiated by centrally generated motor command signals arises from studies in humans and animals that have used motor paralysis and partial neuromuscular blockade. In humans with the muscles of the forearm fully blocked by succinylcholine, an attempt to contract the paralyzed muscle group was accompanied by approximately 50% of the increase in arterial pressure and heart rate reported under normal unblocked conditions (Freyschuss 1970). Therefore in the absence of peripheral feedback (i.e. from immobile muscle) the cardiovascular responses must have been mediated by central command. This suggestion is complemented by studies employing partial neuromuscular blockade using tubocurarine. This drug causes muscle weakness, and therefore in order to produce the same absolute force of muscle contraction after blockade as before, a greater motor command signal is required. In studies in which maximum voluntary contraction (MVC) has been reduced by 50% with tubocurarine, arterial pressure rose more markedly at the same absolute force (Leonard et al. 1985). However, at the same relative force before and after blockade (i.e. the same percent of pre-MVC and post-MVC, and presumably therefore the same degree of motor command) pressure changes were of a similar degree (Leonard et al. 1985).

Mitchell (1990) suggested that the peripheral mataboreflex is also an important mediator of the exercise pressor reflex. This suggestion arose from studies using epidural anaesthesia, which not only reduces muscle strength by partial motor neurone blockade, but also inhibits afferent feedback from the contracting muscle. When repeating the same experimental model described above, it was observed that at the same absolute force the pressor effect was similar. However, at the same relative force cardiovascular responses were less. In attempting to exert the same absolute force, which requires a greater central command signal, the expected elevation of cardiovascular response was not observed. Similarly at the same relative intensity, when central command and therefore the pressor response should have been similar, a reduced cardiovascular response was observed. Given that sensory afferents were inhibited, these studies indicate that the peripheral metaboreflex as well as central command have a role to play in generating the cardiovascular response to exercise.

In response to a powerful isometric contraction there is an immediate increase in arterial pressure and heart rate. The increase in arterial pressure is attributable to an immediate increase in cardiac output resulting from a rapid elevation of heart rate (Martin *et al.* 1974). This tachycardia is governed by the removal of vagal tone rather than an increase in sympathetic activity, as the response is blocked by atropine and not propranolol (Maciel *et al.* 1987). In addition Maciel *et al.* (1987) found that the blockade of parasympathetic activity only influenced the first 10 s of very forceful isometric contractions at 50–70% MVC, whereas sympathetic blockade modified the heart rate response after 10 s.

It is clear, therefore, that central command governs the immediate cardiovascular response to exercise by the removal of vagal inhibition of heart rate. Following the initial 10 s of moderate to intense exercise, this response is increasingly controlled by augmented sympathetic nervous activity. Thus, it appears that central command plays a role in the removal of parasympathetic activity, but not in the activation of the sympathetic nervous system (SNS).

5.3.4 Peripheral command

The metaboreceptors located in muscle have been proposed as possible mediators of the increased activity of the sympathetic nervous system. These receptors are thought to be stimulated by the release of metabolites from exercising muscle in response to a mismatch between blood flow and metabolism. This response can be demonstrated during isometric muscle contraction by occluding the circulation to the muscle during and after exercise. The resultant post-exercise ischaemia maintains both the level of maximum arterial pressure (MAP) (Alam and Smirk 1937) and muscle sympathetic nerve activity (MSNA) (Seals *et al.* 1988) that is observed during exercise. As this response persists, even during passive recovery (and therefore in the absence of any central command), it must be mediated by metabolite activation of muscle metaboreceptors, the leading candidates of which are lactate and changes in pH. The increase in MSNA observed during exercise is delayed for 0.5–2 minutes after the initiation of contraction, a time period required for the accumulation of metabolites needed to activate the metaboreflex. Thus, the current thinking is that cardiovascular responses to isometric exercise are governed by a central command-mediated withdrawal of vagal tone and a peripheral metaboreflex initiation of sympathetic activity.

It was indicated earlier that sympathetic nervous activity (as measured by MSNA and increased concentrations of circulating noradrenaline) begins to increase at a heart rate of approximately 100 beats min^{-1} minute. In sedentary populations, lactate accumulation is not evident until work rates of about 50% $\dot{V}O_{2max}$ are reached. In endurance trained athletes this threshold may be 80% $\dot{V}O_{2max}$. These thresholds correspond to heart rates of approximately 140 and 170 beats min^{-1} respectively. Clearly at heart rates of 100 beats min^{-1} when SNS becomes active, sufficient lactate to stimulate the muscle metaboreceptors will not be present. It is therefore unlikely that the increase in sympathetic nervous activity observed during exercise of a moderate intensity is controlled by such chemoreceptor stimulation.

In summary, central command appears

to govern the cardiovascular response to dynamic exercise at heart rates below 100 beats min[-1] by the withdrawal of vagal tone. At higher work-rates, the haemodynamic response is mediated by the stimulation of peripheral metaboreceptors. The signal that initiates the increase in MSNA at moderate work-rates remains to be established.

5.3.5 Resetting of the arterial baroreflex

The rapid rise in arterial blood pressure and heart rate at the onset of exercise, has led to the conclusion that the arterial baroreflex is inactivated during exercise. This would therefore allow blood pressure to increase, without the baroreflex attempting to return it to a regulated value. Papelier *et al.* (1994) reported that the sensitivity of the baroreflex was unaltered during dynamic exercise in humans, but that the operating point (the value around which pressure is regulated) was shifted upwards in an intensity-dependent manner. That blood pressure may be regulated at a higher level immediately at the onset of exercise is supported by indirect evidence, showing that when the arterial baroreflex is denervated in exercising dogs, blood pressure falls (Melcher and Donald 1981).

Rowell (1993) suggested that the resetting of the arterial baroreflex to a higher operating point during exercise is responsible for the increased activity seen in the sympathetic nervous system and indeed during the past 20 years both animal and human experiments have provided strong evidence of arterial baroreflex resetting during exercise (Raven *et al.* 2006). Immediately at the onset of exercise, central command shifts the operating point of blood pressure to a higher level and withdraws vagal inhibition of heart rate. During mild exercise, the removal of vagal tone is sufficient to allow cardiac output to increase to a level that raises arterial pressure to the new regulated value, and there is therefore no perceived pressure 'error.' During more intense exercise, the

vagally induced increase in cardiac output is not sufficient to counteract the sudden vasodilation occurring in active muscle (i.e. a sudden fall in total peripheral resistance) and therefore according to the equation, $MAP = Q \times TPR$ {where MAP = mean arterial pressure (mmHg), Q = cardiac output (l min[-1]) and TPR = total peripheral resistance (mmHg[-1]min[-1])}, there is a mismatch between the new operating point of arterial pressure and the pressure detected. This pressure 'error' must be corrected by increased sympathetic nervous activity to the heart and vasculature, resulting in increased cardiac output and increased vasoconstrictor tone. Thus above a heart rate of 100 beats min[-1] (when most vagal activity has been withdrawn), increased sympathetic activity is promoted in response to an arterial pressure error, rather than in response to metabolic changes occurring in the active muscle. At higher work rates as lactate begins to accumulate, the muscle metaboreflex may become tonically active and increase sympathetic activity further. (There is a close correlation between muscle sympathetic nerve activity and lactate accumulation.) It is now clear that cardiovascular adjustments observed during dynamic exercise result from pressure-raising reflexes secondary to the detection of arterial pressure errors, rather than a mismatch between blood flow and metabolism, and that both the feedforward mechanism of central command and the feedback mechanism from skeletal muscle afferents are implicated in the resetting of the arterial baroreflex with exercise (Raven *et al.* 2006).

5.4 CONTROL OF BLOOD FLOW AT REST AND DURING EXERCISE

Regional blood flow is adjusted according to functional requirements of the tissue by changes in the resistance to flow through blood vessels. The resistance to flow through a given blood vessel varies inversely with the 4th power of the radius of the vessel, and therefore a relatively small change in the diameter of a resistance vessel initiates a dramatic fluctuation in blood flow through that tissue.

Depending on their functional requirements, tissues have varying ranges of blood flow. The rate of flow through organs such as the brain and liver remain relatively constant even when there are pronounced changes in both arterial blood pressure and cardiac output. In more compliant vascular beds such as skeletal muscle, skin and splanchnic regions, perfusion rates can vary markedly depending on the physiological conditions experienced.

5.4.1 Local regulating mechanisms

There are various substances that are either required for cellular metabolism or are produced as a consequence of it, which have a direct effect on the vasculature of muscle and therefore constitute the metabolic autoregulation of peripheral blood flow. This autoregulatory control is of great significance as it allows the matching of local blood flow to momentary nutritional requirements of the tissue. These local responses can completely override neurogenic constrictor effects, which are mediated centrally. However, the precise identity of a single factor or combination of factors that explain the increase in not only muscle blood flow, but the increase seen in other circulations such as the skin remains unknown (Joyner and Wilkins 2007).

Vasodilatation is evoked by a fall in partial pressure of oxygen in the local vascular bed. Thus, when arterial partial pressure of oxygen decreases as metabolic activity in the region is accelerated, vasodilatation occurs. Various mechanisms have been proposed to explain this process, including a direct effect of oxygen on vascular smooth muscle (Detar 1980). In addition, as regional metabolism increases, there are local increases in the partial pressure of CO_2 and the concentration of H^+, which are also thought to cause vasodilatation. The accumulation of lactate in a vascular bed is associated with vasodilatation, but this

effect is thought to be mediated indirectly by changes in plasma pH. It is unclear how these metabolites promote vasodilatation, but their release during contraction of muscle has a similar time-course to the release of adenosine and its nucleotides, which are known to be potent vasodilators. Furthermore, accumulating evidence now demonstrates that adenosine is released into the venous efflux of exercising muscle and may be responsible for 20–40% of the exercise-induced increase in muscle blood flow (Marshall 2007). In addition, there is much interest focused on the role ATP plays in exercise hyperaemia, since infusion of this nucleotide into the circulation cause an increase in flow (Saltin 2007). Potassium is also a potent vasodilatory substance. Juel et al. (2007) have reported a strong correlation between leg blood flow and potassium concentration during potassium infusion into the femoral artery at rest. Given that during maximal whole-body exercise there are large changes in systemic potassium, increases in this ion may contribute to exercise hyperaemia.

It is now recognized that a substance released from the endothelium acts upon smooth muscle cells to produce relaxation. This substance was originally termed endothelium derived relaxing factor, but has since been identified as nitric oxide (Palmer et al. 1987). It is produced from arginine in endothelial cells and stimulates cyclic guanosine monophosphate (cGMP) in smooth muscle cells to bring about relaxation (Collier and Vallance 1989). Nitric oxide has now been shown to be released continually from the vascular endothelium to exert a profound hypotensive effect.

In addition to a tonic release of nitric oxide from the endothelial cells at rest, blood flow through the lumen of blood vessels has been shown to stimulate the release of nitric oxide (Green et al. 1996). This phenomenon is thought to be caused by shear stress on the endothelial cells, the stimulus for release being proportional to the magnitude of blood flow. With microvascular perfusion coupled to muscle fibre activity, muscle blood flow can be matched to metabolic demands. The resultant hyperaemia would presumably stimulate greater nitric oxide release via shear stress, thereby further increasing blood flow. What is becoming clear is that there is a cocktail of metabolites and paracrine substances that are oblitory in promoting an increase in blood flow. No one single substance can presently be identified as the primary vasodilator. In contrast, it is becoming evident that the substances mentioned above operate in unison to provoke vasodilation.

5.4.2 Neural regulation

The sympathetic nervous system influences vasomotor tone in a number of vascular beds. All blood vessels except capillaries are innervated; with the result of stimulation depending upon the distribution and density of the subclasses of adrenoceptors. The small arteries and arterioles of the skin, kidney and splanchnic regions receive a dense supply of sympathetic noradrenergic vasoconstrictor fibres, whereas those of skeletal muscle and the brain have a relatively sparse supply of these fibres. When stimulated, noradrenaline is released from postganglionic fibres that combine with α adrenoceptors to initiate constriction of the smooth muscle surrounding the lumen of the vessel, leading to increased resistance to blood flow and thereby reduced tissue perfusion.

As previously stated the skeletal muscular, splanchnic, renal and cutaneous vascular beds are the major determinants of changes in systemic vascular resistance, which is under sympathetic noradrenergic control. If sympathetic activity to resting limb muscles is completely abolished there is a two- to three-fold increase in blood flow and, conversely, when noradrenergic activity is maximal, resting blood flow is reduced by 75%. Although these changes only account for a small proportion of those observed during exercise, they nevertheless function to mediate important changes in total systemic vascular resistance due to the large proportion of muscle as a percentage of total body mass. The action of noradrenaline on α adrenoceptors may actually be modulated by the release of local factors from active skeletal muscle. Adenosine, adenine nucleotides, potassium, hydrogen ions and extracellular osmolarity may directly inhibit smooth muscle cell contraction by interrupting vasoconstrictor impulses of sympathetic nerves. Thus, during exercise muscle blood flow may be partially increased by the withdrawal of noradrenergic tone.

The resistance vessels in the arterial circulation of skeletal muscle possess β_2 adrenoceptors, which have a high affinity for circulating adrenaline. As the exercise effort increases in duration and intensity, adrenaline concentration increases. This increase leads to stimulation of β_2 receptors, causing relaxation of the smooth muscle and a reduction of vascular resistance in skeletal muscle and therefore an increase in flow.

Controversy still exists as to the contribution of the cholinergic vasodilator pathway in exercise hyperaemia. Although reflex cholinergic vasodilator responses have been observed in humans during severe mental stress, it remains unclear whether such a mechanism exerts any influence on muscle blood flow during exercise. Cholinergic activity is thought to increase muscle blood flow during the initial 10 s of exercise, existing primarily as an anticipatory response to exercise initiated by the cholinergic vasodilatory pathway in the motor cortex.

5.5 CONTROL OF SKIN BLOOD FLOW DURING EXERCISE

Direct heating of the body or exercising, particularly in a warm environment, raises core temperature and results in a rapid increase in skin blood flow (SkBf) in an attempt to transfer this internal heat convectively away from the body. Such changes in SkBf are thought to be mediated by competition between vasoconstrictor and vasodilatory systems (Johnson, 1992). These systems are in turn regulated by a number of thermoregulatory and non-thermoregulatory reflexes (Gonzalez-Alonso *et al.* 2008).

All cutaneous resistance vessels receive a rich supply of sympathetic fibres, and therefore usually display tonic vasoconstriction. Additionally, the skin of the limbs and body trunk possesses an active vasodilator system. Therefore any increases in SkBf can be mediated by the removal of vasoconstrictor tone, an increase in active vasodilator activity, or both. Indeed, humans are the only species known to be dependent upon active vasodilation and sweating for their heat loss mechanisms. It is still not known whether vasodilation is mediated by specific vasodilator nerve fibres or is secondary to the effects of a neurohumoral compound co-released from sympathetic cholinergic nerve terminals which innervates sweat glands. The close association between active vasodilation and sweating is evident from studies indicating an inability to vasodilate in subjects that have a congenital absence of sweat glands (Brengelmann *et al.* 1981). It has been proposed that sympathetic cholinergic nerves supplying the sweat gland co-release a potent vasodilator, along with acetylcholine. The identity and precise mode of action of this vasodilatory substance remain unknown, but possible candidates include vasoactive intestinal polypeptide and nitric oxide. Although the increases in sweating and SkBf are generally considered to be coincident, the temperature threshold at which both occur has been uncoupled (Kenney and Johnson 1992), indicating that the control of sudomotor and vasodilator activity are independent of each other.

There are many complex interactions between thermoregulatory and non-thermoregulatory reflexes in the control of SkBf. The thermoregulatory reflexes are activated by an increase in both core and skin temperature, leading to the inhibition of vasoconstrictor tone and possibly the initiation of the active vasodilator system.

Non-thermoregulatory reflexes include baroreceptor control of blood pressure and exercise reflexes associated with exercise itself (Rowell 1993).

The cutaneous vascular response to exercise happens like this: Immediately at the onset of exercise there is a vasoconstrictor activity which causes SkBf to decrease below resting baseline values. Having reached its lowest value SkBf returns to pre-exercise values and increases markedly until a core temperature of 38°C is reached. Beyond this temperature SkBf attains a plateau or increases only by a small amount during prolonged endurance exercise (Kenney and Johnson 1992). In addition, during exercise the threshold core temperature at which SkBf begins to increase is much greater than that observed in a warm environment at rest. Therefore during exercise, SkBf at any given core temperature is much lower than at rest. The rate of increase in core temperature, once the threshold for vasodilation has been reached, is unaffected by exercise (Figure 5.2).

Rowell (1983) hypothesized that the rightward shift of the SkBf/ body temperature relationship is caused by a increased sympathetic vasoconstrictor activity during exercise, in response to a fall in resistance to blood flow in skeletal muscle (and therefore in order to maintain MAP, resistance in non-active circulation must be increased). Thus, SkBf was presumed to be limited by increased vasoconstrictor activity rather than a reduction in vasodilator activity, due to the fact that the vasodilator system was thought to be independent of nonthermal control systems (i.e. the baroreflex).

Kellogg *et al.* (1990) have shown that the baroreflex can decrease SkBf by the withdrawal of vasodilator activity. This phenomenon was demonstrated by blocking the release of noradrenaline and therefore vasoconstriction, whilst leaving the active vasodilator mechanism intact. Using this model, Kellogg *et al.* (1991) observed that the usual decrease in SkBf associated with

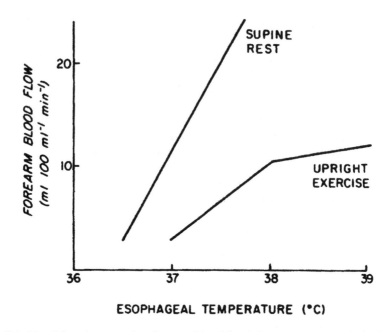

Figure 5.2 Skin blood flow (expressed as forearm blood flow) during passive whole-body heating and during upright exercise (adapted from Rowell 1993).

the onset of exercise was mediated by sympathetic noradrenergic activity and not by the withdrawal of active vasodilation. In addition, it was observed that the delayed increase in SkBf during exercise, compared with heating at rest, was unaffected by adrenergic inhibition, and was therefore caused by a delayed onset in vasodilation outflow to the skin. Furthermore, Kenney and Johnson (1992) reported that the plateau in SkBf observed during prolonged exercise is not mediated by augmented vasoconstriction, but rather by a withdrawal of vasodilator activity. Kenney and Johnson (1992) therefore concluded that the control of SkBf is dominated by active vasodilation and that this system may be under non-thermal baroreflex control in an attempt to preserve arterial blood pressure.

5.6. MEASUREMENT OF BLOOD PRESSURE

Arterial blood pressures are most accurately measured through the use of rapidly responding pressure transducers located in the arterial circulation. Due to the invasive nature of this technique, its use is limited to a clinical environment. For this reason, blood pressure is not usually measured directly, but estimated using the auscultatory technique. This technique requires the use of a sphygmomanometer and stethoscope, and is dependent upon the observer detecting the characteristic 'Korotkoff' sounds that are produced following occlusion of the circulation to the forearm.

A cuff is inflated to supra-systolic pressure around the upper arm and then slowly deflated whilst simultaneously listening for the Korotkoff sounds through a stethoscope which is placed over the brachial artery in the region of the antecubical fossa. At supra-systolic pressures, blood flow to the forearm is completely occluded. When the pressure in the occluding cuff is equal to systolic pressure in the cardiovascular system, blood forces its way back into the artery, creating turbulent flow and producing the so-called 'First Korotkoff' sound. The pressure cuff is connected to a mercury or aneroid manometer, allowing for the estimation of systolic blood pressure at this point. As pressure in the cuff is reduced further, blood flow entering the artery remains turbulent until the diameter of the artery reaches its normal patency. This point reflects diastolic pressure and is indicated by the disappearance of the Korotkoff sounds as the blood flow in the artery is now non-turbulent. When resting environmental conditions and measurement protocol are standardized, this indirect method gives reliable estimations of blood pressures, particularly when used by experienced personnel. In addition, this technique can be used during static and dynamic exercise in steady-state conditions. Indeed, when used to predict mean arterial pressure (diastolic pressure + $^1/_3$ (systolic − diastolic pressure)), this technique has been shown to provide a good estimation of blood pressure measured directly in the brachial artery during exercise (MacDougall *et al.* 1999).

Until recently, beat-to-beat monitoring of blood pressure was only possible using the invasive technique of an intra-arterial catheterization. Since the development of the photoelectric principle, it is now possible to demonstrate the full blood pressure waveform non-invasively from the finger during each cardiac cycle.

This measurement can be performed using the photoplethysmographic technique for measurement of the finger arterial pressure. The instrument (e.g. Ohmeda Finapres 2300, Englewood, Colorado, USA or Portapres, FMS, Amsterdam, Holland) comprises an electropneumatic transducer and an infrared plethysmograph within a small finger cuff. The transducer measures the absorption of light and links the plethysmograph to an air pressure source through a fast reacting servo mechanism. Air pressure in the finger cuff is then rapidly regulated to maintain the finger blood volume and plethysmographic light level equivalent to that detected at zero transmural pressure of the digital artery (unloaded arterial wall), thus reflecting the finger arterial

pressure waveform. Measurement of blood pressure is fully automated using the Finapres device and the equipment is self-calibrating. A volume clamp level is established within 10 heart beats. Thereafter, blood pressure is continuously monitored except for a small interruption every 10 beats initially followed by 70-beat intervals. Such a device allows the immediate assessment of changes in blood pressure in response to various interventions (e.g. upright posture, recovery from exercise), and provides an indication of the real time change in pressure.

5.7 MEASUREMENT OF PERIPHERAL BLOOD FLOW

5.7.1 Strain gauge plethysmography

Limb blood flow may be determined non-invasively by measurement of the volume change in a limb segment. Occlusion of the veins draining a limb to a pressure between venous and diastolic blood pressure allows continued arterial flow into the limb segment resulting in increased venous volume and limb volume. Changes in limb volume during venous occlusion may be determined by the displacement of water or air from a jacket secured around the limb or by the measurement of limb circumference changes using a mercury strain gauge. Whitney (1953) pioneered the mercury strain gauge technique, which is based on Ohm's law of electrical conductance (Voltage = Current × Resistance). The principle of operation is related to the effect of changes in gauge length and diameter on the electrical resistance offered by the mercury thread within a Silastic rubber tube (Whitney 1953). This mercury thread forms one arm of a balanced Wheatstone bridge circuit which is housed within a plethysmograph device (Parks Medical Electronics, Aloha, Oregon, USA). Owing to the good linear correlation between voltage output from the bridge circuit and a change in strain gauge length (Whitney

1953), the change in voltage may be used to reflect the change in limb circumference during venous occlusion (see Figure 5.3).

a) Limb blood flow measurement protocol

The strain gauge is secured around the greatest circumference of the limb. In order to encourage rapid venous drainage during cuff deflation, the elbow and wrist or knee and ankle are comfortably elevated on foam supports to heights of 10 cm and 15 cm respectively. Circulation to the hand or foot is then occluded at a pressure of 200 mmHg for 1 minute before each venous occlusion cycle commences. Venous occlusion is achieved by inflating a collecting cuff, placed around the upper limb (e.g. immediately above the elbow or knee) to a pressure of 50 mmHg in a cycle of 10-s inflation to 5-s deflation for a total of 3 minutes using a rapid cuff inflator (see left arm in Figure 5.3).

b) Calculation of limb blood flow

From the geometry of the circle and cylinder $(2\pi r, \pi r^2, \pi r^2 \times h$, where h = cylinder length), a percentage change in the volume of a cylinder is twice the percentage change in circumference. Although limbs are not cylindrical, their length does not increase upon expansion with blood. The mathematical relationship between percentage changes in circumference and volume therefore holds (Whitney 1953). Following calculation of the slope relating the changes between voltage and time during venous occlusion, the increase in gauge length is determined using the linear regression equation for each individually calibrated strain gauge. The change in gauge length is then expressed as a percentage of limb circumference according to the equation:

$$\text{Bloodflow} = ((\Delta \text{ Gaugelength} \div 10(s) \times 60(s)) \div \text{Girth (mm)}) \times (100 \times 2)$$

For example, for a change in gaugelength of 1 mm in a forearm of girth 20 cm, blood flow = $(1 \div 10 \times 60) \div 200 \times 200 = 6$ ml.100 ml tissue^{-1}.min^{-1}.

The percentage change in limb volume

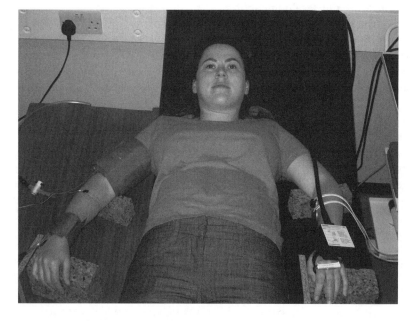

Figure 5.3 Strain gauge plethysmography, laser Doppler flowmetry and beat-to-beat blood pressure measurement in the finger.

over time is then a direct indication of the rate of blood flow, expressed as ml.100 ml tissue^{-1}.min^{-1}.

5.7.2 Skin blood flow

There is no method currently available to quantify total blood flow through the skin. The various techniques used estimate skin blood flow indirectly from variables that are related to flow (Rowell 1993). When blood flow to deeper structures is considered, venous occlusion plethysmography offers a useful indication of skin blood flow (Johnson 1992). Measurements are confined to whole limbs at maximum intervals of 3–4 evaluations per minute. Laser Doppler flowmetry is a new method of skin blood flow measurement with an excellent frequency response that has the capability for continuous, non-invasive monitoring of perfusion to any region of skin or exposed tissue.

a) Theory of laser doppler flowmetry

The use of the laser Doppler technique to measure flow operates on the principle that the frequency shift of laser light reflected from the skin is linearly related to red blood cell flux and thus tissue blood flow. A narrow 2-mW beam of laser-generated monochromatic light is directed at a wavelength of 780 nm through a 2-m optical fibre to a probe (3 mm in diameter) which rests against the skin. Blood cell movement below the illuminated area of skin scatters the light causing a change in wavelength and frequency known as Doppler shift. Since the measurement depth is only 0.5–1.0 mm, there should be no contribution from blood flow in deeper tissues to the laser Doppler signal. Some of the reflected light is returned along another optical fibre to a photodetector in the instrument which converts the frequency differences (Doppler shift) into an electrical signal. Thus, the greater the movement velocity of the blood cells within the measurement area, the greater the Doppler shift. The basic arbitrary unit of laser Doppler measurement is the perfusion unit (PU) which is equivalent to an analogue output of 10 mV (see Figure 5.4).

b) Performance of the laser doppler flow meter

During whole-body heating the changes in skin blood flow in the forearm, measured simultaneously using laser Doppler flowmetry and venous occlusion plethysmography, are linearly related. This relationship (correlation coefficient = 0.94 to 0.98) holds over a range of forearm blood flows. Thus, changes in skin blood flow can be reliably and continuously monitored by means of the laser Doppler method. However, the between-subject variability in laser Doppler values at a given forearm blood flow appears to prevent any possible calibration of the instrument output voltage into conventional blood flow units.

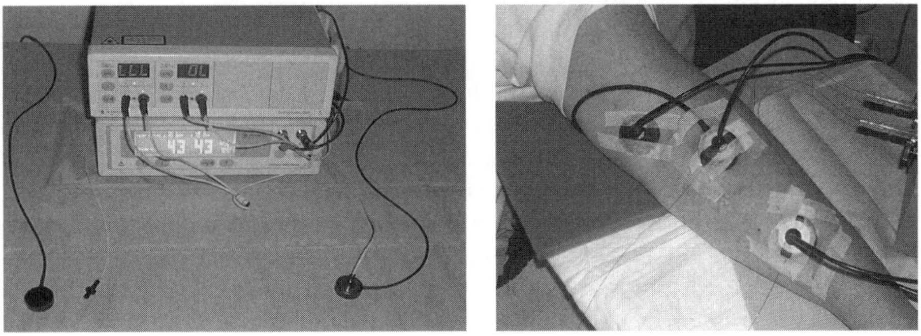

Figure 5.4. Laser Doppler equipment for the measurement of skin blood flow (A) and placement of laser Doppler probes on the skin (**B**).

This source of error is considered to be most likely related to the variable number of capillaries within the illuminated area of the laser Doppler probe.

The changes in skin blood flow throughout the cardiac cycle may be detected by the laser Doppler flow meter. With this degree of sensitivity, skin blood flow changes during rapid challenges to arterial pressure may be followed continuously.

c) Skin blood flow measurement protocol
Skin blood flow can be monitored from any skin surface, the most common being the lateral calf and the anterior aspect of the forearm. It is usually necessary to shave a small area on the leg to gain a good contact. Each probe is secured in a plastic holder and attached onto the limb, using an adhesive disc, so that the probe tip just touched the skin surface.

5.8 PRACTICAL EXERCISES

It is easier to demonstrate cardiovascular responses using single-case studies as examples. Experiments require quiet and controlled laboratory conditions. In addition, Practical 1 requires some modification of environmental temperature.

5.9 PRACTICAL 1: SKIN BLOOD FLOW RESPONSE TO REACTIVE HYPERAEMIA AND EXERCISE

This Practical involves measuring maximal skin blood flow, and the skin blood flow response following exercise in normal and warm conditions.

5.9.1 Aim

To measure maximal skin blood flow and express skin blood flow measured after exercise in different environments as a percentage of this maximum.

5.9.2 Equipment

Sphygmomanometer, stethoscope, pressure cuff, Laser Doppler flow meter and cycle ergometer.

5.9.3 Protocol

The subject lies supine and rests during the placement of the laser Doppler probe on the anterior surface of the forearm. Resting skin blood flow and blood pressures are measured. The subject exercises on cycle ergometer at 70% of the maximal heart rate for 20 min. (If the arm is kept very still during exercise it is possible to measure skin blood flow.) Immediately on cessation of exercise, the subject adopts a supine position for the measurement of skin blood flow and blood pressures for 10 minutes of recovery. Following this recovery, blood flow to the forearm is occluded by inflating the pressure cuff to supra-systolic pressure for 5 minutes. The cuff is released and maximal reactive hyperaemic skin blood flow measured (i.e. peak value for blood flow following cuff release). This protocol can be repeated at varying environmental temperatures (i.e. 16°C vs 30°C).

5.9.4 Results

Tables 5.1 and 5.2 display skin blood flow results expressed in absolute units and as vascular resistance (blood pressure/flow) that can be expected following exercise in normothermic and hyperthermic conditions (see also Figure 5.5). These values are also expressed as a percentage of maximal skin blood flow (see also Figure 5.6). This is derived by dividing SkBf by maximum blood flow measured following circulatory occlusion and multiplying by 100 (e.g. at rest 16°C; $10/100 \times 100 = 10$).

Table 5.1 Skin blood flow data at 16°C. The percentage of maximum Skin blood flow assumes that peak reactive hyperaemic blood flow = 100 Pu (Pu = Perfusion unit).

		Recovery (min)		
	Rest	*2*	*5*	*10*
SkBf (Pu)	10	25	20	12
MAP (mmHg)	90	90	90	90
Skin Vascular Resistance (SkVR)	9	3.6	4.5	7.5
% of Max SkBf	10	25	20	12

Table 5.2 Skin blood flow data at 30°c

		Recovery (min)		
	Rest	*2*	*5*	*10*
SkBf (Pu)	20	60	40	30
MAP (mmHg)	80	80	80	80
Skin Vascular Resistance (SkVR)	4	1.3	2	2.6
% of Max SkBf	20	60	40	30

Values at rest and 2, 5 and 10 min post-exercise

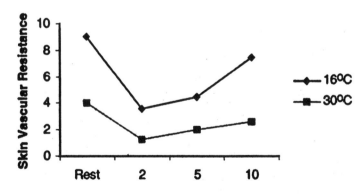

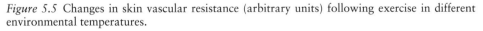

Figure 5.5 Changes in skin vascular resistance (arbitrary units) following exercise in different environmental temperatures.

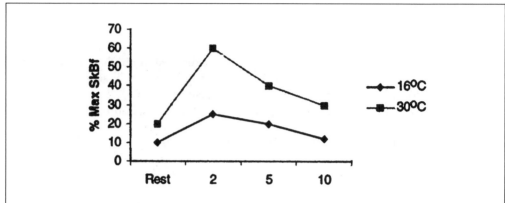

Figure 5.6 Skin blood flow expressed as a percentage of maximum flow following exercise in different environmental temperatures.

5.10 PRACTICAL 2: ACUTE EFFECTS OF EXERCISE ON CARDIOVASCULAR FUNCTION

5.10.1 Aim

To assess the effects of body position and dynamic and static exercise on heart rate, blood pressure, myocardial oxygen demand (an index of cardiac workload), cardiac output, oxygen pulse, total peripheral resistance and oxygen uptake.

5.10.2 Equipment

Sphygmomanometer, stethoscope, oxygen consumption (Douglas Bags or on-line system), handgrip dynamometer and cycle ergometer.

5.10.3 Protocol

1   Resting and static exercise measurements
   i)   Using the data sheet, record the above measurements after:
      Sitting quietly for 2–3 minutes
      Lying quietly for 2–3 minutes
      Standing quietly for 2–3 minutes
   ii) Repeat the standing measurement whilst the subject performs a 50% MVC using a handgrip dynamometer for 1 minute. Blood pressure is measured on the contralateral arm.
   iii) Dynamic exercise with and without static contraction
      1   The subject exercises for 4 minutes at 50, 100 and 150 watts. Measure the $\dot{V}O_2$ and haemodynamic parameters in the fourth minute.
      2   The subject exercises as above, BUT during the fourth minute he/she simultaneously performs a 50% MVC on the handgrip dynamometer.

Assume a-vO$_2$ difference values indicated in Table 5.3.

Some formulae to help

$\dot{V}O_2$ (l.min^{-1}) = Q (l.min^{-1}) × a-vO$_2$ diff (mlO$_2$.100ml^{-1} blood flow)*

*Example: Expression of a-$\dot{V}O_2$ diff in litres where a-$\dot{V}O_2$ diff = 5ml.100ml^{-1} blood flow, equates to 0.05l. Thus, for a typical resting cardiac output of 5 l.min^{-1} and a-$\dot{V}O_2$ diff of 5ml.100ml^{-1} the $\dot{V}O_2$ = 5 1.min^{-1} × 0.05 l = 0.25 l.min^{-1}

Myocardial oxygen demand (RPP) = HR (beats.min^{-1}) × SBP (mmHg)

Oxygen Pulse (ml.beat^{-1}) = $\dot{V}O_2$ ml HR^{-1}

MAP (mmHg) = DBP + (0.33 × (SBP − DBP))

Q = HR × SV

MAP = Q × TPR

Table 5.3 displays expected values for cardiovascular variables during postural change and imposition of exercise stress. Notice that in the upright position MAP and TPR fall. During exercise HR and MAP increase, placing greater demands on the heart (myocardial work). These changes are even greater when handgrip exercise is superimposed on cycling. Notice also, that TPR falls as exercise intensity increases. In this practical the arterial-venous oxygen difference was not measured. The values were assumed to exemplify the relationships between the variables.

Table 5.3 Typical values of cardiovascular function at rest and during dynamic and static exercise.

Power (W)	HR	SBP mmHg	DBP mmHg	MAP mmHg	RPP	$\dot{V}O_2$ $l\,min^{-1}$	Q $l\,min^{-1}$	TPR $(mmHg)/l$ min^{-1}	O_2 Pulse $ml\,bt^{-1}$	$a\text{-}vO_2\,dif$ $(l\,l^{-1})$ assumed	SV (ml)
Sit	60	120	80	93	7200	0.25	5.0	18.6	4.2	0.05	83
Lying	50	125	80	95	6250	0.25	5.0	19	4.2	0.05	100
Stand	70	110	70	83	7700	0.30	6.0	13.8	4.3	0.05	85
50% HG Static stand	85	145	85	105	12325	0.30	6.0	17.5	3.5	0.05	71
50 W	95	130	80	97	12350	0.9	10.0	8.7	9.5	0.09	105
50 W with 50% HG	115	140	90	107	16100	0.9	10.0	10.7	7.8	0.09	87
100 W	120	135	80	98	16200	1.5	12.5	7.8	12.5	0.12	104
100 W with 50% HG	135	150	90	110	20250	1.5	12.5	8.8	11.1	0.12	93
150 W	140	140	80	100	19600	2.1	15.0	6.7	15.0	0.14	107
150 W with 50% HG	150	160	90	113	24000	2.1	15.0	7.5	14.0	0.14	100
5 min Post Ex	100	110	60	77	11000	0.6	8.6	9.0	6.0	0.07	86

HG indicates maximal handgrip force

5.11 PRACTICAL 3: EXERCISE PRESSOR RESPONSE

This practical measures blood pressure during isometric muscle contraction with and without occlusion of blood flow to the exercising limb.

5.11.1 Aim

To demonstrate the importance of peripheral chemoreceptor action in cardiovascular regulation.

5.11.2 Equipment

Sphygmomanometer, stethoscope, pressure cuff and handgrip dynamometer

5.11.3 Protocol

The subject performs a maximal handgrip exercise to establish MVC. Resting blood pressures are then measured, following which the subject performs rhythmical dynamic handgrip exercise at 50%MVC for 2 minutes. Blood pressures are measured in the contralateral limb during the last minute of exercise and at 2-minute intervals during a recovery period of 6 minutes.

After blood pressure has returned to baseline values, the above protocol is repeated, but with blood flow to the exercising limb occluded using supra-systolic pressures (220 mmHg) immediately prior to exercise and for the duration of recovery. Such occlusion, whilst uncomfortable, can be maintained safely for at least 10 minutes.

5.11.4 Results

Figure 5.7 displays an example of blood pressure response with and without occlusion. This clearly highlights the stimulation of peripheral chemoreceptors by trapped metabolites and the maintained or even increased cardiovascular response compared with exercise.

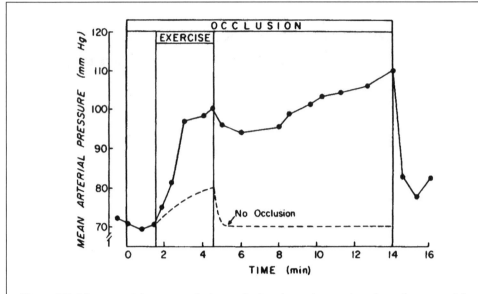

Figure 5.7 Mean arterial pressure during and after dynamic exercise of one forearm with and without circulatory arrest (adapted from Alam and Smirk 1937).

FURTHER READING

Book

Saltin B., Boushel R., Secher N. and Mitchell J. (2000). *Exercise and the Circulation in Health and Disease.* Human Kinetics; Champaign, IL.

Articles

Joyner M. J. and Coyle E. F. (2008) Endurance exercise performance: the physiology of champions. *Journal of Physiology;* **586:** 35–44.

Tanaka H. and Seals D. R. (2008). Endurance exercise performance in Masters athletes: age-associated changes and underlying physiological mechanisms. *Journal of Physiology;* **586** (1): 55–63.

Website

National Center for Chronic Disease Prevention and Rehabilitation; Physical Activity and Health – A report for the Surgeon General. (1999) http://www.cdc.gov/nccdphp/sgr/chap1.htm

REFERENCES

Alam M. and Smirk F.H. (1937) Observations in man upon a blood pressure raising reflex from the voluntary muscles. *Journal of Physiology (London);* 89: 372–83.

Brengelmann G. L., Freund P. L., Rowell L. B., Oleurd J. E. and Kraning K. K. (1981) Absence of active cutaneous vasodilation associated with congenital absence of sweat glands in man. *American Journal of Physiology;* **240:** H571–H575.

Collier J. and Vallance P. (1989) Second messenger role of NO widens to nervous and immune systems. *Trends in Pharmacological Sciences;* **10:** 427–31.

Detar R. (1980) Mechanism of physiological hypoxia-induced depression of vascular smooth muscle contraction. *American Journal of Physiology;* **238:** H761–H769.

Ekblom B., Goldbarg A. N., Kilbom A. and Astrand P. O. (1972) Effects of atropine and propranolol on the oxygen transport system during exercise in man. *Scandinavian Journal of Clinical Laboratory Investigation;* 30: 35–42.

Freyschuss U. (1970) Cardiovascular adjustment of somatomotor activation. *Acta*

Scandinavica Physiologica; **342** (Suppl. 1): 1–63.

Gledhill N., Cox D. and Jamnik R. (1994). Endurance athletes' stroke volume does not plateau; major advantage is diastolic function. *Medicine and Science in Sport and Exercise;* **26**: 1116–21.

Green D. J., O'Driscoll G., Blanksby B. A. and Taylor R.. (1996) Control of skeletal muscle blood flow during dynamic exercise: contribution of endothelium-derived nitric oxide. *Sports Medicine;* **21**: 119–46.

González-Alonso J. (2008) Point: stroke volume does/does not decline during exercise at maximal effort in healthy individuals. *Journal of Applied Physiology;* **104**: 275–6.

González-Alonso J., Crandall C. G, and Johnson J. M. (2008) The cardiovascular challenge of exercising in the heat. *Journal of Physiology;* **586**: 45–53.

Higginbotham M. B., Morris K. G., Williams R. S., Coleman R. E. and Cobb F. R. (1986) Physiologic basis for the age-related decline in aerobic work capacity. *American Journal of Cardiology;* **57**: 1374–9.

Johnson J. M. (1992). Exercise and the cutaneous circulation. *Exercise and Sports Science Reviews;* **20**: 59–97.

Joyner M. J. and Wilkins B. J. (2007) Exercise hyperaemia: is anything obligatory but the hyperaemia? *Journal of Physiology;* **583**: 855–60.

Juel C., Olsen S., Rentsch R. L., González-Alonso J., Rosenmeier J.B. (2007). K+ as a vasodilator in resting human muscle: implications for exercise hyperaemia. *Acta Physiologica Scandinavica;* **190** (4): 311–18.

Kellogg D. M., Johnson J. M. and Kosiba W. A. (1990) Baroreflex control of the cutaneousactive vasodilator system in humans. *Circulation Research;* **66**: 1420–6.

Kellogg D. M., Johnson J. M. and Kosiba W. A. (1991). Competition between the cutaneous active vasoconstrictor and vasodilator systems during exercise in man. *American Journal of Physiology;* **216**: H1184–H1189.

Kenney W. L. and Johnson J. M. (1992) Control of skin blood flow during exercise. *Medicine and Science in Sports and Exercise;* **24**: 303–12.

Leonard B., Mitchell J. H., Mizuno M., Rube N. M., Saltin B. and Secher N. H. (1985) Partial neuromuscular blockade and cardiovascular responses to static exercise in man. *Journal of Physiology (London);* **359**: 365–79.

MacDougall J. D., Brittain M., MacDonald J. R., McKelvie R. S., Moroz D. E., Tarnopolsky M. A. and Moroz J. S. (1999) Validity of predicting mean arterial blood pressure during exercise. *Medicine and Science in Sports and Exercise;* **31**: 1876–9.

Maciel B. C., Gallo L., Marin Neto J. A. and Martins L. E. B. (1987) Autonomic nervous control of the heart rate during isometric exercise in normal man. *Pflugers Archives;* **408**: 173–7.

Marshall J. (2007) The roles of adenosine and related substances in exercise hyperaemia. *Journal of Physiology;* **583**: 835–45.

Martin C. E., Shaver J. A., Leon D. F., Thompson M. E., Reddy P. S. and Leonard J. J. (1974) Autonomic mechanismsin haemodynamic resonses to isometric exercise. *Journal of Clinical Investigation;* **54**: 104–15.

Melcher A. and Donald D. E. (1981). Maintained ability of the carotid baroreflex to regulate arterial pressure during exercise. *American Journal of Physiology;* **241**: H838–H849.

Mitchell J. H. (1990). Neural control of the circulation during exercise. *Medicine and Science in Sports and Exercise;* **22**: 141–54.

Palmer R. M. J., Ferridge A. G. and Moncada S. (1987). Nitric oxide accounts for the biological activity of endothelium-derived relaxing factor. *Nature;* **327**: 524–6.

Papelier Y., Escourrou P., Gauthier J. P. and Rowell L. B. (1994). Carotid baroreflex control of blood pressure and heart rate in men during dynamic exercise. *Journal of Applied Physiology;* **77**: 502–6.

Raven P. B., Fadel P. J., and Ogoh S. (2006) Arterial baroreflex resetting during exercise: a current perspective. *Experimental Physiology;* **91**: 37–49.

Rowell L. B. (1983). Cardiovascular aspects of human thermoregulation. *Circulation Research;* **52**: 367–9.

Rowell L. B. (1993). *Human Cardiovascular Control.* Oxford University Press; New York: pp. 441–83.

Saltin B. (2007). Exercise hyperaemia: magnitude and aspects on regulation in humans. *Journal of Physiology;* **583:** 819–23.

Seals D. R., Victor R. G. and Mark A. L. (1988) Plasma norepinephrine and muscle sympathetic discharge during rhythmic exercise in humans. *Journal of Applied Physiology;* **65:** 940–4.

Warburton D. E. and Gledhill N. (2008) Counterpoint: stroke volume does not decline during exercise at maximal effort in healthy individuals. *Journal of Applied Physiology;* **104:** 276–8.

Whitney R. J. (1953) The measurement of volume changes in human limbs. *Journal of Physiology;* **121:** 1–27.

PART THREE

ASSESSMENT OF ENERGY AND EFFICIENCY

CHAPTER 6

METABOLIC RATE AND ENERGY BALANCE

Carlton B. Cooke

6.1 AIMS

The aims in this chapter are to:
- describe methods of measuring metabolic rate and energy balance;
- describe methods of predicting resting metabolic rate;
- describe methods of measuring energy expenditure using expired air analysis;
- provide examples of the measurement of metabolic rate and energy balance.

6.2 BASAL METABOLIC RATE (BMR)

The main component of daily energy expenditure in the average person is the energy expenditure for maintenance processes, usually called basal metabolic rate (BMR). The BMR is the energy expended for the ongoing processes in the body in the resting state, when no food is digested and no energy is needed for temperature regulation. The BMR reflects the body's heat production and can be determined indirectly by measuring oxygen uptake under strict laboratory conditions. No food is eaten for at least 12 hours prior to the measurement so there will be no increase in the energy required for the digestion and absorption of foods in the digestive system. This fast ensures that measurement of BMR occurs with the subject in the postabsorptive state. In addition, no undue muscular exertion should have occurred for at least 12 hours prior to the measurement of BMR.

Normally, a good time to make a measurement of BMR is after waking from a night's sleep, and in a hospital situation BMR is typically measured at this time. In laboratory Practicals and exercise physiology experiments involving volunteer subjects, it is often impossible to obtain the correct conditions for a true measure of BMR. It is likely that in a laboratory Practical the subject will have eaten a meal in the preceding 12 hours, which will increase metabolism in certain tissues and organs, such as the liver. This is known as the specific dynamic effect. Any measurement not made under the strict laboratory conditions already described is referred to as resting metabolic rate (RMR).

However, if the subject has only eaten a light meal some 3–4 hours prior to the experiment, and is allowed to rest in a supine position for at least 30 minutes, then the measurement of RMR will be elevated only slightly above the true BMR value.

A description of the procedures for the measurement of RMR using the Douglas bag technique is given in Section 6.6. Although the Systeme International (SI) unit for rate of energy expenditure is the Watt (W), RMR and BMR values are typically quoted in kcal min^{-1}. A calorie is defined as the amount of heat necessary to raise the temperature of 1 kg of water 1°C, from 14.5 to 15.5°C. The calorie is therefore typically referred to as the kilocalorie (kcal). To convert kcal into kilojoules (kJ) (the Joule (J) is the SI unit of energy), multiply the kcal value by 4.186. To convert kcal min^{-1} into kilowatts (kW) multiply the kcal min^{-1} by 0.07. (See the Appendix at the end of this book for a full list of conversion factors between different units of measurement.)

Estimates of BMR values can be used to establish an energy baseline for constructing programmes for weight control by means of diet, exercise, or the more effective and healthier option of combining both diet and exercise prescriptions. The measurement of BMR on subjects drawn from a variety of populations provides a basis for studying the relationships between metabolic rate and body size, sex and age.

6.2.1 Body size, sex and age effects on BMR and resting metabolic rate (RMR)

Since the time of Galileo scientists have believed that BMR and RMR are related to body surface area. Rubner (1883) showed that the rate of heat production divided by body surface area was more or less constant in dogs that varied in size. He offered the explanation that metabolically produced heat was limited by ability to lose heat, and was therefore related to body surface area. This relationship between body surface area and basal and resting metabolic rate has since been verified for animals ranging in size from the mouse up to the elephant (Kleiber 1975; McMahon 1984; Schmidt-Nielsen 1984) and is an important consideration when

comparing children and adults. The 'surface area law' therefore states that metabolic rates of animals of different size can be made similar when BMR or RMR is expressed per unit of body surface area.

Table 6.1 shows that, related to body surface area, BMR is at its greatest in early childhood and declines thereafter (Altman and Dittmer 1968; Knoebel 1963). When RMR is based on oxygen uptake values the differences between a 10-year-old boy and a middle-aged man are of the order of 1–2 ml kg^{-1} min^{-1}, which amounts to a 25–35% greater metabolic rate in the child (MacDougall et al. 1979). As can be seen from Table 6.1, BMR values are about 5–10% lower in women than in men. This does not reflect a true sex difference in the metabolic rate of specific tissues, but is largely due to the differences in body composition (McArdle et al. 2006). Women generally have a higher percentage of body fat than men of a similar size, and stored fat is essentially metabolically inert.

If the BMR values are expressed per unit of lean body mass (or fat-free mass) then the sex differences are essentially eliminated. Differences in body composition also largely explain the 2% decrease in BMR per decade observed through adulthood.

6.2.2 Estimation of body surface area and RMR

Using the mean BMR values (kJ m^{-2} h^{-1}) for age and sex from Altman and Dittmer (1968) shown in Table 6.1, it is possible to predict an individual's BMR value using an estimate of body surface area. The procedure is outlined in Section 6.4.

6.3 MEASUREMENT OF ENERGY EXPENDITURE

Energy expenditure can be measured using either direct or indirect calorimetry. Both methods depend on the principle that all the energy used by the body is ultimately degraded into heat. Therefore, the measurement of

Table 6.1 Basal metabolic rate (kJ m-2 h-1) as a function of age and sex (data from Altman and Dittmer 1968)

Age (years)	Females	Males
5	196.7	205.1
10	178	183.3
15	163.2	177.9
20	152.4	165.8
25	151.5	162.0
30	151.1	157.4
35	151.1	155.7
40	151.1	156.1
45	150.3	155.3
50	146.5	154.5
55	142.7	152.4
60	139.4	149.4
65	136.9	146.5
70	135.6	144.0
75	134.8	141.5
80	133.5	139.0

heat produced by the body is also a measure of energy expenditure (direct calorimetry). Direct measures of energy expenditure are made when a subject remains inside a chamber with walls specifically designed to absorb and measure the heat produced. This method is both technically difficult and costly. Since the energy provided from food can only be used as a result of oxidations utilizing oxygen obtained from air, measurement of steady-state oxygen uptake by the body is also used as a measurement of energy expenditure (indirect calorimetry). Detailed procedures for the measurement of oxygen uptake by means of the Douglas bag technique are given in Section 6.6.

6.4 PRACTICAL 1: ESTIMATION OF BODY SURFACE AREA AND RMR

With the mean BMR values (kJ m^{-2} h $^{-1}$) for age and sex from Altman and Dittmer (1968) shown in Table 6.1, it is possible to predict an individual's BMR value using an estimate of body surface area. The most commonly used formula is that of DuBois and DuBois (1916) which requires measures of stature and body mass only.

Subjects should remove their shoes for both the stature and body mass measures. Stature is measured to the nearest mm using a stadiometer. The subject should stand up as tall as he or she can, keeping the heels on the floor and maintaining the head position in the Frankfort Plane (i.e. the straight line through the lower bony orbital margin and the external auditory meatus should be horizontal). Mass should be measured on calibrated weighing scales to the nearest 0.1 kg. The subject should be wearing minimal clothing.

The formula for estimation of body surface area according to DuBois and DuBois

(1916) is:

$$BSA = M^{0.425} \times H^{0.725} \times 71.84 \times 10^{-4}$$

where: BSA is body surface area in m², M is body mass in kg and H is stature in cm.

For example, a subject with a mass of 70 kg and stature of 177 cm will have a body surface area of

$$BSA = 70^{0.425} \times 177^{0.725} \times 71.84 \times 10^{-4}$$
$$= 6.0837 \times 42.6364 \times 71.84 \times 10^{-4}$$
$$= 1.86 \text{ m}^2$$

If the subject is male aged 20 then according to the average values of BMR (kJ m^{-2} h^{-1}) of Altman and Dittmer (1968) (Table 6.1) he would have an approximate BMR value of 165.8 kJ m^{-2} h^{-1} ($\pm$ 10%). This would compute to a resting energy expenditure of 165.8 kJ m^{-2} h^{-1} $\times$ 1.86 m^2 = 308.4 kJ h^{-1}. Over a 24-hour period this would result in an estimated resting energy expenditure of 308.4 kJ h^{-1} $\times$ 24 h = 7401 kJ (1768 kcal).

Other sex-specific formulae based on body mass, stature and age have also been widely used for the estimation of BMR:

- Harris and Benedict (1919)
  103 lean females BMR = 655 + 9.6 (M) + 1.85 (Ht) − 4.68 (age)
  136 lean males BMR = 66 + 13.8(M) + 5.0(Ht) − 6.8(age)
- Owen et al. (1986)
  32 non-athletic females RMR = 795 + 7.2(M)
- Owen et al. (1987)
  60 lean to obese males RMR = 879 + 10.2(M)
- Mifflin et al. (1990)
  247 lean to obese females RMR = − 161 + 10(M) + 6.25(Ht) − 5(age)
  247 lean to obese males RMR = 5 + 10(M) + 6.25(Ht) − 5(age)

  where: M = body mass (kg), Ht = stature (cm), age = age (years), RMR and BMR are expressed in kcal day^{-1}.

Mifflin et al. (1990) provided the most general equations for age and weight. The equations of Harris and Benedict (1919) are shown to predict within 5% of RMR values, with the equations of Owen et al. (1986, 1987) performing even better (Cunningham 1991).

6.5 PRACTICAL 2: ESTIMATION OF RMR FROM FAT-FREE MASS

The resting metabolic rate (RMR) can be estimated from fat-free mass (FFM) according to the following regression equation from Cunningham (1991):

$$RMR \text{ (kcal day}^{-1}) = 370 + 21.6 \times FFM$$

This equation was derived from a review by Cunningham (1991) where all studies measured FFM according to the whole body potassium K^{40} method and RMR, BMR and resting energy expenditure (REE) were considered to be physiologically equivalent. An equation was also presented for FFM estimated from triceps skinfold thickness:

$$RMR \text{ (kcal day}^{-1}) = 261 + 22.6 \times FFM$$
Number of subjects = 77 and variance accounted for E (r^2) = 0.65.

Unfortunately, no reference to the specific source of the estimation of FFM from triceps skinfold thickness was given. However, values of FFM from a variety of methods (see Chapter 1, Eston *et al.* 2009) can be used in the estimation of RMR.

6.6 PRACTICAL 3: MEASUREMENT OF OXYGEN UPTAKE USING THE DOUGLAS BAG TECHNIQUE

Oxygen uptake can be measured using the open circuit Douglas bag technique. With this method the subject breathes from normal air into a Douglas bag while wearing a nose clip. (All valve boxes, valves, tubing and Douglas bags should be routinely checked for wear and tear and leaks.) If subjects are exercising, it is preferable to use a lightweight valve box with low resistance and low dead space, such as that described by Jakeman and Davies (1979). This is attached to lightweight tubing which is at least 30 mm internal diameter (e.g. Falconia tubing), as these provide for some movement of the head and do not require fixed support or the wearing of a headset. During gas collection the subject must also wear a nose clip (Figure 6.1).

Mouthpieces, valve boxes and tubing should be sterilized and dried prior to use by the next subject. Douglas bags must be completely empty before a collection of expired air is made. Ideally, they should be flushed out with a sample of the subject's expired air prior to data collection. For ease of data collection and long life, the Douglas bags should be hung on suitable racks and evacuated by means of vacuum cleaners, rather than rolling them out.

Naïve subjects need habituating to breathing through a mouthpiece prior to data collection. This should be done firstly at rest, and then included in the habituation to ergometry prior to any exercise testing. For steady-state protocols, with 3- or 4-minute stages, the subject need only exercise with the mouthpiece in for 15–20 s before gas collection, as this gives ample time to clear any dead space in the tubing. In ramp protocols and in maximal testing during the latter stages it is necessary to keep the mouthpiece in all the time (Figure 6.2).

Prior to any measurements of gas concentration or volume of expired air, the O_2 and

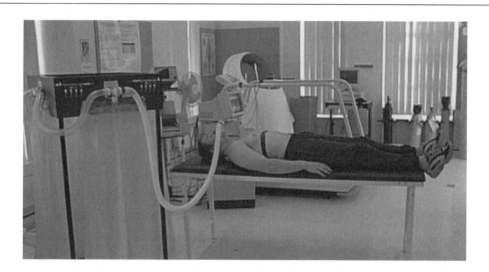

Figure 6.1 Photograph of a subject lying in a supine position in a laboratory practical for the estimation of resting metabolic rate (RMR). Expired air collection is through a mouthpiece attached to a Salford valve and lightweight tubing, which is connected to a Douglas bag. The subject is wearing a nose clip and heart rate data are being recorded by a short-range radio telemeter (Polar, Finland).

Figure 6.2 Photograph showing a subject on a standard Monark cycle ergometer, with expired air collection to a Douglas bag, and heart rate monitored by a short range radio telemeter (Polar, Finland).

CO_2 analyzers should be calibrated and the dry gas meters checked. Gas meters should be calibrated with a minimum of a three-point calibration. This is most conveniently achieved by using 100% nitrogen to set the zero for both analyzers, and two known concentrations of O_2 and CO_2 which span the working range. If Haldane or Micro-Scholander apparatus is available, this can be used to check new standard gases before they are used for routine calibration purposes. Alternatively, more expensive gravimetrically prepared calibration gases can be used which are reported to be within ± 0.0001 of the stated nominal gas fraction, which translates to a precision of $\pm 0.34\%$ for oxygen uptake (James et al. 2007). Outside air is best used as a span gas for setting oxygen to 20.95% (James et al. 2007), with precise measures of atmospheric oxygen concentration varying from 20.945 to 20.952 (Machta and Hughes 1970). The F_IO_2 is the fraction of inspired oxygen (i.e. 0.2095) and $\%O_{2I}$ is the percentage of oxygen in inspired air (i.e. 20.95%). Caution should be exercised in the use of room air for calibration of the oxygen analyzer, as room air has been shown to vary in concentration in a well-ventilated exercise testing laboratory (mean (95% confidence intervals) for oxygen was 20.915% (+ 0.035%) (Sandals 2003). Carbon dioxide was also shown to vary (0.07% ($\pm 0.03\%$). James et al. (2007) reported a systematic error of 0.18% and 0.99% for $\dot{V}O_2$ and $\dot{V}CO_2$, respectively, based on the difference between actual and assumed inspired air fractions. Such systematic errors can be corrected from averaged measured inspired gas concentrations collected over a series of laboratory exercise tests. They compute the precision of $\dot{V}O_2$ and $\dot{V}CO_2$ to be $\pm 0.88\%$ and $+ 0.74\%$, respectively, with the only way of improving on these values being to measured inspired air concentration s for every exercise test. Gas volume meters can be checked with a suitable calibration syringe or a Tissot Spirometer by pumping air through the same calibrated flow system used to remove expired air from the Douglas bags. Care must be taken in calibration of the pumping systems and also that flow rates in terms of volume per unit time do not exceed the specification of gas meters used. Any systematic errors in dry gas meters can be corrected by standard regression techniques to produce an appropriate correction equation. For a more comprehensive consideration of various sources of error and how best to control and account for them in expired air analysis the reader is directed to James et al. (2007).

6.6.1 Simplified estimation of oxygen uptake

The most straightforward estimation of oxygen uptake ($\dot{V}O_2$) only requires the following measures to be made:

- Volume of expired air collected in the Douglas bag = V_E (litres)
- Temperature of air as volume is measured (°C)
- Barometric pressure (mmHg)
- Fraction of oxygen in expired air (F_EO_2 or $\% O_{2E}$)
- Time taken for collection of expired air in Douglas bag (s)

Oxygen uptake ($\dot{V}O_2$) is the volume of oxygen inspired minus the volume of oxygen expired, i.e.:

$$\dot{V}O_2 = [(\dot{V}_I \times F_IO_2) - (\dot{V}_E \times F_EO_2)]$$

where: $\dot{V}O_2$ = oxygen uptake (l min^{-1})
V_I = volume of air inspired (l min^{-1})
F_IO_2 = fraction of oxygen in inspired air = constant value of 0.2095 (i.e. 20.95%)
$\dot{V}_E$ = volume of air expired (l min^{-1})
F_EO_2 = fraction of oxygen in expired air

6.6.2 Timing gas collections and correction of gas volumes

It should be noted that V stands for volume, whereas $\dot{V}$ stands for volume per unit of time, usually per minute.

V_E = volume of air expired in the Douglas bag.
$\dot{V}_E$ = volume of expired air per minute (l min^{-1})
$\dot{V}O_2$ = volume of oxygen consumed per minute (l min^{-1})

Expired air collections should always be timed accurately over a complete number of respiratory cycles, from end expiration to end expiration. Therefore, collection times are rarely equal to 30 s or 1 minute, but can be easily converted into minute ventilation values by the following general calculation:

$\dot{V}_E$ (l min^{-1}) = (volume of expired air collection/60 s)

End expiration can be judged by the following:

• Watching for the closure of the expiratory valve in the valve box;
• Feeling the air flow stop at the tap before turning it to fill the Douglas bag;
• In strenuous exercise, listening for each breath of expired air rushing down the tubing into the Douglas bag.
A stop-watch should be used to time collections.
   Gas volumes obtained in laboratory experiments are typically expressed in one of three ways.

ATPS = ambient temperature, pressure and saturated
STPD = standard temperature, pressure and dry
BTPS = body temperature, ambient pressure and saturated

The conditions at the time of the measurement of the volume of expired air in the Douglas bag are reflected in ATPS. It should be noted that the volume of gas varies with temperature and pressure, and its water content, even though the number of molecules in the gas does not change. More specifically, as the temperature of gas increases the volume increases proportionately and vice versa (i.e. if the pressure is constant then a doubling of the temperature will result in a doubling of the volume). This is known as Charles' Law. However, gas volumes vary inversely with pressure. Thus, an increase in pressure causes a proportionate decrease in volume, and vice versa (i.e. if temperature is constant then a doubling of pressure will cause a halving of volume). This is known as

Boyle's Law. Finally, the volume of a gas increases with the amount of water content.

To compare measures of volume taken under different environmental conditions, there is a need for a standard set of conditions which are defined by STPD and BTPS. Standard temperature and pressure dry (STPD) refers to a gas volume expressed under *Standard Temperature* (273K or 0°C), *Pressure* (760 mmHg) and *Dry* (no water vapour). Volumes corrected to STPD conditions therefore allow comparison between values collected at different temperatures, altitudes and degrees of saturation. Values of $\dot{V}_E$, $\dot{V}O_2$, and $\dot{V}CO_2$ are always expressed at STPD.

The formula for conversion of a volume of moist gas to STPD such as $\dot{V}_E$ is:

$$\dot{V}E_{STPD} = \dot{V}E_{ATPS} \times (273/(273+T°C)) \times ((P_B - PH_2O)/760)$$

where T°C is the temperature of the expired air; P_B is barometric pressure; and P_{H2O} is the water vapour pressure of the sample at the time volume is measured. The P_{H2O} is not measured directly because conversion factors are tabulated for the normal range of temperatures of moist gas samples. Furthermore, none of the correction factors for volumes need to be calculated since tables for converting moist gas volumes into STPD conditions are readily available for the range of values of temperature and pressure normally experienced in most laboratories (Carpenter 1964; McArdle *et al.* 2006).

Body temperature and pressure saturated (BTPS) refers to a gas volume expressed at *Body Temperature* (273 K + 37 K), *Ambient* pressure and *Saturated* with water vapour with a partial pressure of 47 mmHg at 37°C. This is the conventional standard used for assessing lung function volumes (see Eston and Romer, 2009 – Chapter 3 in this book – for more detail).

As with correction from ATPS to STPD, corrections from BTPS to STPD can be achieved by use of tabulated values of correction factors for a broad range of temperatures, or by using the formula:

$$VE_{STPD} = VE_{BTPS} \times (1/\text{Factor to convert ATPS to BTPS}) \times (\text{Factor to convert ATPS to STPD})$$

When using the simplified estimation of $\dot{V}O_2$ the composition of expired air remains relatively constant ($F_IO_2 = 0.2095$, $\%O_2I = 20.95\%$; $F_ICO_2 = 0.00036$, $\%CO_2I = 0.036\%$ and $F_IN_2 = 0.79014$, $\%N_2I = 79.014\%$).

On substituting the value for the fraction of O_2 in inspired air of F_IO_2, the expression becomes:

$$\dot{V}O_2 \text{ STPD } (1 \text{ min}^{-1}) = \dot{V}_E STPD (0.2095 - F_EO_2)$$

For example, given $\dot{V}_E$ ATPS = 60 l min^{-1} (volume measured in Douglas bag), barometric pressure = 754 mmHg (measured by barometer), temperature of gas = 22°C (measured by thermometer as volume is measured), $F_EO_2 = 0.1675$ (measured by oxygen analyzer), then

$\dot{V}_{E\ STPD} = \dot{V}_{E\ ATPS} \times 0.891$ (correction factor taken from Table 6.2)

$\dot{V}_{E\ STPD} = 60 \times 0.891$

$\dot{V}_{E\ STPD} = 53.46$ l min^{-1}

$$\dot{V}O_{2\,STPD} \ (l\ min^{-1}) = 53.46\ (0.2095 - 0.1675)$$
$$\dot{V}O_2 \ (l\ min^{-1}) = 2.25\ l\ min^{-1})$$

In summary, there are two steps to the calculation.

1   Correct the $\dot{V}_E$ value from ATPS to STPD by multiplying by the appropriate correction factor from the appropriate table of values (Table 6.2).

2   Calculate the difference between the concentration of O_2 in inspired and expired air; then all variables on the right of the equation are known and $\dot{V}O_2$ can be calculated.

6.6.3 Calculation of oxygen uptake ($\dot{V}O_2$) using the Haldane transformation

In addition to the measurements required for the simplified calculation of $\dot{V}O_2$ a value for the fraction of carbon dioxide in expired air is also required (F_ECO_2).

Although the concentrations of oxygen (O_2), carbon dioxide (CO_2) and nitrogen (N_2) are constant for inspired air, the values recorded for expired air fractions will vary. The value for F_EO_2 will be less than F_IO_2 as some of the O_2 is extracted from the lungs into the blood capillaries. The F_EO_2 will therefore range between approximately 0.15 and 0.185. The F_ECO_2 will increase in expired air since the body excretes CO_2 with the lungs from the blood by gas exchange. The F_ECO_2 will range from approximately 0.025 to 0.05. Although nitrogen is inert, that is the same number of molecules of N_2 exist in both the inspired and expired air, its concentration will change if the number of O_2 molecules removed from inspired air is not equal to the number of CO_2 molecules excreted in expired air. In simple terms, when the molecules of O_2 removed do not equal the molecules of CO_2 added, then the volume of inspired air (V_I) will not equal the volume of air expired (V_E), and the constant number of N_2 molecules will represent a different fraction or percentage of the inspired and expired volumes.

For example: inspired air constant fractions:

$F_IO_2 = 0.2095$, or $\%O_{2I} = 20.95\%$; $F_ICO_2 = 0.0036$, or $\% CO_{2I} = 0.036\%$; and $F_IN_2 = 0.79014$, or $\%N_{2I} = 79.014\%$
$\%O_{2I} + \%CO_{2I} + \%N_{2I} = 100\%$; $(20.95 + 0.036 + 79.014 = 100)$

Given expired air measured values from experiment:

$\%O_{2E} = 16.75\%$; $\%CO_{2E} = 3.55$
$\%O_{2E} + \%CO_{2E} + \%N_{2E} = 100$
$\%N_{2E} = 100 - (\%O_{2E} + \%CO_{2E})$
$\%N_{2E} = 100 - (16.75 + 3.55)$
$\%N_{2E} = 79.7\%$

Here the fraction of oxygen in inspired air has decreased from a value of 0.2093 to 0.1675 in expired air, whereas the concentration of carbon dioxide in inspired air has increased from a value of 0.00036 to 0.0355 in expired air. The decrease in oxygen concentration is greater than the increase in carbon dioxide concentration in expired air. Therefore the fraction of nitrogen in inspired air ($F_IN_2 = 0.79041$) rises to a value of 0.7970 in expired air (the same number of molecules but increased in concentration).

The constant number of N_2 molecules representing a different percentage or concentration of inspired and expired volumes can be used to calculate V_I from V_E or vice versa. This is possible because the change in volume from inspired to expired is directly proportional to the change in nitrogen concentration:

Mass of N_2 inspired = Mass of N_2 expired

$$\text{As concentration} = \frac{\text{Mass}}{\text{Volume}}$$

$$\%N_{2I} = \frac{\text{Mass of }N_2}{V_I} \text{ and } \%N_{2E} = \frac{\text{Mass of }N_2}{\dot{V}_E}$$

$$\therefore \text{Mass of }N_2 = \%N_{2I} \times V_I = \%N_{2E} \times \dot{V}_E$$

$$\dot{V}_{ISTPD} = \frac{\dot{V}_{ESTPD} \times \%N_{2E}}{\%N2_I}$$

Given the same values as for the simplified calculation, i.e. $V_{E\,ATPS} = 60 \text{ l min}^{-1}$, temperature = 22 °C, barometric pressure = 754 mmHg, correction factor from ATPS to STPD = 0.891, then $\dot{V}_{ESTPD}$ will also be the same: $\dot{V}_{ESTPD} = 53.46 \text{ l min}^{-1}$

Given that $\%N_{2E}$ was calculated from expired $\%O_{2E}$ and $\%CO_{2E}$ as 79.7% and $\%N_{2I}$ is constant at 79.014%, all the values on the right of the equation are known and can be used to calculate $\dot{V}O_{2\,STPD}$.

Oxygen uptake ($\dot{V}O_2$, l min^{-1}) can now be calculated as the volume of oxygen removed from expired air per minute:

$$\dot{V}O_2 = [(V_I \times \%O_{2I}) - (\dot{V}_E \times \%O_{2E})] \div 100$$

Substituting using the Haldane transformation $\dot{V}_I = \dot{V}_E \times \dfrac{\%N_{2E}}{\%N_{2I}}$
we can replace $\dot{V}_I$

by our known expression $\dot{V}_E \times \dfrac{\%N_{2E}}{\%N_{2I}}$

$$\dot{V}O_2 = \frac{[(\dot{V}_E \times \%N_{2E} \times \%O_{2I}) - (\dot{V}_E \times \%O_{2E})]}{\%N_{2I}} \div 100$$

Substituting in constants for inspired air and simplifying the expression:

$$\dot{V}O_2 = \frac{[(\dot{V}_E \times \%N_{2E} \times 20.93 - \%O_{2E})]}{79.014} \div 100$$

Table 6.2 Conversion of gas volumes from ATPS to STPD (data from Carpenter 1964; McArdle et al. 2006)

Barometric reading	Temperature (°C)								
	15	16	17	18	19	20	21	22	23
700	0.855	851	847	842	838	834	829	825	821
702	857	853	849	845	840	836	832	827	823
704	860	856	852	847	843	839	834	830	825
706	862	858	854	850	845	841	837	832	828
708	865	861	856	852	848	843	839	834	830
710	867	863	859	855	850	846	842	837	833
712	870	866	861	857	853	848	844	839	836
714	872	868	864	859	855	851	846	842	837
716	875	871	866	862	858	853	849	844	840
718	877	873	869	864	860	856	851	847	842
720	880	876	871	867	863	858	854	849	845
722	882	878	874	869	865	861	856	852	847
724	885	880	876	872	867	863	858	854	849
726	887	883	879	874	870	866	861	856	852
728	890	886	881	877	872	868	863	859	854
730	892	888	884	879	875	871	866	861	857
732	895	890	886	882	877	873	868	864	859
734	897	893	889	884	880	875	871	866	862
736	900	895	891	887	882	878	873	869	864
738	902	898	894	889	885	880	876	871	866
740	905	900	896	892	887	883	878	874	869
742	907	903	898	894	890	885	881	876	871
744	910	906	901	897	892	888	883	878	874
746	912	908	903	899	895	890	886	881	876
748	915	910	906	901	897	892	888	883	879
750	917	913	908	904	900	895	890	886	881
752	920	915	911	906	902	897	893	888	883
754	922	918	913	909	904	900	895	891	886
756	925	920	916	911	907	902	898	893	888
758	927	923	918	914	909	905	900	896	891
760	930	925	921	916	912	907	902	898	893
762	932	928	923	919	914	910	905	900	896
764	936	930	926	921	916	912	907	903	898
766	937	933	928	924	919	915	910	905	900
768	940	935	931	926	922	917	912	908	903
770	942	938	933	928	924	919	915	910	905

				Temperature (°C)				
24	*25*	*26*	*27*	*28*	*29*	*30*	*31*	*32*
816	812	807	802	797	793	788	783	778
818	814	809	805	800	795	790	785	780
821	816	812	807	802	797	792	787	783
823	819	814	810	804	800	795	790	785
825	821	816	812	807	802	797	792	787
828	824	819	814	809	804	799	795	790
830	826	821	817	812	807	802	797	792
833	828	824	819	814	809	804	799	794
835	831	826	822	816	812	807	802	797
838	833	828	824	819	814	809	804	799
840	836	831	826	821	816	812	807	802
843	838	833	829	824	819	814	809	804
845	840	835	831	826	821	816	811	806
847	843	838	833	829	824	818	813	808
850	845	840	836	831	826	821	816	811
852	847	843	838	833	828	823	818	813
854	850	845	840	836	831	825	820	815
857	852	847	843	838	833	828	823	818
859	855	850	845	840	835	830	825	820
862	857	852	848	843	838	833	828	822
864	860	855	850	845	840	835	830	825
867	862	857	852	847	842	837	832	827
869	864	859	855	850	845	840	834	829
872	867	862	857	852	847	842	837	832
874	869	864	860	854	850	845	839	834
876	872	867	862	857	852	847	842	837
879	874	869	864	859	854	849	844	839
881	876	872	867	862	857	852	846	841
883	879	874	869	864	859	854	849	844
886	881	876	872	866	861	856	851	846
888	883	879	874	869	864	859	854	848
891	886	881	876	871	866	861	856	851
893	888	884	879	874	869	864	858	853
896	891	886	881	876	871	886	861	855
898	893	888	883	878	873	868	863	858
901	896	891	886	881	876	871	865	860

With the most simple form of the equation for computation being:

$$\dot{V}O_2 = \dot{V}_E \times [(\%N_{2E} \times 0.265) - \%O_{2E}] \div 100$$

where $\dot{V}_E$ is measured under ATPS conditions and corrected to STPD conditions before substitution into this equation, $\%O_{2E}$ is measured from O_2 analyzer and $\%N_{2E} = 100 - \%O_{2E} - \%CO_{2E}$ ($\%CO_{2E}$ is measured from CO_2 gas analyzer).
  Inserting the example values into the simplified equation gives:

$$\dot{V}O_2 \ (l \ min^{-1}) = 53.46 \ [(79.7 \times 0.265) - 16.75\%] \div 100$$
$$\dot{V}O_2 \ (1 \ min^{-1}) = 53.46 \ [4.3705] \div 100$$
$$\dot{V}O_2 = 2.34 \ 1 \ min^{-1}$$

6.6.4 Calculation of carbon dioxide production ($\dot{V}CO_2$)

The volume of carbon dioxide produced is calculated according to the following equation:

$$\dot{V}CO_2 = [\dot{V}_E(\%CO_{2E} - \%CO_{2I})] \times 100$$

Where $\dot{V}_E$ is measured and corrected to STPD conditions, $\%CO_{2I} = 0.036\%$ (constant for inspired air) and $\%CO_{2E}$ is measured from CO_2 gas analyzer.
  Since the fraction of CO_2 in inspired air is negligible, the Haldane transformation is unimportant in the calculation of $\dot{V}CO_2$. In many cases the fraction of CO_2 in inspired air is often ignored altogether.
  Using the data from the example calculation of $\dot{V}O_2$.

$$\dot{V}CO_2 \ (l \ min^{-1}) = [53.46 \ (3.55 - 0.036 \ )] \div 100$$
$$\dot{V}CO_2 = 1.88 \ (l \ min^{-1})$$

6.7 PRACTICAL 4: THE RESPIRATORY QUOTIENT

The respiratory quotient (RQ) is calculated as the ratio of metabolic gas exchange:

$$RQ = \frac{\dot{V}CO_2 \ (Volume \ of \ carbon \ dioxide \ produced)}{\dot{V}O_2 \ (Volume \ of \ oxygen \ consumed)}$$

The RQ gives an indication of what combination of carbohydrates, fats and proteins are metabolized in steady-state submaximal exercise or at rest. The specific equation associated with the RQ for oxidation of pure carbohydrates, fats and proteins is as follows:

(a) RQ for carbohydrates (glucose)

$$C_6H_{12}O_6 + 6O_2 + 6CO_2 + 6H_2O$$

During the oxidation of a glucose molecule, six molecules of oxygen are consumed and six molecules of carbon dioxide are produced, therefore:

$$RQ = \frac{6CO_2}{6O_2} = 1$$

The RQ value for carbohydrate is 1.

(b) RQ for fat (palmitic acid)

$$C_{16}H_{32}O_2 = 16CO_2 + 16H_2O$$

$$RQ = \frac{16CO_2}{23O_2} = 0.696$$

Generally, the RQ value for fat is taken to be 0.7.

(c) RQ for protein
The process is more complex for protein to provide energy as proteins are not simply oxidized to carbon dioxide and water, during energy metabolism. Generally, the RQ value for protein is taken to be 0.82.

McLean and Tobin (1987) published equations for the calculation of calorific factors from elemental composition, which included the following equation for respiratory quotient (RQ):

$$RQ = 1/(1 + 2.9789\ f_H/f_C - 0.3754\ f_O/f_C)$$

where 1 g of a substance contains f_C, f_H and f_O g of carbon, hydrogen and oxygen respectively.

Given the formula for the chemical composition of carbohydrate, fat or protein, together with the atomic weights for carbon, hydrogen and oxygen ($a_C = 12.011$, $a_H = 1.008$ and $a_O = 15.999$) it is then possible to calculate f_C, f_H and f_O and solve the equation for RQ.

If we use the example of glucose ($C_6H_{12}O_6$):

C_6 gives $a_C \times 6 = 72.1$
H_{12} gives $a_H \times 12 = 12.1$
O_6 gives $a_O \times 6 = 96.0$

The total is therefore 180.2, which gives fractions for each of 0.4, 0.067 and 0.533 for carbon, hydrogen and oxygen respectively. Substitution of these values in the equation above gives an RQ of 1 as previously derived.

As previously stated, the RQ calculated as the ratio of $\dot{V}CO_2$ and $\dot{V}O_2$ will reflect a combination of carbohydrates, fats and proteins currently being metabolized to provide energy. However, the precise contribution of each of the nutrients can be obtained from the calculation of the non-protein RQ.

(d) Non-protein RQ

This calculation of the non-protein RQ is based upon McArdle *et al.* (2006), where the procedures are discussed in more detail. Although this calculation is typical of the approach in most text books, Durnin and Passmore (1967) described the non-protein RQ as 'an abstraction which has no physiological meaning, as protein metabolism is never zero.' They preferred the four equations set out by Consolazio *et al.* (1963), which are used to define the metabolic mixture and calculate energy expenditure. The four equations are also based on oxidation of carbohydrates, fats and proteins and require the measurement of $\dot{V}CO_2$, $\dot{V}O_2$ and urinary nitrogen. Furthermore, they give the same answer as the classical method using non-protein RQ.

Approximately 1 g of nitrogen is excreted in the urine for every 6.25 g of protein metabolized for energy. Each gram of excreted nitrogen represents a carbon dioxide production of approximately 4.8 litres and an oxygen consumption of about 6.8 litres.

Example calculation:

A subject consumes 3.8 litres of oxygen and produces 3.1 litres of carbon dioxide during 15 minutes of rest, during which 0.11 g of nitrogen are excreted into the urine.

1 CO_2 produced in the catabolism of protein is given by 4.8 l CO_2 g⁻¹ × 0.11 g = 0.53 l of CO_2
2 O_2 consumed in the catabolism of protein is given by 6.0 l O_2 g⁻¹ protein × 0.11 g = 0.66 l of O_2
3 Non-protein CO_2 produced = 3.1 − 0.53 = 2.57 l CO_2
4 Non-protein O_2 consumed = 3.8 − 0.66 = 3.14 l of O_2
5 Non-protein RQ = 2.57 / 3.14 = 0.818

Table 6.3 shows the energy equivalents per litre of oxygen consumed for the range of non-protein RQ values and the percentage of fat and carbohydrates utilized for energy. As Table 6.3 shows 20.20 kJ per litre of oxygen are liberated for a non-protein RQ of 0.82 as calculated above. Thus, 59.7% of the energy is derived from carbohydrate and 40.3% from fat. The non-protein energy production from carbohydrate and fat for the 15-minute period is 63.42 kJ (20.20 kJ ⁻¹ × 3.14 l O_2), whereas the energy derived from protein is 12.71 kJ (19.26 kJ l⁻¹ × 0.66 l O_2). Therefore, the total energy for the 15-minute period is 76.13 kJ (63.42 kJ non-protein + 12.71 kJ protein).

In terms of carbohydrate and fat metabolism, for the non-protein RQ of 0.818, 0.454g of carbohydrate and 0.313g of fat were metabolized per litre of O_2 respectively (Table 6.3). This amounts to 1.43 g of carbohydrate 3.14 l O_2 × 0.455) and 0.98 g of fat (3.14 l O_2 × 0.313) in the 15-minute rest period.

During rest or steady-state exercise such as walking or running slowly, the RQ does not reflect the oxidation of pure carbohydrate or fat, but a mixture of the two, producing RQ values which range between 0.7 and 1.00. As shown by the sample

Table 6.3 Thermal equivalent of O2 for non-protein respiratory quotient, including percentage energy and grams derived from carbohydrate and fat

Non-protein RQ	Energy (kJ) per litre oxygen used	Percentage energy derived from		Grams per litre O_2 consumed	
		Carbohydrate	Fat	Fat	Carbohydrate
0.707	19.62	0	100	0.000	0.496
0.71	19.63	1.1	98.9	0.012	0.491
0.72	19.68	4.8	95.2	0.051	0.476
0.73	19.73	8.4	91.6	0.090	0.460
0.74	19.79	12.0	88.0	0.130	0.444
0.75	19.84	15.6	84.4	0.170	0.428
0.76	19.89	19.2	80.8	0.211	0.412
0.77	19.94	22.8	77.2	0.250	0.396
0.78	19.99	26.3	73.7	0.290	0.380
0.79	20.04	29.9	70.1	0.330	0.363
0.80	20.10	33.4	66.6	0.371	0.347
0.81	20.15	36.9	63.1	0.413	0.330
0.82	20.20	40.3	59.7	0.454	0.313
0.83	20.25	43.8	56.2	0.496	0.297
0.84	20.30	47.2	52.8	0.537	0.280
0.85	20.35	50.7	49.3	0.579	0.263
0.86	20.41	54.1	45.9	0.621	0.247
0.87	20.46	57.5	42.5	0.663	0.230
0.88	20.51	60.8	39.2	0.705	0.213
0.89	20.57	64.2	35.8	0.749	0.195
0.90	20.61	67.5	32.5	0.791	0.178
0.91	20.66	70.8	29.2	0.834	0.160
0.92	20.71	74.1	25.9	0.875	0.143
0.93	20.77	77.4	22.6	0.921	0.125
0.94	20.82	80.7	19.3	0.981	0.108
0.95	20.87	84.0	16.0	1.008	0.080
0.96	20.92	87.2	12.8	1.052	0.072
0.97	20.97	90.4	9.58	1.097	0.054
0.98	21.02	93.6	6.37	1.142	0.036
0.99	21.08	96.8	3.18	1.186	0.018
1.00	21.13	100.0	0	1.231	0.000

calculation of non-protein RQ, protein contributes only a minor amount of the total energy expenditure. For this reason the specific contribution of protein is often ignored, avoiding the monitoring of N_2 excretion together with the more complex and lengthy calculations. In most instances an RQ of 0.82 can be assumed (40% carbohydrate and 60% fat) and the energy equivalent of 20.2 kJ (5.6 kcal) per litre of oxygen can be used in energy expenditure calculations. The maximum error associated with this simplification in estimating energy expenditure from $\dot{V}O_2$ is only of the order of 4% (McArdle *et al.* 1996).

Durnin and Passmore (1967) stated that in most studies of energy expenditure there is no need to find out how much carbohydrate, fat or protein is used. Furthermore, they advocated the use of Weir's (1949) formula for estimation of energy expenditure which negates the need for CO_2 measurement.

$$\text{Energy (kcal min–1)} = \frac{4.92}{100} \dot{V}_{ESTPD} (20.93 - \%O2E)$$

(Note: this equation assumes inspired oxygen percentage is constant at 20.93%)

The advice of Durnin and Passmore (1967) is worth serious consideration given the possible sources of error associated with the Douglas bag technique, gas analysis and volume measurement in unskilled hands.

6.7.1 Respiratory quotient (RQ) and respiratory exchange ratio (RER)

Under steady-state conditions of exercise, the assumption that gas exchange at the lungs reflects gas exchange from metabolism in the cells is reasonably valid. When conditions are other than steady-state, such as in severe exercise, or with hyperventilation, the assumption is no longer valid. Under such conditions the ratio of carbon dioxide production to oxygen consumption is known as RER even though it is calculated in exactly the same way.

6.8 PRACTICAL 5: ESTIMATION OF RMR USING THE DOUGLAS BAG TECHNIQUE

Under ideal conditions RMR should be estimated as soon as the person wakes up from an overnight sleep. This is not possible in most practical situations, but provided that the subject can rest in a supine position for a reasonable period of time a good estimate of RMR can be obtained. During the test the subject lies quietly in a supine position (Figure 6.1), preferably in a temperature-controlled room, thus ensuring a thermoneutral environment. After 30–60 minutes, the subject's oxygen uptake is measured for a minimum of 6–10 minutes, preferably 15 minutes. If O_2 and CO_2 concentrations are measured in expired air then the RQ, energy expenditure, and substrate utilization can be estimated according to the procedures outlined above. Values for oxygen uptake used as an estimate of BMR range between 160 and 290 ml min^{-1} (3.85–6.89 kJ min^{-1}), depending upon a variety of factors, but particularly on body size (McArdle *et al.* 2006).

6.9 PRACTICAL 6: ENERGY BALANCE

This practical introduces the procedures for the measurement of energy balance, incorporating a simplified assessment of energy expenditure and food intake. In simple terms, if the total energy intake is repeatedly greater than the daily energy expenditure, the excess energy is stored as fat. In contrast, if daily energy expenditure is greater than energy intake the subject will lose weight. The aim of the laboratory practical is to calculate the energy expenditure and energy intake for a typical day. An understanding of key concepts in energy expenditure and intake is important for several areas of exercise physiology, such as the use of diet and exercise to alter body composition, thermoregulation and mechanical efficiency. Energy expenditure is calculated by a combination of measurements, using the Douglas bag technique or an automated gas analysis system (Figure 6.3), and estimations using generalized predictive equations and tables for a range of activities. Alternatively, if available, energy expenditure can be recorded for a range of activities using a portable gas analysis system, an example of which is shown in Figure 6.4. (This is a MetaMax II telemetry system [Cortex, Germany]). The estimation of energy intake is based on the energy value of food using standard reference tables. The subject should keep a diary of activities (duration and intensity) and food consumed (quantity and preparation) for a 24-hour period. Energy intake and expenditure can then be calculated from standard tables and from direct measures of energy expenditure completed in the laboratory.

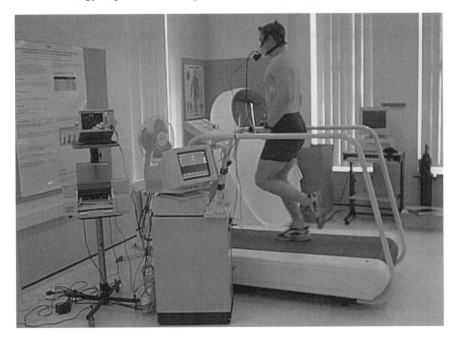

Figure 6.3 A subject running on a motorized treadmill, with expired air analysis through a face mask (Hans Rudolph) connected to an on-line automated breath-by-breath gas analysis system (Oxycon Champion, Jaeger) and a three-lead ECG through an ECG Oscillograph (CR7, Cardiorater).

6.9.1 Energy expenditure

It is possible to measure oxygen uptake for a range of everyday activities, which should be ordered such that the least demanding are completed first. Oxygen uptake should be measured for RMR, and compared with RMR from the predictive formulae in Section 6.4. Oxygen uptake values can then be obtained for sitting, standing, self-paced walking, stair climbing and an appropriate form of exercise for the subject, such as running or cycling. If time permits, duplicate gas collections should be made. Most of the measurements can be made in the laboratory, but some may necessitate access to other buildings, such as stair climbing and descending, and self-paced walking. In such cases, the Douglas bag should be supported in some way. This is where purpose-designed portable gas analysis systems are most useful (Figure 6.4). All gas collections should be made under steady-state conditions for an appropriate length of time to analyze the expired air accurately (minimum of 10 minutes for RMR, dropping to 1 minute for the most strenuous exercise to ensure an accurately quantifiable volume).

Figure 6.4 A portable gas analysis system (MetaMax II, Coretex, Germany) to collect individual energy expenditure values for tennis. The left photograph shows the system being initialized to work via telemetry, sending the signals from the device whilst the subject is playing tennis (right photograph). Alternatively, the device can be used in data logging mode, with the data downloaded to the computer after the game has finished.

Energy expenditure can than be calculated using the $\dot{V}O_2$, $\dot{V}CO_2$ and RQ values and their energy equivalents shown in Table 6.3 or Weir's formula presented in Section 6.7. A comparison of the two forms of calculation will indicate whether the extra precision associated with the measurement of carbon dioxide concentration and the calculation of RQ is warranted if the aim is to calculate energy expenditure.

The directly measured energy expenditure values can then be used in the calculation of the daily energy expenditure from the information recorded in the diary of activities.

Where direct measurement is not possible, values for energy expenditure can be estimated from objective measures of physical activity such as heart rate. Heart rate telemetry systems, typically consisting of a chest strap, or electrodes, to detect heart rate and transmit the signal to a wristwatch receiver with data storage (e.g. Polar, Finland), can be worn throughout the day, with data downloaded through an interface onto a computer for subsequent analysis. To use such heart rate data to estimate energy expenditure requires the relationship between heart rate and oxygen uptake to be established for the subject in the laboratory in a similar fashion to that described above for a range of everyday activities typical for the subject. Oxygen uptake and heart rate are related by a robust linear relationship, which holds true throughout the submaximal range, especially when measured under controlled conditions. The heart rate values recorded throughout a typical day can be affected by a number of other factors, such as state of arousal, emotion, fatigue, stress, fever and other environmental factors, such as temperature and humidity, which limit the validity of using heart rate alone for assessing energy expenditure and physical activity (Rowlands *et al.* 1997). However, the nature of the linear relationship between heart rate and oxygen uptake will be dependent upon the state of training of the subject. Remember that changes in heart rate response to a given workload or energy expenditure constitute a physiological response to endurance training. Heart rate recordings are therefore indicative of the individual, providing they are interpreted in terms of an equation relating heart rate and energy expenditure for that subject. Energy expenditure can then be estimated from the activity diary for the day using energy expenditure values estimated from the appropriate HR-$\dot{V}O_2$ relationship and summed over the time period for which the particular activity was recorded.

Other objective measures of activity are also available, such as movement sensors based on mercury switches or accelerometers. These devices include a large range of relatively inexpensive pedometers to more sophisticated accelerometers which are capable of storing multi-dimensional data for subsequent computer analysis. Many devices will display a cumulative value for energy expenditure, most typically in kcal. However, it should not be assumed that such values are credible. These values are based on equations that link the direct measurement of steps, for example, to an estimate of energy expenditure based on an equation developed and validated on a particular population. It is not always possible to find out the equation used and therefore to understand the limitations of such values produced by the device. It is possible to use the raw data in the form of movement counts or steps, by calibration of the device with subjects prior to use, as exemplified in the study of habitual physical activity in children by Rowlands *et al.* (1999). These, and other methods of estimating physical activity, are described in more detail by Rowlands in Volume 1,Chapter 6.

When either directly determined oxygen uptake or estimated oxygen uptake values are not available, estimates can be taken from mean values of energy expenditure published in the literature (e.g. Durnin and Passmore 1967; Bannister and Brown, 1968; Ainsworth *et al.* 1993, 2000; McArdle *et al.* 2006). (Table 6.4 gives some examples of common activities.) The disadvantage of using mean values of energy expenditure taken from the literature is that they will not be specific to the individual in terms of efficiency, and often are not very sensitive to the intensity of the activity.

Ainsworth *et al.* (1993) have presented a comprehensive compendium of physical activities classified in terms of intensity according to the number of METS of energy

Table 6.4 Energy expenditure values for selected activities

Activity	kcal kg^{-1} min^{-1a}	METSb
Badminton	0.097	4.5 (general)
		7.0 (competitive)
Basketball	0.138	6.0 (general)
		8.0 (competitive)
Cycling	0.100 (15 km h^{-1})	6.0 (16–19 km h^{-1})
	0.169 (racing)	16.0 (racing > 32 km h^{-1})
Dancing (aerobics)	0.135 (intense)	7.0 (high impact)
		5.0 (low impact)
		6.0 (general)
Home (cleaning general)	0.060	3.5 (general)
Home (play with child)		5.0 (run/walk – vig)
		2.5 (sitting)
Home (inactivity – quiet)	0.022 (lying)	1.0 (sitting)
Running	0.163 (cross-country)	9.0 (cross-country)
	0.193 (10.4 km h^{-1})	10.0 (9.6 km h^{-1})
	0.252 (16.0 km h^{-1})	16.0 (16 km h^{-1})
Squash	0.212	12.0
Swimming (crawl)	0.156 (fast)	11.0 (fast)
	0.128 (slow)	8.0 (slow)
Volleyball	0.050	4.0 (competitive)
	3.0 (non-competitive)	
Walking	0.080 (normal pace)	3.5 (4.8 km h^{-1})
		4.5 (6.4 km h^{-1})
		6.0 (backpacking)
		3.0 (downstairs)
		8.0 (upstairs)

[a] Values in kcal kg^{-1} min^{-1} are from McArdle *et al.* (2006) – Appendix C, Student resource CD ROM.
[b] Values in METS are from Ainsworth *et al.* (1993).

Sleep = (57 kg × 0.9 MET × 1 kcal kg^{-1} h^{-1} × 38 (15 min periods)) / 4   = 487 kcal
Walking = (57 × 3.5 × 1 × 11)/4   = 548 kcal
Typing = (57 × 1.5 × 1 × 20)/4   = 428 kcal
Sitting = (57 × 1 × 1 × 11)/4   = 157 kcal
Play = (57 × 5 × 1 × 2)/4   = 143 kcal
Eating E = (57 × 1.5 × 1 × 5)/4   = 107 kcal
Cooking = (57 × 2.5 × 1 × 2)/4   = 71 kcal
Cleaning = (57 × 3.5 × 1 × 2)/4   = 100 kcal
Aerobics = (57 × 6 × 1 × 4)/4   = 342 kcal

Total = 2383 kcal (9975 kJ)

required, which was updated in 2000 (Ainsworth *et al.* 2000). A MET is defined as the energy requirement for RMR. The most accurate way to compute the energy expenditure values for a given individual using their compendium is to measure the RMR and multiply it by the MET value associated with the physical activity of interest. For example, if the oxygen uptake measured as an estimate of RMR for a person of mass 70 kg was 270 ml min^{-1} with an RQ of 0.87 this would equate to an RMR value of 0.27 × 20.46 kJ l $^{-1}$, which equals 5.52 kJ min^{-1} (331 kJ h^{-1} or 7954 kJ day^{-1}) (1900 kcal day^{-1}). This value of RMR would represent one MET and could be multiplied by the appropriate MET value for a given physical activity. According to Ainsworth *et al.* (1993), fencing requires an energy expenditure equivalent to 6 METS. For the 70 kg individual this equates with an energy expenditure value of 6 × 5.52 kJ min^{-1}, which equals 33.1 kJ min^{-1} (7.91 kcal min^{-1}).

In the absence of a measure or prediction of RMR, diaries of self-reported physical activity can be conveniently assessed for energy expenditure based on a mean estimate of RMR of 1 kcal kg^{-1} h^{-1}. For a body mass of 70 kg this value would produce an energy expenditure value of (6 METS × 70 kg × 1 kcal kg^{-1} h^{-1} / 60 min = 7.00 kcal min^{-1} (29.3 kJ min^{-1})) for fencing. This value represents 88% of the value calculated from the measured RMR value.

The diary of physical activities for the day should be broken down into periods of the order of 10–15 minutes, with high intensity activities of a short duration, such as stair climbing, also recorded as these events can have a significant cumulative effect on the total energy expenditure for the day. Table 6.5 shows a proforma for such a diary that has been completed by a fictitious young female (age 24 years; mass 57 kg) who has a sedentary desk job. The data indicate that this person spends much of her time sitting, but walks to work, walks the children home from school, and attends an aerobics class in the evening. Using the appropriate MET values from Ainsworth *et al.* (2000) or Ainsworth *et al.* (1993), the daily energy expenditure can be estimated using a mean estimated RMR of 1 kcal kg $^{-1}$ h^{-1}. For a body mass of 57 kg, this value would produce the following estimates of energy expenditure for Table 6.5:

This fictitious young female subject therefore expended 2383 kcal of energy on this particular day. Table 6.6 shows an example of an alternative data collection form for recording a few physical activities for the same person (57 kg) (Ainsworth *et al.* 1993; Ainsworth *et al.* 2000).

6.9.2 Measuring energy intake

A set of calibrated kitchen weighing scales should be used to weigh all food that is consumed in the 24-hour period under examination. The weight of the food, its form of preparation (e.g. fried, boiled) and the amount and type of fluid drinks should be recorded in the 24 hours food diary. An example of a 24 hours diet for the young female subject for whom a 24 hours activity diary was analyzed is shown in Table 6.7. The diet can then be analyzed for energy intake using standard tables for common foods (e.g. Holland *et al.* 1992; McArdle *et al.* 2006). For the example shown in Table 6.7, using COMPEAT software, the total energy intake is calculated to be 8346 kJ (1994 kcal).

This means that for this particular day the young female subject would be in negative energy balance, expending 1629 kJ (389 kcal) more energy than she consumes. The

Table 6.5 Proforma for recording activity over a 24-hour period.

	15-MINUTE TIME PERIODS			
HOUR	1	2	3	4
1	SLEEP	SLEEP	SLEEP	SLEEP
2	SLEEP	SLEEP	SLEEP	SLEEP
3	SLEEP	SLEEP	SLEEP	SLEEP
4	SLEEP	SLEEP	SLEEP	SLEEP
5	SLEEP	SLEEP	SLEEP	SLEEP
6	SLEEP	SLEEP	SLEEP	SLEEP
7	SLEEP	SLEEP	SITTING	EATING
8	WALKING	WALKING	WALKING	TYPING
9	TYPING	TYPING	TYPING	TYPING
10	SITTING	MEETING	MEETING	MEETING
11	TYPING	TYPING	TYPING	TYPING
12	TYPING	TYPING	TYPING	TYPING
13	WALKING	EATING	EATING	TYPING
14	TYPING	TYPING	TYPING	TYPING
15	TYPING	TYPING	WALKING	WALKING
16	WALKING	SITTING	PLAY CHILD	PLAY CHILD
17	COOKING	COOKING	CLEANING	CLEANING
18	EATING	SITTING	WALKING	SITTING
19	AEROBICS (GENERAL)	AEROBICS	AEROBICS	AEROBICS
20	WALKING	SITTING	EATING	SITTING
21	SITTING	SITTING	SITTING	SITTING
22	SLEEP	SLEEP	SLEEP	SLEEP
23	SLEEP	SLEEP	SLEEP	SLEEP
24	SLEEP	SLEEP	SLEEP	SLEEP

(Short intensive activity should be noted separately)

Table 6.6 Example of recording form for physical activities (Ainsworth et al. 1993)

	Type of activity	METS	Duration hours: min	Energy expended kcal. $kg.^{-1}h^{-1}$
1	Sitting	1.0	8.0	456
2	Walking	3.5	2.0	399
3	Swimming fast	11.0	0:30	313
				Total 1168 (in a 10.5 h period)

dietary analysis can easily be extended to a 7-day weighed food intake, with a more accurate dietary analysis of nutrients and percentages of recommended daily allowances of fat, carbohydrate and protein, which can be performed using commercially available software (e.g. COMPEAT, based on Holland *et al.* 1992).

Table 6.7 Example of a 24-hour diet record sheet

Food description	Mass (g)
Special K	50.0
Skimmed milk	150.0
Water	1700.0
Indian tea	520.0
Meat paste	30.0
Wholemeal bread	76.0
Tomatoes (raw)	65.0
Eating apples (Cox's Pippin)	100.0
Crisps	25.0
Chocolate digestive biscuits	51.0
Cheese and tomato pizza	365.0
Hot cross bun	50.0
Ribena (undiluted)	30.0

6.10 SUMMARY

This chapter has set out a small selection of laboratory Practicals that will give an introduction to the measurement of metabolic rate and energy balance. These procedures form the basis of many aspects of experimental work in a variety of areas of study, such as kinanthropometry, nutrition and exercise physiology, and can easily be adapted to the specific requirements of a large number of experiments using different items of equipment.

FURTHER READING

Books:

Astrand P. O., Rodahl K., Dahl H. A. and Stromme S. B. (2003) *Textbook of Work Physiology: Physiological Bases of Exercise.* Human Kinetics: Champaign, IL.

Foss A and Keteyian M. L. (1998) *Fox's Physiological Basis for Exercise and Sport.* McGraw-Hill; Columbus, OH.

McArdle W. D., Katch F. I. and Katch V. L. (2006) *Exercise Physiology, Energy Nutrition and Human Performance (6th Edition).* Lippincott, Williams and Wilkins; Philadelphia, PA.

Powers S. K. and Howley E. T. (2006) *Exercise Physiology: Theory and Application to Fitness and Performance (6th Edition).* Brown and Benchmark; Madison, WI.

Wilmore J. H. and Costill D. L. (2004) *Physiology of Sport and Exercise.* Human Kinetics; Champaign, IL.

Winter E. M., Jones A. M., Davison R. C. R., Bromley P. D. and Mercer T. H.(eds) (2007) Sport and Exercise Physiology Testing Guidelines. *The British Association of Sport and Exercise Sciences Guide (Volume 1): Sport Testing.* Routledge; Oxon.

Website

The health tools page of the Canadian-based *Preventdisease.com* (http://www.preventdisease.com/healthtools/tools.html#roc) is an excellent website which includes dedicated programmes to calculate personalised basal metabolic rate, active metabolic rate and energy cost of activities. http://preventdisease.com/healthtools/articles/bmr.html

REFERENCES

Ainsworth B. E., Haskell W. L., Leon A. S., Irwin M. L., Swartz A. M., Strath S. J., O'Brien W. L., Bassett D. R., Schmitz K. H., Emplaincourt P. O., Jacobs D. R. and Leon A. S., 1993) Compendium of physical activities: classification of energy costs of human physical activities. *Medicine and Science in Sports and Exercise;* **25**: 71–80.

Ainsworth B. E., Haskell W. L., Whitt M. C., Jacobs D. R., Montoye H. J., Sallis J. F., and Paffenbarger R. (2000) Compendium of physical activities: an update of activity codes and MET intensities. *Medicine and Science in Sports and Exercise;* **32 (9)**: S498–S516.

Altman P. L. and Dittmer D. S. (1968) *Metabolism.* FASBEB; Bethesda, MD.

Bannister E. W. and Brown S. R. (1968) The relative energy requirements of physical activity. In: (H. B. Falls, ed) *Exercise Physiology.* Academic Press; New York.

Carpenter T. M. (1964) *Tables, Functions, and Formulas for Computing Respiratory Exchange and Biological Transformation of Energy (4th Edition).* Carnegie Institution of Washington Publication 303C; Washington, DC.

Consolazio C. F., Johnson R. E. and Pecora L. J. (1963) *Physiological Measurements of Metabolic Functions in Man;* McGraw-Hill; New York.

Cunningham J. J. (1991) Body composition as a determinant of energy expenditure: a synthetic review and a proposed general prediction equation. *American Journal of Clinical Nutrition;* **54**: 963–9.

DuBois D. and DuBois E. F. (1916) Clinical calorimetry: a formula to estimate the approximate surface area if stature and weight are known. *Archives of Internal Medicine;* **17**: 863–71.

Durnin J. V. G. A. and Passmore R. (1967) *Energy, Work and Leisure.* Heinemann; London.

Eston R. G. and Romer L. (2009) Lung Function. In: R. G. Eston and T. Reilly, eds) *Kinanthropometry Laboratory Manual (3rd Edition): Exercise Physiology (Chapter 3).* Routledge; Oxon: pp 75–103.

Eston R. G., Hawes M., Martin A. D. and Reilly T. (2009) Human body composition. In: (R. G. Eston and T. Reilly, eds) *Kinanthropometry Laboratory Manual (3rd Edition): Anthropometry (Chapter 1).* Routledge; Oxon: pp 3–53.

Harris J. and Benedict F. (1919) *A Biometric Study of Basal Metabolism in Man.* Carnegie Institution, Publication 279; Washington, DC.

Holland B., Welch A. A., Unwin I. D., Buss D. H., Paul A. A. and Southgate D. A. T. (1992) *McCance and Widdowson's The Composition of Foods (5th Edition).* The Royal Society of Chemistry and Ministry of Agriculture, Fisheries and Food, Richard Clay Ltd; Bungay, UK.

Jakeman P. and Davies B. (1979) The characteristics of a low resistance breathing valve designed for measurement of high aerobic capacity. *British Journal of Sports Medicine;* **13**: 81–3.

James D. V. B., Sandals L. E., Wood D. and Jones A. M. (2007) Pulmonary gas exchange. In: (E. M. Winter, A. M. Jones, R. Davison, P. D. Bromley and T. H. Mercer, eds) *Sport and Exercise Physiology Testing Guidelines, the British Association of Sport and Exercise Sciences Guide (Volume 1): Sport Testing.* Routledge; Oxon: pp. 101–11.

Kleiber M. (1975) *The Fire of Life. An Introduction to Animal Energetics.* Kreiger; New York.

Knoebel L. K. (1963) Energy metabolism. In: (E. E. Selkurt, ed). *Physiology.* Little, Brown and Co.; Boston, MA: pp. 564–79.

McArdle W. D., Katch F. I. and Katch V. L. (2006) *Exercise Physiology, Energy Nutrition and Human Performance (6th Edition)* (Appendix C Student resource CD ROM.) Lippincott, Williams and Wilkins; Philadelphia, PA.

MacDougall J. D., Roche P. D., Bar-Or O. and Moroz J. R. (1979) Oxygen cost of running in children of different ages; maximal aerobic power of Canadian school children. *Canadian Journal of Applied Sports Sciences;* **4**: 237–41.

Machta L. and Hughes E. (1970) Atmospheric oxygen in 1967 and 1970. *Science;* **168**: 1582–4.

McLean J. A. and Tobin G. (1987) *Animal and Human Calorimetry.* Cambridge University Press; Cambridge.

McMahon T. A. (1984) *Muscles, Reflexes and Locomotion.* Princeton University Press; Princeton, NJ.

Mifflin M. D., St Jeor S. T., Hill L. A., Scott B. J., Daugherty S. A. and Koh Y. O. (1990) A new predictive equation for resting energy expenditure in healthy individuals. *American Journal of Clinical Nutrition;* **51**: 241–7.

Owen O. E., Kavle E. and Owen R. S. (1986) A re-appraisal of the caloric requirements in healthy women. *American Journal of Clinical Nutrition;* **44**: 1–19.

Owen O. E., Holup J. L. and D'Allessio D. A. (1987) A re-appraisal of the caloric requirements of healthy men. *American Journal of Clinical Nutrition;* **46**: 875–85.

Rowlands A. V. (2009) Field methods of assessing physical activity and energy balance. In: (R. G. Eston and T. Reilly, eds) *Kinanthropometry Laboratory Manual (3rd Edition): Anthropometry (Chapter 6).* Routledge; Oxon: pp 163–183.

Rowlands A. V., Eston R. G. and Ingledew D. K. (1997) Measurement of physical activity in children with particular reference to the use of heart rate and pedometry. *Sports Medicine;* **24**: 258–72.

Rowlands A. V., Eston R. G. and Ingledew D. K. (1999). The relationship between activity levels, aerobic fitness, and body fat in 8- to 10-yr-old children. *Journal of Applied Physiology;* **86**: 1428–35.

Rubner M. (1883) Uber den Einfluss der korpergrosse auf Stoff-und Kraftwechsel. *Z. Biology. Munich;* **19**: 535–62.

Sandals L. E. (2003) Oxygen uptake during middle-distance running. Unpublished PhD thesis, University of Gloucestershire. Quoted in: Winter E. M., Jones A. M., Davison R., Bromley P. D. and Mercer T. H. (2007) Sport and exercise physiology testing guidelines. *The British Association of Sport and Exercise Sciences Guide, Volume* **1**: *Sport testing.* Routledge; London: p. 103.

Schmidt-Nielsen K. (1984) *Scaling: Why is Animal Size so Important?* Cambridge University Press; Cambridge.

Weir J. B. De. V. (1949) New methods for calculating metabolic rate with special reference to protein metabolism. *Journal of Physiology;* **109**: 1–9.

CHAPTER 7

MAXIMAL OXYGEN UPTAKE, ECONOMY AND EFFICIENCY

Carlton B. Cooke

7.1 AIMS

The aims in this chapter are to:
- define the measurements of maximal oxygen uptake, economy and efficiency;
- describe procedures for the direct determination of maximal oxygen uptake;
- consider methods and limitations of predicting maximal oxygen uptake;
- describe procedures for assessing the economy of movement;
- discuss the concept of 'efficiency' and describe the limitations of various measurements for assessing the efficiency of human movement;
- describe the effects of load carriage on the economy, posture and kinematics of walking.

7.2 INTRODUCTION

Measurements of maximal oxygen uptake, economy and efficiency of different forms of exercise are important in gaining an understanding of the differences between groups of athletes and the requirements of sporting, recreational and occupational activities. They also serve to help highlight effects of sex, age and size differences.

Maximal oxygen uptake and exercise economy are commonly measured in studies in which the aerobic performances of different individuals or groups of athletes are compared. Defining the current training status of an elite runner, and comparing the physiological profiles of different standards of athletes are examples. Efficiency measures, other than average values for estimating oxygen uptake from external work done, are less often quoted in the literature due to problems of measurement, which are often exacerbated by the use and abuse of different definitions (Cavanagh and Kram 1985).

Load carriage is an activity that provides an appropriate focus for the study of economy, including the need to consider energy expenditure, posture and kinematics. Load carriage is of interest from both an occupational and recreational perspective. The efficacy of rucksacks as a means of load carriage is important for trekkers as well as soldiers, both of which may have to carry relatively heavy loads for prolonged periods of time.

7.3 DIRECT DETERMINATION OF MAXIMAL OXYGEN UPTAKE

7.3.1 Relevance

There is an upper limit to the oxygen that is consumed during exercise requiring maximal effort. This upper limit is defined as maximal oxygen uptake, ($\dot{V}O_{2max}$) which is the maximum rate at which an individual can take up and utilize oxygen while breathing air at sea level (Åstrand et al. 2003). It has traditionally been used as the 'gold standard' criterion of cardiorespiratory fitness, as it is considered to be the single physiological variable that best defines the functional capacity of the cardiovascular and respiratory systems. However, it is more accurate to consider it as an indicator of both potential for endurance performance and, to a lesser extent, training status. Even though the physiological basis of $\dot{V}O_{2max}$ has been established for a considerable time, there has recently been some robust debate based on a challenge of A. V. Hill's paradigm by Noakes (1997, 1998) which has been refuted by Bassett and Howley (1997), Bassett et al. (2000) and others.

At any given time the $\dot{V}O_{2max}$ of an individual is fixed and specific for a given task, for example, running, cycling, rowing and so on. The $\dot{V}O_{2max}$ can be increased with training or decreased with a period of enforced inactivity, such as bed rest. Changes of up to 100% in $\dot{V}O_{2max}$ have been reported after a period of training following prolonged bed rest (Saltin et al. 1968). Pollock (1973) published a review in which the effect of endurance training is reported to have produced changes in $\dot{V}O_{2max}$ which ranged from 0% to 93%. The initial level of fitness (a reflection of an individual combination of endowment and habitual activity), intensity, frequency and duration of training are factors that will influence the effects of endurance training on $\dot{V}O_{2max}$. The age and sex of the individual are relevant considerations also. It is, therefore, not surprising that training studies carried out on habitually active endurance athletes have produced non-significant changes in $\dot{V}O_{2max}$, of the order of only 2–3%, whereas endurance performance has dramatically increased. Training programmes carried out on previously sedentary subjects can produce significant changes in $\dot{V}O_{2max}$ values, usually in the order of 20–30%.

Measurements of $\dot{V}O_{2max}$ indicate aerobic potential and to a lesser extent, training status. The sensitivity of $\dot{V}O_{2max}$ to changes in training or the establishment of regular habitual physical activity is strongly related to the degree of development in $\dot{V}O_{2max}$ that may be ultimately realized, which reflects a combination of endowment and habitual physical activity. Although it is generally agreed that genetic factors play an important role in defining the potential for development of physiological variables such as $\dot{V}O_{2max}$, the extent to which $\dot{V}O_{2max}$ is determined by endowment has been adjusted downwards in more recent studies from 90% to something in the order of 40–70% (Bouchard and Malina 1983).

The maximal oxygen uptake ($\dot{V}O_{2max}$) is also important as a baseline measure to be used with other measures of endurance performance, such as fractional utilization (% $\dot{V}O_{2max}$ that can be sustained for prolonged periods), onset of blood lactate accumulation (OBLA) and running economy (Jones et al. 2009, Chapter 10). Bassett et al. (2000) explained how the variables of $\dot{V}O_{2max}$, the percentage of $\dot{V}O_{2max}$, and running economy can account for the vast majority of the variance in distance running performances. A high $\dot{V}O_{2max}$ may be considered to be a prerequisite for elite performance in endurance sport, but does not guarantee achievement at the highest level of sport. Technique, state of training and psychological factors also has positive and negative modifying effects on performance. It is for these reasons that measures of $\dot{V}O_{2max}$ do not allow an accurate prediction of an individual's performance potential in aerobic power events. Shephard (1984) reviewed 37 studies reporting correlation coefficients between all-out running performance and measured $\dot{V}O_{2max}$ and found coefficients ranging from 0.04 to 0.90.

(a) Age, sex and $\dot{V}O_{2max}$

A combination of cross-sectional and longitudinal studies provides a reasonably clear picture of the development of $\dot{V}O_{2max}$ during childhood and adolescence and its decline during adulthood (Bar-Or 1983; Krahenbuhl et al. 1985; Allied Dunbar National Fitness Survey 1992; Armstrong and Welsman 2001; Åstrand et al. 2003). Absolute $\dot{V}O_{2max}$ values increase steadily prior to puberty with the growth of the pulmonary, cardiovascular and musculoskeletal systems. At the onset of puberty, the curves relating age and $\dot{V}O_{2max}$ values for males and females begin to diverge and continue to do so during adolescence. After the acceleration of $\dot{V}O_{2max}$ values in males at puberty, which reflects the increased muscle mass, and given that $\dot{V}O_{2max}$ in females remains virtually unchanged after early teens, females' $\dot{V}O_{2max}$ values are on average 65–75% of those of males.

In both sexes there is a peak in $\dot{V}O_{2max}$ values at 18–20 years of age followed by a gradual decline with increasing age. The results of the Allied Dunbar National Fitness Survey (1992), where $\dot{V}O_{2max}$ was estimated for over 1,700 men and women, produced average values of 55 and 40 ml kg^{-1} min^{-1} for men and women aged 16–24 years, respectively. After this time, $\dot{V}O_{2max}$ declined steadily with increasing age, resulting in average values of about 30 and 25 ml kg^{-1} min^{-1} for men and women aged 65–74 years, respectively. In contrast, $\dot{V}O_{2max}$ values for elite endurance athletes may exceed 80 ml kg^{-1} min^{-1}. Data from a variety of population studies indicate that at the age of 65 the average $\dot{V}O_{2max}$ value is approximately 70% of that of a 25-year-old of the same sex.

(b) Body size and $\dot{V}O_{2max}$

Comparisons of physiological measurements between subjects of different size are commonplace, especially in the case of children versus adults. These comparisons are made in both cross-sectional and longitudinal studies, which in the latter case include comparisons of the same subjects during the growing years.

In the case of $\dot{V}O_{2max}$ there is a strong positive relationship between body size and absolute $\dot{V}O_{2max}$ (1 min^{-1}). Generally speaking, the larger the subject the larger the $\dot{V}O_{2max}$ in absolute terms (1 min^{-1}). In an attempt to overcome the effects of differences in body mass when comparing $\dot{V}O_{2max}$ values, the latter are often divided by body mass prior to comparison. The $\dot{V}O_{2max}$ (ml kg^{-1} min^{-1}) is therefore considered to be a weight-adjusted expression of $\dot{V}O_{2max}$ where the effects of differences in body mass have been factored out.

However, $\dot{V}O_{2max}$ expressed in ml kg^{-1} min^{-1} correlates negatively with body mass. Far from eliminating the effect of body mass, this form of expression converts a positive relationship between $\dot{V}O_{2max}$ (1 min^{-1}) and body mass into a negative one between $\dot{V}O_{2max}$ (ml kg^{-1} min^{-1}) and body mass. Therefore, this common form of weight correction does not eliminate the effects of body mass or weight at all.

Nevertheless, $\dot{V}O_{2max}$ has probably continued to be related to body mass in the form ml kg^{-1} min^{-1} because body mass is easily obtained. It also correlates well with most measures of cardiorespiratory function. There is also a strong positive relationship with performance in weight-bearing activities such as running, so expressing the power output per kilogram of body mass would seem appropriate where the body mass has to be carried in the activity.

If dividing $\dot{V}O_{2max}$ by body mass does not factor out the effects of body mass on ($\dot{V}O_{2max}$ 1 min^{-1}), then the question arises as to what form of expression of $\dot{V}O_{2max}$ is independent of body mass and can therefore allow meaningful comparisons among individuals differing in body size?

Theoretically, since maximal force in muscle is dependent on cross-sectional area, muscle force will be proportional to length^2 (L^2), the squared function representing an area. Similarly, work or energy is based on force × distance, therefore work done or energy expended is proportional to $F \times L$ or L^3 (on a cubic function). As $\dot{V}O_{2max}$ is an expression of energy expenditure per unit of time or power output, which is $(F \times L)/t$, and time is proportional to L then $\dot{V}O_{2max}$ (1 min^{-1}) is proportional to $L^3 L^{-1}$ or L^2.

Since mass (M) is proportional to volume which is proportional to L^3, then $\dot{V}O_{2max}$ (1 min^{-1}) should be proportional to $M^{2/3}$ (since M is proportional to L^3, $\dot{V}O_{2max}$ is proportional to L^2 and $M^{2/3} = L^2$). A more detailed discussion of the scaling effects of body size and dimensional analysis can be found in Schmidt-Nielson (1984), McMahon (1984) and Åstrand et al. (2003).

The theoretical expectation that $\dot{V}O_{2max}$ (1 min^{-1}) should be proportional to L^2 or $M^{2/3}$ is true for well-trained adult athletes (Åstrand et al. 2003) and recreationally active adult males and females (Nevill et al. 1992). However, longitudinal studies of children's $\dot{V}O_{2max}$ (1 min^{-1}) have identified exponents of L which range from 1.51 to 3.21 (or M from 0.503 to 1.07) (Bar-Or 1983).

In the case of active adults and athletes, expressing $\dot{V}O_{2max}$ in ml kg$^{-2/3}$ min^{-1} would appear to eliminate the confounding effects of body mass on $\dot{V}O_{2max}$ (1 min^{-1}). Therefore, it provides a more meaningful index than the more conventional expression of $\dot{V}O_{2max}$ in ml kg^{-1} min^{-1}, which disadvantages heavier individuals.

Besides demonstrating the superiority of the expression of $\dot{V}O_{2max}$ in ml kg$^{-2/3}$ min^{-1}, in adjusting for differences in body mass, Nevill et al. (1992) also showed that the more conventional expression of $\dot{V}O_{2max}$ in ml kg^{-1} min^{-1} held true in terms of predicting ability to run 5 km expressed as a function of average running speed. This supports the use of the conventional expression of $\dot{V}O_{2max}$ in ml kg^{-1} min^{-1} for weight-bearing activities, which are highly dependent on body size. It is therefore important to be clear on the aim of comparing different forms of expression, since performance and physiological function do not always use the same criteria. Further discussion on the principles of scaling physiological and anthropometric data are presented by Winter and Nevill (2009).

7.3.2 Protocols

There is a large number of protocols reported in the literature for the direct determination of $\dot{V}O_{2max}$. These range from short, single-load protocols performed at so-called 'supra-maximal' workloads lasting no longer than 6 minutes, to relatively long discontinuous protocols where the subject exercises for anything from 3 to 6 minutes at each workload and then rests for about 3 minutes between each increment (Åstrand et al. 2003).

One of the general recommendations for the assessment of $\dot{V}O_{2max}$ is that subjects should perform rhythmic exercise that requires a large muscle mass. This ensures that the cardiorespiratory system is taxed and the test is not limited by local muscular endurance. The muscle mass engaged explains why simulated cross-country skiing produces the highest $\dot{V}O_{2max}$ values, followed by graded treadmill running, flat treadmill running and cycle ergometry. The specificity of the activity of the subject undergoing assessment should take precedence if the aim is to produce meaningful values for interpretation of aerobic potential or current training status. For example, canoeists should be tested on a canoe ergometer, but will generally produce lower $\dot{V}O_{2max}$ values than if they were running on a treadmill. It has been known, in exceptional cases, for a subject only used to strenuous exercise in canoeing to produce a higher $\dot{V}O_{2max}$ value than when running on a treadmill.

Given the plethora of protocols for the direct determination of $\dot{V}O_{2max}$, it is worthwhile to consider attempts at standardization through guidelines such as those published by the British Association of Sports Sciences (1992) in its 'Position Statement on the Physiological

Assessment of the Elite Competitor.' These guidelines contain tables for establishing the appropriate exercise intensities for the direct determination of $\dot{V}O_{2max}$ using leg and arm cycling and graded treadmill running (Tables 7.1 and 7.2).

The British Association of Sports and Exercise Sciences (BASES 1997) has recommended the following criteria for establishing maximal oxygen uptake in adult subjects:

1   A plateau in the oxygen uptake–exercise intensity relationship. This has been defined as an increase in oxygen uptake of less than 2 ml kg^{-1} min^{-1} or 3% with an increase in exercise intensity. If this plateau is not achieved, then the term $\dot{V}O_2$ peak is preferred.

2   A final respiratory exchange ratio of 1.15 or above.

3   A final heart rate of within 10 beats min^{-1} of the predicted age-related maximum.

(Maximum heart rate can be estimated from the formula: Maximal Heart Rate = 220 – age (years) if the maximum value is unknown.)

4   A post-exercise (4–5 minute) blood lactate concentration of 8 mmol l^{-1} or more.

5   Subjective fatigue and volitional exhaustion.

6   A rating of perceived exertion (RPE) of 19 or 20 on the Borg scale.

Given the frequent use of incremental ramp protocols to establish a number of physiological indices in a single test Day et al. (2003) investigated whether a $\dot{V}O_2$ plateau was consistently produced during maximal incremental ramp cycle ergometry in 71 adult subjects and also established the relationship between $\dot{V}O_2$ peak and that determined from maximal constant-load tests. Day et al. (2003) concluded that a plateau in the $\dot{V}O_2$ response is therefore not an obligatory consequence

Table 7.1 Guidelines for establishing exercise intensity for the determination of maximal oxygen uptake during leg or arm cycling in adults

	Warm up (W)	Initial work rate (W)	Work rate increment (W)
Leg cycling (pedal frequency 60 min^{-1})			
Male	120	180–240	30
Female	60	150–200	30
Arm cycling (pedal frequency 60 min^{-1})	60	90	30
Elite cyclists (pedal frequency 90 min^{-1})			
Male	150	200–250	35
Female	100	150	35

Table 7.2 Guidelines for establishing exercise intensity for the determination of maximal oxygen uptake during treadmill running in adults.

	Warm up speed (m s^{-1})	Test speed (m s^{-1})	Initial grade %	Grade increment
Endurance athletes				
Male	3.13	4.47	0	2.5
Female	2.68	4.02	0	2.5
Games players				
Male	3.13	3.58	0	2.5
Female	2.68	3.13	0	2.5

of incremental exercise. Given that the $\dot{V}O_2$ peak value attained was not different from the plateau for the constant-load tests, the $\dot{V}O_2$ peak attained on a maximum-effort incremental test was suggested to be a valid index of $\dot{V}O_{2max}$ despite no evidence of a plateau in the test results. However, Day et al. (2003) did caution that without additional tests, one cannot be certain.

Rossiter et al. (2006), building on the work of Day et al. (2003), sought to determine whether the addition of a step exercise (SE) test at a work rate greater than that achieved in a preceding ramp incremental (RI) test would establish the plateau criterion for $\dot{V}O_2$ using seven adult subjects. Rossiter et al. (2006) concluded that because there was no difference between the $\dot{V}O_2$ peaks established at different work-rate peak values in the RI + SE protocols that the combined RI + SE protocol provides the plateau criterion for verification of maximum $\dot{V}O_2$ in a single test session, even when the $\dot{V}O_2$ data do not themselves evidence a plateau.

Determinants and limitations to maximal oxygen uptake have been the subject of considerable research interest since the original work of Hill which continues in contemporary exercise physiology literature (e.g. Saltin and Calbet 2006 versus Wagner 2006).

The third edition of the BASES guidelines (Winter et al. 2006) has been considerably developed and includes much more useful information than the 2nd edition, including sport-specific guidelines for testing and considerations for testing children. Nevertheless, the tables presented above still provide useful guidance for testing maximal oxygen uptake in adult subjects. Considerations for testing children are also described by Barker et al. (2009).

(a) Example of treadmill protocol (continuous protocol)
The protocol in Table 7.2 is based on that of Taylor et al. (1955) and is suitable for the habitually active and sports participants.

The recommended exercise intensities should produce volitional exhaustion in 9–15 minutes of continuous exercise, following a 5-minute warm-up. Thus, unless steady-state values are required, 2-minute increments are recommended.

(b) Example of cycle ergometer protocol (discontinuous protocol)
A detailed description of such a protocol and associated procedures is given in Section 7.8.

(c) Example of combined two-stage treadmill protocol
A detailed description of a combined protocol for the assessment of running economy, lactate response and maximal oxygen uptake is given in section 7.10 and Chapter 10 by Jones et al. (2009).

7.3.3 Results

Table 7.3 shows a completed proforma for the discontinuous cycle ergometer protocol. It can be used for most protocols involving expired air collection and analysis using the Douglas bag technique, but is easily adapted for variations in data collection or experimental protocols. Figure 7.1 shows the results from a $\dot{V}O_{2max}$ test performed on the treadmill by a trained male runner aged 21. Data for the treadmill test were collected using an Oxycon 5 automated gas analysis system (Mijnhardt, The Netherlands). The test was continuous until volitional exhaustion, after which the subject attempted two further workloads to demonstrate a plateau in oxygen uptake.

7.4 PREDICTION OF MAXIMAL OXYGEN UPTAKE

Although a direct determination of maximal oxygen uptake is feasible with well-conditioned and highly motivated individuals, provided there is access to appropriate laboratory facilities, it is often only possible to conduct either a submaximal exercise test,

Table 7.3 Data collection using a Douglas bag during an intermittent cycle ergometer protocol

Subject: J. Bloggs	Date: 30-9-1993	Time: 2.00	Mass (kg): 81
Age: 21	DoB: 7.12.71	PB (mmHg): 753.5	Ht (cms): 180 Ergometer:
Temp. (°C): 21	Humidity (%) 65	Protocol: Discontinuous	Cycle (3 min work, 3 min rest)

Bag No.	1	2	3	4	5
Work rate (W)	200	250	300	350	400
Exercise time (min)	2–3	5–6	8–9	11–12	14–15
Collection time (s)	60	60	60	60	60
Temperature expired air (°C)	24.0	24.0	23.8	24.0	24.0
Volume (l) (ATPS)	68.60	93.75	125.5	162.1	170.3
Volume of sample (l)	2.0	2.0	2.0	2.0	2.0
$\dot{V}_E$(l) ATPS	70.60	95.75	127.5	164.1	172.3
$\dot{V}_E$ STPD (1 min^{-1})	62.44	84.68	113.1	145.1	152.4
F_EO_2(%)	16.13	17.03	17.37	17.71	17.82
$F_E CO_2$ (%)	4.30	3.46	3.34	3.25	3.22
$\dot{V}O_2$ (1 min^{-1})	3.09	3.41	4.10	4.69	4.73
$\dot{V}CO_2$ (1 min^{-1})	2.66	2.91	3.74	4.69	4.86
RER	0.863	0.852	0.913	1.00	1.03
Borg RPE	13	15	16	19	20
Heart rate (beats min^{-1})	154	168	183	197	198

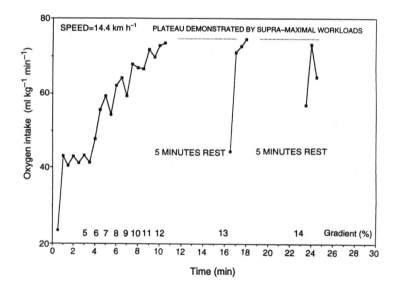

Figure 7.1 Results of a $\dot{V}O_{2max}$ test performed by a 21-year-old male runner on a motorized treadmill.

or a maximum performance test in the field. The results from many such tests are then used to estimate maximal oxygen uptake (Åstrand and Ryhming 1954; Siconolfi et al. 1982; Åstrand et al. 2003; American College of Sports Medicine (ACSM) 2006).

Probably the most widely used procedure for predicting maximal oxygen uptake is the Åstrand–Ryhming (1954) nomogram, now adjusted and renamed as the Åstrand and Åstrand nomogram (Åstrand et al. 2003). Use of the nomogram in submaximal field tests is based on measuring the heart rate response to a quantifiable form of external work for which the mechanical efficiency is known. Thus, the oxygen uptake elicited by the external work can be estimated (i.e. cycle ergometry, treadmill walking and running, and stepping). The nomogram consists of scales for work rate in cycle ergometry, and steps of 33 cm and 40 cm in height, which are located alongside a scale for oxygen uptake. Therefore, if the appropriate step height or cycle ergometry is used, then a prediction of maximal oxygen uptake can be obtained from the measured heart rate response. The value can then be age-adjusted based on empirically derived age-correction factors. Use of the nomogram is endorsed by the ACSM (2006); Shephard (1970) produced an algorithm for a computer solution of the nomogram, which is easily programmed into a spreadsheet.

Åstrand et al. (2003) described a simple submaximal cycle ergometer test, which, when used in conjunction with the nomogram, will provide an estimate of maximal oxygen uptake. For women a work-rate of 75–100 W has been suggested, and for men 100–150 W. If the heart rate exceeds 130 beats. min^{-1} the test is stopped after 6 minutes. If the heart rate is lower than 130 beats min^{-1} after a couple of minutes of exercise, the work rate should be increased by 50 W. The steady-state heart rate response, taken as the mean of the value at 5 and 6 minutes, together with the work-rate can then be used to predict the maximal oxygen uptake. It is acknowledged that there is error associated

with the prediction of $\dot{V}O_{2max}$ using the Åstrand–Ryhming nomogram and associated submaximal test procedures. Some of the reasons for this are: assumptions of linearity in the heart rate-oxygen uptake relationship for all subjects, decline and variation in maximum heart rate with increasing age and variations in mechanical efficiency. In addition, there are factors that affect the heart rate response to a given exercise intensity, but not maximal oxygen uptake, such as anxiety, dehydration, prolonged heavy exercise, exercise with a small muscle mass and exercise after consumption of alcohol (Åstrand et al. 2003).

The standard error for predicting maximal oxygen uptake from the studies used to validate the nomogram is 10% in relatively well-trained individuals of the same age as the original sample, but up to 15% in moderately trained individuals of different ages when the age correction factors are used. Values for untrained subjects are often underestimated, whereas elite athletes are often overestimated (Åstrand et al. 2003). This limitation in accuracy for estimation of maximal oxygen uptake is an important consideration, especially when dealing with repeated measures of subjects participating in a training study. The authors concluded that, 'this drawback (in accuracy) holds true for any submaximal cardiopulmonary test'. (Astrand et al. 2003, p 287).

Another common form of submaximal test using a step or a cycle ergometer is to exercise the subject at four different exercise intensities and measure the heart rate and oxygen uptake at each work-rate (Wyndham et al. 1966; Harrison et al. 1980). Using linear regression, the HR-$\dot{V}O_2$ relationship is extrapolated to a predicted maximum heart rate value (e.g. maximum heart rate = 220 – age in years) to obtain an estimate of maximal oxygen uptake.

More recently, Faulkner and Eston (2007) have observed that $\dot{V}O_{2max}$ can be predicted with reasonable accuracy by extrapolation of the RPE–$\dot{V}O_2$ relationship in fit and unfit participants. It is also possible to manipulate workload *in response* to the RPE. Application of RPE-regulated exercise tests (e.g. perceptually-regulated exercise at RPE 9, 11, 13, 15) enables prediction of $\dot{V}O_{2max}$ in trained and untrained adults (Eston *et al.*, 2006, 2008; Faulkner *et al.* 2007). In these studies it was noteworthy that each stage of an RPE-regulated test elicited a change in workload equivalent to around 1–2 METs in untrained individuals, which is in accordance with standard guidelines for the submaximal testing of healthy individuals (ACSM 2006). These studies are described in more detail by Eston *et al.* (2009) – Chapter 9.

The Physical Work Capacity (PWC) test is also a popular form of submaximal exercise test, and was adopted as the cycle ergometer test for use with children in the Eurofit initiative (Council of Europe, 1988). The relationship between heart rate and work-rate is established using three or four submaximal work-rates and the PWC is calculated by extrapolation to a specific heart rate, which is most commonly 170 beats min^{-1}; hence the score is called a PWC_{170}. However, if the oxygen uptake can be measured directly, then it is preferable to do so as the PWC procedure takes no account of individual variations in mechanical efficiency. This test has also been used with adults in an adjusted form where the target heart rate for the final workload was 85% of predicted maximum heart rate. Whether or not this heart rate value is achieved during the test, it is used as the criterion value for the extrapolation or interpolation of the PWC value.

There is also a large number of field tests which include an equation for the prediction of maximal oxygen uptake, such as a one-mile walk test (Kline *et al.* 1987), a 20 m multistage shuttle test (Leger and Lambert, 1982; Paliczka *et al.* 1987; Boreham *et al.* 1990), and Cooper's 12-minute walk/run test (Cooper, 1968). All these tests are maximal in that the subjects have to go as fast as possible in the walk and run tests, and for as long as possible in the multistage shuttle

test. They are therefore dependent on subjects being well motivated and used to strenuous exercise. However, they are acceptable as indicators of current training status as they are all performance tests, irrespective of their accuracy in the prediction of maximal oxygen uptake. The reliability and validity of run-walk tests have been reviewed by Eston and Brodie (1985).

In conclusion, whatever form of sub-maximal test is adopted, whether it is based on either the relationship between work rate and heart rate or the oxygen uptake–heart rate relationship, extreme caution should be used in the interpretation of predicted maximal oxygen uptake values.

7.5 ECONOMY

7.5.1 Introduction

Economy of energy expenditure is important in any endurance event that makes demands on aerobic energy supply and it continues to be a major focus of research interest since the last edition of this chapter was produced. If a lower oxygen uptake can be achieved through the optimization of skill and technique for a given exercise intensity, be it cross-country skiing, kayaking or running, then, all other things being equal, performance can be maintained for a longer period of time at a given exercise intensity, or at a slightly increased exercise intensity for the same period of time. Although the measurement of economy of energy expenditure described here is that of running economy, similar principles, procedures and protocols also apply to other activities. One such activity that is also considered is that of load carriage, which may have an effect on economy, kinematics and efficiency of movement.

Running economy can be defined as the metabolic cost, measured as oxygen uptake per kilogram per minute for a given treadmill speed and slope. A lower oxygen uptake for a given running speed is therefore interpreted as a better running economy.

There is a strong correlation between $\dot{V}O_{2max}$ and distance running performance in studies based on a wide range of running capabilities (Cooper 1968; Costill *et al.* 1973). This relationship is not evident in a homogeneous sample of elite runners (Conley and Krahenbuhl 1980). However, running economy is correlated significantly with distance running performance (Costill 1972; Costill *et al.* 1973; Conley and Krahenbuhl 1980) and therefore may, in part, account for why $\dot{V}O_{2max}$ is not a good predictor in a group homogenous in competitive level and performance.

7.5.2 Methodology

Running economy is measured by means of establishing the oxygen cost to running speed (or speed and gradient) relationship. Many of the studies in the literature have entailed comparisons of measures of running economy for a single running speed of 4.44 m s^{-1} at 1% gradient (Jones 2007) or equivalent to race pace and/or training pace. Nevertheless, there is value in measuring oxygen uptake over a range of running speeds, especially if comparing the performance of children and adults.

In order to obtain a 'true' measure of running economy at a range of running speeds the oxygen uptake must be measured under steady-state conditions. The subject should be exercising in the aerobic range (i.e. no significant contribution to metabolic energy from anaerobic sources). Åstrand *et al.* (2003) suggested that $\dot{V}O_{2max}$ protocols based on work rates where a steady-state of oxygen uptake is achieved have the advantage of simultaneously establishing relationships between submaximal oxygen cost and speed of performance. Similarly, measures of running economy can be made at the same time as the establishment of blood lactate responses (Jones *et al.* 2009 – Chapter 10). When the $\dot{V}O_{2max}$ of the subject is known, it is common practice to select four running speeds which are predicted to elicit 60%, 70%, 80% and 90% of $\dot{V}O_{2max}$.

(a) Protocol

A protocol for measurement of running economy is described in Section 7.9. This protocol and associated procedures can easily be adapted for other forms of ergometry. An alternative protocol used to assess middle- and long-distance runners by UK athletics is described as stage 1 in Section 7.9.

7.5.3 Results

Figure 7.2 shows the relationships between oxygen cost and running speed for three groups of adult male runners: 10 elite, 10 club and 10 recreational runners. There was a significant increase ($P < 0.001$) in the oxygen cost of running over the range of speeds analyzed (2.67–4.00 m s^{-1}) in all three groups. Linear regression equations for the three groups are:

Elite $\dot{V}O_2$ (ml kg^{-1} min^{-1}) = 8.07 ×
    SPEED (m s^{-1})
+8.87 (r= 0.99; r^2 = 0.98
(variance accounted for))
Club $\dot{V}O_2$ (ml kg^{-1} min^{-1}) = 8.27 ×
    SPEED (m s^{-1})
+13.27 (r= 0.99; r^2 = 0.98
(variance accounted for))
Rec $\dot{V}O_2$ (ml kg^{-1} min^{-1}) = 7.80 ×
    SPEED (m s^{-1})
+14.35 (r= 0.99; r^2 = 0.98
(variance accounted for))

There was a significant difference ($P < 0.001$) in the oxygen cost of running in the three groups. The elite group required significantly lower ($P < 0.001$) oxygen uptakes than either the club or recreational runners (mean difference of 4.7 ml kg^{-1} min^{-1}; 11.5%). The recreational runners appeared to have slightly better running economy at the higher running speeds than the club runners (Figure 7.2). Blood lactate values revealed that not all the recreational runners were meeting the energy requirements by aerobic sources alone, which would account for the less steep slope of their regression line. It is therefore important to ensure that comparisons of running economy are made on subjects who are exercising aerobically so that steady-state oxygen uptake values reflect the energy requirements of the exercise.

Jones (2007) reported the average $\dot{V}O_2$ in well-trained adult runners as 52 ml kg^{-1} min^{-1} . The following are then presented as a basis for a rough assessment of male or female $\dot{V}O_2$ values at 4.44 m s^{-1}: 44–47 ml kg^{-1} min^{-1} is excellent, 47–50 ml kg^{-1} min^{-1} is very good, 50–54 ml kg^{-1} min^{-1} is average and 55–58 ml kg^{-1} min^{-1} is poor. Using the three equations for the elite, club and recreational runners, above, at a speed of 4.44 m s^{-1} produces values that are classified as excellent, borderline average to very good and very good, respectively. An alternative expression for running economy is in ml kg^{-1} km^{-1}, which is an expression per unit distance. The typical value for running economy using this measure is 200 ml kg^{-1} km^{-1}, which is independent of running speed, with values of 170–180 ml kg^{-1} km^{-1} categorised as excellent, 180–190 ml kg^{-1} km^{-1} as very good, 190–200

ml kg^{-1} km^{-1} as above average, 200–210 ml kg^{-1} km^{-1} as below average and 210–220 ml kg^{-1} km^{-1} as poor (Jones 2007). The equation for conversion of running economy expressed as ml kg^{-1} min^{-1} to ml kg^{-1} km^{-1} is:

$$\dot{V}O_2 \,(\text{ml kg}^{-1}\,\text{km}^{-1}) = \dot{V}O_2 \,(\text{ml kg}^{-1}\,\text{min}^{-1}) / (\text{speed (km h}^{-1}) / 60) \,(\text{Jones, 2007})$$

Figure 7.3 shows the relationships between oxygen cost and running speed for two groups of male runners: adults aged $21.3 \pm 2.3 >$ years and children aged 11.9 ± 1.0 years (Cooke *et al.* 1991). There was a significant increase ($P < 0.001$) in the oxygen cost of running over the range of speeds studied (2.67, 3.11, 3.56 and 4.0 m s^{-1}) in both the children and adults. The children required a significantly greater ($P < 0.001$) $\dot{V}O_2$, on average 7 ml kg^{-1} min^{-1} (18.5%), for any given running speed. The divergence of the two regression lines shows the significant difference (analysis of covariance (ANCOVA); $P < 0.05$) in the $\dot{V}O_2$ response of the children and the adults over the range of speeds. Slopes of 10.87 for the

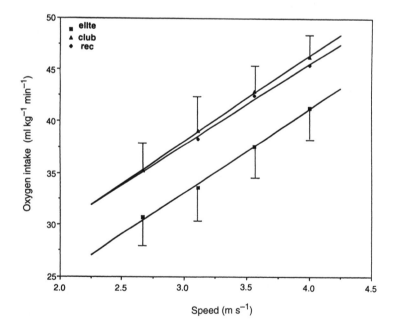

Figure 7.2 Oxygen cost to running speed relationship for three groups of 10 adult male runners: elite, club and recreational.

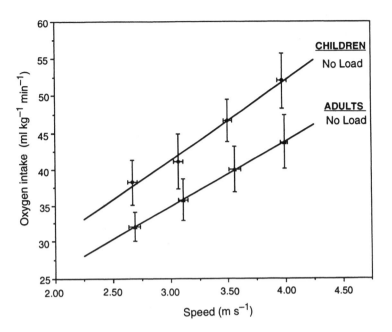

Figure 7.3 Oxygen cost ml kg^{-1} min^{-1} to running speed relationship for two groups of well-trained male runners: eight boys and eight men (Cooke *et al*. 1991).

children and 9.05 for the adults equate to a difference of 5.8 ml kg^{-1} min^{-1} at 2.67 m s^{-1} and 8.6 ml kg^{-1} min^{-1} at 4.0 m s^{-1}.

As the correlation between oxygen uptake and body mass is non-significant when oxygen uptake is expressed in ml kg$^{-0.75}$ min^{-1} (Kleiber, 1975), the ANCOVA was repeated with $\dot{V}O_2$ expressed in ml kg$^{-0.75}$ to establish whether the group differences in the oxygen cost of unloaded running could be accounted for by differences in body mass. Figure 7.4 shows that there was no significant difference between the groups as the regression lines became similar. For an explanation of the analysis of covariance procedure and its application, see Winter and Nevill (2009).

7.5.4 Discussion

(a) Adult running economy values

The running economy results for the three groups of adult male runners reflect that elite runners have trained themselves in the technique of running, optimizing their running style to produce significantly lower oxygen uptake values for any given running speed. This finding is in agreement with other cross-sectional studies, which have generally reported that highly-trained distance runners have better running economy than runners of club and recreational standard, but there is variation in economy within each standard of running (Costill and Fox 1969; Costill 1972; Pollock 1973; Bransford and Howley 1977; Conley and Krahenbuhl 1980; Morgan *et al.* 1995). Longitudinal studies have also shown that running economy can be improved with training (Conley *et al.* 1981).

It is fairly well established that there is a U-shaped relationship between stride length or stride frequency and energy cost at a given unloaded walking or running speed (Cavanagh and Williams 1982). Moreover, it appears that the curve is relatively flat near to the optimum stride length-stride frequency combination. As a result small deviations from the normal pattern have little or no effect on energy cost. Freely chosen stride length-stride frequency combinations are known to be close to optimum (Cavanagh

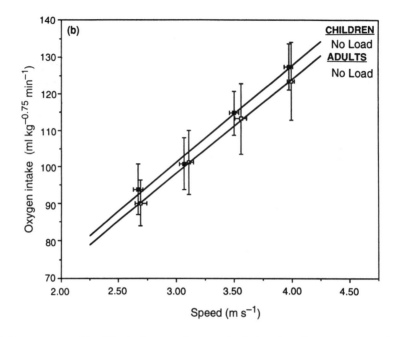

Figure 7.4 Oxygen cost ml kg$^{-0.75}$ min^{-1} to running speed relationships for two groups of well-trained male runners: eight boys and eight men (Cooke *et al.* 1991).

and Williams 1982). However, variations in stride length and stride frequency have been shown to increase the oxygen uptake for a given running speed, thereby making the movement less economical. This has been found in experiments where runners have made acute adjustments to their running technique by either deliberately overstriding or understriding. Both forms of adjustment therefore decrease economy, which led researchers to the conclusion that runners adopt a stride length-stride frequency combination that best suits them in terms of running economy. However, the research that has led to this viewpoint is based on experiments that incorporate acute rather than chronic changes to running kinematics. In the case of competitive athletes, the stride length-stride frequency combination has developed as a result of long-term training. The effect of stride manipulation on running economy can be demonstrated easily in the laboratory.

The effect of posture on running economy can be assessed by altering head position. In one study, runners were required to run with their eyes focused on a target 2 m in front of them at eye level, to produce an upright posture, or 1 m in front of them at floor level to induce a bent-over posture. Running economy was lower in the bent-over position (Jordan and Cooke 1998). The protocol outlined in Section 7.9 can be used to evaluate the effects of the adjustments of either head position or stride length. When altering stride length it is necessary to measure stride frequency using a stop watch to time a set number of stride cycles. Changes in stride length (SL) can then be calculated from the stride frequency (SF) and speed of the treadmill, using the formula SL (m) = (m.s^{-1}/str.s^{-1}). If required, a video camera can be set up perpendicular to the line of running to record the runner. This allows the changes in posture to be checked by simple measurements taken from the video images.

It is well established in the animal literature that mammals use the elastic properties of their legs, specifically tendons, ligaments, and muscles, to run economically, while maintaining consistent running mechanics across various surfaces. Kerdok et al. (2002) conducted an experiment with eight male adult runners to examine how leg stiffness and metabolic cost are affected by changes in running surface stiffness (five different surface stiffnesses: 75.4, 97.5, 216.8, 454.2, and 945.7 kN m^{-1}) using experimental platforms with adjustable stiffness on a force-plate-fitted treadmill. The 12.5-fold decrease in surface stiffness resulted in a 12% decrease in the runner's metabolic rate and a 29% increase in their leg stiffness. The results of this study showed that surface stiffness affects running economy without affecting running support mechanics. Kerdok et al. (2002) postulated that an increased energy rebound from the compliant surfaces studied contributed to the enhanced running economy. This study demonstrates the importance of considering a variety of mechanical factors which influence running economy.

One criticism of comparing weight-corrected oxygen uptake values between individuals or groups is that oxygen uptake per kilogram body mass is not itself independent of body mass. Since the elite subjects had a lower mean body mass, the differences between the elite, club and recreational runners would be increased only slightly if oxygen uptake was expressed in ml kg$^{-0.75}$ min^{-1}.

(b) Child and adult running economy values

The mass-specific equations relating oxygen uptake to running speed for both children and adults shown in Figure 7.3 are similar to others reported in the literature (Åstrand 1952; Margaria et al. 1963; Davies 1980). Some variation in equations due to population bias, treadmill type, and measurement techniques is to be expected. However, the mean difference between children and adults of 8 ml kg^{-1} min^{-1} in oxygen uptake is similar to that of other studies.

Smaller animals are metabolically more active than larger ones. This difference is also apparent in a comparison of mass-specific resting metabolic rates of children and adults. If the estimated resting metabolic rate is subtracted from the gross oxygen cost of running shown in Figure 7.3 then the difference between the regression lines decreases by 1.8 ml kg^{-1} min^{-1} (25%). Resting metabolic rate was estimated from the data of Altman and Dittmer (1968) using the formula of DuBois and DuBois (1916) for estimating body surface area.

The correlation between metabolic rate per unit of body size and body mass is non-significant when metabolic rate is divided by body mass to the power of 0.75 (Kleiber 1975). The data for boys and men shown in Figure 7.4 are consistent with this established comparative measure of metabolic body size.

The data also agree closely with a power function developed to predict the mass-specific oxygen cost of running from body mass and running speed in over 50 animal species (Taylor et al. 1982). The power function was indicated by:

$$\frac{\dot{V}O_2}{M} = 0.533 \times M^{-0.316} \times V + 0.300 \times M^{-0.303}$$

where $\dfrac{\dot{V}O_2}{M}$ = oxygen cost (ml kg^{-1} s^{-1})

V = velocity (m s^{-1})
M = body mass (kg)

The analogy between animals of different mass (from the flying squirrel with a mass of 0.063 kg to the Zebu cattle with a mass of 254 kg) would appear to suggest that differences in the relationship between oxygen cost and running speed in children and adults might be expected. However, Eston et al. (1993) showed that when body mass was used as a covariate (i.e. the dependent variable of oxygen uptake was linearly adjusted such that comparisons were made as if all subjects had the same body mass) differences between the oxygen uptake of boys and men running at the same speeds were non-significant. The use of scaling techniques to partition out the effects of size is an area of considerable interest and investigation (Rowland 2005; Welsman and Armstrong 2007, and is discussed in greater detail in Winter and Nevill (2009).

Rowland (1990) has suggested a number of factors which might explain the differences in running economy between children and adults:

1   Ratio of surface area to mass: as discussed previously, differences in basal metabolic rate (BMR) may account for something of the order of 25% of the greater oxygen cost of running in children compared with adults. This difference in BMR is based on the surface area law as described in Chapter 6 (Volume 2) of this text.

2   Stride frequency: the higher oxygen uptake for a given running speed in children may be partly explained by the necessarily higher stride frequency, resulting in the more frequent braking and acceleration of the centre of mass of the body, and the increased metabolic cost of producing more muscle contractions (Unnithan and Eston 1990).

3   Immature running mechanics: the running styles of children are different from those of adults, with changes occurring through the growing years to adulthood (Wickstrom 1983). However, the extent to which variations in running style with age might explain the differences between adults and children in the relationship between oxygen uptake and running speed are as yet unknown.

4   Speed–mass mismatch: the speed at which a muscle contracts is inversely related to the force generated. Thus, as muscles contract more quickly they produce less force (Hill 1939). Davies (1980) suggested that an imbalance of these two factors might help to explain the differences between children and adults in running economy. This suggestion was based on observations that when children were loaded with a weight jacket their oxygen uptake per kilogram total mass decreased, and approached adult values. However, similar experiments have revealed different results, suggesting that children and adults may be equally efficient at running with different forms of loading (Thorstensson 1986; Cooke et al. 1991).

5   Differences in anaerobic energy: it is well established that children are unable to produce anaerobic energy as effectively as adults. It is therefore important that subjects are exercising aerobically to prevent any inflation of child–adult differences in running economy values due to anaerobic energy contributions in the adult subjects.

6   Less efficient ventilation: children need to ventilate more than adults for each litre of oxygen consumed (i.e. $V_E/\dot{V}O_2$, the ventilatory equivalent for oxygen is greater in children). These differences in ventilation patterns in children and adults may contribute to the differences in economy, since during maximal exercise the oxygen cost of ventilation may reach 14–19% of total oxygen uptake.

Sex differences in the running economy of 6-year-old children have been reported in terms of absolute and mass specific oxygen uptake values, but oxygen uptake values expressed relative to fat free-mass were not different. The conclusion was that the sex differences in running economy may reflect an increase in aerobic energy demands associated with the greater muscle mass of the boys (Morgan et al. 1999). For anyone interested in running economy it is worthwhile to read the collection of papers from a symposium on this topic which was introduced by Morgan (1992).

More recently McCann and Adams (2003) reported on whether differences in running economy among 36 children, 23 adolescents and 24 adults can be explained by differences in resting metabolism, mass, and stature. In their study they used a dimensionless index called the size independent cost (SIC), which was defined as the net oxygen cost to move a mass of 1 kg a distance equal to stature. They concluded that when resting metabolism and the dimensional effects of mass and stature are controlled, the running economy of adolescents is greater than in children and adults, which are similar. Therefore, differences in oxygen cost of running among children, adolescents, and adults do not solely reflect qualitative differences in running performance.

There are very few studies in the literature which have tracked changes in running economy on a longitudinal basis. One such study by Welsman and Armstrong (2000) monitored longitudinal changes in young people's submaximal oxygen uptake responses during horizontal treadmill running at 8 $km.h^{-1}$. The 236 participants (118 boys, 118 girls) were aged 11.2 ± 0.4 years (mean $\pm$ s) at the onset of the study. Submaximal $\dot{V}O_2$, peak $\dot{V}O_2$ and anthropometry were recorded annually for 3 consecutive years. Their results confirmed that the conventional ratio standard $ml.kg^{-1}.min^{-1}$ does not adequately describe the relationship between body mass and submaximal $\dot{V}O_2$ during the period of growth studied. The effects of maturity and age were non-significant, but girls consumed significantly less $\dot{V}O_2$ than boys running. Submaximal $\dot{V}O_2$ responses were explained predominantly by changes in body mass and skinfold thicknesses, with no additional maturity-related increments. However, when differences in body mass and skinfolds were controlled for, a difference in submaximal $\dot{V}O_2$ remained between the sexes, with girls becoming increasingly more economical with age.

7.6 EFFICIENCY

7.6.1 Introduction

Efficiency is defined as:

$$\% \text{ Efficiency} = \frac{\text{Output}}{\text{Input}} \times 100$$

In order to produce an efficiency ratio, both the numerator and the denominator have to be measured. With regard to activities such as walking, running and load carriage, there are several definitions of efficiency, which are based on different forms of numerator and denominator in the efficiency equation (Whipp and Wasserman 1969; Gaesser and Brooks 1975). However, the numerator is always based on some measure of work done (either internal, external or both) and the denominator is based on some measure of metabolic rate (oxygen uptake).

These efficiency ratios are defined as:

Gross efficiency

$$\% \text{Efficiency} = \frac{\text{Work accomplished} \times 100}{\text{Energy expended}}$$

$$= \frac{W \times 100}{E}$$

Net efficiency

$$\% \text{Efficiency} = \frac{\text{Work accomplished} \times 100}{\text{Energy expended above}}{\text{than at rest}}$$

$$= \frac{W \times 100}{E - e}$$

Apparent or work efficiency

$$\% \text{Efficiency} = \frac{\text{Work accomplished} \times 100}{\text{Energy expended above}}{\text{unloaded}}$$

$$= \frac{W \times 100}{EL - EU}$$

Delta efficiency

$$\% \text{Efficiency} = \frac{\text{Delta work accomplished}}{\text{Delta energy expended}}$$

$$= \frac{DW \times 100}{DE}$$

where: W = caloric equivalent of mechanical work done
E = gross caloric output
e = resting caloric output

EL = caloric output loaded condition
EU = caloric output unloaded condition
DW = caloric equivalent of increment in work performed above previous work-rate
DE = increment in caloric output above that at previous work-rate.

These definitions of efficiency are not a complete set and have received criticism by several authors (e.g. Stainsby *et al.* 1980; Cavanagh and Kram 1985).

Muscle efficiency is the efficiency of the conversion of chemical energy into mechanical energy at the cross-bridges and is based on phosphorylative coupling and contraction coupling, which are essentially linked in series. Phosphorylative coupling efficiency, which is defined as:

$$\frac{\text{Free energy conserved as ATP}}{\text{Free energy of oxidized food}} \times 100$$

has been estimated to be between 40% and 60% (Krebs and Kornberg 1957). Contraction coupling, the conversion of energy stored as phosphates into tension in the muscle is of the order of 50% efficient, giving an overall theoretical maximum muscle efficiency of 30% (Whipp and Wasserman 1969; Wilkie 1974; Gaesser and Brooks 1975). Given a maximum value of only 30% for muscle efficiency, it is of interest to examine why gross efficiency values quoted in the literature for activities such as running are often considerably higher, and can even exceed 100% using certain forms of calculation in the estimation of mechanical work done (Norman *et al.* 1976).

Measures of whole-body efficiency or implied changes based on the different $\dot{V}O_2$ responses of children and adults to unloaded running (Davies 1980) do not indicate the efficiency of muscle. The different definitions of efficiency quoted above are therefore important when trying to compare values from various sources.

The efficiency experiment, which will be described in detail, is that originally proposed

by Lloyd and Zacks (1972). It was designed to measure the mechanical efficiency of running against a horizontal impeding force.

7.6.2 Methodology

The problem of accurately measuring external work in horizontal running was overcome, to a large extent, by Lloyd and Zacks (1972) who reported an experimental procedure in which they used a quantifiable external workload, in the form of a horizontal impeding force, on adult subjects running on the treadmill. Loaded running efficiency (LRE) was then calculated for a given running speed from the linear relationship between metabolic rate (oxygen uptake) and external work rate. The value of LRE is therefore consistent with apparent or work efficiency as defined by Whipp and Wasserman (1969). This method was also used by Cooke *et al.* (1991) to test the hypothesis that there are differences in LRE between children and adults.

(a) Protocol
The protocol and procedures for the LRE experiment are described in detail in Section 7.11.

7.6.3 Results

The results presented here are from a comparison of LRE values between a group of well-trained boys and men (Cooke *et al.* 1991). Figure 7.5 shows that no significant differences were found between the two groups in terms of LRE and the effects of speed. The mean LRE was 43.8% for the boys and 42.9% for the men.

7.6.4 Discussion

The major finding from the horizontal impeding force experiment on boys and men is that there is no significant difference between the LRE values. The mean LRE values quoted in the results fall between the small number of values published in the literature (36%, Lloyd

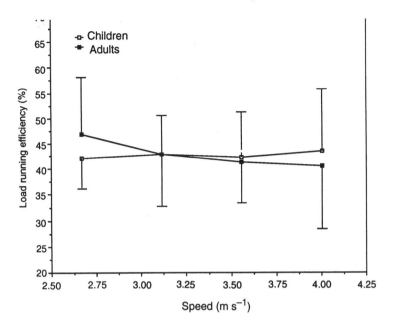

Figure 7.5 Loaded running efficiency values (means ± SD) for two groups of well-trained male runners: eight boys and eight men (Cooke *et al.* 1991).

and Zacks 1972; 39.1%, Zacks 1973; 53.8%, Asmussen and Bonde-Peterson 1974). These data support the hypothesis that there is no significant difference in efficiency between children and adults in the performance of external work.

Measures of mechanical efficiency for other forms of ergometry, such as the cycle or the step are necessary for the estimation of energy expenditure from mechanical work done when $\dot{V}O_2$ is not measured. For example, such values form the basis of the Åstrand–Ryhming (1954) nomogram, when only the mechanical work done is known. Oxygen uptake is estimated from the work performed in stepping or cycling, which together with the heart rate response can be used to estimate $\dot{V}O_{2max}$. A description of how to measure mechanical efficiency in both stepping and cycle ergometry is given in Section 7.12.

7.7 LOAD CARRIAGE

7.7.1 Effects on economy

Load carriage is an activity that provides an appropriate focus for the study of economy, including the need to consider energy expenditure, posture and kinematics. Load carriage is of interest from both an occupational and recreational perspective, where relatively heavy loads are carried for prolonged periods of time. The physiology of load carriage has been extensively studied, with the effect of the position of the carried load on energy expenditure receiving particular attention.

Carrying loads on the head is a common method of load carriage in both Africa and Asia (Datta and Ramanathan 1970; Maloiy *et al.*, 1986). Maloiy *et al.* (1986) found that African women could carry loads of up to 20% body weight with no increase in energy cost and that thereafter oxygen uptake rose proportionately with added load (i.e. an added load of 30% body weight produced a 10% increase in oxygen uptake, an added load of

40% body weight produced an increase in oxygen uptake of 20%).

It would seem then that the energy cost of carrying loads is not fixed but can be affected by the position of the load. This fact may have implications for different load carriage systems. Again many comparative studies have been undertaken. Datta and Ramanathan (1971) compared seven modes of carrying loads. The results indicated the best economy for a double pack system, where the load was shared between the back and front of the trunk. The order in terms of energy cost from lowest to highest was: double pack, load carried on basket on head, rucksack, load supported by strap on forehead, rice bag, yoke and finally load in canvas bags carried by hands. The oxygen uptake associated with the double pack was significantly lower than that associated with all of the other methods except for the load carried in a basket on the head. Legg and Mahanty (1985) compared five modes of carrying loads close to the trunk. No significant differences were found between any of the load carriage systems, but there was a consistent trend for the double pack to be associated with the lowest physiological cost. Lloyd and Cooke (2000) also observed that the economy of level and inclined walking was greater when wearing a rucksack which distributed the weight around the front and back of the trunk, compared to a traditional rucksack.

Kirk and Schneider (1992) compared the performance of internal and external frame packs. The results indicated no significant difference in economy between the two packs, although there was a consistent trend for the internal frame pack to elicit lower oxygen uptake values than the external frame pack. The postulated advantage for the internal frame pack is that the load can be carried closer to the body.

7.7.2 Effects on stride pattern

The majority of previous studies relating to the kinematics of load carriage have been concerned with alterations to stride length and frequency. Theoretically, changes in stride length-stride frequency associated with acute responses to load carriage, may lead to an increased energy cost, therefore changing both economy and efficiency. However, the studies reported all deal with acute perturbations to the walking gait. The effect of chronic changes are less well known, but given the long-term changes in stride length-stride frequency achieved by athletes it is possible that adaptation may take place.

There is no consensus concerning the effect of load carriage on stride length to stride frequency. Martin and Nelson (1986) observed an increase in stride frequency, 2% for men and a 5% for women, when carrying a load of 36 kg, made up of military clothing, waist belt and rucksack, at 6.34 km.h^{-1}. Cooke et al. (1991) reported a significant difference in stride frequency when loads of 5% and 10% body weight were carried around the trunk. The magnitudes of the increases were 1.5% and 5% above the unloaded condition. Thorstensson (1986) found significant differences in stride frequency for both boys and men when carrying a load of 10% body weight around the trunk at 10 km.h^{-1} for the boys and 11 km.h^{-1} for the men. The percentage increases were 1.5% and 1.9% for the men and boys respectively. Kram et al. (1987) reported a significant increase in stride frequency when 60% body weight was carried at 10.8 km.h^{-1} using a method in which the load is attached to either end of a bamboo pole, which is then carried across the shoulders. They found no significant difference in stride frequency when the same load was carried in a traditional rucksack. A number of other studies, covering a wide range of loading conditions and speeds, have reported no significant changes in stride frequency. These include Robertson et al. (1982) (loads of 0–15% body weight carried at speeds between 3.2 and 8.1 km h^{-1}), Maloiy et al. (1986) (34 kg carried on the head) and Kinoshita (1985) (loads of 20% and 40% body weight carried at 4.5 km h^{-1} in a traditional rucksack and a double pack system).

7.7.3 Effects on trunk angle

It would seem that the alterations to stride length to stride frequency elicited by load carriage are relatively small and, on their own, unlikely to have a significant effect on energy cost. However, it is possible that these small alterations may either contribute to, or combine with, changes in other variables and thus have a significant effect on the economy of load carriage. One of the most important changes in kinematics associated with load carriage is an alteration in trunk angle. This is an aspect of load carriage that has received scant attention.

Kinoshita (1985) found that both back and front/back load carriage systems were associated with increased forward lean but that the forward lean associated with the back system, (11°), was considerably greater than for the double pack system. Bloom and Woodhull-McNeal (1987) observed increased forward lean while standing for both an internal and an external frame pack loaded with 27% body weight, but did not quantify it. Martin and Nelson (1986) showed that forward lean increased when a load was carried on the back but not when distributed about the waist. When carrying a total of 36 kg (19 kg on the back) forward lean was increased by approximately 10°. Gordon et al. (1983) also noted that forward lean increased with the addition of load, but did not quantify this.

Another form of measurement that has been used to make comparisons between different load carriage systems, loads, speeds and gradients is the extra load index (ELI) (Taylor et al. 1980). This is a measure of relative economy, which is calculated by dividing the oxygen consumption when carrying a load (ml.kg total mass^{-1}min^{-1}) by the oxygen consumption for no load (ml kg body mass^{-1}.min^{-1}). An ELI of 1 indicates that the energy cost of carrying 1 kg of extra load is the same as that of 1 kg of live mass; a value >1 indicates a reduction in the economy of load carriage; a value <1 indicates an increased economy. Using this technique, the results of Lloyd and Cooke (2000) suggested that the energy cost of carrying a kilogram of extra load is greater than that of carrying a kilogram of live mass.

7.7.4 Methodology

Numerous protocols have been used to assess the effects of load carriage on economy and efficiency. Various treadmill walking and running speeds and both uphill and downhill gradients have been used to compare a variety of different forms of load carriage. The methodology for assessing the effects of load carriage on economy is very similar to that described for running economy in Section 7.5. The protocols typically consist of steady-state exercise, walking or running at each speed and gradient combination for a period of a minimum of 3 minutes.

a) Protocol

A protocol for investigating the effects of load carriage on efficiency is described in detail in Section 7.11.

The experimental protocol and results presented here are based on the work of Lloyd and Cooke (2000). The protocol involved walking downhill at a speed of 3 km h^{-1} for 3 min at gradients of 27%, 22%, 17%, 12% and 5% . Subjects were then given a rest of 20 minutes, after which they walked uphill at a speed of 3 km h^{-1} for 3 minutes at gradients of 0%, 5%, 10%, 15% and 20%. Expired air was collected throughout both the downhill and uphill sections. The protocol was completed three times. On each occasion the subjects completed one of three conditions in randomized order: unloaded, loaded with a traditional rucksack, and loaded with a rucksack that incorporated front pockets. This distributed the load around the front and back of the trunk. The mass of both 65 litre packs and contents was 25.6 kg. All the treadmill tests were filmed with a video camera.

7.7.5 Results

a) Economy

Statistical analysis (3×10 repeated measures of analysis of variance (ANOVA)) of the data indicated that unloaded walking requiring a significantly lower ($P < 0.05$) $\dot{V}O_2$ than either of the loaded conditions. On average the extra oxygen cost, above that for unloaded walking, associated with the front and back loading rucksack was 5.4 ml.kg^{-1}min^{-1} (45.1%), whilst that associated with the traditional rucksack was 6.3 ml.kg^{-1}min^{-1} (52.8%). The $\dot{V}O_2$ was also about 8% lower ($P < 0.05$) for the front and back loading rucksack on the uphill gradients (Figure 7.6)

b) Stride length

Mean values of stride length (m) and percentage changes from the unloaded condition at each gradient are shown in Table 7.4. Changes in stride length were greater in the loaded condition ($P < 0.05$). Across the whole protocol, the traditional rucksack and the front and back loading rucksack were associated with, on average, 3.2 cm (3%) and 5.1 cm (5%) shorter stride lengths, respectively, although there was no significant difference ($P > 0.05$) in stride length for the two conditions. The reduction in stride length associated with both rucksacks was slightly more marked during the uphill section than the downhill section.

c) Trunk angle

The increase in forward lean was greater whilst wearing the traditional rucksack when standing still and walking ($P < 0.001$). The increases amounted to about 4° and 14° for the front and back loading and traditional rucksacks, respectively. The extra forward lean induced by traditional rucksack also tended to increase as the slope increased, whereas it remained relatively constant in the front and back loaded condition.

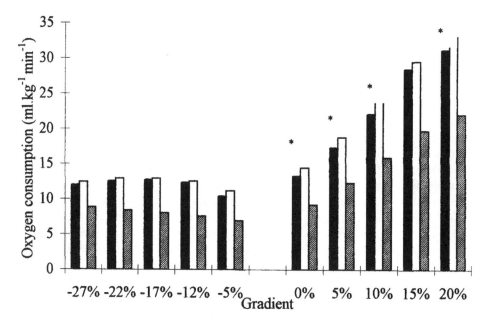

Figure 7.6 Oxygen uptake values (means + SD) for walking with rucksack with front and back pockets (■), traditional rucksack (□) and unloaded conditions (▨) (* denotes P < 0.05 between the two rucksacks).

Table 7.4. Mean (±s) stride length (m) and mean (±s) percentage change from the unloaded condition at each gradient

		-27%	-22%	-17%	-12%	- 5%	0%	5%	10%	15%	20%
AARN	Mean (±s)	0.86	0.88	0.89	0.95	1.04	1.12	1.12	1.14	1.11	1.08
		0.07	0.06	0.07	0.08	0.08	0.08	0.09	0.12	0.11	0.11
	Mean (±s)	-5.4	-5.4	-5.8	-4.0	0.1	0.5	-5.7	-5.0	-5.7	-7.8
	%Change	5.8	5.4	5.9	5.8	4.6	4.2	5.5	4.1	5.7	5.6
Traditional	Mean (±s)	0.86	0.89	0.91	0.99	1.06	1.14	1.17	1.15	1.12	1.08
		0.07	0.07	0.06	0.12	0.10	0.11	0.15	0.14	0.13	0.13
	Mean (±s)	-5.1	-4.3	-3.7	-0.4	1.9	1.6	-2.0	-3.6	-4.8	-7.6
	%Change	6.5	4.5	4.4	4.8	7.1	7.2	6.0	8.3	8.0	5.9
Unloaded	Mean (±s)	0.91	0.93	0.95	0.99	1.04	1.12	1.19	1.20	1.18	1.18
		0.07	0.08	0.08	0.11	0.11	0.09	0.13	0.13	0.13	0.13

7.8 PRACTICAL 1: DIRECT DETERMINATION OF $\dot{V}O_{2MAX}$ USING A DISCONTINUOUS CYCLE ERGOMETER PROTOCOL

7.8.1 Protocol

1   Warm-up: cycle for 3 minutes at 50 W for females or 100 W for males.
2   Rest: 2 minutes,
3   Initial work rate: 50–150 W for females, 100–200 W for males, depending on type of subject, e.g. lighter less active subjects would be set lower work rates (heart rate response during warm up is a good guide to selection of appropriate work rate). Record heart rate every 30 s. Collect expired air for last 30 s of work rate.
4   Rest: 3 minutes (during which time team members can analyze expired air).
5   Increase work-rate by 50 W and repeat stages 3 and 4 of the protocol.
6   At higher workloads increments of 25 W may be used. If the subject cannot complete a 3 minutes workload then a gas collection can be made on a signal from the subject (minimum 30 s, preferably 1 minute).
7   Recovery: at the end of the test the subject should continue to pedal gently at a low work rate of the order of 25–50 W.

The subject should be closely monitored at all times, both during the test and recovery, since the probability of some sort of cardiac episode occurring is higher at exercise intensities above 80% of age-related maximum heart rate and during the 20 min or so following the cessation of the test. The subject may need verbal encouragement to complete the later stages of the test in order to attain a maximal oxygen consumption.

Although heart rate can be monitored effectively by radio telemetry, it is preferable to use chest electrodes linked to an oscilloscope and/or chart recorder. This enables the shape of the electrocardiogram (ECG) to be observed. In the event of a gross abnormality or arrhythmia occurring, the test can be stopped and the hard copy of the ECG examined by a qualified person. Clearly the more sophisticated the ECG equipment used, the more objective will be the ECG analysis. It is possible to see arrhythmias such as ventricular ectopics with a simple three-lead system, which is available in most laboratories.

7.8.2 Procedures

The procedures for the cycle ergometer protocol are as described, but they can be generalized in most cases to any direct determination of $\dot{V}O_{2max}$ using the Douglas bag technique.

1   The procedures and protocol should be explained to the subject, and should include a statement that he or she can stop the test at any time.
2   The subject should sign an informed consent form.
3   The name, age and sex of the subject should be recorded.
4   The stature (m) and body mass (kg) of the subject should be measured.
5   The heart rate measuring device or ECG electrodes should be attached and a check made that a good signal is being recorded or displayed.
6   The handlebar and saddle positions should be adjusted to suit the size of the subject, especially as subjects can become uncomfortable during the later stages of the test, resulting in the premature cessation of the test. If the saddle is too low, the subject may experience undue fatigue in the quadriceps muscles and possibly pain in the knee joint. If the saddle is too high, the subject will have to raise and lower his/her left and right hips repeatedly in order to maintain effective contact with the pedals. The recommended position is obtained by placing the middle of the foot on the pedal at the bottom of its travel. If the saddle height is correct the leg will be very slightly flexed. More sophisticated guidelines are available in the literature, but the simple procedure described here works well in most cases. Competitive cyclists will have their own measures for obtaining an optimal saddle height and handlebar position. They also prefer their own bicycles mounted on turbo-trainers. More sophisticated examples, such as the King Cycle™ have gained wide acceptance in exercise physiology laboratories.
7   The respiratory value and mouthpiece should be connected to allow room air to be inspired and then expired into the Douglas bag.
8   The nose clip should be placed on the subject's nose so that all the expired air passes into the Douglas bag.
9   The warm-up and the test proper should be completed according to the protocol described above.

With respect to the control of cycle ergometers, the following points should be considered.

a) All cycle ergometers should be calibrated regularly according to the manufacturers' instructions.
b) Recommended pedalling frequencies for mechanically braked cycle ergometers are traditionally of the order of 50–60 rev min⁻¹. Although a frequency of 60 rev min⁻¹ is comfortable and efficient for low work-rates, it is recommended that the pedal frequency be increased above work-rates of the order of 200 W to 70–80 rev min⁻¹. This will decrease the force required per pedal revolution, thus decreasing the strength component of the pedalling action and the probability of cessation of the test due to fatigue in the quadriceps .
c) It is always important to inform the subject in advance of alterations in work rate in continuous protocols. This is especially important in the use of electronically braked cycle ergometers, which automatically alter the resistance at the pedals

to accommodate changes in pedalling frequency, thus keeping the power output constant. A tired subject pedalling at 200 W with an unexpected increase of 50 W who is already pedalling at the lower end of the pedalling frequency range (approximately 50 rev min^{-1}) may well let the cadence drop still further with the increase in load. This will result in a further increase in resistance offered at the pedals. The result could then be that the subject terminates the test, so a warning of pending increases in workload should always be given, together with encouragement to pedal faster to accommodate the increase in work-rate on an electronically braked cycle ergometer.

d) Mechanically braked cycle ergometers of the type used in most laboratories require the subject to pedal at a constant frequency in order to maintain a constant power output. To help maintain a constant pedalling frequency the subject may pedal in time to a metronome and/or use a digital display of pedalling frequency, which is now fitted to most new cycle ergometers. Another alternative is to mount small mechanical cams or opto-electric devices on the flywheel to count the number of revolutions during each workload. Use of these suggestions should help ensure that quantification of external power output is as objective as possible.

7.8.3 Calculations

Gas analysis, volume measurement, $\dot{V}O_2$, $\dot{V}CO_2$ and RER calculations should be performed in accordance with the procedures outlined in Chapter 6 of this text.

7.8.4 Results

Table 7.3 shows a completed proforma for the discontinuous cycle ergometer test described above.

Some questions to consider for the measurement of maximum oxygen uptake:

1   What day to day variability might you expect in repeated measures of maximum oxygen uptake and what might be the factors that contribute to this variability?

2   What are the ethical implications and methodological limitations of using direct measurements of maximal oxygen uptake on subjects who are not well accustomed to strenuous exertion?

3   What are the apparent contradictions in considering the general principles of testing for maximal oxygen uptake, such as using a large muscle mass in a rhythmic movement pattern, and testing sports performers from a particular sport?

4   Should maximal oxygen uptake be considered the criterion 'gold standard' measure of aerobic or endurance fitness?

5   What are the practical and theoretical factors that might effect whether a plateau in oxygen consumption is measurable or not?

7.9 PRACTICAL 2: MEASUREMENT OF RUNNING ECONOMY

7.9.1 Protocol

The protocol outlined here is recommended by The British Association of Sport and Exercise Sciences (1992). Where the $\dot{V}O_{2max}$ of the subject is known, an appropriate generalized equation relating $\dot{V}O_2$ to running speed can be used to predict the running speeds that should elicit 50–90% of $\dot{V}O_{2max}$. For example, PE Students (British Association of Sport Sciences, 1992):

Males $n = 58$ $Y = 11.6 \times + 0.72$
Females $n = 44$ $Y = 10.7 \times + 3.30$
where: $Y = \dot{V}O_2$ (ml kg^{-1} min^{-1}) and $\times$ = running speed (m s^{-1})

or those cited in Section 7.5.3. However, the selection of the running speeds should take into account the state of training of the subjects since only well-conditioned athletes can cope with running speeds that elicit 90% of $\dot{V}O_{2max}$.

1   Warm-up: no warm up other than gentle jogging and stretching is required since the first workload represents a running speed approximately equivalent to 60% $\dot{V}O_{2max}$. Ideally, naïve subjects should be habituated to treadmill running on a previous occasion so $\dot{V}O_2$ values will be a true reflection of running economy.

2   Test: the protocol consists of 16 minutes of running on a level treadmill during which running speed is increased every 4 minutes. For children aged less than 15 years, a 3-minute interval is recommended.

3   Expired air should be collected for the 4th, 8th 12th and 16th minute for adults and for the 3rd, 6th, 9th and 12th minute for children.

7.9.2 Data collection, gas analysis and calculations

Follow the procedures outlined in Chapter 6 for the collection and analysis of expired air using the Douglas bag technique, and the calculation of oxygen uptake. Alternatively an automated gas analysis system can be used to collect and analyze the expired air (as in Figure 6.3).

7.9.3 Results

The results from the experiment should be plotted with oxygen uptake on the y axis and running speed on the x axis. The method of least squares can then be used to establish the extent to which the data conform to the expected linear relationship, with the production of a linear regression equation, correlation coefficient (r) and coefficient of determination (r^2 = variance accounted for) (see Nevill and Atkinson 2009). Group data can then be compared using appropriate statistical techniques, such as ANOVA or ANCOVA. Examples of group comparisons for both equations and graphs appear in Sections 7.5.3 and 7.5.4.

Some questions to consider on running economy and related areas of study include:

1   Is it appropriate to be totally confident in extrapolating forwards or backwards

using an individual subject's equation that allows you to predict oxygen uptake from running speed?

2   What applications might make use of extrapolations from such equations?

3   What happens to the oxygen uptake-speed relationship when the subject walks instead of runs?

7.10 PRACTICAL 3: COMBINED MEASUREMENT OF RUNNING ECONOMY, LACTATE THRESHOLD AND TURNPOINT, AND $\dot{V}O_{2MAX}$

7.10.1 Protocol

This treadmill test protocol is one of the tests adopted for use in the physiological evaluation of middle-distance and long-distance runners by UK athletics (Jones 2007). It combines, normally in two parts, the measurement of running economy, lactate threshold and turnpoint, and $\dot{V}O_{2max}$ in the same test, taking no more than 1 hour including, a 15 minute recovery between part 1 and 2.

Part 1

This is a multi-stage incremental test for the measurement of oxygen uptake, heart rate, and blood lactate responses to a range of running speeds and to establish heart rate training zones.

1   Take a resting blood lactate sample

2   Athlete completes their warm up

3   Heart rate or ECG monitor fitted/connected

4   Set the treadmill gradient at 1% (Jones and Doust 1996)

5   Test starts as treadmill speed increased gradually to first stage:

World class performance male	4.18 m s^{-1} (15.0 km h^{-1})
World class performance female	3.61 m s^{-1} (13.0 km h^{-1})
World class potential male	3.89 m s^{-1} (14.0 km h^{-1})
World class potential female	3.33 m s^{-1} (12.0 km h^{-1})
Regional junior male	3.61 m s^{-1} (13.0 km h^{-1})
Regional junior female	3.06 m s^{-1} (11.0 km h^{-1})

6   Each stage is 3 minutes in duration and each increment in speed is 0.28 m s^{-1} (1.0 km h^{-1})

7   Athletes should complete between 5 and 9 stages, inclusively.

8   After 90 s of each stage the athlete should be handed a mouthpiece and nose clip, or face mask, and expired air should be collected either in a Douglas bag using standard procedures, or using an automated gas analysis system.

9   The average heart rate during the last 30 s of each stage should be recorded.

10 At the end of the stage the athlete uses the hand rails to support his/her weight and move the legs astride the treadmill belt.

11 A fingertip blood sample should then be taken as quickly as possible (no more than 30 s) using standard procedures as described in Chapter 4 (Maughan *et al.* 2009).

12 When the blood sample has been taken the athlete should use the hand rails

to resume running on the treadmill belt, at which point the speed should be increased by 0.28 ms^{-1} (1.0 kmh^{-1}) and the clocks reset to record the next 3-minute stage.

13 This part of the test should be stopped when the athlete feels they could only complete one more 3-minute stage. Their heart rate will usually be about 5–10 beats min^{-1} away from their maximum and blood lactate concentration will be greater than 4 mM.

14 For athletes who compete in 10 km or further, where precise $\dot{V}O_{2max}$ determination is less crucial, this test can be continued to exhaustion. The $\dot{V}O_{2max}$ achieved in the final stage is usually within 5% of the value measured in a more traditional $\dot{V}O_{2max}$ test. Also the speed increments can be halved for these longer distance athletes to give better resolution in the determination of speeds at lactate threshold and turnpoint.

15 On completion of part 1 the athletes should be allowed about 15 minutes of self-paced active recovery on the treadmill or round the laboratory, if room allows.

Part 2

This part of the test is used to measure $\dot{V}O_{2max}$.

1   The athlete should be asked to give a maximal effort and keep going for as long as possible.

2   Speed is set at 0.56 m.s^{-1} (2 km h^{-1}) less than the speed at the end of part 1 and remains the same throughout part 2 of the test.

3   The gradient is set at 1%.

4   The athlete starts the test by moving steadily up to the desired speed over a 1- to 2-minute period.

5   When the start speed is reached the clocks are reset and timing begins again.

6   Treadmill gradient is increased by 1% every minute.

7   This part of the test will normally last between 5 and 10 minutes.

8   The athlete runs for the first 3 minutes without mouthpiece and noseclip or mask, but once the athlete has them in place they remain until the end of the test. A timed gas collection of at least 30 s in the last 45 s of each minute stage should be made using a Douglas bag, or the whole of the remainder of the test can be recoded using an automated gas analysis system.

A fingertip blood sample should be taken immediately post-exercise and then at 1, 3, 5, 7 and 10 minutes of recovery, if peak blood lactate concentration is required.

The data for heart rate and blood lactate response to stage 1 of the protocol can be plotted against running speed to prescribe training heart rate zones based on lactate threshold and turnpoint indices. Full details of all the tests and measurements used in the assessment of middle-distance and long-distance runners for the UK athletics can be found in Jones (2007).

7.10.2 Procedures

Follow the procedures outlined in Chapter 6 for the collection and analysis of expired air using the Douglas bag technique, and the calculation of oxygen uptake. Alternatively an automated gas analysis system can be used to collect and analyze the expired air (as in Figure 6.3). Follow the procedures in Chapter 4 for the collection and analysis of fingertip blood samples.

7.10.3 Results

The running economy results can be treated in the same way as for the protocol for the separate assessment of running economy in Section 7.9. The blood lactate and heart rate data can be treated in the same way as for the graph shown in Figure 10.10 (Jones *et al.* 2009, Chapter 10), which facilitates identification of training zones based on heart rate and blood lactate concentration. The interpretation of the $\dot{V}O_{2max}$ data can be performed using the same criteria as outlined in Section 7.3.2.

A question to consider in terms of the use of this protocol is: what are the strengths and weaknesses of using this combined protocol versus the separate protocols for the assessment of each measurement?

7.11 PRACTICAL 4: MEASUREMENT OF LOADED RUNNING EFFICIENCY

7.11.1 Protocol

For each running speed the subject should run unloaded for 3 minutes. A horizontal impeding force is then exerted via weights attached to the subject by a cord running over a pulley (Figure 7.7). A total of three increasing loads can then be added to the system, one every 3 minutes (a total of 12 minutes continuous running including the 3 minutes unloaded), followed by 5 minutes rest. Weights should be individually selected such that the maximum external load applied to the system does not elicit a $\dot{V}O_2$ greater than 85% of $\dot{V}O_{2max}$ in well-trained subjects. (This value would have to be adjusted down for less active individuals as it is important that the energy expenditure is derived from aerobic metabolism and therefore reflected in the measured $\dot{V}O_2$ values.) Even increments in $\dot{V}O_2$ can be achieved by predicting the increase in $\dot{V}O_2$ per kilogram of mass added to the pulley, on the basis of a mean LRE value from the literature of approximately 40%. Running speeds and weight increments can then be individually tailored to the subject in terms of $\dot{V}O_{2max}$ and running economy. Where subjects represent a homogeneous sample it is better in terms of experimental design to have all subjects run at the same speeds with the same increments. Typical values for weights to be added to the pulley would be 1 kg, 2 kg and 3 kg for adults and 0.5 kg, 1 kg and 1.5 kg for children.

7.11.2 Procedures

Collection and analysis of expired air can be performed either according to the procedures outlined for the Douglas bag technique in Chapter 6, or using an automated gas analysis system. The data presented in Figure 7.5 and discussed in section 7.6.4 were collected using an Oxycon 4 system (Mijnhardt, The Netherlands). A full description of the experimental procedures can be found in Cooke *et al.* (1991).

7.11.3 Calculation of LRE

Metabolic work-rate is calculated from steady-state $\dot{V}O_2$ for each load condition. A value of 20.9 kJ (5.0 kcal min^{-1}, 348.8 W) can be used as the energy equivalent for one

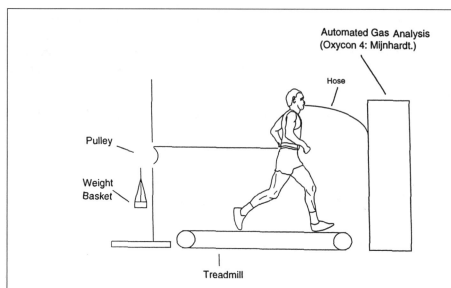

Figure 7.7 A diagram of the horizontal impeding force experiment used to calculate loaded running efficiency (Lloyd and Zacks 1972).

litre of oxygen since this will cause no more than a 4% variation based on observed respiratory exchange ratios.

External work rate is calculated by the product of the force exerted by the weight over the pulley and the distance moved per unit of time by the treadmill belt. A linear regression equation is then fitted to the data, with metabolic rate as the dependent variable and external work rate as the independent variable. Apparent efficiency of running against a horizontal load, or LRE is then calculated for each speed of running by taking the inverse of the slope of the regression equation, as shown in Figure 7.7

For example, given the raw data which form the basis for Figure 7.7, the calculations are as follows.

Running speed constant at 11.2 km h^{-1} (11.2 × 1000//600/60 = 3.11 m s^{-1})

The calculation of metabolic work rate (MWR) in watts is given by:

MWR (W) $\dot{V}O_2$ (l min^{-1}) × 348.8
where: $\dot{V}O_2$= measured oxygen uptake for each load condition
= 20.9 kJ = 348.8 W = 5 kcal min^{-1} = 1 litre of oxygen

The calculation of external work-rate (EWR) in watts is given by:

EWR (W) = M (kg) × g (m s^{-2}) × D (m s^{-1})
where: M is mass applied to runner acting over pulley, g is acceleration due to gravity, D is distance moved by treadmill belt in 1 s = velocity of treadmill (m s^{-1})

Given the following oxygen uptake values for each of four external loads measured as mass applied to the pulley the metabolic work-rate and external work-rate can be calculated according to the formulae above:

Mass on pulley (kg)	EWR (W)	$\dot{V}O_2$ ($1\ min^{-1}$)	MWR (W)
0	0	2.01	699.4
1	30.51	2.22	772.6
2	61.02	2.43	845.8
3	91.53	2.63	919.1

The EWR and MWR values are plotted in Figure 7.8, which also shows the linear regression equation fitted by the method of least squares. Given that EWR is the independent variable it has to be plotted on the x axis, and the dependent variable, MWR, is plotted on the y axis. Loaded running efficiency expressed as a percentage is therefore given by the reciprocal of the gradient of the linear regression equation multiplied by 100:

% Loaded running efficiency = $1/2.4 \pm 100 = 41.8$ %

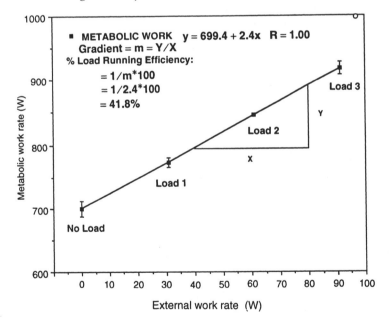

Figure 7.8 Calculation of loaded running efficiency (LRE) in the horizontal impeding force experiment for a subject running at 11.2 km h[-1]. Values are means ± SD for data collected in two experiments completed by the same subject on different days (Cooke *et al.* 1991)

Some questions to consider:

1   What are the limitations involved in the measurement of loaded running efficiency?
2   The example discussed in the text for this Practical is concerned with a comparison of children and adults. What other applications and research questions can this procedure be used to investigate?

7.11.4 Results

The results can be reported in terms of individual LRE values for each speed of running, and combined in a variety of ways depending on the aim of the experiment (e.g. either to investigate the effects of running speed on LRE or to compare the apparent efficiency of horizontal treadmill running against other forms of ergometry).

7.12 PRACTICAL 5: MEASUREMENT OF THE EFFICIENCY OF CYCLING AND STEPPING

7.12.1 Cycle ergometry

In mechanical cycle ergometry the external power output (W) or mechanical work rate is quantified as the product of the frictional force (N) or resistance applied to the flywheel and the distance travelled (m) by one point on the circumference of the flywheel, which gives the work done (J), divided by the time to do the work (s):

$$\text{External power output (W)} = \frac{\text{Force (N)} \times \text{Distance (m)}}{\text{Time (s)}}$$

Most cycle ergometers allow the work-rate to be set in watts, whether they are mechanically or electronically braked.

As with the LRE experiment metabolic work-rate is calculated from steady-state $\dot{V}O_2$:

$$\text{Metabolic work-rate (W)} = (\dot{V}O_2 \, l \, min^{-1}) \times 348.8$$

A gross measure of efficiency can then be calculated by dividing the external power output by the metabolic power output:

$$\%\,\text{Gross efficiency} = \frac{[(\text{Force} \times \text{Distance}) \, \text{Time}]}{\dot{V}O_2 \, l \, min^{-1}) \times 348.8} \times 100$$

Net efficiency can be calculated by dividing the external power output by net metabolic power, the latter being obtained by subtracting an estimate of resting $\dot{V}O_2$ from the gross measured value (see Chapter 6). Provided that both the numerator and denominator are in the same units (Watts kJ min^{-1} or kcal min^{-1}) the correct ratio will be calculated and when multiplied by 100 will give percentage net efficiency.

7.12.2 Stepping

For stepping, the external work-rate (W) is calculated as a function of the vertical height that the centre of mass of the body is raised (m). This is estimated by multiplying the step height (m) by the number of complete step cycles performed. The total vertical height is then multiplied by the force (body weight (N)), and divided by the duration (s) of the stepping exercise:

$$\text{External power output (W)} = \frac{\text{Step height (m)} \times \text{No. steps} \times \text{Weight (N)}}{\text{Time (s)}}$$

The gross and net efficiency ratios can then be calculated using the external work-rate and metabolic work-rate as for cycle ergometry.

The net efficiency of stepping is of the order of 16% (Shephard *et al.* 1968).

7.12.3 Experimental procedures and protocols

Gross and net efficiency ratios can be calculated over the submaximal range of exercise intensities, provided that the energy demands of the exercise are matched by a steady-state of oxygen uptake. Efficiency values calculated for high intensity exercise, where anaerobic sources make a significant contribution to the energy demands, will be higher than expected since under such conditions oxygen uptake will not reflect the energy demands of the exercise.

For stepping on a double 'nine-inch' step (total vertical height 45 cm) the oxygen uptake can be estimated to be:

$$\dot{V}O_2(\text{ml kg}^{-1} \text{ min}^{-1}) = 1.34 \times n$$

where n = number of step cycles per minute.

For example stepping on a double step requires a six beat cadence. Therefore stepping to a metronome set at 120 beats per minute would result in the completion of 20 step cycles per minute, giving an estimated oxygen uptake of 26.8 ml kg^{-1} min^{-1}.

A suitable submaximal range of work-rates for the above step would consist of four by 3-minute work rates with metronome cadences set at 60, 90, 120 and 150 beats min^{-1}. Expired air can be collected during the third minute of each work-rate and analyzed according to the methods described in Chapter 6.

Although stepping is considered to be a simple, inexpensive form of ergometry, every effort must be made to ensure that the subject keeps in time with the metronome and that he/she stands up straight on a flat foot with full knee extension.

For cycle ergometry a suitable range of submaximal exercise intensities would consist of 50–150 W depending on the age, sex and condition of the subjects. As a guide, heart rate response should not exceed 85% of age-related maximum heart rate during a submaximal test. Traditionally a pedal frequency of 50 rev min^{-1} has been used in submaximal exercise tests using mechanically braked cycle ergometers. However, 60 rev min^{-1} is often a more comfortable pedalling frequency.

Shephard *et al.* (1968) showed that over a range of submaximal loads the mean net mechanical efficiency for stepping and cycle ergometry were 16% and 23% respectively.

7.12.4 Discussion

The values quoted from Shephard *et al.* (1968) represent group means for subjects performing repeated experiments in both stepping and cycling to a randomized design. There was more variability in stepping (coefficient of variation approximately 10%) than cycling (coefficient of variation approximately 7%). There was also some variation in mechanical efficiency values associated with loading.

Individual values for mechanical efficiency can be used as calibration factors for estimating oxygen uptake from work done, rather than having to use estimates from the literature. There are several experiments that can be conducted with either stepping or cycle ergometry to investigate variations in mechanical efficiency values. For example, the effects of pedalling frequency, stepping frequency, work rate, saddle height, single or double step, step height and leg length in relation to step height can all be investigated.

Consider the effects that the variability in efficiency across subjects might have on estimating energy expenditure for a given task, predicting fitness (e.g. maximum oxygen uptake) and predicting performance without reference to measures of economy, based on assumptions of constant mechanical efficiency.

7.13 PRACTICAL 6: THE EFFECTS OF LOAD CARRIAGE ON THE ECONOMY OF WALKING

7.13.1 Protocol

The experimental protocol involves walking at a speed of 3 km.h^{-1} for 3 min at each selected gradient. The gradients used in the study discussed above were downhill at 27%, 22%, 17%, 12% and 5%, which was completed first. Subjects were then given a rest of 20 minutes. After the rest subjects walked uphill at a speed of 3 km.h^{-1} for 3 minutes at gradients of 0%, 5%, 10%, 15% and 20%. This gives a total test time of 50 minutes (30 minutes walking and 20 minutes resting) per subject per load condition, but allows the data to be compared directly to the results presented above. In terms of a single practical, reasonable results could be obtained for one subject using one downhill gradient of 20%, level walking and one uphill gradient of 20%. For the purpose of comparing unloaded and loaded walking it is only necessary to use two conditions, one without a rucksack and one carrying a loaded rucksack. Clearly, different rucksacks, load carriage systems or loads can be used, but this would only be practical for project work. The Practical could also be adapted by looking at different walking speeds, or running with a daysack.

7.13.2 Measurements

Follow the procedures outlined in Chapter 6 for the collection and analysis of expired air using the Douglas bag technique, and the calculation of oxygen uptake. Alternatively use an automated gas analysis system, making sure that you calibrate either system carefully before you start your testing. If you are using an automated gas analysis system it is worthwhile ensuring that you include minute ventilation, breathing frequency and tidal volume in your configuration of the system as well as oxygen consumption and carbon dioxide production.

Although not essential for the comparison of economy between unloaded and loaded walking, it is also worthwhile timing a set number of stride cycles at each workload using a stopwatch to assess whether there is any difference in stride length and frequency between the two conditions. If you have a video camera available it is also worthwhile setting one up with the axis of the lens perpendicular to the plane of walking (about 5–6 m away from the side of the treadmill should suffice). This will facilitate measurement of the forward lean of the trunk (touch down, toe-off and mid-stance are good points for comparison) in both conditions, as well as allowing checks on the stride length and stride frequency calculations. Rating of perceived exertion and heart rate can also be recorded for each stage of the protocol.

7.13.3 Results

Draw a graph of the results for the following variables for every stage of the protocol for each of the two (or more) loading conditions (use mean and standard deviations if you have more than one subject): oxygen consumption, minute ventilation, breathing frequency, tidal volume, heart rate, stride length, stride frequency, stride length and forward lean. Use values from the Douglas bag collected in the third minute, or the last two 30-s values from the automated gas analysis system for expired air variables.

Calculate ELI values for your data and compare them with the mean values presented above.

Compare all of your results with those presented above and, more importantly, evaluate the differences between the results for the two loading conditions.

It may be worthwhile considering whether there are any associations between changes in certain variables with loading, which might suggest some explanation of some of the physiological effects of load carriage.

Consider the implications, in terms of different types of validity and reliability, for designing an appropriate protocol to be used in comparing different load carriage systems.

Some questions to consider:

1   What would you need to add to the experiment in order to measure the efficiency of different load carriage systems?
2   How might you go about doing this?

FURTHER READING

Books:

American College of Sports Medicine. (2006). *ACSM's Guidelines for Exercise Testing and Prescription (7th Edition)*. Lippincott Williams & Wilkins; Philadelphia, PA.Maud P. J. and Foster C. (2006) *Physiological Assessment of Human Fitness*, Human Kinetics; Champaign, IL.

McArdle W. D., Katch F. I. and Katch V. L. (2006) *Exercise Physiology, Energy Nutrition and Human Performance (6th Edition)*. Lippincott, Williams and Wilkins; Philadelphia, PA.

Winter E. M., Jones A. M., Davison R. C. R., Bromley P. D. and Mercer T. H. (eds) (2007) *Sport and Exercise Physiology Testing Guidelines*. The British Association of Sport and Exercise Sciences Guide, Volume **1**: Sport Testing. Routledge; Oxon.

REFERENCES

American College of Sports Medicine (2006) *ACSM's Guidelines for Exercise Testing and Prescription* (7th Edition). Lippincott, Williams and Wilkins; Philadelphia, PA.

Allied Dunbar National Fitness Survey (1992) *Main Findings*. Sports Council and Health Education Authority; London.

Altman P. L. and Dittmer D. S. (1968) *Metabolism*. FASBEB; Bethesda, MD.

Armstrong N. and Welsman J. (2001) Peak oxygen uptake in relation to growth and maturation in 11- to 17-year-old humans. *European Journal of Applied Physiology*; **85**: 546–51.

Asmussen E. and Bonde-Peterson F. (1974) Apparent efficiency and storage of elastic energy in human muscles during exercise. *Acta Physiologica Scandinavica*; **92**: 537–45.

Åstrand P. O. (1952) *Experimental Studies of Physical Working Capacity in Relation to Sex and Age*. Munksgaard; Copenhagen.

Åstrand P. O. and Ryhming I. (1954) A nomogram for the calculation of aerobic capacity (physical fitness) from pulse rate during submaximal work. *Journal of Applied Physiology*; **7** (**2**): 218–21.

Åstrand P. O., Rodahl K., Dahl H. A. and Stromme S. B. (2003) *Textbook of Work Physiology:Physiological Bases of Exercise (4th Edition)* Human Kinetics; Champaign, IL.

Barker A., Boreham C. A., Van Praagh E. and Rowlands A. V. (2009) Special considerations for assessing performance in young children. In: (R. G. Eston and T. Reilly, eds.) *Kinanthropometry Laboratory Manual (3rd Edition): Anthropometry (Chapter 8)*. Routledge; Oxon: pp 197–230.

Bar-Or O. (1983) Pediatric sports medicine for the practitioner. In: *Physiological Principles to Clinical Application*. Springer; New York.

Bassett D. R. and Howley E. T. (1997) Maximal oxygen uptake: 'classical' versus 'contemporary' viewpoints. *Medicine and Science in Sports and Exercise*; **29**: 591–603.

Bassett D. R., Howley J. R. and Howley E. T. (2000) Limiting factors for maximum oxygen uptake and determinants of endurance performance. *Medicine Science in Sports and Exercise*; **32**: 70–84.

Bloom D. and Woodhull-McNeal A. P. (1987) Postural adjustments while standing with two types of loaded backpack. *Ergonomics*; **30**: 1425–30.

Boreham C. A. G., Paliczka V. J. and Nichols A. K. (1990) A comparison of PWC_{170} and 20-MST tests of aerobic fitness in adolescent schoolchildren. *Journal of Sports Medicine and Physical Fitness*; **30**: 19–23.

Bouchard C. and Malina R. M. (1983) Genetics of physiological fitness and motor performance. *Exercise and Sport Sciences Reviews*; **11**: 306–39.

Bransford D. R. and Howley E. T. (1977) Oxygen cost of running in trained and untrained men and women. *Medicine and Science in Sports and Exercise*; **9**: 41–4.

British Association of Sport and Exercise Sciences (1997) *Guidelines for the Physiological Testing of Athletes* (S. Bird and R. Davison, eds). British Association of Sport and Exercise Sciences; Leeds, UK.

British Association of Sports Sciences (1992) *Position Statement on the Physiological Assessment of the Elite Athlete*. British Association of Sports Sciences (Physiology Section).

Cavanagh P. R. and Williams K. R. (1982) The effect of stride length variation on oxygen uptake during distance running. *Medicine and Science in Sports and Exercise;* **14:** 30–5.

Cavanagh P. R. and Kram R. (1985) The efficiency of human movement – a statement of the problem. *Medicine and Science in Sports and Exercise;* **17:** 304–8.

Conley D. L. and Krahenbuhl G. (1980) Running economy and distance running performance of highly trained athlete. *Medicine and Science in Sports and Exercise;* **12:** 357–60.

Conley D. L., Krahenbuhl G. and Burkett, L. (1981) Training for aerobic capacity and running economy. *Physician and Sportsmedicine;* **9** (4): 107–15.

Cooke C. B., McDonagh M. J. N., Nevill A. M. and Davies C. T. M. (1991) Effects of load on oxygen intake in trained boys and men during treadmill running. *Journal of Applied Physiology;* **71:** 1237–44.

Cooper K. H. (1968) A means of assessing maximal oxygen intake, correlation between field and treadmill testing. *Journal of American Medical Association;* **203:** 201–4.

Costill D. L. (1972) Physiology of marathon running. *Journal of the American Medical Association;* **221:** 1024–9.

Costill D. L. and Fox E. L. (1969) Energetics of marathon running. *Medicine and Science in Sports;* **1:** 81–6.

Costill D. L., Thomson H. and Roberts E. (1973) Fractional utilisation of the aerobic capacity during distance running. *Medicine and Science in Sports and Exercise;* **5:** 248–52.

Council of Europe (1988) *Testing Physical Fitness.* Eurofit; Strasbourg.

Datta S. R. and Ramanathan N. L. (1970) Ergonomical studies on load carrying up staircases. Part **1:** Effect of external load on energy cost and heart rate. *Indian Journal of Medical Research;* **58:** 1629–35.

Datta S. R. and Ramanathan N. L. (1971) Ergonomic comparison of seven modes of carrying loads on the horizontal plane. *Ergonomics;* **14:** 269–78.

Davies C. T. M. (1980) Metabolic cost of exercise and physical performance in children with some observations on external loading. *European Journal of Applied Physiology;* **45:** 95–102.

Day J. R., Rossiter H. B., Coats E. M., Skasick

A. and Whipp B. J. (2003) The maximally attainable $\dot{V}O_2$ during exercise in humans: the peak vs. maximum issue. *Journal of Applied Physiology;* **95:** 1901–7.

DuBois D. and DuBois E. F. (1916) Clinical calorimetry: a formula to estimate the approximate surface area if height and weight are known. *Archives of Internal Medicine;* **17:** 863–71.

Eston R. E. and Brodie D. A. (1985) The assessment of maximal oxygen uptake from running tests. *Physical Education Review;* **8** (1), 28–36.

Eston R. G., Robson S. and Winter E. (1993) A comparison of oxygen uptake during running in children and adults. In: (W. Duquet and J. A. P. Day, eds) *Kinanthropometry IV.* E. & F. N. Spon; London: pp. 236–41.

Eston R. G., Faulkner J. A., Parfitt C. G. and Mason E. (2006) The validity of predicting maximal oxygen uptake from a perceptually regulated graded exercise tests of different durations. *European Journal of Applied Physiology;* **97:** 535–41.

Eston R. G., Shepherd K., Lambrick D. and Parfitt G. (2008) The validity of predicting maximal oxygen uptake ($\dot{V}O_{2max}$) of sedentary individuals using a perceptually regulated sub-maximal graded exercise test. *Journal of Sports Sciences;* **26:** 131–9.

Eston R. G., Williams J. G. and Faulkner J. (2009) Control of exercise intensity using heart rate, perceived exertion and other non-invasive procedures. In: (R. G. Eston and T. Reilly, eds) *Kinanthropometry and Laboratory Manual (3rd Edition): Exercise Physiology (Chapter 9).* Routledge; Oxon: pp. 237–270.

Faulkner J. A. and Eston R. G. (2007) Overall and peripheral ratings of perceived exertion during a graded exercise test to volitional exhaustion in individuals of high and low fitness. *European Journal of Applied Physiology;* **101:** 613–20.

Faulkner J. A., Parfitt G. and Eston R.G. (2007) Prediction of maximal oxygen uptake from the ratings of perceived exertion and heart rate during a perceptually-regulated sub-maximal exercise test in active and sedentary participants. *European Journal of Applied Physiology;* **101:** 397–407.

Gaesser G. A. and Brooks G. A. (1975) Muscular efficiency during steady-rate exercise: effects of speed and work rate. *Journal of Applied Physiology*; **38**: 1132–9.

Gordon M. J., Goslin B. R., Graham T. and Hoare J. (1983) Comparison between load carriage and grade walking on a treadmill. *Ergonomics*; **26**: 289–98.

Harrison M. H., Bruce D. L., Brown G. A. and Cochrane L. A. (1980) A comparison of some indirect methods of predicting maximal oxygen uptake. *Aviation Space and Environmental Medicine*; **51** (10): 1128–33.

Hill A. V. (1939) The mechanical efficiency of frog's muscle. *Proceedings of the Royal Society of London*; **127**: 434–51.

Jones A. M. (2007) Middle- and long-distance running. In: (E. M. Winter, Jones, A. M., Davison, R. C., Bromley, P. & Mercer, T. eds). *Sport and Exercise Physiology Testing Guidelines: The British Association of Sport and Exercise Sciences Guide*. Routledge; Oxon: pp. 147–54.

Jones A. M. and Doust J. H. (1996) A 1% treadmill grade most accurately reflects the energetic cost of outdoor running. *Journal of Sports Sciences*; **14**: 3231–327.

Jones A. M., Vanhatalo A. T. and Doust J. (2009) Aerobic exercise performance. In: (R. G. Eston and T. Reilly, eds) *Kinanthropometry Laboratory Manual(3rd Edition): Exercise Physiology (Chapter 10)*. Routledge; Oxon: pp. 271–306.

Jordan C. D. and Cooke C. B. (1998) The effects of upper posture on horizontal running economy. *Journal of Sports Sciences*; **16**: 53–4.

Kerdok A. E., Biewener A. A., McMahon T. A., Weyand P. G. and Herr H. M. (2002) Energetics and mechanics of human running on surfaces of different stiffnesses. *Journal of Applied Physiology*; **92**: 469–78.

Kinoshita H. (1985) Effects of different loads and carrying systems on selected biomechanical parameters describing walking gait. *Ergonomics*; **28**: 1347–62.

Kirk J. and Schneider D. A. (1992). Physiological and perceptual responses to load carrying in female subjects using internal and external frame backpacks. *Ergonomics*; **35**: 445–55.

Kleiber M. (1975) *The Fire of Life: An Introduction to Animal Energetics*. Kreiger; New York.

Kline G. M., Porcari J. P., Hintermeister R., Freedson P. S., Ward A., McCarron R. F., Ross J. and Rippe J. M. (1987) Estimation of $\dot{V}O_{2max}$ from a one-mile track walk, gender, age, and body weight. *Medicine and Science in Sports and Exercise*; **19**: 253–9.

Krahenbuhl G. S., Skinner J. S. and Kohrt W. M. (1985) Developmental aspects of maximal aerobic power in children. *Exercise and Sport Sciences Reviews*; **13**: 503–38.

Kram R., McMahon T. A. and Taylor C. R. (1987) Load carriage with compliant poles: physiological and/or biomechanical advantages. *Journal of Biomechanics*; **20**: 893.

Krebs H. A. and Kornberg H. L. (1957) *Energy Transformations in Living Matter*. Springer; Berlin.

Leger L. and Lambert J. (1982) A maximal multistage 20 m shuttle run test to predict $\dot{V}O_{2max}$. *European Journal of Applied Physiology*; **49**: 1–12.

Legg S. J. and Mahanty A. (1985) Comparison of five modes of carrying a load close to the trunk. *Ergonomics*; **28**: 1653–60.

Lloyd B. B. and Zacks R. M. (1972) The mechanical efficiency of treadmill running against a horizontal impeding force. *Journal of Physiology (London)*; **223**: 355–63.

Lloyd R. and Cooke C. B. (2000) The oxygen consumption with unloaded walking and load carriage using two different backpacks. *European Journal of Applied Physiology*; **81**: 486–92.

McCann D. J. and Adams W. C. (2003) The size-independent oxygen cost of running. *Medicine and Science in Sports and Exercise*; **35**: 1049–56.

McMahon T. A. (1984) *Muscles, Reflexes and Locomotion*. Princeton University Press; Princeton, NJ.

Maloiy G. M. O., Heglund N. C., Prager L. M., Cavagna G. A. and Taylor C. R. (1986) Energetic cost of carrying loads: have African women discovered an economic way? *Nature*; **319**: 668–9.

Margaria R., Cerretelli P., Aghemo P. and Sassi G. (1963) Energy cost of running. *Journal of Applied Physiology*; **18**: 367–70.

Martin P. E. and Nelson R. C. (1986) The effects of carried loads on the walking patterns of men and women. *Ergonomics;* **29**: 1191–202.

Maughan R., Leiper J. and Shirreffs S. (2009) Haematology. In: (R. G. Eston and T. Reilly, eds.) *Kinanthropometry Laboratory Manual (3rd Edition): Exercise Physiology (Chapter 4).* Routledge; Oxon: pp. 104–123.

Morgan D. W. (1992) Introduction: economy of running: a multidisciplinary perspective. *Medicine and Science in Sports and Exercise;* **24**: 454–5.

Morgan D. W., Bransford D. R., Costill D. L., Daniels J. T., Howley E. T. and Krahenbuhl G. S. (1995) Variation in the aerobic demand of running among trained and untrained subjects. *Medicine and Science in Sports and Exercise;* **27**: 404–9.

Morgan D. W., Tseh W., Caputo J. L., Craig I. S., Keefer D. J. and Martin, P. (1999) Sex differences in running economy of young children. *Pediatric Exercise Science;* **11**: 122–8.

Nevill A. M., Ramsbottom R. and Williams C. (1992) Scaling physiological measurements for individuals of different body size. *European Journal of Applied Physiology;* **65**: 110–17.

Nevill A. M., Atkinson G. and Scott M. A. (2009) Statistical methods in kinanthropometry and exercise physiology. In: (R. G Eston and T. Reilly, eds.) *Kinanthropometry Laboratory Manual (3rd Edition): Anthropometry (Chapter 10).* Routledge; Oxon: pp. 250–299.

Noakes T. D. (1997) Challenging beliefs: ex Africa semper aliquid novi. *Medicine and Science in Sport and Exercise;* **29**: 571–590.

Noakes T. D. (1998) Maximal oxygen uptake: 'classical' versus 'contemporary' viewpoints: a rebuttal. *Medicine and Science in Sport and Exercise;* **30**: 1381–98.

Norman R., Sharrat M., Pezzack J. and Noble E. (1976) Re-examination of the mechanical efficiency of horizontal treadmill running. *Biomechanics;* **7**: 87–98.

Paliczka V. J., Nichols A. K. and Boreham C. A. G. (1987) A multi-stage shuttle run test as a predictor of running performance and maximal oxygen uptake in adults. *British Journal of Sports Medicine;* **21**: 163–5.

Pollock M. L. (1973) The quantification of endurance training programmes. In: (J. H. Wilmore, ed) *Exercise and Sport Sciences Reviews.* Academic Press; New York: pp. 155–88.

Robertson R. J., Caspersen C. J., Allison T. G., Skrinar G. S., Abbott R. A. and Metz K. F. (1982) Differentiated perceptions of exertion and energy cost of young women while carrying loads. *European Journal of Applied Physiology and Occupational Physiology;* **49**: 69–78.

Rossiter H. B., Kowalchuk J. M. and Whipp B. J. (2006) A test to establish maximum O_2 uptake despite no plateau in the O_2 uptake response to ramp incremental exercise. *Journal of Applied Physiology;* **100**: 764–70.

Rowland T. W. (1990) *Exercise and Children's Health.* Human Kinetics; Champaign, IL.

Rowland T. W. (2005) *Children's Exercise Physiology.* Human Kinetics; Champaign, IL.

Saltin B. and Calbet J. A. L. (2006) Point: In health and in a normoxic environment, $\dot{V}O_{2max}$ is limited primarily by cardiac output and locomotor muscle blood flow. *Journal of Applied Physiology;* **100**: 744–8.

Saltin B., Blomquist G., Mitchell J. H., Johnson, R. L., Wildenthal, K. and Chapman, C. B. (1968) Response to exercise after bed rest and after training. *Circulation;* **38** (Suppl. 7): 1–78.

Schmidt-Nielsen K. (1984) *Scaling: Why is Animal Size so Important?* Cambridge University Press; Cambridge.

Shephard R. J. (1970) Computer programs for solution of the Åstrand nomogram and calculation of body surface area. *Journal of Sports Medicine and Physical Fitness;* **10**: 206–12.

Shephard R. J. (1984) Tests of maximum oxygen intake: a critical review. *Sports Medicine;* **1**: 99–124.

Shephard R. J., Allen C., Benade A. J. S., Davies C. T. M., di Prampero P. E., Hedman R., Merriman J. E., Myhre K. and Simmons, R. (1968) Standardization of submaximal exercise tests. *Bulletin of the World Health Organization;* **38**: 765–75.

Siconolfi J. F., Cullinane E. M., Carleton R. A. and Thompson P. D. (1982)

Assessing $\dot{V}O_{2max}$ in epidemiologic studies: modifications of the Astrand–Ryhming test. *Medicine and Science in Sports and Exercise;* **14**: 335–8.

Stainsby W. N., Gladden L. B., Barclay J. K. and Wilson B. A. (1980) Exercise efficiency: validity of baseline subtractions. *Journal of Applied Physiology;* **48**: 518–22.

Taylor C. R., Heglund N. C., McMahon T. A. and Looney T. R. (1980) Energetic cost of generating muscular force during running. *Journal of Experimental Biology;* **86**: 9–18.

Taylor C. R., Heglund N. C. and Maloiy G. M. O. (1982) Energetics and mechanics of terrestrial locomotion I: metabolic energy consumption as a function of speed and body size in birds and mammals. *Journal of Experimental Biology;* **97**: 1–22.

Taylor H. L., Buskirk E. and Henschel A. (1955) Maximal oxygen uptake as an objective measure of cardiorespiratory performance. *Journal of Applied Physiology;* **8**: 73–77.

Thorstensson A. (1986) Effects of moderate external loading on the aerobic demand of submaximal running in men and 10–year-old boys. *European Journal of Applied Physiology and Occupational Physiology;* **55**: 569–74.

Unnithan V. B. and Eston R. G. (1990) Stride frequency and submaximal treadmill running economy in adults and children. *Pediatric Exercise Science;* **2**: 149–55.

Wagner P. D. (2006) Point: In health and in a normoxic environment, $\dot{V}O_{2max}$ is not limited primarily by cardiac output and locomotor muscle blood flow. *Journal of Applied Physiology;* **100**: 744–8.

Welsman J. R. and Armstrong N. (2000) Longitudinal changes in submaximal oxygen uptake in 11- to 13-year-olds. *Journal of Sports Sciences;* **18**: 183–9.

Welsman J. R. and Armstrong N. (2007) Interpreting performance in relation to body size. In: (N. Armstrong, ed) *Paediatric Exercise Physiology.* Elsevier; London. pp. 27–46.

Whipp B. J. and Wasserman K. (1969) Efficiency of muscular work. *Journal of Applied Physiology;* **26**: 644–8.

Wickstrom R. L. (1983) *Fundamental Motor Patterns.* Lea and Febiger; Philadelphia, PA.

Wilkie D. R. (1974) The efficiency of muscular contraction. *Journal of Mechanochemistry and Cell Motility;* **2**: 257–67.

Winter E. M., Jones, A. M., Davison R. C., Bromley P. D. and Mercer T. M. (eds) (2006) *Sport and Exercise Physiology Testing Guidelines.* Routledge; Oxon: pp. 120–9.

Winter E. M. and Nevill A. M. (2009) Scaling: adjusting for differences in body size. In: (R. G. Eston and T. Reilly, eds) *Kinanthropometry Laboratory Manual (3rd Edition): Anthropometry (Chapter 11).* Routledge; Oxon: pp. 300–320.

Wyndham C. H., Strydom N. B., Leary W. P. and Williams C. G. (1966) Studies of the maximum capacity of men for physical effort. *Internationale Zeitschrift fur Angewandte Physiologie;* **22**: 285–95.

Zacks R. M. (1973) The mechanical efficiencies of running and bicycling against a horizontal impeding force. *Internationale Zeitschrift für Angewandte Physiologie;* **31**: 249–58.

CHAPTER 8

THERMOREGULATION

Thomas Reilly and Tim Cable

8.1 AIMS

- To provide students with an understanding of human thermoregulation, at rest and during exercise;
- To describe the relevance of anthropometric factors in maintaining heat balance;
- To outline practical exercises for the acquisition of techniques to monitor physiological responses to heat loads.

8.2 INTRODUCTION

The human is homeothermic, meaning that body temperature is maintained within narrow limits independently of fluctuations in environmental temperature. For thermoregulatory purposes the body can be regarded as consisting of a core within which the temperature is 37°C and an outer shell where the ideal average temperature is 33°C, although this value is largely dependent on environmental factors and clothing worn. The precise temperature gradient from core to skin depends on the body part, but generally speaking the size of the gradient that exists between the skin and the environment will determine the amount of heat that is lost or gained by the body.

8.3 PROCESSES OF HEAT LOSS/HEAT GAIN

Normally the body is maintained in thermoequilibrium or heat balance. Heat is produced by metabolism and the level of heat production can be increased dramatically by physical exercise. The processes of conduction, convection and radiation allow for either heat loss or heat gain (depending on environmental conditions) with evaporation being a major avenue of heat loss when body temperature is rising.

The heat of basal metabolism is about 1 kcal kg^{-1} h^{-1}. One kcal (4.186 kJ) is the energy required to raise 1 litre of water through 1°C. The specific heat of human tissue is less than this figure, 0.83 kcal of energy being needed to raise 1 kg of tissue through 1°C. Thus if there were no avenue of heat loss, the temperature of the body would rise by 1°C per hour in an individual with body mass of about 72 kg, and within 4–6 hours death from overheating would follow. The process would be accelerated during exercise when energy expenditure might approach 25 kcal min⁻¹ (105 kJ min⁻¹). This value might include 1 kcal min⁻¹ for basal metabolism and 6 kcal min⁻¹ for producing muscular work. The remaining 18 kcal is dissipated as heat, which builds up within the body. In this instance the theoretical rise in body temperature would be 20°C in just over 1 hour. Obviously maintaining life depends on the ability to exchange heat with the environment.

A number of factors contribute to heat production and heat loss (Figure 8.1). The maintenance of a relatively constant core temperature is frequently expressed in the form of a heat balance equation:

Heat stored = Metabolic rate – Evaporation
± Radiation ± Convection
± Conduction – Work done

Heat may be gained from terrestrial sources of radiation or from solar radiation, but the body also radiates heat to its immediate environment. In physical terms, the human body can be regarded as a black box: the body surface being a good absorber of radiant heat and also a good radiator. Convection refers to transfer of heat by movement of gas or fluid. The barriers to convective heat exchange include subcutaneous adipose tissue, clothing and films of stationary air or water in immediate contact with clothing. Conduction describes heat transfer from core through body fluids to the surface of the body

and exchange with the environment by direct contact of the skin with objects, materials or surfaces.

Evaporative heat loss includes vaporisation of water from moist mucous membrane of the upper respiratory tract with breathing, insensible perspiration through the skin and evaporation of sweat from the surface of the body. When water evaporates from any surface, that surface is cooled. When sweat drops directly from the skin, no heat is exchanged. At rest in a room temperature of 21°C the heat lost by a nude human would be about 60% from radiation, 25% evaporation from lungs and skin, 12% by means of convective air currents and 3% by means of conduction from the feet. During exercise the main mechanism for heat loss is evaporation of sweat. This mechanism will be less effective when the air is highly humid, 100% relative humidity meaning that the air is totally saturated already with water vapour and can take up no more at the prevailing temperature.

The rate of evaporative heat loss depends on the vapour pressure gradient across the film of stationary air surrounding the skin and on the thickness of the stationary film. It is influenced also by air movement over the skin surface. Evaporative loss from the lungs depends on minute ventilation, dryness of the atmosphere and the barometric pressure. Consequently, dry nose and throat are experienced at altitude where the atmospheric pressure is lower than at sea level.

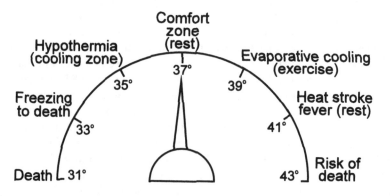

Figure 8.1 The body temperature range.

8.4 CONTROL OF BODY TEMPERATURE

Body temperature is regulated by temperature-sensitive neurons located in the anterior and posterior hypothalamus. These cells detect the temperature of the circulating blood, with the cells in the anterior hypothalamus responding to an increase in body temperature and those in the posterior portion triggering the effector response to a decrease. These areas also receive afferent input from peripheral warm and cold receptors located in the skin and therefore receive information about changes in the body's immediate environment. Warm receptors in the skin are stimulated in the temperature range of 28–45°C. Paradoxically, above this level the cold receptors begin to fire, particularly if the skin is subjected to a rapid increase in temperature. This is called paradoxical inhibition and gives the sensation of cold in very hot surroundings (e.g. in a shower).

During exposure to cold, or when body temperature decreases, the posterior hypothalamus initiates a number of responses. This activity will be neurally mediated via the sympathetic nervous system, and will result in a generalised vasoconstriction of the cutaneous circulation. Blood will be displaced centrally away from the peripheral circulation, promoting a fall in skin temperature, which will ultimately increase the temperature gradient between the core and the skin. However, it is important to note that this reduction in skin temperature will decrease the gradient that exists between the skin and the environment, and therefore reduce the potential for heat loss from the body. Superficial veins are also affected, such that blood returning from the limbs is diverted from them to the vena comitantes that overlie the main arteries. The result is that arterial blood is cooled by the venous return almost immediately it enters the limb by means of the countercurrent heat exchange mechanism.

The reduction in blood flow is not uniform throughout the body, with its effects being most pronounced in the extremities. Severe cold may decrease blood flow to the fingers to 2.5% of its normal value whereas, in contrast, blood flow to the head remains unaltered. There are no vasoconstrictor fibres to the vessels of the scalp which seem to be slow in responding to the direct effect of cooling (Webb 1982). As heat loss from the head can account for up to 25% of the total heat production, the importance of covering the head to protect against the cold is clear. This would equally apply to the underwater swimmer moving headfirst through the water and to the jogger or skier in winter weather. There is a linear relationship between heat loss through the head and ambient temperature within the range –20°C to +32°C, emphasizing the need to insulate the top of the head in extreme cold (Froese and Burton 1957).

Paradoxically, if the environment is extremely cold, there may be a delayed vasodilation of the blood vessels in the skin, which alternates with intense vasoconstriction in cycles of 15–30 minutes and leads to excessive heat loss. This has been described as a hunting reaction in the quest for an appropriate skin temperature to achieve the best combination of gradients between core, shell and environment. The vasodilation may be the result of accumulated vasoactive metabolites arising from the endothelium whose activity is associated with the reduced blood flow. The smooth muscle in the walls of peripheral blood vessels are effectively paralyzed at temperatures of 10°C; as the muscles cannot then respond to noradrenaline released by vasoconstrictor nerves, the muscles relax to allow a return of blood flow through the vessels, thus completing the cycle. This alternation of high and low blood flow to local tissue produced by ice-pack application is exploited in the treatment of sports injuries by physiotherapists. It is also the principle underlying the iced-baths used by some athletes post-exercise to accelerate recovery processes. The phenomenon of hunting is well recognized by runners and cyclists if they train in cold conditions without wearing gloves; initially the fingers are white, but become a ruddy colour as blood enters the digits in increased volumes. Blood flow to the skin may also be influenced by alcohol, which has a vasodilator effect. Though alcohol can make a person feel more comfortable when exposed to cold, it will increase heat loss and so may endanger the individual. Consequently, drinking alcohol is not recommended when staying outdoors overnight in inclement weather conditions; similarly, the customary hip-flask of whiskey serves no useful protective function for recreational skiers or mountaineers.

Shivering represents a response of the autonomic nervous system to cold. It constitutes involuntary activity of skeletal muscles and the resultant heat production may be as large as three times the basal metabolic rate. Indeed, metabolic rates five times that at rest have been reported (Horvath 1981), though such values are rare. Shivering tends to be intermittent and persists during exercise until the exercise intensity is sufficient on its own to maintain core temperature. The piloerection response to cold that is found in animals is less useful to the human who lacks the furry overcoat to the skin that cold-dwelling animals possess. Contraction of the small muscles attached to hair roots causes air to be trapped in the fur and this impedes heat loss. The pilomotor reflex in humans has little thermal impact, but is reflected in the appearance of goose pimples. Paradoxically, the 'gooseflesh syndrome' is sometimes found in marathon runners during heat stress when heat loss mechanisms begin to fail, with the condition being accompanied by a sensation of coldness (Pugh 1972).

Elevation of basal heat production may be brought about by the neuroendocine system in conditions of long-term cold exposure. The hypothalamus stimulates the pituitary gland to release hormones that affect other target organs, notably the thyroid and adrenal glands. Thyroxine causes an increase in metabolic rate within 5–6 hours of cold exposure.

This elevation will persist throughout a sojourn with the metabolic rate at rest being greater in cold than in temperate climates and elevated over that of tropical residents. Adrenaline and adrenocortical hormones may also cause a slight increase in metabolism, though the combined hormonal effects are still relatively modest. Brown fat, so-called because of its iron-containing cytochromes active in oxidative processes, is a potential source of thermogenesis. This form of fat is located primarily in and around the kidneys and adjacent to the great vessels, beneath the shoulder blades and along the spine. It is evident in abundance in infants, but its stores decline during growth and development.

The anterior hypothalamus initiates vasodilation of the cutaneous circulation in response to an increase in body temperature. This results in an expansion of the core and ultimately increases the temperature gradient between the skin and the environment, allowing for greater heat exchange. Cutaneous vasodilation is initiated by a removal of vasoconstrictor tone in the skin, and enhanced by the release of vasodilator substances (bradykinin and vasoactive intestinal polypeptide) from the sweat glands following stimulation via sympathetic cholinergic fibres. These substances are thought to cause the smooth muscle of the cutaneous blood vessels to relax and allow total peripheral resistance to decrease, thereby increasing blood flow. Evidence for this response comes from individuals with a congenital lack of sweat glands, who are not able to increase skin blood flow when body temperature increases. The role and context of nitric oxide released from endothelial cells in provoking vasodilation are considered by Cable (2009, Chapter 5)

It is evident, therefore, that the process of thermoregulation is subserved by the cardiovascular system. That is to say, heat is gained or lost by changes in blood flow. Such changes in blood flow must obviously have ramifications for the control of blood pressure. If total peripheral resistance is increased (i.e. when body temperature falls and skin blood flow is restricted), blood pressure will also increase. Conversely, skin blood flow is enhanced with peripheral vasodilation and blood pressure may fall. Thus thermoregulatory responses can initiate changes in non-thermal control mechanisms. Examples of this include the increased diuresis that occurs in cold weather. As total peripheral resistance increases, secretion of antidiuretic hormone is reduced and therefore less fluid is reabsorbed from the kidney; ultimately some blood volume is lost, which returns blood pressure to normal. Conversely, the soldier that stands on parade for a number of hours in the heat will, following increases in skin blood flow, no longer be able to maintain blood pressure sufficiently to perfuse the cerebral circulation, and therefore may faint to allow blood flow to return to normal.

Disturbances in cerebral neurotransmitter substances have been implicated in the negative mental states characterizing central fatigue during heat exhaustion (Reilly et al. 2006). An experimental model that employed active and passive heating allowed Low et al. (2005) to compare the impact of either hyperthermia or hypotension on central fatigue, with prolactin as a marker. With core and skin temperature held constant, but blood pressure and cutaneous blood flow markedly different, the prolactin response was unaltered, suggesting that thermal adjustments are key to the genesis of central fatigue. Others have shown that performance can be enhanced in the heat, and core temperature raised further by use of

dopamine-noradrenaline reuptake inhibitors, a class of drug used to treat depression (Watson et al. 2005). The effect of such drugs (not evident at temperatures of 18°C) could increase the risk of developing heat injury, whether used as a putative ergogenic aid or when medically prescribed for an athlete experiencing depression.

8.5 THERMOREGULATION AND OTHER CONTROL SYSTEMS

During exercise, particularly in the heat, sweating becomes the main mechanism for losing heat. Sweat is secreted by corkscrew-shaped glands within the skin and it contains a range of electrolyes as well as substances, such as urea and lactic acid. Its concentration is less than in plasma, so sweat is described as hypotonic. Altogether there are about 2 million eccrine sweat glands in the human body, though the number varies between individuals; the other type, apocrine sweat glands are found mainly in the axilla and groin and are not important in thermoregulation in the human. While exercising hard in hot conditions, the amount of fluid lost in sweat may exceed $2\,l\,h^{-1}$ so athletes may lose 5–6% of body weight as water within 2 hours of heavy exercise. This loss would amount to over 8% of body water stores and represent a serious level of dehydration. The normal body water balance is illustrated in Table 8.1.

As thermoregulatory needs tend to override the physiological controls over body water, sweat secretion will continue and exacerbate the effects of dehydration

Table 8.1 The 24-hour water balance in a sedentary individual

Intake (ml)		Output (ml)	
Solid and semi-solid food	1200	Skin	350
Water released in metabolism	300	Expired air	500
Drinks (water, tea, fruit juice, Coffee, milk and so on)	1000	Urine	1500
Total	2500	Faeces	150
		Total	2500

until heat injury is manifest. Costill (1981) quantified the distribution of water losses among body water pools during prolonged exercise. Muscle biopsies were taken before, during and after exercise in active and non-active muscles and blood samples were also obtained. It was calculated that extracellular and intracellular and total body water values decreased by 9%, 3% and 7.5%, respectively. The conclusion was that electrolye losses in sweat did not alter the calculated membrane potential of active and inactive muscles sufficiently to be the cause of cramp suffered in such conditions.

Effects of dehydration are manifest at a water deficit of 1% of body weight in a feeling of thirst. This sensation is due to a change in cellular osmolarity and to dryness in the mucous membrane of the mouth and throat. The sensation can be satisfied long before the fluid is replaced so that thirst is an imperfect immediate indicator of the body's needs. As fluid may be lost at a greater rate than it can be absorbed, regular intakes of water, say 150 ml every 10–15 minutes, are recommended in events such as marathon running. This recommendation can help to reduce the rise in heart rate and body temperature towards hyperthermic levels that might otherwise have resulted. Energy drinks have little added value for thermoregulatory purposes, though hypotonic solutions that include sodium have marginal benefits in terms of the speed at which the ingested fluid is absorbed. Indeed, it is a sound practice to start contests in hot conditions well hydrated and then take small amounts of fluid frequently en route. However, in prolonged endurance events care must be taken not to over-hydrate as this can lead to the development of hyponatraemia or water toxicity, which, if severe, may need hospitalization. This condition usually only presents itself in avid water drinkers, but is becoming more common during events such as 'ironman' triathlons, 'ultra marathons' and in the slower runners in marathon races (Almond et al. 2005).

Boxers and wrestlers are known to use dehydrating practices to lose weight before their events and stay within the limit of their particular weight categories. In many cases the use of diuretics for the purpose of body water loss has been suspected. The practice is dangerous, especially if the impending contest is to be held in hot conditions and severe levels of dehydration have been induced prior to weighing-in.

Effects of dehydration on performance vary with the amount of fluid lost and the nature of the activity being performed. These are compounded when accompanied by imminent hyperthermia due to a combination of high humidity and high ambient temperature. Throughout the history of sport there are many dramatic examples of competitors suffering from heat stress. The casualties of heat injury during endurance events at the Summer Olympics have been catalogued by Peiser and Reilly (2004). An example of death due to heat stress was a Danish cyclist (Knud Jensen) at the Rome Olympics in 1960. Later, the British professional cyclist, Tommy Simpson died during a stage of the Tour de France cycle race. In both cases the use of amphetamines was allegedly implicated, these having an enhanced effect on performance, but a deleterious effect on thermoregulatory mechanisms.

The fact that body water content is variable should be taken into account when body composition is assessed from measurements of body water. This applies to chemical methods for measuring body water and predicting body fat values from the measurements. It applies also to the use of bioelectric impedance analysis (BIA) methods, which record conductance or resistance of the whole body in response to a low voltage electrical signal administered to the subjects. The resistance is dependent on water content and estimates of body fat will be affected by the state of the subject's hydration (Lemmey et al. 2000).

Women are often reputed to have inferior thermoregulatory functions to men during exercise in the heat. It seems that the early studies reporting women to be less tolerant of exercise in the heat ignored the low fitness levels of the women who were studied. Though women tend to have more body fat than men, and therefore greater insulation properties, their larger surface area relative to mass gives them an advantage in losing heat. There appears to be no sex difference in acclimatization to heat; for example, the frequency of heat illness in road races in the USA is approximately the same for each sex (Haymes 1984).

However, there are differences between the sexes that should be considered when body temperature is concerned. The greater subcutaneous tissue layers in females should provide them with better insulation against the cold. In females the set point is not fixed at 37°C but varies with the menstrual cycle. In mid-cycle there is a sharp rise of about 0.5°C, which is due to the influence of progesterone and this elevation is indicative of ovulation.

There is also a circadian rhythm in body temperature, which is independent of the environmental conditions (Reilly 1990). The body is in heat-gain mode in the morning and in heat-loss mode in the evening, the promotion of heat loss being due to the vasodilatory effects of melatonin. Core temperature is at a low point during sleep and is at its peak at about 18.00 hours (Figure 8.2). The peak to trough variation is about 0.6°C and applies to both males and females. The amplitude is less than this in aged individuals (Reilly *et al.* 1997). Peripheral circulation deteriorates with age and there is evidence that warming the feet before bedtime helps old people sleep (Raymann *et al.* 2007). There is some evidence that melatonin can improve performance due to its vasodilatory effects by attenuating heat gain during exercise (Atkinson *et al.* 2005). There is a wealth of evidence intimating that many types of human performance follow a curve during the day that is closely linked to the rhythm in body temperature (Reilly *et al.* 2000).

8.6 MEASUREMENT OF BODY TEMPERATURE

Core temperature refers to the thermal state of essential internal organs, such as

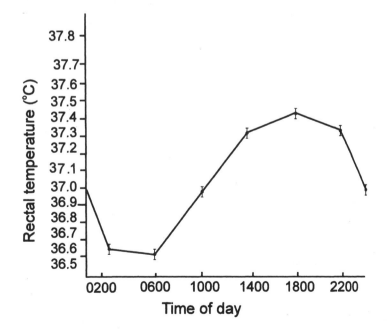

Figure 8.2 Circadian variation in core temperature.

heart, liver, viscera and brain. Although it is normally considered that core temperature is regulated about an internal temperature of 37°C, this value varies depending on the site of measurement. There are also rhythmic changes in the temperature set point which varies during exercise and in fever.

Rectal temperature is the most commonly used site for indicating core temperature in athletes. The probe should be inserted to a depth of 8 cm beyond the sphincter ani if reliable measures are to be obtained. Care is also necessary that probes are sterilized and treated with HIV risk in mind. Rectal temperature is not the best measure of core temperature in situations where temperature is changing rapidly. For this reason oesophageal temperature is preferred in some exercise experiments. This entails inserting a probe through the nose and threading it into the oesophagus.

An alternative is tympanic temperature where a sensor is placed adjacent to the tympanic membrane. Caution is necessary as it is easy to damage the membrane and also the ear must be completely insulated to avoid environmental influences. The temperature of the external auditory meatus can also be measured by inserting a probe 1 cm inside the ear canal and insulating the ear. However, with this measurement and those of rectal and oesophageal temperatures, it is best to represent data as a change from baseline since a temperature gradient exists down these tissues.

In more recent years, intestinal temperature has gained acceptance in sport and exercise settings (Byrne and Lim 2007). A temperature-sensitive pill is ingested and transmits a signal to a receiver worn as a bum-bag by the subject. Data collection can be commenced after 3–4 hours once the pill has passed through the stomach into the intestines and may continue until it has passed through the intestinal tract. The data can be downloaded subsequently, but the pills are not retrieved. The method demonstrates close agreement with oesophageal and rectal temperatures

and has excellent utility for ambulatory field-based applications (Byrne and Lim 2007). For example, the method has proved suitable for measuring continuous core temperature responses to unrestrained outdoor exercise such as distance running (Byrne et al. 2006) and in circadian studies whereas axillary temperature has not (Edwards et al. 2002).

Oral or sublingual temperatures, typically measured with a mercury thermometer, are used in clinical rather than exercise contexts and give values about 0.4°C lower than rectal temperature. Oral temperature is of little use in swimmers, for example, whose mouths are affected by surrounding water and high ventilation rates. Similarly measurement of axilla or groin temperatures in athletic subjects gives a poor indication of their thermal status. Another option is to measure the temperature of mid-stream urine, which gives a reasonable indication of internal body temperature.

Skin temperature has conventionally been measured by thermistor and thermocouples. Optoelectronic devices are now also available. The common method is to place thermistors over the surface of the skin and tape over them. From measurements of a number of designated skin sites, a mean skin temperature may be calculated. The formulae that require the least number of observations are:

$$MST = 0.5\ T_c + 0.36\ T_l + 0.14\ T_a$$
$$(Burton\ 1935)$$

$$MST = 0.3\ T_c + 0.3\ T_a$$
$$+ 0.2\ T_t + 0.2\ T_l$$
$$(Ramanathan\ 1964)$$

where MST is mean skin temperature, T_c is temperature of the chest juxta nipple, T_l is leg temperature measured over the lateral side of the calf muscle, T_a is lower arm temperature and T_t is anterior thigh temperature. Mean body temperature (MBT) may then be calculated by weighting rectal temperature (T_r) and MST in the ratio 4:1. In other words: $MBT = 0.8\ T_r + 0.2\ MST$.

Thermistors, thermocouples and platinum resistance sensors are used to measure the required combination of skin and core temperatures. Current systems are incorporated into dataloggers, which offer appropriate ranges for each type of sensor. Squirrel dataloggers (Grant Instruments, Cambridge Ltd) provide different options in a multi-channel device. Comprehensive data handling, automatic calibration and wireless data logging are combined in some monitoring systems (e.g. Ellab, Kings Lynn, Norfolk) that include channels for oesophageal and muscle temperature.

8.7 THERMOREGULATORY RESPONSES TO EXERCISE

Exercise implies activity of skeletal muscle and this demands energy. Most of the energy utilized is dissipated as heat, a small amount contributing towards mechanical work. The muscular efficiency represents the work performed as a percentage of the total energy expenditure. For cycle ergometry this value is about 22% depending on whether or not the resting energy expenditure is taken into consideration. In swimming, this figure is much lower; in weight lifting, it has been calculated to be about 12% (Reilly 1983). It is acknowledged that the mechanical efficiency is difficult to estimate in activities such as running.

During sustained exercise the cardiac output supplies oxygen to the active muscles, but also distributes blood to the skin to cool the body. In cases where cardiac output is maximal, the exercise performance is impaired by thermoregulatory needs. Since the maximal cardiac output determines how well blood can be distributed for peripheral cooling, the heat load induced by exercise is a function of the percentage of maximal oxygen uptake rather than the absolute work rate engaged.

The body acts as a heat sink in the early minutes of exercise and blood is shunted from viscera and other organs to the exercising muscles. Blood flow to the brain remains intact although there seems to be differential distribution to areas within the brain. If exercise imparts a severe heat load, the sweat glands are activated and droplets appear on the skin surface after about 7 minutes. The extent to which body temperature rises then depends on the exercise intensity, the fitness of the individual and the environmental conditions.

Thermoregulatory responses to exercise can be altered by cooling the body beforehand rather than performing the traditional warm-up, a procedure referred to as precooling (Reilly et al. 2006). Due to the high rate of cooling, immersion in cold water is usually used as a cooling manoeuvre to lower core body temperature by about 0.5°C. This strategy is relevant in sports that occur over an extended duration under high environmental temperatures and where rules permit limited opportunities to consume fluids. The ergogenic effect is ascribed to a combination of factors that include an increased heat storage, a delay in the time to reach a critical core temperature, and an improved thermal comfort (see Figure 8.3).

8.8 ENVIRONMENTAL FACTORS

Heat exchange with the environment is influenced by a number of environmental variables as well as individual characteristics. The clothing and equipment used also affect heat exchange. Thus some background is provided on relevant interactions with the environment in this section before progressing to anthropometric considerations in the next.

Athletic contests are sometimes held in conditions that challenge the body's thermoregulatory system. Cold is less of a problem than heat since athletes usually choose to avoid extremes of cold. Exceptions are winter sports, such as mountaineering, where it is imperative to protect the individuals against the cold. Outdoor games, such as

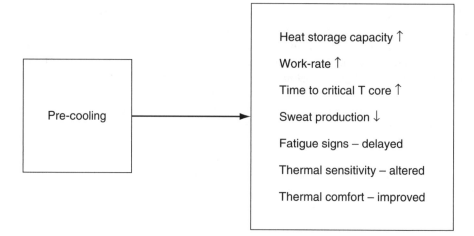

Figure 8.3 Causes thought to contribute to the ergogenic effect of precooling (adapted from Reilly *et al.* 2006).

American football, are also sometimes played in freezing conditions.

Experiments in cold air close to freezing have not consistently shown a significant effect on the maximal oxygen uptake. The effects are more marked in the periphery of the body where the drop in temperature of tissues is more pronounced. Normally the mean skin temperature is about 33°C and extreme discomfort is felt when this drops below 25°C. As skin temperature of the hand falls below 23°C, movements of the limb begin to get clumsy and finger dexterity is severely affected at skin temperatures between 13°C and 16°C. This is especially critical in winter sport activities that require fine manipulative actions of the fingers which are impaired because of numbness in those digits. Tactile sensitivity of the fingers is also affected for the worse to the extent that an impact on the skin at 20°C has to be about six times greater than normal for usual sensations to be felt. The skeletal muscles function at an optimal internal temperature and when this drops to about 27°C, the muscle's contractile force is much impaired. This impairment can be demonstrated by the progressive decline in grip strength with increased cooling of the arm. In sports such as downhill skiing, the performer could be cooled during the chair lift to the top of the ski-run and must therefore take steps to keep the limb muscles warm prior to skiing. Synovial fluid in the joints also becomes colder and more viscous, thus increasing the stiffness of the joints. The fatigue curve of muscle also deteriorates due to a combination of factors, such as impaired strength, lower blood flow, increased resistance of connective tissue and increased discomfort.

One of the most important consequences of sports participation outdoors in the cold is the poorer neuromuscular co-ordination that may result. As temperature in nervous tissue falls, conduction velocity of nerve impulses is retarded and this slows reaction time. If the slide in temperature is not reversed, eventually complete neural block occurs. Co-ordination is also impaired by the effect of cold on the muscle spindles which, at 27°C, respond to only 50% of normal to a standardized stimulus. Consequently, the stumbling and poor locomotion of climbers in the cold may be due to impairments in peripheral nerves.

Such an effect is particularly evident during cold water immersion. When swimming in water temperatures below 10°C there is a progressive reduction in swimming efficiency that appears to be related to local cooling in the arm muscles, rather than whole-body hypothermia. Arm cooling tends to result in local muscle weakness and even paralysis, which results in increasing drag and risk of sinking. This, coupled with the hyperventilation often seen during cold immersion, makes a co-ordinated swimming stroke virtually impossible, and may be a reason why many drowning deaths occur in cold water, even in cases where the victim is very close to land and safety (Tipton *et al.* 1999).

Some protection against this risk is offered by a greater subcutaneous fat layer around the arm muscles to restrict heat loss. In addition, lean individuals acutely exposed to cold water immersion, should restrict body movement in order to prevent hypothermia. While this manoeuvre may limit heat production, it will allow heat loss to be markedly restricted. This effect is because both fat and inactive muscle act as good insulators. However, when muscle becomes active, blood flow is dramatically increased, which ultimately changes a good insulator under resting conditions into a very effective heat conductor.

Frostbite is one of the risks of recreational activities in extreme cold. This condition can occur when the temperature in the fingers or toes falls below freezing and at –1°C ice crystals are formed in those tissues. The results can be a gangrenous extremity often experienced by mountaineers in icy conditions when their gloves or boots fail to provide adequate thermal insulation. Recent clinical experience is that amputation of damaged tissue is not a necessary consequence of frostbite and prognosis tends to be more optimistic than thought in previous decades. Of more serious consequence is a fall in the body's core temperature. The cold stress is progressively manifested by an enlargement of the area of the shell while the area of the core becomes smaller until its temperature ultimately begins to fall dangerously. Ainslie and Reilly (2003) demonstrated how quickly the core temperature of hill walkers can drop during breaks for snacks on the mountains. A core temperature of 34.5°C is usually taken

as indicative of grave hypothermic risk, though there is no absolute consensus of a critical end point. Some researchers assume that a rectal temperature of 32–33°C is a critical end point, though the exact value of hypothalamic temperature for fatality is subject to controversy.

Scientists have used metaphorical models to predict survival time by extrapolating from initial rates of decline in core temperature to an arbitrary value of 30°C (Ross *et al.* 1980). This avoids the need to take subjects too close to a risk of hypothermia. Researchers in Nazi concentration camps were not so considerate to their prisoners who were cooled to death at core temperatures of about 27°C. Holdcroft (1980) described an alcoholic woman exposed overnight in Chicago to subfreezing temperatures and whose rectal temperature was reported to be 18°C when she was found in a stupor. In hindsight it is doubtful if this was representative of core temperature in these conditions. Happily, she survived after being re-warmed in a hospital room temperature of 20°C. Death usually occurs at a much higher core temperature than that reported for the fortunate Chicago woman, with shivering usually being replaced by permanent muscle rigidity, then loss of consciousness at core a temperature of 32°C and heart failure may follow. The range of clinical symptoms associated with hypothermia is presented in texts such as Holdcroft (1980), and the details of the experiments on hypothermia in the Nazi concentration camps are open to scrutiny from accredited researchers.

Behavioural strategies and proper clothing can safeguard individuals in cold environments. Enormous strides have been made in the provision of protective equipment against the cold for sports participants. Major advances have been made in clothing design for outdoor conditions, protective suits for cases of accidental immersion in water and in the reliability and durability of tents. A similar systematic improvement is noted in the provision of first-aid and rescue services for most outdoor pursuits. The specially treated sheets of foil paper readily availed of by recreational marathon runners to safeguard against rapid heat loss on cessation of activity serve as an example.

Existence of good rescue facilities is no excuse for climbing parties to take risks in inclement weather. Early warning systems used by rangers on mountainsides must be heeded if they are to be effective and this inevitably means consumer education. Otherwise, the safety of the rescue team, in addition to that of the climbing party, may be jeopardized if weather conditions further deteriorate. Assessment of the risk involves some calculations of the magnitude of cold stress. On the mountainside the wind velocity may be the most influential factor in cooling the body so that the ambient temperature alone would grossly underestimate the prevailing risk. The wind-chill index originally designed by Siple and Passel (1945), and still widely used by mountaineers and skiers, provides a method of comparing different combinations of temperature and wind speed. The values calculated correspond to a caloric scale for rate of heat loss per unit body surface area; they are then converted in to a sensation scale ranging from hot (about 80) through cool (400) to bitterly cold (1200) and on to a value where exposed flesh freezes within 60 s. The cooling effects of combinations of certain temperatures and wind speeds are expressed as 'temperature equivalents' and are estimated with a nomogram. Use of the wind-chill index enables sojourners to evaluate the magnitude of cold stress and take appropriate precautions. Wet conditions can exacerbate cold stress, especially if the clothing worn begins to lose its insulation. Attention to safety may be even more important in water sports since, apart from the risk of drowning, body heat is lost much more rapidly in water than in air.

The formula of Siple and Passel (1945) for calculating heat loss is:

$$K_o = (\sqrt{100}\ V + 10.5 - V)\ (33 - T)$$

Where K_o = heat loss in kcal m^{-2} h^{-1}

V = wind velocity in m s^{-1}
T = environmental temperature in °C
10.5 = a constant
33 = assumed normal skin temperature in °C

For example, if wind velocity is 14 m.s^{-1} and the ambient temperature is 2°C, the rate of heat loss is:

$$(\sqrt{100 \times 4} + 10.5 - 14)\ (33-2)\ 37.4 +$$
$$10.5 - 14 = (33.9)\ (31)$$
$$= 1051\ \text{kcal m}^{-2}\ \text{h}^{-1}$$

Water has a much greater heat conduction capacity than air and so heat is readily exchanged with the environment when the human body is immersed. Though mean skin temperature is normally about 33°C, a bath at that temperature feels cold, yet if the water temperature is elevated by 2°C, the temperature of the body will begin to rise. This suggests that the human is poorly equipped for spending long spells in the water. Finding the appropriate water temperature is important for swimming pool managers who have to cater for different levels of ability. The preferred water temperature for inactive individuals is 33°C, for learners it is about 30°C, for active swimmers it is in the range of 27–29°C, whereas competitive swimmers are more content with temperatures around 25°C. Generally, the water is regulated to suit the active users. Indeed, the whole environment of the swimming pool must be engineered for the comfort of users. Condensation in the arena may not be welcomed by spectators, but the high humidity in the swimming pool militates against heat loss when the swimmer is out of the water. Engineering usually involves double glazing of the surround to avoid losing radiant heat outwards from the building as well as provision of supplementary radiant heating. Permissible indoor dew points can be calculated from temperature differences between outdoors and inside the pool to avoid high condensation risks – these being the points where moisture is deposited. Air ventilation rates inside the building may reduce the moisture content of indoor areas to decrease the discomfort of spectators, but this will cool the bather and call for increased heating costs. A practical compromise is to have air temperatures in the region of 28–30°C, which are much warmer than normal office room temperatures.

In hot conditions, heat stroke is a major risk and should be classed as an emergency. It reflects failure of normal thermoregulatory mechanisms. It is characterized by a body temperature of 41°C or higher, cessation of sweating and total confusion. Once sweating stops, the body temperature will rise quickly and soon cause irreversible damage to liver, kidney and brain cells. In such an emergency immediate treatment is essential.

Calculating the risk of heat injury requires accurate assessment of environmental conditions. The main factors to consider are dry bulb temperature, air velocity and cloud cover. Dry bulb temperature can be measured with a mercury glass thermometer, whereas relative humidity can be calculated from data obtained from a wet bulb thermometer used in either a sling psychrometer or a Stevenson screen. It can also be measured using a hair hygrometer. The dew point temperature – the point at which the air becomes saturated – is a measure of absolute humidity and it can be measured with a whirling hygrometer. Radiant temperature is measured by a globe thermometer inserted into a hollow metal sphere coated with black matt paint. Air velocity can be measured by means of a vane anemometer or an alcohol thermometer coated with polished silver. Cloud cover may provide some intermittent relief to the athlete from radiant heat stress but does not independently determine performance in marathon races (Ely et al. 2007). More details of the measuring devices and their operations are contained in the classical publication by Bedford (1946).

A problem for the sports scientist is to find the proper combination of factors to reach an integrated assessment of the environmental heat load. Many equations have been derived for this purpose over the last century of research. Most of the formulae incorporate composites of the environmental measures, whereas some, such as the predicted 4-hour sweat rate (P4SR), predict physiological responses from such measures. Probably the most widely used equation in industrial and military establishments has been the WBGT Index; WBGT standing for wet bulb and globe temperature. The US National Institute of Occupational Safety and Health recommended it as the standard heat stress index in 1972. The weightings (beta weights) underline the importance of considering relative humidity:

$$WBGT = 0.7\,WBT + 0.2\,GBT + 0.1\,DBT$$

Where   WB represents wet bulb
        G indicates globe
        DB represents dry bulb
        T indicates temperature

A comprehensive selection of indices derived in the United Kingdom and the USA was given by Lee (1980). A later development is the Botsball, which was validated by Beshir et al. (1982). It combines the effects of air temperature, humidity, wind speed and radiation into a single reading. It got its name from its designer, Botsford, and the WBGT can be reliably predicted from it if necessary.

Heat stress indices provide a framework for evaluating the risk of competing in hot conditions and for predicting the casualties. The American College of Sports Medicine (1984) originally set down guidelines for distance races, recommending that events longer than 16 km should not be conducted when the WBGT Index exceeds 28°C. This value is often exceeded in competitive races in Europe and in the USA during the summer months, and in many marathon races in Asia and Africa. However, it is imperative in all cases that the risks be understood and that symptoms of distress are recognized and promptly attended to. The plentiful provision of fluids en route and facilities for cooling participants are important precautionary steps.

8.9 ANTHROPOMETRY AND HEAT EXCHANGE

The exchange of heat between the human and the environment is affected by both body size and weight composition. Age, sex and physique of the individual are also relevant considerations.

The exchange of heat is a function of the body surface area relative to body mass. The dimensional exponent for this relation is 0.67. The smaller the individual the easier it is to exchange heat with the environment. Consequently children gain and lose heat more quickly than do adults, and marathon runners on average tend to be smaller than those specializing in shorter running events. It is important to recognize that children are more vulnerable than adults in extremes of environmental conditions.

It is thought that elderly people living alone prefer warmer environments than younger individuals, due to their lower metabolic rate. This is countered by a decrease in insensible perspiration due to a change in the vapour diffusion resistance of the skin with age. There is a higher incidence of death from hypothermia in old people living alone in the European winter than in the general population. These deaths are more likely to be due to socioeconomic conditions and physical immobility than to thermoregulatory changes with age. The older population is also susceptible to death from hyperthermia during unexpected summer heat waves.

Physiological thermoregulatory responses to heat stress – notably skin blood flow and sweat rates – tend to diminish with increasing age. This is probably due to age-related changes in the skin. Nevertheless, changes in core temperature and heat storage often show only marginal age-related effects if healthy men and women preserve a high degree of aerobic fitness. The ability to exercise in hot conditions is more a function of the status of the oxygen transport system (especially maximal oxygen uptake and cardiac output) than of chronological age.

Differences between the sexes in heat exchange are largely explained by body composition, physique and surface-to-volume ratios. These factors predominate once differences in fitness levels are taken into account. There is some empirical evidence that the decrement in performance in female marathon runners is greater than observed in males when conditions are hot, but the mechanism for this impairment is unclear (Ely *et al.* 2007).

Adipose tissue layers beneath the skin act to insulate the body and are protective in cold conditions. The degree of muscularity or mesomorphy can add to this. Ross *et al.* (1980) demonstrated that prediction of survival time in accidental immersion in water should take both endomorphy and mesomorphy into consideration and the best prediction was when the entire somatotype was taken into account. Pugh and Edholm (1955), in their classical studies of English channel swimmers, showed that the leaner individuals suffered from the cold much earlier than did those with high proportions of body adiposity. They compared responses of two ultra-distance swimmers in water of 15°C. The larger and fatter individual showed no decrease in rectal temperature for 7 hours, after which his radial pulse was impalpable for 50 minutes. The lighter and leaner swimmer was taken from the water after half an hour when his rectal temperature had dropped from 37°C to 34.5°C. In their studies in a swimming flume, Holmer and Bergh (1974) found that oesophageal temperature was constant at a water temperature of 26°C in subjects operating at 50% $\dot{V}O_{2max}$, except for a decrease in those with low body fat. They would be at an even greater disadvantage in colder water.

Racial differences in thermoregulatory response to heat seem to reflect physiological adjustments to environmental conditions more than genetic factors. Acclimatization to heat occurs relatively rapidly, with a good degree of adaptation being achieved within 2 weeks. Sweating capacity is increased, concentrations of electrolytes in sweat are reduced due to an influence of aldosterone and there is an expansion of plasma volume. The sensitivity of the sweat glands is altered so that more sweat is produced for a given rise in core temperature. It is less clear how genetic and acclimatization factors are separated for cold exposure, since diet, activity, living conditions and so on are confounding factors. Studies of the Ama, professional pearl divers of Korea and Japan, suggest a mild adjustment to chronic cold water exposure occurs (Rahn and Yokoyama, 1965). Thermal conductance in a given water temperature was found to be lower for diving than for non-diving women matched for skinfold thickness. These divers were also reported to have higher resting metabolic rates, which would help them to preserve heat. A similar vasoconstriction to reduce thermal conductance of tissues was reported by Skreslet and Aarefjord (1968) in subjects diving with self-contained underwater breathing apparatus (SCUBA) in the Arctic for 45 days.

The elevation of metabolic rate is also found in Eskimos when their thermal values are compared to Europeans. To what extent this difference can be attributed to diet and the specific dynamic activity of food is not clear. Adaptive vasoconstriction is most pronounced in Aborigines sleeping semi-naked in near-freezing temperatures in the Australian 'outback.' By restricting peripheral circulation, they can tolerate cold conditions that would cause grave danger to sojourners similarly exposed. This circulatory adjustment occurs without an increase in metabolic rate.

8.10 PRACTICAL EXERCISES

It is easier to demonstrate thermoregulatory factors using single-case studies as examples. Experiments require controlled laboratory conditions and usually prolonged exercise is involved. In the absence of an environmental chamber, three different laboratory demonstrations are suggested.

8.11 PRACTICAL 1: MUSCULAR EFFICIENCY

This practical entails exercise under steady-rate conditions on a cycle ergometer with work-rate being controlled and metabolic responses measured. From these measurements the muscular efficiency of exercise can be calculated.

8.11.1 Aim

To examine the efficiency of various cycling cadences.

8.11.2 Equipment

Electrically braked cycle ergometer.
    Oxygen consumption (e.g. on-line system or Douglas bags and oxygen and carbon dioxide analyzers).

8.11.3 Protocol

An electronically braked ergometer maintains work-rate (power output) independent of changes in pedal cadence. In this instance the work-rate chosen was 120 W. The subject has $\dot{V}O_2$ measured whilst sitting still, then commences exercise pedalling at a frequency of 50 rev min^{-1} for 20 minutes with $\dot{V}O_2$ measured during the last 2 minutes. This is followed by a 10-minute rest period and then this regimen is performed twice more using exactly the same work-rate but with new pedalling frequencies of 70 and 100 rev min^{-1}.

8.11.4 Calculations

Work efficiency = $\dfrac{\text{Work done (kJ min-1)}}{\text{Energy expended (kJ min}^{-1})}$

Where 1 Watt = 0.06 kJ min^{-1}
Energy expended = $\dot{V}O_2$ (1 min^{-1}) × Caloric equivalent (see Table 6.3 (Cooke, 2009)).

Net efficiency; as above except that resting $\dot{V}O_2$ must be subtracted from the exercise value. (Note: If an electrically braked cycle ergometer is not available, use a mechanically braked ergometer and exercise entailing a steady-state protocol.)

8.11.5 Examples of calculations

Efficiency   e.g. Work-rate = 120 W
                          = 7.2 kJ min^{-1}

                          Resting $\dot{V}O_2$ = 0.24 1 min^{-1}
                          Exercise $\dot{V}O_2$ = 2.0 1 min^{-1}
                          RER = 0.85

Energy equivalent for 2.0 1 min^{-1} at RER = 0.85 = 20.3 kJ min^{-1}

Therefore Gross efficiency = $\dfrac{7.2}{2.0 \times 20.3} \times 100$

= 17.74%

Net efficiency = $\dfrac{7.2}{(2.0 - 0.25) \times 20.3} \times 100$

= 20.3%

8.12 PRACTICAL 2: THERMOREGULATORY RESPONSES TO EXERCISE

The laboratory exercise involves recordings of rectal and skin temperatures at regular intervals during sustained performance. Exercise may be undertaken on either a motor-driven treadmill or a cycle ergometer. The purpose is to demonstrate physiological responses to exercise using thermoregulatory variables.

An example is shown in Figure 8.4. The exercise intensity was 210 W sustained for 60 minutes. Rectal temperature and skin temperatures were calculated. The rectal temperature rose by 2°C during the experiment.

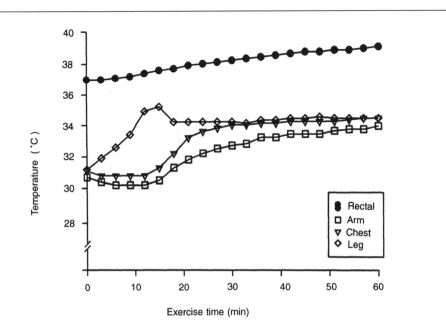

Figure 8.4 Temperature changes during exercise.

8.12.1 Aim

To investigate the thermoregulatory response to steady-state and incremental exercise.

8.12.2 Equipment

- Cycle ergometer
- Weighing scales
- Rectal thermistor (e.g. Yellow Springs, Squirrel Datalogger or Ellab)
- Analogue or digital temperature monitor or data logger
- Electrocardiogram or short-range radio telemetry (e.g. Polar Electro, or Activo)

8.12.3 Protocol

The subjects should place the rectal thermistor 10 cm beyond the external anal sphincter and attach skin thermistors on the sternum, on the medial forearm midway between elbow and wrist, on the anterior surface of the thigh midway between hip and knee and on the lateral surface of the lower leg between knee and ankle. Measure the subject's body mass immediately prior to exercise. One subject exercises at 70% maximum heart rate for 60 minutes with measurements of all variables taken at 5-minute intervals. The other subject exercises at 60 W for 5 minutes with the work rate increased by 30 W each subsequent 5 minutes until exhaustion. Variables should be measured every minute. At the completion of exercise subjects should be weighed immediately (without drying the skin) to obtain an index of sweat evaporation rate.

8.12.4 Cleaning of probes

Rectal probes should be washed in warm soapy water and then immersed in a 1:20 concentration of Milton solution (sterilization fluid) for at least 30 minutes. On removal from the solution, the probes should be left to dry completely in room air before further use. Skin probes can be washed and immersed in a 1:40 solution of Milton for 10 minutes and left to dry.

8.13 PRACTICAL 3: ESTIMATION OF PARTITIONAL HEAT EXCHANGE

8.13.1 Aim

To examine the effect of different environmental conditions on evaporative and partitional heat exchange during exercise.

8.13.2 Equipment

- Cycle ergometer
- Weighing scales
- Rectal thermistor (e.g. Yellow Springs, Squirrel Datalogger or Ellab)
- Four skin thermistors (e.g. Yellow Springs, Squirrel Datalogger, or Ellab)
- Analogue or digital temperature monitor or data logger

8.13.3 Protocol

The same subject exercises on two separate occasions, once in normal ambient conditions (21°C) and again in a hotter environment at the same work-rate. Immediately prior to exercise the individual is weighted (with all probes and clothes) and then completes 30–60 minutes of exercise followed by rapid re-weighing. All temperatures are measured every 5 minutes and $\dot{V}O_2$ at 20-minute intervals.

8.13.4 Calculations

Heat balance equation

$$HS = M \pm (R \pm C \pm C) - E - W$$

Where

$$\text{Metabolism} = \frac{\dot{V}O_2 \ (1 \ \text{min}^{-1}) \times \text{caloric equivalent} \times 60}{\text{Body surface area (BSA)}}$$

$$\text{Evaporation} = \frac{(\text{pre-exercise mass} - \text{post-exercise mass}) \ (\text{kg}) \times 2430 \ (\text{kJ.1}^{-1} \ \text{sweat loss})}{\text{Time of exercise (h)} \times \text{BSA}}$$

$$\text{Work} = \frac{\text{Work-rate (kJ min}^{-1} \times 60)}{\text{BSA}}$$

$$\text{Stored heat} = \frac{(\text{post-exercise } T_B - \text{pre-exercise } T_B) \times 3.47 \text{ (kJ kg}^{-1} \text{ h}^{-1} \times \text{mass})}{\text{Time (h)} \times \text{BSA}}$$

All units are kJ m^{-2} h^{-1}

Examples of calculations using the following data:

$\dot{V}O_2 = 2.0$ 1 min^{-1}

RER = 0.85

Pre-exercise rectal temperature = 36.5°C

Post-exercise rectal temperature = 38.0°C

Pre-exercise skin temperature = 33.0°C

Post-exercise skin temperature = 33.9°C

Pre-exercise body mass = 72.0 kg

Post-exercise body mass = 71.5 kg

Body surface area = 1.8 m^2

Work-rate = 120 W

Duration of exercise = 60 min

$$\begin{aligned}
\text{Metabolism} &= \frac{\dot{V}O_2 \times \text{caloric equivalent} \times 60}{\text{BSA}} \\
&= \frac{2.0 \times 20.3 \times 60}{1.8} \\
&= 1353.33 \text{ kJ m}^{-2} \text{ h}^{-1}
\end{aligned}$$

$$\begin{aligned}
\text{Evaporation} &= \frac{\text{Weight loss} \times 2430}{\text{Time} \times \text{BSA}} \\
&= \frac{(72.0 - 71.5) \times 2430}{1 \times 1.8} \\
&= 675 \text{ kJ m}^{-2} \text{ h}^{-1}
\end{aligned}$$

$$\begin{aligned}
\text{Work} &= \frac{\text{Work-rate} \times 60}{\text{BSA}} \\
&= \frac{7.2 \times 60}{1.8} \quad \text{i.e. } 7.2 \text{ kJ min}^{-1} \\
&= 240 \text{ kJ m}^{-2} \text{ h}^{-1}
\end{aligned}$$

$$\text{Stored heat} = \frac{(\text{post-exercise } T_B - \text{pre-exercise } T_B) \times 3.47}{\text{Time} \times \text{BSA}}$$

Where $T_B = (0.65 \text{ rectal}) + (0.35 \text{ skin})$

$$\begin{aligned}
&= \frac{(36.57 - 35.28) \times 3.47 \times 72}{1 \times 1.8} \\
&= 179.1 \text{ kJ m}^{-2} \text{ h}^{-1}
\end{aligned}$$

Heat balance HS = M − E ± (R ± C ± C) − W

Therefore rearranging the equation:

Partitional heat exchange $= HS − M + E + W$
$$= 179.1 − 1353.3 + 675 + 240$$
$$= −259.2 \text{ kJ m}^{-2} \text{ h}^{-1}$$

Therefore in the above example 259.2 kJ m^{-2} h^{-1} is lost from the body by the combined processes of radiation, conduction and convection.

FURTHER READING

Golden F. and Tipton M. (2002) *Essentials of Sea Survival.* Human Kinetics; Leeds.

Parsons K. (1993) *Human Thermal Environments: the Principles and the Practice.* Taylor and Francis; London.

Reilly T. and Waterhouse J. (2005) *Sport, Exercise and Environmental Physiology.* Elsevier; Edinburgh.

REFERENCES

Ainslie P. N. and Reilly T. (2003). Physiology of accidental hypothermia in the mountains: a forgotten story. *British Journal of Sports Medicine;* 37: 548–50.

Almond C. S., Shin A. Y., Fortescue E. B., Mannix R. C., Wypij D., Binstadt B. A., Duncan C. N., Olson D., Salerno A. E., Newburger J. W. and Greenes D. S. (2005). Hyponatremia among runners in the Boston Marathon. *New England Journal of Medicine;* 352: 1550–6.

American College of Sports Medicine (1984) Position Statement. Prevention of thermal injuries during distance running. *Physician and Sportsmedicine;* 12 (7): 43–51.

Atkinson G., Holder A., Robertson C., Gant N., Drust B., Reilly T. and Waterhouse J. (2005). Effects of melatonin on the thermoregulatory responses to intermittent exercise. *Journal of Pineal Research;* 39: 353–9.

Bedford T. (1946) Environmental warmth and its measurement. *Medical Research Council War Memorandum no. 17.* HMSO; London.

Beshir M. Y., Ramsey J. D. and Burford C. L. (1982) Threshold values for the Botsball: a field study of occupational heat. *Ergonomics;* 25: 247–54.

Burton A. L. (1935) Human calorimetry. *Journal of Nutrition;* 9: 261–79.

Byrne C. and Lim C. L. (2007). The ingestible telemetric body core temperature sensor: a review of validity and exercise applications. *British Journal of Sports Medicine;* 41: 126–33.

Byrne C., Lee K. W., Chew S. A. N., Lim C. L. and Tan E. Y. M. (2006). Continuous thermoregulatory responses to mass-participation distance running in heat. *Medicine and Science in Sports and Exercise;* 38: 803–10.

Cable N. T. (2009) Cardiovascular function. In: (R. G. Eston and T. Reilly, eds) *Kinanthropometry and Exercise Physiology Laboratory Manual (3rd Edition): Exercise Physiology (Chapter 5).* Routledge; Oxon.

Cooke C. (2009) Metabolic rate and energy balance. In: (R. G. Eston and T. Reilly, eds) *Kinanthropometry Laboratory Manual (3rd edition): Physiology (Chapter 6).* Routledge; London: pp. 147–173.

Costill D. L. (1981) Muscle water and electrolye distribution during prolonged exercise. *International Journal of Sports Medicine;* 2: 130–4.

Edwards B., Waterhouse J., Reilly T. and Atkinson G. (2002). A comparison of suitabilities of rectal, gut and insulated axilla temperatures for measurement of the circadian rhythm of core temperature in field studies. *Chronobiology International;* 19: 579–97.

Ely M. R., Cheuvront S. N. and Montain S. J. (2007). Neither cloud cover nor low solar loads are associated with fast marathon performance. *Medicine and Science in Sports and Exercise;* **39**: 2029–35.

Froese G. and Burton A. C. (1957) Heat loss from the human head. *Journal of Applied Physiology;* **10**: 235–41.

Haymes E. M. (1984) Physiological responses of female athletes to heat stress: a review. *Physician and Sportsmedicine;* **12** (3): 45–55.

Holdcroft P. (1980) *Body Temperature Control.* Bailliere Tindall; London.

Holmer I. and Bergh U. (1974) Metabolic and thermal responses to swimming in water at varying temperatures. *Journal of Applied Physiology;* **37**: 702–5.

Horvath S. M. (1981) Exercise in a cold environment. *Exercise and Sport Science Reviews;* **9**: 221–63.

Lee D. H. K. (1980) Seventy five years of searching for a heat index. *Environmental Research;* **22**: 331–56.

Lemmey A., Eston R. G., Moloney S. and Yeomans J. (2000) The effects of hydration state and rehydration method on bioelectrical impedance analysis. *South African Journal of Sports Medicine;* **7**: 8–12.

Low D., Purvis A. J., Reilly T. and Cable N. T. (2005). The prolactin response to active and passive heating in man. *Experimental Physiology;* **90**: 909–1017.

Peiser B. and Reilly T. (2004). Environmental factors in the summer Olympics in historical perspective. *Journal of Sports Sciences;* **22**: 981–1002.

Pugh G. (1972) The gooseflesh syndrome in long distance runners. *British Journal of Physical Education;* March: ix–xii.

Pugh L. G. C. and Edholm O. G. (1955) The physiology of channel swimmers. *Lancet;* ii: 761–8.

Rahn H. and Yokoyama T. (eds) (1965) *Physiology of Breathold Diving and the Ama of Japan.* National Academy of Sciences; Washington, DC.

Ramanathan N. L. (1964) A new weighting system for mean temperature of the human body. *Journal of Applied Physiology;* **19**: 531–3.

Raymann J. E. M., Swaab D. F. and Van Someren E. W. (2007). Skin temperature and sleep-onset latency: changes with age and insomnia. *Physiology and Behavior;* **90**: 257–66.

Reilly T. (1983) The energy cost and mechanical efficiency of circuit weight training. *Journal of Human Movement Studies;* **9**: 39–45.

Reilly T. (1990) Human circadian rhythms and exercise. *Critical Reviews in Biomedical Engineering;* **18**: 165–80.

Reilly T., Waterhouse J. and Atkinson G. (1997) Aging, rhythms of physical performance, and adjustment to changes in the sleep-activity cycle. *Occupational and Environmental Studies;* **54**: 812–16.

Reilly T., Atkinson G. and Waterhouse J. (2000) Chronobiology and physical performance. In: (W. E. Garrett Jr. and D. T. Kirkendall, eds) *Exercise and Sport Science.* Lippincott, Williams and Wilkins; Philadelphia, PA: pp. 351–72.

Reilly T., Drust B. and Gregson W. (2006). Thermoregulation in elite athletes. *Current Opinion in Clinical Nutrition and Metabolic Care;* **9**: 666–71.

Ross W. R., Drinkwater D. T., Bailey D. A., Marshall G. W. and Leahy R. M. (1980) Kinanthropometry; traditions and new perspectives. In: (M. Ostyn, G. Beunen and J. Simons, eds) *Kinanthropometry II.* University Park Press; Baltimore, MD: pp. 3–27.

Siple P. A. and Passel C. F. (1945) Measurement of dry atmospheric cooling in sub-freezing temperatures. *Proceedings of the American Philosophical Society;* **89**: 177–99.

Skreslet S. and Aarefjord F. (1968) Acclimatisation to cold in man induced by frequent scuba diving in cold water. *Journal of Applied Physiology;* **24**: 177–81.

Tipton M., Eglin C., Gennser M. and Golden F. (1999) Immersion deaths and deterioration in swimming performance in cold water. *Lancet;* **354**: 626–9.

Watson P., Hasegawa H., Roelands B., Piacentini M. F., Looverie R. and Meeusen R. (2005). Acute dopamine/noradrenaline reuptake inhibition enhances human exercise performance in warm, but not temperate conditions. *Journal of Physiology;* **565**: 873–83.

Webb P. (1982) Thermal problems. In: (O. G. Edholm and J. S. Weiner, eds) *The Physiology and Medicine of Diving.* Bailliere Tindall; London: pp. 297–318.

PART FOUR

ASSESSMENT AND REGULATION OF ENERGY EXPENDITURE AND EXERCISE INTENSITY

CHAPTER 9

CONTROL OF EXERCISE INTENSITY USING HEART RATE, PERCEIVED EXERTION AND OTHER NON-INVASIVE PROCEDURES

Roger Eston, John G. Williams and James Faulkner

9.1 AIMS

- To review and apply common non-invasive methods of determining exercise intensity;
- To review relationships between heart rate, rating of perceived exertion, oxygen uptake and exercise intensity;
- To assess the reliability of ratings of perceived exertion and evaluate the validity of such methods in controlling exercise intensity.

9.2 INTRODUCTION

People participate in physical exercise to improve general health, performance-related fitness for a particular sport, and/or for recreation and relaxation. Improved fitness results from adaptation and improvement of cardiovascular, respiratory, and metabolic function as well as local responses in the muscle groups engaged. The nature and magnitude of any training effect are influenced by the frequency, duration and intensity of exercise (for a comprehensive review see American College of Sports Medicine, ACSM, 2006). The process of determining and controlling appropriate exercise intensity presents a challenge, which has implications related to both physiological changes and to individual compliance within an exercise programme.

An important principle to be assimilated at the outset is that intensity is interpreted by the person engaged in the exercise. No matter how sophisticated the physiological measurements, the psychological interpretation of cardiorespiratory, metabolic and musculoskeletal functions will play a major role in this process. The psychological component of how 'hard' or 'easy' people perceive their physical efforts to be has been emphasized by Gunnar Borg for exercise testing and prescription since the 1960s (e.g. Borg 1962). The application of Borg's Ratings of Perceived Exertion (RPE) scales (see Section 9.4.2) are included in mainstream guidelines for the conduct of exercise testing and prescription (ACSM 2006; British Association of Sport and Exercise Sciences, BASES 2007).

However perceptive an individual's judgements of exercise intensity may be, accurate determination is enhanced by assessing and monitoring functional capacity to ensure that an optimal intensity is prescribed. The acquisition of such data is only possible in a fully equipped exercise physiology laboratory using trained personnel. The ACSM (2006) and BASES (2007) have provided concise guidelines for the conduct of such assessments.

9.3 USING OXYGEN CONSUMPTION AND HEART RATE TO PRESCRIBE EXERCISE INTENSITY

Several measurements for gauging exercise intensity for various exercise modalities have been devised and applied. These include proportion of maximal oxygen uptake (% $\dot{V}O_{2max}$), proportion of maximal heart rate (HR$_{max}$), proportion of maximal heart rate reserve (HRR$_{max}$), and blood lactate (La) indices. The following sections cover the main principles of predicting and controlling exercise intensity by extrapolation of the relationships between oxygen uptake ($\dot{V}O_2$), heart rate (HR), power output and running speed. For a detailed review of the application of metabolic and ventilatory measures for controlling exercise intensity, refer to Jones *et al.* (2009, Chapter 10).

9.3.1 Using oxygen consumption to prescribe exercise intensity ($\dot{V}O_2$)

Exercising at a high (or moderate) intensity for a sustained period of time requires the ability to deliver oxygen to the active muscles. The most frequently cited criterion of maximal functional capacity for sustained exercise is maximal oxygen uptake ($\dot{V}O_{2max}$). Its measurement requires appropriately equipped facilities and expert personnel as well as a high degree of compliance on the part of the participant due to the exhaustive nature of the testing procedures. The method is explained in Chapter 7 Cooke (2009a). Ideally, proportions of the $\dot{V}O_{2max}$ are used to specify exercise intensity levels. The recommended intensity range is normally between 40% and 85% depending on the health and training status of the individual (ACSM 2006).

(a) Prediction of oxygen consumption levels using a multi-stage test

Maximal oxygen uptake is considered to be one of the best indicators of cardiovascular fitness and is often directly assessed during a graded exercise test (GXT). However, practical and ethical concerns arise when adopting exhaustive exercise tests in non-athletic or patient populations. Although the measurement of $\dot{V}O_2$ is preferred, it is possible to predict $\dot{V}O_{2max}$ using equations (ACSM 2006) for walking, running, leg cycling, arm cycling and stepping. The $\dot{V}O_2$ can be predicted for any speed of walking and running on level or inclined surfaces, as well as for cycling, stepping and rowing at specific work rates. In this way, the submaximal, predicted $\dot{V}O_2$ values can be compared against the subject's heart rate and extrapolated to the maximal heart rate to predict $\dot{V}O_{2max}$. With knowledge of the $\dot{V}O_{2max}$ it is then possible to prescribe speeds and/or work rates, which correspond to a given exercise intensity (% $\dot{V}O_{2max}$ values), and which are appropriate for the subject. The following examples are for running and cycling.

The formula used to predict $\dot{V}O_2$ at any given speed and gradient is:

$$\dot{V}O_2 \, (ml \, kg^{-1} \, min^{-1}) = horizontal \, component + vertical \, component + resting \, component$$

For running

$$\dot{V}O_2 \, (ml \, kg^{-1} \, min^{-1}) = (Speed \, (m \, min^{-1}) \times 0.2 \, ml \, kg^{-1} \, min^{-1}) + (gradient \times m \, min^{-1} \times 0.9 \, ml \, kg^{-1} \, min^{-1}) + 3.5 \, ml \, kg^{-1} \, min^{-1}$$

For cycling

$$\dot{V}O_2(ml) = (Work \, rate \, (kg \, m \, min^{-1}) \times 2 \, ml \, kgm^{-1} \, min^{-1}) + (Mass \times 3.5 \, ml \, kg^{-1} \, min^{-1})$$

(Note: 1 W = 6.12 kgm min^{-1}; an alternative and simpler formula is:
$$\dot{V}O_2 \, (ml) = (12 \times W) + 300$$

In a multi-stage test the subject runs or cycles at two levels. When two submaximal $\dot{V}O_2$ values are calculated, the slope of the $\dot{V}O_2$ regression line is obtained and this is used to predict the $\dot{V}O_{2max}$ by extrapolation of one of the multi-stage $\dot{V}O_2$:HR values.

Calculation of the 'slope' of the $\dot{V}O_2$:HR relationship is determined by:

Slope $(b) = (\dot{V}O_2 \text{ stage } 2 - \dot{V}O_2 \text{ stage } 1)$ / (HR stage 2 – HR stage 1)

$\dot{V}O_{2max} = \dot{V}O_2 \text{ stage } 2 + b \{(220\text{-age}) - HR \text{ stage } 2\}$

It is important to note that HR values must be at steady-state. For adults, this typically means exercising for at least 3 minutes to achieve steady-state (for children it could be much less with steady-state being achieved in 1–2 minutes depending on age), although the exercise intensity (low, moderate, high) and the ensuing time constant of a subjects $\dot{V}O_2$ kinetics may alter this duration (shorter or longer), and should therefore be considered. If the HR is not at steady-state (i.e. it is still increasing) it will predict an unrealistic overestimation of the $\dot{V}O_{2max}$ and be inaccurate for prescription of subsequent exercise intensity. What follows is an example of the method used to predict $\dot{V}O_{2max}$ using actual data derived from an exercise test. The formulae below uses the equation 220 – age to predict HR_{max}. An alternative and potentially more accurate technique may be the more recently derived equation of HR_{max} = 207 – (0.7 × age) (Gellish *et al.* 2007). The data are from a fit and healthy male (RGE, age 38, weight 86 kg).

(i) Prediction of $\dot{V}O_{2max}$ (treadmill protocol)

Treadmill data

	Stage 1	Stage 2
Speed (mph)	6	8
Gradient (%)	4	8
HR	134	172

Calculation of submaximal $\dot{V}O_2$

Stage 1

$\dot{V}O_2$ (ml kg^{-1} min^{-1}) = (160.8 m min^{-1} × 0.2 ml kg^{-1} min^{-1} + (0.04 × 160.8 m min^{-1} × 0.9 ml kg^{-1} min^{-1}) + 3.5 ml kg^{-1} min^{-1} = 41.4 ml kg^{-1} min^{-1}

Stage 2

$\dot{V}O_2$(ml kg^{-1} min^{-1}) = (214.4m min^{-1} × 0.2 ml kg^{-1} min^{-1}) + (0.08 × 214.4 m min^{-1} × 0.9 ml kg^{-1} min^{-1}) + 3.5 ml kg^{-1} min^{-1} = 61.8 ml kg^{-1} min^{-1}

(*Note*: 1 mph = 26.8 m min^{-1} = 0.45 m s^{-1})

Calculation of slope (b)

$b = (61.8 – 41.4)/(172 – 134) = 0.54$

Calculation of $\dot{V}O_{2max}$

$\dot{V}O_{2max}$ (ml kg^{-1} min^{-1}) = 61.8 + 0.54 ((220 – 38) – 172)

$\dot{V}O_{2max}$ l kg^{-1} min^{-1}) = 67

(ii) Prediction of $\dot{V}O_{2max}$ (cycle ergometry protocol)

Cycle ergometry data

	Stage 1	Stage 2
Work rate (kgm min–1)	900 (147 W)	1200 (196 W)
Heart rate	124	138

Calculation of submaximal $\dot{V}O_2$

Stage 1

$\dot{V}O_2$(ml) = (900 kg·m·min^{-1} × 2ml kgm^{-1} min^{-1}) + (86 kg × 3.5 ml kg^{-1} min^{-1})

$\dot{V}O_2$(ml) = 2101

$\dot{V}O_2$(ml kg^{-1} min^{-1}) = 2101 ml/86 kg = 24

Stage 2

$\dot{V}O_2$(ml) = (1200 kg·m·min^{-1} × 2 ml kgm^{-1} min^{-1}) + (86 kg × 3.5 ml kg^{-1} min^{-1})

$\dot{V}O_2$(ml) = 2701

$\dot{V}O_2$(ml kg^{-1} min^{-1}) = 2701 ml/86 kg = 31

Calculation of slope (b)
b = (31.4 – 24.4)/(138 – 124) = 0.50

Calculation of $\dot{V}O_{2max}$ for cycle ergometry
$\dot{V}O_2$(ml kg^{-1} min^{-1}) = 31.4 + 0.50 ((220 – 38) – 138)

$\dot{V}O_{2max}$(ml kg^{-1} min^{-1}) = 53

b) Determining the exercise prescription

Once a maximal aerobic capacity has been determined, it is possible to prescribe a running speed/work rate that corresponds to a given exercise intensity. In the following example, the exercise intensity corresponding to 70% $\dot{V}O_{2max}$ is determined, for running and for cycling for RGE.

(i) For running

In the above example the $\dot{V}O_{2max}$ was determined to be 67 ml kg^{-1} min^{-1}; 70% of this is 46.9 ml kg^{-1} min^{-1}
    By substitution into the formula:

$\dot{V}O_2$ = (m min^{-1} × 0.2 ml m^{-1} min^{-1}) + 3.5

The running speed (m min^{-1})
= ($\dot{V}O_2$ – 3.5)/0.2
= (46.9 – 3.5)/0.2
= 217 m min^{-1} (3.61 m s^{-1})

This equates to a running speed of 13 km h^{-1} (8.1 mph) or a running pace of 4 minutes 36 s per km or 7 minuntes 24 s per mile (60 min/8.1 mph) on a level gradient.

(ii) For cycling on a basket loaded ergometer (e.g. Monark 812)

In the above example the $\dot{V}O_{2max}$ was determined to be 53 ml kg^{-1} min^{-1}; 70% of the this is 37.4 ml kg^{-1} min^{-1}. This value is multiplied by mass (86 kg) to give an absolute $\dot{V}O_2$ = 3216 ml

By substitution into the formula
$\dot{V}O_2$(ml) = (kgm min^{-1} × 2 ml kgm^{-1} + (3.5 ml kg^{-1} min^{-1} × Mass)

The work rate (kgm min^{-1})
= ($\dot{V}O_2$ – (3.5 × Mass))/2 = (3216.4 – (3.5 × 86))/2 = 1457.7 kgm min^{-1} (238 W)

The next thing to decide is the preferred cycling frequency. As power output (Watts) is a function of the pedal frequency and cycle load (Power output = pedal frequency × cycle load), the higher the pedal frequency, the lower the load. If we assume that one pedal revolution is equal to a forward motion of 6 m (as per a Monark cycle ergometer), the loading can be calculated by the formula:

Load (kg) = (kgm min^{-1}) / (6 m × rev min^{-1})

Thus, for a pedal frequency of 50 rev min^{-1} the loading will be 4.86 kg and for a pedal frequency of 70 rev min^{-1} it would be 3.47 kg. At both pedaling speeds, the power output = 1457 kgm min^{-1} or 238 W

c) Estimation of energy expenditure

The concept of energy expenditure and metabolic rate is reviewed in chapter 6 (Cooke, 2009b). The total energy expenditure can be calculated on the basis that 1 MET (3.5 ml kg^{-1} min^{-1}) is equivalent to an energy expenditure of approximately 4.2 kJ kg h^{-1} (1 kcal kg^{-1} h^{-1}). Thus, an 86 kg person would expend approximately 361 kJ min^{-1} (86 kcal min^{-1}) at rest. In the above example, to run at a pace equal to 70% $\dot{V}O_{2max}$, the metabolic equivalent is about 13.4 METs. Thus, the energy expenditure per hour is 86 kg × 13.4 kcal kg^{-1} h^{-1} = 1154 kcal h^{-1} (4831 kJ h^{-1}). If the person runs for 30 minutes, the theoretical energy expenditure at this level can be calculated by the appropriate time proportion, i.e. 30/60 = 577 kcal (2415 kJ). This method is sometimes used to estimate a predicted weight loss. For example, on the basis that

1 g of substrate of mixed carbohydrate and fat (assuming a respiratory exchange ratio of 0.85) yields an energy content of 7.2 kcal (30 kJ), the weight loss in the above example was approximately 2415 kJ/30 kJ g^{-1} (577 kcal/7.2 kcal.g^{-1}) which equals 80 g. This may not seem much for all that effort, but an energy deficit of this magnitude for 7 days a week over 1 month would lead to a weight loss of (5 d × 80 g × 4.2 week) approximately 2.4 kg (5.3 lb).

9.3.2. Using heart rate to prescribe exercise intensity

Since heart rate and oxygen uptake share a positive, linear relationship regardless of age and sex, target heart rate ranges may be selected to correspond with $\dot{V}O_{2max}$ values (Karvonen and Vuorimaa 1988). This method is used in a variety of field tests and exercise protocols to approximate and monitor exercise intensity.

As a general rule, maximal aerobic power improves if exercise is sufficiently intense to increase heart rate to about 70% of maximum; equivalent to about 50–55% of $\dot{V}O_{2max}$. This is a level of intensity thought to be the minimal stimulus required to produce a training effect (Gaesser and Rich 1984), which will vary according to initial fitness status. Estimation of $\dot{V}O_{2max}$ from %HR_{max} is subject to error in all populations because of the need for a true maximal heart rate value. This can be attained from 2–4 minutes of 'all-out' exercise in the activity of interest. Such a procedure demands sound health coupled with a high level of commitment from an individual and is only really appropriate for competitive athletes. For this reason, maximal heart rate is usually predicted from equations (e.g. 220 – age) regardless of sex and age.

As all people of the same age (or sex) do not possess the same maximal heart rate, the variance for any given age (1 SD ± 10 beats min^{-1}) is considerable (ACSM 2006). The large standard errors of estimate from

formulae that predict maximal heart rate may result in inaccuracy when applied to general populations (Robergs and Landwehr 2002). Caution is therefore required with this procedure because, within normal variation, 68% of 20-year-olds will have a maximal heart rate between 190 and 210 beats min^{-1} (i.e. 220–20 ± 10 beats min^{-1}). This formula is also inappropriate for certain activities and for individuals on certain medication (e.g. *beta* blockers; Eston and Connolly 1996). For swimming, flotation in the supine position and the cooling effect of water may elicit heart rate values to be on average 10–13 beats min^{-1} lower than those observed during running. The assessment of intensity for swimming should therefore be at least 10 beats min^{-1} lower than the age-predicted maximal heart rate (McArdle *et al.* 1991).

A preferred method to prescribe exercise intensity is the percentage maximal heart rate reserve method (% HRR_{max}) as described by Karvonen and Vuorimaa (1988). This method uses the percentage difference between resting and maximal heart rate added to the resting heart rate. When compared to the % HR_{max} method, % HRR_{max} yields at least a 10 beat min^{-1} higher training heart rate when calculated for exercise intensities between 60% and 85% $\dot{V}O_{2max}$. This method equates more closely with given submaximal $\dot{V}O_{2max}$ values in both healthy adults and cardiac patients (Pollock *et al.* 1982).

The procedure for calculating % HRR_{max} values to determine exercise heart rates and the method of calculating % HRR_{max} from exercise heart rates are shown below.

RHR = Resting heart rate
HRR = Heart rate reserve
%HRR_{max} = Percentage maximal heart rate reserve
HR_{max} = 220 – age (e.g. at age 25 the predicted HR_{max} = 195 beats min^{-1})
HRR = HR_{max} – RHR (e.g. if RHR = 60 then HRR=195 – 60 = 135 beats min^{-1})
%HRR_{max} = (Training intensity (% of

maximum) × HRR) + RHR

The training intensity at 70% of HRR_{max} is therefore $((0.7 \times 135) + 60) = 154$ beats min^{-1}.

To calculate $\%HRR_{max}$ from an exercising heart rate the following formula is used:

$$\%HRR_{max} = \frac{\text{Exercise HR} - \text{RHR}}{HR_{max} - \text{RHR}}$$

e.g. $\dfrac{154-60}{195-60} = 70\% \ HRR_{max}$

Table 9.1 provides data in support of the $\%HRR_{max}$ method. Oxygen uptake and HR data were collected on RGE during a graded exercise test to maximum for treadmill running. The $\%HRR_{max}$ values (column 1) correspond very closely to the $\% \dot{V}O_{2max}$ values (column 7), and may be used to prescribe exercise intensity at a given $\% \ \dot{V}O_{2max}$. The $\%HR_{max}$ values tend to underestimate the $\% \dot{V}O_{2max}$ values (column 4), as exemplified in Figure 9.1.

9.4 USING THE RATING OF PERCEIVED EXERTION TO PRESCRIBE EXERCISE INTENSITY

9.4.1 The concept of effort perception

Physical performance emanates from the complex interaction of perceptual, cognitive and metabolic processes (see discussion by Borg 1998). The relationship of human

Table 9.1 A comparison of $\% \dot{V}O_{2max}$ at equivalent $\%HRR_{max}$ and $\%HR_{max}$ levels

%HR level	HR at% HR$_{max}$	$\dot{V}O_2$ (ml kg^{-1} min^{-1})	$\%\dot{V}O_{2max}$	HR at% HRR$_{max}$	$\dot{V}O_{2max}$ (ml kg^{-1} min^{-1})	$\%\dot{V}O_{2max}$
40	73	8	13	105	26	41
50	91	21	33	118	33	52
60	109	28	44	131	38	60
70	127	37	59	144	46	73
80	140	43	68	157	52	82
90	164	56	89	169	58	92
100	182	63	100	182	63	100

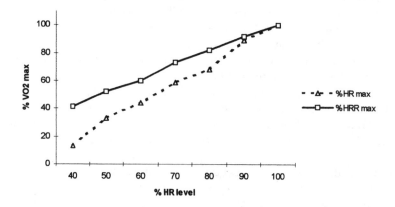

Figure 9.1. A comparison of $\% \dot{V}O_{2max}$ values at equivalent $\%HRR_{max}$ and $\%HR_{max}$ levels for RGE.

performance and perceived exertion has been an area of considerable interest over the last 40 years and remains a focus of extensive research in exercise and sport science. The perception of exertion may be defined as the subjective intensity of effort, strain, discomfort, and/or fatigue that is experienced during physical exercise (Robertson and Noble 1997). The Borg 6–20 RPE scale (Borg 1998) is an established equidistant interval tool that is commonly used to complement the objective physiological markers of the exercise response and to aid the prescription of exercise intensity in healthy adult populations and some criterion groups (Borg 1998; ACSM 1998, 2006).

The reasoning behind the use of what appears to be 'cardboard technology' is that humans possess a well-developed system for sensing the strain involved in physical effort. This system is in constant use. A person can sense whether he/she is able to continue during vigorous exercise. Furthermore, during a bout of exercise, one is able to report both current, overall feelings of exertion and the locus of particular strain (say, in the chest or arms). With some experience of various levels of exercise, people have little difficulty in numerically scaling or at least ordering samples of exercise to which they have been subjected.

9.4.2 Rating of perceived exertion scales

Attempts have been made to establish a basis for interpreting bodily sensations during exercise. By applying established principles of psychophysics (Stevens 1957; Ekman, 1961) to gross motor action, Borg determined relative stimulus-response (S-R) functions and then developed two rating scales, the *6–20 Category Scale* (RPE, Borg 1970) and the *Category-Ratio 10 Scale* (CR10, Borg 1982). Both Scales have been revised since their inception. By far, the most commonly used device is the Borg 6–20 RPE Scale (RPE, Table 9.2). This scale was designed

to assess sensations of exertion in relation to physiological (heart rate, oxygen uptake) and physical (power output) markers that rise commensurately with increments in exercise intensity. The RPE has been repeatedly validated against measures of physiological strain, such as heart rate, oxygen uptake, blood lactate and power output during graded exercise tests (Morgan and Borg 1976; Eston *et al.* 1987; Chen *et al.* 2002; Faulkner and Eston 2007). The CR10 Scale (Table 9.3) was constructed by Borg to take advantage of the properties of Stevens' ratio scaling (Stevens 1957, 1971) and category scaling, so that verbal expressions and numbers could be used in a way that is congruent with the non-linear characteristics of sensory perception and physical stimulation. Basically, the psychophysical characteristics of the relationship between perceived exertion (Response, R) and exercise intensity (Stimulus, S) can be described as $R = c \times S^n$, where *n* is the exponent that reflects the growth function. The CR10 Scale may therefore be considered more appropriate to reflect the psychophysical characteristics of those variables which increase as a curvilinear function of power output (positively accelerating), such as blood lactate and ventilation.

In both scales, numbers are anchored to verbal expressions. However, in the CR10 Scale, unlike the Borg 6–20 RPE Scale, the numbers are not fixed. Half numbers or decimals can be used, e.g. 0.7 or 2.3. The numerical values also have a fixed relation to one another. For example, an intensity (I) judgement of 5 would be gauged to be half that of 10. It is important to note that a rating of 10 is not truly maximal with the CR10 Scale. As the scale does not have a fixed endpoint, subjects have the option to choose a rating of perceived exertion that is greater than that previously experienced. Borg (1998, p. 51) indicated that a rating of 10 equates to a feeling which is 'as hard as most people have ever experienced before in their lives.' If during the exercise test the subjective intensity exceeds this level, the person is free

Table 9.2 The Borg 6–20 RPE Scale (Borg 1998)	
6	No exertion at all
7	
	Extremely light
8	
9	Very light
10	
11	Light
12	
13	Somewhat hard
14	
15	Hard (heavy)
16	
17	Very hard
18	
19	Extremely hard
20	Maximal exertion

Table 9.3 The Borg CR10 Scale (Borg 1998)		
0	Nothing at all	'No I'
0.3		
0.5	Extremely weak	Just noticeable
0.7		
1	Very weak	
1.5		
2	Weak	Light
2.5		
3	Moderate	
4		
5	Strong	(heavy)
6		
7	Very strong	
8		
9		
10	**Extremely strong**	**'Max I'**
11	Maximal	
!	Absolute maximum	Highest possible

to choose any number in proportion to 10 which describes the proportionate growth in the sensation of effort. For example if the exercise intensity feels 20% harder than 10, the RPE would be 12. Instructions and rationale for using the two RPE Scales are provided in more detail by Borg (1998). The use of the Borg 6–20 Scale is shown in Figure 9.2.

9.4.3 Exercise intensity and effort perception

The RPE and indices of relative exercise intensity (%$\dot{V}O_{2max}$, % HR_{max}, La, etc) are highly correlated. (r > 0.85). For example, Faulkner and Eston (2007), observed that undifferentiated RPE was almost as highly correlated with $\dot{V}O_2$ as heart rate during GXTs terminated at volitional exhaustion (R^2 = ~ 0.96 and R^2 = 0.98, respectively). This is exemplified in Figure 9.3, which shows a strong linear relationship between the RPE and power output for the individual in this study.

This relationship holds for cycling, running, walking, and arm ergometry. Furthermore, criterion group differences (such as trained vs untrained, lean vs obese, men vs women) observed at equivalent absolute work rates diminish at the same % $\dot{V}O_{2max}$. These results apply to both intermittent and continuous protocols. For example, although women often report a higher RPE when exercising at the same absolute intensity (i.e. $\dot{V}O_2$, heart rate), those differences disappear or are minimized when men and women are tested at the same relative exercise intensity (Noble et al. 1981; DeMello et al. 1987, Ueda and Kurokawa, 1995; Faulkner and Eston 2007). Thus, given the robust association between RPE, HR, $\dot{V}O_2$ and La, if the relationship for an individual is known, it is eminently feasible to use the RPE as a guide to individualized exercise intensity prescription.

A simple example of the efficacy of the RPE for tracking changes in HR and La is

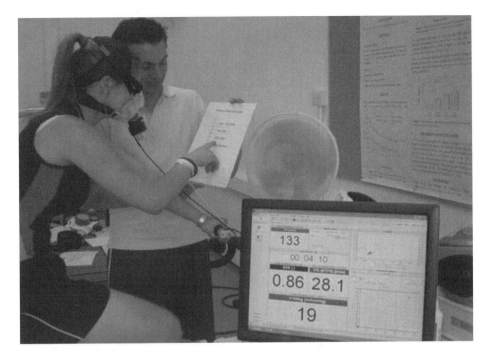

Figure 9.2. Measurement of the rating of perceived exertion using the Borg 6–20 RPE Scale during an incremental exercise test.

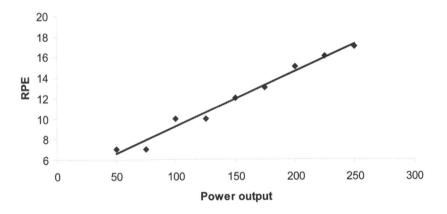

Figure 9.3 Linear relationship between power output and the rating of perceived exertion (using the 4-minute data from Table 9.5).

shown in Figure 9.4 using data from a young fit male (age 24) during a graded exercise test to maximal volitional exhaustion. For this individual, a heart rate ~150 and RPE ~15 corresponds to a lactate turnpoint (about 4mM), which may be recommended as a guide to elicit a target training intensity.

9.4.4 Reliability of RPE production and estimation procedures

Evidence to support the notion that the regulation of exercise intensity is a psycho-physiological process led to the assertion that the RPE alone could be a sufficient basis for gauging exercise intensity (Borg 1971).

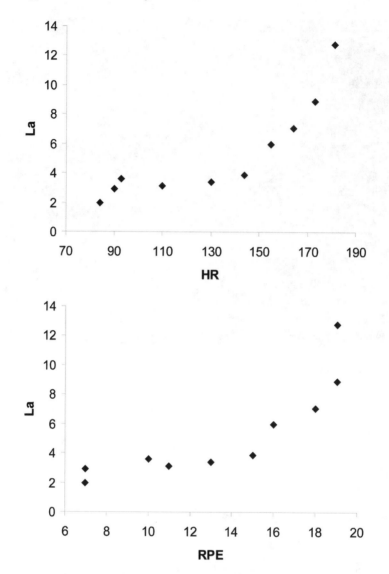

Figure 9.4 Example of the efficacy of the RPE for tracking changes in heart rate and blood lactate in a 24-year-old healthy male during a graded exercise test to volitional exhaustion on a cycle ergometer (commencing at 60 W with increments of 30 W every 4 minutes).

Since then, a number of studies have used the RPE as a frame of reference for regulating exercise intensity. Such an approach is clearly applicable to endurance training in various sports, but also applies to the attainment of general fitness and rehabilitation. It seems sensible to encourage people to 'tune' to their effort sense and develop sufficient awareness for determining an appropriate

exercise intensity without recourse to external devices.

Research has confirmed the validity of self-regulation guided by effort rating procedures. This has been demonstrated for treadmill running (Smutok *et al.* 1980; Eston *et al.* 1987; Dunbar *et al.* 1992; Glass *et al.* 1992), cycling (Eston and Williams 1988; Dunbar *et al.* 1992; Buckley *et al.*

2000), wheelchair exercise in children (Ward et al. 1995), cycling in children (Eston and Williams 1986; Williams et al. 1991; Eston et al. 2000; Robertson et al. 2002) and stepping in children (Williams et al. 1993, 1994; Parfitt et al. 2007).

The production procedure is considered an 'active' process, as participants must be attuned to their bodies to produce a certain rating of perceived exertion. As such, individuals are required to actively produce an exercise intensity based upon his/her interpretation of the effort sense and the cognition and understanding of the RPE prescribed. Several studies have supported the application of the ratings of perceived exertion within an active production procedure (Eston et al. 1987; Eston and Williams 1988; Dunbar et al. 1992; Glass et al. 1992; Parfitt et al. 1996; Eston and Thompson 1997; Faulkner et al. 2007a; Eston et al. 2008). The strong relationship between perceived exertion and physiological variables during effort production tests has been shown regardless of sex (Eston et al. 1987; Kang et al. 2003; Faulkner et al. 2007a) or the exercise modality (Eston et al. 1987; Eston and Williams 1988).

A conventional application to assess perceived exertion is an *estimation-production* procedure. An estimation-production procedure is considered to be an appropriate method to regulate exercise intensity, as it resembles the prescription process that is typically used with active, sedentary or clinical populations (e.g. McArdle's disease, chronic obstructive pulmonary disease and cardiac rehabilitation patients). Historically, the procedure involves prescribing a rating of perceived exertion to a given heart rate, oxygen uptake or blood lactate value (production mode) reported from a prior graded exercise test (estimation mode). Research has demonstrated that the estimation-production procedure is a physiologically valid method of regulating exercise intensity with individuals of varying age, gender, fitness and health (Smutok et al. 1980; Eston et al. 1987; Eston and Williams

1988; Ceci and Hassmen 1991; Dunbar et al. 1992; Glass et al. 1992; Buckley et al. 2000; Kang et al. 2003).

An important consideration of the plausibility of determining exercise intensity through perceived exertion is that much of the research in this area has been undertaken in controlled laboratory conditions, where the target production mode RPE levels were determined from a passive estimation protocol measured during an initial GXT. Byrne and Eston (1997) recommended caution when inferring a target production RPE from GXT estimation mode responses. They reported a mismatch of exercise intensities at a given RPE between estimation and production modes. Noble (1982) stated that the different procedures produce different psychophysical functions as an effort intensity from memory (production) is not identical to the process of estimating effort intensity during continuous exercise. Eston and Williams (1988) evaluated the reliability of multiple-trial production mode using pre-selected, randomly assigned RPEs of 9, 13 and 17 during cycle ergometry, and concluded that the accuracy of effort perception is dependent on familiarization and practice for both production and estimation procedures.

9.4.5 Prediction of maximal oxygen uptake using the RPE

Evidence suggests that the RPE elicited from estimation procedures can provide predictions of $\dot{V}O_{2max}$ that are as good as, or better than heart rate (Morgan and Borg 1976; Noble et al. 1981; Wilmore et al. 1985; Eston et al. 1987; Faulkner and Eston 2007; Faulkner et al. 2007b). Morgan and Borg (1976) measured the RPE during progressive maximal exercise to exhaustion for measurement of $\dot{V}O_{2max}$ in a group of healthy, physically active and sedentary men. They observed that RPE increased linearly with increases in work rate enabling extrapolation to a theoretical end point, which in turn makes possible the prediction of maximal work capacity.

Specifically, they observed that sub-maximal RPE predicted maximal work capacity with less error (1%) compared to heart rate (15%). Faulkner and Eston (2007) demonstrated no differences between measured $\dot{V}O_{2max}$ (43.3 ± 10.0 ml kg^{-1}min^{-1}) and $\dot{V}O_{2max}$ predicted from sub-maximal RPE ranges up to 13, 15 and 17 (42.1 ± 12.5, 43.4 ± 11.5, 44.2 ± 11.3 ml kg^{-1}min^{-1}, respectively) during a graded exercise test (estimation procedure). Although they observed a slight improvement in the prediction of $\dot{V}O_{2max}$ when utilizing age-predicted maximal heart rate in conjunction with sub-maximal RPE, the difference was only 1–1.5 ml·kg^{-1}min^{-1} (2 %).

An alternative application of the estimation-production procedure has been proposed and tested by Eston *et al.* (2005, 2006, 2008) and Faulkner *et al.* (2007a). Using repeat-production procedures, high- and low-active participants exercised at perceptually-regulated intensities prescribed at specific submaximal RPE (e.g. 9, 11, 13, 15, 17), for either 2, 3 or 4 minutes. In all cases the order of the RPE was the same as it was felt that this approach was conceptually appropriate as it would resemble the approximate increases in exercise intensity during a GXT. No differences were observed in these studies between measured $\dot{V}O_{2max}$ from a GXT to volitional exhaustion (estimation), and $\dot{V}O_{2max}$ predicted from sub-maximal, perceptually-guided GXTs (production). Furthermore, the predictions of $\dot{V}O_{2max}$ were not moderated by sex (Eston *et al.* 2005; Faulkner *et al.* 2007a), and were typically more accurate when extrapolating to the peak RPE (i.e. RPE 19 not RPE 20) from five (RPE 9–17), rather than from four (RPE 11–17, 9–15) or three (RPE 9–13) perceptual intensities. Estimates of $\dot{V}O_{2max}$ were improved following practice. This was demonstrated by the presence of smaller 95% Limits of Agreement (LoA) for the second and third trials, and increased between-trial correlation coefficients between the estimated and measured $\dot{V}O_{2max}$.

An interesting observation from several of these studies (Eston *et al.* 2006; Faulkner and Eston 2007; Faulkner *et al.* 2007a, b) was that participants typically reported an RPE of 18 or 19 at maximal volitional exhaustion. This finding has also been reported by others (St Clair Gibson *et al.* 1999; Kay *et al.* 2001).

The observation that $\dot{V}O_{2max}$ could be predicted from relatively low perceptual ranges (Faulkner *et al.* 2007a,b) has obvious importance for sedentary or clinical populations. Faulkner *et al.* (2007a) predicted $\dot{V}O_{2max}$ with reasonable accuracy by extrapolation of submaximal $\dot{V}O_2$ values (up to and including RPE 13) from a single GXT and perceptually-regulated protocol in men and women of low-fitness. This is important because the affective state may become increasingly negative with increasing exercise intensity in such populations (Hardy and Rejeski 1989; Parfitt *et al.* 1996), and potentially reduce the inclination to continue exercising.

A further important observation from the studies by Eston *et al.* (2008) and Faulkner *et al.* (2007a) was that the prescribed changes in RPE were successful in eliciting step changes in exercise intensity and metabolic cost of 1–2 METS (3.5 – 7.0 ml.kg^{-1}min^{-1}) in the sedentary or low-fitness groups. This is commensurate with standard submaximal graded exercise tests for healthy individuals (ACSM 2006).

9.4.6 Overall and local feelings of exertion

The overall perception of exertion is based on the complex 'gestalt' of cognitively integrated sensations from the working muscles and joints, respiratory and circulatory systems and the higher centres of the brain. It has been reported that *local factors are the dominant sensation of exertion* (Pandolf *et al.* 1975; Shephard *et al.* 1992). This has been shown irrespective of the size of the muscle mass recruited (Pandolf and Noble 1973), although it is typically assumed that the smaller the muscle mass, the greater the perception of exertion (Berry *et al.* 1989). The classic study by Ekblom and Goldbarg (1971) which differentiated between *local* and *central* effort percepts showed that the RPE for a given submaximal oxygen uptake or heart rate was higher for cycling compared to running. It has been suggested that cycling initiates the activation of a greater amount of fast twitch fibres than during running, thus stimulating a greater afferent input from perceptual pain receptors, muscle spindles and golgi tendons (Pandolf *et al.* 1975).

Research has also demonstrated that slower pedal rates initiate significantly higher local sensations (muscle pain/knee pain) on mechanically-braked cycle ergometers. (Jameson and Ring 2000). These investigators observed a greater localized RPE at 50 rpm compared to 70 and 90 rpm at work rates of 100, 150 and 200 W. Overall RPE and central sensations (breathlessness and heart beat intensity) were not affected by changes in cadence. Consequently, if exercise prescription is to be based on RPE, then the exercise mode must be specified because the source of the effort percept varies and influences the magnitude of the rating (Pandolf 1983). Dunbar *et al.* (1992) observed that there was greater test–retest reliability when RPE was estimated during cycle ergometry compared to treadmill running. This was attributed to the greater localization of muscle fatigue during cycle ergometry, allowing for a more accurate assessment of the intensity of the peripheral signal. They reported that a comparatively greater attentional focus on these intense regionalized perceptual signals might sharpen input to the perceptual cognitive framework. It follows from this finding that the production of a target RPE on the cycle should be facilitated. Another possible explanation advanced by Dunbar *et al.* (1992) was that the more stable position of the subject during cycle ergometry results in greater consistency in the RPE estimation. They postulated that the task of maintaining balance on a moving belt as in treadmill running may distract the individual from the quantity and intensity of the perceptual signals.

9.4.7 Dissociative strategies and RPE

Although the process is not the same, the role of *dissociation*, as a method of alleviating the discomfort associated with exercise-induced fatigue has been the subject of interest for some time (Benson *et al.* 1978). It has been claimed to be a useful coping mechanism (Morgan *et al.* 1983), although Rejeski (1985) has reported that theoretical explanations of why and how it works are lacking. He suggested that dissociative strategies provide a relief from fatigue by occupying limited channel capacity critical to bringing a percept into focal awareness.

9.4.8 Preferred exercise intensity, perceived exertion and affect

The association between RPE and preferred exercise intensity was included in Borg's published PhD thesis (Borg 1962). Parfitt *et al.* (2000) investigated the differences in psychological affect and interest-enjoyment between a prescribed treadmill intensity (based on 65% $\dot{V}O_{2max}$) session and a preferred intensity session, each of 20 minutes. In their study, participants exercised at a higher intensity in the preferred versus the prescribed exercise condition, although there were no differences in RPE. It seems that the participants perceived that they were exercising at the same level in both conditions. This study indicated a positive perception for the preferred exercise condition as the participants worked harder, but reported similar RPEs. When individuals are allowed to self-select their exercise intensity, they choose intensities which are close to the ventilatory or lactate threshold and the intensity is increased across the duration of the bout (Lind *et al.* 2005; Parfitt *et al.* 2006; Rose and Parfitt 2007). In conjunction, although intensity increases across time with commensurate increases in RPE, the individuals feel generally positive about the exercise intensity (Eston *et al.* 1998).

Maximizing the affective response to exercise may be the first link in a chain between exercise and adherence (Van Landuyt *et al.* 2000). Exercise intensities that lead to the individual feeling good are more likely to facilitate future adherence, while those that do not are more likely to lead to withdrawal from exercise (Parfitt *et al.* 2006). These authors confirmed that self-selected intensity with sedentary individuals promotes positive affective responses. However, there is no guarantee that using the RPE scale to self-regulate (e.g. instructing the individual to produce a perceptually-regulated exercise intensity at RPE 13) ensures a positive affective response. The RPE scale is a valid measure of the heaviness and strain of physical work; it is not a measure of the affective response of pleasure/displeasure (Hardy and Rejeski 1989).

It has therefore been proposed that one approach to control exercise intensity is to allow the individual to self-regulate his/her exercise intensity to produce a positive affective response (Rose and Parfitt 2009). The Feeling Scale (FS) developed by Hardy and Rejeski (1989) has been recommended by Ekkekakis and Petruzzello (2002) to measure the valence (pleasure-displeasure, good-bad) component of affect. This is an 11-point bipolar scale anchored from very good (+5) through neutral (0) to very bad (-5). Individuals are asked to report how they feel at specific time points.

Rose and Parfitt (2009) assessed the efficacy of using the FS as a means of regulating exercise intensity. In their study, 17 sedentary women (mean age 44.8 ± 8.9 years) completed eight 30-minute laboratory-based treadmill exercise sessions. In four consecutive sessions, participants exercised at an intensity they perceived corresponded to an FS value of 1 (Fairly Good) and the other four sessions, at an intensity corresponding to a FS value of 3 (Good). They observed that to achieve an affective state of Good (FS 3) individuals exercised at a lower intensity (64% HR_{max}) compared to an affective state of Fairly Good (FS 1), which elicited an exercise intensity of 68% HR_{max}. These FS conditions equated to mean RPE values of 11.4 and 12.0, respectively, and exercise intensities corresponding to ~ 6 METS for both conditions. These intensities were 7–8% above the individuals' ventilatory threshold. Across the four bouts of exercise at each condition, individuals consistently selected the same intensity to elicit a feeling state of Good and Fairly Good. Across the 30 minutes in all of the exercise sessions, individuals also increased the intensity of exercise in order to maintain the required affective state. Whilst this is an isolated study, the principle is worthy of further investigation as it offers considerable scope for exercise prescription for those who are most likely to drop out.

9.4.9 The RPE Scales with time and distance in open and closed loop tasks

Recently, a number of research groups has observed a scalar linear relationship between the ratings of perceived exertion and the duration of exercise (Noakes 2004; Eston *et al.* 2007; Joseph *et al.* 2008; Faulkner *et al.* 2008; Crewe *et al.* 2008). This relationship was originally described by Horstman *et al.* (1979). In their study, with the purpose of describing a generalizable pattern of change in effort sense and the potential for predicting the work end point, 26 healthy young men walked or ran at 80% $\dot{V}O_{2max}$ to self-imposed exhaustion. As work continued during both tasks, significant increases in ventilation, ventilatory equivalent for oxygen, and heart rate were observed, whilst $\dot{V}O_2$ and respiratory exchange ratio remained constant. Notably, the RPE was identical for both conditions, increasing in a linear fashion from a value of about 12.9 at 25% work time to 18.9 at exhaustion, and rising as a linear function of the percentage of total exercise duration. They reported that the early pattern of change in RPE during prolonged work can be used as a sensitive predictor of the point of self-imposed exhaustion. To our knowledge these were the first authors to observe the rate of change in RPE during prolonged constant work could be used as a sensitive predictor of the point of self-imposed exhaustion.

Renewed interest in this area was sparked by a letter to the editor of the *Journal of Applied Physiology* from Tim Noakes (2004) who observed that in subjects exercising at a fixed work rate while either carbohydrate-replete or partially carbohydrate depleted (from the study by Baldwin *et al.* 2003), the RPE appeared to rise as a linear function of the duration of exercise that remained. Noakes (2004) proposed that perceived exertion is set in an anticipatory manner from the start of the exercise bout, implying that the brain increases the RPE as a proportion of the time that has been completed, or the percentage of time that remains. These observations have been verified in two 'open loop' exercise tests involving a constant load. Figure 9.5 shows the pattern of response in RPE against time and %time to self imposed exhaustion during a pre-fatigued and fresh condition whilst cycling at constant load set at 70% $\dot{V}O_{2max}$ in 10 young men. Intrigued by this phenomenon, Eston *et al.* (2007) conducted a similar study on a separate group of 10 young men and produced identical results, which confirmed that the RPE increased as linear function of the duration of exercise that remained. Joseph *et al.* (2008) provided further support for these observations during a 'closed loop' task involving cycling time-trials of either 2.5 km, 5 km or 10 km. They showed that RPE increases in relation to relative distance, regardless of the distance performed, suggesting that the perception of effort has a scalar relationship with the distance remaining during closed-loop exercise tasks.

Based on these findings, Faulkner *et al.* (2008) explored whether the scalar time properties of perceived exertion were evident during competitive distance running in the field. As research within the domain of teleoanticipation had focused on cycle ergometry in a laboratory environment (Kay *et al.* 2001; Albertus *et al.* 2005; Eston *et al.* 2007; Joseph *et al.* 2008), they were interested in determining whether the distance, course elevation (gradient), and variations in pacing strategy, coupled with the greater cardio-pulmonary sensations of exertion experienced during running, altered the RPE-time relationship that had been previously demonstrated. They hypothesized that if the scalar teleoanticipatory theory of RPE was correct, the brain would take into account the environmental conditions (i.e. distance, course elevation) and manipulate the absolute RPE-duration relationship, but maintain the relative scalar relationship between performance and RPE.

In their study, nine men and women competed in a 7-mile (11.2 km) road race (7-MR) and the Great West Run half-marathon (GWR; 13.1 miles). Heart rate, split mile time and RPE were recorded throughout the races. The RPE was regressed against time and %time to complete the 7-MR and GWR and distance and %distance. Although the rate of increase in RPE was greater in the 7-MR, there were no differences when expressed against %time or against %distance. They concluded that as the course elevation, distance, pacing strategy and heart rate response varied between conditions, the perceptual response may have distinct temporal characteristics during distance running.

The results from the varied studies of Horstman *et al.* (1979), Eston *et al.* (2007), Crewe *et al.* (2008), Joseph *et al.* (2008) and Faulkner *et al.* (2008) provide further confirmation that the RPE scales with time and distance in both open and closed-loop exercise tasks. These results have implications for the utility of the RPE to predict the end point of exhaustion. Further studies on the use of this concept are recommended in both healthy and clinical populations.

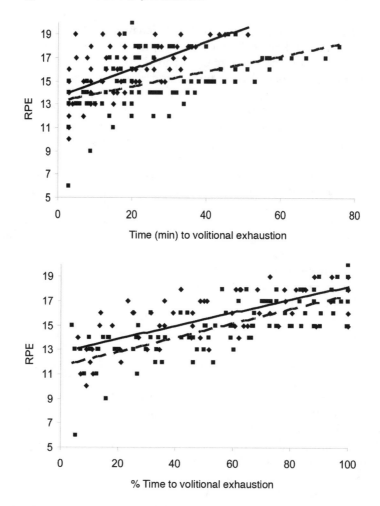

Figure 9.5 Rate of increase in RPE in 10 University students during constant load exercise at 65% $\dot{V}O_{2max}$ in a fresh and fatigued state when RPE is expressed against time to volitional exhaustion and when RPE is expressed relative to time remaining. Application: An RPE of 15 indicates that the time at this point marks ~60% of the time completed. (Macombie 2005; unpublished data).

9.5 EFFORT PERCEPTION IN CHILDREN

There have been important advances in the study of effort perception in children in the last 20 years which are described in greater detail elsewhere (Eston and Parfitt 2007; Lamb *et al.* 2008). Bar Or (1977) and Borg (1977) recognized that the age, reading ability, experience, and conceptual understanding of the child has to be taken into account when developing an appropriate perceptual scale.

For a child to perceive effort accurately, and subsequently to produce an exercise intensity level from a predetermined RPE, it is logical to assume that learning must occur. Learning is a more or less permanent change in behaviour, which is reflected by a change in performance brought about by practice as well as maturation (Buskist and Gerbing 1990). Thus, the child must have developed the relevant cognitive capacity to comprehend the task as well the direct experience and practice of the activity.

According to Piaget's (1972) stage model of development, children around the age of 7–10 years can understand categorization, but find it easier to understand and interpret pictures and symbols rather than words and numbers. Williams *et al.* (1993) found that very young children aged 6–8 years were unable to gauge intermediate levels of exercise intensity. Contemporary paediatric exercise research has addressed this problem.

The idea for a simplified perceived exertion scale which was more suitable for use with children emanated from the study by Williams *et al.* (1991) on 40 boys and girls aged 11–14 years. In their study, although the children seemed to accept and understand the purpose of Borg's 6–20 RPE Scale, the authors were not convinced with its utility with children and proposed the idea for a 1–10 scale anchored with more developmentally appropriate expressions of effort. This led to a significant development in the measurement of children's effort perception in 1994 with two publications that proposed and validated an alternative child-specific rating scale – the Children's Effort Rating Table (CERT, Eston *et al.* 1994; Williams *et al.* 1994; Table 9.4). Compared to the Borg Scale, the CERT has five fewer possible responses, a range of numbers (1–10) more familiar to children than the Borg 6–20 Scale and verbal expressions chosen by children as descriptors of exercise effort.

The CERT initiative for a simplified scale containing more 'developmentally-appropriate' numerical and verbal expressions, led to the development of scales that combined numerical and pictorial ratings of perceived exertion scales, which were used to portray increased states of physical exertion. Like the CERT, the scales have embraced a similar, condensed numerical range and words or expressions which are either identical to (PCERT, Yelling *et al.* 2002), abridged from (CALER, Eston *et al.* 2000; BABE, Parfitt *et al.* 2007) or similar in context to the CERT (OMNI, Robertson 1997; Robertson *et al.* 2000). All the above pictorial scales have

Table 9.4 Children's Effort Rating Table (CERT) (Williams *et al.* 1994)

1	Very, very easy
2	Very easy
3	Easy
4	Just feeling a strain
5	Starting to get hard
6	Getting quite hard
7	Hard
8	Very hard
9	Very, very hard
10	So hard I am going to stop

been used successfully to regulate exercise intensity in children (see Eston and Parfitt 2007 and Lamb *et al.* 2008 for detailed reviews). Studies comparing the validity of derivatives of the CERT (P-CERT, Roemmich *et al.* 2006; CALER, Barkley and Roemmich, 2008) with the OMNI have shown that the scales can be used with equal utility. As with adults, studies have also shown that repeated practice improves the reliability of effort production when using the CALER (Eston *et al.* 2000; Parfitt *et al.* 2007) and the BABE scales (Parfitt *et al.* 2007). The latter study also showed that the two scales, which are pictorially quite different, could be used interchangeably to regulate exercise intensity in 30 children aged 7–11 years. Specifically, they observed that the CALER scale could be used to regulate stepping and the BABE scale could be used to regulate cycling.

Other variants, including a four effort level scale anchored with versions of the well known 'smiley' face and scaled directly from CERT and RPE, have been developed. Research with 7-year-olds has shown that children readily identify and discriminate effort level with the various facial expressions (Williams and O'Brien 2000).

All the pictorial scales considered above have used either a horizontal line or one that has a linear slope. A curvilinear scale has been proposed (E-P Scale, Eston and Parfitt, 2007; Figure 9.6) for consideration and evaluation. The rationale for exploring the use of such a scale was originally founded on its inherently obvious face validity. It is readily conceivable that a child will recognize from previous learning and experience that the steeper the hill, the harder it is to ascend. This may also be helpful in the process of 'anchoring' effort perceptions.

The premise for such a scale was highlighted by Barkley and Roemmich (2008) in a study to assess the validity of the CALER and OMNI-Bike ratings of perceived exertion scale. In their study, 16 boys and girls aged 9–10 years performed a progressive exercise test on a cycle ergometer to exhaustion. They observed that the proportions of the maximal CALER (75%) and OMNI (74%) scales were significantly less than the peak percentage of the predicted maximal heart rate (95%). They indicated that although both scales appear to illustrate effort during submaximal exercise successfully, they could benefit from modifications to their upper range. They suggested that a change in the linearity of the scales so that the final stages increase at a greater rate or increase in a curvilinear fashion could improve the agreement with physiological measures at peak exercise intensities.

A recent study on 13 boys and girls aged 7–8 years indicates that this approach is valid (Lambrick *et al.* 2008). In this study the children performed an intermittent, incremental test (10 W min^{-1}) on a cycle ergometer, to exhaustion. Cardiorespiratory data were collected continuously. Each child estimated their RPE at the end of each 1-minute exercise bout by pointing to or sliding a marker along the numerical range of the E-P Scale. They also placed an unlimited number of marbles into a separate jar to indicate their perceived exertion (Figure 9.7). There were highly significant increases in $\dot{V}O_2$, HR and RPE estimates using the E-P Scale and marbles task with increasing work rate. It was also noted that the correlation coefficients were higher for the curvilinear compared to the linear relationships between the perceptual data and work rate, for the E-P scale ($R^2 = 0.83 - 0.99$ and $0.73 - 0.99$) and Marbles ($R^2 = 0.83 - 0.99$ and $0.58 - 0.97$), respectively. The increase in perceptual response with increasing exercise intensity indicates that children readily understand the nature of the E-P Scale. Furthermore, the novel perceptual 'marble' task gave rise to some encouraging findings and demonstrated that a child's perception of effort rises curvilinearly with equal increments in work rate. Such visual representation may facilitate a child's understanding and thus their ability to use the scale. Future studies should focus on the reliability of the E-P Scale, and its utility in the production mode.

Eston and Parfitt (2007) have also shown that children can use the scale to self-regulate exercise intensities. In their study, 20 8- to 11-year-old children were requested to bench step for 3-minutes at an exercise intensity corresponding to RPEs of 2, 5 and 8, continuously, in that order, and without reference to objective feedback measures. Intraclass-correlations of R = 0.71, 0.75 and 0.76 for RPEs 2, 5 and 8 were reported for HR data collected in the final 15 s of each 3-minute bout, across the six experimental trials.

The next stage for the reader is to gain practical experience of determining exercise intensity which involves the measurement of perceived exertion and heart rate. Three practical exercises, an *effort estimation,* a *heart rate production,* and *effort production* protocol, are described. The data shown in Tables 9.5, 9.6 and 9.7 were taken on RGE over 3 consecutive days in 1994.

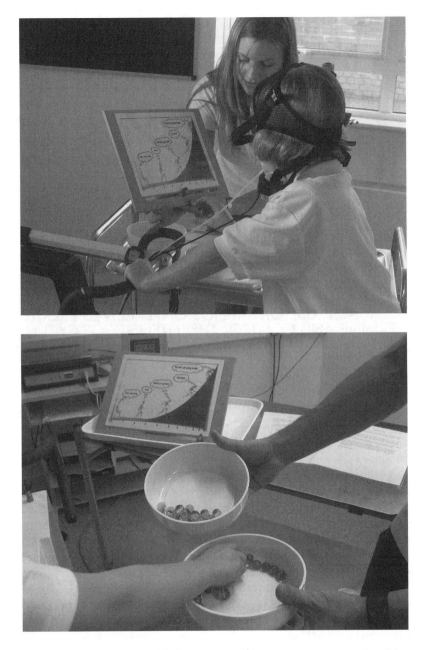

Figure 9.6 Measurement of perceived exertion using the Eston-Parfitt (E-P) Curvilinear Pictorial Scale. The children in this study were also requested to place an unlimited number of marbles into a separate jar to indicate their perceived exertion.

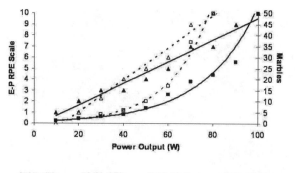

Figure 9.7 The rating of perceived exertion of two girls (aged 8) during an exercise task of progressively increasing intensity using the Eston-Parfitt (E-P) RPE Scale and a task that involved placing any number of marbles into a bowl. Data are from the study of Lambrick *et al.* (2008) (solid line is girl A; dashed line is girl B). Most of the children in this study were able to use the E-P Scale and marbles task to accurately reflect changes in the proportion of peak oxygen uptake.

9.6 PRACTICAL 1: USE OF RATINGS OF PERCEIVED EXERTION TO DETERMINE AND CONTROL THE INTENSITY OF CYCLING EXERCISE

9.6.1 Estimation protocol

(a) Purpose

To determine the relationships between heart rate (HR), rating of perceived exertion (RPE), and power output for cycle ergometry.

(b) Procedure

The subject is prepared for exercise with a heart rate monitoring device and informed that consecutive bouts of exercise will be performed on a cycle ergometer for 4 minutes. In the last 15 s of each 2-minute period the HR is recorded and the subject is requested to provide a rating of how hard the exercise feels. After the 4-minute period the resistance is increased by 25 W and the procedure repeated. The subject continues exercising in this way until 85% of the predicted maximal heart rate (220 minus age) is reached. At this point the resistance is removed and the subject is allowed a 5-minute warm-down period. All data are recorded as in Table 9.5.

Immediately prior to exercising, each subject is introduced to Borg's 6–20 Rating of Perceived Exertion Scale. It is essential that the subjects clearly understand that an accurate interpretation of the overall feeling of exertion brought about by the exercise is required when requested by the investigator. To do this, the participant uses the verbal expressions on the scale to provide a numerical rating of effort during exercise. It is recommended that standardized instructions are used to introduce the scale, as described in Borg (1998) and that complete comprehension of the process is checked during a brief warm-up period. Customized instructions may be needed for special applications of RPE. We have found that the perceptual 'anchoring' of the scale can be facilitated by manipulating the work rates so that the participant experiences how hard the exercise feels at RPEs of 8–9 and RPEs of 16–17.

9.6.2 Production protocol

(a) Purpose

To use heart rate and a given perceived exertion rating to produce exercise intensity levels on a cycle ergometer.

(b) Procedure

The subjects, apparatus, exercise mode and general organization remain the same as in task 1. However, in this task the approach is quite different. Two protocols are followed. Both are representative of procedures used in the determination of exercise intensity. The investigator should register the results into a record as shown in Tables 9.6 and

Table 9.5 RPE estimation protocol

| Name Roger Eston | | Age 38 | | HT 1.78 m | |
| Body mass 83 kg | | Date 21st Sept '94 | | Rest HR 45 beats min^{-1} | |
Power (W)	Time (min)	HR	RPE	$\%HR_{max}$	$\%HRR_{max}$
50	2	67	6	37	16
	4	73	7	40	20
75	2	81	7	44	26
	4	82	7	45	27
100	2	86	9	47	30
	4	92	10	50	34
125	2	96	10	53	37
	4	97	10	53	38
150	2	117	11	64	53
	4	122	12	67	56
175	2	135	12	74	66
	4	140	13	77	69
200	2	148	14	81	75
	4	153	15	84	79
225	2	157	15	86	82
	4	160	16	88	84
250	2	163	16	90	86
	4	165	17	91	88

9.7 which also serves as a guide to each step in the process.

(c) HR Production Test: use of heart rate to produce selected levels of exercise intensity (Table 9.6)

The subject is allowed a brief period to habituate and warm-up for exercise. Following this the investigator increases power output in a randomized manner to elicit steady-state heart rate levels of 110, 130, 150 and 170 beats min^{-1} for between 3 and 4 minutes. The RPE (Category Scale) is applied in the final 15 s of the exercise period.

(d) RPE Production Test: use of RPE to produce selected levels of exercise intensity (Table 9.7)

The subject uses Borg's 6–20 category scale as a frame of reference to determine selected levels of exercise intensity using only his or her bodily sensations arising from

Table 9.6 Using heart rate to control exercise intensity

HR	Power output (W)	RPE	%HRR$_{max}$
110	159	11	47
130	188	12	62
150	223	14	77
170	260	18	91

Table 9.7 Using RPE to control exercise intensity

RPE	Power output(W)	HR	%HRR$_{max}$
11	105	107	45
13	182	135	66
15	217	150	77
17	253	165	88

the exercise. All visual (except pedalling frequency, which is constant) and auditory information feedback is removed. The subject exercises and self-adjusts power output until steady-state levels of RPE 11, 13, 15 and 17 are established and maintained for between 3 and 4 minutes. The investigator records power output at steady-state and heart rate in the final 15 s of exercise, when the subject is confident that he or she is exercising at a constant RPE.

(e) Tasks/Questions

1   Using linear regression analysis on data from the estimation protocol at minute 4, comment on the relationship between power output, heart rate and the rating of perceived exertion.

2   Using related t tests, compare the HR and RPE data from minute 2 and 4. How could this difference affect the prediction of maximal values for power output and HR?

3   Draw a simple graph to compare the relationship between HR and RPE for each of the three protocols. Put HR on the $\times$ axis so that the relationships can be directly compared.

4   Compare/correlate the power output and RPE values predicted from the estimation test at HR 110, 130, 150, 170 to the actual RPE and power output values produced in the HR production test.

5   Using RPEs of 19 and 20, predict the HR$_{max}$ from both the estimation and production protocol. How does this compare to 220 – age?

9.7 PRACTICAL 2: ANALYSIS OF THE EFFORT ESTIMATION AND PRODUCTION TEST DATA SHOWN IN TABLES 5, 6 AND 7

9.7.1 RPE estimation test

Table 9.5 contains an example of data collected during an 'estimation test' on one of the authors (RGE). It is possible to determine relationships between power output, heart rate and the rating of perceived exertion. It is evident from these data that there is a strong correlation between HR, RPE and power output with correlations around 0.98. The importance of allowing sufficient time to adapt to the work rate is also evident. A related t-test indicates a significantly lower HR and RPE at minute 2 compared to minute 4 ($P < 0.01$).

Figure 9.3 shows the strong linear relationship between power output and RPE. From this relationship it is theoretically possible to predict the maximal power output that the participant can sustain for 4 minutes from the submaximal ratings of perceived exertion. Using all the 4-minute values up to and including RPE 17 (250 W), RPE 15 (200 W) and RPE 13 (175 W) with the RPE entered as the independent (prediction) factor, the resulting linear regression equations are:

Eq. 1 Power Output (W) = 18.4 (RPE) – 68 (up to and including RPE 17) (R = 0.99)

Eq. 2 Power Output (W) = 17.9 (RPE) – 61 (up to and including RPE 15) (R = 0.98)

Eq. 3 Power Output (W) = 18.2 (RPE) – 67 (up to and including RPE 13) (R = 0.97)

If we assume that RGE's maximal power output will occur at RPE 20 (the theoretical maximal RPE) which, as indicated previously is not always the case, the predicted maximal power outputs can be predicted by inserting RPE 20 into each of the equations. Using this approach, predicted maximal power outputs of 300 W, 297 W and 297 W are predicted from the submaximal RPE : power output ranges, which have included values up to 17, 15 and 13, respectively. As there is such a strong linear relationship between RPE and PO for RGE, it is therefore possible to gain an estimation of his maximal power output from a submaximal load which equates to an RPE of 13. Clearly, if this approach was valid for individuals who are not used to exercising at very high intensity levels, it could have considerable potential for estimating maximal functional capacity.

The data from the estimation test can be compared to data derived from the production test. As already indicated above, the high correlations between HR, power output and RPE allow predictions of HR and power output to be made from RPE in both the estimation protocol (Table 9.6) and the effort production test (Table 9.7). The following section provides an example of such calculations. Note that only steady-state values have been used. The RPE data for each protocol could also be graphed against HR to compare the relationship.

In the estimation test, the regression equation for HR and power output is: power output = 1.9 (HR) – 79 ($r = 0.99$, SEE = 12 W). Thus, with prescribed heart rates of 110, 130, 150 and 170 beats min^{-1} the predicted power output values are 130, 168, 206 and 244 W, respectively. A similar analysis on HR : RPE reveals that the predicted RPEs at these heart rates are 10.8, 12.9, 14.9 and 17 (RPE = 0.102 (HR) – 0.4; $r = 0.98$, SEE = 0.7). These values compare fairly well to the obtained values in the production test.

9.7.2 RPE production test

To compare how well the manipulation of RPE in the effort production protocol was at producing target heart rates, it is necessary to recompute the linear regression equation for RPE : HR, with RPE as the predictor variable. The regression equation for RPE and HR is: HR = 9.47 (RPE) + 7.8 ($r = 0.98$, SEE = 11 beats min^{-1}). Thus, for an RPE 11, 13, 15 and 17, the predicted HR values are 112, 131, 150 and 169, which compare extremely well with the target heart rates used to prescribe exercise intensity in Table 9.6. A similar analysis reveals that the predicted power output values at these RPEs is 134 W, 171 W, 208 W and 244 W, respectively. The regression equation for this prediction is: power output = 18.4 (RPE) – 68.4 ($r = 0.99$, SEE = 22 W). The reliability of the predicted versus actual HR and power output values at the prescribed RPEs is 0.99 and 0.98, respectively. Related t tests revealed no significant difference between the means.

As subjects rarely report a maximal RPE of 20, it is recommended that RPE values of 19 and 20 are inserted into the regression equation to predict a HR_{max} range. The predicted HR_{max} is 188 to 197 for RPE 19 and 20, respectively. A HR_{max} of 192 (RPE19) was recorded on RGE 1 year later during a graded exercise test on the treadmill. This value compares to an age-predicted HR_{max} of (220 – 38) = 182. For this individual therefore, the RPE estimation of maximal heart rate is closer.

For RGE the exercise test provided useful data which enabled him to regulate subsequent exercise intensities using both RPE and HR information obtained in the estimation test. However, one should remember that the subject was an experienced user of the RPE scale and that practice improves the reliability of RPE for prescribing exercise intensities (Eston and Williams, 1988; Buckley *et al.* 2000, Eston *et al.* 2000, 2005, 2006).

9.8 PRACTICAL 3: RELATIONSHIP BETWEEN POWER OUTPUT, PERCEIVED EXERTION (CR10), HEART RATE AND BLOOD LACTATE

9.8.1 Purpose

The purpose of this experiment is to determine the relationship between perceived exertion (R), using Borg's CR10 Scale, with equal and gradual increments in exercise intensity (Stimulus, S) of 30–40 W. The psychophysical characteristics of the relationship can primarily be described as $R = c \times S^n$, where ^{n} is the exponent that reflects the growth function.

9.8.2 Protocol

After explanation of the procedures, exercise intensity commences at 30–40 W and increase by similar increments until the participant responds at about 8 on the CR10 Scale. The participant should be reminded that he/she does not have to stick to the numbers on the scale. The scale is continuous and decimals (e.g. 0.8 or 2.3) can be used. If the participant is able, he/she should continue to maximal volitional exhaustion. The predicted maximal work rate from extrapolation of the 'curve of best fit' can then be compared to the actual maximal work rate.

To do

1   Plot the raw values of power output against the CR10 Scale on the vertical axis. You should observe that the relationship is curvilinear in nature.
2   *Calculation of the exponent by log-log regression analysis.*
The curve of best fit can be calculated by performing a simple linear regression analysis on the natural log values (ln) from the CR10 Scale and the power output values. The following is an example which uses the sample class data:

Stimulus (S in Watts)	Response (R, CR10)
40	0.8
80	2.0
120	3.5
160	5.5
200	8.0

The ln:ln regression equation for the above data is R = -5.496 + S (1.42). In this case, the exponent is 1.42.
3   *Prediction of maximal* work rate *using CR10 as the independent variable*
Using a similar procedure, it should be possible to predict the maximal work rate from the above submaximal data by entering a CR10 value of 10. The ln:ln regression equation for the above, using R as the $\times$ value is: S = 3.872 + 0.703(R). The antilog of 3.872 is 48.04. The exponent is 0.703.

Then from the equation $y = bx^a$:

Maximal power output at CR10 = b . CR10$^{0.703}$
$$= 48.04 \times (CR10)^{0.703} = 242 \text{ W}$$

As a check, enter ln 250 into the equation in paragraph 2, which uses PO as the independent factor, i.e. R = -5.496 + 1.42 (5.52) = ln 2.344. Antilog of 2.344 = 10!

1   It would be interesting to compare the predicted maximal power output to the actual maximum obtained. The data in Table 9.8 was derived from a female participant (Elaine) during a workshop with Gunnar Borg at the University of Wales, Bangor, in April 2000. You could compare the power output versus lactate relationship using similar procedures.

Ln: Ln regression equation (of values up to CR 7.5) to calculate exponent:

R = -4.871 + S (1.18)   Exponent = 1.18

Ln: Ln regression equation using CR10 as the independent variable:

Max S at CR10 = 4.271 + R (0.64)   Exponent = 0.64
                                              Antilog of intercept = 71.6

Equation of the curve to predict maximal power output (POmax) at CR10 $(y=bx^a)$:

$71.6 \times CR10^{0.64}$ Predicted POmax at CR10 = 313 W

Table 9.8. Relationship between power output, perceived exertion (CR10), heart rate and blood lactate. (Female aged 24, 182 cm, 78 kg)

W	CR10 value	HR	La
40	0.5	94	2.5
80	1.0	102	2.4
120	2.5	135	1.9
160	3.5	154	3.9
200	4.5	166	4.1
240	7.5	184	6.1
280	9.5	191	10.1
320	11.0	193	12.9
3 min post			12.1

Actual POmax at CR11 = 320 W

What does this indicate about the efficacy of the CR10 Scale to predict maximal functional capacity?

9.9 PRACTICAL 4: THE BORG CYCLING STRENGTH TEST WITH CONSTANT LOAD

9.9.1 Purpose:

The purpose of the following experiment is to determine the maximal power output that can be sustained for a period of 30 s, using the Borg RPE Scale. The rationale and development of this test, which could be considered as the forerunner to the well established Wingate Test (described by Winter and MacLaren 2009, Chapter 11) is presented in greater detail by Borg (1998).

9.9.2 Protocol

In this laboratory experiment, the participant cycles for a series of 30 s bouts at constant work rates of 50, 100, 150, 200, 250, 300 ....W, to an RPE of about 16–17. Pedaling speed should be kept constant at 60 or 70 rpm. The work intervals are separated by 2 minutes rest/active recovery. Both RPE and HR are recorded in the final 5 s. The predicted maximal work rate range is calculated by extrapolating to RPE 19–20. This could be done by linear regression or pen and paper. After 5 minutes the subject cycles at the predicted work rate (W1) that he/she can sustain for 30 s. The time is recorded. This is T1. The load is then adjusted using time to exhaustion (T1) at W1 using the formula below.

To do

1   Plot the raw values of PO versus RPE and HR for each increment.
2   Extrapolate the PO:RPE and the PO:HR relationships to RPE = 20 and HR = maximal heart rate, respectively.
3   Compare the predicted work rates from the perpendicular at RPE (20) and the predicted HR_{max}.
4   The equation describing the curvilinear relationship for this kind of exercise is:

$$\text{Time on task} = c \times W^{-4} \text{ (see Borg 1998 pp 57–58)}$$

5   In Borg's example (1998: p. 58), the predicted maximal work rate that can be sustained for 30 s is 275 W. This is W1. The subject now pedals at this level for as long as possible, which in Borg's example is 44 s (T1). The power output is then corrected according to the formula:

$$W2 = W1 \times (T1/30s)^{0.25}.$$
$$\text{i.e. } W2 = 275 \times (44s/30s)^{0.25} = 302 \text{ W}.$$

After a rest of 5 minutes the subject pedals at close to the desired 30-s PO (W2) and the time is recorded. Table 9.9 contains data from a female participant (Elaine, age 24, ht 182 cm, 78 kg) collected during the RPE Symposium at Bangor in April 2000 to exemplify the procedure.

Regression analysis for RPE (x) and W (y) produced the following equation:

W = –231 + 40 (RPE) r = 0.96   Predicted POmax at RPE 19–20 = 529 – 569W

Regression analysis for HR (x) and W (y) produced the following equation:

W = –446 + 4.95 (HR) r = 0.98   Predicted POmax at HR_{max} (196) = 524 W

Trial 1. Time (s) at predicted POmax using RPE = 46 s

Trial 2. Time (s) at 'corrected POmax' based on formula: $W2 = W1 \times (T1/T2)^{0.25}$

Table 9.9: Data example from the Borg Cycling Strength Test with constant load

Power Output (W)	RPE value	HR
50	7	94
100	7	109
150	11	131
200	11	134
250	13	146
300	14	151
350	14	152
400	15	170
450	16	178

W2 = $569 \times (46/30)^{0.25}$ = 633 W

After a 5-minute recovery, Elaine managed to sustain the above power output for 29 s. For Elaine, therefore, the procedure seems to have worked well.

9.10 SUMMARY

1   Beneficial effects of exercise accrue when individuals engage in activity with appropriate frequency, duration and intensity. The interplay of all three dimensions is important, but the determination of appropriate intensity requires careful consideration because of the impact of numerous variables.

2   One approach to determining intensity is to base judgements on physiological information. The usual method is to recommend intensity levels relative to actual or predicted maximal capacity based on measures of heart rate response, oxygen utilization, ventilation and blood lactate.

3   A comprehensive approach to setting exercise intensity is desirable. This requires the coupling of indices of bodily response during exercise with information on how hard the individual perceives the exercise to be. The most commonly used perceived exertion device is the Borg 6–20 RPE Scale (Borg 1998), although the Category-Ratio 10 Scale is also a useful tool when monitoring or regulating certain markers of exercise intensity (blood lactate, ventilation). For young children, the Children's Effort Rating Table (CERT) has been recommended. More recently, pictorial scales such as the CALER, OMNI and E-P Scales have been suggested.

4   Perceived exertion ratings have historically been used in two ways: estimation and production procedures. In the former, the participant provides a rating of perceived exertion for a given exercise intensity. In the latter, the participant is requested to produce a given exercise intensity, which is judged to correspond with a given RPE.

5   The predictions of exercise intensity and maximal functional capacity using the RPE must consider the process by which it is used, owing to the essential differences in the process of estimation and production. Recent research utilizing an estimation-production procedure has shown that perceptually-

regulated exercise, prescribed at specific submaximal RPE, provide accurate predictions of $\dot{V}O_{2max}$.

6   Until recently, it appears that a fundamental relationship between the ratings of perceived exertion and the duration of exercise that remains until exhaustion has been overlooked. A number of very recent studies have demonstrated that the RPE scales with time and distance in open and closed-loop tasks in the laboratory setting and in a competitive, real world environment.

7   A further unique approach to control exercise intensity is to allow the individual to self-regulate his/her exercise intensity to produce a positive affective response using the Feeling Scale – an 11-point bipolar scale ranging from -5 (very bad) through 0 (neutral) to +5 (very good).

8   Whilst the correlation between physiological information and perceived exertion ratings measured in an exercise physiology laboratory for both *response* and *production* methods is usually high, 25% of the variance in the relationship between the two methods remains unaccounted for. The remnant is probably due to individual differences, which predispose people to modulate their interpretation of intensity. Thus, the fine-tuning of exercise intensity within an exercise programme comes down to individual decision-making emanating from effort sense. The exercise scientist's role is to arrive at a balanced judgement from a psychophysiological perspective by taking into account the variables discussed.

The purpose of this chapter has been to introduce the reader to the concept of exercise intensity determination as a multifaceted process, which requires consideration of both physiological and psychological information about the individual relative to specific activities. Through reading the introductory material, following up some of the primary reference material and undertaking the practical tasks which were suggested, a sound knowledge base for decision-making in this area should have been acquired.

FURTHER READING:

Books

American College of Sports Medicine (2006) *Guidelines for Exercise Testing and Prescription (7th Edition)*. Williams and Wilkins; Baltimore, MD.

Borg G. A. V. (1998) *Borg's Perceived Exertion and Pain Scales*. Human Kinetics; Champaign, IL.

Noble B. and Robertson R. (1996) *Perceived Exertion*. Human Kinetics; Champaign, IL.

Journal articles

Faulkner J. A. and Eston R. G. (2008) Perceived exertion research in the 21st century: developments, reflections and questions for the future. *Journal of Exercise Science and Fitness*; 6 (1): 1–12.

Hampson D. B., St Clair Gibson A., Lambert M. I. and Noakes T. D. (2001). The influence of sensory cues on the performance of effort during exercise and central regulation of exercise performance. *Sports Medicine*; 31: 935–52.

St Clair Gibson A., Lambert E. V., Rauch L. H. G., Tucker R., Baden D. A., Foster C. and Noakes,, T. D. (2006). The role of information processing between the brain and peripheral physiological systems in pacing and perception of effort. *Sports Medicine*; 36: 705–22.

Ulmer H. V. (1996). Concept of an extracellular regulation of muscular metabolic rate during heavy exercise in humans by psychophysiological feedback. *Experientia*; 52: 416–20.

Williams J. G. and Eston R. G. (1989) Determination of the intensity dimension in vigorous exercise programmes with particular reference to the use of the Rating of Perceived Exertion. *Sports Medicine*; 8: 177–89.

Website

The health tools page of the Canadian-based *Preventdisease.com* (http://www.preventdisease.com/healthtools/tools.html#roc) is an excellent website which contains a number of useful resources and dedicated programmes to calculate personalised metabolic rate, energy cost of activities and fitness.

ACKNOWLEDGEMENT

We are grateful to Danielle Lambrick for her help with some of the Figures.

REFERENCES

Albertus Y., Tucker R., St Clair Gibson A., Lambert E. V., Hampson D. B. and Noakes T. D. (2005). Effect of distance feedback on pacing strategies and perceived exertion during cycling. *Medicine and Science in Sports and Exercise*; 37: 461–8.

American College of Sports Medicine (2006) *Guidelines for Exercise Testing and Prescription (7th Edition)*. Williams and Wilkins; Baltimore, MD.

American College of Sports Medicine Position Stand (1998). The recommended quantity and quality of exercise for developing and maintaining cardiorespiratory and muscular strength and flexibility in healthy adults. *Medicine and Science in Sports and Exercise*; 30: 975–91.

Baldwin J., Snow R. J., Gibala M. J., Garnham A., Howarth K. and Febbraio M. A. (2003) Glycogen availability does not affect the TCA cycle or TAN pools during prolonged fatiguing exercise. *Journal of Applied Physiology*; 94: 2181–7.

Bar-Or O. (1977) Age-related changes in exercise perception. In: (G. Borg, ed) *Physical Work and Effort*. Pergamon Press; Oxford: pp. 255–66.

Barkley J. E. and Roemmich J. N. (2008) Validity of the CALER and OMNI bike ratings of perceived exertion. *Medicine and Science in Sports and Exercise*; 40: 760–66.

Benson H., Dryer T. and Hartley H. (1978) Decreased $\dot{V}O_2$ consumption during exercise with elicitation of the relaxation response. *Journal of Human Stress*; 4: 38–42.

Berry M. J., Weyrich A. S., Robergs R. A. *et al.* (1989) Ratings of perceived exertion in individuals with varying fitness levels during walking and running. *European Journal of Applied Physiology*; 58: 494–9.

Borg G. A .V. (1962) Physical performance and perceived exertion. *Studia Psychologica et Paedagogica. Series altera, Investigationes XI.* Gleerup; Lund, Sweden.

Borg G. A. V. (1970) Perceived exertion as an indicator of somatic stress. *Scandinavian Journal of Rehabilitation Medicine*; 2: 92–8.

Borg G. A. V. (1971) La sensation de fatigue consécutive au travail physique. *Psycholigie Médicale*; 3: 761–73.

Borg G. A. V. (1977) *Physical Work and Effort*. Pergamon Press; Oxford: pp. 289–93

Borg G. A. V. (1982) Psychophysical basis of perceived exertion. *Medicine and Science in Sports and Exercise*; 14: 377–81.

Borg G. A. V. (1998) *Borg's Perceived Exertion and Pain Scales*. Human Kinetics; Champaign, IL: pp. 2–6 and 57–8

British Association of Sports & Exercise Sciences. (2007) *Physiological Testing Guidelines, Volume two; Exercise and Clinical Testing*, (E. M. Winter, A. M. Jones, R. Davison, P. D. Bromley and T. H. Mercer, eds) BASES; Leeds, UK.

Buckley J. P., Eston R. G. and Sim J. (2000) Ratings of perceived exertion in Braille: validity and reliability in 'production' mode. *British Journal of Sports Medicine*; 34: 297–302.

Buskist W. and Gerbing D. W. (1990) *Psychology: Boundaries and Frontiers.* Harper Collins; New York: pp. 376–414.

Byrne C and Eston R. G. (1997) Use of ratings of perceived exertion to regulate exercise intensity: a study using effort estimation and effort production (abstract). *Journal of Sports Sciences*; 16: 15P.

Ceci R. and Hassmen P. (1991) Self-monitored exercise at three different RPE intensities in treadmill vs field running. *Medicine and Science in Sports and Exercise*; 23: 732–8.

Chen M. J., Fan X. and Moe S. T. (2002) Criterion-related validity of the Borg ratings of perceived exertion scale in healthy individuals: A meta analysis. *Journal of Sport Sciences*; 20: 873–99.

Cooke C. (2009a) Maximal oxygen uptake, economy and efficiency. In: (R. G. Eston and T. Reilly, eds) *Kinanthropometry Laboratory Manual (3rd Edition): Exercise Physiology (Chapter 7)*. Routledge; Oxon: pp. 147–173.

Cooke C. (2009b) Metabolic rate and energy balance. In: (R. G. Eston and T. Reilly, eds) *Kinanthropometry Laboratory Manual (3rd Edition): Exercise Physiology (Chapter 6)*. Routledge; Oxon: pp. 174–212.

Crewe, H., Tucker, R., and Noakes, T. D. (2008) The rate of increase in rating of perceived exertion predicts the duration of exercise to fatigue at a fixed power output in different enviromental conditions. *European Journal of Applied Physiology*; **103**: 569–577.

DeMello J. J., Cureton K. J., Boineau R. E. and Singh M. M. (1987) Ratings of perceived exertion at the lactate threshold in trained and untrained men and women. *Medicine and Science in Sports and Exercise*; **19**: 354–62.

Dunbar C. C., Robertson R. J., Baun R., Blandon, M. F., Metz, K., Burdett, R., and Goss, F. L. 1992) The validity of regulating exercise intensity by ratings of perceived exertion. *Medicine and Science in Sports and Exercise*; **24**: 94–9.

Ekblom B. and Goldbarg A. N. (1971) The influence of physical training and other factors in the subjective rating of perceived exertion. *Acta Physiologica Scandinavica*; **83**: 399–406.

Ekkekakis P. and Petruzzello S. J. (2002) Analysis of the affect measurement conundrum in exercise psychology: IV. A conceptual case for the affect circumplex. *Psychology of Sport and Exercise*; **3**: 35–63.

Ekman G. (1961) A simple method for fitting psychophysical power functions. *Journal of Psychology*; **51**: 343–50.

Eston R., Davies B. and Williams J. G. (1987) Use of perceived effort ratings to control exercise intensity in young, healthy adults. *European Journal of Applied Physiology*; **56**: 222–4.

Eston R. G. and Williams J. G. (1986) Exercise intensity and perceived exertion in adolescent boys. *British Journal of Sports Medicine*; **20**: 27–30.

Eston R. and Williams J. G. (1988) Reliability

of ratings of perceived effort for the regulation of exercise intensity. *British Journal of Sports Medicine*; **22**: 153–4.

Eston R. G., Lamb K. L., Bain A., Williams M. and Williams J. G. (1994) Validity of a perceived exertion scale for children: a pilot study. *Perceptual and Motor Skills*; **78**: 691–7.

Eston R. and Connolly D. (1996) The use of the ratings of perceived exertion for exercise prescription inpatients receiving beta-blocker therapy. *Sports Medicine*; **21**: 176–90.

Eston R. G. and Thompson M. (1997) Use of ratings of perceived exertion for prediction of maximal exercise levels and exercise prescription in patients receiving atenolol. *British Journal of Sports Medicine*; **31**: 114–19.

Eston R. G. and Parfitt C. G. (2007) Effort Perception. In: (N. Armstrong, ed) *Paediatric Exercise Physiology*. Elsevier; London: pp. 275–98.

Eston R. G. Parfitt G. and Tucker R. (1998) Ratings of perceived exertion and psychological affect during preferred exercise intensity in high- and low-active men. *Journal of Sports Sciences*; **16**: 77P.

Eston R. G., Parfitt C. G., Campbell L. and Lamb K. L. (2000) Reliability of effort perception for regulating exercise intensity in children using the Cart and Load Effort Rating (CALER) Scale. *Pediatric Exercise Science*; **12**: 388–97.

Eston R. G., Lamb K. L., Parfitt C. G. and King N. (2005) The validity of predicting maximal oxygen uptake from a perceptually regulated graded exercise test. *European Journal of Applied Physiology*; **94**: 221–7.

Eston R. G., Faulkner J. A., Parfitt C. G. and Mason E. (2006) The validity of predicting maximal oxygen uptake from a perceptually regulated graded exercise tests of different durations *European Journal of Applied Physiology*; **97**: 535–41.

Eston R., Faulkner J., St Clair Gibson A., Noakes T. and Parfitt G. (2007) The effect of antecedent fatiguing activity on the relationship between perceived exertion and physiological activity during a constant load exercise task. *Psychophysiology*; **44**: 779–86.

Eston R. G., Lambrick D., Sheppard K. and

Parfitt G. (2008) Prediction of maximal oxygen uptake in sedentary males from a perceptually-regulated, sub-maximal graded exercise test. *Journal of Sport Sciences*; **26**: 131–9.

Faulkner J. A. and Eston R. G. (2007) Overall and peripheral ratings of perceived exertion during a graded exercise test to volitional exhaustion in individuals of high and low fitness. *European Journal of Applied Physiology*; **101**: 613–20.

Faulkner J. A., Parfitt G. and Eston R. G. (2007a) Prediction of maximal oxygen uptake from the ratings of perceived exertion and heart rate during a perceptually-regulated sub-maximal exercise test in active and sedentary participants. *European Journal of Applied Physiology*; **101**: 397–407.

Faulkner J. A., Lambrick D., Rowlands A. V., Parfitt G. and Eston R. G. (2007b) Prediction of maximal oxygen uptake from the Astrand-Ryhming nomogram and ratings of perceived exertion. *6th Conference on Sport, Leisure and Ergonomics*, Burton Manor, UK.

Faulkner J., Parfitt G. and Eston R. G (2008). The rating of perceived exertion during competitive running scales with time. *Psychophysiology*. 45, Published online ahead of print: doi: 10.1111/j.1469–8986.2008.00712.x

Gaesser G. A. and Rich E. G. (1984) Effects of high performance and low intensity training on aerobic capacity and blood lipids. *Medicine and Science in Sports and Exercise*; **16**: 269–74.

Gellish R. L., Goslin B. R., Olson R. E., McDonald A., Russi G. D. and Moudgil V. K. (2007) Longitudinal modeling of the relationship between age and maximal heart rate. *Medicine and Science in Sports and Exercise*; **39**: 822–9.

Glass S., Knowlton R. and Becque M. D. (1992) Accuracy of RPE from graded exercise to establish exercise training intensity. *Medicine and Science in Sports and Exercise*; **24**: 1303–7.

Hardy C. J. and Rejeski W. J. (1989) Not what, but how one feels: The measurement of affect during exercise. *Journal of Sport and Exercise Psychology*; **11**: 304–17.

Horstman D. H., Morgan W. P., Cymerman A. and Stokes J. (1979). Perception of effort during constant work to self-imposed exhaustion. *Perceptual and Motor Skills*; **48**: 1111–26.

Jameson C. and Ring C. (2000) Contributions of local and central sensations to the perception of exertion during cycling: Effects of work rate and cadence. *Journal of Sport Sciences*; **18**: 291–8.

Jones A. M., Vanhatalo A. T. and Doust J. (2009) Limitations to submaximal exercise performance. In: (R. G. Eston and T. Reilly, eds) *Kinanthropmetry Laboratory Manual(3rd Edition): Exercise Physiology (Chapter 10)*. Routledge; Oxon: pp. 271–306.

Joseph T., Johnson B., Battista R. A., Wright G., Dodge C., Procari J. P., De Koning J. J. and Foster C. (2008) Perception of fatigue during simulated competition. *Medicine and Science in Sports and Exercise*; **40**: 381–6.

Karvonen J. and Vuorimaa T. (1988) Heart rate and exercise intensity during sports activities. *Sports Medicine*; **5**: 303–12.

Kang J., Hoffman J. R., Walker H., Chaloupka E. C., and Utter A. C. (2003) Regulating intensity using perceived exertion during extended exercise periods. *European Journal of Applied Physiology*; **89**: 475–82.

Kay D., Marino F. E., Cannon J., St Clair Gibson A., Lambert M. I. and Noakes T. D. (2001) Evidence for neuromuscular fatigue during cycling in warm humid conditions. *European Journal of Applied Physiology*; **84**: 115–21.

Lamb K. L., Parfitt G. and Eston R. G. (2008) Effort Perception. In : (N. Armstrong and W. Van-Mechelen, eds), *Paediatric Exercise Science and Medicine*. Oxford University Press: pp. 145–154.

Lambrick D., Rowlands A. and Eston R (2008) Assessing the perceptual response to exercise with children 7–8 years: validation of a pictorial curvilinear ratings of perceived exertion scale. *European College of Sport Science Annual Conference*. Estoril, Portugal.

Lind E., Joens-Matre R. R., Ekkekakis P. (2005) What intensity of physical activity do previously sedentary middle-aged women select? Evidence of a coherent pattern from physiological, perceptual, and affective markers. *Preventive Medicine*; **40**: 407–19.

McArdle W. D., Katch F. and Katch V. L. (1991) *Exercise Physiology: Energy, Nutrition and Human Performance.* Lea & Febiger; Philadelphia, PA.

Macombie M. (2005) Changes in the rate of increase of perceived exertion to a constant-load exercise task in a fatigued and fresh state. Unpublished MSc dissertation. University of Exeter.

Morgan W. P. and Borg G. (1976) Perception of effort in the prescription of physical activity. In: T. Craig (ed) *The Humanistic Aspects of Sports, Exercise and Recreation;* American Medical Association; Chicago: pp. 126–9.

Morgan W. P., Horstman D. J., Cymerman A. and Stokes J. (1983) Facilitation of physical performance by means of a cognitive strategy. *Cognitive Therapy and Research;* 7: 251–64.

Noakes, T. D. (2004) Linear relationship between the perception of effort and the duration of constant load exercise that remains. *Journal of Applied Physiology,* 96: 1571–1573, (Letter to the editor).

Noble B. J. (1982) Clinical applications of perceived exertion. *Medicine and Science in Sports and Exercise;* 14: 406–11.

Noble B. J., Maresh C. M. and Ritchey M. (1981) Comparison of exercise sensations between females and males. In: (J. Borms, M. Hebbelinck and A.Venerando, eds) *Women and Sport.* S. Karger; Basel: pp. 175–9.

Pandolf K. D. (1983) Advances in the study and application of perceived exertion. In: (R. L. Terjung, ed) *Exercise and Sport Sciences Reviews.* Franklin Institute Press; Philadelphia, PA: pp. 118–58.

Pandolf K. B. and Noble B. J. (1973) The effect of pedalling speed and resistance changes on perceived exertion for equivalent power outputs on a cycle ergometer. *Medicine and Science in Sports and Exercise;* 5: 132–6.

Pandolf K. B., Burse R. L. and Goldman R. F. (1975) Differentiated ratings of perceived exertion during physical conditioning of older individuals using leg-weight loading. *Perceptual and Motor Skills;* 40: 563–74

Parfitt G., Eston R. G. and Connolly D. A. (1996) Psychological affect at different ratings of perceived exertion in high- and low-active women: a study using a production protocol. *Perceptual and Motor Skills;* 82: 1035–42.

Parfitt G., Rose E. and Markland D. (2000) The effect of prescribed and preferred intensity exercise on psychological affect and the influence of baseline measures of affect. *Journal of Health Psychology;* 5: 231–40.

Parfitt G., Rose E. A. and Burgess W. M. (2006) The psychological and physiological responses of sedentary individuals to prescribed and preferred intensity exercise. *British Journal of Health Psychology;* 11: 39–53.

Parfitt G., Shepherd P. and Eston R. G. (2007) Reliability of effort production using the children's CALER and BABE perceived exertion scales. *Journal of Exercise Science and Fitness;* 5: 49–55.

Piaget J. (1972) Intellectual evolution from adolescence to adulthood. *Human Development;* 15: 1–12.

Pollock M. L., Foster C., Rod J. L. and Wible G. (1982) Comparison of methods of determining exercise training intensity for cardiac patients and healthy adults. In: (J. J. Kellermann, ed) *Comprehensive Cardiac Rehabilitation.* S Karger; Basel: pp. 129–33.

Rejeski W. J. (1985) Perceived exertion: an active or a passive process. *Journal of Sport Psychology;* 7: 371–8.

Robergs R. A. and Landwehr R. (2002) The surprising history of the 'HRmax = 220–age' equation. *Journal of Exercise Physiology Online;* 5: 1–10.

Robertson R. J. (1997) Perceived exertion in young people: future directions of enquiry. In: (J. Welsman, N. Armstrong and B. Kirby, eds) *Children and Exercise XIX (Volume II).* Washington Singer Press; Exeter: pp. 33–9.

Robertson R. J. and Noble B. J. (1997) Perception of physical exertion: methods, mediators and applications. *Exercise and Sport Science Reviews;* 25: 407–52.

Robertson R. J., Goss F. L., Boer N. F., Robertson R. J., Goss F. L., Boer, N. F., Peoples J. A., Foreman A. J., Dabayebeh I. M., Millich N. B., Balasekaran G., Riechman S. E., Gallagher J. D. and Thompkins T. (2000) Childrens OMNI Scale of perceived exertion: mixed gender and race validation. *Medicine and Science in Sports and Exercise;* 32: 452–8.

Robertson R. J., Goss J. L., Bell F. A., Dixon C. B., Gallagher K. I., Lagally K. M., Timmer J. M., Abt K. L, Gallagher J. D. and Thompkins T. (2002) Self-regulated cycling using the Children's OMNI Scale of Perceived Exertion. *Medicine and Science in Sports and Exercise*; **34**: 1168–75.

Roemmich J. N., Barkley J. E., Epstein L. H. (2006) Validity of the PCERT and OMNI-walk/run ratings of perceived exertion scales. *Medicine and Science in Sports and Exercise*; **38**: 1014–19.

Rose E. A. and Parfitt G. (2007) A quantitative analysis and qualitative explanation of the individual differences in affective responses to prescribed and self-selected exercise intensities. *Journal of Sport and Exercise Psychology*; **29**: 281–309.

Rose E. A. and Parfitt G. (2009) Can the Feeling Scale be used to regulate exercise intensity? *Medicine and Science in Sports and Exercise*; In Press.

Shephard R. J., Vandewalle H., Gil V., Bouhlel E. and Monod H. (1992) Respiratory, muscular and overall perceptions of effort: the influence of hypoxia and muscle mass. *Medicine and Science in Sports and Exercise*; **24**: 556–7.

Smutok M. A., Skrinar G. S. and Pandolf K. B. (1980) Exercise intensity: subjective regulation by perceived exertion. *Archives of Physical Medicine and Rehabilitation*; **61**: 569–74.

St Clair Gibson A., Lambert M. I., Hawley J. A., Broomhead S. A. and Noakes T. D. (1999) Measurement of maximal oxygen uptake from two different laboratory protocols in runners and squash players. *Medicine and Science in Sports and Exercise*; **31**: 1226–9.

Stevens S. S. (1957) On the psychophysical law. *The Psychological Review*; **64**: 153–81.

Steven S. S. (1971) Issues in psychophysiological measurement. *The Psychological Review*; **78**: 426–50.

Ueda T. and Kurokawa T. (1995) Relationships between perceived exertion and physiological variables during swimming. *International Journal of Sports Medicine*; **16**: 385–9.

Van Landuyt L. M., Ekkekakis P., Hall E. E. and Petruzzello S. J. (2000) Throwing the mountains into the lakes: On the perils of nonthetic conceptions of exercise – affect relationship. *Journal of Sport and Exercise Psychology*; **22**: 208–34.

Ward D. S., Bar-Or O., Longmuir P. and Smith K. (1995) Use of RPE to control exercise intensity in wheelchair-bound children and adults. *Pediatric Exercise Science*; **7**: 94–102.

Wilmore J. H., Roby F. B., Stanforth M. J., Buono M. J., Constable S. H., Tsao Y. and Lowdon B. J. (1985) Ratings of perceived exertion, heart rate and power output in predicting maximal oxygen uptake during submaximal bicycle riding. *The Physician and Sports Medicine*; **14**: 133–43.

Williams J. G. and O'Brien M. (2000) A Children's Perceived Exertion Picture Scale. *Unpublished data*, University of West Chester, PA.

Williams J. G., Eston R. and Stretch C. (1991) Use of the Rating of Perceived Exertion to control exercise intensity in children. *Pediatric Exercise Science*; **3**: 21–7.

Williams J. G., Furlong B., Mackintosh C. and Hockley T. J. (1993) Rating and regulation of exercise intensity in young children. *Medicine and Science in Sports and Exercise*; **5** (Suppl. 25): S8.

Williams J. G., Eston R. and Furlong B. A. F. (1994) CERT: a perceived exertion scale for young children. *Perceptual and Motor Skills*; **79**: 1451–8.

Winter E. M. and MacLaren D. (2009) Maximal intensity exercise. In: (R. G. Eston and T. Reilly, eds) *Kinanthropometry Laboratory Manual (3rd Edition): Exercise Physiology (Chapter 11)*. Routledge; Oxon: pp. 307–333.

Yelling M., Lamb K. and Swaine I. L. (2002) Validity of a pictorial perceived exertion scale for effort estimation and effort production during stepping exercise in adolescent children. *European Physical Education Review*; **8**: 157–75.

CHAPTER 10

AEROBIC EXERCISE PERFORMANCE

Andrew M. Jones, Anni T. Vanhatalo and Jonathan H. Doust

10.1 AIMS

- To describe the four 'domains' of exercise intensity in terms of changes in acid-base status and respiratory gas exchange dynamics;
- To review the methods that have been used to delineate the transition from moderate to heavy intensity exercise, in particular the lactate and gas exchange thresholds;
- To review the methods that have been used to delineate the transition from heavy to severe intensity exercise, in particular the maximal lactate steady-state and critical power;
- To highlight the importance of knowledge of the exercise domains in predicting the physiological response to exercise, and in prescribing and regulating exercise intensity within endurance training programmes;
- To provide a series of practical exercises which explore the methods that have been used to identify the boundaries between the various domains of exercise intensity.

10.2 INTRODUCTION

'Maximal exercise' can be defined as exercise of an intensity that requires 100 % of the maximal oxygen uptake ($\dot{V}O_{2max}$). It follows that exercise that has an oxygen requirement above an individual's $\dot{V}O_{2max}$ max can be described as 'supramaximal,' while exercise that requires an oxygen uptake below $\dot{V}O_{2max}$ can be termed 'submaximal.' The work-rate associated with 100 % $\dot{V}O_{2max}$ can be sustained for about 4–8 minutes (Billat *et al.* 1994). The $\dot{V}O_{2max}$ can be attained during exhaustive high-intensity submaximal exercise, during step or ramp incremental exercise to volitional exhaustion, and during prolonged all-out sprint exercise (Poole *et al.* 1988; Day *et al.* 2003; Burnley *et al.* 2006). Whether the $\dot{V}O_2$ projects towards maximum or a submaximal steady-state during an exercise bout has important implications for exercise tolerance and performance (Burnley and Jones 2007). The attainment (or not) of steady-state $\dot{V}O_2$ during constant-work-rate exercise is reflected in the response dynamics of blood lactate concentration (blood lactate).

Most forms of recreational exercise, and indeed many sports, can be considered to be submaximal; that is, performed below $\dot{V}O_{2max}$. Continuous submaximal exercise can also be termed endurance exercise. The causes of fatigue during submaximal exercise are manifold and complex, but may depend, in part, upon whether the exercise is of a sufficiently low intensity that ATP resynthesis is almost completely aerobic, or whether supplementary anaerobiosis is required, reflected in a progressive accumulation of muscle and blood lactate. For low-intensity submaximal exercise, fatigue may result from substrate depletion, dehydration, hyperthermia, or loss of motivation associated with central fatigue (Newsholme et al. 1992). At higher intensities of exercise, fatigue may result, in part, from the effects of acidosis on muscle contractile function (Edwards 1981), although other factors including changes in phosphocreatine, inorganic phosphate, and potassium concentrations are likely also of considerable importance (Allen et al. 2008; McKenna et al. 2008). Understanding the physiological limitations of submaximal exercise is important in developing training programmes to enhance endurance performance.

10.3 EXERCISE INTENSITY DOMAINS

Four domains of exercise intensity have been identified based on the characteristic responses of blood acid-base status and pulmonary gas exchange (Jones and Poole 2005; Whipp and Mahler, 1980; Whipp and Ward, 1990). In this chapter, these will be termed moderate, heavy, severe, and extreme exercise (Hill et al. 2002; Wilkerson et al. 2004; Jones and Poole 2005; Figure 10.1); however, it should be appreciated that other authors use different terms to describe essentially the same domains (e.g. Ozyener et al. 2001). The metabolic, physiological and perceptual responses to exercise differ considerably according to the exercise domain that is studied. The boundaries between these different domains can be demarcated by the physiological

'landmarks' of the lactate threshold (or gas exchange/ventilatory threshold), the maximal lactate steady-state or critical power, and the $\dot{V}O_{2max}$. The lactate threshold (Tlac), which marks the transition between moderate and heavy intensity exercise, can be defined as the $\dot{V}O_2$ above which blood lactate exceeds the resting concentration during incremental exercise (Wasserman et al. 1973). The maximal lactate steady-state (MLSS) or critical power (Pcrit), which marks the transition between heavy and severe intensity exercise, can be defined as the highest exercise intensity that allows blood lactate and $\dot{V}O_2$ to be sabilized during long-term exercise (Poole et al. 1988; Beneke and von Duvillard, 1996). The upper limit of the severe intensity domain occurs at the work rate above which exercise tolerance is extremely limited and voluntary exhaustion ensues before the $\dot{V}O_2$ can reach maximal values (Hill et al. 2002; Wilkerson et al. 2004). Considering the distinct physiological response profiles associated with different intensity domains, it is of importance in both research and applied settings that exercise intensity is prescribed with regard to the physiological landmarks demarcating these domains.

If constant-work-rate *moderate* exercise (below the Tlac) is commenced from a resting baseline, pulmonary $\dot{V}O_2$ rises to attain a steady-state value within 2–3 minutes. The deficit between the energy demand and the oxygen uptake during this initial period of exercise is covered by intramuscular oxygen stores, depletion of phosphocreatine and, perhaps, a small and transient increase in the rate of anaerobic glycolysis resulting in 'early lactate.' This lactate is rapidly cleared as exercise proceeds so that blood lactate will remain at or close to resting values during continuous moderate intensity exercise.

If constant-work-rate *heavy* exercise (i.e. above the Tlac, but below the MLSS) is commenced from a resting baseline, $\dot{V}O_2$ rises to attain its predicted steady-state value within 2–3 minutes. However, as exercise is sustained, $\dot{V}O_2$ continues to rise until it reaches a steady-

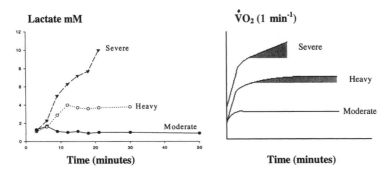

Figure 10.1: Blood lactate and oxygen uptake responses during moderate, heavy, and severe intensity submaximal exercise. The shaded areas in the oxygen uptake panel represent the increase in VO₂ above the expected steady-state level.

state value that is higher than the expected value. This continued increase in $\dot{V}O_2$, until a delayed and elevated steady-state is attained, is due to the emergence of the $\dot{V}O_2$ 'slow component' (Whipp and Wasserman 1972). The physiological mechanisms responsible for this reduction in efficiency (i.e. an increased oxygen cost for the same external power output) during sustained exercise above Tlac are not known with certainty. However, it has been demonstrated that ~ 86% of the $\dot{V}O_2$ slow component can be attributed to increased oxygen utilization in the exercising limbs (Poole *et al.* 1991). It has therefore been suggested that the recruitment of type II muscle fibres with an increased energetic cost of contraction might be important in eliciting the $\dot{V}O_2$ slow component (Whipp 1994; Barstow *et al.* 1996). If serial blood samples are taken during continuous heavy exercise, blood lactate will eventually sabilize at an elevated level of around 2–5 mM.

In the transition from rest to *severe* exercise (i.e. above the MLSS or Pcrit), the development of the $\dot{V}O_2$ slow component after 2–3 minutes also causes $\dot{V}O_2$ to rise above the expected steady-state value. However, in contrast to heavy exercise, during severe exercise, $\dot{V}O_2$ will not attain a steady-state, but will continue to rise until $\dot{V}O_{2max}$ is attained and exercise is terminated (Poole *et al.* 1988; Wilkerson *et al.* 2004). The $\dot{V}O_2$ slow component can account for as much as 0.5–1.0 l min^{-1} of $\dot{V}O_2$

and result in the attainment of $\dot{V}O_{2max}$ during high intensity (but ostensibly *submaximal*) exercise. The attainment of $\dot{V}O_{2max}$ and the limited and predictable time to exhaustion during constant work-rate exercise are unique characteristics of the severe intensity domain (Hill and Ferguson 1999; Fukuba and Whipp 1999; Whipp and Rossiter 2005). If severe exercise is continued, and blood lactate is determined at regular intervals, it can be observed that blood lactate never attains a steady-state, but continues to increase with time. Typically, the exercise is volitionally terminated by the subject at a blood lactate of 8–12 mM.

The upper limit of the severe domain has only relatively recently received attention in the literature (Özyener *et al.* 2001; Hill *et al.* 2002; Wilkerson *et al.* 2004; Hill and Stevens 2005). If the severe intensity domain is defined by the attainment of $\dot{V}O_{2max}$ then it follows that it must have an upper limit, because at extremely high work rates voluntary exhaustion occurs before $\dot{V}O_{2max}$ is attained. The highest work rate for which $\dot{V}O_{2max}$ is attained (the upper limit of the severe domain) is determined by first establishing the hyperbolic relationships between work rate and time to exhaustion and work rate and time to $\dot{V}O_{2max}$ for severe intensity exercise, and by determining the intersect between the two curves (Hill *et al.* 2002). Above this boundary, within the *extreme* domain, the

$\dot{V}O_2$ slow component is no longer manifested, exercise time is very limited and blood lactate accumulates rapidly. The severe-extreme domain boundary has been reported to occur at a work rate of approximately 170% Pcrit (Hill et al. 2002; Hill and Stevens 2005).

The profound differences in the physiological responses to moderate, heavy, severe and extreme exercise make it essential that the boundaries that demarcate these intensities can be accurately measured. This is important not only in terms of exercise and training prescription, but also for the prediction of functional or performance capability. It should be recognized that setting exercise intensity in relation to $\dot{V}O_{2max}$ alone may result in very different physiological responses to exercise even in individuals with identical $\dot{V}O_{2max}$ values (Katch et al. 1978). This is because exercise at, for example, 65% $\dot{V}O_{2max}$ may be above the Tlac in some subjects, but below this threshold in others. Likewise, exercise at 85% $\dot{V}O_{2max}$ will be above Tlac in most subjects but it could be above the MLSS in some subjects and below MLSS in others. Therefore, setting exercise intensity relative to $\dot{V}O_{2max}$ alone is unlikely to adequately 'normalize' exercise stress across a group of subjects. If an equivalent exercise intensity is required in a group of subjects, then this should, ideally, be calculated using measurements of Tlac, MLSS or Pcrit, and $\dot{V}O_{2max}$. This point is being increasingly recognized by exercise physiologists, as is evident in the numerous methods that have been proposed to determine the boundaries between moderate, heavy and severe exercise in different population groups and in different settings (for example, field vs laboratory).

10.4 FROM MODERATE TO HEAVY EXERCISE: THE LACTATE/ GAS EXCHANGE THRESHOLD

10.4.1 The lactate threshold (TLac)

Tlac was originally defined as the first increase in blood lactate above close-to-resting values during incremental exercise (Figure 10.2; Wasserman et al. 1973). The Tlac is associated with a non-linear increase in both $\dot{V}CO_2$ and $\dot{V}_E$ (the gas exchange or ventilatory threshold, Tvent) due to bicarbonate buffering of the lactic acidosis (see below). As outlined previously, constant-intensity exercise below Tlac can be sustained without an appreciable increase in blood lactate. Heart rate and ventilation reach an early steady-state and subjects perceive the exercise to be relatively easy. Exercise below Tlac can be sustained for several hours, but will eventually be terminated by substrate depletion, dehydration, musculo-skeletal injury or by psychological factors. If exercise at a constant intensity just above the Tlac is performed, blood lactate increases above resting levels, eventually sabilizing at 2–5 mM. Exercise above Tlac is associated with a non-linear increase in metabolic, respiratory and perceptual stress (Katch et al. 1978; Whipp and Ward 1990). Furthermore, exercise above Tlac is associated with more rapid fatigue, either through the effects of metabolic acidosis on contractile function or through an accelerated depletion of muscle glycogen (Jones et al. 1977; Roberts and Smith 1989). However, it should be noted, that while blood lactate accumulation is *associated* with the fatigue process, the relationship is not necessarily causal (e.g. Westerblad et al. 2002).

The exercise intensity at the Tlac/Tvent is a powerful predictor of endurance exercise performance (Farrell et al. 1979; Fay et al. 1989). Numerous studies also testify to the sensitivity of the Tlac and Tvent to endurance training. A rightward shift of the Tlac/Tvent to a higher power output or running speed is characteristic of successful endurance training programmes (Henritze et al. 1985; Weltman et al. 1992; Carter et al. 1999b). This adaptation allows a higher absolute (running speed or power output) and relative (%$\dot{V}O_{2max}$) exercise intensity to be sustained without the accumulation of blood lactate. In athletes who have trained for competition for

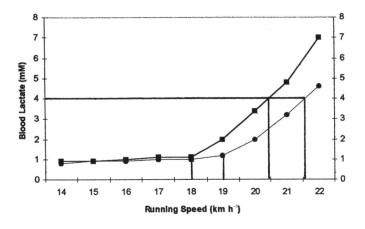

Figure 10.2: Determination of exercise intensity at lactate threshold (Tlac, first increase in blood lactate above resting values) and at 4 mM blood lactate ('OBLA') from an incremental treadmill test before (squares) and after (circles) a period of endurance training.

several years, the Tlac (and performance) may continue to improve despite a relatively stable $\dot{V}O_{2max}$ (Pierce *et al.* 1990; Coyle 2005; Jones 2006). Furthermore, endurance training is associated with a reduction in the degree of lactacidaemia for any given absolute or relative exercise intensity. This means the power output or running speed corresponding to arbitrary 'blood lactate reference values' such as 2 mM or 4 mM blood lactate is increased following a period of endurance training (Farrell *et al.* 1979; Hurley *et al.* 1984). An improvement in the Tlac/Tvent with training is therefore a clear marker of an enhanced endurance capacity. The Tlac/Tvent is typically found at 60–80 % $\dot{V}O_{2max}$ even in highly trained subjects, and therefore, it occurs at a lower exercise intensity than is maintained by athletes during most forms of endurance competition. The MLSS, which is the highest exercise intensity at which blood lactate does not accumulate over time, may be of more importance to success in these events.

Several authors have hypothesized that Tlac represents the optimal intensity for improvement of endurance fitness (Weltman *et al.* 1990; Mader 1991). Training at Tlac should provide a high-quality aerobic training stimulus without the accumulation of lactate

that might otherwise compromise training duration (Weltman 1989). In general, it appears that training at intensities close to or slightly above the existing Tlac/Tvent is important in eliciting significant improvements in this parameter (Henritze *et al.* 1985; Acavedo and Goldfarb 1989; Weltman *et al.* 1992; Londeree 1997). For example, increasing training intensity through the use of fartlek training on three days per week (Acavedo and Goldfarb 1989) or adding a 20-minute run at speed corresponding to Tlac to the weekly training programme (Sjodin *et al.* 1982) caused an improvement in Tlac with no change in $\dot{V}O_{2max}$ in runners.

The physiological mechanisms responsible for the increase in blood lactate at the Tlac have been much debated (Walsh and Banister 1988). It was originally considered that muscle hypoxia was the main cause of this increase (Wasserman *et al.* 1973). Despite the possibility that there may be regional inequalities in muscle perfusion, many find it hard to accept that O_2 availability may be limited at the submaximal exercise intensities associated with the Tlac. Indeed, some studies have demonstrated an increase in lactate production without any evidence for the existence of hypoxic loci in the contracting muscle tissue (Jobsis and Stainsby 1968;

Connett et al. 1984). It has been proposed that lactate produced in muscle during submaximal exercise may be important as a cytosolic reserve for carbohydrate and reducing equivalents, thereby maintaining optimal coupling of cytosolic supply to mitochondrial utilization (Connett et al. 1985; Honig et al. 1992). The effect of catecholaminergic stimulation of glycolysis should also be considered. Some studies have shown similar patterns of increase and simultaneous 'thresholds' in plasma lactate and plasma catecholamines (Mazzeo and Marshall 1989). Greater oxidative enzyme activity following training may reduce lactate production by limiting the ability of lactate dehydrogenase (LDH) to compete with the mitochondria for pyruvate and reducing equivalents. Also, an augmented rate of entry of pyruvate into the mitochondria would diminish the possibility of a mass action effect. It is possible that Tlac represents a transient imbalance between mechanisms of lactate production and lactate removal from the blood (Brooks 1991). Certainly, the rate of blood lactate accumulation should be considered to be the difference between the rate of muscle lactate production and the rate of lactate clearance in tissues such as red skeletal muscle fibres, and the heart, liver and kidneys (Donovan and Pagliassotti 1990; MacRae et al. 1992). It should also be considered that lactate produced in type II muscle fibres might be used as a fuel by adjacent type I muscle fibres before it ever reaches the bloodstream, and that net lactate release by less active muscle during exercise may provide a convenient method to distribute carbohydrate stores from glycogen-replete to glycogen depleted areas (Talmadge et al. 1989; Brooks 1991). Finally, the close correlation between the percentage of type I fibres in the active muscles and the Tlac (Ivy et al. 1980) suggests that Tlac may coincide with a greater recruitment of type II fibres as exercise intensity increases (Nagata et al. 1981).

The notion of a 'threshold' in blood lactate accumulation is not universally accepted. Some groups have argued that blood lactate increases as a continuous function of exercise intensity (Hughson et al. 1987). However, although lactate may increase exponentially above Tlac, an exponential curve does not provide a good fit to exercise lactate data in the region of interest (1–4 mM) (Wasserman et al. 1990). The exercise protocol is also of importance if a clear identification of Tlac is required. Firstly, it is critical that the exercise test is started at a sufficiently low exercise intensity so that the baseline blood lactate can be established. If precision is required in the identification of Tlac then numerous stages (7–9) with small increments between stages is recommended (Jones and Doust 1997a). The $\dot{V}O_2$ at Tlac is independent of the rate at which the exercise intensity is increased during incremental or ramp exercise tests. Yoshida (1984) demonstrated that the $\dot{V}O_2$ at Tlac was the same when exercise was increased by 25 W every 1 minute or by 25 W every 4 minutes. However, the power output or running speed at the Tlac depends upon the incremental rate used (Ferry et al. 1988), so if the identification of power output or running speed at Tlac is required for training prescription then a protocol using 'steady-state' stages of at least 3–4 minutes duration is recommended. The 'actual' exercise intensity at Tlac can be estimated from ramp or incremental tests if the data are corrected for the lag time in $\dot{V}O_2$ at the onset of exercise. This is generally equivalent to subtracting ¾ of the ramp rate from the measured value. For example, if the power output at Tlac is 200 W when using a ramp exercise test with a ramp rate of 20 $W.min^{-1}$, then the 'corrected' power output at Tlac = 200 − (0.75 × 20) = 185 W.

The Tlac is routinely used in laboratory based physiological assessments of endurance capacity. Subjects commonly perform a single incremental protocol involving a number of short (3- to 5-minute) stages of increasing intensity. Blood samples for the determination of blood lactate are obtained at the end of

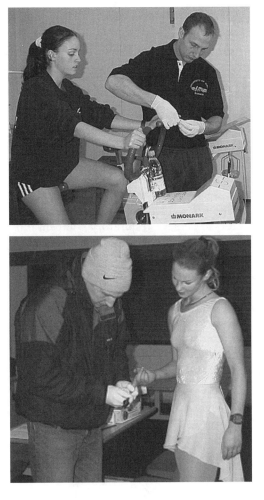

Figure 10.3a and 10.3b: Lactate measurement in the laboratory and in the field on two members of the British Figure Skating team.

each stage before the exercise intensity is increased. Assessment of Tlac is usually by scrutiny of data plots by one or more reviewers. While this practice has been shown to be highly reliable both within and between reviewers (Davis 1985), some authors have criticised this approach for its subjectivity (Yeh *et al.* 1983). Until relatively recently, the measurement of blood lactate was confined to the exercise laboratory. However, the introduction of portable and robust blood lactate analyzers has enabled blood lactate and the Tlac to be assessed in field conditions. (Figures 10.3a and 10.3b)

10.4.2 Reference blood lactate concentrations

To circumvent problems associated with the subjective assessment of Tlac, some authors have chosen to define Tlac as the $\dot{V}O_2$, power output or running speed at which an absolute blood lactate concentration is reached. Examples of this are interpolation to blood lactate of 2 mM (Lafontaine *et al.* 1981), 2.5 mM (Hurley *et al.* 1984) and 1 mM above resting values (Coyle *et al.* 1983). It should be borne in mind that absolute blood lactate concentrations are affected by factors such as the incremental rate used in the exercise protocol (Foxdal *et al.* 1994), muscle glycogen levels (Hughes *et al.* 1982), the blood sampling site (artery, vein, or fingertip) and the choice of assay (whole blood, lysed blood, or plasma), (Robergs *et al.* 1990; Williams *et al.* 1992). Despite these limitations, the reduction in blood lactate for a given absolute exercise intensity following endurance training means that this method can be useful in demonstrating an improved endurance capacity, provided that the same methods are used longitudinally. Another method that has been used to increase objectivity of Tlac assessment is the Dmax method (Cheng *et al.* 1992). This procedure involves fitting a curve to the blood lactate response to exercise and then drawing a line between the first and the last data points. The 'Tlac' is defined as the running speed that is furthest away from this line. However, a problem with the Dmax method is that determination of the 'Tlac' may be skewed by error in either the first or last blood lactate measurement.

10.4.3 The gas exchange or ventilatory threshold

The Tlac can be assessed non-invasively by consideration of the gas exchange responses to exercise. Due to its low pK, lactic acid will be almost completely dissociated on formation. The liberated protons will be buffered predominantly by intracellular and plasma bicarbonates, resulting in the liberation of large amounts of 'non-metabolic' CO_2. This is detected by the peripheral chemoreceptors and causes a disproportionate increase in $\dot{V}CO_2$ and $\dot{V}_E$ at what is known as the gas exchange or ventilatory threshold (Tvent), (Figure 10.4). The most sensitive approaches to the measurement of the Tvent is the disproportionate increase in $\dot{V}CO_2$ relative to $\dot{V}O_2$ known as the V-slope method (Beaver *et al.* 1986), and the increase in the ventilatory equivalent for O_2 ($\dot{V}_E/\dot{V}O_2$) without a concomitant increase in the ventilatory equivalent for CO_2 ($\dot{V}_E/\dot{V}CO_2$) (Caiozzo *et al.* 1982).

The Tvent can be measured during multistage exercise protocols with stage durations of 3–4 minutes, but ventilatory breakpoints are sharper when fast incremental or ramp protocols are used to bring subjects to exhaustion in around 10 minutes. It is possible to measure Tvent by collecting expired air into Douglas bags during each stage of an incremental test but breath-by-breath gas analysis allows a greater density of respiratory gas exchange measures and a more reliable assessment of the Tvent. During fast incremental or ramp exercise tests, a second ventilatory breakpoint known as the respiratory compensation threshold can be identified. For a short period of time during incremental exercise above the Tvent, there is an 'isocapnic buffering' region in which $\dot{V}_E$ increases in direct proportion to $\dot{V}CO_2$. Above this point, $\dot{V}_E$ increases at a faster rate than $\dot{V}CO_2$ to achieve respiratory compensation for the metabolic acidosis. The respiratory compensation threshold can be observed as a second breakpoint in $\dot{V}_E$ when plotted against $\dot{V}O_2$, or, more easily, as a single breakpoint when $\dot{V}_E$ is plotted against $\dot{V}CO_2$. While measurement of the Tvent can be convenient, the requirement for sensitive gas analysis equipment means that it is essentially limited to laboratory use.

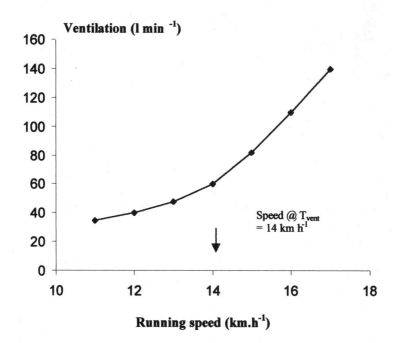

Figure 10.4: Determination of exercise intensity at ventilatory threshold (Tvent) from an incremental treadmill test.

10.4.4 Breathing frequency threshold

The increase in $\dot{V}_E$ during incremental exercise is caused by changes in tidal volume (breathing depth) and ventilatory frequency (breathing rate). Tidal volume typically attains a plateau at ~ 50% $\dot{V}O_{2max}$, so that further increases in $\dot{V}_E$ are mediated mainly by changes in ventilatory frequency. It has been suggested that a nonlinear increase in ventilatory frequency might be used to determine Tvent without the requirement for the analysis of expired air (James *et al.* 1989). This would allow for the Tlac/Tvent to be determined non-invasively outside the laboratory and for exercise intensity to be prescribed and/or monitored using ventilatory frequency. However, factors such as the entrainment of ventilatory frequency to exercise rhythm (cadence) and disruption of the ventilatory pattern by coughing, swallowing, and speech limit the utility of monitoring breathing frequency to give information on the proximity to Tvent in the field situation (Jones and Doust 1998a).

10.5 FROM HEAVY TO SEVERE EXERCISE: THE MAXIMAL LACTATE STEADY-STATE AND CRITICAL POWER

10.5.1 The maximal lactate steady-state

MLSS, the exercise intensity above which blood lactate (and $\dot{V}O_2$) will rise continuously during continuous exercise, demarcates the boundary between heavy and severe exercise and it is considered by some to be the criterion measure of endurance fitness. Measurement of the MLSS requires that subjects perform a series of prolonged constant-intensity exercise bouts with blood lactate determined serially over a range of exercise intensities. As an example, a subject may be required to complete five treadmill runs each of 30-minutes duration at different running speeds on separate days (see Figure 10.5). The MLSS is defined as the highest running speed or power output at which blood lactate will sabilize during prolonged exercise (Beneke and von Duvillard 1996; Jones and Doust, 1998b). However, measurement of MLSS is not suitable for routine diagnostic use. It is time-consuming and requires several days to complete the series of exercise bouts. Additionally, a large number of blood samples must be taken in order to define MLSS accurately (e.g. 30 samples for 5×30-minute exercise bouts with blood samples taken at rest and then every 5 minutes during exercise). This is inconvenient for the subject and is expensive in costs of consumables. Another problem is the precise definition of MLSS. While several methods have been used to define MLSS, Londeree (1986) recommended an increase of no more than 1 mM in blood lactate measured between 10 and 30 minutes of a sustained exercise bout and this criterion has been applied by other authors (Snyder *et al.* 1994; Beneke and von Duvillard 1996; Jones and Doust 1998b). This criterion would appear to be reasonable given the small error inherent in capillary blood sampling and assay and the changes in muscle substrate and plasma volume that might be expected with exercise of this duration and intensity (Beneke 2003).

For exercise above the MLSS, the time to exhaustion will be a function of the rate at which $\dot{V}O_2$ increases towards $\dot{V}O_{2max}$ and the rate at which muscle and blood lactate rises to values associated with fatigue. Therefore, it is not surprising that the MLSS has been shown to be an important predictor of endurance exercise performance (Billat *et al.* 2004). Jones and Doust (1998b) demonstrated that the MLSS was better correlated with 8 km running performance (r = 0.92) than a number of other physiological measures including Tlac, Tvent, blood lactate reference values, and $\dot{V}O_{2max}$. Theoretically, the exercise intensity at the MLSS can be sustained for one hour during competition but under laboratory conditions an exercise duration of

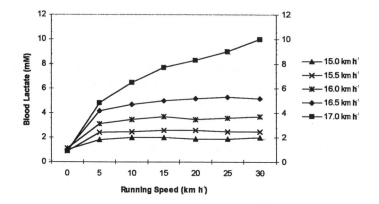

Figure 10.5: Determination of the running speed at the maximal lactate steady-state (MLSS) from five treadmill runs of 30 minutes duration at different speeds. In this example, the MLSS occurs at 16.5 km.h⁻¹.

40–50 minutes is more common. Therefore, it appears that the MLSS is closely related to the running speed that can be sustained during competition in running races at distances of 10 km to 10 miles.

Despite the great theoretical and practical interest in the direct determination of the MLSS, the requirement for several laboratory sessions and numerous blood samples has led exercise physiologists to devise simpler tests for estimation of the MLSS.

10.5.2 Critical power

Monod and Scherrer (1965) observed that when a series of fatiguing constant work-rate tests were performed, a linear relationship was established between work done and the time to exhaustion. The slope of this regression was termed critical power (Pcrit), which was considered to represent the highest exercise intensity that could be sustained for long periods without fatigue (Monod and Scherrer 1965; Moritani *et al.* 1981). This interpretation has since been revised, as several investigations have shown that exercise at Pcrit can only be sustained for 20–45 minutes under laboratory conditions (Poole *et al.* 1988; Housh *et al.* 1989; Jenkins and Quigley 1990; Overend *et al.* 1992; Brickley *et al.* 2002). The work-time relationship can be expressed

as two mathematically equivalent functions: the hyperbolic power-time relationship where Pcrit is indicated by the power-asymptote, and the linear power-inverse of time (1/t) relationship where Pcrit is the y-intercept (Figure 10.6, panel A).

The measurement of Pcrit requires that subjects exercise to exhaustion at several (ideally 4–6) constant power outputs on separate days. The Pcrit is most commonly established for cycling exercise, but the concept has also been applied to other activities including running (Hughson *et al.* 1984; Smith and Jones 2001) and swimming (Wakayoshi *et al.* 1992; Dekerle *et al.* 2005) where the term 'critical speed' is used. Poole *et al.* (1988) demonstrated that blood lactate and $\dot{V}O_2$ attained steady-state values during exercise at Pcrit but rose over time during exercise performed above the Pcrit. Recently, Jones *et al.* (2008) provided the first evidence that the Pcrit demarcates those work rates for which steady-state muscle metabolic responses can be attained from those work rates where exercise results in continuous depletion of phosphocreatine and significant accumulation of fatigue related metabolites (i.e. Pi, H⁺). The Pcrit is known to be sensitive to endurance training (Gaesser and Wilson 1988; Poole *et al.* 1990; Jenkins and Quigley 1992).

The critical power protocol has not been strictly standardized on the assumption that any exercise bout performed to volitional exhaustion can be included in critical power modelling. However, the duration of predicting trials can have a considerable effect on the parameter estimates and it has been noted that exercise times of less than ~ 2 minutes do not conform to the linear work-time relationship (Monod and Scherrer 1965; Bishop et al. 1998). The times to exhaustion used to model the critical power should therefore range from ~ 2 to 12 minutes, and the same end-exercise $\dot{V}O_2$ should be attained in all trials (i.e. $\dot{V}O_{2max}$). The Pcrit estimate can be deemed accurate when the associated SEE is less than 5% (Hill 1993; Hill and Smith 1994).

Although, in theory, the Pcrit should represent the same exercise intensity as the MLSS, experimental studies have shown that the Pcrit typically occurs in a close proximity, but slightly (~5%) above MLSS (Smith and Jones 2001; Pringle and Jones 2002; Dekerle et al. 2005). However, the definition of MLSS as the highest work-rate where blood lactate *stabilizes* during prolonged exercise would imply that the MLSS lies within the heavy intensity domain. The Pcrit differs from all other proposed demarcators of exercise intensity domains in that it is not based on the measurement of physiological responses during exercise but on the measurement of mechanical work done and exercise tolerance. It should also be noted that the blood lactate is not the only index by which the transition from heavy to severe intensity exercise is classified and indeed may be considered a secondary index to the behaviour of $\dot{V}O_2$. Importantly, the Pcrit signifies a boundary above which constant-work-rate exercise results in the attainment of $\dot{V}O_{2max}$ (Hill *et al.* 2002; Hill and Ferguson 1999; Poole et. al. 1988).

The critical power has obvious relevance as a theoretical construct. However, the necessity for subjects to perform a number of exhaustive efforts on separate days

has precluded its routine use as means of identifying the boundary between heavy and severe exercise.

10.5.3 The 3-minute all-out test

Recently, it has been proposed that the Pcrit can also be established in a single 3-minute bout of all-out cycling against a fixed resistance (Burnley et al. 2006; Vanhatalo et al. 2007). An integral assumption on which the estimation of Pcrit from all-out exercise relies is the finite nature of the work capacity above Pcrit denoted by the curvature constant of the power-time relationship (W'; Monod and Scherrer 1965; Fukuba et al. 2003). During any exercise bout above Pcrit this finite work capacity is gradually expended and cannot be replenished until work-rate falls below Pcrit or exercise is terminated (Coats et al. 2003; Morton 2006). Therefore, once the W' has been entirely utilized during a bout of all-out exercise, the highest work rate that can be elicited must equal Pcrit (Vanhatalo et al. 2007).

Burnley et al. (2006) demonstrated that in a 3-minute all-out test the power output attained a plateau within ~2–2.5 min. The end-test power output (EP), calculated as the mean over the final 30 s of the test, was highly reproducible. Prolonged constant-work-rate exercise at 15 W below EP yielded steady-state $\dot{V}O_2$ and blood lactate responses indicative of heavy exercise, whereas at 15 W above EP, exercise tolerance was limited, blood lactate increased continually and $\dot{V}O_{2max}$ was attained (Burnley et al. 2006). Subsequently, the same investigators reported a remarkably close agreement between the 3-minute test EP and a conventionally estimated Pcrit (SEE 6 W, r = 0.99; Vanhatalo et al. 2007). The protocol robustness of the 3-minute test has been assessed by manipulating the power profile and the pedal rate (by altering the fixed resistance; Vanhatalo et al. 2008). The EP was unaffected by minor variations in cadence, although higher than standard pedal rate (+10 rpm) tended to yield reduced EP estimates. This finding is consistent with the reduction observed in the conventional Pcrit estimates at high cadences as a result of increased 'internal' work (i.e. loss of efficiency; McNaughton and Thomas 1996; Barker *et al.* 2006). In the same study, the EP was unaffected by pacing when power output was fixed at either 100% or 130% of the ramp test maximum over the initial 30 s of the test followed by a 2.5-minute all-out effort (Vanhatalo *et al.* 2008). Recent work (Vanhatalo *et al.*, in press) has shown the EP to be sensitive to change as a result of a training intervention, with EP demonstrating a similar change to the conventionally measured Pcrit.

These findings confirm the notion of the fixed 'work capacity above critical power' and lend significant support to the theoretical validity of the application of the critical power concept to all-out exercise. The evidence presented thus far suggests that the 3-minute all-out test may provide a valid and reliable measure of Pcrit.

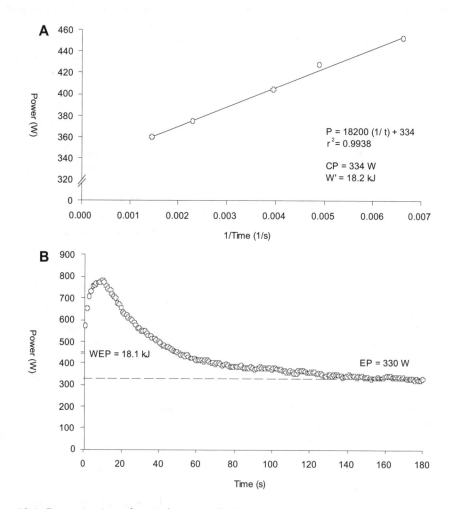

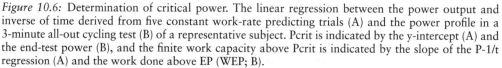

Figure 10.6: Determination of critical power. The linear regression between the power output and inverse of time derived from five constant work-rate predicting trials (A) and the power profile in a 3-minute all-out cycling test (B) of a representative subject. Pcrit is indicated by the y-intercept (A) and the end-test power (B), and the finite work capacity above Pcrit is indicated by the slope of the P-1/t regression (A) and the work done above EP (WEP; B).

10.5.4 Neuromuscular fatigue threshold

The neuromuscular fatigue threshold (NFT) was first described by de Vries et al. (1982). Determination of the NFT requires subjects to exercise at a number of severe and extreme power outputs while electromyographic activity (EMG) in the working muscles is measured continuously. The slope of the increase in the integrated EMG (iEMG) over time in each of these exercise bouts is recorded. Subsequently, the slope of the iEMG is plotted against the respective power output and the intercept of this relationship is defined as the NFT (i.e. the NFT therefore represents the highest power output at which iEMG will theoretically remain stable over time; Moritani et al. 1993). Constant load exercise at NFT has been shown to reflect the parallel steady-state profiles in blood lactate and ventilatory responses (Hanon et al. 1998; Hug et al. 2003) and the NFT has been shown to occur at a similar power output to the Pcrit (Housh et al. 1991a; Housh et al. 1991b). This coincidence may indicate that the transition from heavy to severe exercise is associated with an increased firing frequency of already recruited muscle fibres or with a progressive recruitment of low-efficiency type II muscle fibres as fatigue ensues.

Measurement of the NFT has not proved popular as a method for defining the boundary between the heavy and severe exercise intensity domains due to the requirement for subjects to complete several exercise bouts and for equipment to measure and analyze electromyographic activity. Moreover, significant problems with actually defining NFT have been reported (Pringle and Jones 2002).

10.5.5 Lactate turnpoint

During incremental exercise tests, some authors have identified two lactate thresholds from plots of blood lactate against $\dot{V}O_2$ or exercise intensity (Ribeiro et al. 1986;

Aunola and Rusko 1992; Hofmann et al. 1994). These correspond to the traditional 'first' lactate threshold where blood lactate first increases above baseline, and a 'second' 'sudden and sustained' lactate threshold or lactate turnpoint at around 2.5–4.0 mM. Skinner and McLellan (1980) first argued for the existence of two transition points in both the blood lactate and ventilatory responses to incremental exercise, and these authors also speculated on the possible physiological mechanisms that may underpin these phenomena. It has been noted that the lactate turnpoint may be more meaningful in terms of the endurance race performance capabilities of highly trained subjects than is the Tlac (Ribeiro et al. 1986; Aunola and Rusko 1992; Hoffman et al. 1994). It is not known whether any similarity between the exercise intensity at the lactate turnpoint and the Pcrit/MLSS is coincidental or whether both are related to the same underlying mechanism. If incremental exercise tests utilize stage durations that are sufficiently long and intensity increments that are sufficiently small to allow the measured blood lactate to reflect entry of lactate into and its removal from the blood, it is possible that the lactate turnpoint can provide a reasonable estimate of the MLSS. Several investigations have indeed shown that the LTP provides an adequate estimate of the MLSS work-rate (Aunola and Rusko 1992; Hofmann et al. 1994; Smith and Jones 2001; Kilding and Jones 2005). However, it should be noted that the visual determination of breakpoints (and especially the second breakpoint) from blood lactate-work-rate plots is a subjective process which can affect the repeatability and inter-evaluator reliability of parameter estimates (Gladden et al. 1985; Yeh et al. 1983).

10.5.6 Fixed blood lactate concentrations (OBLA)

Mader et al (1976) defined the 'aerobic-anaerobic transition' as the point at which blood lactate reached 4 mM in an incremental exercise test (Figure 10.2). The rationale for this may have been based on the suggestion that muscle lactate transporters become saturated at approximately 4 mM muscle lactate (Jorfeldt *et al.* 1978). Support for the 4mM concept was provided by Kindermann *et al* (1979) and Heck *et al* (1985) who demonstrated that the *mean* blood lactate at MLSS was 4.0 ± 0.7 mM (range: 3.1–5.5 mM). Jones and Doust (1998b) also reported that the mean blood lactate at MLSS in a group of runners was close to 4 mM, but noted that individual values could be as low as 2.5 mM or as high as 6.0 mM. There is some evidence that the blood lactate at the MLSS might be related to the muscle mass involved in the exercise (Beneke *et al.* 2001; Almarwaey *et al.* 2004). The 4 mM blood lactate reference value evaluated during incremental exercise was termed the 'onset of blood lactate accumulation' (OBLA) by Sjodin and Jacobs (1981). However, this is a misnomer given that 4 mM blood lactate value is reached at a significantly higher exercise intensity than the Tlac.

The use of OBLA, and other fixed values such as 3 mM (Borch *et al.* 1993) certainly improve the objectivity with which exercise blood lactate data can be evaluated and may be useful in demonstrating a reduced reliance on non-oxidative metabolism during submaximal exercise following training. However, this procedure takes no account of inter-individual differences in the rate of blood lactate accumulation. Moreover, the dependency of blood lactate on substrate availability (Ivy *et al.* 1981), exercise protocol (Ferry *et al.* 1988), and on the site of blood sampling and the assay medium (Williams *et al.* 1992) brings the validity of this practice into question. Coincidentally, the exercise intensity at 4mM blood lactate may be similar in some subjects to the exercise intensity at the lactate turnpoint which, in turn, may provide a good estimate of the MLSS. However, it should be remembered that blood lactate responses during incremental exercise tests rarely allow the blood lactate response during prolonged exercise at a constant intensity to be predicted (Orok *et al.* 1989; Aunola and Rusko 1992). For example, if subjects are asked to exercise continuously at the exercise intensity corresponding to 4 mM blood lactate derived from an incremental test, blood lactate rises throughout the exercise bout and exhaustion occurs relatively quickly (Mognoni *et al.* 1990; Oyono-Enguille *et al.* 1990). This suggests that, in most subjects, the exercise intensity at which 4 mM blood lactate is reached in an incremental test overestimates the exercise intensity at the MLSS. This may be especially true in elite subjects who may not increase their blood lactate to greater than 4 mM until they reach ≥ 95% $\dot{V}O_{2max}$ (Coyle 2005; Jones 2006).

10.5.7 Individual anaerobic threshold

Investigations by Stegmann *et al.* (1981) and Stegmann and Kindermann (1982) into individual blood lactate kinetics during exercise and recovery led to the concept of the individual anaerobic threshold (IAT). The calculation of IAT involves the measurement of blood lactate during a standard incremental exercise test and during the subsequent recovery period. The IAT concept makes several important assumptions including that the lactate clearance kinetics during recovery reflect those that are operating during exercise. An exponential curve is fitted to the blood lactate response to exercise and a third order polynomial is fitted to the data for lactate during the recovery period. Then, a horizontal line is drawn to connect the peak exercise lactate value to the equivalent lactate value in recovery. A second line is then drawn from this point on the 'recovery lactate curve' tangential to the 'exercise lactate curve.' The point at which this line transects the 'exercise lactate curve' is defined as the IAT and is assumed to represent the exercise intensity at which the elimination of blood lactate is both maximal and equal to the rate of diffusion of lactate from working muscle to blood

(Stegmann *et al.* 1981). The physiological rationale for this approach has never been transparent and misgivings exist as to the validity of a number of the assumptions made in the IAT concept, including that the rate of blood lactate clearance reaches a plateau during submaximal exercise. Although the IAT is sensitive to endurance training (Keith *et al.* 1992), the time to exhaustion and physiological responses at IAT work rate have varied considerably in different studies. Some have reported times to exhaustion as long as 50–60 minutes and steady-state responses at the IAT (Stegmann *et al.* 1981; McLellan and Cheung 1992), while Orok *et al.* (1989) found that exercise at IAT could only be sustained for 3–36 minutes. Jones and Doust (1998c) reported that in well-trained runners, the IAT overestimated the running speed at both Tlac and at 4 mM blood lactate. The differences between studies may be explained by subsequent findings that the IAT estimate is affected by the incremental rate and stage duration during the incremental phase (Coen *et al.* 2001), whether the incremental test is continued until exhaustion, as well as the selection of either active or passive recovery (McLellan and Jacobs 1993).

The requirement for complex data analysis in the determination of IAT precludes its routine use by athlete and coach, and due to concerns over its theoretical bases, the IAT method cannot be recommended for the estimation of the heavy-severe domain boundary.

10.5.8 Lactate minimum speed

Tegtbur *et al.* (1993) suggested that the point at which blood lactate reached a minimum before beginning to rise during an incremental exercise test initiated during lactacidosis provided a valid estimate of MLSS. The lactate minimum speed test requires subjects to perform: (1) two supramaximal exercise bouts for 60 s and 45 s (separated by a 60 s recovery period) at an intensity of ~ 120 % $\dot{V}O_{2max}$; (2) an 8-minute walk to allow

lactate to reach a peak in the blood; and (3) an incremental exercise test using ~ 3-minute stages with blood lactate measured at the end of each stage. The blood lactate response during the incremental portion of the test, which should be described using a cubic spline function, is characteristically U-shaped and the nadir on this curve can be termed the lactate minimum speed (LMS), (Figure 10.7). Tegtbur *et al.* (1993) suggested that the decreasing blood lactate during the early stages of the incremental test indicated that the rate of blood lactate clearance was greater than the rate of lactate production, while the increasing blood lactate during the latter part of the test indicated that lactate production outstripped its removal. On this basis, the point at which lactate reaches a minimum should reflect the point at which lactate production and lactate clearance rates are equal (i.e. the MLSS). Tegtbur *et al.* (1993) showed that when 25 endurance runners ran for 8 km at the LMS they exhibited elevated but stable blood lactate, whereas when the subjects ran at a speed just above the LMS, there was a significant accumulation of blood lactate which caused 11 subjects to terminate the exercise bout before 8 km had been completed. Similar results were reported by MacIntosh *et al.* (2002) for cycling exercise.

Several studies indicate that the LMS may not be valid for the estimation of MLSS. Jones and Doust (1998b) reported that the LMS was not significantly different to the running speed at Tlac but that it was significantly lower than the running speed at the directly-determined MLSS in 10 trained runners. The LMS had poor discriminatory power between subjects, was poorly correlated with MLSS, and provided the worst estimate of the MLSS out of a range of other physiological measures including Tlac, Tvent, and OBLA. Carter *et al.* (1999a) have shown that the LMS is profoundly influenced by the exercise intensity at which the incremental portion of the lactate minimum test is started. These authors reported a positive linear relationship between the starting speed used in the incremental test

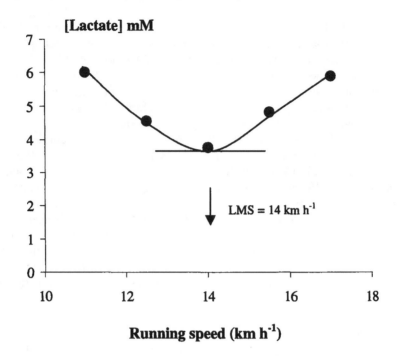

Figure 10.7: Determination of the lactate minimum speed (LMS). In this example, an incremental treadmill test involving five exercise stages has been completed following prior sprint exercise. The blood lactate data are fitted with a cubic spline and the minimum point on the curve is termed the LMS.

and the speed at which the lactate minimum was found. Although it would be possible to choose a starting speed that would provide a reasonable value for LMS, this requirement for manipulating the test protocol to achieve the 'correct' result questions the validity of the LMS concept. In another study, Carter *et al.* (1999b) measured Tlac and the blood lactate response to a standard incremental treadmill test, the LMS, and $\dot{V}O_{2max}$ in 16 subjects before and after they completed a 6-week endurance training programme. There were significant improvements in the running speeds at Tlac and 3 mM blood lactate, and a significant increase in $\dot{V}O_{2max}$. Despite this clear evidence of improvement in endurance fitness with training, the LMS was not significantly different before or after training. This lack of sensitivity to training along with the protocol-dependency of the lactate minimum test clearly question the validity of the LMS test.

10.5.9 Heart rate deflection point

Conconi *et al.* (1982) reported that the speed at which the linearity in the heart rate (HR) – running speed relationship was lost in an incremental field test in runners, that is, the heart rate deflection point, was highly correlated with (r = 0.99) and not significantly different from the running speed at Tlac. Droghetti *et al.* (1985) confirmed this relationship in a number of other sports and activities. Conconi *et al.* (1982) proposed that the $\dot{V}O_2$ spared by the increased anaerobic contribution to the total energy cost of exercise beyond Tlac would be reflected by a reduced rate of increase in HR above Tlac. Conconi's original method required subjects to run around an athletics track initially at a slow speed. Thereafter, there was a progressive increase in running speed every 200 m. Heart rate was recorded telemetrically at the end of each stage and athletes continued until exhaustion. When HR is plotted against running speed, a deviation of heart rate at high speeds can sometimes be seen (Figure 10.8). Conconi *et al.* (1982) reported that the deflection point in HR could be observed in all subjects and that it occurred at the same running speed as the Tlac. However, the protocol used to assess Tlac was unusual and it was later suggested that the deflection in HR corresponded to the lactate turnpoint (Ribeiro *et al.* 1985) or the MLSS (Hofmann *et al.* 1994). The original Conconi test protocol has recently been modified (Grazzi *et al.* 1999).

The interest in the possibility of a non-invasive field test for MLSS led to a large number of investigations into the validity of Conconi's method. The majority of these studies have questioned the validity, reliability, and mechanistic bases of the Conconi test (Kuipers *et al.* 1988; Tokmakidis and Leger 1992; Jones and Doust 1995; Jones and Doust, 1997b) although other groups have maintained that the test is valid and useful (Hofmann *et al.* 1994; Bunc *et al.* 1995). The physiological rationale for the existence of a deflection in heart rate and for its mechanistic link to increased blood lactate accumulation has never been clear. Conconi's original hypothesis that increased anaerobic metabolism spares $\dot{V}O_2$ is, however, untenable. The increased rate of ATP resynthesis through anaerobic glycolysis above the Tlac appears to supplement rather than spare the rate of ATP production through oxidative metabolism. During incremental tests that bring subjects to exhaustion in 8–12 minutes, a reduced rate of increase in $\dot{V}O_2$ during submaximal exercise has never been demonstrated (aside from the plateau in $\dot{V}O_2$ at maximal exercise). Rather, with

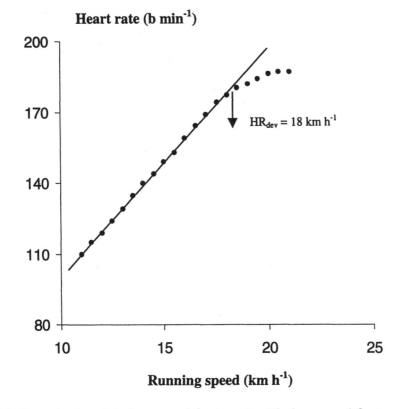

Figure 10.8: Determination of the heart rate deflection point. The heart rate deflection point is the running speed at which heart rate begins to deviate from linearity.

longer stage durations, $\dot{V}O_2$ may demonstrate an upward curvilinearity as the $\dot{V}O_2$ slow component develops, reflecting a reduction in muscle efficiency (Jones *et al.* 1999). It has therefore been suggested that the deflection in heart rate is an artefact of the specifics of the Conconi test protocol (Jones and Doust 1997b). The increase in running speed every 200 m means that the time between increases in exercise intensity becomes progressively shorter as the test proceeds. This may have two important effects. Firstly, measurements of HR become more frequent as HR approaches its maximum. When plotted against running speed, this will elongate the region at HR max and lead to the artificial appearance of a deflection point. Secondly, the decreasing exercise stage durations in the face of similar or slowed HR response kinetics may not allow sufficient time for HR to rise to its 'steady-state' level.

Difficulty in observing a deflection in HR in all subjects has been recognized as a limitation to the Conconi test (Kuipers *et al.* 1988; Jones and Doust 1995; Jones and Doust, 1997b) and these difficulties persist even when mathematical approaches to the identification of a deflection in HR are utilized (Tokmakidis and Leger 1992). Jones and Doust (1995) assessed the test-retest reliability of the Conconi test in 15 subjects and reported that a deflection in HR was found in both tests in only 6 individuals. The deflection in HR has also been shown to occur at rather high submaximal exercise intensities; that is, 90–95% HR max, much higher than the Tlac and OBLA (Tokmakidis and Leger 1992; Jones and Doust, 1997b). Two studies in running (Jones and Doust 1997b) and cycling (Heck and Hollmann 1992) have shown that the exercise intensity at the deflection in HR can not be sustained without appreciable accumulation of blood lactate and premature fatigue. These studies suggest that a deflection in HR, when it can be determined, overestimates the exercise intensity at MLSS in most subjects.

10.5.10 Other estimates

Other approaches have been used to estimate the boundary between heavy and severe exercise. Snyder *et al.* (1994) proposed that the exercise intensity at 85% HR max provides a close estimate of the exercise intensity at MLSS. While this may be generally true, dangers in non-individual evaluation of the physiological response to exercise have been highlighted previously (Katch *et al.* 1978). For example, in elite distance runners, exercise at the MLSS requires approximately 90 % HR max (Jones 1998). Billat *et al.* (1994) estimated the power output at MLSS during cycling by analyzing the change in blood lactate between 20 and 30 minutes at two intensities corresponding to ~ 65% and ~ 80% $\dot{V}O_{2max}$. Effectively, these authors interpolated between a power output which resulted in decreased or constant blood lactate with time, and a power output which resulted in an increased blood lactate with time, to predict a power output at which blood lactate would be maximal but stable. However, a subsequent investigation by Kilding and Jones (2005) indicated that the accuracy of 'characteristic exercise intensity' proposed by Billat *et al.* (1994) was affected by inter-individual variability in blood lactate responses at the given intensities and that the proposed method significantly underestimated the running speed at the MLSS. Another method for 'single-visit' MLSS assessment based on a combination of heart rate, rating of perceived exertion, breathing frequency and race pace, was introduced by Palmer *et al.* (1999) and supported by Kuphal *et al.* (2004). Although promising, this method appears to be unlikely to estimate the MLSS accurately in all subjects.

It has also been proposed that the *second* ventilatory threshold (or the 'respiratory compensation point', RCP, see above) during ramp incremental exercise would coincide with the Pcrit and/or the MLSS. Pouilly *et al.* (2005) claimed that the Pcrit could be estimated from a single ramp incremental test based on the assumption that Pcrit was equal to the RCP. However, Simon *et al.* (1983) demonstrated that exercise marginally below the RCP resulted in non-steady-state blood lactate profiles, with only three out of five subjects completing 30 minutes of exercise. More recently, the RCP has been shown to occur at a significantly higher work-rate than the MLSS in swimming (Dekerle *et al.* 2003) and in cycling (Laplaud *et al.* 2006). Estimation of the Pcrit work-rate from ventilatory and/or gas exchange responses during incremental exercise should be approached with great caution.

10.6 FROM SEVERE TO EXTREME EXERCISE: $\dot{V}O_{2MAX}$

10.6.1 $\dot{V}O_{2max}$ and exercise economy

Although the $\dot{V}O_{2max}$ is typically measured in an incremental exercise test where the maximum is reached at or near exhaustion, it is important to note that the attainment of $\dot{V}O_{2max}$ is not associated with any single work rate. As discussed above, the severe exercise intensity domain is characterized by the attainment of $\dot{V}O_{2max}$ during constant work-rate exercise and as such the severe domain may well be characterized as the 'maximal domain.' Because the $\dot{V}O_{2max}$ can still be attained at work-rates up to approximately 120% $\dot{V}O_{2max}$, the work-rate associated with 100% $\dot{V}O_{2max}$ by definition lies within the severe domain.

The $\dot{V}O_{2max}$, nevertheless, remains the customary demarcator between submaximal and supramaximal exercise. Numerous studies have shown that $\dot{V}O_{2max}$ is an excellent predictor of endurance performance in heterogeneous groups (e.g. Costill *et al.* 1973). Although a high $\dot{V}O_{2max}$ (> 70 ml.kg^{-1}min^{-1} for males, > 60 ml.kg^{-1} min^{-1} for females) is necessary for elite-level performance, other factors, such as Tlac, MLSS, and exercise economy, can discriminate performance differences in athletes with similar $\dot{V}O_{2max}$

values. In terms of the control of physical training, and the definition of exercise intensity domains, however, it is not the absolute or relative value of $\dot{V}O_{2max}$ (in units of l.min^{-1} or ml.kg^{-1}min^{-1}) that is important but rather the 'functional expression' of $\dot{V}O_{2max}$ in units of velocity or power output. In order to estimate the running velocity at $\dot{V}O_{2max}$ (V–$\dot{V}O_{2max}$) it is necessary to make measurements of both $\dot{V}O_{2max}$ and the running economy characteristics of the subject. The latter is best done by measuring the steady-state $\dot{V}O_2$ at several sub-Tlac running speeds. A regression equation describing the relationship between $\dot{V}O_2$ and submaximal running speed can then be solved for $\dot{V}O_{2max}$ to give the estimated V–$\dot{V}O_{2max}$ (Morgan *et al.* 1989). Two individuals with the same $\dot{V}O_{2max}$ values may have different V–$\dot{V}O_{2max}$ values if one subject is more economical than the other (Figure 10.9). In this example, the subject with the better economy would be able to run at a higher speed for the same exercise intensity such as 100 % $\dot{V}O_{2max}$. The V–$\dot{V}O_{2max}$ is highly correlated with endurance performance (Jones 1998; Jones and Doust 1998b). This is, in part, due to the fact that athletes sustain similar percentages of their $\dot{V}O_{2max}$ for given durations of exercise (Londeree 1986). The V–$\dot{V}O_2$ has been shown to be sensitive to endurance training (Jones, 1998; Billat *et al.* 1999). It has been suggested that the V–$\dot{V}O_{2max}$ represents an important exercise intensity if the goal is to improve $\dot{V}O_{2max}$ (Billat and Koralsztein 1996; Hill and Rowell, 1997).

10.7 CONCLUSION

This chapter has reviewed the 'domains' of exercise intensity (Figure 10.1). Moderate exercise is that performed below the Tlac. During moderate exercise, $\dot{V}O_2$ attains an early steady-state and blood lactate remains close to resting levels. Heavy exercise is that above the Tlac but below the MLSS or Pcrit. In this domain, both $\dot{V}O_2$ and blood lactate will attain a delayed but elevated steady-

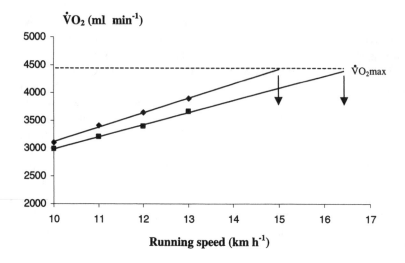

Figure 10.9: Determination of the running velocity at maximal oxygen uptake (V–$\dot{V}O_{2max}$). This involves regressing $\dot{V}O_2$ on exercise intensity for submaximal exercise and extrapolating this relationship to $\dot{V}O_{2max}$. The V–$\dot{V}O_{2max}$ can differ in two individuals with the same $\dot{V}O_{2max}$ (in ml.kg^{-1}.min^{-1}) if exercise economy differs in the two individuals.

state. In the severe domain, above the MLSS or Pcrit, both $\dot{V}O_2$ and blood lactate will rise continuously over time until $\dot{V}O_{2max}$ is reached and exercise is terminated. In the severe exercise domain, the time to exhaustion is predictable based upon the Pcrit concept. In the extreme intensity domain, exercise tolerance is extremely limited so that the $\dot{V}O_2$ remains below maximum at exhaustion.

In order to define exercise intensity accurately, it is important to delineate the boundaries between the various intensity domains. In this chapter, the various methods that have been employed to measure or estimate the physiological parameters that define the transition from one domain to another have been reviewed. These methods differ in the degree to which the scientific literature supports their validity, reliability and sensitivity to change following physical training. The possible advantages of practicality and simplicity of a method must be secondary to sound scientific measurement procedures. None of the methods reviewed above has received universal acceptance but the weight of evidence suggests that the Tlac/Tvent, the MLSS/Pcrit, and the

$\dot{V}O_{2max}$ are the 'gold standards' in terms of defining the boundaries between the exercise intensity domains. The following Table 10.1 summarises the validity, reliability, sensitivity, objectivity, practicality, and acceptability of the methods that are most commonly used for evaluating endurance fitness.

Direct measurements (or estimates) of Tlac, MLSS, Pcrit and V–$\dot{V}O_{2max}$ in an individual athlete allows for endurance performance capability and/or times to exhaustion at particular running speeds or power outputs to be estimated. This information can also be used to help in the prescription of a structured, balanced and appropriate training programme. For example, an individual who is new to regular exercise may initially be prescribed only moderate-intensity exercise because higher intensities (> Tlac) may be perceived to be unpleasant and stressful and this experience may adversely affect adherence to the exercise programme (but see O'Donovan *et al.* 2005). In contrast, elite endurance athletes will generally perform exercise sessions at moderate, heavy and severe intensities during a normal training week. The relative proportions of these

Table 10.1 The validity, reliability, sensitivity, objectivity, practicality and acceptability of the methods that are most commonly used for evaluating endurance fitness

Test	Strong evidence for validity?	Strong evidence for reliability?	Strong evidence for sensitivity?	Objective?	OK for field testing?	Athlete friendly?
Tlac	✓	✓	✓	✗	✓	✓
Tvent	✓	✓	✓	✗	✗	✓
MLSS	✓	✓	✓	✓	✓	✗
Pcrit	✓	✓	✓	✓	✓	✗
EP (Pcrit)	✓	✓	?	✓	?	✓
LTP	?	?	?	✗	?	✓
OBLA	✗	✗	✓	✓	✓	✓
IAT	✗	?	✓	✓	✗	✓
LMS	✗	✓	✗	✓	✓	✓
HRD	✗	✗	✗	✗	✓	✓
V–$\dot{V}O_{2max}$	✓	✓	✓	✓	✗	✓

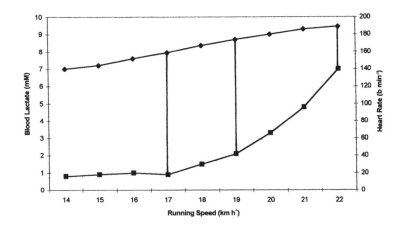

Figure 10.10: Use of heart rate to regulate training intensity. The vertical lines represent the heart rate at lactate threshold, the heart rate at the lactate turnpoint (which may provide a reasonable estimate of the maximal lactate steady-state) and the maximal heart rate. These heart rates and the corresponding running speeds can be used to prescribe and regulate training intensity within the moderate, heavy, severe and supramaximal domains.

sessions will depend on current fitness status, age, aspirations, training preferences, the time in the training macrocycle and the specialist event. Excessive severe intensity exercise may impair recovery and eventually contribute to overtraining, while if moderate intensity exercise is performed almost exclusively in a training programme then 'underperformance' may result. The training intensity can be regulated if an athlete has a portable heart rate monitor and knows his or her heart rate at Tlac and at MLSS as well as the maximal heart rate (Figure 10). The balance of training intensities (and hence durations) in a training programme can be specified and controlled with this systematic approach. Over time, this should maximize the effectiveness of training and result in improved performance.

10.8 PRACTICAL EXERCISES

10.8.1 General guidelines

Subject Preparation: Subjects should be well rested and hydrated to ensure that the responses to exercise are not influenced by acute changes in physiological status. The following procedure is recommended.

48 Hours Before Testing: Refrain from heavy exercise. Light exercise can be undertaken. A high carbohydrate diet should be consumed.

24 Hours Before Testing: No exercise should be undertaken. A high carbohydrate diet should be consumed.

The Day of Testing: No exercise should be undertaken. A light carbohydrate meal 2–4 hours before testing should be consumed, but nothing thereafter. Adequate fluids should be taken, but no caffeine or high (>12%) carbohydrate drinks should be consumed in the 4 hours prior to testing.

Subjects should wear appropriate athletic clothing and training shoes. The laboratory should be well ventilated and at a comfortable temperature for exercise (17–20°C). Appropriate informed consent and pre-exercise health questionnaires should be completed (see Jones and Doust 1997a).

Estimating Capability
In a number of the experiments, an estimate of the subject's likely performance is required to guide the intensity of exercise in an incremental test. Prior testing for maximal oxygen uptake provides the best guidance, although estimations can be made based on knowledge of the subject's sporting performance. Table 10.2 offers guidance:

Table 10.2 Estimation of speed and work-rate increments for graded exercise testing according to fitness status

STANDARD	RUNNING (male) (km.h⁻¹)	RUNNING (female) (km.h⁻¹)	CYCLING (male) (Watts)	CYCLING (female) (Watts)
Fair	9, 10.5, 12, 13.5, 15	7, 8.5, 10, 11.5, 13	50, 80, 110, 140, 170	50, 75, 100, 125, 150
Average	11, 12.5, 14, 15.5, 17	9, 10.5, 12, 13.5, 15	110, 140, 170, 200, 230	80, 110, 140, 170, 200
Good	13, 14.5, 16, 17.5, 19	11, 12.5, 14, 15.5, 17	180, 210, 240, 270, 300	110, 140, 170, 200, 230
Excellent	15, 16.5, 18, 19.5, 21	13, 14.5, 16, 17.5, 19	250, 280, 310, 340, 370	140, 170, 200, 230, 260

Fair would be a typical student who keeps fit but does not take part in competitive sport.
Average would be a typical student who plays team sports.
Good would be a typical student endurance athlete.
Excellent would be a competitive endurance athlete.

10.8.2 General methods

Heart rate is best obtained from a portable heart rate telemeter (Polar Sport Tester, Polar Electro, Oy, Finland) or similar device set to 5-s recording intervals for immediate playback after exercise. Interpretation of data can be enhanced if the subject is instructed to press the electronic marker button at the commencement of each level of a staged protocol.

Oxygen uptake can be obtained from an on-line system or from Douglas bags. The former allows observation in real time. If using Douglas bags, expired air should be collected for a whole number of breaths over a timed period of about 45 s during the final minute of each level of a staged protocol. Rating of perceived exertion can be obtained during the period of expired air collection.

Blood sampling can take place immediately after collection of air is completed. During treadmill running, blood sampling is most easily achieved by the subject jumping astride the moving belt at the end of each stage. This allows a finger to be held stable for sampling. During the sampling period the treadmill speed can be increased to the next level and once sampling is complete the subject can re-commence running. The advantages of achieving a quick and neat sample from a stationary hand outweigh the disadvantages of the short (~ 30 s) interruption to exercise, which, given the slow kinetics of lactate change, is unlikely to significantly influence the data (Gullstrand et al. 1994). In cycling exercise, a finger can easily be sabilized and no interruption to exercise is required.

Fingertip capillary sampling is the most convenient method for blood collection although the earlobe is preferred by some. Lactate concentration is affected by the site of sampling and the post-sampling treatment (see Williams et al. 1992). The general pattern of change will be similar whatever the method used but absolute values will differ.

Treadmill grade should be set to 1% to reflect the energetic cost of outdoor running (Jones 2007). An electronically-braked cycle ergometer, where power is kept constant even if pedalling rate changes, will allow superior results to those obtained with a friction-braked cycle ergometer.

Where a laboratory practical is being undertaken with inexperienced students to show the basic phenomena, the use of larger increments (1.5 km.h^{-1} or 30 W) will provide clear data and allow easy understanding but poor precision. More precise identification of the Tlac requires smaller step changes and the guidance given in the Guidelines of the British Association of Sport and Exercise Sciences (Jones, 2007) should be followed.

10.8.3 General further analysis opportunities

If more than one of the following practicals can be completed over the course of a teaching unit, the running speed or power output obtained by the different methods can be ranked and cross-correlated. This would allow discussion of how the data fit into the theoretical framework (see main text) and the extent of similarity between the parameters.

Confirmation, or otherwise, of the validity of any of the parameters can be shown by a 'verification' test. Following identification of the running speed or power output at Tlac, subjects may undertake continuous exercise at this intensity on a separate day.

Heart rate, oxygen uptake and lactate can be determined at 5-minute intervals. This test can be undertaken on a running track with heart rate monitored continuously and a blood sample taken every 800 m (running) or 2400 m (cycling) for analysis of lactate.

10.9 PRACTICAL 1: THE TLAC (LACTATE THRESHOLD) AND OBLA (ONSET OF BLOOD LACTATE ACCUMULATION)

10.9.1 General protocol (cycling or running)

Following a 5-minute jogging or cycling warm-up, the subject completes an incremental test of five 4-minute stages. Oxygen uptake is measured over the final minute of each stage. A blood sample is taken at the end of each stage for the determination of lactate concentration. The intensities can be estimated from Table 10.2.

10.9.2 Additional hints

This Practical can be performed equally well on a treadmill or a cycle ergometer.

Only a short warm-up is required due to the early, sub-threshold stages of the protocol.

10.9.3 Data analysis

Blood lactate should be plotted against exercise intensity (speed or power output). The data points may be joined by straight lines.

The OBLA is determined as the exercise intensity at a blood lactate of 4 mM. The lactate threshold is judged by visual inspection as the exercise intensity at which the lactate data show a sudden and sustained increase above baseline levels.

10.9.4 Further analysis opportunities

Determine inter-reviewer reliability by coding plots. Each person in a class can then be asked to identify Tlac.

Does lactate at Tlac = lactate at OBLA?

10.10 PRACTICAL 2: GAS EXCHANGE AND VENTILATORY THRESHOLD

10.10.1 General protocol (cycling or running)

Following a 5-minute jogging or cycling warm-up, the subject completes an incremental test comprising seven 2-minute stages. Oxygen uptake is measured over the final minute of each stage. The exercise intensities can be estimated from Table 10.2.

10.10.2 Additional hints

This Practical can be performed equally well on a treadmill or a cycle ergometer.

Only a short warm-up is required due to the early, sub-threshold stages of the protocol.

A ramp protocol can be used (20 W.min^{-1} or 1 km.h^{-1}.min^{-1}) with gas exchange and ventilation being measured continuously with an on-line system or with sequential Douglas bag collections each over 45 s.

10.10.3 Data analysis

Ventilation (l min^{-1} STPD) should be plotted against exercise intensity (running speed or cycling power output). The data points may be joined by straight lines.

Ventilatory threshold is assessed as the intensity at which the linear relationship between V_E and exercise intensity is lost.

10.10.4 Further analysis opportunities

Plotting the ventilatory equivalent for oxygen (that is $\dot{V}_E/\dot{V}O_2$) against exercise intensity may make the threshold clearer.

Ventilatory parameters may be plotted against $\dot{V}O_2$ as well as speed or power output.

Plotting three lines ($\dot{V}_E$, RER and $\dot{V}CO_2$) against exercise intensity offers the opportunity to discuss potential underlying physiological mechanisms.

Determine inter-reviewer reliability by coding plots. Each person in a class can then be asked to identify Tvent.

10.11 PRACTICAL 3: CRITICAL POWER

10.11.1 General protocol (cycle)

Three tests to exhaustion are completed on three separate days. Each test is undertaken at a constant intensity and cadence. The intensity is set so that time to exhaustion is between 2 and 12 minutes. After a 5-minute submaximal warm-up, the intensity is increased to the desired value and the subject continues until unable to maintain the required cadence (> 5 rev min^{-1} decrease for > 5 s). Since the tests are maximal, strong verbal encouragement is appropriate.

The intensities can be judged from the Table 10.2 by taking the fifth stage intensity and cycling at this intensity (likely duration about 10 min), + 15 % (likely duration about 6 minutes), and + 25 % (likely duration about 2 minutes).

10.11.2 Additional hints

Attempting to complete three tests on one day will not yield reliable results.

The accuracy of the Pcrit estimate is improved by administering more than three trials, which is strongly recommended when Pcrit is established for research purposes.

Note the saddle height so this may be kept constant between tests.

The exact intensities chosen for the three bouts are not critical since, in principle, exhaustion times anywhere between 2 and ~15 minutes will be linearly related. However, the variability in time to exhaustion is greater with durations above 10 minutes.

Ideally, the intensities should be presented in random order. If little is known about the subject, give the middle intensity first and the intensities for the subsequent two bouts can be adjusted to ensure the data spans an adequate range of times to exhaustion.

The equivalent to critical power, the critical velocity (Vcrit), can be determined on the treadmill or in a swimming pool using three bouts of exhaustive exercise at different speeds. However, running to exhaustion on a fast-moving treadmill is a potentially dangerous procedure and not advisable as a student practical. For swimming, since the velocity is under the swimmer's control, the assessment of Vcrit will only work well with experienced swimmers who are able to pace themselves and sustain a similar efficiency throughout an exhaustive bout of swimming.

10.11.3 Data analysis

The inverse of time to exhaustion (that is, $1/t$) is plotted against power output and a linear regression line is fitted. The intercept of the line gives critical power (Pcrit) and the slope of the line gives the finite work capacity above Pcrit (W′).

10.11.4 Further analysis opportunities

Adjusting one of the times to exhaustion by ~ 10% and recalculating Pcrit and W′ will allow discussion of the sensitivity of these parameters to methodological variation due to the subject's motivation to exercise to exhaustion.

Transform the power -$1/t$ relationship to work-time relationship and compare the Pcrit and W′ estimates between the two models. If the data fit is good, the two models should return very similar estimates. Discrepancy between parameter estimates from different models is usually associated with a random error in predicting trial data.

10.12 PRACTICAL 4: LACTATE MINIMUM SPEED

10.12.1 General protocol (running)

The subject should warm up with 5 minutes of jogging, some stretching and three acceleration sprints where the treadmill speed is raised over 30 s from slow jogging to sprinting speed and back down again.

The test begins with two pre-test sprints at a speed which is 120% of the running speed at $\dot{V}O_{2max}$. The subject should stand with legs astride the treadmill belt. The treadmill speed is increased to the required level and the subject lets go carefully and begins running. The first sprint is for 60 s and the second is for 45 s with a 60-s rest given between sprints. The treadmill speed is lowered to 4 km h^{-1} and the subject walks for 8 minutes with a capillary blood sample taken after 7 minutes for the determination of lactate concentration. Five 3-minute incremental stages are then completed. The intensities can be judged from the Table 10.2.

A capillary sample is obtained at the end of each stage for the determination of lactate concentration.

10.12.2 Data analysis

Capillary lactate concentration is plotted against running speed for the five incremental stages. A cubic spline is fitted and the lactate minimum speed determined as the speed at which the lowest point occurs (i.e. a zero gradient tangent) by visual inspection or mathematically. If a spline fitting algorithm is not available the data may be connected by straight lines.

10.12.3 Additional hints

The lactate concentration after walking for 7 minutes allows confirmation that the pre-test sprints have induced a significant lactacidosis. If the value is < 5 mM the sprints were insufficiently intense and the test should be stopped and repeated on another day.

The exact sprinting speed and the exact lactate concentration after the sprints is not important in illustrating the principle of the lactate minimum speed test.

If running speed at $\dot{V}O_{2max}$ is not known, the speeds for the initial sprints can be estimated by adding 4 km h^{-1} to the fifth stage speed shown in Table 10.2.

It is not recommended that any form of best-fit polynomial curve is used since there is no physiological justification for such an approach.

The test can be undertaken on a cycle ergometer. The sprint power can be estimated as 125% of the fifth stage power output in Table 10.2 The same table gives estimates for the power output during the subsequent five stages.

The test can be undertaken in the field using a running track. A pre-recorded tape and loudspeaker system is needed to control the running pace (see Tegtbur *et al*. 1993)

10.13 PRACTICAL 5: HEART RATE DEFLECTION POINT (CONCONI TEST)

10.13.1 General protocol (running)

Following a 3-minute warm-up jog and some stretching, the subject completes an incremental protocol to maximal effort. The starting intensity is the lowest intensity shown in Table 10.2. Treadmill velocity is increased by 0.5 km.h^{-1} every 200 m. Heart rate is recorded throughout using a short-range radio telemeter (Polar Sport Tester, Polar Electro Oy, Finland) or similar device set to 5-s recording intervals for immediate playback after exercise. The subject should press the electronic marker button on the telemeter at the end of each stage.

10.13.2 Data analysis

Heart rate at the end of each 200-m stage is plotted against running speed. Heart rate deflection point is identified as the running speed at which linearity is lost in the HR-speed relationship.

10.13.3 Additional hints

The test can be undertaken in the field using a running track. A pre-recorded tape and loudspeaker system is needed to control the running pace. The intensity should be increased according to distance covered (i.e. every 200 m), not according to time, to remain true to Conconi's original work.

10.13.4 Further analysis opportunities

Determine inter-reviewer reliability by coding plots. Each person in a class can then be asked to identify the heart rate deflection point.

A deflection point may not be seen since there are questions about the underlying rationale of the Conconi test. With a student group, examine how many individuals demonstrate a deflection point and use this to discuss both the usefulness of the test and the cardiovascular responses to increasing intensity of exercise (see text).

Compare the heart rate deflection point determined by visual inspection with the same point determined using the software provided with the Polar Sport Tester radio telemetry unit.

FURTHER READING

Books

Jones A. M. and Poole D. C. (Eds). (2005). *Oxygen Uptake Kinetics in Sport, Exercise and Medicine*. Routledge; Oxon: pp. 1–405.

Spurway N. C. and Jones A. M. (2007). Lactate testing. In: (E. M. Winter, A. M. Jones, R. R. C. Davison, P. Bromley and T. Mercer, eds). *Sport and Exercise Science Testing Guidelines: The British Association of Sport and Exercise Sciences Guide*. Routledge; Oxon: pp. 112–19.

Journals

Burnley M. and Jones A. M. (2007). Oxygen uptake kinetics as a determinant of sports performance. *European Journal of Sports Sciences*; 7: 63–79.

Jones A. M. and Poole D. C. (2005). Oxygen uptake dynamics: from muscle to mouth.

Medicine and Science in Sports and Exercise; 37: 1542–50.

REFERENCES

Acavedo E. O. and Goldfarb A. H. (1989) Increased training intensity effects on plasma lactate, ventilatory threshold, and endurance. *Medicine and Science in Sports and Exercise*; 21: 563–8.

Allen D. G., Lamb G. D. and Westerblad,, H. (2008) Skeletal muscle fatigue: cellular mechanisms. *Physiological Reviews*; 88: 287–332.

Almarwaey O. A., Jones A. M. and Tolfrey K. (2004) Maximal lactate steady state in trained adolescent runners. *Journal of Sports Sciences*; 22: 215–25.

Aunola S. and Rusko H. (1992) Does anaerobic threshold correlate with maximal lactate steady state? *Journal of Sports Sciences*; 10: 309–23.

Barker T., Poole D. C., Noble L. M. and

Barstow T. J. (2006). Human critical power-oxygen uptake relationship at different pedalling frequencies. *Experimental Physiology*, **91**: 621–32.

Barstow T. J., Jones A. M., Nguyen P. and Casaburi R. (1996) Influence of muscle fiber type and pedal frequency on oxygen uptake kinetics of heavy exercise. *Journal of Applied Physiology*; **81**: 1642–50.

Beaver W. L., Wasserman K. and Whipp B. J. (1986) A new method for detecting anaerobic threshold by gas exchange. *Journal of Applied Physiology*; **60**: 2020–7.

Beneke R. (2003). Methodological aspects of maximal lactate steady state-implications for performance testing. *European Journal of Applied Physiology*; **89**: 95–9.

Beneke R. and von Duvillard S. P. (1996) Determination of maximal lactate steady state response in selected sports events. *Medicine and Science in Sports and Exercise*; **28**: 241–6.

Beneke R., Leithäuser R. M. and Hütler M. (2001) Dependence of the maximal lactate steady state on the motor pattern of exercise. *British Journal of Sports Medicine*; **35**: 192–6.

Billat V. L., Dalmay F., Antonini M. T. and Chassain A. P. (1994) A method for determining the maximal steady state of blood lactate concentration from two levels of submaximal exercise. *European Journal of Applied Physiology*; **69**: 196–202.

Billat V. L. and Koralsztein J. P. (1996) Significance of the velocity at $\dot{V}O_{2max}$ and time to exhaustion at this velocity. *Sports Medicine*; **22**: 90–108.

Billat V. L., Renoux J. C., Pinoteau J., Petit B. and Koralsztein J. P. (1994) Times to exhaustion at 100% of velocity at $\dot{V}O_{2max}$ and modelling of the time-limit / velocity relationship in elite long-distance runners. *European Journal of Applied Physiology*; **69**: 271–3.

Billat V., Blondel N. and Berthoin S. (1999) Determination of the longest time to exhaustion at maximal oxygen uptake. *European Journal of Applied Physiology*; **80**: 159–61.

Billat V., Sirvent P., Lepretre P. M. and Koralsztein J. P. (2004) Training effect on performance, substrate balance and blood lactate concentration at maximal lactate steady state in master endurance-runners. *Pflugers Archives*; **447**: 875–83.

Bishop D., Jenkins D. G. and Howard A. (1998). The critical power function is dependent on the duration of the predictive exercise tests chosen. *International Journal of Sports Medicine*; **19**: 125–9.

Borch K. W., Ingjer F., Larsen S. and Tomten S. E. (1993) Rate of accumulation of blood lactate during graded exercise as a predictor of 'anaerobic threshold.' *Journal of Sports Sciences*; **11**: 49–55.

Brickley G., Doust J. and Williams C. A. (2002) Physiological responses during exercise to exhaustion at critical power. *European Journal of Applied Physiology*; **88**: 146–51.

Brooks G. A. (1991) Current concepts in lactate exchange. *Medicine and Science in Sports and Exercise*; **23**: 895–906.

Bunc V., Hofmann P., Leitner H. and Gaisl G. (1995) Verification of the heart rate threshold. *European Journal of Applied Physiology*; **70**: 263–9.

Burnley M. and Jones A. M. (2007) Oxygen uptake kinetics as a determinant of sports performance. *European Journal of Sports Sciences*; **7**: 63–79.

Burnley M., Doust J. H. and Vanhatalo A. (2006) A 3-min all-out test to determine peak oxygen uptake and the maximal steady state. *Medicine & Science in Sports & Exercise*; **38**: 1995–2003.

Caiozzo V. L., Davis J. A., Ellis J. F., Azus J. L., Vandagriff R., Prietto C. A. and McMaster W. C. (1982) A comparison of gas exchange indices used to detect the anaerobic threshold. *Journal of Applied Physiology*; **53**: 1184–9.

Carter H., Jones A. M. and Doust J. H. (1999a) Effect of incremental test protocol on the lactate minimum speed. *Medicine and Science in Sports and Exercise*; **31**: 837–45.

Carter H., Jones A. M. and Doust J. H. (1999b) Effect of six weeks of endurance training on the lactate minimum speed. *Journal of Sports Sciences*; **17**: 957–67.

Cheng B., Kuipers H., Snyder A. C., Keizer H. A., Jeukendrup A. and Hesselink M. (1992) A new approach for the determination of ventilatory and lactate thresholds. *International Journal of Sports Medicine*;

13: 518–22.

Coats E. M., Rossiter H. B., Day J. R., Miura A., Fukuba Y. and Whipp B. J. (2003). Intensity-dependent tolerance to exercise after attaining V̇O₂max in humans. *Journal of Applied Physiology*; 95: 483–90.

Coen B., Urhausen A. and Kindermann W. (2001). Individual anaerobic threshold: methodological aspects of its assessment in running. *International Journal of Sports Medicine*; 28: 300–5.

Conconi F., Ferrari M., Ziglio P. G., Droghetti P. and Codeca L. (1982) Determination of the anaerobic threshold by a noninvasive field test in runners. *Journal of Applied Physiology*; 52: 869–73.

Connett R. J., Gayeski T. E. J. and Honig C. R. (1984) Lactate accumulation in fully aerobic, working, dog gracilis muscle. *American Journal of Physiology*; 246: 120–8.

Connett R. J., Gayeski T. E. J. and Honig C. R. (1985) Energy sources in fully aerobic work-rest transitions: a new role for glycolysis. *American Journal of Physiology*; 248: 922–9.

Costill D. L., Thomason H. and Roberts E. (1973) Fractional utilisation of the aerobic capacity during distance running. *Medicine and Science in Sports*; 5: 248–52.

Coyle E. F. (2005). Improved muscular efficiency displayed as Tour de France champion matures. *Journal of Applied Physiology*; 98: 2191–6.

Coyle E. F., Martin W. H., Ehsani A. A., Hagberg J. M., Bloomfield S. A., Sinacore D. R. and Holloszy J. O. (1983) Blood lactate threshold in some well-trained ischemic heart disease patients. *Journal of Applied Physiology*; 54: 18–23.

Davis J. A. (1985) Anaerobic threshold: review of the concept and direction for future research. *Medicine and Science in Sports and Exercise*; 17: 6–18.

Day J. R., Rossiter H. B., Coats E. M., Skasick A. and Whipp B. J. (2003). The maximally attainable V̇O₂ during exercise in humans: the peak vs. maximum issue. *Journal of Applied Physiology*; 95: 1901–7.

Dekerle J., Baron B., Dupont L., Vanvelcenaher J. and Pelayo P. (2003). Maximal lactate steady state, respiratory compensation threshold and critical power. *European Journal of Applied Physiology*; 89: 281–8.

Dekerle J., Pelayo P., Clipet B., Depretz S., Lefevre T. and Sidney M. (2005). Critical swimming speed does not represent the speed at maximal lactate steady state. *International Journal of Sports Medicine*; 26: 524–30.

de Vries H. A., Moritani T., Nagata A. and Magnussen K. (1982) The relation between critical power and neuromuscular fatigue as estimated from electromyographic data. *Ergonomics*; 25: 783–91.

Donovan C. M. and Pagliassotti M. J. (1990) Enhanced efficiency of lactate removal after endurance training. *Journal of Applied Physiology*; 68: 1053–8.

Droghetti P., Borsetto C., Casoni I., Cellini M., Ferrari M., Paolini A. R., Ziglio P. G. and Conconi F. (1985) Non-invasive determination of the anaerobic threshold in canoeing, cross-country skiing, cycling, roller and iceskating, rowing and walking. *European Journal of Applied Physiology*; 53: 299–303.

Edwards R. H. T. (1981) Human muscle function and fatigue. In: (R. Porter and J. Whelan, eds) *Human muscle Fatigue: Physiological Mechanisms*. CIBA Foundations Symposium No. 82, Pitman Medical; London: pp. 1–18.

Farrell P. A., Wilmore J. H., Coyle E. F., Billing J. E. and Costill D. E. (1979) Plasma lactate accumulation and distance running performance. *Medicine and Science in Sports*; 11: 338–44.

Fay L., Londeree B. R., Lafontaine T. P. and Volek M. R. (1989) Physiological parameters related to distance running performance in female athletes. *Medicine and Science in Sports and Exercise*; 21: 319–24.

Ferry A., Duvallet A. and Rieu M. (1988) The effect of experimental protocol on the relationship between blood lactate and workload. *Journal of Sports Medicine and Physical Fitness*; 28: 341–7.

Foxdal P., Sjodin B., Sjodin A. and Ostman B. (1994) The validity and accuracy of blood lactate measurements for prediction of maximal endurance running capacity: dependency of analysed blood media in combination with different designs of the exercise test. *International Journal of Sports Medicine*; **15**: 89–95.

Fukuba Y. and Whipp B. J. (1999). A metabolic limit on the ability to make up for lost time in endurance events. *Journal of Applied Physiology*; **87**: 853–61.

Fukuba Y., Miura A., Endo M., Kan A., Yanagawa K. and Whipp B.J. (2003). The curvature constant parameter of the power-duration curve for varied-power exercise. *Medicine & Science in Sports & Exercise*; **35**: 1413–18.

Gaesser G. A. and Wilson L. A. (1988). Effects of continuous and interval training on the parameters of the power-endurance time relationship for high-intensity exercise. *International Journal of Sports Medicine*; **9**: 417–21.

Gladden L.B., Yates J.W., Stremel R.W. and Stanford B.A. (1985). Gas exchange and lactate anaerobic thresholds: inter- and intra-evaluator agreement. *Journal of Applied Physiology*, **58**: 2082–9.

Grazzi G., Alfieri N., Borsetto C., Casoni I., Manfredini F., Mazzoni G. and Conconi F. (1999) The power output / heart rate relationship in cycling: test standardization and repeatability. *Medicine and Science in Sports and Exercise*; **31**: 1478–83.

Gullstrand L., Sjodin B. and Svedenhag J. (1994) Blood sampling during continuous running and 30-second intervals on a treadmill: effects on the lactate threshold results? *Scandinavian Journal of Science and Medicine in Sports*; **4**: 239–42.

Hanon C., Thepaut-Mathieu C., Hausswirth C. and Le Chevalier J. M. (1998). Electromyogram as an indicator of neuromuscular fatigue during incremental exercise. *European Journal of Applied Physiology*; **78**: 315–23.

Heck H. and Hollmann W. (1992) Identification, objectivity, and validity of Conconi threshold by cycle stress tests. *Osler Journal Sportsmedizin*; **22**: 35–53.

Heck H., Mader A., Hess G., Mucke S., Muller R. and Hollmann W. (1985) Justification of the 4 mmol/l lactate threshold. *International Journal of Sports Medicine*; **6**: 117–30.

Henritze J., Weltman A., Schurrer R. L. and Barlow K. (1985) Effects of training at and above the lactate threshold on the lactate threshold and maximal oxygen uptake. *European Journal of Applied Physiology*; **54**: 84–8.

Hill D. W. (1993). The critical power concept: a review. *Sports Medicine*; **16**: 237–54.

Hill D. W. and Smith J. C. (1994). A method to ensure accuracy of estimates of anaerobic capacity derived using the critical power concept. *Journal of Sports Medicine and Physical Fitness*; **34**: 23–37.

Hill D.W. and Rowell A. L. (1997) Response to exercise at the velocity associated with $\dot{V}O_{2max}$. *Medicine and Science in Sports and Exercise*; **29**: 113–16.

Hill D. W. and Ferguson C. S. (1999). A physiological description of critical velocity. *European Journal of Applied Physiology*; **79**: 290–3.

Hill D.W. and Stevens E. C. (2005). $\dot{V}O_2$ response profiles in severe intensity exercise. *Journal of Sports Medicine and Physical Fitness*; **45**: 239–47.

Hill D. W., Poole D. C. and Smith J. C. (2002). The relationship between power and the time to achieve $\dot{V}O_{2max}$. *Medicine & Science in Sports & Exercise*; **34**: 709–14.

Hofmann P., Bunc V., Leinter H., Pokan R. and Gaisl P. (1994) Heart rate threshold related to lactate turnpoint and steady-state exercise on a cycle ergometer. *European Journal of Applied Physiology*; **69**: 132–9.

Honig C. R,. Connett R. J. and Gayeski T. E. J. (1992) O_2 transport and its interaction with metabolism: a systems view of aerobic capacity. *Medicine and Science in Sports and Exercise*; **24**: 47–53.

Housh D. J., Housh, T. J. and Bauge S. M. (1989) The accuracy of the critical power test for predicting time to exhaustion during cycle ergometry. *Ergonomics*; **32**: 997–1004.

Housh T. J., DeVries H. A., Housh D. J., Tichy M. W., Smyth K. D. and Tichy A. M. (1991a) The relationship between critical power and the onset of blood lactate accumulation. *Journal of Sports Medicine and Physical Fitness*; **31**: 31–6.

Housh T. J., Johnson G.,O., McDowell S. L., Housh D. J. and Pepper M. (1991b). Physiological responses at the fatigue threshold. *International Journal of Sports Medicine*; **12**: 305–8.

Hug F., Faucher M., Kipson N. and Jammes Y.

(2003). EMG signs of neuromuscular fatigue related to the ventilatory threshold during cycling. *Clinical Physiology and Functional Imaging*; **23**: 207–14.

Hughes E. F., Turner S. C. and Brooks G. A. (1982) Effects of glycogen depletion and pedalling speed on 'anaerobic threshold.' *Journal of Applied Physiology*; **52**: 1598–1607.

Hughson R. L., Cook C. J. and Staudt L. E. (1984) A high velocity treadmill running test to assess endurance running potential. *International Journal of Sports Medicine*; **5**: 23–5.

Hughson R. L., Weisiger K. H. and Swanson G. D. (1987) Blood lactate concentration increases as a continuous function in progressive exercise. *Journal of Applied Physiology*, **62**: 1975–81.

Hurley B. F., Hagberg J. M., Allen W. K., Seals D. P., Young J. C., Cuddihee R. W. and Holloszy J. O. (1984) Effect of training on blood lactate levels during submaximal exercise. *Journal of Applied Physiology*; **56**: 1260–4.

Ivy J. L., Withers R. T., Van Handel P. J., Elger D. H. and Costill D. L. (1980) Muscle respiratory capacity and fiber type as determinants of the lactate threshold. *Journal of Applied Physiology*; **48**: 523–7.

Ivy J. L., Costill D. L., Van Handel P. J., Essig D. A. and Lower R. W. (1981) Alteration in the lactate threshold with changes in substrate availability. *International Journal of Sports Medicine*; **48**: 523–7.

James N. W., Adams G. M. and Wilson A. F. (1989) Determination of the anaerobic threshold by breathing frequency. *International Journal of Sports Medicine*; **10**: 192–6.

Jenkins D. G. and Quigley B. M. (1990). Blood lactate in trained cyclists during cycle ergometry at critical power. *European Journal of Applied Physiology*; **61**: 278–83.

Jenkins D. G. and Quigley B. M. (1992) Endurance training enhances critical power. *Medicine and Science in Sports and Exercise*; **24**: 1283–9.

Jobsis F. F. and Stainsby W. N. (1968) Oxidation of NADH during contractions of circulated mammalian skeletal muscle. *Respiration Physiology*; **4**: 292–300.

Jones A. M. (1998) A five year physiological case study of an Olympic athlete. *British Journal of Sports Medicine*; **32**: 39–43.

Jones A. M. (2006). The physiology of the world record holder for the women's marathon. *International Journal of Sports Science and Coaching*; **2**: 101–16.

Jones A. M. and Doust J. H. (1995) Lack of reliability in Conconi's heart rate deflection point. *International Journal of Sports Medicine*; **16**: 541–4.

Jones A. M. and Doust J. H. (1996) A 1% treadmill grade most accurately reflects the energetic cost of outdoor running. *Journal of Sports Sciences*; **14**: 321–7.

Jones A. M. and Doust J. H. (1997a) Specific considerations for the assessment of middle distance and long distance runners. In: (S. Bird and R. Davison, eds). *British Association of Sport and Exercise Sciences Physiological Testing Guidelines (3rd Edition)*. BASES; Leeds, 108–11.

Jones A. M. and Doust J. H. (1997b) The Conconi test is not valid for estimation of the lactate turnpoint in runners. *Journal of Sports Sciences*; **15**: 385–94.

Jones A. M. and Doust J. H. (1998a) Assessment of the lactate and ventilatory thresholds by breathing frequency in runners. *Journal of Sports Sciences*; **16**: 667–75.

Jones A. M. and Doust J. H. (1998b) The validity of the lactate minimum test for determination of the maximal lactate steady state. *Medicine and Science in Sports and Exercise*; **30**: 1304–13.

Jones A. M. and Doust J. H. (1998c) The relationship between the individual anaerobic threshold, the lactate threshold, and the 4 mM blood lactate reference value during incremental treadmill exercise (abstract). *Journal of Sports Sciences*; **16**: 53.

Jones A. M. and Poole D. C. (2005). Introduction to oxygen uptake kinetics and historical development of the discipline. In: (A. M. Jones and D. C. Poole, eds) *Oxygen Uptake Kinetics in Sport, Exercise and Medicine*. Routledge; Oxon: pp 3–35.

Jones A. M., Carter H. and Doust J. H. (1999). A disproportionate increase in $\dot{V}O_2$ coincident with lactate threshold during treadmill exercise. *Medicine and Science in Sports and Exercise*; **31**: 1299–1306.

Jones A. M., Wilkerson D. P., Dimenna F., Fulford J. and Poole D. C. (2008). Muscle metabolic responses to exercise above and below the 'critical power' assessed using 31P-MRS. *American Journal of Physiology: Regulatory, Integrative and Comparative Physiology*; **294**: R585–93.

Jones A. M. (2007). Middle and long distance running. In: (E. M. Winter, A. M. Jones, R. C. C. Davison, P. Bromley and T. Mercer, eds). *Sport and Exercise Science Testing Guidelines: The British Association of Sport and Exercise Sciences Guide*. Routledge; Oxon: pp. 147–154.

Jones N. L., Sutton J. R., Taylor R. and Toews C. J. (1977) Effect of pH on cardiorespiratory and metabolic responses to exercise. *Journal of Applied Physiology*; **43**: 959–64.

Jorfeldt L., Juhlin-Dabbfelt A. and Karlsson J. (1978) Lactate release in relation to tissue lactate in human skeletal muscle during exercise. *Journal of Applied Physiology*; **44**: 350–2.

Katch V., Weltman A., Sady S. and Freedson P. (1978) Validity of the relative percent concept for equating training intensity. *European Journal of Applied Physiology*; **39**: 219–27.

Keith S. P., Jacobs I. and McLellan T. M. (1992) Adaptations to training at the individual anaerobic threshold. *European Journal of Applied Physiology*; **65**: 316–23.

Kilding A. E. and Jones A. M. (2005). Validity of a single-visit protocol to estimate the maximum lactate steady state. *Medicine & Science in Sports & Exercise*; **37**: 1734–40.

Kindermann W., Simon G. and Keul J. (1979) The significance of the aerobic-anaerobic transition for the determination of work load intensities during endurance training. *European Journal of Applied Physiology*; **42**: 25–34.

Kuipers H., Keizer H. A., De Vries T., van Rijthoven P. and Wijts M. (1988) Comparison of heart rate as a non-invasive determinant of anaerobic threshold with the lactate threshold when cycling. *European Journal of Applied Physiology*; **58**: 303–6.

Kuphal K. E., Potteiger J. A., Frey B. B. and Hise M. P. (2004). Validation of a single-day maximal lactate steady state assessment protocol. *Journal of Sports Medicine and Physical Fitness*; **44**: 132–40.

Lafontaine T. P., Londeree B. R. and Spath W. K. (1981) The maximal stady state versus selected running events. *Medicine and Science in Sports and Exercise*; **13**: 190–3.

Laplaud D., Guinot M., Favre-Juvin A. and Flore P. (2006). Maximal lactate steady state determination with a single incremental test exercise. *European Journal of Applied Physiology*; **96**: 446–52.

Londeree B. R. (1986) The use of laboratory test results with long distance runners. *Sports Medicine*; **3**: 201–13.

Londeree B. R. (1997) Effect of training on lactate/ventilatory thresholds: a meta-analysis. *Medicine and Science in Sports and Exercise*; **29**: 837–43.

MacIntosh B. R., Esau S. and Svedahl K. (2002). The lactate minimum test for cycling: estimation of the maximal lactate steady state. *Canadian Journal of Applied Physiology*; **27**: 232–49.

McKenna M. J., Bangsbo J. and Renaud J. M. (2008). Muscle K+, Na+, and Cl disturbances and Na+-K+ pump inactivation: implications for fatigue. *Journal of Applied Physiology*; **104**: 288–95.

MacRae H., Dennis S. C., Bosch A. N. and Noakes T. D. (1992) Endurance training vs lactate production and removal. *Journal of Applied Physiology*; **73**: 2206–7.

McLellan T. M. and Cheung K. S. Y. (1992). A comparative evaluation of the individual anaerobic threshold and the critical power. *Medicine & Science in Sports & Exercise*; **24**: 543–50.

McLellan T. M. and Jacobs I. (1993) Reliability, reproducibility and validity of the individual anaerobic threshold. *European Journal of Applied Physiology*; **67**: 125–31.

McNaughton L. and Thomas D. (1996). Effects of differing pedalling speeds on the power-duration relationship of high intensity cycle ergometry. *International Journal of Sports Medicine*; **17**: 287–92.

Mader A. (1991) Evaluation of the endurance performance of marathon runners and theoretical analysis of test results. *Journal of Sports Medicine and Physical Fitness;* **31:** 1–19.

Mader A., Liesen H., Heck H., Phillipy H. and Rost R. (1976) Zur Beurteilung der sportartspezifischen Ausdauerleistungsfähigkeit im labor. *Sport und Medizin;* **27:** 80–112.

Mazzeo R. S. and Marshall P. (1989) Influence of plasma catecholamines on the lactate threshold during graded cycling. *Journal of Applied Physiology;* **67:** 1319–22.

Mognoni P., Sirtori M. D., Lorenzelli F. and Cerretelli P. (1990). Physiological responses during prolonged exercise at the power output corresponding to the blood lactate threshold. *European Journal of Applied Physiology;* **60:** 239–43.

Monod H. and Scherrer J. (1965) The work capacity of a synergic muscle group. *Ergonomics;* **8:** 329–38.

Morgan D. W., Baldini F. D., Martin P. E. and Kohrt W. M. (1989) Ten kilometer performance and predicted velocity at $\dot{V}O_{2max}$ among well-trained male runners. *Medicine and Science in Sports and Exercise;* **21:** 78–83.

Moritani T., Nagata A., DeVries H. A. and Muro M. (1981) Critical power as a measure of physical work capacity and anaerobic threshold. *Ergonomics;* **24:** 339–50.

Moritani T., Takaishi T. and Matsumoto T. (1993). Determination of maximal power output at neuromuscular fatigue threshold. *Journal of Applied Physiology;* **74:** 1729–34.

Morton R.H. (2006). The critical power and related whole-body bioenergetic models. *European Journal of Applied Physiology;* **71:** 379–380.

Nagata A., Muro M., Moritani T. and Yoshida T. (1981) Anaerobic threshold determination by blood lactate and myoelectric signals. *Japanese Journal of Physiology;* **31:** 585–97.

Newsholme E. A., Blomstrand E. and Ekblom B. (1992) Physical and mental fatigue: metabolic mechanisms and importance of plasma amino acids. *British Medical Bulletin;* **48:** 477–95.

O'Donovan G., Owen A., Bird S. R., Kearney E. M., Nevill A. M., Jones D. W. and Woolf–May K. (2005). Changes in cardiorespiratory fitness and coronary heart disease risk factors following 24 wk of moderate- or high–intensity exercise of equal energy cost. *Journal of Applied Physiology;* **98:** 1619–25.

Orok C. J., Hughson R. L., Green H. J. and Thomson J. A. (1989) Blood lactate responses in incremental exercise as predictors of constant load performance. *European Journal of Applied Physiology;* **59:** 262–7.

Overend T. J., Cunningham D. A., Paterson D. H. and Smith W. D. F. (1992) Physiological responses of young and elderly men to prolonged exercise at critical power. *European Journal of Applied Physiology;* **64:** 187–93.

Oyono-Enguille S., Heitz A., Marbach J., Ott C. and Gartner M. (1990) Blood lactate during constant-load exercise at aerobic and anaerobic thresholds. *European Journal of Applied Physiology;* **60:** 321–30.

Özyener F., Rossiter H. B., Ward S. A. and Whipp B. J. (2001). Influence of exercise intensity on the on- and off-transient kinetics of pulmonary oxygen uptake in humans. *Journal of Physiology;* **533:** 891–902.

Palmer A. S., Potteiger J. A., Nau K. L. and Tong R. J. (1999). A 1-day maximal lactate steady-state assessment protocol for trained runners. *Medicine and Science in Sports and Exercise;* **31:** 1336–41.

Pierce E. F., Weltman A., Seip R. L. and Snead D. (1990) Effects of training specificity on the lactate threshold and $\dot{V}O_2$ peak. *International Journal of Sports Medicine;* **11:** 267–72.

Poole D. C., Ward S.A., Gardner G. W. and Whipp B. J. (1988). Metabolic and respiratory profile of the upper limit for prolonged exercise in man. *Ergonomics;* **31:** 1265–79.

Poole D. C., Ward S. A. and Whipp B. J. (1990). The effects of training on the metabolic and respiratory profile of high-intensity cycle ergometer exercise. *European Journal of Applied Physiology;* **59:** 421–9.

Poole D. C., Schaffartzik W., Knight D. R., Derion T., Kennedy B., Guy H. J., Prediletto R. and Wagner P. D. (1991) Contribution of exercising legs to the slow component of oxygen uptake kinetics in humans. *Journal of Applied Physiology;* **71:** 1245–53.

Pouilly J.-P. Chatagnon M., Thomas V. and Busso T. (2005). Estimation of the parameters of the relationship between power and time to exhaustion from a single ramp test. *Canadian Journal of Applied Physiology*; 30: 735–42.

Pringle J. S. M. and Jones A. M. (2002). Maximal lactate steady state, critical power and EMG during cycling. *European Journal of Applied Physiology*; 88: 214–26.

Ribeiro J. P., Fielding R. A., Hughes V., Black A., Bochese M. A. and Knuttgen H. G. (1985) Heart rate breakpoint may coincide with the anaerobic and not the aerobic threshold. *International Journal of Sports Medicine*; 6: 224–34.

Ribeiro J. P., Hughes V., Fielding R. A., Holden W., Evans W. and Knuttgen H. G. (1986) Metabolic and ventilatory responses to steady state exercise relative to lactate thresholds. *International Journal of Sports Medicine*; 6: 220–4.

Robergs R. A., Chwalbinska-Moneta J., Mitchell J. B., Pascoe D. D., Houmard J. and Costill D. L. (1990) Blood lactate threshold differences between arterialised and venous blood. *International Journal of Sports Medicine*; 11: 446–51.

Roberts D. and Smith D. J. (1989) Biochemical aspects of peripheral muscle fatigue: a review. *Sports Medicine*; 7: 125–38.

Simon J., Young J. L., Gutin B., Blood D. K. and Case R. B. (1983). Lactate accumulation relative to the anaerobic and respiratory compensation thresholds. *Journal of Applied Physiology*; 54: 13–17.

Sjodin B. and Jacobs I. (1981) Onset of blood lactate accumulation and marathon running performance. *International Journal of Sports Medicine*, 2: 23–6.

Sjodin B, Jacobs I. and Svedenhag J. (1982) Changes in onset of blood lactate accumulation (OBLA) and muscle enzymes after training at OBLA. *European Journal of Applied Physiology*; 49: 45–57.

Skinner J. S. and McLellan T. H. (1980) The transition from aerobic to anaerobic metabolism. *Research Quarterly for Exercise and Sports*; 51: 234–48.

Smith C. G. M. and Jones A. M. (2001). The relationship between critical velocity, maximal lactate steady-state velocity and lactate turnpoint velocity in runners. *European Journal of Applied Physiology*; 85: 19–26.

Snyder A. C., Woulfe T., Welsh R. and Foster C. (1994) A simplified approach to estimating the maximal lactate steady state. *International Journal of Sports Medicine*; 15: 27–31.

Stegmann H. and Kindermann W. (1982) Comparison of prolonged exercise tests at the individual anaerobic threshold and the fixed anaerobic threshold of 4 mmol/l lactate. *International Journal of Sports Medicine*; 3: 105–10.

Stegmann H., Kindermann W. and Schnabel A. (1981) Lactate kinetics and individual anaerobic threshold. *International Journal of Sports Medicine*; 2: 160–5.

Talmadge R. J., Scheide J. I. and Silverman H. (1989) Glycogen synthesis from lactate in a chronically active muscle. *Journal of Applied Physiology*; 66: 2231–8.

Tegtbur U., Busse M. W. and Braumann K. M. (1993) Estimation of an individual equilibrium between lactate production and catabolism during exercise. *Medicine and Science in Sports and Exercise*. 25: 620–7.

Tokmakidis S. P. and Leger L. (1992) Comparison of mathematically determined blood lactate and heart rate 'threshold' points and relationship with performance. *European Journal of Applied Physiology*; 641: 309–17.

Vanhatalo A., Doust J. H. and Burnley M. (2007). Determination of critical power using a 3-min all-out cycling test. *Medicine and Science in Sports and Exercise*; 39: 548–55.

Vanhatalo A., Doust J. H. and Burnley M. (2008). Robustness of a 3-min all-out cycling test to manipulations of power profile and cadence in humans. *Experimental Physiology*; 93: 383–90.

Vanhatalo A., Doust J. H. and Burnley M. (2008, in press). A 3-min all-out cycling test is sensitive to a change in critical power. *Medicine and Science in Sports and Exercise*.

Wakayoshi K., Yoshida T., Udo M., Harada T. and Moritani T. (1992) The determination and validity of critical speed as an index of swimming performance in the competitive swimmer. *European Journal of Applied Physiology*; **64**: 153–7.

Walsh M. L. and Banister E. W. (1988) Possible mechanisms of the anaerobic threshold – a review. *Sports Medicine*; **5**: 269–302.

Wasserman K., Whipp B. J., Koyal S. N. and Beaver W. L. (1973) Anaerobic threshold and respiratory gas exchange during exercise. *Journal of Applied Physiology*; **35**: 236–43.

Wasserman K., Beaver W. L. and Whipp B. J. (1990) Gas exchange theory and the lactic acidosis (anaerobic) threshold. *Circulation*; **81** (Suppl II): 14–30.

Weltman A. (1989) The lactate threshold and endurance performance. *Advances in Sports Medicine and Fitness*; **2**: 91–116.

Weltman A., Snead D. and Seip R. (1990). Percentages of maximal heart rate, heart rate reserve and $\dot{V}O_{2max}$ for determining endurance training intensity in male runners. *International Journal of Sports Medicine*; **11**: 218–22.

Weltman A., Seip R. L., Snead D., Weltman J. V., Haskvitz E. M., Evans W. S., Veldhuis J. D. and Rogol A. D. (1992) Exercise training at and above the lactate threshold in previously untrained women. *International Journal of Sports Medicine*; **13**: 257–63.

Westerblad H., Allen D. G. and Lännergren J. (2002). Muscle fatigue: lactic acid or inorganic phosphate the major cause? *News in Physiological Sciences*; **17**: 17–21.

Whipp B. J. (1994). The slow component of O_2 uptake kinetics during heavy exercise. *Medicine and Science in Sports and Exercise*; **26**: 1319–26.

Whipp B. J. and Wasserman K. (1972). Oxygen uptake kinetics for various intensities of constant-load work. *Journal of Applied Physiology*; **33**: 351–6.

Whipp B. J. and Mahler M. (1980) Dynamics of pulmonary gas exchange during exercise. In: (J. B. West, ed) *Pulmonary Gas Exchange (Volume II)*. Academic Press; New York: pp. 33–96.

Whipp, B.J. and Ward S. A. (1990) Physiological determinants of pulmonary gas exchange kinetics during exercise. *Medicine and Science in Sports and Exercise*; **22**: 62–71.

Whipp B.J. and Rossiter H. B. (2005). The kinetics of oxygen uptake: physiological inferences from parameters. In: (A. M. Jones and D. C. Poole, eds) *Oxygen Uptake Kinetics in Sport, Exercise and Medicine*. Routledge; Oxon.

Williams J. R., Armstrong N. and Kirby B. J. (1992) The influence of the site of sampling and assay medium upon the measurement and interpretation of blood lactate responses to exercise. *Journal of Sports Sciences*; **10**: 95–107.

Wilkerson D. P., Koppo K., Barstow T. J. and Jones A. M. (2004). Effect of work-rate on the functional 'gain' of Phase II pulmonary O_2 uptake response to exercise. *Respiratory Physiology & Neurobiology*, **142**: 211–23.

Yeh M. P., Gardner R. M., Adams T. W., Yanowitz F. G. and Crapo R. O. (1983) 'Anaerobic threshold': problems of determination and validation. *Journal of Applied Physiology*; **55**: 1178–86.

Yoshida T. (1984) Effect of exercise duration during incremental exercise on the determination of anaerobic threshold and the onset of blood lactate accumulation. *European Journal of Applied Physiology*; **53**: 196–9.

CHAPTER 11

ASSESSMENT OF MAXIMAL-INTENSITY EXERCISE

Edward M. Winter and Don P. MacLaren

11.1 AIMS

The fundamental aim of this chapter is to develop knowledge and understanding of what constitutes maximal-intensity exercise and how this type of exercise can be assessed. Specifically it will:

- provide students with an understanding of techniques for assessing maximal intensity exercise;
- outline appropriate uses of mechanical constructs to describe maximal intensity exercise;
- describe the development of cycle-ergometer-based assessments of peak power output;
- describe the concept of anaerobic capacity;
- describe techniques for direct (invasive) and indirect (non-invasive) estimation of anaerobic metabolism.

11.2 INTRODUCTION

Maximal-intensity exercise refers to exercise that is performed 'all-out'. It should not be confused with intensities of exercise that elicit a maximal physiological response. For instance, maximal oxygen uptake ($\dot{V}O_{2max}$) can be elicited by intensities of exercise that are only a third or quarter of maximal-intensity exercise (Williams 1987).

It should also be acknowledged that movement does not always occur during maximal-intensity exercise. The scrum in rugby and maintenance of the crucifix and balance in gymnastics are examples where maximal force production can occur during isometric muscle activity. Durations of exercise are short and range from approximately 1–2 seconds in discrete activities like the shot putt and golf swing to 20–45 seconds of sprinting during running and cycling. Even in these latter activities, there is probably an element of pacing rather than genuinely all-out effort. Also, associated mechanisms of energy release are predominantly anaerobic but they are not exclusively so. During 30 s of 'flat-out' cycling for example, 13–29% of energy provision could come from aerobic sources (Inbar *et al.* 1976; Bar-Or, 1987).

The purpose of this chapter is to outline considerations in assessments of maximal intensity exercise. Special attention is given to those that use cycle ergometry, and to investigations into accompanying metabolism.

11.3 TERMS AND NOMENCLATURE

Maximal-intensity exercise can be assessed in several ways and care should be taken to ensure that descriptions of performance adhere to principles of mechanics. These descriptions can be categorised into one of three broad groups. First and the most basic, are scalar quantities such as time (t), distance (s) and speed (m s^{-1}). In the field, time is probably the most widely used measure and is employed to assess performance in activities such as running, swimming and cycling; distance is used to assess performance in activities that involve throwing and jumping – either for height or distance – and speed can be used to assess performance when both time taken and distance moved are known.

Second are vector quantities such as force (F), velocity (v), impulse (Ns) and momentum (mv) that are assessments that tend to be laboratory rather than field-based. Care should be taken with the use of 'velocity.' For example, mean velocity for a 400-m runner who runs in the inside lane of a 400-m track or a 100-m swimmer in a 50-m pool is 0.

Third are measures of energy that also tend to be laboratory-based and concern either energy expended (J) or mechanical power output (W). Clearly, power output is only one measure of maximal intensity exercise, yet there is a tendency to assume that this type of exercise must be synonymous with power output. Indeed, Adamson and Whitney (1971) and Smith (1972) addressed this point in detail and suggested that in explosive activities such as jumping, the use of power is meaningless and unjustified.

It is worth exploring why this is so. The principal factor that determines how far a projectile travels is its velocity at release. As velocity is a vector quantity, this accommodates direction and hence angle of release and the like. From Newton's second law:

$$F \propto a$$

where F = force in N and a = acceleration

This proportionality can be turned into the equation:

$$F = ma$$

where is the mass of the projectile

Acceleration is the difference between initial velocity (u) and final velocity (v) so our expression can be represented as:

$$F = m (v - u)/t$$

If initial velocity is zero, for instance in the javelin throw, shot putt or Sargent-type vertical jump, the expression becomes:

$$F = mv/t$$

This can be rearranged to:

$$Ft = mv$$

mv is the projectile's momentum and Ft is known as impulse. This is why Newton's second law is sometimes called the impulse-momentum relationship. Importantly, velocity at release – the principal determinant of performance – is given by impulse divided by the projectile's mass.

It is the magnitude of preceding impulse that determines a projectile's velocity at release and hence, the distance it travels. What the athlete has to do is maximize this impulse by refining their technique. What is still not known is precisely how to manipulate force and the duration over which this force is applied so as to achieve this maximization. Too high a force might lead to injury as muscle, tendon or ligament are challenged and too great a duration might compromise stretch-shortening cycles in muscle.

The same applies to activities such as side-stepping, swerving and cutting in field games. Performers change direction, and hence impulse, as quickly as possible to outwit their opponents.

Horizontal velocity in sprinting and vertical velocity in jumping are determined by impulse. Consequently, it is the impulse-generating capability of muscle, not its power-producing capability that is the determinant of effective performance.

Unless the units of performance are watts, performance cannot be described as power. Even when these units are used and the description appears to be sound, underlying theoretical bases might not be sustainable.

These considerations are important and not just academic minutiae because they influence the purpose of assessments. Performance *per se* could be the focus in studies that investigate the effects of training. An assessment could also be used to investigate changes in metabolism brought about by training or growth. The integrity of the procedure has to be sound otherwise insights into underlying mechanisms could be obscured. An understanding of principles of mechanics is a prerequisite for effective test selection and subsequent description of measures.

11.4 HISTORICAL BACKGROUND

Concerted interest in maximal-intensity exercise has a long history that can be traced back to 1885 when Marey and Demeney introduced a force platform to investigate mechanisms that underpinned jumping (Cavagna 1975). Investigations into how muscle functions were based on studies of isolated mammalian and amphibian tissue (Hill, 1913). Attention turned to humans and investigations into $\dot{V}O_2$ at running speeds that were in excess of those that could be maintained at steady-state (Hill and Lupton 1922; Sargent 1926; Furusawa *et al.* 1927) and attempts to determine mechanical efficiency and equations to describe motion during maximal intensity exercise (Lupton 1923; Best and Partridge 1928, 1929).

In 1921, D. A. Sargent introduced a jump test that is still used today. Shortly afterwards, L. W. Sargent (1924) suggested that the test could be used as a measure of power and the Lewis nomogram (Fox *et al.* 1988) has been suggested as a means to estimate power output from vertical jump data in spite of the forcible objections stated earlier by Adamson and Whitney (1971) and Smith (1972).

Investigations into the mechanics of bicycle pedalling during high-intensity exercise also have a long history (Dickinson 1928; Fenn 1932; Hill 1934). So too, have attempts to increase the sensitivity of assessment in this type of exercise. Kelso and Hellebrandt (1932) introduced an ergometer that used a direct current generator to apply resistive force and Tuttle and Wendler (1945) modified the design so that alternating current could be used. It was not until Fleisch (1950) and Von Döbeln (1954) introduced the forerunners that inexpensive friction-braked devices became available commercially. It was a further 20 or so years later before these types of ergometer had a marked impact on studies into maximal-intensity exercise when microprocessor-based data logging systems (McClenaghan and Literowitch 1987) presented new opportunities.

In 1938, Hill published one of the most influential reports on muscle function ever written in which he described the relationship between the force a muscle can exert and the accompanying speed with which it can shorten. This relationship has become known as the muscle force-velocity curve. Hill was remarkably modest about this work and claimed later that he 'stumbled upon it' (Hill 1970, p. 3) and that Fenn and Marsh (1935) had actually outlined a similar relationship already. A major point to be emphasized here is that peak power output is produced by an optimum load; if the load is either too great or too small, a muscle or group of muscles will not exert peak power output. This presents major implications for meaningful assessments of peak power output during maximal-intensity exercise.

11.5 SCREENING

Tests of maximal-intensity exercise are strenuous and might produce feelings of nausea of giddiness. It is important that participants are screened carefully before they are recruited (Winter et al. 2007).

11.6 PROCEDURES FOR ASSESSING MAXIMAL INTENSITY EXERCISE

There is a variety of procedures for assessing maximal intensity exercise. Cycle ergometer tests are the most common and these can be categorised into one of four groups: a) 'Wingate' type procedures; b) optimization procedures; c) correction procedures; and d) isokinetic procedures. The first three of these procedures use friction-braked devices whereas the isokinetic group uses more elaborate control systems that restrain pedalling to constant speed. Other procedures include other forms of isokinetic testing, treadmill and field assessments. Details of laboratory procedures for the above tests are outlined at the end of this chapter.

11.6.1 Wingate-type procedures

The Wingate Anaerobic Test, so named because it was developed at the Wingate Institute in Israel, was introduced as a prototype by Ayalon et al. (1974). Since then it has been refined and a comprehensive description was published later (Bar-Or 1981) and subsequently reviewed (Bar-Or 1987). Its use has become widespread. Participants have to pedal flat out for 30 s on a cycle ergometer against an external resistive load that usually is equivalent to 7.5% of body weight for Monark type ergometers and 4% on Fleisch systems (see Practical 1).

In the original Wingate anaerobic test, three measures of performance were recorded: these were peak power output, mean power output and power decay. For the purposes of recording, the test was subdivided into six 5-second blocks and peak power output invariably occured in the first 5 seconds. Although mean power output was demonstrated to be a robust measure and could withstand variations above and below the proposed optimum (Dotan and Bar-Or 1983), reservations were expressed about the integrity of peak power output. Sargeant et al. (1981) suggested that the fixed load of 7.5% of bodyweight was unlikely to satisfy Hill's force-velocity relationships, so casting doubt on this particular measure. Later, Bar-Or (1987) acknowledged that this might be the case and confirmation was provided by Winter et al. (1987 and 1989). Consequently, it is advisable to omit this measure from data summaries.

Time to peak power can be of interest although the importance placed upon this measure depends to a large extent on the timing system that is used. With rolling starts, the precise beginning of the test is difficult to identify. While a stationary start would resolve this issue, it is difficult to set the system in motion from standstill.

After the highest value of power output is produced, and although maximal effort is continued, performance begins to deteriorate as fatigue sets in. At first sight it is tempting to suggest that mechanisms of adenosine triphosphate (ATP) synthesis are being demonstrated and that performance can be partitioned into alactic and lactacid phases. Studies that have used muscle biopsy techniques have demonstrated clearly that lactic acid is produced from the moment all-out exercise begins, not when phosphocreatine stores are depleted (Boobis 1987). Consequently, use of the terms alactacid and lactacid should be avoided.

Blood lactate concentration [HLa] provides some insights into underlying metabolism, although there are some points of caution that have to be considered. Peak HLa occurs some minutes after exercise has ended and, coincidentally, tends to correspond with feelings of nausea. Efflux of lactic acid from muscle cells into interstitial fluid and then into blood takes time and not all of the lactic acid that is produced enters the circulation. Some of it is used by muscle cells as substrate (Brooks 1986) and some is removed from the circulation before subsequent sampling occurs. This is a timely reminder that although blood lactate can be a useful indicator of metabolism, when non-steady-state exercise is under examination, it might well provide a less than clear window through which mechanisms can be viewed.

Differences in performance are partly attributable to differences in body size between participants, so ways to partition out size have to be introduced. This scaling, as it is called, is currently an area of interest (Nevill *et al.* 1992; Winter 1992; although early considerations date back more than 40 years ago (Tanner 1949). It is now appreciated that the construction of straightforward ratio standards in which a performance variable is simply divided by an anthropometric characteristic such as body mass, probably misleads by distorting the data under investigation. Comparisons between participants, especially when there are marked differences in size—say between men and women or adults and children—should be based on *power function ratios* (Nevill *et al.* 1992; Welsman *et al.* 1993; Winter *et al.* 1993; Eston *et al.* 1997) that are obtained from the allometric relationship between performance and anthropometric variables (Schmidt-Nielsen 1984). This issue is discussed in more detail by Winter and Nevill (2009).

Another feature that appears to be clear, but upon further investigation is seen to be more complicated, is the expression of fatigue profiles. It is tempting to suggest that after training, the difference between peak power output and the succeeding lowest value would decrease, but this is not necessarily the case (Bird and Davison 1997). Training can produce a higher peak so that fatigue appears actually to increase and there is no clear explanation for this observation. Possibilities could be a change in force-velocity characteristics of muscle that are not accommodated by the fixed resistive load, technicalities over the way in which performance is expressed or other as yet unidentified factors associated with the skill required to perform the test. This is a rich area for further research.

In summary, the Wingate Anaerobic Test is a useful laboratory procedure to demonstrate how fatigue occurs. The fixed external resistive force might not satisfy muscle force-velocity relationships, so values of peak power output are probably affected adversely. Blood lactate does not necessarily provide a full insight into the underlying metabolism. Fatigue profiles are ambiguous. Differences in the size of participants should be scaled out using allometry (see Winter and Nevill 2009). It is also acknowledged that even the test's name might be a misnomer; because of the contribution of aerobic mechanisms to performance, the adjective 'anaerobic' is misplaced.

11.6.2 Optimization procedures

Anxieties about the potential inability of fixed external loads to satisfy muscle force-velocity relationships led to the development of alternative procedures that provide theoretically sound indications of peak power output. The concern is not simply with a single isolated muscle, but groups of muscles *in vivo* whose leverage characteristics undergo constant change throughout a complete mechanical cycle.

The availability of 'drop-loading' basket ergometers has played a key role in developments whose origins date back almost 80 years to when Dickinson (1929) identified an inverse linear relationship between peak pedalling rate and applied load. Vandewalle *et al.* (1985) and Nakamura *et al.* (1985) used the principle to calculate optimized peak power output on the basis of flywheel-derived data. Acknowledging the reservations about the use of instantaneous values of power output expressed by Adamson and Whitney (1971) and Smith (1972), Winter *et al.* (1991) modified the protocol and recorded movements of the pedals.

The relationship between peak pedalling rate in rev·min^{-1} (R) and applied load (L) is in the form:

R = a + bL
Where:
a = intercept of the line of best fit
b = slope of the line of best fit

On Monark ergometers, one revolution of the pedal crank moves a point on the flywheel a distance of 6 m. Consequently, an expression for power output (W) can be produced as:

$$1\ W = 1\ J\,s^{-1} = 1\ Nm\,s^{-1}\ then\ W = R/60 \times 6\ m \times L\ (newtons)$$

$$\therefore W = \frac{(a + bL)}{60} \times 6m \times L\ (newtons)$$

$$\therefore W = \frac{aL}{10} + \frac{bL^2}{10}$$

Differential calculus can help us interpret the relationship. By differentiating the power/load expression, which is a quadratic relationship, the gradient at any point on the curve can be identified:

$$\frac{dW}{dL} = a + 2bL$$

At the top of the curve, the gradient is zero:

$$\therefore 0 = a + 2bL$$

$$\therefore L = \frac{-a}{2b}$$

Substitution of this value of L in the original equation yields the optimized peak power output i.e.:

Optimized peak power output =

$$= \frac{a\left(\dfrac{-a}{2b}\right)}{10} + \frac{b\left(\dfrac{-a}{2b}\right)^2}{10}$$

Thus, three key measures of performance can be identified: optimized peak power output; the load corresponding to this peak power output; and the pedalling rate that corresponds to optimized peak power output. Assessment of these measures is exemplified in Practical 2.

Seemingly, optimization procedures are useful and they increase the sensitivity with which maximal intensity exercise can be assessed. However, the protocols are considerably longer than the Wingate anaerobic test, even if, as Nakamura *et al.* (1985) suggested, only three loads are used to establish the regression equation that provides the basis for calculating optimized peak power output. Furthermore, while peak values are identified, the protocols don't assess fatigue profiles and this is a distinct limitation. Nevertheless, the protocols have one distinct advantage: because body weight is supported, they isolate activity to the legs and remove potentially contaminating effects from the trunk, head and arms. Similarly, they can be applied to investigations of performance characteristics of the arms (Smith and Price 2007). Coupled with this is an old although still especially useful anthropometric technique that can assess the total and lean volume of the leg (Jones and Pearson 1969) and meaningful comparisons of performance capabilities between groups can be made.

Winter *et al.* (1991) and Eston *et al.* (1997) compared maximal-intensity exercise of men with women and found that there were distinct differences in performance that were independent of differences in the size of the leg. These studies also demonstrated the importance of applying correct scaling procedures. Similarly, the techniques have been used to compare children and adults (Winter *et al.* 1993) where it is suggested that traditional ratio standard measures overestimate children's maximal intensity exercise.

In summary, optimization procedures appear to satisfy muscle force-velocity relationships and produce theoretically sound assessments of peak power output. Useful studies can be performed when optimization is coupled with anthropometric procedures that assess limb volumes. Optimization procedures do not produce valid fatigue profiles.

11.6.3 Correction procedures

Optimization procedures are not the only tests that have been proposed for friction-braked cycle ergometers. The completeness of calculations that are used to determine the optimized peak power output has been questioned by Lakomy (1986) who pointed out that the external resistive load does not account for all the forces applied to the pedals and transmitted to an ergometer's flywheel. Clearly, as the flywheel is accelerated, a force greater than the resistive load is applied to the system and this extra force is ignored in traditional calculations of mechanical work done and hence power output.

Lakomy (1986) determined an 'acceleration balancing load' (EL) which was identified by plotting deceleration of the flywheel from 150 rev min⁻¹ against the conventional resistive force. As a result, the effective load (i.e. the actual force applied) could be calculated as:

Effective Load (F) = Resistive Load (RL) + Excess Load (EL)

The value of F could then be multiplied by the velocity of the flywheel to provide an instantaneous value of power output. By introducing this correction, Lakomy (1985) demonstrated that the lightest loads produced peak power output. A commercially available kit (Concept II), which contains a flywheel mounted generator and related computer software, can be used with Monark friction

braked ergometers. A similar system was developed by Bassett (1989). By using the kit, data can be logged simultaneously from the flywheel to calculate corrected peak power output, and from the pedals to calculate the optimized peak power output.

As can be seen from the data generated in Practical 3, although the relationship between performance-measures in optimization and correction procedures is high, the two methods can produce different absolute results. The explanation for this could be technical in that it is associated with the precision of measurement, but the sensitivity of measurement procedures suggests that this is unlikely. The reason could still be technical because of the procedures for calculating power output that are, of course, distinctly different. The value for optimized peak power output is calculated at peak angular velocity for a complete mechanical cycle of activity, whereas the corrected peak power output is based on products of force and instantaneous velocity. This latter procedure has been questioned by Adamson and Whitney (1971) and Smith (1972). While these products yield the units of power, the meaningfulness of using W is still not clear. Correction procedures are based on systems in which acceleration occurs and in Section 11.3, it was pointed out that acceleration and hence change in momentum is attributable not to power but to preceding impulse. Hence, it is the impulse-generating capability of muscle that is manifest, but it is described in terms of power. Nevertheless, although there is a difference between the optimized peak power output and the corrected peak power output, the difference is systematic and the association between the variables is particularly strong.

Clearly, this unresolved debate impacts directly on our understanding of how muscle functions, and in particular, how it functions in concert with skeletal, neurophysiological and metabolic systems *in vivo*. Winter *et al.* (1996) compared optimized and corrected peak power outputs but no studies have been undertaken to compare the way in which these values reflect changes in performance brought about by training. From a practical point of view, correction procedures are easier to administer than optimization tests because only one bout of exercise has to be performed. On the other hand optimization procedures satisfy muscle force-velocity relationships and appear to be sound theoretically. This area is still a rich field for further investigation.

11.6.4 Isokinetic systems

Before the advent of optimization and correction procedures, isokinetic systems were introduced to assess peak power output in a way that satisfied muscle force-velocity relationships. Sargeant et al. (1981) designed an ergometer in which the pedals were driven at constant angular velocity by an external electric motor and forces applied to the pedals were detected by strain gauges attached to the pedal cranks. By altering pedalling rate externally, force-velocity relationships were explored. McCartney et al. (1983) developed a similar system but in this case, the pedals of the ergometer are driven by the participant until an electric motor restricts any further acceleration of the system.

The acquisition of data from these systems is demanding. Signals have to be transmitted from a rotating device via a slip ring and this can introduce noise into the signals that can be difficult to suppress. Also, previously questioned instantaneous values of power output are calculated from the products of force and velocity. Conversely, calibration is easier than in friction-braked systems. In the latter, frictional losses from the chain and bearing assemblies are not usually considered whereas in the former, especially with the motor-driven version, these losses are irrelevant. The assessment of peak power output using a conventional isokinetic dynamometry system has also been compared to the traditional Wingate test (Baltzopoulos et al. 1988).

11.6.5 Non-motorized treadmills

While cycle ergometry has several key advantages, there is one major limitation: it is task specific and does not necessarily reflect performance in running. Within the last decade attempts have been made to redress this problem by means of non-motorized treadmills in which the participant drives the belt of the treadmill. These systems can used to assess power output whilst running horizontally (Lakomy 1984; Tong et al. 2001). Participants are tethered to the apparatus by a suitable harness that contains a force transducer fitted in series. Horizontal force and treadmill speed provide the basis for calculation.

It has been reported that substantial periods of habituation are required before valid data can be obtained (Gamble et al. 1988). Nevertheless, this type of assessment has been used successfully to examine mechanical characteristics of running (Cheetham and Williams, 1985; Cheetham et al. 1986: Tong et al. 2001).

Developments in the design of treadmills have maintained interest in the use of this form of ergometry to assess exercise capabilities of humans (Jaskólska et al. 1996; Jaskólska et al. 1999). Jaskólska et al. (1996) attempted to identify optimal resistances that maximized external peak power output and Jaskólska et al. (1999) compared muscle force-velocity relationships during treadmill running and cycling. The improved sensitivity of these systems and their continued development suggest that they will be used in further studies of exercise performance and underlying metabolism. Certainly, interest in adaptations to maximal- and high-intensity exercise shows little sign of waning (Burgomaster et al. 2008).

11.6.6 Multiple-sprint type protocols

Maximal-intensity exercise might have to be performed in repeated bouts interspersed with periods of rest. This intermittent form of exercise is typified in what have been termed multiple-sprint sports (Williams 1987) such as soccer, hockey and racket games and is probably the most common type of activity in sport. Common though it is, this type of activity is difficult to model, but the challenge has been met by proposals of field-based and laboratory-based procedures.

Léger and Lambert (1982) devised a shuttle running-type protocol in which participants ran 20-m lengths in time to a metronome. Running speed increased progressively until volitional exhaustion occurred. Since then this system has been commercialized (Brewer *et al*. 1988) and is widely used.

Wootton and Williams (1983) used cycle ergometry and participants performed five bouts of exercise each of which lasted 6 s with a 30 s rest between each bout. Bird and Davison (1997) suggested 10 × 6-s sprints and outlined other field-and laboratory-based procedures. Non-motorized treadmills have been used (Hamilton *et al*. 1991; Nevill *et al*. 1993) in which up to 30 repeated sprints are required. However, there have been concerted attempts to develop protocols that model multiple-sprint activities in controlled ways.

Studies have investigated the effects of: hot environments on shuttle-running performance (Morris *et al*. 1998); creatine supplementation in repeated sprint swimming (Peyrebrune *et al*. 1998); and branched-chain amino acids and carbohydrate on fatigue during intermittent, high-intensity running (Davis *et al*. 1999). Muscle soreness resulting from shuttle running has also been examined (Thompson *et al*. 1999) as has the effect of intermittent high-intensity exercise on neuromuscular performance (Mercer *et al*. 1998). It is likely that these types of assessment will be used increasingly as investigations into metabolism and mechanisms of fatigue continue.

11.7 ASSESSMENT OF METABOLISM

There have been developments in procedures for assessing maximal-intensity exercise

and both the sensitivity and integrity of measures have been improved in recent years. While performance can be quantified and underlying metabolic processes demonstrated, quantification of this underlying metabolism is still a considerable challenge. By way of comparison, the 'gold standard' for aerobic exercise is maximum oxygen uptake ($\dot{V}O_{2max}$), but as Williams (1990) asked: why should this be so?

The problem is to measure the contribution from anaerobic energy releasing mechanisms up to and including the maximum contribution (i.e. a person's anaerobic capacity). Immediately a dilemma is presented: anaerobic capacity could be expressed as an amount, but the concern is more likely to be with the rate at which energy can be released and the length of time for which this release can be sustained. Furthermore, it was reported in Section 11.6.1 that even in a short duration test like the Wingate anaerobic test, aerobic mechanisms account for ~ 20 % of total energy provision. We have also already seen that previous suggestions that maximal intensity exercise could be partitioned into alactacid and lactacid phases are now known to be simplifications; energy release from high energy phosphagens and glycolysis occurs simultaneously not sequentially.

In spite of these difficulties, techniques that attempt to assess anaerobic capacity have been devised and can be categorized into 'direct' and 'indirect' determinations (Bangsbo 1997). The direct measures include the use of muscle biopsies before and immediately after any form of muscle contractions, or the use of ^{31}P magnetic resonance spectroscopy if the muscle is electrically stimulated or made to perform isometrically. Indirect measures on the other hand are based on the concept of the oxygen deficit.

11.7.1 Direct estimation of anaerobic metabolism

During maximal and high intensity exercise, decreases in muscle ATP and in creatine phosphate (PCr) are observed along with an increase in lactate. It is possible therefore to quantify the anaerobic energy production if determinations of the changes in these metabolites are made immediately following the exercise. This quantification has only been made possible after the introduction of the muscle biopsy technique (Bergström, 1962). In essence, the process requires the muscle under investigation to be identified before a small area on the surface is sterilized and then a local anaesthetic injected beneath the surface of the skin. A small incision of the skin and subcutaneous tissue is made initially before cutting through the muscle fascia. A hollow biopsy needle can then be inserted through the incision to the depth required before aspiration is applied. Aspiration causes a small portion of the muscle to 'bulge' into a small window at the side of the biopsy needle where it is cut by a sharp blade inside the hollow of the needle. The needle is then withdrawn and the sample is immediately frozen in liquid nitrogen. When this process is used for the determination of phosphagen stores (i.e. ATP + PCr) following high-intensity exercise, speed of sampling and freezing the muscle tissue is necessary since some re-synthesis is possible.

Table 11.1 provides data from selected studies in which the muscle biopsy technique has been used for the estimation of anaerobic energy production from phosphagens and glycolysis before and immediately after maximal intensity exercise of varying time periods.

The findings are based on calculations of the decrease in muscle ATP and PCr, and the increase in muscle lactate from muscle samples taken both at rest and immediately after exercise. The highest rates of anaerobic energy production for PCr and for glycolysis during dynamic exercise lasting up to 10 s are 5·1 and 9·3 mmol kg^{-1}·s^{-1} respectively. When the dynamic exercise is increased to 30 s, the highest rates of ATP produced anaerobically from PCr and glycolysis are 2·0 and 5·9 mmol kg^{-1} s^{-1} respectively. These values are mean rates over the 10- or 30-s exercise bouts, and that actual peak rates would be expected to occur within the first second or so. Indeed, the change in power output during a 30-s Wingate test reflects the maximal rates of ATP being engendered within the muscle from these anaerobic sources as well as the aerobic contribution.

Table 11.1 Estimated total anaerobic ATP production, rate of anaerobic ATP production and % contribution from PCr and glycolysis during dynamic exercise

Reference	Type of exercise	Duration (s)	Total ATP produced (mmol·kg^{-1})	Rate of ATP produced (mmol·kg^{-1}·s^{-1})		% Contribution	
				PCr	Glycolysis	PCr	Glycolysis
Boobis *et al.* (1982)	Cycle	0–6	63	4.9	4.8	47	53
		0–30	189	1.9	4.0	30	64
Jones *et al.* (1985)	Isokinetic cycle 60 rpm	0–10	166	5.1	8.0	42	58
		0–30	291	1.4	5.8	21	79
	140 rpm	0–10	173	4.4	9.3	35	65
		0–30	240	0.7	6.5	11	89
McCartney Isokinetic *et al.* (1986)	Isokinetic cycle 100 rpm	0–30	228	1.4	5.9	23	77
Cheetham *et al.* (1986)	Run	0–30	183	1.9	3.8	38	62
Nevill *et al.* (1989)	Run	0–30	186	1.9	4.1	33	67

There are problems with the estimations calculated from the muscle biopsy data. First, there is the time delay in getting the muscle sample frozen following exercise. This procedure involves stopping the activity, immobilising the leg, taking the biopsy, and then transferring the sample to the liquid nitrogen; a series of events that can take between 10 and 20 s. Nevertheless, Soderlund and Hultman (1986) have shown that ATP and PCr concentrations in muscle biopsy samples are not markedly affected by a delay in freezing. A second problem is the difficulty in determining the muscle mass involved in whole-body exercise, and therefore the metabolic response of the biopsied muscle could not be representative of all those muscles engaged in the exercise. Finally, the amount of energy related to the release of lactate into the blood from the muscle is not taken into account in the calculations presented in Table 11.1 so the anaerobic energy production from glycolysis is underestimated. It is difficult to determine the volume in which lactate is diluted. Bangsbo (1997) suggested that the likely underestimation for a 75-kg individual is between 5.2% and 25.6% for maximal intensity exercise of 30-s duration. The lower value is based on a dilution volume of 6 litres (i.e. blood volume) whereas the higher value based on a dilution volume of 30 litres (i.e. total body fluids). Even these calculations do not take account of the lactate metabolized by inactive muscles and by the heart.

In spite of the limitations outlined above, there is a consistency in the data on rates of anaerobic ATP production during maximal-intensity exercise from the various studies. Indeed, the data from a recent study involving 20 electrically evoked maximal isometric actions of the anterior tibialis muscle using both magnetic resonance spectroscopy and muscle biopsy demonstrated that there was little difference in the muscle concentration of PCr, although differences were found in the estimates of ATP and changes in lactate (Constantin-Teodosiu et al. 1997). The notable higher muscle lactate concentrations

estimated using magnetic resonance spectroscopy accounted for ~ 30% greater estimation of ATP turnover.

All the studies reported so far have documented the metabolic response of mixed muscle to maximal-intensity exercise without recourse to possible variations in fibre type. Some investigations have separated single fibres and measured ATP, PCr, and glycogen of one fibre type at rest, during muscle action and in recovery (Soderlund et al. 1992; Greenhaff et al. 1994; Casey et al. 1996). The conclusions from these studies are that during maximal-intensity exercise, type II fibres compared with type I fibres produce a greater rate of PCr degradation, a greater rate of glycolysis and a slower rate of resynthesis of PCr.

As many sports can be classified as multiple-sprint sports, there have been developments in assessing the metabolic requirements of repeated high-intensity exercise. Casey et al. (1996) reported metabolic responses of different fibre types during repeated bouts of maximal isokinetic cycling. Exercise consisted of two bouts of 30-s cycling with a 4-minute passive recovery between bouts. The authors reported that a 4-minute recovery period was insufficient to allow total resynthesis of ATP and PCr in type II muscle fibres although recovery was complete in type I fibres. Furthermore, utilization of ATP and PCr was less in type II fibres during the second bout of exercise without a corresponding change in type I fibres. Performance was also markedly reduced.

A major reason for performing tests of anaerobic capacity, speed, power output and the like is to examine the effect of training on these measures. Sprint training normally results in an increase in the ability to perform maximal-intensity exercise. Are these performance changes reflected in an enhanced capacity for generation of anaerobic ATP production? Boobis et al. (1983) trained participants for 8 weeks by means of sprinting on a cycle ergometer and analyzed muscle samples at rest and after

30 s of maximal cycling before and after the training programme. Training increased the mean power output by 8%, a change mirrored by an increase in anaerobic energy production from glycolysis. The energy produced anaerobically from PCr and ATP was not significantly affected. Similar results were obtained in a study in which recreational runners were sprint-trained for 8 weeks (Nevill *et al.* 1989). A 6% increase in mean power output was matched by a 20% increase in anaerobic energy production from glycolysis, but not from the phosphagen stores.

11.7.2 Indirect estimations of anaerobic metabolism

Direct measures of metabolites in muscle are needed to determine anaerobic capacity accurately, but owing to the invasive nature of this approach an alternative technique is often desirable. The most commonly used indirect estimation of anaerobic capacity is maximal accumulated oxygen deficit (MAOD) during short, intense exercise. This measure arose from the original idea of the oxygen deficit and was first proposed by Hermansen (1969). The method requires establishing a linear relationship between oxygen uptake and exercise intensity over a number of visits (since oxygen uptake is measured over a period of 4–10 minutes for each intensity), then extrapolating the line beyond maximal oxygen uptake to a value corresponding to 120% $\dot{V}O_{2max}$. The participant then exercises at this intensity to exhaustion. The MAOD is calculated as the difference in oxygen estimated as needed to exercise at that intensity (from the extrapolated data) and the actual oxygen consumed during the exercise corresponding to 120% $\dot{V}O_{2max}$ (see Medbø *et al.* 1988). Although there appears to be similarity in the estimation of anaerobic energy provision between the MAOD and data from muscle biopsies in isolated muscle groups (Bangsbo *et al.* 1990), there are conflicting views about

the implications for whole-body exercise. For details of opposing views in the literature, readers are advised to consult Bangsbo (1996a, 1996b) and Medbø (1996a, 1996b). Practical 4 provides a modified version of the MAOD assessment procedure.

11.7.3 Aerobic contribution

The data presented above are exclusively concerned with rates of anaerobic energy production with no recourse to aerobic contribution. Indirect estimates of the anaerobic and aerobic contribution to intense isolated knee extension exercise of 30 s are 80% and 20%, respectively (Bangsbo *et al.* 1990). These values change to 45%:55% and 30%:70% anaerobic:aerobic as the exercise duration increases from 60–90 s and 120–192 s. During the first 10 s of a 30-s Wingate test, the estimated contribution from aerobic metabolism is 3% (Serresse *et al.* 1988), whereas the mean values of the aerobic contribution for the 30-s Wingate test have been reported as being between 16% and 28% (Serresse *et al.* 1988; Smith and Hill 1991). Even if a participant does not breathe, existing air in the lungs, myoglobin and haemoglobin stores can provide oxygen for aerobic energy provision and assessment of anaerobic capacity needs to take account of the likely aerobic energy contribution.

11.7.4 Possible relationship between metabolism and fatigue

The power output profile of an individual undergoing a 30-s Wingate test shows a peak in the first few seconds followed by a decline. This profile has a parallel in the decrease in rate of ATP production from both PCr and glycolysis (Table 11.1). It should also be recognized that aerobic contribution increases with time. The greatest rate of decrease in energy production is attributable to the depletion of PCr stores. This is noticeable in the type II muscle fibres where after 10 s of activity 70% of these stores are used and after 20 s they are nearly depleted. The maximal rate of ATP production from glycolysis probably occurs at around 20 s and is maintained thereafter until the build up of lactate and inorganic phosphate inhibit glycolytic enzyme activity. The switch from generation of ATP from PCr predominantly to glycolysis and then to aerobic metabolism necessitates a decrease in the maximal rate of ATP production. If ATP can only be generated at given (reducing) rates, then power output must decrease in a like manner. So the power output profile over 30 s is a function of maximal rate of ATP production from a changing energy source and is unlikely to be due solely to increases in lactate production and concomitant increases in hydrogen ions.

11.8 SUMMARY AND CONCLUSION

There has been considerable progress in assessments of maximal intensity exercise that involve brief single and repeated bouts of exercise. Similarly, successful field- and laboratory-based attempts have been made to model multiple-sprint type sports. Unequivocal quantification of accompanying metabolism is a challenge that has yet to be met.

11.9 PRACTICAL 1: WINGATE TEST

The aim of this practical is two-fold: (a) to describe external power output characteristics during the Wingate anaerobic test; and (b) to examine changes in blood lactate concentration.

11.9.1 Equipment

A Monark 814E basket-loading cycle ergometer with microprocessor linked data-logging facilities is used to record movements of either the flywheel or pedals; a separate ergometer can be used for use during the warm up. Figure 11.1 shows the general arrangement for the test and Figures 11.2 and 11.3 illustrate detection systems for logging data from movements of the flywheel and pedals, respectively.

11.9.2 Methods

1   Take a finger prick blood sample at rest. Collect the blood in duplicate i.e. in two micro capillary tubes. One tube is labelled *a* the other *b*. [See Maughan *et al.* 2009)

2   Participants have a 5-minute warm up at 100 W with a flat out sprint for 5 s at 3 minutes, followed by 5 minutes of rest.

3   During this time participants transfer to the test machine. Seat height is adjusted for comfort (Hamley and Thomas 1967; Nordeen-Snyder 1977), toe clips are secured (La Voie *et al.* 1984), the resistive load is positioned and a restraining harness should be fixed to ensure that the participant cannot rise from the saddle.

4   Participants pedal at 50–60 rev min^{-1} with the external load supported. Upon the command, '3, 2, 1 go!' the load is applied abruptly, participants begin to pedal flat out and data logging is started.

5   Participants pedal for 30 s.

6   At the end of the test participants undertake a suitable warm down; e.g. 2 minutes

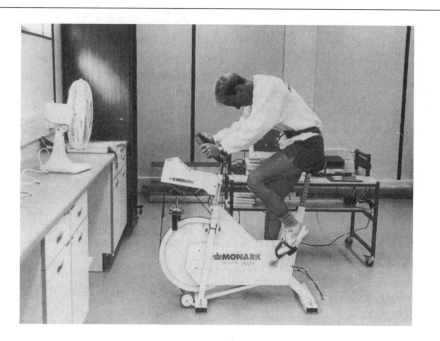

Figure 11.1 General layout of the equipment used in the Wingate Anaerobic Test. The cycle ergometer is bolted to the floor and has a modified load hanger. Note also the use of toe clips and a restraining belt.

Figure 11.2 Data logging from the flywheel by means of a precision DC motor (Lakomy 1986).

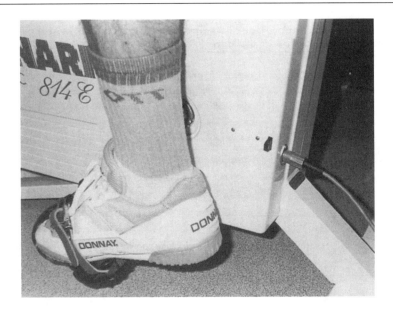

Figure 11.3 Data logging from the passage of the left pedal by means of a photo-optic sensor housed in the chain guard (Winter *et al.* 1991, 1996).

of cycling at 100 W.

7   Take blood samples as in (1) immediately at the end of exercise, 7.5 minutes and 12.5 minutes later and determine blood lactate concentration (HLa). This can be done by means of fast response analyzers, but this practical uses Maughan's (1982) fluorimetric technique, which has greater control over the precision of measurement.

8   Complete the results sections (Tables 11.2, 11.3, 11.4, 11.5, 11.6 and 11.7).

11.9.3 Sample results

Mean power output ranges from 400–900 W, although differences in size account for

Table 11.2 Raw data for WAnT on a small sample of 20-year-old male college students

Subject	Time to peak power (s)	Mean power (W)	Decay (W)
1	4.50	635	456
2	2.87	806	538
3	3.45	745	426
4	5.34	813	562
5	3.83	830	446
Mean	4.00	765.8	485.6
SD	0.96	79.8	60.4

Table 11.3 Calibration data for blood lactate (HLa). This is a six point calibration, i.e. a blank and five standards are used. Each is analyzed in duplicate.

Standards (mmoll $^{-1}$)

Tube	Blank	2.5	5.0	7.5	10.5	12.5
1	0	18	35	53	70	91
2	0	18	37	54	72	90
Mean	0	18.0	36.0	53.5	71.0	90.5

Plot the calibration curve including the regression analysis.

The regression equation for the above, which minimizes the sum of squares of residuals about the regression line in a *horizontal* direction, is equal to:

$x = 0.015 + 0.139 \, y$

Table 11.4 Samples (fluorimeter reading); note how each of the capillary tubes is analyzed in duplicate

	Rest		0		7.5 min PE		12.5 min PE	
Tube	a	b	a	b	a	b	a	b
1	5	6	64	66	75	75	68	61
2	5	6	62	64	76	75	70	62

Table 11.5 Blood lactate values in mmol $^{-1}$. Use the regression data from Table 11.3 to convert the instrument readings in Table 11.4. Note how each blood sample is analyzed in quadruplicate.

	Rest		0		7.5 min		12.5 min	
Tube	a	b	a	b	a	b	a	b
1	0.71	0.85	8.92	9.19	10.45	10.45	9.47	8.50
2	0.71	0.85	8.64	8.92	10.58	10.45	9.75	8.64
Mean	0.71	0.85	8.78	9.06	10.52	10.45	9.61	8.57
Mean	0.78		8.92		10.49		9.09	

Table 11.6 Sample results for WAnT

	Mean	SD	Range
Time to peak power (s)	3.6	1.2	2–6
Mean power (W)	650	80	400–900
Decay (W)	300	50	150–500

Table 11.7 Sample results for blood lactate following performance of the Wingate Anaerobic Test (values are mean, SD)

	Blood lactate (mmol $^{-1}$)
Rest	0.70, 0.15
Immediately after exercise	9.6, 2.1
7.5 min after exercise	12.5, 2.4
12.5 min after exercise	11.0, 2.1

some of the difference. Time to peak power output ranges from approximately 2–6 s, very early in the test, and decay, the difference between the highest value of peak power output and the subsequent lowest value is approximately 40–60 % of the mean value. Blood lactate concentrations tend to peak some 7–8 minutes after exercise has ended.

11.10 PRACTICAL 2: OPTIMIZATION PROCEDURES

The purposes of this practical are to (a) assess optimized peak power output, optimized load and the optimized pedalling rate; (b) compare these measures with Wingate-derived data; and (c) establish the extent to which muscle force-velocity relationships are not satisfied by the Wingate Anaerobic Test.

11.10.1 Equipment

The same as for the the Wingate anaerobic test.

11.10.2 Methods

1 Dress, warm up and screening procedures are the same as for the Wingate anaerobic test.
2 After a 5-minute warm up, participants perform four bouts of all-out exercise against randomly assigned loads. Each bout lasts 10 s and is followed by 1 minute of warm down. A period of rest is allowed such that each exercise bout is separated in total by 5 minutes. Each bout is started in the same way as for the Wingate anaerobic test.
3 Loads are assigned according to body mass and guidelines are given in Table 11.8. These loads should produce peak pedalling rates within the range 100–200 rev·min^{-1}.
4 The order for applying the loads is: Wingate (i.e. 7.5% of body weight), load 2, load 4 and finally load 1.
5 Record peak pedalling rate for each load and calculate the optimized peak power output, optimized load and optimized pedalling rate.
6 Compare the Wingate-derived values of peak power output and peak pedalling rate with the optimized values.

11.10.3 Sample results

Table 11.9 gives peak pedalling rate and applied load data for a female sports studies student. Pearson's product moment correlation coefficient and regression data are as follows:

$r = -0.998$
R = 212.5 – 1.969L

Table 11.8 Suggested loads in newtons according to body mass for the optimization procedure

	Body mass (kg)					
Load	< 50	50–59.95	60–69.95	70–79.95	80–89.95	> 90
1	20.0	25.0	25.0	25.0	30.0	30.0
2	30.0	35.0	37.5	40.0	45.0	47.5
3	Wingate	Wingate	Wingate	Wingate	Wingate	Wingate
4	50.0	55.0	62.5	70.0	75.0	82.5

(9.81 N = 1 kg)

Table 11.9 Sample results for peak pedalling rate and applied load

Load (N)	Peak pedalling rate (rev min^{-1})	Peak power output (W)
44.1	128	564
34.3	144	493
53.9	105	566
24.5	164	402

i.e. a = 212.5
b = − 1.97

Substituting these values of a and b :

$$\text{Optimized peak power output} = \frac{-0.025a^2}{b} = 573 \text{ W}$$

$$\text{Optimized load} = \frac{-a}{2b} = 53.9 \text{ N } (5.49 \text{ kg})$$

$$\text{Optimized pedalling rate} = a + bL = 106.2 \text{ rev min}^{-1}$$

The relationship between peak pedalling rate, applied load and power output is illustrated in Figure 11.4. Tables 11.10 and 11.11 illustrate some typical results.

Table 11.10 Sample results for optimized and WAnT-derived data in men, n = 19. Values are mean, SEM (Winter et al. 1987).

	Optimum	Wingate	r	t	V%
Peak power (W)	1012, 30	883, 21	0.898[a]	−9.029[a]	5.8
Pedal rate (rev·min^{-1})	118.4, 1.8	155.9, 2.5	0.589[b]	−19.078[a]	5.4

[a] P < 0.001; [b]P < 0.01.

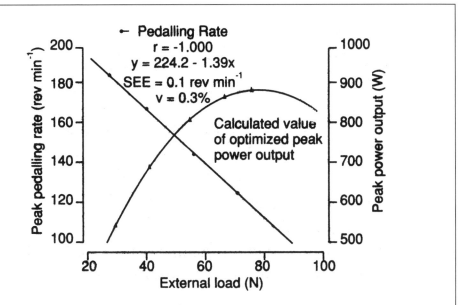

Figure 11.4 An example of the way in which peak pedalling rate and power output are related to the applied braking force.

Table 11.11 Sample results for optimized and WAnT-derived data in women, $n = 28$. Values are mean, SEM (Winter *et al.* 1987).

	Optimum	Wingate	r	t	V%
Peak power (W)	640, 20	579, 17	0.918[a]	9.22[a]	6.8
Pedal rate	103.8, 1.6	134.5, 1.7	0.582[b]	–22.571[a]	6.7

[a]$P < 0.001$; [b]$P < 0.01$.

The calculation of the optimized peak power output, optimized load and optimized pedalling rate depends on the linearity of the relationship between peak pedalling rate and applied load. In this example, r was -0.996 ± 0.005 for the men and -0.996 ± 0.006 for the women so the required linearity is clearly illustrated. Values of peak power output derived from the Wingate Anaerobic Test were only ~ 88% of the optimized peak power output in men and ~ 90% in women. In addition, the reductions were not consistent. Although values of r indicated a relationship ($P < 0.001$), ~ 20% of the variance of the optimized peak power output in men and ~ 16% in women is not accounted for by the relationship with Wingate-derived peak power output values.

The results demonstrate clearly that the optimized peak power output is greater than Wingate-derived peak power output (WPP) and that the pedalling rate that accompanied WPP is greater than the pedalling rate that accompanied the optimized peak power output. Consequently, these data confirm the suggestion (Sargeant *et al.* 1981) that the Wingate load of 7.5% of body weight does not necessarily satisfy muscle force-velocity relationships. Optimized pedalling rate is ~ 115 rev min[-1] in men (Sargeant *et al.* 1984; Nakamura *et al.* 1985; Winter *et al.* 1991) and ~ 105 rev min[-1] in women (Sargeant *et al.* 1984; Winter *et al.* 1991). Pedalling rate at WPP is some 15–20% higher in each case. The higher pedalling rate is at the expense of effective force production and hence power output. This reduction in effectiveness is also illustrated by optimized load which is ~ 11% of body weight in both men and women, and considerably higher than the Wingate value.

11.11 PRACTICAL 3: CORRECTION PROCEDURES

The purpose of this practical is to compare optimized peak power output values to corrected values for peak power output, as suggested by Lakomy (1985).

11.11.1 Methods

1 Warm-up procedures as for Practical 1.
2 Participants perform the optimization procedure outlined previously.
3 During the 'Wingate Load' bout, i.e. bout one, data are also recorded using the Concept II system and the corrected peak power output is calculated.
4 Record the corrected peak power output, the optimized peak power output and the pedalling rates for both.

11.11.2 Sample results

Table 11.12 Sample data for optimized and corrected peak power output in men, $n = 19$. Values are mean, SEM (Winter *et al.* 1996)

	Optimized	Corrected	r	t	V%
Men					
Peak power (W)	915, 35	1005, 32	0.92[a]	−6.79[a]	5.4
Pedal rate (rev min⁻¹)	110.6, 1.2	127.9, 1.9	0.64[b]	−11.77[a]	5.1
Women					
Peak Power (W)	673, 33	777, 39	0.96[a]	-9.38[a]	5.8
Pedal rate (rev min⁻¹)	101, 1	111, 2	0.51[b]	−4.71[a]	5.1

[a]$P < 0.001$; [b]$P < 0.01$.

The important points to note are that the corrected peak power output is greater than the optimized peak power output and similarly, pedalling rate is higher for the corrected peak power values.

The value for the corrected peak power output is ~10% greater than the optimized peak power output although the relationship between the measures is strong with 85% of the variance in the corrected peak power output accounted for by its relationship with the optimized peak power output. Similarly, the pedalling rate for the corrected peak power output is ~15% greater, but in this case only 41% of the variance in this value is accounted for by its relationship with the optimized equivalent. However, the coefficient of variation is smaller than for the optimized peak power output and this is a good example of the caution that has to be taken when r is interpreted. The magnitude of r is influenced by the range in the data and it does not necessarily give a clear indication of the relationship between variables. This is a reminder of the care that has to be taken when using r (Sale 1991).

11.12 PRACTICAL 4. ASSESSMENT OF MAXIMAL ACCUMULATED OXYGEN DEFICIT (MAOD)

The original method for the determination of MAOD as described by Medbo et al. (1988) required participants to perform ~20 runs on a treadmill at varying speeds up to a speed corresponding to maximal oxygen uptake. Each run lasted for 10 minutes, with the treadmill gradient set at 10.5%. Oxygen uptake was determined in the last 2 minutes of each run, and because only one run was performed on a particular day, the whole process took three weeks. Clearly this would be impractical for testing athletes or for student laboratory classes. However, to illustrate the principles a scaled-down version can be used over two testing sessions as follows:

11.12.1 Methods

1   The participant runs at four submaximal speeds on a treadmill with a gradient set at 10.5% for 4 minutes each during which oxygen uptake is measured in the last 2 minutes. From these data, it is possible to establish a linear relationship between oxygen uptake and running speed.

2   After the final 4-minute run, the treadmill speed is progressively increased every minute until volitional exhaustion occurs so that maximal oxygen uptake can be determined.

3   Produce a graph of $\dot{V}O_2$ vs Running Speed and determine the oxygen demand and running speed equivalent to 120% of $\dot{V}O_{2max}$. This is achieved by extrapolating the straight line relationship beyond $\dot{V}O_{2max}$. Alternatively, it may be predicted from the regression equation derived from the relationship between oxygen uptake (x) and running speed (y).

4   On a separate day, the participant runs to exhaustion on the treadmill (set at 10.5% gradient) at the speed corresponding to 120% $\dot{V}O_{2max}$. Oxygen uptake is monitored throughout this test, which normally results in fatigue between 2 and 6 minutes.

5   The MAOD is calculated from the difference between the oxygen demand for that running speed (i.e. time to fatigue × $\dot{V}O_2$ extrapolated to 120% $\dot{V}O_{2max}$) and the actual total oxygen consumption during the run.

Using this brief method, it is possible to distinguish between sprint-trained and endurance-trained populations, but it is probably not sensitive enough to distinguish subtle changes due to training. The use of four 4-minute bouts of running in one session as well as continuing to $\dot{V}O_{2max}$ might account for this lack of sensitivity.

11.12.2 Sample results

The following data provide an example of oxygen uptake values collected on a male college sprinter using the above protocol.

i) Day One (Table 11.13)
Regression equation for $\dot{V}O_2$ (x) versus speed (y) :

$$\text{Speed (m min}^{-1}\text{)} = 23.2 + 2.758 \, (\dot{V}O_2) \quad r = 0.99$$

Therefore, the speed corresponding to 120% $\dot{V}O_{2max}$ = 251.5 m min^{-1}

Table 11.13 Running speeds and equivalent oxygen uptake values

	Speed (m min^{-1})	$\dot{V}O_2$ (ml kg^{-1}min^{-1})
Run		
1.	161	49
2.	174	56
3.	188	60
4.	201	64
Speed at $\dot{V}O_{2max}$	214	69

120% of $\dot{V}O_{2max}$ (1.2 × 69) = 83 ml kg^{-1}min^{-1}

ii) Day Two (Treadmill speed = 251.5 m min^{-1} at a gradient of 10.5%) (Table 11.14)

$$\text{Calculation of MAOD} = (2.5 \text{ min} \times 83 \text{ ml/kg}) - ((27+49+55+60+62)/2) =$$
$$= 207.5 - 126.5 = 81 \text{ ml kg}^{-1}$$

$$\text{Aerobic contribution} = (126.5/ 207.5) \times 100 = 61\%$$

Table 11.14 Oxygen uptake at specific times while running at 251.5 m·min^{-1} at a gradient of 10.5%

Time (s)	$\dot{V}O_2$* ml kg^{-1}min^{-1}
30s	27
60s	49
90s	55
120s	60
150s	62

Following are typical values for MAOD (Table 11.15):
Values of 55 ml kg^{-1} and 72 ml kg^{-1} have been observed for endurance-trained and sprint-trained men in the exercise physiology laboratory in Don MacLaren's laboratory.

Table 11.15 Typical values for MAOD (ml·kg⁻¹)

	ml kg⁻¹
Before training (males)	66.4
After training (males)	79.8
Before training (females)	69.6
After training (females)	80.9
(Ramsbottom *et al.* 1991)	

FURTHER READING:

Books

Smith P. M. and Price M. J. (2007) Upper-body exercise. In: (E. M. Winter, A. M. Jones, R. C. R. Davison, P. D. Bromley and T. H. Mercer, eds) *Sport and Exercise Physiology Testing Guidelines Volume One Sport Testing*. Routledge; Oxford: pp. 138–44.

Website

Escola de Educação Física e Esporte – University of Sao Paulo, Brazil (Laboratory of Biophysics) http://lob.incubadora.fapesp.br/portal/t/glossary.

REFERENCES

Adamson G. T. and Whitney R. J. (1971) Critical appraisal of jumping as a measure of human power. In: (J. Vredenbregt and J. Wartenweiler, eds) *Medicine and Sport 6, Biomechanics II*. S. Karger; Basel: pp. 208–11.

Ayalon A., Inbar O. and Bar-Or O. (1974) Relationships among measurements of explosive strength and anaerobic power. In: (R. C. Nelson and C. A. Morehouse, eds) *International Series on Sport Sciences Volume I, Biomechanics IV*. University Press; Baltimore, MD: pp. 572–7.

Baltzopoulos V., Eston R. G. and Maclaren D. A. (1988) A comparison of power measures between the Wingate test and tests of using an isokinetic device. *Ergonomics; 3*: 1693–9.

Bangsbo J. (1996a) Oxygen deficit: a measure of the anaerobic energy production during intense exercise? *Canadian Journal of Applied Physiology*; **21**: 350–63.

Bangsbo J. (1996b) Bangsbo responds to Medbo's paper. *Canadian Journal of Applied Physiology*; **21**: 384–8.

Bangsbo J. (1997) Quantification of anaerobic energy production during intense exercise. *Medicine and Science in Sports and Exercise*; **30**: 47–52.

Bangsbo J., Gollnick P. D., Graham T. E., Juel C., Kiens B., Mizuno M. and Saltin B. (1990) Anaerobic energy production and the O deficit-debt relationship during exhaustive exercise in humans. *Journal of Physiology*; **422**: 539–59.

Bar-Or O. (1981) Le test Anaérobie de Wingate: caractéristiques et applications. *Symbioses*; **13**: 157–72.

Bar-Or O. (1987) The Wingate anaerobic test: an update on methodology, reliability and validity. *Sports Medicine*; **4**: 381–94.

Bassett D. R. (1989) Correcting the Wingate Test for changes in kinetic energy of the ergometer flywheel. *International Journal of Sports Medicine*; **10**: 446–9.

Bergström J. (1962) Muscle electrolytes in man. *Scandinavian Journal of Clinical Laboratory Investigation*; **14** (Suppl. 68): 110.

Best C.H. and Partridge R.C. (1928) The equation of motion of a runner exerting maximal effort. *Proceedings of the Royal Society Series B*; **103**: 218–25.

Best C. H. and Partridge R. C. (1929) Observations on Olympic athletes. *Proceedings of the Royal Society Series B*; **105**: 323–32.

Bird S. and Davison R. (1997) *Physiological Testing Guidelines (3rd Edition)*. British

Association of Sport and Exercise Sciences; Leeds.

Boobis L. H. (1987) Metabolic aspects of fatigue during sprinting. In: (D. Macleod, R. Maughan, M. Nimmo, T. Reilly and C. Williams, eds) *Exercise: benefits, limitations and adaptations*. E. and F. N. Spon; London: pp. 116–43.

Boobis L. H., Williams C. and Wootton S.A. (1982) Human muscle metabolism during brief maximal exercise. *Journal of Physiology*; **338**: 21P–22P.

Boobis L. H., Williams C. and Wootton S. A. (1983) Influence of sprint training on muscle metabolism during brief maximal exercise in man. *Journal of Physiology*; **342**: 36P–37P.

Brewer J., Ramsbottom R. and Williams C. (1988) *Multistage Fitness Test – a Progressive Shuttle-run Test for the Prediction of Maximum Oxygen Uptake*. National Coaching Foundation; Leeds.

Brooks G. A. (1986) The lactate shuttle during exercise and recovery. *Medicine and Science in Sports and Exercise*; **18**: 355–64.

Burgomaster K. A., Howarth K. R., Phillips S. M., Rakobowchuk M., MacDonald M. J., McGee S. L. and Gibala M. J. (2008) Similar metabolic adaptations during exercise after low volume sprint interval and traditional endurance training in humans. *Journal of Physiology*; **586**: 151–60.

Casey A., Constantin-Teodosiu D., Howell S., Hultman E. and Greenhaff P. L. (1996) Metabolic response of type I and II muscle fibres during repeated bouts of maximal exercise in humans. *American Journal of Physiology*; **271**: E38–E43.

Cavagna G. A. (1975) Force platforms as ergometers. *Journal of Applied Physiology*; **39**: 174–9.

Cheetham M. E. and Williams C. (1985) Blood pH and blood lactate concentrations following maximal treadmill sprinting in man. *Journal of Physiology*; **361**: 79 (Abstract).

Cheetham M.E., Boobis L. H., Brooks S. and Williams C. (1986) Human muscle metabolism during sprint running in man. *Journal of Applied Physiology*; **61**: 54–60.

Constantin-Teodosiu D., Greenhaff P. L., McIntyre D. B., Round J. M. and Jones D. A. (1997) Anaerobic energy production in human skeletal muscle in intense contraction: a comparison of ^{31}P magnetic resonance spectroscopy and biochemical techniques. *Experimental Physiology*; **82**: 593–601.

Davis J. M., Welsh R. S., DeVolve K. L. and Alderson N.A. (1999) Effects of branched-chain amino acids and carbohydrate on fatigue during intermittent, high-intensity running. *International Journal of Sports Medicine*; **20**: 309–14.

Dickinson S. (1928) The dynamics of bicycle pedalling. *Proceedings of the Royal Society Series B*; **103**: 225–33.

Dickinson S. (1929) The efficiency of bicycle pedalling as affected by speed and load. *Journal of Physiology*; **67**: 242–55.

Dotan R. and Bar-Or O. (1983) Load optimization for the Wingate anaerobic test. *European Journal of Applied Physiology*; **51**: 409–17.

Eston R. G., Winter E. and Baltzopoulos V. (1997) Ratio standards and allometric modelling to scale peak power output for differences in lean upper leg volume in men and women. *Journal of Sports Sciences*; **15**: 29.

Fenn W. O. (1932) Zür Mechanik des Radfahrens im Vergleich zu der des Laufens. *Pflügers Archiv für die gesamte Physiologie*; **229**: 354–66.

Fenn W. O. and Marsh B. S. (1935) Muscular force at different speeds of shortening. *Journal of Physiology*; **85**: 277–97.

Fleisch A. (1950) Ergostat a puissances constantes et multiples. *Helvetica Medica Acta Series A*; **17**: 47–58.

Fox M. L., Bowers R. W. and Foss M. L. (1988) *The Physiological Basis of Physical Education and Athletics (4th Edition)* Saunders;Philadelphia, PA.

Furusawa K., Hill A. V. and Parkinson J. L. (1927) The energy used in 'sprint' running. *Proceedings of the Royal Society Series B*; **102**: 43–50.

Gamble D. J., Jakeman P. M. and Bartlett R. M. (1988) Force velocity characteristics during non-motorised treadmill sprinting. *Journal of Sports Sciences*; **6**: 156.

Greenhaff P. L., Nevill M. E., Soderlund K., Bodin K., Boobis L. H., Williams C. and Hultman E. (1994) The metabolic responses of human type I and II muscle fibers during maximal treadmill sprinting. *Journal of Physiology*; **478**: 149–55.

Hamilton A. L., Nevill M. E., Brooks S. and Williams C. (1991) Physiological responses to maximal intermittent exercise: differences between endurance-trained runners and games players. *Journal of Sports Sciences*; **9**: 371–82.

Hamley E. J. and Thomas V. (1967) Physiological and postural factors in the calibration of the bicycle ergometer. *Journal of Physiology*; **193**: 55P–57P.

Hermansen L. (1969) Anaerobic energy release. *Medicine and Science in Sports*; **1**: 32–8.

Hill A. V. (1913) The absolute mechanical efficiency of the contraction of an isolated muscle. *Journal of Physiology*; **46**: 435–69.

Hill A. V. (1934) The efficiency of bicycle pedalling. *Journal of Physiology*; **82**: 207–10.

Hill A. V. (1938) The heat of shortening and the dynamic constants of muscle. *Proceedings of the Royal Society Series B*; **126**: 136–95.

Hill A. V. (1970) *First and Last Experiments in Muscle Mechanics*. Cambridge University Press; London.

Hill A. V. and Lupton H. (1922) The oxygen consumption during running. *Journal of Physiology*; **56**: xxxii–xxxiii.

Inbar O., Dotan R. and Bar-Or O. (1976) Aerobic and anaerobic components of a thirty-second supramaximal cycling task. *Medicine and Science in Sports*; **8**: 51 (Abstract).

Jaskólska A., Veenstra B., Goossens P., Jaskólska A. and Skinner J. S. (1996) Optimised resistance for maximal power during treadmill running. *Sports Medicine and Training Rehabilitation*; **7**: 17–30.

Jaskólska A., Goossens P., Veenstra B., Jaskólski A. and Skinner J. S. (1999) Comparison of treadmill and cycle ergometer measurements of force-velocity relationships and power output. *International Journal of Sports Medicine*; **20**: 192–7.

Jones N. L., McCartney N., Graham T., Spriet L. L., Kowalchuk J. M., Heigenhauser G. J. F. and Sutton J. R. (1985) Muscle performance and metabolism in maximal

isokinetic cycling at slow and fast speeds. *Journal of Applied Physiology*; **59**: 132–6.

Jones P. R. M. and Pearson J. (1969) Anthropometric determination of leg fat and muscle plus bone volumes in young male and female adults. *Journal of Physiology*; **204**: 63P–66P.

Kelso L. E. A. and Hellebrandt F. A. (1932) The recording electrodynamic brake bicycle ergometer. *Journal of Clinical and Laboratory Medicine*; **19**: 1105–13.

Lakomy H. K. A. (1984) An ergometer for measuring the power generated during sprinting. *Journal of Physiology*; **354**: 33P (Abstract).

Lakomy H. K. A. (1985) Effect of load on corrected peak power output generated on friction loaded cycle ergometers. *Journal of Sports Sciences*; **3**: 240 (Abstract).

Lakomy H. K. A. (1986) Measurement of work and power output using friction loaded cycle ergometers. *Ergonomics*; **29**: 509–17.

La Voie N., Dallaire J., Brayne S. and Barrett D. (1984) Anaerobic testing using the Wingate and Evans-Quinney protocols with and without toe stirrups. *Canadian Journal of Applied Sport Sciences*; **9**: 1–5.

Léger L. A. and Lambert J. (1982) A maximal multistage 20m shuttle run test to predict O_{2max}. *European Journal of Applied Physiology*; **49**: 1–5.

Lupton H. (1923) An analysis of the effects of speed on the mechanical efficiency of human muscular movement. *Journal of Physiology*; **57**: 337–53.

Maughan R. J. (1982) A simple rapid method for the determination of glucose, lactate, pyruvate, alanine, b hydroxybutyrate and acetoacetate on a single 20 ml blood sample. *Clinica Chimica Acta*; **122**: 231–40.

Maughan R., Leiper J. and Shirreffs S. (2009) Haematology. In: (R. G. Eston and T. Reilly, eds.) *Kinanthropometry Laboratory Manual (3rd Edition): Exercise Physiology (Chapter 4)* Routledge; Oxon: pp. 104–123.

McCartney N., Heigenhauser G. J. F., Sargeant A. J. and Jones N. L. (1983) A constant-velocity cycle ergometer for the study of dynamic muscle function. *Journal of Applied Physiology*; **55**: 212–17.

McCartney N., Spriet L. L., Heigenhauser G. J. F., Kowalchuk J. M., Sutton J. R. and Jones

N. L. (1986) Muscle power and metabolism in maximal intermittent exercise. *Journal of Applied Physiology;* **60**: 1164–9.

McClenaghan B. A. and Literowitch W. (1987) Fundamentals of computerised data acquisition in the human performance laboratory. *Sports Medicine;* **4**: 425–45.

Medbø J. I. (1996a) Medbo responds to Bangsbo's paper. *Canadian Journal of Applied Physiology;* **21**: 364–9.

Medbø J. I. (1996b) Is the maximal accumulated oxygen deficit an adequate measure of the anaerobic capacity? *Canadian Journal of Applied Physiology;* **21**: 370–83.

Medbø J. I., Mohn A., Tabata I., Bahr R., Vaage O. and Sejersted O. (1988) Anaerobic capacity determined by the maximal accumulated oxygen deficit. *Journal of Applied Physiology;* **64**: 50–60.

Mercer T. H., Gleeson N. P., Claridge S. and Clement S. (1998) Prolonged intermittent high intensity exercise impairs neuromuscular performance of the knee flexors. *European Journal of Applied Physiology;* **77**: 560–2.

Morris J. G., Nevill M. E., Lakomy H. K. A., Nicholas C. and Williams C. (1998) Effect of a hot environment on performance of prolonged, intermittent, high-intensity shuttle running. *Journal of Sports Sciences;* **16**: 677–86.

Nakamura Y., Mutoh Y. and Miyashita M. (1985) Determination of the peak power output during maximal brief pedalling bouts. *Journal of Sports Sciences;* **3**: 181–7.

Nevill A. M., Ramsbottom R. and Williams C. (1992) Scaling measurements in physiology and medicine for individuals of different size. *European Journal of Applied Physiology;* **65**: 110–17.

Nevill M. E., Boobis L. H., Brooks S. and Williams C. (1989) Effect of training on muscle metabolism during treadmill sprinting. *Journal of Applied Physiology;* **67**: 2376–82.

Nevill M. E., Williams C., Roper D., Slater C. and Nevill A. M. (1993) Effect of diet on performance during recovery from intermittent sprint exercise. *Journal of Sports Sciences;* **11**: 119–26.

Nordeen-Snyder K. (1977) The effect of bicycle seat height variation upon oxygen consumption and lower limb kinematics. *Medicine and Science in Sports and Exercise;* **9**: 113–17.

Peyrebrune M. C., Nevill M. E., Donaldson F. J. and Cosford D. J. (1998) The effect of oral creatine supplementation on performance in single and repeated sprint swimming. *Journal of Sports Sciences;* **16**: 271–9.

Ramsbottom R., Nevill A. M., Nevill M. E. and Williams C. (1991) Effect of training on maximal accumulated oxygen deficit and shuttle run performance. *Journal of Sports Sciences;* **9**: 429–30.

Sale D. G. (1991) Testing strength and power. In: (J. D. MacDougall, H. A. Wenger and H. A. Green, eds) *Physiological Testing of the High-Performance Athlete (2nd Edition).* Human Kinetics; Champaign, IL: pp. 21–106.

Sargeant A. J., Hoinville E. and Young A. (1981) Maximum leg force and power output during short term dynamic exercise. *Journal of Applied Physiology;* **53**: 1175–82.

Sargeant A. J., Dolan P. and Young A. (1984) Optimal velocity for maximal short-term (anaerobic) power output in cycling. *International Journal of Sports Medicine;* **5**: 124–5.

Sargent D. A. (1921) The physical test of a man. *American Physical Education Review;* **26**: 188–94.

Sargent L. W. (1924) Some observations on the Sargent test of neuromuscar efficiency. *American Physical Education Review;* **29**: 47–56.

Sargent R. M. (1926) The relation between oxygen requirement and speed in running. *Proceedings of the Royal Society Series B;* **100**: 10–22.

Schmidt-Nielsen K. (1984) *Scaling: why is animal size so important?* Cambridge University Press; Cambridge.

Serresse O., Lortie G., Bouchard C. and Boulay M. R. (1988) Estimation of the contribution of the various energy systems during maximal work of short duration. *International Journal of Sports Medicine;* **9**: 456–60.

Smith A. J. (1972) *A study of the forces on the body in athletic activities, with particular reference to jumping.* Unpublished Doctoral

Thesis, University of Leeds.

Smith J. C. and Hill D. W. (1991) Contribution of energy systems during a Wingate power test. *British Journal of Sports Medicine*; **25**: 196–9.

Smith P. M. and Price M. J. (2007) Upper-body exercise. In: (E. M. Winter, A. M. Jones, R. R. R. Davison, P. D. Bromley and T. H. Mercer, eds) *Sport and Exercise Physiology Testing Guidelines Volume One Sport Testing*. Routledge; Oxford: pp. 138–44.

Soderlund K. and Hultman E. (1986) Effects of delayed freezing on content of phosphagens in human skeletal muscle biopsy samples. *Journal of Applied Physiology*; **61**: 832–5.

Soderlund K., Greenhaff P. L. and Hultman E. (1992) Energy metabolism in type I and II human muscle fibres during short term electrical stimulation at different frequencies. *Acta Physiologica Scandinavica*; **144**: 15–22.

Tanner J. M. (1949) Fallacy of per-weight and per-surface area standards and their relation to spurious correlation. *Journal of Applied Physiology*; **2**: 1–15.

Thompson D., Nicholas C. W. and Williams C. (1999) Muscular soreness following prolonged intermittent high-intensity shuttle running. *Journal of Sports Sciences*; **17**: 387–95.

Tong R. J., Bell W., Ball G. and Winter E. M. (2001). Validity and reliability of power output measurements during treadmill sprinting in rugby players. *Journal of Sports Sciences*; **19**: 289–97.

Tuttle W. W. and Wendler A. J. (1945) The construction, calibration and use of an alternating current electrodynamic brake bicycle ergometer. *Journal of Laboratory and Clinical Medicine*; **30**: 173–83.

Vandewalle H., Pérès G., Heller J. and Monod H. (1985) All out anaerobic capacity tests on cycle ergometers: a comparative study on men and women. *European Journal of Applied Physiology*; **54**: 222–29.

Von Döbeln W. (1954) A simple bicycle ergometer. *Journal of Applied Physiology*; **7**: 222–4.

Welsman J., Armstrong N., Winter E. and Kirby B. J. (1993) The influence of various scaling techniques on the interpretation of developmental changes in peak O_2. *Pediatric Exercise Science*; **5**: 485 (Abstract).

Williams C. (1987) Short term activity. In: (D. Macleod, R. Maughan, M. Nimmo, T. Reilly and C. Williams, eds) *Exercise: Benefits, Limits and Adaptations*. E and F. N. Spon; London: pp. 59–62.

Williams C. (1990) Metabolic aspects of exercise. In: (T. Reilly, N. Secher, P. Snell and C. Williams, eds) *Physiology of Sports*. E. and F. N. Spon; London: pp. 3–40.

Winter E. M. (1992) Scaling: partitioning out differences in body size. *Pediatric Exercise Science*; **4**: 296–301.

Winter E. M., Brookes F. B. C. and Hamley E. J. (1987) A comparison of optimized and non-optimized peak power output in young, active men and women. *Journal of Sports Sciences*; **5**: 71 (Abstract).

Winter E. M., Brookes F. B. C. and Hamley E. J. (1989) Optimized loads for external power output during brief, maximal cycling. *Journal of Sports Sciences*; **7**: 69–70.

Winter E. M., Brookes F. B. C. and Hamley E. J. (1991) Maximal exercise performance and lean leg volume in men and women. *Journal of Sports Sciences*; **9**: 3–13.

Winter E. M., Brookes F. B. C. and Roberts K. W. (1993) The effects of scaling on comparisons between maximal exercise performance in boys and men. *Pediatric Exercise Science*; **5**: 488 (Abstract).

Winter E. M., Brown D., Roberts N. K. A., Brookes F. B. C. and Swaine I. L. (1996) Optimized and corrected peak power output during friction-braked cycle ergometry. *Journal of Sports Sciences*; **14**: 513–21.

Winter E. M., Jones A. M., Davison R. C. R., Bromley P. D. and Mercer T. H. (2007) *Sport and Exercise Physiology Testing Guidelines Volume One Sport Testing*. Routledge; Oxford.

Winter E. M. and Nevill A. M. (2009) Scaling: adjusting for differences in body size. In: (R. G. Eston and T. Reilly, eds.) *Kinanthropometry Laboratory Manual (3rd Edition): Anthropometry (Chapter 11)* Routledge; Oxon: pp. 300–320.

Wootton S. and Williams C. (1983) The influence of recovery duration on repeated maximal sprints. In: (H. G. Knuttgen, J. A. Vogel and J. Poortmans, eds) *Biochemistry of Exercise*. Human Kinetics; Champaign, IL: pp. 269–73.

RELATIONSHIPS BETWEEN UNITS OF ENERGY, WORK, POWER AND SPEED

Table A.1 Energy and work units

1 joule[a] (J)	=	1 Newton-metre (Nm)
1 kilojoule (kJ)	=	1000 J
	=	0.23889 kcal
1 megajoule (MJ)	=	1000 kJ
1 kilocalorie (kcal)	=	4.186 kJ = 426.8 kg-m

[a]The joule is the SI unit for work and represents the application of a force of 1 newton (N) through a distance of 1 metre. A newton is the force producing an acceleration of 1 metre per second every second (1 m s^{-2}) when it acts on 1 kg.

Table A.2 Relationships between various power units

	W	kcal min^{-1}	kJ min^{-1}	kgm min^{-1}
1 watt (W)[a]	1.0	0.014	0.060	6.118
1 kcal min^{-1}	69.77	1.0	4.186	426.78
1 kJ min^{-1}	16.667	0.2389	1.0	101.97
1 kgm min^{-1}	0.1634	0.00234	0.00981	1.0

[a] The watt is the SI unit for power and is equivalent to 1 J s^{-1}.

Table A.3 Conversion table for units of speed

km h⁻¹	m s⁻¹	mph
1	0.28	0.62
2	0.56	1.24
3	0.83	1.87
4	1.11	2.49
5	1.39	3.11
6	1.67	3.73
7	1.94	4.35
8	2.22	4.98
9	2.50	5.60
10	2.78	6.22

* m s⁻¹ is the SI unit for speed

INDEX